MULTINATIONAL
COLLECTIVE BARGAINING
ATTEMPTS

Major Industrial Research Unit Studies

The Wharton School's Industrial Research Unit has been noted for its "relevant research" since its founding in 1921. The IRU is now the largest academic publisher of manpower and collective bargaining studies. Publications include the Major Industrial Research Unit Studies, listed below, and monographs in special series, such as the Labor Relations and Public Policy Series, Manpower and Human Resources Studies, and Multinational Industrial Relations Series.

No. 45   William N. Chernish, *Coalition Bargaining: A Study of Union Tactics and Public Policy* (1969).*

No. 46   Herbert R. Northrup, Richard L. Rowan, et al., *Negro Employment in Basic Industry: A Study of Racial Policies in Six Industries*, Studies of Negro Employment, Vol. I (1970).*

No. 49   Herbert R. Northrup et al., *Negro Employment in Southern Industry: A Study of the Racial Policies in the Paper, Lumber, Tobacco, Bituminous Coal, and Textile Industries*, Studies of Negro Employment, Vol. IV (1971).*

No. 50   Herbert R. Northrup et al., *Negro Employment in Land and Air Transport: A Study of Racial Policies in the Railroad, Airline, Trucking, and Urban Transit Industries*, Studies of Negro Employment, Vol. V (1971) $13.50.

No. 51   Gordon F. Bloom, Charles R. Perry, and F. Marion Fletcher, *Negro Employment in Retail Trade: A Study of Racial Policies in the Department Store, Drugstore, and Supermarket Industries*, Studies of Negro Employment, Vol. VI (1972).*

No. 53   Charles R. Perry, Bernard E. Anderson, Richard L. Rowan, Herbert R. Northrup, *The Impact of Government Manpower Programs*, Manpower and Human Resources Studies, No. 4 (1975) $18.50.

No. 54   Herbert R. Northrup and Howard G. Foster, *Open Shop Construction* (1975) $15.00.

No. 55   Stephen A. Schneider, *The Availability of Minorities and Women for Professional and Managerial Positions, 1970-1985*, Manpower and Human Resources Studies, No. 7 (1977) $25.00.

No. 56   Herbert R. Northrup, Ronald M. Cowin, Lawrence G. Vanden Plas, et al., *The Objective Selection of Supervisors*, Manpower and Human Resources Studies, No. 8 (1978) $25.00.

No. 57   Herbert R. Northrup et al., *Black and Other Minority Participation in the All-Volunteer Navy and Marine Corps*, Studies of Negro Employment, Vol. VIII (1978).*

No. 58   Herbert R. Northrup and Richard L. Rowan, *Multinational Collective Bargaining Attempts: The Record, the Cases, and the Prospects*, Multinational Industrial Relations Series, No. 6 (1979) $27.50.

Order from the Industrial Research Unit
The Wharton School, University of Pennsylvania
Philadelphia, Pennsylvania 19104

* Order these books from University Microfilms, Inc. Attn: Books Editorial Department, 300 North Zeeb Road, Ann Arbor, Michigan 48106.

MULTINATIONAL COLLECTIVE BARGAINING ATTEMPTS

The Record, the Cases, and the Prospects

by

HERBERT R. NORTHRUP AND RICHARD L. ROWAN

INDUSTRIAL RESEARCH UNIT
The Wharton School, Vance Hall/CS
University of Pennsylvania
Philadelphia, Pennsylvania 19104
U.S.A.

Foreword

This book culminates seven years of research designed to determine the status of and prospects for multinational collective bargaining. In the course of this work, we have traveled several times each year to Europe, visited Japan and Asia twice, and sent our researchers to Latin America and Australia. The book is long and is meant as an analytic documentary and reference work upon which future studies in this area can build.

Multinational Collective Bargaining: The Record, the Cases, and the Prospects is part of the Wharton Industrial Research Unit's ongoing research project dealing with the international activities of trade unions and the potential for multinational bargaining. This research has resulted in the publication of the sixteen articles listed at the end of this foreword and several other publications. In addition, a Multinational Information Service has been established based upon the numerous contacts developed in Europe, Asia, Australia, and North and South America; the materials collected are, we believe, the most complete extant on international union and multinational corporation contacts and relationships. The project is under the joint direction of the undersigned.

Another aspect of the Industrial Research Unit's multinational industrial relations project is the examination of the labor relations situation and climate in various countries. Thus, as listed on the dust jacket, studies have been published for Brazil, Mexico, Peru, and Venezuela. Others are in progress for Colombia, India, Spain, the Philippines, and Hong Kong.

A third aspect of the Wharton Industrial Research Unit's multinational industrial relations project is the comparative analysis of policies and practices in different countries. Earlier in 1979, the Unit published *Profit Sharing, Employee Stock Ownership, Savings, and Asset Formation Plans in the Western World*, by Geoffrey W. Latta. Projected studies will deal with shift practices, hours of work on an annual basis, layoffs, and plant closings and, like the profit sharing study, will compare the situation among the major industrialized countries.

The Industrial Research Unit also conducts special unpublished studies of labor conditions in various countries by request. The Unit's capability in this field has been greatly enhanced as a result of the Chase Manhattan Bank's gift of its international industrial relations library and extensive files. The Chase files, now carefully and continuously updated, were developed over a twelve-year period and are on a country-by-country basis from Abu Dhabi to Zambia. In addition to the industrialized countries, these files also include materials on all underdeveloped areas, with extensive coverage of current industrial relations developments, legislation, labor conditions, policies, and practices. These complement the Industrial Research Unit's extensive and unique materials on companies and unions.

It would be impossible to list the great number of company, employer association, union, international trade secretariat, and government officials who have given so freely of their time and provided extensive documentation for our work. For this assistance, we remain very grateful. Without such extensive help, this study clearly could not have been accomplished. We wish also to thank the editors and publishers of the journals listed on the following pages for their cooperation in permitting us to reproduce information first published as articles.

Within our organization, we also received considerable help. Mr. Philip Miscimarra, Research Assistant, wrote the first draft of chapter XVI; Ms. Mary J. Immediata, a former assistant, did the same for chapter XVII. Ms. Rae Ann O'Brien, Research Specialist, helped in fact gathering on several occasions, as did Messrs. Mario Gobbo, Rajiva Singh, and Jaime Infante, and Ms. Gracie Hemphill, all research assistants. Ms. Lois A. Rappaport, Senior Research Specialist—Multinational, and Professor Janice R. Bellace, Senior Faculty Research Specialist—Legal, provided continuing support. Our French and German translators and research specialists, Dr. Betty J. Slowinski and Mr. Christian F. Schneider, made numerous documents available to us from French, German, and Dutch.

Mr. Robert E. Bolick, Jr., Chief Editor of the Industrial Research Unit, edited the final manuscript; Ms. Judy Webster made up the index; and Mrs. Margaret E. Doyle, Office Manager, handled the various administrative matters involved in the work. The manuscript was typed by our secretarial staff: Mrs. Nancy E. Chiang, Ms. Carolyn W. Free, Ms. Kathryn Hunter, and Ms. Judith A. Pepper. The study was financed between 1972 and 1975 by the unrestricted funds provided by the Wharton Labor Relations Council and the Industrial Research Unit's American Research Advisory Group. Since 1975, financing has been largely provided by the contributions of the Industrial Research Unit's Multinational Research Advisory Group members and Information Service subscribers. Such funds are also unrestricted, although it is understood that they will be utilized for multinational industrial relations studies. A portion of the unrestricted grant from the John M. Olin Foundation, Inc., was also utilized to complete this work. The authors are, of course, solely responsible for the study's content and for the research and views expressed, which should not be attributed to the University of Pennsylvania.

HERBERT R. NORTHRUP, *Director*
RICHARD L. ROWAN, *Co-Director*
Industrial Research Unit
The Wharton School
University of Pennsylvania

Philadelphia
October 1979

Acknowledgments

Material from the following previously published articles (by Herbert R. Northrup and Richard L. Rowan, unless otherwise noted) has been utilized in this book by permission of the editors and publishers.

"Multinational Collective Bargaining Activity: The Factual Record in Chemicals, Glass, and Rubber Tires," Parts I and II, *Columbia Journal of World Business*, spring 1974 and summer 1974, pp. 112-24 and 49-63.

"Multinational Bargaining in Food and Allied Industries: Approaches and Prospects," *Wharton Quarterly*, Vol. VII, No. 4, spring 1974, pp. 32-40.

"The ICF-IFPCW Conflict," *Columbia Journal of World Business*, winter 1974, pp. 109-20.

"Multinational Bargaining in Metals and Electrical Industries: Approaches and Prospects," *Journal of Industrial Relations* (Australia), Vol. 17, No. 1, March 1975, pp. 1-29.

"Multinational Bargaining in the Telecommunications Industry," *British Journal of Industrial Relations*, Vol. XIII, No. 2, July 1975, pp. 257-62.

"Multinational Bargaining Approaches in the Western European Flat Glass Industry," *Industrial and Labor Relations Review*, Vol. 30, No. 1, October 1976, pp. 32-46. Copyright Cornell University. All rights reserved.

"Multinational Union Activity in the 1976 U.S. Rubber Tire Strike," *Sloan Management Review*, Vol. 18, No. 3, spring 1977, pp. 17-28.

"Australian Maritime Unions and the International Transport Workers' Federation," by Kingsley Laffer, *Journal of Industrial Relations* (Australia), Vol. 19, No. 2, June 1977, pp. 113-32.

"Multinational Union-Management Consultation: The European Experience." Reproduced, by permission, from *International Labour Review* (Geneva), Vol. 116, No. 2, September-October 1977, pp. 153-70. Copyright International Labour Organisation 1977.

"International Enforcement of Union Standards in Ocean Transport," by Richard L. Rowan, Herbert R. Northrup, and Mary J. Immediata, *British Journal of Industrial Relations*, Vol. XV, No. 3, November 1977, pp. 338-55.

"Multinational Union Activities and Plant Closings: The Case of Akzo," *Industrial Relations Journal* (U.K.), Vol. 9, No. 1, spring 1978, pp. 27-36.

"Why Multinational Bargaining Neither Exists Nor Is Desirable," *Labor Law Journal*, Vol. 29, No. 6, June 1978, pp. 330-42.

"The Socio-Economic Environment and International Union Aspirations," *Columbia Journal of World Business*, winter 1978, pp. 111-21.

"Activités syndicales multinationales au sein de l'industrie papetière," *Relations Industrielles* (Canada), Vol. 34, No. 4, December 1979.

"Multinational Union-Management Contacts in the Graphical and Publishing Industries," *British Journal of Industrial Relations*, Vol. XVII, No. 3, November 1979.

TABLE OF CONTENTS

PART FOUR

THE FOOD, BEVERAGE, AND TOBACCO INDUSTRIES

PART FIVE

THE SERVICES AND COMMUNICATIONS INDUSTRIES

LIST OF TABLES

LIST OF FIGURES

PART ONE

Background

CHAPTER I

Introduction

This study had its genesis in 1971, when one of the authors planned a sabbatical at Cambridge University in England. At that time, as now, the Wharton Industrial Research Unit was deeply committed to the study of American industrial relations developments. Coalition or coordinated bargaining had been one of our subjects for research,[1] and the idea was being broached that such bargaining could be extended across national borders,[2] especially in Europe as a result of the integration that followed the formation and expansion of the European Community. We were aware that some claims of multinational union action could not be squared with the facts,[3] but our knowledge was almost totally limited. It was therefore agreed that one author would devote six months in Europe to fact finding on the potential and extent, if any, of multinational bargaining, while the other would pursue the same investigation on this side of the Atlantic. It was hoped that an article or two would result.

We soon found ourselves engulfed in information. Field surveys of the subject were conspicuous largely by their absence. We found corporations, international trade union secretariats,[4] and government officials, with few exceptions, delighted to share information. Returning to Europe usually twice annually since then and making trips to Japan and Asia, we have continually discovered new sources of information or have found serious questions concerning reports of action that were long accepted as fact. Some of our research results have been set forth in the seventeen articles listed in the prefatory materials. This book incorporates these articles with an equal amount of information not heretofore published.

---

[1] See William N. Chernish, *Coalition Bargaining*, Industrial Research Unit Major Study, No. 45 (Philadelphia: Industrial Research Unit, The Wharton School, University of Pennsylvania, 1969).

[2] See, e.g., chapter III for the ideas of the late Walter Reuther on this subject.

[3] See, e.g., the American Cyanamid case in chapter VIII.

[4] These organizations are defined in chapter II.

3

RESEARCH METHODOLOGY AND FINDINGS

As noted, this study is based primarily upon extensive fieldwork. We have interviewed several hundred corporate, government, employer association, union, and international trade union secretariat personnel on three continents and a dozen countries to obtain information. Wherever possible, we acquired documentation to support our findings. Our library, greatly augmented by the gift of the books and files from the Chase Manhattan Bank and by subscriptions to publications from all over the world, has provided much additional documentation. In support of the facts, we have traveled widely and dug deeply.

Our findings do not support the belief that multinational bargaining is either widespread or imminent. Indeed, it is almost nonexistent, with a form alive in the European recording, radio, and television industries and some approaches elsewhere. There have also been some international activities in transport and in a few other industries that may be termed approximations or approaches. For the most part, claims of greater activity are unsupported by the facts.

Nevertheless, the potential is there, and several organizations, usually making good use of international governmental agency support, continue to look for the opportunity to effectuate a breakthrough. How great that potential is, the reader may assess for himself by examining the carefully documented case histories that make up the bulk of this book. Our own assessments are made in the concluding chapter and in analyses that comment upon previously described cases.

ORGANIZATION OF THE STUDY

Chapter II briefly describes the organizational setting for the major multinational corporations and the international trade union movement. The bulk of the book is then divided into five major parts, which in turn are broken up into industry chapters. Thus, Part Two deals with the metal and electrical industries; Part Three with the glass, chemical, rubber, and petroleum and related products industries; Part Four with the food, beverage, and tobacco industries; Part Five with services and communications; and Part Six with transport. The final section of the book sums up our findings, evaluates the potential for multinational bargaining and the activities and organizations that support it, and assesses its future potential in the light of our findings.

CHAPTER II

The Multinational Corporations and Union Organizations

Multinational collective bargaining envisions organizations on both sides of the table that operate across national boundaries, and they do exist both on the corporate and the union side. As a preclude to our main discussion, we examine briefly in this chapter some of the corporate and union organizations that could play a role in multinational bargaining. The final section of this chapter points out some problems that either inhibit or make difficult the effectuation of multinational bargaining. This should enable the reader to evaluate more realistically some of the quoted claims and rhetoric discussed in the following chapters.

THE MULTINATIONAL CORPORATION

Much has been written about the multinational corporation in recent years,[1] but actually, there is no general agreement as to what makes a company "multinational." Our definition is a pragmatic one: if a company produces or operates functionally in more than one country, we would deem it a multinational concern. Merely selling abroad is not sufficient. Thus, Hertz is a multinational because it has rental car branches in many countries; but a large plane manufacturer that sells products abroad but builds them only in its home country is not.

---

[1] See, e.g., Nasrollah S. Fatemi and Gail W. Williams, *Multinational Corporations* (New York: A. S. Barnes and Company, 1975); Mira Wilkins, *The Maturing of Multinational Enterprise* (Cambridge, Mass.: Harvard University Press, 1974); C. Fred Bergsten, Thomas Horst, and Theodore H. Moran, *American Multinationals and American Interests* (Washington, D.C.: The Brookings Institution, 1978). There are many others, including a more radical treatment, Richard L. Barnet and Ronald E. Müller, *Global Reach* (New York: Simon and Schuster, 1974).

5

The multinational companies with which we are concerned are mostly very large companies, but there are many others that are in fact quite small. Moreover, some very large concerns are either not multinational or have very limited operations abroad. The major steel and shipbuilding concerns of the world, as well as many aerospace companies, are found in the latter category. In a real sense also, the major airlines and ocean shipping concerns are not multinational companies, although they operate around the world. We shall find in chapters IV, XVII, and XVIII, however, that multinational union activity may impact upon companies that are technically not multinational by our pragmatic definition.

Neither New Nor Unitary

It is important to note at the outset that multinational corporations are neither a new nor a unitary phenomenon. Dr. Wilkins has traced multinational business operations to the Sumerian merchants, 2500 B.C., and modern-type organizations to the Industrial Revolution or before.[2] Each rising industrial country adds to the list of concerns that transverse national boundaries. Thus, prior to World War I, European companies were most commonly abroad. Post-World War II was the epochal American expansion period, so much so that, to many, the multinational corporation and the American corporation are synonymous—a thoroughly false concept. More recent years have seen the strong push of Japanese companies and the resurgence of the Germans and, very recently, the emergence of huge combines from South Korea. Rising industrialization leads to corporate expansion. Small countries often have a number of large multinational concerns. In order to grow, such companies must jump across national boundaries. Switzerland, for example, is home to companies with only a small percentage of their sales—for Nestlé but 3 percent—in their headquarters country.

Private vs. State-Owned

It is common to think of multinational concerns as private aggregations of capital. Most are, but some are not. Thus, Renault, the French auto maker, is wholly government owned, as is its lagging competitor, British Leyland. Volkswagen is 40

---

[2] Mira Wilkins, *The Emergence of Multinational Enterprise* (Cambridge, Mass.: Harvard University Press, 1970).

percent in the hands of government. Such petroleum concerns as Elf-Acquitaine and Française des Pétroles (France), ENI (Italy), National Iranian Oil, Petróleos de Venezuela, and Petróleo Brasileiro are totally owned or controlled by governments. All of these companies were among the fifty largest industrial concerns in 1978 for which data were available (see Table II-1).

No record is available for another type of multinational corporation—the agencies of the Soviet Union and its satellites which operate industrial concerns. Some of these organizations operate far beyond their home bases, but data regarding them are neither usually available nor comparable if available.

Size and Structure

The nature of a company's business is crucial in determining its size and structure. Table II-1 shows the *Fortune* list for 1978 of the fifty largest industrial companies in the world by sales (for which data are available). Of these, eighteen are petroleum companies, ten are automobile concerns, eight are primarily in electrical and electronic businesses, six are chemical concerns, four are in food and related products, three are in steel, and one is in glass and building materials. The dominance of the petroleum group is directly related to the size and cost of investments that the companies must make to acquire, refine, and sell products, and in varying degrees, this can be said for each product group included in Table II-1. Other factors, such as management capability, source of product (National Iranian Oil), or success of marketing, are also important.

Table II-1 also tells much about a country's industrial progress. Twenty-one of the Table II-1 companies are United States-based; seven, West Germany; six, Japan; five, France; three, the United Kingdom; two, a combination of the United Kingdom and the Netherlands; and one each in the Netherlands, Switzerland, Italy, Iran, Venezuela, and Brazil. Those in the last four countries are state-owned. If one looks back to *Fortune*'s lists for previous years, one finds that Japanese and West German company representation has been growing; the British, declining; and the United States, also falling off.

Managements

No generalization can be made about the managements of multinational corporations. To a large extent, they reflect man-

TABLE II-1

The Fifty Largest Industrial Companies in the World, 1978

RANK '78	'77	COMPANY	HEADQUARTERS	SALES ($000)	NET INCOME ($000)
1	1	General Motors	Detroit	63,221,100	3,508,000
2	2	Exxon	New York	60,334,527	2,763,000
3	3	Royal Dutch/Shell Group	London/The Hague	44,044,534	2,084,653
4	4	Ford Motor	Dearborn, Mich.	42,784,100	1,588,900
5	5	Mobil	New York	34,736,045	1,125,638
6	6	Texaco	Harrison, N.Y.	28,607,521	852,461
7	8	British Petroleum	London	27,407,620	853,057
8	9	Standard Oil of California	San Francisco	23,232,413	1,105,881
9	7	National Iranian Oil	Tehran	22,789,650	15,178,157
10	10	International Business Machines	Armonk, N.Y.	21,076,089	3,110,568
11	12	General Electric	Fairfield, Conn.	19,653,800	1,299,700
12	14	Unilever	London/Rotterdam	18,893,176	531,337
13	11	Gulf Oil	Pittsburgh	18,069,000	791,000
14	13	Chrysler	Highland Park, Mich.	16,340,700	(204,600)
15	15	International Tel. & Tel.	New York	15,261,178	661,807
16	17	Philips' Gloeilampenfabrieken	Eindhoven (Netherlands)	15,121,166	327,117
17	16	Standard Oil (Ind.)	Chicago	14,961,489	1,076,412
18	20	Siemens	Munich	13,864,726	322,021
19	21	Volkswagenwerk	Wolfsburg (Germany)	13,332,059	275,671
20	28	Toyota Motor	Toyota City (Japan)	12,768,821	529,933
21	25	Renault	Paris	12,715,866	2,222
22	22	ENI	Rome	12,565,727	(367,892)
23	19	Françiase des Pétroles	Paris	12,509,942	60,305
24	18	Atlantic Richfield	Los Angeles	12,298,403	804,325
25	34	Daimler-Benz	Stuttgart	12,090,806	295,054

26	24	Hoechst	Frankfurt	12,068,207	107,559
27	30	Bayer	Leverkusen (Germany)	11,392,483	203,857
28	23	Shell Oil	Houston	11,062,883	813,623
29	27	U.S. Steel	Pittsburgh	11,049,500	242,000
30	36	Nestlé	Vevey (Switzerland)	11,001,848	416,131
31	31	BASF	Ludwigshafen on Rhine	10,732,452	210,170
32	35	Peugeot-Citroën	Paris	10,620,992	300,200
33	29	E.I. du Pont de Nemours	Wilmington, Del.	10,584,200	787,000
34	48	Matsushita Electric Industrial	Osaka (Japan)	10,020,545	416,695
35	44	Nissan Motor	Yokohama (Japan)	9,751,661	371,790
36	32	Nippon Steel	Tokyo	9,521,847	56,937
37	41	Western Electric	New York	9,521,835	561,200
38	33	Continental Oil	Stamford, Conn.	9,455,241	451,340
39	42	Mitsubishi Heavy Industries	Tokyo	9,200,492	79,975
40	37	Thyssen	Duisburg (Germany)	9,182,135	61,238
41	39	Hitachi	Tokyo	9,153,283	304,390
42	26	Petróleos de Venezuela	Caracas	9,137,238	1,449,209
43	38	Petrobrás (Petróleo Brasileiro)	Rio de Janeiro	9,131,228	1,214,516
44	43	Elf-Aquitaine	Paris	9,115,703	332,336
45	45	Tenneco	Houston	8,762,000	466,000
46	40	Imperial Chemical Industries	London	8,701,411	577,791
47	46	Procter & Gamble	Cincinnati	8,099,687	511,668
48	47	Union Carbide	New York	7,869,700	394,300
49	50	B.A.T. Industries	London	7,750,092	411,061
50	●	Saint-Gobain-Pont-à-Mousson	Paris	7,598,170	91,783
		TOTALS		829,165,291	49,337,496

Source: *Fortune*, Vol. 100 (August 13, 1979), p. 208. Reproduced by permission.

agerial policies in their home countries, particularly with regard to such matters as degree of centralization and decentralization, attitudes toward unions and social legislation, and other matters. Moreover, managements from the same country often have quite different styles, approaches, and attitudes. Thus, there is no single mold for multinational corporation executives and managers except that they must be capable of operating and managing large, far-flung organizations, which can succeed—or fail—as a result of the decisions that they make.

Industries Involved

Much of this book deals with labor relations situations or alleged ones involving the industries represented by the companies in Table II-1: automobiles, electrical and electronic, petroleum, chemicals, glass, and food. Other industries studied include rubber tires, various metals, transport, and services, in which very large companies also exist. These are industries in which are found the large, highly visible companies that one pictures when the multinational corporation is considered. And, of course, such companies are the natural targets of the international labor movement.

Employer Associations

There are national and international associations of employers in nearly every industry, but except for broad policy, we shall find few involved in labor or employee relations. There is an International Organization of Employers and an International Chamber of Commerce. These organizations help coordinate employer policies and representation before such bodies as the International Labour Organisation and the Organization for Economic Cooperation and Development and, therefore, help to coordinate labor and social policies of employers. They take no part, however, in a particular company's or industry's relationship with employee organizations.

With a few notable exceptions (e.g., the graphic and printing industry—chapter XI—or recording, radio, and television—chapter XVI), therefore, the relationships or lack thereof discussed in this book involve union coalitions and/or coordinating bodies on the one hand and single multinational corporate enterprises on the other. Although, in Europe, employer associations commonly represent companies in collective bargaining, there has apparently been no serious consideration to having multinational employer associations act on behalf of companies or national employer associations in an employee relations capacity. A single meeting between the Western European Metal Trades Employers' Organization and the European Metalworkers' Federation ended in dispute (see chapter IV) and is not likely to be repeated in the near future.

On the other hand, under the aegis of the European Community, tripartite European meetings are encouraged and have been held in a number of industries. Where an industry is seriously depressed (e.g., shipbuilding—chapter IV), the potential for multinational union-management relationships, joint action, and even bargaining through a multinational association or cooperating national associations and a multinational union or a coordinated committee of national unions could be enhanced, especially within the European Community.

THE INTERNATIONAL TRADE UNION MOVEMENT

It is perhaps incorrect to use the term *movement* in describing multinational trade union activities. Unions on the international scene are split by ideology between Communist dictatorship-oriented organizations and those that operate as free institutions in democratic or in authoritarian but not totalitarian countries. A group that originated from Catholic teachings but has since become both "deconfessionalized" and considerably radicalized adds to the diversity. Then there are regional groups, some affiliated with central bodies, some not. A brief review of the principal international labor organizations will assist in understanding the developments described in the following chapters.[3]

The Global Organizations

There are three "global" organizations, or central groups, of international unions: the World Federation of Trade Unions (WFTU), headquartered in Prague, and the International Confederation of Free Trade Unions (ICFTU), and the World Confederation of Labour (WCL), both headquartered in Brussels. Although they all are centers for internationalism, their

---

[3] A more complete outline of the international trade union movement will be found in the handbook being currently prepared by the authors for publication by Management Centre Europe, Brussels. A thorough analysis will be published by the Industrial Research Unit in 1980.

TABLE II-2
International Trade Union Movement:
The Global Organizations
1979

World Federation of Trade Unions (WFTU)

Vinohradska 10
Prague 2, Czechoslovakia

| President: | Sandor Gaspar, Hungary |
| General Secretary: | Enrique Pastorino, Uruguay |

International Confederation of Free Trade Unions (ICFTU)

Rue Montagne aux Herbes Potagères, 37-41
1000 Brussels, Belgium

| President: | P. P. Narayanan, Malaysia |
| General Secretary: | Otto Kersten, Germany |

World Confederation of Labour (WCL)

Rue Joseph II, 50
B-1040 Brussels, Belgium

| President: | Marcel Pépin, Canada |
| General Secretary: | Jan Kulakowski, Belgium |

---

actual operations are quite different. Table II-2 lists the two top principal officers and addresses of these organizations.

The WFTU. The WFTU was organized in 1945 during the World War II euphoria when cooperation between East and West was widely advocated. The then split American labor movement did not fully cooperate. The Congress of Industrial Organizations was a founding member; the American Federation of Labor did not join. From the beginning, the Soviets worked to dominate the organization. After the Communist coup in Czechoslovakia and the denunciation of the Marshall Plan for European recovery by the WFTU, the non-Communist unions withdrew from the organization. Since then, the WFTU has been completely dominated by the Soviet Union, whose state-controlled unions are a major portion of its affiliated membership. The Soviets have been very successful, however, in having nominal leadership placed in the hands of trustworthy affiliates from other countries. Thus, for many years, France's largest union federation, the Confédération Générale du Travail (CGT), which is Communist-dominated, supplied the general secretary, the key administrative post in all international labor organizations. (The president of nearly all international labor bodies serves the international part-time and is typically the head of a major affiliate.) At the April 1978 congress, however, the CGT, in an ostentatious display of independence, closely related to the defeat of the left in the preceding French elections, refused to put forward a candidate; a Uruguayan exile in Eastern Europe was then placed in the post. CGT officials continue, however, to be prominent in WFTU-controlled bodies, and the CGT remains actively affiliated to the WFTU.

The Confederazione Generale Italiana del Lavoro (CGIL), the Italian Communist-dominated labor federation, disaffiliated from the WFTU at the same 1978 congress, but CGIL delegates continue to attend WFTU-controlled meetings as "observers." The CGIL is anxious to demonstrate such "independence" to maintain its role as part of the European trade union movement, which is discussed below. Two other Western union groups affiliated with the WFTU are the Spanish Comisiones Obreras and the Portuguese Confederação Geral de Trabalhadores Portugueses Intersindical. Both are Communist-controlled.

At the present time, the WFTU is concentrating its apparently considerable funds and energies on Third World countries—in Africa, the Middle East, Latin America, and Asia. The WFTU has established regional bodies for this purpose, often in conjunction with European satellite countries or Cuba. At its 1978 congress, for example, Eastern bloc countries dominated the gathering, but the largest number of attendees were unionists from Third World countries whose expenses were funded by the WFTU. The WFTU claims 190,000,000 affiliated members, but two-thirds are accounted for by the Soviet unions.

After its organization, the WFTU made strenuous efforts under Communist leadership to take over the international trade union "secretariats" (ITS), which had been organized for many years along industry or craft lines as international coordinating bodies for national industrial or craft unions. The ITS, however, retained their independence and do today, as we point out below. Thereupon, the WFTU organized its own secretariats, or "trade unions internationals" (TUI) as it calls them. A list of the TUI is found in Table II-3.

Unlike the independent free labor secretariats, the Communist TUI are departments of the WFTU, completely under the latter's central direction. Their significance varies, with those in the metals, chemicals, food, agriculture, journalism, and teaching fields being most visible. Often these TUI will be bypassed

TABLE II-3
*The Trade Unions Internationals
of the World Federation of Trade Unions*

Metal and Engineering

Oil, Chemical and Allied Industries

Food, Tobacco, Hotel and Allied Industries

Teachers

Journalists

Forestry and Plantations

Textiles, Clothing, Leather and Fur

Commerce, including Offices and Banks

Construction, Wood and Building Materials

Mining

Transport and Fisheries

---

and special committees established to attempt to accomplish an objective, such as to establish an international union-coordinating committee with Western nation unions for an industry or company, such as has been done for Solvay, the Belgian chemical company (chapter VIII), or for the paper industry (chapter XI).

The ICFTU. Organized in 1949 by the union confederations of the West following their withdrawal from the WFTU, the ICFTU affiliated the trade union centers of the democratic and prodemocratic countries of the world. It was extremely active during its first two decades, providing leadership to the international activities of the free world, providing a conduit of funds through its solidarity fund to assist the international trade union secretariats in their work and funding the less wealthy among them, and assisting union centers in the Third World. Beginning in 1969, however, the ICFTU suffered two damaging blows: the disaffiliation of the AFL-CIO and the formation of the European Trade Union Confederation (ETUC).

The AFL-CIO's disaffiliation in 1969 cost the ICFTU the loss of 25 percent of its membership and a considerable drop in its funding. Even before then, the ICFTU had been under financial stress as trade union centers in the United Kingdom, Germany, and the United States began shifting their aid programs away from the ICFTU to their own specially created organizations or to regional groups.[4] The AFL-CIO's disaffiliation was triggered by the threat of the ICFTU to permit the United Automobile, Aerospace and Agricultural Implement Workers (UAW) to affiliate with the ICFTU directly after the UAW had disaffiliated from the AFL-CIO. The AFL-CIO was then (as now) also concerned about the ICFTU's support of contacts with the WFTU and about its continuing propensity to concentrate criticisms against breaches of freedom in the West while giving little or no attention to deprivation of human rights in the Communist bloc.[5] Today, the ICFTU claims about fifty-two million affiliated members.

The ICFTU has established regional organizations in the Americas, Asia, and Africa, which are active in varying degrees depending upon the support engendered from principal trade union centers. In Europe, the formation of the ETUC in 1973, discussed below, has quite clearly put the ICFTU in a secondary role there. In the Americas, the Organización Regional Interamericano de Trabajadores is controlled more by the AFL-CIO than by the ICFTU; the Organization for African Trade Union Unity has greatly restricted ICFTU activities in that continent; and an Asian Trade Union Council is being considered by Southeast Asian countries even though the ICFTU maintains an Asian Regional Organization and P. P. Narayanan of Malaysia is president of the ICFTU.

The Secretariats (ITS). The most important labor organizations for the study of multinational collective bargaining attempts, with the possible exception of the European regional unions, are the international trade union secretariats (ITS). Many were organized prior to World War I and managed to reconstruct themselves after two disruptive world wars; others are of much more recent vintage. The older ones were originally totally European, emphasizing a socialist creed. Today, most of the secretariats have large North American and Japanese affiliated memberships, plus other affiliates from most continents. Table II-4 lists the secretariats.

---

[4] For an account of the state of the ICFTU, its finances, and the issues involved at the time of the AFL-CIO disaffiliation, see John P. Windmuller, "Internationalism in Eclipse: The ICFTU After Two Decades," *Industrial and Labor Relations Review*, Vol. 23 (July 1970), pp. 510-27.

[5] For compelling evidence on this point, see John P. Windmuller, "Realignment in the I.C.F.T.U.: The Impact of Detente," *British Journal of Industrial Relations*, Vol. XIV (November 1976), pp. 247-60.

TABLE II-4
International Trade Union Secretariats

International Federation of Building and Woodworkers (IFBWW)

27-29, rue de la Coulouvrenière
CH-1204 Geneva
Switzerland

President: Abraham Buys, The Netherlands
General Secretary: John Löfblad, Sweden
Membership: 3,500,000 (as of January 1977)

International Federation of Chemical, Energy and General Workers' Unions (ICEF)

58, rue de Moillebeau
CH-1211 Geneva 19
Switzerland

President: Karl Hauenschild, Germany
General Secretary: Charles Levinson, Canada
Membership: 4,573,987 members, 114 unions, 38 countries
                   (as of 1978)

International Federation of Commercial, Clerical and Technical Employees (FIET)

15, avenue de Balexert
CH-1210 Geneva (Châtelaine)
Switzerland

President: Günter Stephan, Germany
General Secretary: Heribert Maier, Austria
Membership: 6,359,833 in 179 unions in 80 countries
                   (as of May 1979)

Universal Alliance of Diamond Workers (UADW)

Plantin-en-Moretuslei 66-68
Antwerp
Belgium

President: G. Maters, The Netherlands
General Secretary: Albert Buelens, Belgium
Membership: 10,880 (as of December 1971, appears to be
                   defunct)

International Secretariat of Entertainment Trade Unions (ISETU)

c/o Gewerkschaft Kunst, Medien, Freie Berufe
Maria-Theresien Strasse, 11
A-1090 Vienna
Austria

President: J. Schweinzer, Austria
General Secretary: not presently known
Membership: 500,000 in 33 countries reported in May 1976
                   (as of July 1979, ISETU appeared to be inactive)

TABLE II-4 (continued)

International Union of Food and Allied Workers' Associations (IUF)

Rampe du Pont-Rouge 8
CH-1213 Petit-Lancy (Geneva)
Switzerland

President:	Sigvard Nyström, Sweden
General Secretary:	Dan Gallin, Switzerland
Membership:	2,082,289 (as of 1977)

International Graphical Federation (IGF)

Monbijoustrasse 73
CH-3007 Berne
Switzerland

President:	Leonard Mahlein, Germany
General Secretary:	Heinz Göke, Germany
Membership:	810,285 (as of December 1975)

International Federation of Journalists (IFJ)

I.P.C., Bd Charlemagne 1
1041 Brussels
Belgium

President:	Paul Parisot, France
General Secretary:	Theo Bogaerts, Jr., Belgium
Membership:	84,244 (as of 1977)

International Metalworkers' Federation (IMF)

54 bis, Route des Acacias
P. O. Box 325
CH-1227 Geneva
Switzerland

President:	Eugen Loderer, Germany
General Secretary:	Herman Rebhan, United States
Membership:	13,506,587 (end of 1976)

Miners' International Federation (MIF)

75-76 Blackfriars Road
London SE1 8HE
England

President:	Adolf Schmidt, Germany
General Secretary:	Peter Tait, United Kingdom
Membership:	1,269,825 (as of December 1973)

International Federation of Petroleum and Chemical Workers (IFPCW)

435 South Newport Way
Denver, Colorado 80224

President:	George Sacre, Lebanon (as of 1975)
General Secretary:	Curtis Hogan, United States
Membership:	Ceased all activities June 1975

TABLE II-4 (continued)

International Federation of Plantation, Agricultural and Allied Workers (IFPAAW)

> 17, rue Necker
> CH-1201 Geneva
> Switzerland
>
>> President: Tom S. Bavin, United Kingdom
>> General Secretary: Stanley G. Correa, Malaysia
>> Membership: 1,573,888 members in 76 unions in 50 countries (as of December 1976)

Postal, Telegraph and Telephone International (PTTI)

> 36, avenue du Lignon
> CH-1219 Le Lignon-Geneva
> Switzerland
>
>> President: Ernst Breit, Germany
>> General Secretary: Stefan Nedzynski, Switzerland
>> Membership: 2,770,183 members in 192 unions in 56 countries (as of 1977)

International Federation of Free Teachers' Unions (IFFTU)

> 111, avenue Bergmann
> 1050 Brussels
> Belgium
>
>> President: Eric Frister, Germany
>> Secretary General: André Braconier, Belgium
>> Membership: 2,445,089 members (as of January 1978)

International Textile, Garment and Leather Workers' Federation (ITGLWF)

> 8, rue Joseph Stevens
> B-1000 Brussels
> Belgium
>
>> President: Karl Buschmann, Germany
>> General Secretary: Charles Ford, United Kingdom
>> Membership: approximately 5,500,000 (as of July 1979)

International Transport Workers' Federation (ITF)

> 133-135 Great Suffolk Street
> London SE1 1PD
> England
>
>> President: Fritz Prechtl, Austria
>> General Secretary: Harold Lewis, United Kingdom
>> Membership: 4,409,883 in 378 trade unions in 83 countries (as of December 1976)

Public Services International (PSI)

> Hallström House
> Central Way
> Feltham, Middlesex
> England
>
>> President: Heinz Klunker, Germany
>> General Secretary: Carl W. Franken, The Netherlands
>> Membership: 4,772,068 (as of 1976)

The ITS vary considerably in size, strength, and activity. Largest and most important is the International Metalworkers' Federation (IMF), whose affiliates include such powerful unions as the German Industriegewerkschaft Metall, the United States United Automobile Workers, United Steelworkers, and International Association of Machinists and Aerospace Workers, plus large Japanese automobile, steel, and electrical unions. In size, caliber of staff, or by any other reasonable criterion, the IMF is literally in a class by itself.

Another secretariat to which we shall devote considerable attention is the International Federation of Chemical, Energy and General Workers' Unions (ICEF), which has probably received more press attention than any other secretariat thanks to the astute public relations of its secretary general. We shall find, however, that claims of action by the ICEF against multinational companies are usually not supportable by factual evidence.

A third but smaller ITS, the International Union of Food and Allied Workers, has been quite active in attempting contacts with multinational corporations, and the International Federation of Commercial, Clerical and Technical Employees is becoming increasingly active under its vigorous new leadership. The International Transport Workers' Federation, by reason of its strategically placed dock workers' affiliates, has been able to force shipowners to deal directly with it. A number of other secretariats figure in our analyses involving specific industries or incidents.

In ideology, the ITS have a socialist-liberal orientation, are non-Communist, and, with rare exception, do not affiliate Communist-controlled unions. They work with the ICFTU; most ITS general secretariats meet with ICFTU officials regularly and share much in common. The ITS general secretaries are, however, totally independent of the ICFTU, as already noted, and each answers only to his own affiliated union membership.

Related Internationals. There are, besides the secretariats, international organizations that are similar to the ITS in many respects but also quite different in others. These organizations are found principally in the air transport and communications and entertainment industries. These organizations are listed in Table II-5. Foremost among these is the International Federation of Air Line Pilots' Associations, which is primarily concerned with safety and technical matters but also with labor relations, as we shall discuss in chapter XVIII. Two of the communications and entertainment unions listed in Table II-5 have come closest

TABLE II-5
The Air Transport and Entertainment and Communications International Federations

I. AIR TRANSPORT

International Federation of Air Line Pilots' Associations (IFALPA)

Interpilot House
116 High Street
Egham, Surrey TW20 9HQ
England

President: Captain Derry F. Pearce, Hong Kong
Executive Secretary: Captain Laurie Taylor, United Kingdom

International Federation of Air Traffic Controllers' Associations (IFATCA)

6 Longlands Park
Ayshire KA7 LRJ
Scotland

President: Harry H. Henschler, Canada
Executive Secretary: E. Bradshaw, United Kingdom

Flight Engineers International Association (FEIA)*

905 16th Street, N.W.
Washington, D.C. 20006

President: William A. Gill, Jr., United States
Secretary-Treasurer: Karl F. Anderson, United States

II. RADIO, TELEVISION, AND ENTERTAINMENT

International Federation of Musicians (FIM)

Hofackerstrasse 7
8032 Zurich
Switzerland

President: John Morton, United Kingdom
General Secretary: Rudolf Leuzinger, Switzerland

International Federation of Actors (FIA)

30 Thayer Street
London WIM 5LJ
England

President: France Delahalle, France
General Secretary: Gerald Croasdell, United Kingdom

International Federation of Unions of Audio-Visual Workers (FISTAV)

14-16 Rue des Lilas
75019 Paris
France

President: Alan Sapper, United Kingdom
General Secretary: René Janelle, France

---

* This is an American union, affiliated to the AFL-CIO, which bargains for its American members as a national union but affiliates foreign unions and serves as a secretariat for them.

to multinational collective bargaining of any of the international labor organizations. Their experience is discussed in chapter XVI.

Like the secretariats, the organizations listed in Table II-5 affiliate national unions within their industries. Unlike the secretariats, however, they attempt a nonpolitical approach and affiliate unions both from the Communist bloc and from the Western democracies. How this works in practice is discussed in separate Wharton Industrial Research Unit studies.[6]

Another separate group is composed of "cadres"—managers and professionals who have formed organizations to ensure that they will receive their fair share of economic benefits. The cadres have an international federation that affiliates both national centers and specific professional or managerial groups. It is a strictly European group, headquartered in Brussels and known as the Confédération Internationale des Cadres.

The WCL. The World Confederation of Labour developed out of the European Christian (largely Catholic) labor movement. Originally the International Federation of Christian Trade Unions, which was founded in 1920, the WCL deconfessionalized and took its present name in 1968. It now expounds a strident anti-multinational corporation and leftist line and often is as Marxist as the WFTU.

The WCL has steadily lost membership in Europe. The latest blow was the disaffiliation of the French Confédération Française Démocratique du Travail, the deconfessionalized French federation. The recent merger of Catholic and socialist unions in the Netherlands could cause further losses for the WCL. Although it claims more, the WCL's affiliated membership is probably five million at most.

Like the WFTU, the WCL has announced that it will concentrate its efforts in the Third World. Its largest membership is in Latin America, but even there, its affiliate, the Central Latinoamericana de Trabajadores (CLAT), is not the leading federation in any country. The WCL has other affiliates in Quebec and Asia.

The WCL's secretariats are mostly quite small and not very significant. They are part of the central organization or of the CLAT, not independent. They do not figure except peripherally in any of our case studies.

---

[6] A separate study of the International Federation of Air Line Pilots' Associations will be published early in 1980; the study of the entertainment unions is now in progress.

Regional Unions

The formation of the European Trade Union Confederation in 1973 brought into being a significant organization of European trade union centers that is now recognized as the official spokesman for labor by the European Community. The ETUC affiliates not only the social-democratic unions but also the European Christian ones and the Italian Communist CGIL. The French CGT, however, remains outside its pale. The ETUC now claims forty million affiliated members.

The ETUC has no direct link with the secretariats. Moreover, it has established industry committees, most of which are separate from the secretariats also, thus weakening the latter in a key area of influence and power. Most important of these committees is the European Metalworkers' Federation (EMF), which has no direct link to the International Metalworkers' Federation. The EMF has pushed hard for multinational bargaining, as is discussed in chapters IV and V.

Another regional organization that should be noted is the Organization for African Trade Union Unity (OATUU). Established by the Organization for African Unity, the OATUU is intended to reduce the influence of the international labor movement in Africa. The WFTU has made strenuous efforts to influence the OATUU and has had several "fraternal" meetings with it.

Table II-6 lists these principal regional unions. Others which either exist now or have existed in Latin America and elsewhere are not significant for our analysis.

OBSTACLES TO MULTINATIONAL
COLLECTIVE BARGAINING

Before turning to multinational bargaining attempts in various industries, it seems prudent to note some obstacles to such bargaining. We merely list them here to put the discussion which follows in proper perspective. In the closing part of the book, they are analyzed in greater depth.

Different Legislation

No two countries have the same labor laws or practices; they differ even in such small neighboring lands as the Netherlands, Belgium, and Luxembourg. This means that bargaining rights,

TABLE II-6
Principal Independent Regional Union Centers

European Trade Union Confederation (ETUC)

    Rue Montagne aux Herbes Potagères, 37-41
    1000 Brussels, Belgium

        President: Wim Kok, The Netherlands
        General Secretary: Mathias Hinterschied, Luxembourg

European Metalworkers' Federation (EMF)
(Committee of the ETUC)

    Rue Fossé-aux-Loups, 38 (Bte. 4)
    1000 Brussels, Belgium

        President: Terry Duffy, United Kingdom
        General Secretary: Hubert Thierron, Belgium

Organization of African Trade Union Unity (OATUU)

    Accra, Ghana

        President: Alhaji Issifu, Ghana
        General Secretary: J. Dennis Akumu, Kenya

---

requirements and duties, union structure, bargaining structure, extent of rival or multiple unions, and a host of other factors are very different and difficult to reconcile from one country to another.

Employer Opposition

Employers see nothing to gain from multinational bargaining but rather further pressures and costs. Hence, they almost universally oppose it.

Union Questions

Union officials often verbally support multinational bargaining but, in practice, have questions. One significant fear is that such bargaining will result in a transfer of power from national union officials to those who lead multinational organizations. Another problem is how and by whom can autonomous national unions be committed to an agreement?

Employee Attitudes

There is little in the literature or practice to lead one to believe that employees in one country will happily lose wages to support workers in another. Although such action is not unknown, it has been rare.

CONCLUSION

The management and labor organizations on the international scene constitute a diverse group. There are formidable obstacles in the path of multinational collective bargaining. Yet much has occurred in a variety of industries which has been, or can be, portrayed as a step in the direction of such bargaining. In the next sixteen chapters, we examine the record on an industry-by-industry basis, sort out the facts, and then, in the final part of the book, analyze this record and the prospects for multinational collective bargaining.

PART TWO

The Automobile, Metals, and Electrical Industries

CHAPTER III

The Automobile Industry

The automobile industry is particularly important in a study of multinational industrial relations because it encompasses some of the world's largest employers and some of the most professional and financially sound international trade secretariats.[1] Table III-1 shows the major automobile-producing firms in the United States, Europe, and Japan. The labor organizations involved in the industry are the International Metalworkers' Federation (IMF), the largest and one of the oldest "international trade secretariats"[2] based in Geneva, Switzerland, and a relatively new organization—with which the IMF is often confused but with which it has no formal ties—the European Metalworkers' Federation in the Community (EMF), a Brussels-based European regional group.

THE IMF ORGANIZATION FOR MULTINATIONAL BARGAINING

Despite the fact that it dates back to 1894 and was officially organized in 1904, the IMF did not move toward multinational bargaining approaches until the post-World War II years. Prior thereto, it was a socialist-oriented organization devoted to the exchange of information among European unions. As late as 1959, a history of the IMF, written under the auspices of the United States Department of Labor, devoted only two paragraphs to the potential for bargaining coordinated across national boundaries.[3]

---

[1] For an earlier discussion, see Richard L. Rowan and Herbert R. Northrup, "Multinational Bargaining in Metals and Electrical Industries: Approaches and Prospects," *Journal of Industrial Relations*, March 1975, pp. 1-29.

[2] For succinct explanations of the organization of the world trade union movement and the role of the international trade secretariats, see the works cited in chapter II.

[3] U.S. Department of Labor, Office of International Labor Affairs, *The International Metalworkers' Federation* (Washington, D.C.: Government Print-

TABLE III-1

The Sixteen Largest Automotive Companies, 1978

Company	Headquarters	Sales ($000)	Assets ($000)	Net Income ($000)	Employees
General Motors	Detroit, Mich.	63,221,100	30,598,300	3,508,000	839,000 [k]
Ford Motor Company	Dearborn, Mich.	42,784,100	22,101,400	1,588,900	506,531 [k]
Chrysler Corporation	Highland Park, Mich.	16,340,700	6,981,200	204,600 [i]	157,958 [k]
Volkswagenwerk	Wolfsburg	13,332,059	9,978,630	275,671	206,948
Toyota Motor [a]	Toyota City	12,768,821 [g]	8,763,130 [g]	529,933 [g]	60,846 [g]
Renault [b]	Boulogne-Billancourt	12,715,866	9,815,903	2,222	239,447
Daimler-Benz	Stuttgart	12,090,806	7,066,451	295,054	167,165
Peugeot-Citroën	Paris	10,620,992	8,831,545	300,200	190,170
Nissan Motor [c]	Tokyo	9,751,661	8,407,754	371,790	93,652
British Leyland [b]	London	5,898,224	4,408,919	72,329 [i]	191,853
Fiat	Turin	5,323,540 [h]	5,705,507 [h]	88,062 [h]	124,320 [h]
Volvo	Gothenburg, Sweden	4,236,598	4,132,541	69,042	61,650
Honda Motor [d]	Tokyo	3,725,256	2,741,903	105,852	31,067
Toyo Kogyo [e]	Hiroshima	3,294,627	3,716,111	17,728	29,782
BMW	Munich	3,085,307	1,703,646	76,034	37,581
American Motors [f]	Southfield, Mich.	2,585,428	994,071	36,690 [j]	27,517 [k]

Source: *Fortune*, Vol. 99 (May 7, 1979), pp. 270-75; Vol. 100 (August 13, 1979), pp. 194-95.

a Figures are for fiscal year ending June 30, 1978.

b Government owned.

c Figures are for fiscal year ending March 31, 1978.

d Figures are for fiscal year ending February 28, 1978.

e Figures are for fiscal year ending October 31, 1978.

f Figures are for fiscal year ending September 30, 1978.

g Also includes certain subsidiaries owned 50 percent or less, either fully or on a prorated basis.

h Parent only.

i Loss.

j Reflects an extraordinary credit of at least 10 percent.

k Average for the year.

In 1949, however, the direction of the IMF began to shift. By then, American unions were playing a key role in the IMF for the first time. Under the leadership of Konrad Ilg, who in that year was both general secretary of the IMF and head of the Swiss Metal and Watchmakers' Union (and backed energetically by the late Walter Reuther, then the newly elected president of the United Automobile, Aerospace and Agricultural Implement Workers of America), the IMF was restructured into industry departments. From its inception until his death in 1970, Reuther headed the IMF Automotive Department, which, like those for iron, steel, and nonferrous metals; shipbuilding; and mechanical engineering, was organized in 1950.[4] A department covering electrical industry employees was established in 1967 and a department of occupational health and safety was organized in 1978.[5]

The Automotive Department and the Auto Councils

Since its formation, the IMF Automotive Department has been influenced heavily by the United Automobile Workers (UAW) in leadership and financial support. Personnel attached to the Automotive Department were originally led by Daniel Benedict, a former General Electric Company employee, who worked first as a UAW-IMF representative in South America and then, after serving as executive of the Automotive Department, became assistant general secretary of the IMF until his retirement in 1976. The election in 1974 of Herman Rebhan, formerly coordinator of the IMF world auto councils in Geneva and director of the UAW's International Affairs Department, as general secretary of the IMF has continued the UAW's influence in the Automotive Department.

In 1962, the UAW established a Free World Labor Defense Fund, which has been used in part to support IMF activities.

---

ing Office, 1959), p. 64. See also Everett M. Kassalow, "The International Metalworkers' Federation and the World Automotive Industry: The Early Years, Another View of the Forest" (Paper presented at the International Industrial Relations Association Third World Congress, London, September 3-7, 1973); and Karl F. Trechel, "The World Auto Councils and Collective Bargaining," *Industrial Relations*, Vol. II (February 1972), pp. 72-79.

[4] U.S. Department of Labor, *The International Metalworkers' Federation*, p. 14.

[5] Kassalow, "The International Metalworkers' Federation and the World Automotive Industry," p. 19, n.16.

The fund was created by a constitutional provision and financed by earnings on the investment of strike funds during 1962-74. By the end of 1964, a total of $4,346,221.49 had accumulated in the fund, and the UAW International Executive Board decided to suspend further additions because income from strike funds exceeded the Free World Labor budget. Disbursements continued to be made from the fund, and a deficit was finally created in 1970 coinciding with the depletion of the UAW treasury after a long strike in the United States automobile industry. Deficit spending occurred from 1970 until the end of 1973. The financial report for the year ended December 31, 1973, shows a beginning deficit of $1,521,308.19 in the Defense Fund, financed by a transfer from the General Funds in the amount of $1,948,345.98. Disbursements for 1973 were at the lowest point since 1963 at $409,780.25. Confusion over the financing and disbursing of the fund led to its abolishment at the 1974 UAW Convention. Disbursements for international affairs have since been made through the General Funds.[6]

From the beginning, Reuther urged the Automotive Department to organize itself for multinational bargaining by setting up separate subgroups for each major automotive concern and thereby increasing communications and cooperation among unions dealing with a common employer. Thus, at the 1953 Vitznau, Switzerland, meeting, he submitted a memorandum proposing "sub-councils to facilitate the exchange of data" that could "lay the basis for international coordination of collective bargaining with international companies."[7] This proposal was adopted but acted upon very slowly. Studies were made, largely through UAW efforts, of labor conditions in Ford and General Motors plants throughout the world. European unions, however, appeared considerably less interested in multinational bargaining than did the UAW—perhaps fearful that it was a device to reduce the foreign threat to American car makers by raising their standards to American levels and thus equalizing American and European wage costs. At the 1957 IMF Automotive Department Conference, the UAW succeeded in getting a number of foreign unions to send representatives to the United States,

---

[6] Financial data contained in *Solidarity* (UAW), for years stated. See report of Emil Mazey in *Solidarity*, July-August 1974, pp. 5, 7; and *Solidarity*, September 1974, p. 9.

[7] Kassalow, "The International Metalworkers' Federation and the World Automotive Industry," p. 8.

partly at its expense, to be present during the 1958 American collective bargaining negotiations and to inspect American practices and conditions in the automotive industry.[8] It was not, however, until the mid-1960s that the automotive councils were formally organized and began to operate as Reuther might have envisioned fifteen years earlier.

THE WORLD AUTO COUNCILS IN ACTION

The IMF finally gave its formal commitment for the creation of world auto councils at the 1964 IMF Fifth Automotive Conference in Frankfurt. Permanent councils were created for General Motors, Ford, and Chrysler at a meeting in Detroit in 1966, and subsequently, councils were organized for Volkswagen-Daimler-Benz (1966), British Leyland (1969), Fiat (1969), Renault-Peugeot (1971), Toyota (1973), Nissan (1973), and Volvo-DAF-Saab (1974). Renault became a separate council in 1974, and a Peugeot-Citroën Council was also formed in the same year. Some consideration is being given to the establishment of a Honda Council.[9] The world auto councils have been coordinated in Geneva by Herman Rebhan, now general secretary of the IMF; Burton Bendiner, who retired in 1977; and Collin Gonze, who was previously an assistant to Rebhan in the International Affairs Department of the UAW in Washington, D.C.

Reuther made it clear at the 1966 Detroit meeting that the purpose of the councils was to further international union cooperation that would eventually lead to multinational collective bargaining:

> When a GM worker discusses a problem at the bargaining table in Brazil or in Great Britain, in Canada, in Australia, in Germany, or in any other part of the world, he ought to know precisely what GM is doing about that kind of problem in every part of the world. He should not be talking about vacation pay as though he were the only one dealing with that problem; he ought to know precisely what everybody else is doing about that demand. What is true about vacation pay is true about every other basic collective bargaining demand whether it concerns pensions, holidays, wage rates, production standards, etc. because only as we can bring our collec-

---

[8] U.S. Department of Labor, *The International Metalworkers' Federation*, p. 17.

[9] International Metalworkers' Federation, *The IMF World Auto Councils* (Geneva, n.d.), p. 3.

tive effort to bear upon these practical collective bargaining problems can we really begin to give meaning and purpose to the slogans of international trade union solidarity.[10]

Prior to the meeting, the UAW research department, with the cooperation of the IMF and other unions, had prepared detailed analyses of the leading automobile corporations' production, profits, plant locations, and union contract provisions. These company booklets have served as guides for automotive bargaining throughout the world. Company officials interviewed attest to their significance. They point out that, especially among unions in underdeveloped countries, these booklets have led to increased aspirations and greater sophistication in demands and bargaining and that evidence of a "Detroit psychology" and UAW and/or IMF advice is generally present, particularly in South American countries' negotiations and those in various Asian countries as well.[11]

Since the 1966 conclave, the IMF Automotive Department and the world auto councils have met on a periodic basis. The Turin conference in 1968 emphasized the need for regional coordination and the UAW commitment to raise standards in Latin American plants, and the general IMF support for harmonization of plants in the European Economic Community and Britain. Detailed data on production, bargaining, labor conditions, and collective bargaining agreement provisions were distributed to unions in the industry and, as noted, have influenced union demands and bargaining ever since.

At the 1971 London conference, chaired by Leonard Woodcock, who succeeded to the presidency of the UAW upon Reuther's death, the delegates emphasized the need for common expiration dates of contracts, "so that the full weight of the totality of the firm's organized workers can be brought to bear upon each corporation, under conditions when all unions involved are free of contractual restrictions."[12] This call for common contract termination dates for all unions within a multinational auto-manufacturing company has been one of the auto councils' most fundamental and necessary goals. It is obvious, however,

---

10 IMF Automotive Department, *World Company Councils; Auto Workers' Answer to World Company Power* (Geneva, 1967), p. 7.

11 Major American automobile company officials, interviews, 1972-79.

12 "Declaration of London IMF World Auto Company Councils, 23-25 March 1971," *Reports of the Secretariat and National Affiliates 1968-1971, 22nd International Metalworkers' Congress* (Geneva, 1971), p. 137.

that multinational auto firms have been reluctant to permit this type of coordinated action and that they will undoubtedly continue to resist this IMF objective. Moreover, the different national bargaining systems make its realization difficult. In Germany, national bargaining in the metals industries encompasses the automobile industry; in Britain, a variety of disparate unions are involved; in Australia, procedures under the arbitration laws must be considered; and in several countries, the systems of bargaining involve not only national or multiplant arrangements but also local ones with local unions, works councils, or stewards' committees. A sorting out of these arrangements to achieve common bargaining arrangements would be difficult even if the major automobile concerns were inclined to cooperate.

The problems on the union side are further illustrated by the dissimilarity in priorities among the various auto council subgroups' objectives, which were enunciated at the 1971 conference. The General Motors Council, for instance, listed hours of work and security of employment as its primary concerns, while the Ford Council was more concerned with pension systems and health benefits. The Renault-Peugeot Council, on the other hand, was more interested in safety control and rest periods. This lack of uniformity was evident in every council except Chrysler, whose first priority was the same as that of General Motors, all of which serves to demonstrate further the immense problems involved in seeking a multinational agreement.

The 1971 London conference was held during the eighth week of a nine-week strike by fifteen unions against Ford in England. Leonard Woodcock, president of the UAW, joined pickets outside the Ford Dagenham stamping and body plant for a brief appearance. On the last day of the conference, a declaration of solidarity with the strikers was issued.[13]

Ford management in Britain was not able to detect any immediate effects of the IMF conference or of the declaration on the strike.[14] The parties reached a settlement at the end of the week following the IMF conference.

Several meetings of the world auto councils have been held since the 1971 London conference. Some of these meetings

---

[13] "Declaration of Solidarity for the Strike of British Ford Workers," issued by the International Metalworkers' Federation, Geneva, March 25, 1971.

[14] Interviews in London, England, and Dearborn, Michigan, 1972-73.

are discussed below and serve to illustrate the primary functions of the councils.

FORD

Ford Motor Company is the second largest automobile manufacturer in the United States and one of the largest multinational firms in the world. In 1979, the company employed 506,531 people and had sales of over $42 billion (see Table III-1).

At a Ford World Auto Council meeting in Geneva on June 14, 1972, sixteen union representatives from England, Germany, Belgium, the Netherlands, France, and Ireland concluded that they would propose a meeting with the management of Ford of Europe to discuss items such as short- and medium-term investment, production plans of Ford Motor Company in Europe, differences in working conditions and fringe benefits, and the feasibility of common expiration dates for collective bargaining contracts in European Ford operations. Representatives were urged to do everything possible to bring the dates of regional and plant contracts in line with one another.[15]

The then IMF general secretary, Ivar Norén, wrote a letter to the president of Ford of Europe requesting a meeting between management of Ford's European automotive operations, the IMF, and trade union representatives.[16] Ford of Europe declined the request, emphasizing the efforts that Ford national companies make to assure effective collective bargaining and consultative relationships at the national company level and expressing the belief that such meetings would hinder and confuse local and national company relationships.[17]

In December 1972, several months after Ford of Europe declined to meet with the IMF, the UAW requested a meeting with representatives of the UAW, IMF, and trade unions in Belgium, Britain, and Germany that represent Ford's employees to discuss production planning as it affects jobs and working conditions in Ford's European plants. Management at Ford's world headquarters in Dearborn, Michigan, refused this request,

---

[15] *IMF News*, No. 24 (June 1972), p. 2.

[16] IMF Auto Councils Press Release, No. 37 (June 1972) ; see also *Times* (London), June 15 and 16, 1972.

[17] Company interviews; and Robert Copp, "The Labor Affairs Function in a Multinational Firm," *Labor Law Journal*, Vol. 24 (August 1973), especially pp. 457-58. Copp is Ford's liaison manager in international labor relations.

stating that it would not have ongoing meetings with the IMF. It was agreed, however, that Ford's management in Dearborn would meet with representatives from the IMF secretariat for the purpose of affording IMF officials an opportunity to present their reasons for believing that Ford's interest would be served by following a different course than the one it had announced. The meeting was held on February 9, 1973, at Ford world headquarters. Representatives at this meeting included the IMF general secretary, assistant general secretary, and the coordinator of the world automotive councils; the UAW representatives included the vice-president for labor relations, the director of the Labor Affairs Office, and the liaison manager in overseas industrial relations.

The Dearborn meeting was brief, with most of the time spent by the IMF in an attempt to explore Ford's intentions in regard to investments abroad. No commitment was made by Ford to hold such further meetings.[18] Subsequent to this meeting, Ford of Europe was approached in May 1974 by the trade union side of the British "Ford" National Joint Negotiating Committee on behalf of the IMF to discuss the company's European investment strategy and, in particular, the anticipated effects of building a new plant in Spain. Ford's British management responded to the request by maintaining the view that the matter could be discussed by British union/company representatives in the joint negotiating committee. The chairman of Ford of Europe agreed to meet informally with local union and company managers in preparation for a profferred meeting by Ford of Britain's managing director with the National Joint Negotiating Committee.

Burton Bendiner, coordinator of the IMF world auto councils, announced at the IMF congress in Stockholm in July 1974 that "in Europe trade unionists will meet the director of Ford European subsidiaries. . . . The discussion at Ford's will concentrate on investments by this multinational in dictatorships."[19] An IMF Ford Auto Council meeting was held on November 4 and 5, 1974, in London, and the IMF states in its September 1974 *News* that

> high on the agenda will be a discussion of the Company's increased investment in a new plant now under construction in Spain, where

---

[18] Copp, "The Labor Affairs Function."

[19] *IMF News*, No. 23 (July 1974), p. 4.

the repressive government is making collective bargaining difficult. There is a possibility of an informal meeting with Ford of Europe management to discuss long term production policies of the company in Europe, as these affect members jobs and income security.[20]

The "informal meeting" did not materialize, and the next Ford Council meeting was held in October 1978.

The October 1978 meeting occurred at a time when Ford of United Kingdom was on strike. Thirty-two delegates from eleven affiliated unions in Germany, the United Kingdom, Spain, Switzerland, Belgium, and France attended the meeting, including General Secretary Herman Rebhan, Collin Gonze, head of the Automotive Department, and Press Secretary David Fowler from the IMF. A statement of solidarity was issued by the IMF which read in part:

> We delegates of IMF-affiliated Unions representing Ford Workers in Western Europe, have gathered here in London to demonstrate with our presence our solidarity with the 57,000 Ford UK workers, striking for decent wage increases, improved working conditions and better pensions. . . . We have met here today to examine the impact of this integration on our own jobs and on our production and assembly facilities. Some of us have already been laid off or had their worktime cut back. What we have learned we can bring back to our own unions to counteract the propaganda of Ford/Europe, for we are indissolubly linked together in a vast chain of labour solidarity.[21]

Delegates were asked to monitor any transfer of work or additional overtime work caused by the strike in their countries. As far as we can determine, no coordinated activity resulted from the meeting. The German delegates could not agree to a ban on overtime because IG Metall had actively fought for it in the most recent past and other delegates, such as the ones from Belgium, knew that their own national employee interests had to be protected. One can conclude, however, that the meeting did give moral support to the striking United Kingdom workers, and it provided the delegates a further opportunity to review Ford's policy of product integration. National union reports also provided a means of communication and enlightened the delegates on the general status of Ford of Europe's employee relations problems.

[20] *IMF News*, No. 28 (September 1974), p. 1.

[21] "Declaration," issued by the IMF Ford Auto Council, Geneva, October 19, 1978; see also "IMF's 'solidarity' in Ford strike," *Industrial Relations Europe*, Vol. VI (November 1978), pp. 1-2.

NISSAN MOTOR CO., LTD.

Nissan Motor Company, Ltd., is the second largest Japanese automobile concern. In 1978, it had sales of $9.8 billion and 93,652 employees (see Table III-1). Nissan has a number of joint ventures with local principals in such countries as Taiwan, Thailand, Singapore, and Malaysia and operates major facilities in Australia and Mexico.

Nissan World Council and International Union Relations

The IMF extended its automotive world council program to Japan in 1973 with the organization of such councils for Nissan and for Toyota, Nissan's larger rival (see Table III-1). Generally, the two councils meet together and then separate for some discussions. Among the activities that the Nissan Council adopted as its aims were "to cooperate in founding trade unions and strengthening them, and contribute from the angle of labour management relations to the improvement of the lives of the people of a country." [22] The enterprise union at Nissan and the Confederation of Japan Automobile Workers' Union (Jidosha Soren) have followed that policy with the much weaker unions in Southeast Asian countries and have also had direct contact with Australian automotive and Mexican automotive unions.

For example, in December 1973, intervention by Jidosha Soren and the Nissan enterprise union personnel succeeded in obtaining reinstatement for a union official at a parts plant serving the Nissan joint venture in Taiwan. A few years later, complaints were received from workers at the Nissan facility in Singapore. The Japanese union officials investigated and found that the management decisions were correct and so advised their Singapore correspondents. Jidosha Soren maintains an international department, which gives such assistance to unions in Southeast Asian countries and advises them, when requested, on negotiating, organizing, and other problems.[23]

Requests for assistance from unions in Southeast Asia come directly to the enterprise union or Jidosha Soren. At other times, aid is requested from the Japanese Council of Metalworkers' Unions (IMF-JC), to which all major electrical and

---

22 Ichiro Shioji, president of Jidosha Soren, keynote address at IMF Nissan and Toyota World Council Meeting, held in Japan, September 27, 1973, p. 7.

23 Jidosha Soren officials, interviews in Tokyo, July 1977.

metal-manufacturing company unions and/or confederations in Japan are affiliated. The IMF-JC coordinates IMF activities not only in Japan but also throughout eastern and Southeast Asia. In any case, the IMF-JC is kept informed, but the basic decision-making and action organization is the enterprise union, often with the assistance of the confederation's international department. Since the Nissan enterprise union is stronger and more aggressive than its Toyota counterpart,[24] it seems to have engaged in more international activities.

The contact with Australian automotive unions occurred in 1976-77, when Nissan was in the process of purchasing the former Volkswagen facilities there. After talking with Nissan company officials, confederation and Nissan enterprise union leadership conveyed the company's assurance to their Australian counterparts that the sale and purchase would involve no dismissals. This secured Australian union support for the transaction. Contacts made at IMF world council meetings were credited by Japanese unionists with encouraging and facilitating this exchange.[25]

The Nissan Mexicana Strikes

Nissan Mexicana, located in Cuernavaca, suffered strikes in 1974 and 1976 that illustrate both the increasing labor militancy in Mexico and the relations of Mexican labor with international labor groups.[26]

The 1974 strike began on April 1 and ended twenty-one days later. The principal issue was wages. The union demanded an

---

[24] This view was shared by union officials both from Toyota and Nissan. Interviews in Toyota City and Tokyo, July 1977. The practice of union officials rotating in and out of jobs with the union and back to the company at Toyota, and the relative isolation of Toyota in a company-dominated community are likely to be the contributing factors. For an interesting account of the evolution of Toyota and the community surrounding it, see Gary D. Allison, *Japanese Urbanism* (Berkeley, California: University of California Press, 1975).

[25] Jidosha Soren officials, interviews in Tokyo, July 1977.

[26] This strike has been commented upon in the *IMF News* by Professor Koshiro, Yokohoma National University, and by the coordinator of the IMF world auto councils. Because of some factual discrepancies, the Industrial Research Unit discussed the facts and issues with officials of Nissan and the Confederation of Japan Automobile Workers' Unions in Tokyo, July 1977, and with officials of Nissan Mexicana in Mexico City, August 1977. The facts as agreed on by these company and union officials are the basis of this account.

80 percent increase, the company offered 17 percent, and the
settlement provided for a 22 percent increase. The labor agreement was for two years, and when it expired on April 1, 1976,
the union again struck, this time for forty-seven days. Again,
the basic issue was wages, with the union demanding a 40
percent increase, the company offering 15 percent, and this
time a settlement of 20 percent.

The moving force behind these strikes was the Authentic
Workers Federation (FAT), which had won control of the Nissan Mexicana local union prior to the 1974 strike and which
also controls the locals at Volkswagen and at DINA Nacional.
The FAT is a Marxist, Christian-Democratic, radical group and
is affiliated with the Confederación Latinoamericana Sindical
Cristiana, headquartered in Venezuela, and with the World Confederation of Labour, headquartered in Brussels. The FAT
opposes Mexico's labor hierarchy and relationships with the secretariats, including the IMF. Nevertheless, it has maintained
at least a nominal membership in the IMF Nissan World Council. The FAT is aggressively antagonistic toward multinational
firms.

There are several accounts of the 1974 strike. Professor
Koshiro wrote:

> The union of Nissan Mexicana used to be affiliated to the IMF,
> but the left-wing faction within the union manipulated its secession
> from both IMF and the Mexican TUC, demanding a tremendous
> wage increase of 80 percent. Since the union still remained a mem-
> ber of the NWAC [Nissan World Auto Council], however, Ichiro
> Shioji, president of the JAW [Japan Autoworkers] and the NWAC,
> took advantage of this situation to mediate in the dispute. As a
> result, a 22 percent increase was accepted.[27]

The IMF also claimed considerable involvement in the 1974
strike:

> Coordinated efforts through the IMF Nissan World Auto Council
> in Geneva, by Ichiro Shioji, President of Jidosha Soren, the Con-
> federation of Japan Automobile Unions, Ivar Norén, IMF General
> Secretary and Fernando Melgosa, IMF Regional Representative
> for Latin America, resulted in a settlement including a 22 percent
> increase for Nissan workers in the Cuernavaca plant in Mexico. An

---

[27] Kazutoski Koshiro, "Comment," in *Multinationals, Unions and Labor
Relations in Industrialized Countries*, ed. Robert F. Banks and Jack Stieber
(Ithaca, New York: Cornell University Press, 1977), pp. 140-41. Koshiro
stated that Mexican Ford and Volkswagen had already reached an agreement for a 20 percent increase. Actually, Ford did have a negotiation in 1974,
and Volkswagen settled three months after Nissan for 24 percent.

unreasonable stance by the Company, in first making a contemptuous offer of only 1 per cent increase [*sic*] in the face of the union's demand for a 20-30 percent wage rise [*sic*], was overcome by the efforts of all concerned, spearheaded by the union leaders in the plant itself.[28]

A later IMF publication corrects the account to note that the company offered 15 percent, not 1 percent.[29] The coordinator of the IMF world auto councils summarized the series of events involving the 1974 strike as follows:

> The Coordinator's Office in Geneva was informed by cable by the IMF representative in Mexico City that the union at the Cuernavacos plant was on strike, involving about 13,000 workers. A wage increase was the chief issue; the union and management were far apart and an impasse had developed. In addition, there were complicating factors in the local situation: a group of dissidents was determined to embarrass the local union leadership.
>
> A first step was to inform Ichiro Shioji, president of the Confederation of Japanese Auto Workers and head of the Nissan Auto Workers' Union in Japan. Shioji helped the IMF inform the Nissan and Toyota councils. When the issues were made clear to him, Shioji discussed the Mexican union's demands with the parent company's industrial relations department and with the top management dealing with the company's Mexican subsidiary. Shioji had the backing of his own union and of the confederation, but he also had to listen to the Tokyo office's side of the story and to the version that it had received from the local management in Mexico City. This information was sent to the Geneva office and relayed to Cuernavacos. After denials, further explanations, clarifications, and eventual concessions on both sides, a final settlement was made 7 percent above the local management's original offer.
>
> Although it was not global union agreement, it was coordinated collective bargaining—Mexico City, Geneva, and Tokyo. A settlement would have been possible without the IMF Nissan World Auto Council, but undeniably it would have been a lot more difficult for the weaker Mexican affiliate of the IMF to reach satisfactory terms with the company. Also, it would have taken a good deal longer were it not for the assistance of the stronger Japanese union.[30]

Our investigation indicates that the IMF's role, as Bendiner reported, was limited but that of the Confederation of Japan Automobile Workers' Unions was more extensive. The FAT

---

28 *IMF News*, No. 16 (May 1974), p. 1.

29 *IMF News*, No. 22 (June 1974), p. 7.

30 Burton Bendiner, "World Automotive Councils: A Union Response to Transnational Bargaining," in *Multinationals, Unions and Labor Relations in Industrialized Countries*, pp. 187-88.

group has been more ready to permit the Japanese confederation a role than to deal through the IMF. Moreover, the Japanese confederation officials did not take a strong position in the situation but primarily attempted to ascertain the facts and to inform Nissan headquarters of what they learned and of their position regarding the dispute. They were an information channel but certainly not a part of a coordinated bargaining effort. There was no action or threats of action against Nissan plants in Japan or against those in any other part of the world. The dispute settlement, although very high, was in line with previously agreed upon bargains by Ford, Volkswagen, and other companies in the Mexican automobile industry.

The 1976 Strike

There appears to have been no IMF involvement in the 1976 strike. No mention of this strike appears in the 1976 issues of the *IMF News*. No Mexican union delegation attended the Nissan World Council meeting in Japan in 1975.[31] This could be because of lack of funds, as well as ideological differences, but the FAT group was still in control of the Nissan Mexicana local in 1976 and led the strike, which produced approximately the same results as the 1974 strike. The Confederation of Japan Automobile Workers' Unions maintained some contact with the local union during the strike, as they still do; but again, the contact was informational and limited by ideological differences. One additional factor that might explain the lack of IMF involvement in the 1976 strike is the apparent difficult relationship between the IMF regional representative for Latin America, Fernando Melgosa, headquartered in Mexico City, and General Secretary Herman Rebhan. Melgosa supported Daniel Benedict when Rebhan was elected general secretary of the IMF, and this has restricted Rebhan's ability to move as strongly as he would like in Mexico.

As these strikes illustrate, Mexican labor is beset with divisions, and in some areas, radical groups are in ascent. This both complicates international union relationships and requires that claims of international union action be carefully scrutinized.

---

[31] Revised list of participants for Nissan and Toyota World Auto Councils' second meeting, Japan, October 13-15, 1975, issued by the International Metalworkers' Federation, Geneva.

VOLKSWAGEN

Volkswagenwerk, headquartered in Wolfsburg, Germany, is the world's fourth largest automobile manufacturer. In 1978, it had sales of $13.3 billion and 206,948 employees (see Table III-1). The company was established by the Hitler regime as a state-owned enterprise. In 1972, 60 percent of the shares were sold to private stockholders. The remaining 40 percent is now equally divided between the German federal government and the state of Lower Saxony. In addition, one of the major private stockholders is the labor union-owned Bank für Gemeinwirtschaft. Support of government and bank representatives on the twenty-member Volkswagen Supervisory Board have aided Eugen Loderer, vice-chairman of that board and president of IG Metall and the IMF, in becoming a very powerful influence on Volkswagen policy decisions. In fact, Loderer chaired the latest annual meeting of the company's stockholders in West Berlin on July 4, 1979, because of the illness of Heinz Birnbaum, chairman of Volkswagen's Supervisory Board.[32]

Volkswagen has historically been a German company with limited multinational operations. There are five Volkswagen plants in Germany in addition to the huge complex in Wolfsburg, plus two more German plants of the company's NSU-Audi subsidiary. Outside of Germany, Volkswagen's largest affiliate is in Brazil. It also manufactures or assembles cars in Belgium, Mexico, and South Africa and, through a minority interest in firms, in Nigeria, Yugoslavia, and Indonesia. In 1976, Volkswagen sold its manufacturing facility in Australia to Nissan and disposed of a minority interest held in a firm in Spain. In 1978, it began operations in a plant near Pittsburgh, Pennsylvania, and has been plagued by labor problems ever since employees voted on June 9, 1978, to accept the UAW to represent them in collective bargaining. Disputes, strikes, and charges of unfair labor practices have arisen over such issues as disciplinary action, wages, and the allotment of workers' relief time.[33]

---

[32] See Alfred L. Thimm, "Decision-Making at Volkswagen, 1972-1975," *Columbia Journal of World Business*, Vol. XI (spring 1976), pp. 94-103. See also "A Former Blue-Collar Worker Will Preside at VW's Meeting," *New York Times*, June 22, 1979, p. D2.

[33] Information from Volkswagenwerk Aktiengesellschaft, *Report for the Year 1976* (Wolfsburg, 1977). For an account of the latest labor strife, see "UAW Charges VW with Unfair Labor Practices at Pennsylvania Plant," *Wall Street Journal*, June 22, 1979, p. 10.

The opening of Volkswagen's United States facility in 1978 and its announcement in July 1979 to expand facilities in the United States, Canada, and Mexico add a major dimension to its multinational status.[34] In the long discussion over whether the United States plant should be initiated, there was considerable communication between leaders of IG Metall and the United Automobile Workers. It remains to be seen whether the growth of the United States plant and other plants will induce IG Metall leadership to encourage multinational union-management meetings involving Volkswagen.

An IMF world auto council has existed for Volkswagen in combination with Daimler-Benz since 1966 and has met on various occasions.[35] Perhaps because the German union leadership may not desire it, there seems to have been little or no pressure for meetings with management. Since Eugen Loderer, president of both IG Metall and the IMF, is vice-chairman of Volkswagen as well, such a meeting could presumably be arranged, but apparently none has occurred. Moreover, there seems to have been no international involvement in the strikes that have occurred in the company's Mexican subsidiary.[36] The only international union-management meetings to which Volkswagen personnel have been a party involved the German and Belgian works councils and a meeting in Wolfsburg, Germany, from June 12 to 14, 1979.

Volkswagen considers the Brussels assembly plant a part of the same group as the German facilities. As a result of major cutbacks following the oil crisis, the Belgian works council, fearing (incorrectly) that its plant was being subject to more cutbacks than others, asked for meetings with the central management and works councils. Two such meetings were held—one in 1974 and one in 1976. The Belgian group visited Wolfsburg for one of these meetings, was given a plant tour, and talked to the top management and the German works council members. No international union personnel were involved. Future meetings are not being encouraged by Volkswagen management but will presumably be agreed to if one of the works councils strongly de-

---

[34] Leslie Colitt, "VW plans $2.7 bn expansion as sales leap in U.S.," *Financial Times*, July 4, 1979, p. 1.

[35] See, e.g., *IMF News*, No. 23 (July 1974), p. 4.

[36] See James L. Schlagheck, *The Political, Economic, and Labor Climate in Mexico*, Multinational Industrial Relations Series, No. 4B (Philadelphia: Industrial Research Unit, The Wharton School, University of Pennsylvania, 1977), pp. 34, 107, 134.

sires it. None has been held since 1976. The fact that the workers in the Belgian assembly plant are predominantly adherents of a Christian federation union (Confédération des Syndicats Chrétiens—CSC), which is not affiliated with the IMF, rather than a socialist one (Fédération Général du Travail de Belgique— FGTB), may be a factor in the apparent lack of enthusiasm for such meetings on the part of their German coworkers.[37]

The latest meeting of the VW World Auto Council was held in Wolfsburg from June 12 to 14, 1979. Approximately eighty delegates from Belgium, Brazil, South Africa, the United States, and West Germany attended the meeting "to compare wages, working conditions and the social and political conditions of their home countries." [38] General Secretary Rebhan opened the session and explained that

> The task of the IMF VW Council is to create a tight network of unions capable of coming to each other's assistance in ordinary day to day activities and for emergencies. . . . The effectiveness of your response will, in part, be a function of the degree of cooperation and trust you will have reached among yourselves . . . cooperation on broad bargaining goals; cooperation on health and safety questions; cooperation on a hundred issues concerning the destiny of VW workers as individuals and as members of IMF-affiliated unions.[39]

The meeting provided an opportunity for some union members to visit the company's headquarters for the first time and to meet their fellow unionists. Emphasis at the meeting was, as usual, on exchange of information and the need for cooperation and solidarity. There was no discussion of multinational bargaining as such; however, harmonization of working conditions continues to be a major concern and one that the IMF hopes to facilitate through sophisticated development and exchange of company information that can be used in a meaningful bargaining context in a given country.

One of the highlights of this meeting was the appearance of Volkswagen's president, Toni Schmücker, and personnel director, Karl-Heinz Briam. Both company officials addressed the delegates and answered questions. The IMF considered this a successful meeting and would obviously like to include management

---

[37] Volkswagen personnel officials, interview in Wolfsburg, September 12, 1977.

[38] IMF Press Release, No. 15 (June 1, 1979), p. 1.

[39] IMF Press Release, No. 18 (June 12, 1979), p. 1.

participation as part of their general strategy for world council meetings in the future.

PEUGEOT-CITROËN/CHRYSLER

On August 10, 1978, the Paris-based Peugeot-Citroën Company announced its intention to take over Chrysler's European operations, including major facilities in Britain and Spain.[40] The takeover has resulted in Peugeot-Citroën's becoming the largest automobile producer in Europe. It has been predicted that the establishment in Britain of manufacturing subsidiaries of a multinational company not based in England or the United States will have a major effect on both the British and European automobile industry as a whole.

The anouncement of the merger provoked the unions immediately to express a fear that Chrysler's twenty-three thousand employees in Britain and fourteen thousand employees in Spain would have their job security threatened.[41] The unions indicated that they would resist any efforts on the part of the merged company to make the British and Spanish operations merely assembly plants for parts produced in France.

An emergency meeting of the Chrysler World Auto Council of the IMF brought together union delegates from Spain, France, the United States, Britain, and Australia in Geneva on August 30, 1978, to discuss the merger and what appeared to them to be an absence of any job security commitments. They said:

> We pledge as IMF unions organizing at Chrysler and Peugeot-Citroën, to prepare ourselves for international solidarity action up to and including industrial action in case of attempted plant closures or other significant rationalization of production resulting in loss of jobs.[42]

The IMF also requested the French, Spanish, and British governments to demand several assurances from the company before approving the merger. These included "(1) guarantees that the jobs of 14,000 Spanish and 23,000 British workers and workers in French factories will be maintained; (2) guarantees . . . to pre-

---

[40] "Chrysler Quits Europe, Peugeot-Citroën picks up the bits," *Economist,* August 12, 1978, p. 69.

[41] "Union leaders of five countries pledge to protect Chrysler jobs," *Times* (London), August 31, 1978.

[42] "Unions threaten 5-nation attack over Chrysler," *Daily Telegraph* (London), August 31, 1978.

vent plants from becoming purely sites of robot assembly operations for Peugeot-Citroën." [43]

Subsequent to the union meetings, Jean-Paul Parayre, chairman of Peugeot-Citroën, attempted to minimize the possible employment effects of the merger and agreed to meet with the British unions to discuss the matter upon the intervention of Eric Varley, Britain's industrial secretary, but IMF-sponsored talks were rejected.[44]

The meeting between Peugeot-Citroën management and the British unions was held in London on September 13, 1978, without Parayre, who apparently wished to remain uninvolved. Union leaders, including Gavin Laird of the Amalgamated Union of Engineering Workers (AUEW) and Granville Hawley of the Transport and General Workers' Union (TGWU), were reported to be "reasonably satisfied" with the French management's assurances that no plant closures or loss of job opportunities were contemplated at present; however, a further meeting was refused, and the British government approved the merger on September 28, 1978.[45] It is expected that the company will move toward rationalization of its operations, and job protection will no doubt be tied to employee/union participation in increased productivity schemes. A second IMF meeting on Peugeot-Citroën/Chrysler was held in London on October 18, 1978, to review developments since the August meeting. The meeting established a permanent council of trade unions from France, Spain, Belgium, and the United Kingdom "to vigilantly monitor actions and promises of the company so as to guarantee job security and extend democratic trade union representation in all plants." [46] The IMF was successful through its council meetings in obtaining initial pledges from the company to provide job security for Chrysler's United Kingdom employees. On the other hand, the company has indicated that, "initially, we plan only to continue with the Chrysler operations as they are. But the next step is ration-

---

[43] *Ibid.*

[44] "Unions to meet Peugeot President," *Financial Times*, September 13, 1978.

[45] "Peugeot Pledge on Chrysler's Future," *Financial Times*, September 14, 1978; and "Government Agrees Peugeot takeover of Chrysler U.K.," *Financial Times*, September 29, 1978, p. 1.

[46] IMF Press Release, No. 28 (October 20, 1978).

alization, and that will be the key to profitability." [47] The IMF world council will have a difficult road ahead if British employees persist in strike threats and do not cooperate in the productivity schemes that their new French employer may have in mind. It should also be noted that the IMF has limited impact on the French union situation since the large Confédération Générale du Travail (CGT) is not an affiliate of the IMF, and there is an independent union situation in the Peugeot/Chrysler (Simca) operation.

VOLVO-DAF-SAAB

Volvo is the largest Swedish automobile manufacturer, with sales in 1978 of $4.2 billion and 61,650 employees (see Table III-1). The merger with DAF, the Dutch automobile manufacturer, effective January 1, 1975, and proposals for a merger with Saab in 1977 led to the formation of the Volvo-DAF-Saab World Auto Council.[48] There have been several meetings of the council, including one with Volvo management.

The Founding of the Council

The founding meeting of the Volvo-DAF Council occurred on December 9, 1974, in Amsterdam when union representatives from Svenska Metallindustriarbetareförbundet (Sweden), Industriebond-NVV (the Netherlands), and the Centrale des Métallurgistes de Belgique (Belgium) met at NVV headquarters to discuss problems associated with the takeover of DAF by Volvo. The stated objectives of the meeting were

—the formation of the IMF Volvo-DAF World Auto Council, the tenth such body formed on an automobile company basis by the International Metalworkers' Federation;

—a discussion of unemployment and layoffs in the two companies;

—and the question of an additional union representative on the DAF Board of Supervisors.[49]

---

[47] "Europe; Peugeot-Citroën's bold bid to be No. 1," *Business Week*, August 28, 1978, p. 44; see also Terry Dodsworth, "Chrysler Europe losses 'to show significant rise,'" *Financial Times*, July 4, 1979, p. 1.

[48] *IMF News*, No. 38 (December 1974), p. 1; "Facts and Figures About Volvo" (Report prepared for the meeting of the IMF Volvo-DAF-Saab World Auto Council, Geneva, September 27, 1977.

[49] *IMF News*, No. 38 (December 1974), p. 1.

The union members agreed that there was a "need for information and analysis of developments in collective bargaining in Volvo and DAF outside their home countries." [50] In addition, the delegates agreed to exchange information in regard to plant practices and workers' participation. Burton Bendiner, IMF coordinator, explained the work of the other world auto councils. The establishment of the council provided a liaison among the unions involved in Volvo's operations, and it has facilitated further meetings, held on September 27, 1977, and October 7, 1977.[51]

Council Meetings in 1977

The council arranged a meeting of twenty-five representatives of trade unions organized in the Volvo company and the Dutch and Belgian subsidiaries of Volvo at the IMF headquarters in Geneva on September 27, 1977.[52] The purpose of the meeting was to discuss the employment situation particularly in the Dutch and Belgium plants of the company. It was agreed that a meeting with top Volvo management should be held to discuss the company's investment policy and future production planning as it might affect employment and the use of subsidies from national government to curtail the loss of jobs. Unions represented at the meeting from Sweden were the Swedish Metalworkers, the Union of Clerical and Technical Employees in Industry (Svenska Industritjänstemannaförbundet—SIF), and the Swedish Foremen's and Supervisors' Association (Sveriges Arbetsledareförbund—SALF). The Dutch and Belgian unions represented were the Centrale des Métallurgistes de Belgique (CMB) and Industriebond-NVV. A special committee of representatives of the unions affiliated to the IMF, led by General Secretary Herman Rebhan, was selected to meet with the Volvo management, including Gert Gunnarsson, Svenska Metallindustriarbetareförbundet (Svenska Metall); Michel Cossaer, CMB; Bart v.d. Steenhoven, Industriebond-NVV; Stig Svensson, SIF; Arne Jonsson, SALF; Herman Rebhan, IMF general secretary; and Burton Bendiner, IMF world auto councils coordinator. The agenda for the planned meeting with management included the following subjects: the investment policy of Volvo as it affects employment; possibility

---

[50] *Ibid.*

[51] IMF Press Release, No. 7 (September 28, 1977); No. 10 (October 13, 1977); and Release from the IMF World Auto Councils, October 10, 1977.

[52] IMF Press Release, No. 7 (September 28, 1977).

of government subsidies to maintain operations and employment; production planning; production of the model 343; production of automatic and manual transmissions; and developments in the Volvo-Saab merger.[53]

On October 7, 1977, the union committee met in Eindhoven, Holland, in the presence of Pehr Gyllenhammar, president of Volvo, to discuss the production problems pertaining to the Volvo 343 model, which is manufactured in Born, Holland. Gyllenhammar and his associates indicated that the commercial prospects for the revised model of the automobile were good, and they indicated the need for the Dutch government to provide a substantial subsidy for the manufacture of the automobile.[54]

Volvo Agreement with Dutch Government

Volvo later held meetings with the Dutch government, both of which are shareholders in Volvo Car B.V., on the financial situation of the company. Early in 1978, Volvo and the Dutch government concluded an agreement on the financing of Volvo Car B.V. through the years 1978-80. According to Volvo, the agreement included the following items:

> 1) An increase of the share capital with app[roximately] 165 million-Scr with the Dutch National Investment Bank as shareholder. This reduced Volvo's ownership of the company from 75% to 55%; and 2) A temporary contribution to the result of the company by the Dutch government with app[roximately] 230 million-Scr for the period 1978-1980, repayable when the company has reached a sufficient level of profitability. During the same period Volvo will contribute app[roximately] 185 million-Scr.[55]

As the above indicates, the deal negotiated between the Dutch government and Volvo is more of "an act of mutual responsibility from the shareholders of the company" rather than an explicit act on the part of the government to subsidize the company.[56]

The Volvo/Ghent Strike

The IMF and the council have also been active at Volvo as the result of a strike at the company's Ghent operation.

---

53 *Ibid.*

54 IMF Press Release, No. 10 (October 13, 1977).

55 Letter from Volvo to the author, March 14, 1978.

56 *Ibid.*

In February of 1978, a new contract at Volvo/Ghent was negotiated and approved by all parties, including the unions and the government. Shortly after the agreement, a local strike broke out on March 28, 1978, in the car and light truck operations and spread to the warehouse locations.[57] When the Swedish unions heard about the strike, they indicated that they would refuse to handle the goods being produced in the Ghent operation while the strike was being conducted. The IMF also telexed the Swedish unions asking for their support of the Belgian workers.[58]

In response to the sympathy action announced by the Swedish unions, Gyllenhammar at Volvo said that the unions were acting irresponsibly and that their action broke the agreement the company had with the unions in Sweden. The Swedish unions in turn indicated that they would postpone sympathy action pending a decision on the part of the court, which ruled on April 14, 1978, that, since the Belgian strike was legal, the sympathy action on the part of the Swedish unions would be legal. The local strike in Belgium ended while the matter was pending in the Swedish court, and the Swedish unions did not have to conduct sympathy action.

Apparently, the IMF was unable to do very much in the strike situation, except for sending a telex supporting the union members, since it was not informed about the strike activity until it had been under way for several weeks. It is interesting to note, however, that the Volvo situation was used as an illustration of the principle of solidarity among automobile workers by General Secretary Rebhan in his speech before the World Automotive Conference held in Detroit during May 30-June 1, 1978. Rebhan said:

> The principle of solidarity among automobile workers, the right to refuse work from a struck plant, is so entrenched amongst auto workers that we believed it to be a basic right. Yet, when striking Volvo workers in Ghent, Belgium, recently called on Swedish Volvo workers in Göteborg to boycott work transferred from Belgium, they found themselves faced with a court case. Fortunately, subsequent proceedings in a labor court vindicated the Swedish metalworkers' stand, ruling that Swedish trade unions have the right to refuse to handle goods from the struck plant.[59]

---

[57] Letter from Volvo to the author, July 7, 1978.

[58] Interviews at IMF, May 17, 1978.

[59] Herman Rebhan, remarks before the IMF World Auto Conference, Detroit, May 30-June 1, 1978, pp. 6-7.

Rebhan concluded that "this only illustrates the need to draw our links so tight that the multinational corporations are made plainly aware that the IMF auto workers see an attack on auto workers anywhere as an attack on auto workers everywhere." [60]

Sympathy Action and the Swedish Court Decision

With the hope of clarifying the legality of sympathy action in Sweden, Volvo challenged the provisional court decision, and the Labor Court issued a verdict on December 6, 1978.[61]

Two questions were before the court: (a) whether members of Svenska Metall (the Swedish metalworkers' union) at AB Volvo were entitled to adopt measures in sympathy to the advantage of the strike at the Belgian subsidiary of the company and (b) whether the employees of the Swedish company were unhindered legally when they refused to accept work transferred from the Belgian subsidiary to the company plants in Sweden.

The Swedish Labor Court rejected the company's position in regard to (a) and rejected the union's position in regard to (b). The Swedish Labor Court found "that the Swedish metalworkers' union was entitled to use conflict measures to support CMB and CCMB [the Belgian unions] in connection with the conflict that occurred at Volvo Europa NV, Ghent, during the period March 30-April 20, 1978." [62] In this part of the verdict, it appears clear that the court found the use of sympathy action supportable under the law provided the strike is legal in the country of origin and the employees engaged in the sympathy action are acting as a union under Swedish law.

It is interesting to note that the Swedish union emphasized the importance of the international trade secretariats in pursuing its case. It stated:

> The international trade union organizations (EMF and IMF) are seriously active organizations. It must be assumed that they do not request support for illegal conflict measures in countries where strikes and other trade union conflict measures on the part of the employees are permitted. . . . The international trade unions have better resources than the Swedish trade union to determine whether a conflict measure is permitted according to the system of rules in

---

[60] *Ibid.*

[61] Swedish Labor Court Verdict No. 160/78, Case No. A66/78, December 6, 1978. See also *European Industrial Relations Review*, No. 61 (February 1979), for a review of the effectiveness of the Swedish Labor Court.

[62] *Ibid.*, p. 19.

a certain country. The Swedish trade unions should therefore depend on information from these international organizations as to whether a conflict measure is permissible and should not need to carry out its own survey into this matter. A survey of this type takes some time to carry out and sympathy measures lose their value if they cannot be adopted quickly.[63]

The employer parties responded as follows:

A request from an international trade union organization for sympathy measures cannot be sufficient in order to make such measures permissible. It is not always possible to presume that an organization of this type carries out a specially thorough investigation as to the permissible aspect of a conflict measure.[64]

The significance of the court decision lies in the fact that it supports the Swedish law permitting sympathy strikes across national borders and that it recognizes a perceived strength and competence in the international trade secretariats.

OTHER IMF ACTIVITIES IN THE AUTOMOBILE INDUSTRY

In addition to the work of the world auto councils, as illustrated in the preceding section, the IMF has conducted other activities in the automobile industry. Seminars, special conferences, solidarity messages, and assistance to unions in the developing world have all been used in an effort to focus on problems related to automobile workers. Some of these activities are discussed briefly in the following section.

Publicity and Australian Intervention

At the IMF's 1966 Detroit meeting, Reuther forged another tactic that has been utilized not only by IMF groups but also by other secretariats: amplification of the significance of meetings with company officials to give the impression that multinational bargaining is close at hand. Arrangements were made for the delegates to tour facilities and to meet with the top labor relations personnel at Ford and General Motors. According to an IMF account:

Although these were not collective bargaining sessions as such, delegates took the opportunity to make known a number of the

---

[63] *Ibid.*, pp. 4-5.

[64] *Ibid.*, p. 9.

stronger grievances, particularly those arising from the anti-union attitudes, unfair practices and reluctance to bargain on the part of company officials in various countries.[65]

The companies' version is that they agreed to the meetings most reluctantly and only on the clear understanding that there would be no collective bargaining discussion. When the delegates began discussing issues at various foreign plants, the United States industrial relations personnel referred them to their respective home plants.[66] The net effect of the 1966 conclave was a propaganda coup for the IMF auto councils and a basic wariness on the part of General Motors and Ford in meeting with international union groups.

Even before the 1966 meeting, the UAW evidenced its international concern by sending officials to Australia to support the case of the union representing employees of General Motors-Holden's Pty. Ltd., General Motors' Australian affiliate. The Australian union demanded "a prosperity loading of $6 p.w. for some 17,000 employees of the company" in a case before Australia's Commonwealth Arbitration Court.[67] The court denied the union position:

> The union case had some unfortunate aspects: it followed the American precedent, especially observable in the vehicle industry, of "picking off" either the most vulnerable or the most prosperous employer in the field, obtaining a contract from that employer, and then following this up by claims for a similar contract with other employers in the same field. The origin of the dispute was a claim, backed by strike action, against G.M.-H. two years ago and this was reinforced by calling in aid the evidence of the regional director of the United Automobile Workers Union most directly concerned with that union's relations with General Motors Corporation in the U.S., Mr. E. S. Patterson. Mr. Patterson's evidence was obviously meant to be the lynch-pin of the union's case, but it was bypassed by the Commission on the ground that the internal affairs of General Motors, whether in Australia or the U.S., were no concern of the Commission: its main concern was with the principle of uniformity between employees doing the same class of work, the principle of comparative wage justice.[68]

---

[65] International Metalworkers' Federation, *World Company Councils: Auto Workers' Answer to World Company Power* (Geneva, 1967), p. 28.

[66] Interviews with company officials, and company transcript of meetings in authors' possession.

[67] The decision was handed down on September 12, 1966, and is found in 1966 A.I.L.R. Rep. 323.

[68] See "Legislation and Decisions," *Journal of Industrial Relations* (Australia), Vol. 8 (November 1966), pp. 301-2.

General Motors's corporate officials did not participate directly in the case, although they undoubtedly supplied information to their Holden affiliate from the wings. Their concern was that any appearance before the Commonwealth Commission would lend credence to the UAW claim that strings were pulled from Detroit and that, if the commission were to consider the total corporation profit picture, not just the Australian operation, in making its award, as the UAW and the Australian Vehicle Builders desired, a big step toward multinational bargaining might occur.[69]

"Flying Seminars," 1974

In the fall of 1974, the IMF world auto councils conducted a series of meetings, known as "flying seminars," to assist local union leaders in the Latin American countries of Venezuela, Brazil, Argentina, Colombia, and Mexico.[70] Topics covered during the seminars included preparation of collective bargaining, grievance handling, union structure, and training methods for shop stewards. Lectures were given by representatives from the UAW in the United States, IG Metall in West Germany, Confédération Générale Démocratique du Travail (CFDT) and Force Ouvrière (FO) in France, as well as staff from the IMF offices in Mexico City and Geneva.

These seminars were intended to develop and strengthen the ability of local union members to conduct their affairs more effectively on a day-to-day basis. The union team had an opportunity to visit several plant locations, including Volkswagen do Brazil in São Bernardo do Campo and General Motors and Peugeot outside Buenos Aires; further, a meeting was arranged with the industrial relations director of SOFASA, a Colombian subsidiary of the Renault Company.

At the conclusion of the sessions held in each country, a working meeting was conducted in Mexico City, where results of the seminars were summarized and the political situation in the countries discussed. The IMF has attempted to follow up some of the activities begun in the seminars, and there has been a particular effort made to assist Brazilian trade unionists in

---

[69] These views are ascribed to General Motors by the authors after discussions with GM personnel.

[70] Documentation on this section is found in *IMF News*, No. 27 (September 1974), p. 3; and No. 32 (October 1974), pp. 1-2.

the strikes of 1978 and 1979. It is an extremely expensive operation, however, to assist Latin American affiliates who are generally unable to pay dues. This fact, of course, limits the work of all secretariats attempting to manage programs in Latin America, and many times, support must be sought through agencies such as the American Institute for Free Labor Development (AIFLD).

Latin American Automotive Conference, 1976

The IMF held its second Latin American and Caribbean Automobile and Agricultural Implement Conference in Valencia, Venezuela, from September 27 to 29, 1976.[71] Approximately sixty-five delegates attended the meeting from Brazil, Mexico, Argentina, Venezuela, Peru, Colombia, Chile, Panama, the Dominican Republic, Jamaica, and Curaçao. Most of the conference was taken up with reports of delegates who explained "conditions in the automobile plants in their countries and emphasized the special problems relating to confrontation with governments and management."[72] For example, José Rodriguez, vice-president of the IMF for Latin America and secretary general of SMATA in Argentina, "analysed in detail the political situation in Argentina, describing the dangerous and difficult position in which the trade unions now find themselves with intervention by the military in their administration"; "the Venezuelan and Peruvian delegates reported on employee benefits in the automobile plants in their countries"; and "the Chilean and Brazilian representatives described the policy of their unions in handling non-political matters strictly within their province."[73]

Two reports were produced for the conference. Report I contains statistical data that, according to the IMF,

> [provides] the union organizations defending the rights and interests of the Latin American auto workers with all necessary information to give them a growing knowledge of the industry in which they work, which is marked by a constantly shrinking number of powerful multinational giants, especially the data on production, sales and earnings in worldwide operations; investment, employment, production and sales in operations of their affiliates and

---

[71] Documentation for this section is found in *IMF News*, No. 20 (November 1976), pp. 2, 6.

[72] *Ibid.*, p. 2.

[73] *Ibid.*

subsidiaries in the various regional countries; to locate exactly for a worker in an auto company his place with regard to his compatriots working in other companies and his brothers who are employed by the same multinational corporation, in other countries of this continent and the rest of the world; and finally, to achieve an ever-upward parity, at the highest levels, of wages, working conditions, etc., using the examples of the best gains in each contract in different countries.

The periodic publication of the up-dated comparative tables has meant a very important saving in time and effort for the auto unions and their leaders, who no longer have to ask in person or by mail, as they used to do, to have each contract, pact, agreement and effective law in each country sent to them, and then proceed to interpret and compare them, with the obvious difficulties involved. The IMF tables and statistics have been used in a practical way at educational seminars for training union negotiators, and have been a useful tool in their hands when the time comes to sit down and talk with management representatives about new contracts or renewal of old ones.[74]

Report II of the conference contains information on

the relations between Latin American subsidiaries and parent companies with respect to investment policy and production planning. . . . In addition to covering production and investment there is a summary of the essential work conditions in the plants of parent companies. Information is also given, where it exists, on programs for worker participation in decision-making and work humanization.[75]

These reports represent the IMF's extensive efforts in attempting to provide to affiliates information that can be used in bargaining and toward achieving the overall objective of harmonizing working conditions across national boundaries in particular industries.

European Automobile Conference, 1976

Approximately 270 delegates from national union affiliates attended the IMF European Automobile Conference in Munich, West Germany, from May 10 to 13, 1976. In addition to the European delegates, observers from the United States and Japan attended the meeting. The major themes of the conference were

---

74 Report I (Prepared for the Second IMF Latin American and Caribbean Automobile and Agricultural Implement Conference, Valencia, Venezuela, September 27-29, 1976), pp. 1-2.

75 "Latin American Automotive Subsidiaries," Report II (Prepared for the Second IMF Latin American and Caribbean Automobile and Agricultural Implement Conference, Valencia, Venezuela, September 27-29, 1976), p. 1.

"Employment, Work Humanisation, Industrial Democracy, and The Future of the European Automotive Industry." [76]

The conference concept permits the IMF to bring together unionists on an occasional basis to share information and to become better acquainted with regional and/or worldwide labor problems in a particular industry. As the IMF points out: "The Conference afforded an excellent opportunity for coordination of activities among the unions on a company basis, involving significant separate meetings between representatives of unions in Volvo and DAF as well as important private talks between representatives of British and Japanese auto workers unions." [77] The declaration of the European conference calls upon the IMF "to intensify the activities of the existing world auto councils, which should in particular follow very closely the actions of the multinational companies." [78] In general, because of personnel and financial limitations, a conference declaration does not lead to increased activity at the IMF level; for example, the world auto councils have always been coordinated by one staff person, who would find it extremely difficult to carry out extensive new demands emanating from conferences that are regularly conducted by the secretariat. The 1979 IMF Calendar of Activities shows only one meeting of the world auto councils scheduled; however, emergency meetings will likely be held to respond to immediate problems that may arise.

One of the most important aspects of the conferences appears to be that of informing not only union members but also government officials about the concerns of the secretariat. Prominent governmental officials generally attend and address the conferences. Jack A. Peel, director of industrial relations for the European Commission, addressed the 1976 conference on work humanization and listened to the delegates' views. Views expressed by union officials before governmental representatives are usually considered very carefully and, many times, are translated into public policy proposals.

---

[76] *IMF News*, Special Edition, No. 10/11 (May 1976); "What's Ahead for the European Auto Industry: Employment, Work Humanisation and Industrial Democracy," Report I; "What's Ahead for the European Auto Industry: Its Position in the World and Main Social and Structural Problems," Report II (Prepared for the European Automotive Conference, Munich, May 10-13, 1976).

[77] *IMF News*, Special Edition, No. 10/11 (May 1976), p. 7.

[78] *Ibid.*, p. 8.

The 1978 World Auto Conference

An IMF world auto conference was held in Detroit, Michigan, from May 30 to June 1, 1978, on the theme "Auto Workers and the Future of the World Auto Industry." Four background volumes were prepared by the IMF and presented to the delegates. These were *Worldwide Developments, Role of the Auto in Society; International Comparisons of Wages and Working Conditions; National Industry Profiles, Pollution and Energy, Company Reports;* and *What's Ahead?* (which includes an analysis of important elements of national and company competition affecting the livelihood and security of autoworkers).[79] Company reports were prepared and circulated for Peugeot-Citroën, Renault, Nissan Motors, Toyota Motors, Volkswagen, British Leyland, Chrysler, Ford, and General Motors.

The conference was attended by approximately 130 union representatives from twenty-five countries.[80] There was some concern on the part of conference planners that the leaders of some of the major trade union affiliates were not present. Seated at the speakers' platform for the conference were Douglas Fraser, president of the UAW and the IMF Automotive Department and chairman of the conference; Pat Greathouse, vice-president of the UAW and principal negotiator for the United States agricultural implement industry; Herman Rebhan, general secretary of the IMF; Hans Mayr, vice-president of IG Metall; Collin Gonze, coordinator of the IMF world auto councils; David Fowler, press officer of the IMF; Karl Casserini, assistant general secretary of the IMF; and Ichiro Shioji of the IMF-Japan Council.

Some of the trade union leaders who attended the meeting were Len Townsend, Australian Vehicle Builders Employees' Federation; Robert White, new head of the UAW in Canada; Michel Faure of the FO in France; Bernard Poirier of the CFDT in France; Hans Mayr of IG Metall in Germany; Reg Birch of the AUEW in Great Britain; Gren Hawley of the TGWU in Great Britain; Yoshiyuki Ishikawa of Jidosha Soren in Japan; Carlos Pardo of the Unión General de Trabajadores in Spain;

---

[79] All volumes published by the International Metalworkers' Federation, Geneva, 1970.

[80] "IMF World Auto Conference," IMF Press Release, No. 11 (May 12, 1978).

Jesus Perez of the Venezuelan Metalworkers; and Yngve Lind of Svenska Metall in Sweden.[81]

The conference agenda included presentations on the following topics: "Auto Workers and the Future of the Industry"; "The Motor Vehicle, 1980-2000—Can Needs be Met?" presented by Dr. Lars Brising, member of the Royal Swedish Academy of Engineering Sciences; "The World Auto Industry—What's Ahead for Companies and Unions?" by Michael Hinks-Edwards of the Economic Research Department of Eurofinance S.A. in Paris; "New Directions in Collective Bargaining," by Karl Casserini of the IMF; and "What's Ahead for the World Auto Councils?" by Collin Gonze of the IMF.[82]

On the afternoon of the second day of the conference, the delegates representing workers employed by General Motors, Ford, and Chrysler in their respective countries assembled and were transported to company headquarters for brief meetings with management in the companies.[83] For example, approximately twenty delegates went to Ford world headquarters for lunch and for brief presentations by Ford's vice-president of labor relations, executive director of the labor relations staff, director of the Labor Relations Services Office, assistant director of the Hourly Benefits Planning and Administration Office, and international labor affairs manager. Ford's managers discussed briefly the relationship between Ford and the UAW in the United States, programs for employment and training, programs for employment and income security, and some of Ford's announced plans for additional investment.[84] The meeting was cordial and was followed by a few questions from the delegates. Similar brief meetings were held at the General Motors and Chrysler headquarters. Meetings with the companies were closed to the press, and the UAW appeared to be pleased with the conduct of the meetings.

---

[81] List of participants for IMF World Auto Conference, Detroit, May 30-June 1, 1978, issued by the International Metalworkers' Federation, Geneva.

[82] Provisional agenda for IMF World Auto Conference, Detroit, May 30-June 1, 1978, issued by the International Metalworkers' Federation, Geneva.

[83] Ralph Orr, "World Auto Unions Eye Multinationals," *Detroit Free Press*, May 31, 1978, pp. A3, A14; and Mark Lett, "Ford hosts unionist from German plant," *Detroit News*, June 1, 1978.

[84] Information supplied by Ford Motor Company, June 1, 1978.

The conference declaration emphasizes the work of the IMF in developing strong unions and in seeking harmonization of working conditions:

> Our fundamental task remains to help to establish strong unions capable of meeting the challenge of multinational corporations at the national and international level.
> In this task we seek . . .—to harmonize internationally our conditions of employment to the highest possible level, erasing the gap between workers in industrial and developing countries.[85]

By 1978, it was clear that the IMF was considering a communication and assistance program to affiliated unions leading toward harmonization of working conditions as a major objective.

Conclusion

The IMF world auto councils and conferences have provided an effective means to stimulate interest and to disseminate information among trade union affiliates. Company studies prepared by the IMF have been generally well done and professional. These activities may be viewed as serving the IMF objective of facilitating harmonization of working conditions in the automobile industry. On the other hand, there is little or no evidence of any actual multinational bargaining having taken place between the IMF and a multinational firm. This is clearly summarized in a speech by UAW President Douglas Fraser, who chaired the 1978 Detroit World Auto Conference on the future of the world auto industry:

> Some day it's possible we'll see some form of worldwide collective bargaining, but that day appears to be far off. . . . Workers around the world have common goals and aspirations even though the implementation varies based on the situation facing each group. We must continue the progress which has been made toward harmonization of working conditions, wages, and benefits.[86]

Fraser and Rebhan, of course, will continue to push for meetings between trade unions and corporate management on a worldwide basis. There appears, however, to be no inclination on the part of management to receive international trade secretariat representatives except during exceptional periods, such as at a time when a world conference is in session and the IMF arranges

---

[85] "Declaration of the IMF World Auto Conference," issued by the International Metalworkers' Federation, Geneva, pp. 1-2.

[86] *News from UAW*, May 30, 1978, p. 2.

a company visit through a national union affiliate. Worldwide collective bargaining does, indeed, appear to be "far off" in the automobile industry.

THE EMF AND THE AUTOMOBILE INDUSTRY

The European Metalworkers' Federation was formed in 1971 and affiliates metalworkers' unions from nine European Community countries, Norway, and Sweden and has admitted Greek, Spanish, and Finnish metal unions to associate status. Although its founding members were all IMF affiliates, the EMF did not directly affiliate to the IMF. Today, the EMF is a recognized committee of the European Trade Union Confederation, and its relationship to the IMF is that of a cooperating but independent body. Regular communications occur between the two metalworkers' groups, and the officers of each attend the executive committee meetings of the other. Eugen Loderer serves as president of IG Metall and the IMF, respectively, and as vice-president of the EMF, and it appears that he has acted as a restraining influence over EMF initiatives with respect to certain industries and multinational companies.

The EMF Executive Committee contains special committees and working groups to generate discussion and studies and to coordinate activities in special areas, in branches of the European metals industry, and with certain European companies. The EMF maintains a working group for the automobile industry, among others. This group was originally structured as two company committees for Fiat-Citroën-Berliet and KHD-Savien-Volvo-DAF. Never truly operative, soon obsolete as these companies developed new corporate structures, and conflicting directly with IMF policy regarding its responsibility for world auto councils, both EMF committees were dissolved, and a sector committee oriented strictly toward European Community affairs was established.

The EMF's attempts to meet with the Association of European Automobile Manufacturers have so far been blocked by the Western European Metal Trades Employers' Organization (WEM). Nevertheless, the working group meets to exchange information and to formulate positions that are then submitted to the European Commission; the commission, in turn, has requested the EMF to submit a report on working conditions in the automobile industry in Europe. This report was completed in 1977 and presented jointly by the IMF to the commission.[87]

CONCLUSION

The International Metalworkers' Federation and the European Metalworkers' Federation have been among the most professional and effectively led international trade secretariats in the world. Multinational collective bargaining has not been achieved by either group; however, harmonization of working conditions has become a more realistic goal. Support of national union affiliates through information exchange and solidarity actions has been effectuated in many instances. In the most recent past, IMF officers have been elected to supervisory boards in West Germany, and this is likely to enhance the position of the secretariats further in dealing with multinational firms. Employers in the metals industries will continue to find the IMF and the EMF organizations to be reckoned with in the future.

In addition to the work of the free trade union movement, the Communist organizations have also been active in the metals field. The Trade Unions International of Workers in the Metal Industries (TUI Metal), which belongs to the World Federation of Trade Unions, held its eighth international meeting in Warsaw, Poland, from November 19 to 23, 1978. The conference was claimed to have brought together 172 representatives of seventy national trade union organizations from forty-nine countries.[88] As indicated in statements made at the 1978 conference, TUI Metal, of course, views the multinational firm in a far different light than that in which the IMF and the EMF view it: "It is not enough generally to speak about negative effects of multinational corporations. It is time to ACT against EACH corporation separately. The struggle against financial and industrial domination means the struggle with imperialism itself." [89]

---

[87] Commission of the European Communities, Employment and Social Affairs Directorate, *Report on the Working Conditions in the European Automobile Industry* (Presented by the EMF and IMF: First Part: changes in the working conditions; organisation and humanisation of work; economic and industrial democracy; Second Part: comparative tables concerning the structure of employment, wage systems, working hours and complementary systems of social security) V./900./77-E, and V./900./77-EN, respectively.

[88] *Informations* (Union Internationale des Syndicats des Travailleurs de la Metallurgie), Special Issue, No. 10 (November 1978), p. 1.

[89] *Ibid.*, p. 3.

The basic document prepared for the 1978 conference of TUI Metal, "Metalworking unions in Action," denounces the "brutal exploitation" [90] by the multinational firm and indicates that the EMF, through discriminatory practices against certain national organizations, will not "become the real instrument of united trade union action which all in this part of the world would like." [91] Communist influence is more heavily felt in the under-developed areas, and the free trade unions constantly feel the competitive menace of the Communist groups.

---

[90] World Federation of Trade Unions, Trade Unions International of Workers in the Metal Industries, *Metalworking Unions in Action*, Bulletin No. 3, December 1978, Special Issue (Adopted by the VIIIth International Trades Conference of Metalworkers, Warsaw, Poland, November 19-23, 1978), p. 43.

[91] *Ibid.*, p. 5.

CHAPTER IV

Other Metals and Mining Industries

The International Metalworkers' Federation (IMF) and the European Metalworkers' Federation (EMF) have been active in several industries in addition to automobiles as discussed in chapter III. This chapter analyzes the activities of the secretariats in the aerospace, agricultural equipment and construction machinery, metal can, nickel, aluminum, ball bearings, steel, and shipbuilding industries.

THE AEROSPACE INDUSTRY

The aerospace industry has been dominated by United States companies since World War II. Today, the Boeing Company of Seattle, Washington, has a commanding lead in the number of commercial transport planes in operation and on order, while McDonnell Douglas, Lockheed, the Convair Division of General Dynamics, the Aerospace Division of Rockwell International, Grumman, and Northrop are other worldwide leaders. Similarly, the aircraft engine business is led by two American companies— the Pratt & Whitney Division of United Technologies and the aircraft engine divisions of the General Electric Company.[1]

Europe also boasts a significant number of aircraft concerns, but all much smaller than their American counterparts. These include British Aerospace, an amalgam of companies nationalized by the Labour government in the mid-1970s; Rolls-Royce, a strong competitor of Pratt & Whitney and General Electric in engines;

---

[1] For information on the industry, see *Aerospace Facts and Figures* (Annual compilation published for the Aerospace Industries Association of America, Inc., by *Aviation Week and Space Technology*); "Aerospace," *Financial Times*, June 4, 1979, pp. I-XII; "Aeronautics Industry; Statistics on the Labour Market," *Europe*, June 30, 1979, p. 10; and "Trade Unions and Collective Bargaining in the Aerospace Industry," "Aerospace Company Profiles, Co-Production, and Country Profiles," "The World Aerospace Industry Today" (Prepared for the IMF World Aerospace Conference, Seattle, Washington, May 22-24, 1979).

Avions Marcel Dassault-Bréguet and Aerospatiale (SNIAS), two French concerns; the soon-to-be-dissolved German-Dutch union, VFW-Fokker; the Germany company Messerschmitt-Bölkow-Blohm (MBB) ; and Aeritalia, Italy's largest aerospace company. Finally, Japan, through its Civil Transport Development Corporation, has created a consortium of the aircraft-manufacturing divisions of three companies—Mitsubishi Heavy Industries, Kawasaki Heavy Industries, and Fuji Heavy Industries. Table IV-1 contains relevant information on the leading aerospace companies.

The dominant American companies are not multinational in that they do not manufacture aerospace bodies or engines outside of the United States, except for some Canadian operations. Several, however, have minority interests in European companies. Northrop has significant minority interests in three Spanish, one Japanese, and one French company and a 20 percent interest in VFW-Fokker. Moreover, to satisfy national aspirations, joint ventures or subcontracting across national borders are not infrequent. The General Dynamics production of the F-16 military plane is coproduced in several European countries that have ordered it, and Boeing has subcontracted parts of planes being produced for the 1980s to Aeritalia and to the Japanese consortium.

The EMF Role

As the data in Table IV-1 demonstrate, aerospace is a major employer, but it is also one that features wide fluctuations. Employment in the American industry has peaked at nearly 1.5 million and fallen below 900,000 in recent years. The fear that the domination of the United States industry would cause the European one virtually to disappear has been a concern of governments, managements, and unions there for many years. This in turn has led to joint ventures among European companies and to considerable agitation on behalf of a European aerospace industry by the European Metalworkers' Federation. The former includes the prestigious, but financially disastrous, Concorde project of the French and British; the much more successful, but still not profitable, Airbus Industrie Consortium of several countries, as discussed below; and the apparently abortive VFW-Fokker merger. The EMF, which has long agitated for a European aerospace industry and a "buy European" policy for

TABLE IV-1

Eight Major Aerospace Companies, 1978

Companies [a]	Headquarters	Sales ($000)	Assets ($000)	Net Income ($000)	Employees
United Technologies [b]	Hartford, Conn.	6,265,318	4,074,325	234,144	152,213
Boeing	Seattle	5,463,000	3,573,200	322,900	81,200
General Dynamics [b]	St. Louis	3,205,205	1,778,723	48,088 [d]	77,100
Aerospatiale [c]	Les Mureaux, France	2,114,646 [e]	3,731,739 [e]	19,238 [d,e]	33,152 [e]
Northrop	Los Angeles	1,829,839	931,049	88,417	31,200
British Aerospace	Weybridge, U.K.	1,717,040	1,466,642	54,786	70,160
Rolls-Royce [c]	London	1,464,601	1,331,270	13,746	59,283
Avions M. Dassault-Bréguet	Vaucresson, France	1,404,566	3,167,171	55,093	1,557

Source: *Fortune*, Vol. 99 (May 7, 1979), pp. 272-77; Vol. 100 (August 13, 1979), pp. 196-98.
[a] Other major aerospace companies are the divisions of General Electric and Rockwell International.
[b] Data include substantial nonaerospace businesses.
[c] Government owned.
[d] Loss.
[e] Parent only.

members of the European Community,[2] began its multinational program with VFW-Fokker.

The EMF and VFW-Fokker

The experience of VFW-Fokker with the EMF provides a good illustration of how unions seek informational meetings as a prelude (in this case unsuccessful) to bargaining relationships. VFW-Fokker is an international aerospace company created by a merger in January 1970 of Germany's Vereinigte Flugtechnische Werke (VFW) and the Royal Netherlands Aircraft Factories Fokker. In 1978, the company, which has its central office in Düsseldorf, Germany, employed 17,710 workers in eight Dutch and nine German plants. VFW-Fokker also jointly controls the Belgian firm SABCA with the French aircraft company Dassault-Bréguet.[3]

There were six meetings between VFW-Fokker and the EMF between 1970 and 1974. In contrast to the Philips case discussed in the following chapter, the IMF was represented at two of these meetings, and in addition, a representative of the European metalworkers' organization of the World Confederation of Labour attended the session on October 17, 1973.[4] The company did not refuse to meet with IMF representatives present, but it did question the propriety thereof.

These meetings considered a variety of matters, such as medium-term investment plans and personnel planning, but major emphasis by the union in all sessions was on the harmonization of working conditions between the Dutch and German plants and the regularization of a contract structure between multinational management and worker representatives. Neither of these latter two union claims was ever resolved by the parties.[5] On the matter of harmonization, which was raised at the fourth

---

2 See, e.g., "Workers in the European Aerospace Industry Defending Employment," EMF Press Release, May 10, 1974.

3 Philip Sickman, "Europe's Love Affair with Bigness," *Fortune*, Vol. LXXXI (March 1970), p. 168; also *IMF News*, No. 41 (December 1970), p. 2, and No. 46 (December 1973), p. 3. See also "Racing to Build Fighter Planes Worth $20-Billion," *Business Week*, August 10, 1974, p. 156; and *Fortune*, Vol. 100 (August 13, 1979), p. 201.

4 *IMF News*, No. 16 (April 1973), p. 1, and No. 46 (December 1973), p. 3. The World Confederation of Labour's European metalworkers' organization later dissolved, and its affiliates joined the EMF.

5 *IMF News*, No. 16 (April 1973), p. 1.

meeting on April 13, 1973, the IMF stated: "This was rejected outright by management on various grounds, a particularly interesting one being that they saw no reason for so much international concern when the workers affected had not been creating any serious problems in the shop over this matter in the first place." [6] In regard to regularizing meetings and recognizing "a permanent trade union committee representing the workers of all Fokker-VFW plants," the company replied that "it was considering its own plan for improved communications and hoped to have it ready in 'a few months.' " [7] The company again rejected harmonization at the fifth meeting on October 17, 1973, but agreed to have better communications between national works councils in Germany and in the Netherlands.

It appeared for a time that VFW-Fokker would provide an innovative example of transnational bargaining even though the company insisted that bargaining relationships should be between national unions and company managements in various countries, if for no other reason than that existing national legal systems make multinational bargaining neither possible nor desirable.[8] Nevertheless, the company's dependence on government and the relationships of the unions with various European governments and political parties at least raised the question whether it could fend off the obvious EMF push for a formal bargaining relationship.

In fact, however, the company fended off the EMF quite successfully. The "improved communications" between national works councils referred to above meant actually the substitution of joint Dutch-German works council meetings for those with the EMF. The last EMF-VFW-Fokker meeting occurred on May 22, 1974. A meeting scheduled for October 1974 "could not be held because of date conflicts." [9] Meanwhile, the German (Gesamtbetriebsrat der Vereinigten Flugtechnischen Werke-Fokker GmbH) and the Dutch (Centrale Ondernemingsraad der Fokker-VFW B.V.) enterprise works councils (GBR and COR) began joint meetings with company officials on June 24, 1974, and con-

---

[6] *Ibid.*

[7] *Ibid.*

[8] Letter from Dr. Sadtler, general secretary, VFW-Fokker, to the authors, January 23, 1974.

[9] Letters from Dr. Sadtler to the authors, September 29, 1975, and October 14, 1976.

tinued on a twice per year basis through at least 1976. Discussions centered on balancing work among the plants of the enterprise and the possibility of doing so by transferring work across borders. Employee representatives on the works councils may invite union representatives to attend such meetings. Representatives of IG Metall participated in all meetings, but the Dutch unions were not represented.

According to the company, "it is not intended that EMF representatives should participate in meetings of the enterprise management and COR and GBR. Separate discussions with the EMF are possible in which only questions of mutual interest are discussed and clarified and concerning which there have not already been consultations with COR and GBR." [10] No such EMF discussions, however, ever occurred after 1974. The company clearly preferred meetings with the works councils "since the council members are entirely from the plants and not from union headquarters." [11]

The VFW-Fokker merger did not stand the test of time. By 1977, the VFW part was in a poor financial situation and a drain on Fokker. Meanwhile, the German government has been advocating a VFW-MBB merger to form a unified German aerospace concern. By mid-1979, the only question was the time and terms for the merger dissolution.[12] Under these circumstances, the EMF leadership, already squeezed out of the scene, agreed that there would be no purpose to another VFW-Fokker meeting.[13]

Other EMF Activities

The EMF continues to be active on the European aerospace scene despite its failure to achieve status with VFW-Fokker. Its principal effort today concerns Airbus Industrie, for which it plans a permanent committee by the beginning of 1980. Airbus Industrie is a consortium of Aerospatiale (SNIAS), MBB, VFW-Fokker, CASA (Spain), and British Aerospace, which coproduces the A-300 Airbus. The EMF has had an Airbus/Concorde "work-

---

[10] Letter from Dr. Sadtler to the authors, September 29, 1975.

[11] Dr. Sadtler, telephone interview, May 4, 1976.

[12] Charles Batchelor, "Delays in break-up of Fokker continue," *Financial Times*, May 23, 1979, p. 4; Roger Boyes, "VFW Fokker returns to black," *Financial Times*, June 7, 1979, p. 21.

[13] Hubert Thierron, general secretary, EMF, interview in Brussels, May 10, 1979.

ing party," which has had meetings since 1974 and has been a part of the EMF's general program to support the European industry and its employment.[14]

Given the national involvements in the Airbus program and the association of different plants in different countries, it seems likely that the EMF will move toward joint discussions on a multinational basis. Once the permanent EMF Airbus Industrie Committee is organized, this is a likely prospect.

The IMF Role

In addition to the role played by the EMF in the European aerospace industry, the IMF has asserted itself on a worldwide basis. An IMF World Aerospace Conference was held in Seattle, Washington, from May 22 to 24, 1979. The conference was jointly hosted by the International Association of Machinists and Aerospace Workers (IAM), an IMF affiliate, and the keynote address was given by IAM President William Winpisinger. According to the IMF, seventy-five delegates from fourteen countries attended the meeting, which focused on "the future of the industry between now and the year 2000 and on ways in which workers and their IMF-affiliated unions can cooperate to win fair shares of the consequences of this growth." [15]

Documentation for the conference was prepared by the IMF and included "Trade Unions and Collective Bargaining in the Aerospace Industry," "Aerospace Company Profiles, Co-Production and Country Profiles," and "The World Aerospace Industry Today." General Secretary Herman Rebhan indicated that "these three short documents . . . should represent an important step forward in the promotion of mutual understanding and international labour solidarity in the aerospace industry." [16] During the conference, the Boeing Company hosted a tour of the 747 facility for Winpisinger, a local IAM union president, and eighty-five

[14] Memorandum of the European Metalworkers' Federation on the Aerospace Industry in Europe, November 28, 1975; see also "Workers in the European Aerospace Industry."

[15] "World Aerospace Workers to Meet in Seattle," IMF Press Release, No. 10 (May 1, 1979). A similar meeting was held by the IMF Aerospace Committee in London at the end of March 1977. See International Metalworkers' Federation, *Report of Activities to the 24th World Congress*, Munich, October 24-28, 1977, Vol. 1, p. 34.

[16] "Trade Unions and Collective Bargaining in the Aerospace Industry," p. i.

union delegates. Two Boeing officials also addressed the plant visitors about particular airplane programs.[17]

One interesting development at the conference was the apparent concern on the part of the European delegates that the Americans were taking over too much of the aerospace business. Divisiveness among the delegates seems to arise when, for example, they observe Boeing's plans to produce twenty-eight planes per month compared to Airbus Industrie's plans to produce only eight planes a month by the end of 1983.[18] This situation, of course, places national union interests in potential conflict with the international trade union objectives. Winpisinger, as president of the American IAM, can hardly afford to give up jobs to the Europeans or agree to a plan that might call for a "balancing" of production between American and European firms. Of course, the IMF can realistically push for greater harmonization of working conditions on a worldwide basis, but any significant striving for reallocation of production in the industry across national boundaries is likely to provoke strong negative responses from national union leaders, particularly when such moves would suggest that a country restrain production and thereby eliminate jobs.

Conclusion

Given the diversity of interests between European and American unionists, it seems likely that effective international union relationships in the aerospace industry will remain largely a European prospect under EMF leadership.

AGRICULTURAL EQUIPMENT AND CONSTRUCTION MACHINERY INDUSTRIES

This section analyzes the activities in the agricultural equipment and construction machinery industries. As noted in Table IV-2, the four largest companies in these industries, and discussed herein, are Caterpillar Tractor, International Harvester, John Deere, and Massey-Ferguson.

---

[17] Jerry Bergsman, "Trade unionists hear call to unite," *Seattle Times,* May 23, 1979, p. C10; "Boeing official sees SST in America's future," *ibid.,* May 24, 1979, p. C13; "Economic Myth: What Free Market," *Aero Mechanic,* May 30, 1979, p. 8; and confidential interviews.

[18] Interviews with Boeing, June 4, 1979; and "Airbus Industrie Plans Production Expansion to Eight Jets Monthly," *Wall Street Journal,* June 11, 1979, p. 5.

TABLE IV-2

The Four Largest Companies
in the

Agricultural Implements and Construction Machinery Industry [a]

Company	Headquarters	Sales ($000)	Assets ($000)	Net Income ($000)	Employees
Caterpillar Tractor	Peoria, Ill.	7,219,200	5,031,100	556,300	84,004 [d]
International Harvester [b]	Chicago, Ill.	6,664,347	4,316,105	186,680	95,450
John Deere [b]	Moline, Ill.	4,154,953	3,866,616	264,813	59,208
Massey-Ferguson [b]	Toronto, Canada	2,925,494	2,547,185	256,709 [c]	57,983

Source: *Fortune:* Vol. 99 (May 7, 1979), pp. 270-71; Vol. 100 (August 13, 1979), p. 196.
[a] Ford Motor Company is one of the top tractor manufacturers, and General Motors, Fiat, Hitachi and others are major construction machinery manufacturers.
[b] Figures are for fiscal year ending October 31, 1978.
[c] Loss.
[d] Average for the year.

Caterpillar

Caterpillar Tractor Company, headquartered in Peoria, Illinois, is the leading world producer of earth-moving machinery. Although Caterpillar has produced no agricultural implements since the 1930s, its collective bargaining in the United States is tied in with agricultural implement producers, particularly John Deere and International Harvester, whose wage employees, like those of Caterpillar, are mainly represented by the United Automobile, Aerospace and Agricultural Implement Workers (UAW). In Europe, Caterpillar's plants are located in Glasgow, Scotland; Newcastle and Leicester, England; Gosselies, Belgium; and Grenoble, France, plus a warehouse and office in Grimbergen, Belgium. In late 1974, Caterpillar acquired a foundry near Paris. It also operates in Japan, Australia, and other parts of the world, as well as having numerous plants in the United States.[19]

Direct National Union Contacts. Multinational union activity involving Caterpillar is relatively new, an early instance being a visit by UAW Vice-President Pat Greathouse and three other UAW staff personnel to the plant in Gosselies, Belgium, on May 14, 1972. They toured the plant and met with Belgian unionists. Thereafter, they participated, together with then UAW President Leonard Woodcock, in the plans for the formation of a World Agricultural Implement Council, which met later in Brussels.

In March 1973, a strike at Gosselies involving new contract terms occurred, but over a three-week period, it collapsed as a large percentage of the workers returned. Toward the end of the stoppage, the Gosselies unionists of the Fédération Générale du Travail de Belgique (FGTB) were attempting to have the unionists at Glasgow "blacken" diesel engines supplied by Gosselies. Also, union members in Grenoble, France, posted a complete list of the FGTB's bargaining demands at Gosselies.

These international visits continued with Jean Gayetot, general secretary of the FGTB in Brussels, visiting Peoria in August while on a tour sponsored by the State Department, and Leonard

---

[19] Information in this section is based on that supplied by company interviews and letters, plus *IMF News*, No. 20 (May 1972), pp. 2-3 and appendix; No. 29 (July 1973), pp. 3-4; and "A 'First' Scored in Agricultural Implement Company Negotiations as Union Participant Observers Attend Caterpillar Negotiations from Overseas Plants," IMF World Auto Councils Press Release, Circular No. 47 (July 13, 1973); also "Towards European Unity" (translated), issued by the Confédération Générale du Travail, Grenoble, France, December 2, 1974; *Journal De Charleroi* (Belgium), October 29, 1974; and local papers, Gosselies, Belgium, November 4, 1974.

Woodcock and other UAW officials visiting Gosselies in June 1974 on their way to the IMF congress in Stockholm. In each case, there were discussions between company officials and American and Belgian unionists concerning general company information, not bargaining matters.

Prior to the 1973 contract negotiations between the UAW and Caterpillar (like those between the same union and Deere and International Harvester), the UAW advised the company that it had invited foreign unionists as visitors for the opening session and requested that they be given a plant tour. Those present at the Caterpillar negotiations included representatives from the metalworker affiliate of the FGTB, the French General Federation of Metalworkers; the national officer for the metal industry of the British General and Municipal Workers' Union (GMWU); and the IMF coordinator of the world auto councils. The visitors were given a plant tour and departed, taking no part in the negotiations, but the IMF's press release signaled a greater interest in Caterpillar than had been the case heretofore.[20]

In October 1974, thirteen UAW employee delegates from three United States Caterpillar plants participated in an international union conference in London at which there were about seventy participants. Four Caterpillar union delegates also toured the Glasgow plant, visited in the Glasgow area and elsewhere, and met with other British union officials. This visit was apparently organized by Robert Johnston, director of UAW Region 4, in cooperation with the British Amalgamated Union of Engineering Workers.[21]

Two weeks later, a one-day meeting occurred at Gosselies between representatives of the FGTB, which is a socialist-oriented organization, and representatives of the French Communist Confédération Générale du Travail (CGT) from Grenoble. Local plant and full-time union representatives from the national FGTB and regional CGT were involved. Emphasis was on establishing a full-time coordinating committee and planning to involve Glasgow employees in the coordinating committee.

IMF Conference. From May 6 to 8, 1975, the UAW hosted an IMF Tri-Company (Caterpillar, Deere, and International Harvester) World Agricultural Implement Conference in Chicago. Delegates attended from Argentina, Australia, Belgium, Brazil,

20 See IMF World Auto Councils Press Release, Circular No. 47 (July 13, 1973).

21 See *AUEW Journal*, January 1975, p. 2.

France, Germany, Japan, Mexico, South Africa, the United Kingdom, and Venezuela, in addition to the United States and Canada. Pat Greathouse, UAW vice-president, chaired the meeting, which was addressed by Leonard Woodcock, UAW president, and Herman Rebhan, IMF general secretary. Burton Bendiner, then IMF world auto council coordinator, who, like Rebhan, was a UAW staff member on leave, also participated.

Greathouse requested the three companies to receive the unionists and had an early commitment from Caterpillar to do so. Deere also agreed. The visitations to both companies occurred on May 8, with Greathouse accompanying the Caterpillar group to Peoria and his administrative assistant and Bendiner going to Deere at Moline, both sites located in Illinois south of Chicago. Both visitations were handled politely but expeditiously. They included lunch, a short plant tour, answers to general questions, and either talks or movies. Questions centered on such matters as foreign investment, transfer of work from one plant to another, sales to Eastern Europe and OPEC countries, and central office relations to local or national plant labor policy. There seemed little doubt that the IMF was attempting to increase information exchange and possibly to eventually obtain more coordination of bargaining than has heretofore occurred in these companies.

Harvester took a different approach. Its vice-president for industrial relations and two staff members hosted the union delegates at a cocktail party in a Chicago hotel, exchanged pleasantries, and departed. Requests for a plant tour were turned over to the Public Relations Department. A group toured the plant in Melrose Park (near Chicago) and was treated like any other plant tour group, with no discussions, luncheon, etc.

The UAW's monthly journal gives a much more expansive report, in which general answers to general questions become "frank discussions":

> Climax of the conference was a series of frank discussions with the multinationals' management in which the delegates learned first hand how executives in the agricultural implement companies' board rooms determine labor-management relations policy in every country in which they operate.[22]

Greathouse enunciated IMF and UAW policy regarding the meeting, declaring that companies are "affecting us all" by moving jobs around internationally "just as they have been moved

---

[22] *Solidarity* (UAW), June 1975, p. 5.

from one plant to another" in the United States. He said that the UAW does not desire to export its policies, but "we must work harder in coordinating our activities . . . and it is important that we exchange information and that we work toward a common program." [23]

EMF Meeting. Following this meeting, the European Metalworkers' Federation, at the request of the Belgian FGTB, hosted a European Caterpillar union conference at FGTB headquarters in Brussels from June 5 to 6, 1975. Present were Bendiner representing the IMF and Hubert Thierron, then assistant general secretary of the EMF, plus representatives of both the FGTB and the Belgian Confédération des Syndicats Chrétiens (CSC), three representatives of the Confédération Française Démocratique du Travail (CFDT), one from the French CGT, and one from the British GMWU. Excepting some Belgian union officials, Thierron, and Bendiner, all delegates were Caterpillar employees. Prior to the meeting, the unions at various Caterpillar plants involved had requested detailed information on such issues as products by plant, production and sales forecasts, and safety records, but this was not supplied except as already available in the annual reports or other published data. A request for a plant visit at Gosselies was handled by the Public Relations Department and treated like any group plant tour, although Caterpillar Belgium shop stewards and their friends in the plant made those who were touring known to the workers.

Implications. From this recitation of events, it appears that two efforts were under way that could have presaged a multinational union coalition against Caterpillar. One is the world council approach being pushed by the IMF and the UAW. This involves, thus far, largely reciprocal visits of unionists, informal discussions with Caterpillar officials, and heavy reliance on exchanges of information among union groups to coordinate strategy, demands, and other union activities.

The second effort, which could have involved more direct confrontation, may have been blunted by the increased UAW and IMF involvement. The FGTB at Gosselies has called a number of strikes that have failed to obtain either strong employee support or union objectives. It is this FGTB group, which, although socialist, sought the support of the Communist CGT in the French plant and, more recently, the British at Glasgow. The June 1975 conference at Brussels, coordinated by the EMF and, unlike many

---

[23] *Ibid.*

EMF activities, with IMF cooperation, may well have been an effort to place the direct FGTB-CGT contacts within an IMF framework and therefore to develop a coordinated union policy in Europe against Caterpillar. Presumably, this would include less strikes at Gosselies aimed at challenging management's shop control and more concentration on wage bargaining. Although the union communication links seem to have been forged for some serious coordination of action against Caterpillar, nothing of substance seems to have occurred since 1975.

Deere

Deere and Company, headquartered in Moline, Illinois, is the world's largest manufacturer of farm implements. The company maintains a sales organization covering some forty-five countries and production operations in seven.[24]

There is no permanent organization of unions on an international basis from the Deere plants. As noted in the preceding analysis of Caterpillar, union officials from Force Ouvrière (FO) in France, IG Metall, and the Amalgamated Union of Engineering Workers (AUEW) in Britain attended the opening day session of the 1973 UAW-Deere negotiations. The visitors observed the opening ceremonies and departed to take a plant tour. Following the May 1975 IMF Tri-Company Conference in Chicago, discussed previously, three overseas union representatives, including Burton Bendiner of the UAW staff on loan to the IMF, met at Deere with six Deere executives. Deere acted as host to the overseas union officials, who were given a tour of the assembly area for combines at the John Deere Harvester Works.

In addition to these activities, contacts between the Mannheim (Germany) Works Council and union delegates of the Saran Works (Orléans, France) have existed since 1970. Annual meetings are arranged on an alternating basis in Mannheim and Orléans with four to five members participating from each group.

The initiative for meetings has come from the German side, with the first one being held in France when the chairman of the Mannheim Works Council and three members of his negotiating committee visited union delegates of the Saran plant. IG Metall, the CGT, and the CFDT coordinated and paid for the

---

[24] See "Deere Tunes Up to Take on Caterpillar," *Business Week*, June 1, 1974, pp. 66-67.

visit, including translator services for a two-day meeting. Meetings have served the purpose of exchanging notes and experiences in the following areas:

a) communications and negotiations with management (practices, techniques, and union assistance) ;

b) general employment conditions (hours of work, overtime requirements, employee services, and interrelationship of operations between Mannheim and Saran) ;

c) compensation packages (wage rates, hourly and incentive earnings, benefits, and social security provisions).[25]

Cautious efforts have also been made to explore possibilities for promoting and agreeing on common union objectives within the "John Deere family" and to harmonize employment conditions and compensation practices in both locations. The push for this type of harmonization has not been strong since the German workers' employment situation is generally superior to that of their French counterparts.

It does not appear to the company that the meetings held over the past years have resulted in common programs or action plans. The meetings have included only the two Deere plants, with those at Zweibrücken (Germany) and Arc-les-Gray and Senonches (France) not represented in the annual visits.

There is no doubt, however, that, if an action plan is worked out by the Mannheim and Saran representatives, it would have an impact on the company's other plants. Interestingly enough, neither the IMF nor the EMF has been involved in the transnational union contacts. There was some "leaflet action" in France by the IMF during a 1973 strike in Germany, but this did not result in any substantive support by the French for the German workers. In a similar strike situation in 1972, the strikers in France were denied assistance by the German works council.

International Harvester Company

International Harvester Company is a major producer of trucks and engines, as well as farm equipment and construction machinery. Harvester has long manufactured overseas. Today, besides its many American facilities, it has three plants in the United Kingdom, in addition to that of its newly acquired

---

[25] Correspondence and interviews with Deere (Mannheim), April 17, 1975, and September 10, 1975.

English subsidiary, the Sedden Diesel Vehicle Company, which is a truck and bus manufacturer; three plants in France and two in Germany; and additional ones in Canada, Mexico, Australia, New Zealand, the Philippines, and South Africa. Harvester also owns a one-third interest in the Dutch DAF Trucks, which is now totally separate from the Volvo-controlled DAF automobile concern.[26]

As noted in the previous Caterpillar discussion, union officials from the FO, IG Metall, and the AUEW were present at the opening of the 1973 UAW-Harvester negotiations in Chicago. They were introduced by Pat Greathouse, UAW vice-president, silently observed the opening ceremonies, and left to tour a plant. A Harvester employee, and chief steward for the Transport and General Workers' Union at the main plant in Britain, also attended the IMF Tri-Company Conference in Chicago in 1975 (see discussion on page 75). After his return, he acquainted fellow employees with the pension and holiday provisions of the UAW-Harvester contract and the requirements therein for the payment in certain instances of average hourly earnings instead of base rates when employees are unable to work under the incentive pay system. He apparently felt these provisions were superior to British conditions.

In 1973, prior to the union appearances at the UAW negotiations, a UAW national representative, Carl Shier, who was assigned to service the contract at the Harvester Melrose Park plant, visited Britain apparently on his own initiative but with official UAW approval. He contacted the AUEW and, through it, made contacts with various Harvester plant stewards and exchanged information about plant conditions. No apparent developments resulted from this visit.

The British Harvester unionists do not seem to have developed contacts with their German and French counterparts. A member of the Harvester Neuss Works Council did attend an IMF Agricultural World Council Meeting in Brussels in 1972, but no one from either the French or German plants was a delegate to the IMF Tri-Company meeting in Chicago in 1975. The first overt American-French contact occurred in 1963 after an IMF meeting. A UAW delegation visiting Europe asked, through a Force Ouvrière group, to visit a French Harvester plant, and did so.

---

[26] This and the following information are based primarily on interviews in Chicago, London, Paris, and Neuss, Germany, June, July, and September 1975, and April 1976, plus union documents relating to the 1973 negotiations, and the 1975 IMF Chicago meeting, cited in the preceding Caterpillar discussion.

In addition, there have been regular unofficial meetings since 1973 between works council groups from the Harvester French plant at Saint Dizier and the German one at Heidelberg. These are left-wing groups, and the contacts were probably initiated by the Communist CGT in France. The other plants, including Neuss, Germany, have not been involved, although Neuss manufactures engines and Saint Dizier manufactures transmissions for all European plants. They are thus linked together industrially more closely than are Heidelberg and Saint Dizier. Recently, a Heidelberg unionist, now chairman of the German Harvester enterprise works council, has urged participation by Neuss workers in these meetings, but without success. Those involved in the Saint Dizier and Heidelberg meetings have also requested Harvester officials to set up a joint committee of the two groups for discussions, but it is doubtful that the company will give serious consideration to doing so.

There has been no other overt push for joint bargaining; the only possible transnational factors entering negotiations have occurred during strikes. For example, one at Neuss in 1973 shut off the engine supply to Saint Dizier. The company agreed to counter the layoffs that resulted at Saint Dizier by overtime when engines again became available, and no international implications resulted then or at any other time. A strike at Saint Dizier in March 1976 did not lead to any union contacts between the French and Germans. Similar strikes in British plants have upset production schedules at Neuss or caused reductions in overtime, again without international union or works council relationships evolving.

Massey-Ferguson

Massey-Ferguson, second only to Deere as a farm implement producer, first in the world in tractor production and also a manufacturer of construction machinery and diesel engines, is a Toronto-based company, with more of its employees found outside of North America than within Canada and the United States.[27] In 1975, Massey-Ferguson had approximately 5,500 employees in Canada, 3,500 in the United States, but 13,500 in the United Kingdom and additional concentrations in Europe, South Africa, Rhodesia, Australia, Turkey, and Latin America. The name of the company was changed from Massey-Harris after

---

[27] This section is based on confidential interviews in the United Kingdom and Toronto, May 1975 and January 1976.

merger with Harry Ferguson, Ltd., in the 1950s. In 1959, the company purchased the Perkins Engines Group, a United Kingdom-based producer of diesel engines. Since 1977, the company has reduced its commitments in Third World countries because of severe losses. (See Table IV-2.)

Despite its significance in the farm equipment industry, international union activity affecting Massey-Ferguson has been confined largely to relations involving Canadian and American unionists. The UAW represents most Massey-Ferguson blue-collar employees in both countries. There has never been a joint meeting of unionists representing Massey-Ferguson plants, except for those in Canada and the United States, nor have there been visitors to negotiations with this company, such as occurred in 1973 in the cases of Caterpillar, Deere, and International Harvester. The May 1975 conference sponsored by the IMF in Chicago also involved only the latter three companies.

The UAW Canadian director, who negotiates with Massey-Ferguson, participated in the formation of the IMF World Agricultural Implement Council in Brussels in 1972 and, while on this trip, visited fellow unionists and Massey-Ferguson plants. In 1975, an official of the AUEW visiting Canada with his family arranged to meet and talk to manufacturing officials at a company plant. There have been inquiries from French unionists to those in the United States and interest on the part of British unionists concerning company policies in Spain, South America, and South Africa, but none of these matters involved either international union activity or the beginning of direct relations between national unions.

Conclusion

Thus, beyond meetings and occasional contacts between national unions, coordination at the international level in these countries has been quite limited. It is likely to remain at this stage, barring a dramatic incident or the assignment of a permanent IMF staff member to encourage cooperation and meetings.

THE METAL CAN INDUSTRY

The expensive technology and equipment required by the metal can industry, plus marketing and transportation economics that emphasize plant locations near customers, have created an industrial structure of a small number of key companies, each with a large number of plants. Each plant in turn features expensive equipment operated by a relatively small number of employees. Thus, the total worldwide employment of the industry's largest company by sales—American Can—is only 52,900, including that company's employees in non-metal packaging and other industries (see Table IV-3).

Although can companies are capital intensive rather than labor intensive, the high-speed manufacturing lines, the need to deliver cans where the customer requires them, and the high cost and the difficulties of warehousing finished products provide tremendous leverage to employees and unions. The results are threefold: very high wages and excellent benefits for employees; continuous emphasis on improved technology, materials, and methods by the companies; and increasing competition both from substitute materials and from customer integration. Thus, metal cans compete with glass, plastic, and paper containers. Metal has won over much of the beverage markets from glass but, in turn, lost to paper such volume products in the United States as frozen orange juice concentrate and motor oil. Continental and American Can have major paper and plastic divisions, but a switch in can material composition usually means a switch in plant location, employment, and conditions, even if the business remains in the same company.

In recent years, also, more can-using companies have built their own can facilities; thus, Campbell Soup Company may be the third largest metal can manufacturer in the United States, producing largely for its own consumption. Likewise, major beer producers in the United States are increasing their captive canneries. In such cases, of course, the work shifts to a new labor force often compensated at the lesser rate prevalent in the user industry.

Another factor is that Reynolds Aluminum entered the field to promote the use of aluminum cans, again creating intensified competitive pressures. With these pressures, and with many plant closings and relocations to meet customer needs, the industry has been in considerable flux in recent years. The employment problems associated with these developments have attracted the attention of the IMF, as is set forth below. Prior thereto, as a result of developments within the European Community, the EMF began a series of meetings with Continental Can's European company.

TABLE IV-3

The Six Largest Metal Canning Companies, 1978

Company	Headquarters	Sales ($000)	Assets ($000)	Net Income ($000)	Employees
American Can	Greenwich, Conn.	3,981,000	2,478,100	105,600 [b]	52,900 [c]
Continental Group	New York	3,943,900	2,997,200	126,200	56,532 [c]
Metal Box, Ltd. [a]	Reading, U.K.	1,452,473	973,215	62,232	60,312
Crown, Cork & Seal	Philadelphia	1,260,235	744,407	64,319	17,288
National Can	Chicago	1,107,172	542,267	19,846	11,241 [c]
J. J. Carnaud	Boulogne-sur-Seine, France	747,411	582,912	8,867	12,972

Source: *Fortune*, Vol. 99 (May 7, 1979), pp. 272-73, 278-79; and Vol. 100 (August 13, 1979), pp. 198, 202.

[a] Figures are for fiscal year ending March 31, 1978.
[b] Reflects an extraordinary change of at least 10 percent.
[c] Average for the year.

Continental and the EMF

Continental, the world's largest packaging company, has been active in multinational operations since 1930, but prior to the late 1960s, such activity was confined to licensing arrangements. Continental sold its can-making technology to European, Latin American, Asian, and Australian concerns and received royalties in return. According to *Fortune*:

> Continental has never been aggressive about acquiring equity interests in its licensees; it has, in fact, invested in them only at their invitation. In some cases this happened when a licensee ran into financial difficulties and asked Continental to accept stock in place of license fees. Other investments came about when the foreign company seeking capital for expansion invited Continental to become a minority partner. Continental . . . [in 1972 earned] $5.1 million a year in royalties on its technology and $918,000 in dividends from minority interests.[28]

In the late 1960s, Continental Can and some of its licensees agreed to form a new company, Europemballage (now the Continental Group of Europe), which would take over much of the can business in Britain, France, Germany, Italy, Austria, the Netherlands, Belgium, and Luxembourg. Under the planned arrangements, Continental would have a controlling interest in Europemballage. Prior, however, to the announcement of the plan, J. J. Carnaud et Forges de Basse-Inche, the French licensee, withdrew as the result of a major stockholder's objection. Then the Commission of the European Community warned that a violation of the Treaty of Rome's antitrust provision was involved. This caused Metal Box Company, Ltd., the British firm, to decline to participate. Continental went ahead with its plans, acquiring Thomassen & Drijver-Verblifa N.V., a Dutch company, and J. A. Schmalbach-Lubeca-Werke AG, a German concern. Thomassen & Drijver, in turn, controls Sobemi, the Belgian concern, while Schmalbach has an Austrian subsidiary and has since acquired a plastic-packaging company in Germany. All these holdings were placed in Europemballage, headquartered in Brussels.[29]

---

28 See Peter Vanderwicken, "Continental Can's International Tribulations," *Fortune*, Vol. LXXXVIII (August 1973), p. 78.

29 *Ibid.*, pp. 74-79, 116, 118. Carnaud, in which Continental has an 8 percent interest, controls 50 percent of the French can market; Metal Box, in which Continental held a 3.1 percent interest, holds 85 percent of the British market. Continental has since sold its interest in Metal Box.

The European Commission filed charges of market domination in 1971, but the European Court of Justice ruled that other forms of packaging, plus the large size of Europemballage customers (Unilever is the largest), prevented market domination. The decision, in effect, left Europemballage in place but precluded additional acquisitions or combinations in metal can manufacturing.[30]

The filing of the charge and Continental's desire to safeguard Europemballage against attacks of a political nature both made Europemballage a target of international unionism and created a reluctance on the part of the company to do anything that might encourage union attacks on its existence. Following the charge of the European Commission, the EMF announced on November 16, 1971, that a coordinating committee would be established to negotiate with Continental Can on a European basis.[31] A meeting organized by the EMF in Brussels was held on February 10, 1972, chaired by Günter Köpke, then general secretary of the EMF, at which representatives of the metal unions and the works councils for the Dutch and German subsidiaries were present. It was decided to request a meeting with Europemballage management, and a letter to that effect was received by Europemballage on March 15, 1972, requesting a discussion of union problems and the pending commission case.

On April 21, 1972, the president of Europemballage, Ben ter Haar, and one associate, R. C. Hietink, met with Gustav Wallaert, then president of the EMF, and Köpke. Ter Haar discussed the pending case and promised that, after the case was resolved, he would decide whether to have meetings with the EMF.

Meanwhile, the Christian union metal federation (Organisation Europiénne de la Métallurgie) also asked for a meeting. After an exchange of letters, ter Haar met with Hubert Thierron, then secretary of this organization, on May 31, 1972. Thierron asked for further meetings dealing with union problems but did not discuss the pending case.

On March 28, 1973, ter Haar and Hietink met with Wallaert, Köpke, and Thierron in a joint meeting to discuss possible fu-

---

30 *Ibid.*

31 The balance of the Continental Can story is based on interviews with Europemballage and EMF officials in Brussels, July 1974 and February 1975, plus correspondence and documents supplied by each. See also, for the EMF version, European Metalworkers' Federation, *Report of Activities, 1971-74* (Brussels, 1974).

ture meetings and their content. Although it was tentatively planned to have a meeting the following month to discuss an agenda for a formal meeting in May or June, that meeting did not occur, in part because of a metalworkers' strike in the Netherlands but apparently also because the company was concerned about the EMF's obvious attempts to push toward a bargaining situation. Moreover, the EMF's press releases tended to give an impression that the meetings were in fact moving in that direction.

The next meeting occurred in December 1973 with the same participants as in March. The company rejected the EMF's request for bargaining or discussion of national terms of employment, and it confined the meeting to a discussion of items appearing in the annual report of Europemballage, talking generally about company plans for expansion, closing of obsolete plants (which it has successfully effectuated in a number of cases despite the European worker-union opposition to plant closings in general),[32] and other matters that were mostly already available in company reports. To emphasize that the meetings should not cover matters bargainable at the national or plant levels, the company's personnel executive never participated.

Meetings between the EMF and what is now the Continental Group of Europe occurred in August and November 1974 and in February 1976. Prior to these meetings, the Christian unions dissolved their European metal organization and affiliated with the EMF. Thierron became assistant general secretary of the EMF and, in that capacity, participated in the meetings.[33]

The 1976 meeting proved to be the last in the series. The company had always rejected the EMF's suggestions that national union officials be present at the meetings and insisted that the union representatives be confined to the president and secretaries of the EMF. Nevertheless, in February 1976, representatives from the Dutch and German metal unions accompanied Köpke and Thierron to the meetings. When the Continental executive pointed out that this was contrary to their understand-

---

[32] By mid-1973, Schmalbach had closed four plants, Thomassen & Drijver, three, but the Dutch company agreed to a three-year moratorium on plant closings. Vanderwicken, "Continental Can's International Tribulations," p. 118. It should be emphasized that plant closings were handled as a national, not Europemballage, matter.

[33] In July 1978, Thierron was elected general secretary of the EMF, following the resignation of Köpke, who had been previously elected managing director of the European Trade Union Institute.

ing, Köpke declared that, because the EMF president (then Hugh Scanlon, president of the AUEW) and various EMF vice-presidents were unavailable, he had requested representatives of these unions to accompany him. The Continental executive responded that the Dutch and German representatives could remain only as individuals, that employment and related matters in Germany and the Netherlands would not be discussed and should be taken up with management in these countries, and finally that, in any future meetings, only the president and secretaries of the EMF should participate.

No meetings have been held since February 1976, nor has either party sought one. Now that the International Metalworkers' Federation has exhibited its interest in the industry, the EMF initiative may be ended.

The IMF World Can Meeting

The IMF held its first can industry conference in London from April 5 to 6, 1978, under the direction of Karl Casserini, assistant general secretary and head of the IMF Department for the Iron and Steel and Nonferrous Metals Industries. Approximately sixty trade unionists from plant and national levels in the can-manufacturing industry from Europe, the United States, Venezuela, and Australia attended the conference. The conference was called in response to the IMF's continuing concern about job security in the can industry. This concern apparently grows out of the union's perception of the ability of the industry to close down plant facilities quickly and to relocate in a minimum amount of time.

There were two background documents prepared for the conference. "Collective Bargaining, Wages and Social Achievements in the Can Industry" includes a survey of collective agreements in the United States, Canada, Great Britain, Germany, the Netherlands, France, Belgium, and Mexico; an overall survey of wages and their evolution, with data on wages for the United States, Great Britain, Germany, the Netherlands, France, Belgium, Sweden, Spain, Israel, Australia, Japan, and Mexico; and a list of documentation available at the IMF secretariat—including the latest available collective agreements for companies operating in the United States, Canada, Great Britain, Germany, France, Belgium, and Mexico; health and safety documents; economic documentation; and company reports. These materials were furnished for the purpose of "practical use of affiliates in their daily activities, collective bargaining and negotiations on industry problems, particularly regarding employment and to provide general knowledge for short and long term union policy in the can industry." [34] It is obvious that the IMF information has been prepared to pursue the principle of harmonization of wages and working conditions.

"The Can Industry in the World" includes sections on structure, market trends, and technology; social problems; can making in developing countries; company reports for Continental Group Incorporated, American Can Company, National Can, Crown, Cork and Seal, Metal Box Limited, and Toyo Seikan Company Limited; and trade union conclusions, including the IMF action program in the can industry.

The IMF declaration of common action in the can industry, contained in "The Can Industry," changed in several important respects when finalized after the conference. We present below the amended conference declarations, with the postconference changes italicized:

> A tripartite analysis within the framework of the ILO World Employment Programme should be carried out about the role and potential of the can making industry in developing countries, particularly in the field of food preservation and processing of agricultural products for exports;
>
> policy and behavior of multinational can companies should be constantly surveyed on the basis of the ILO Tripartite Declaration of Multinational Enterprises, particularly with regard to security and creation of employment as well as trade union freedom and social standards; a complaint machinery must provide for corrective measures. In a similar way, other codes on multinational companies like the one of the OECD and that of the European Community for South Africa as well as any future code of the United Nations should find practical application.
>
> Employers in the can making industry when deciding plant locations must be compelled through negotiation with state authorities and unions, to accept fully their social obligations to the community.
>
> Cooperation between can manufacturers, public authorities and trade unions should ensure sound development of this industry with full consideration for environmental protection and stable employment prospects;
>
> worldwide action is to be undertaken through research and development, legislation, control measures, and *collective bargaining* to

---

[34] "Collective Bargaining, Wages and Social Achievements in the Can Industry" (Prepared for the First IMF World Can Industry Conference, London, April 5-6, 1978), p. 1.

eradicate health and safety risks in the metal container industry. These hazards are to be eliminated at the source, concentrating on healthy and secure work places. *Effective government and trade union action in the areas of health and safety can only be fully successful with the trade union participating at all levels.* Special efforts are urgently needed to reach a low noise level and emission free work environment. *The recently created IMF Department for Health and Safety should address itself to this problem as soon as possible.*[35]

Included in the priorities for the common direct trade union efforts are the following:

Guaranteed employment and income throughout the can industry;

Progressive working and social conditions;

Upward-harmonization of these conditions, wages and benefits, particularly for the rapid advancement of can workers in developing countries;

More advanced working and social conditions in the basic raw material sectors of steel and aluminum should be obtained by negotiations also for can workers;

Determined union action against *excessive* overtime and, in accordance with the action programme of IMF affiliates, strong emphasis on efforts to reduce working time with special consideration for the difficult conditions of environment and shift work;

Limitation of night work to the absolute minimum required;

Strict observation of limits on shift work as obtained in socially progressive plants;

Through collective bargaining, shift work and work schedule arrangements designed to alleviate the possible harmful effects of shift work, particularly the avoidance of work schedules which have the effects of harmfully lengthening the workday as well as;

Orderly preparations of shift workers for their possible adjustment to regular work; and

Effective measures for full trade union participation for maximum health and safety protection.[36]

In discussions with Karl Casserini at the IMF headquarters in Geneva on May 17, 1978, it was indicated that the can conference was a good beginning of the IMF's work toward providing greater job security for the employees in the can industry and toward attempting to harmonize conditions of work in that industry. To

---

[35] "The Can Industry" (Prepared for the First IMF World Can Industry Conference, London, April 5-6, 1978), p. 19; and "Declaration for Common Action," issued by the International Metalworkers' Federation, Geneva, n.d.

[36] *Ibid.*

what extent this beginning will be pursued and at what pace remain to be determined.

THE NICKEL INDUSTRY

The nickel industry was once almost synonymous with the International Nickel Company of Canada, Ltd., now Inco, Ltd. In 1978, Inco had sales in excess of $2 billion and 52,581 employees.[37] This includes some 15,000 employees of ESB Incorporated (formerly Electric Storage Battery Company), the largest battery manufacturer in the world, which was acquired by Inco through a tender offer in 1974. ESB, which is headquartered in Philadelphia, has fifty-three plants in the United States and thirty-five in various parts of the world, including Canada, plus a minority interest in sixteen others. Inco has its major operations, except for ESB, in Canada and its headquarters in Toronto. It also operates a rolling mill in West Virginia and a rolling mill and refinery in the United Kingdom and has developed nickel production operations in Indonesia and Guatemala.

Inco's biggest concentration of employment is in Sudbury, Ontario, 250 miles north of Toronto, where twelve mines, nickel and copper refineries, various smelters and mills, and an iron ore plant have employed 14,000 hourly and 3,400 salaried workers on a forty square-mile complex. In other Canadian operations, another 4,200 hourly and 1,600 salaried workers have been employed. In contrast, in the United States, exclusive of ESB, Inco has 4,000 employees in its metal business, including both hourly and salaried, and about the same number in the United Kingdom.

In location of the bulk of its facilities, as well as its share ownership, Inco is a Canadian company. It is in Canada that the world's supply of sulphide nickel ores is most abundant, although the Soviet Union and Australia are also major sources. Lateritic ores are found in tropical and subtropical countries. Laterite lies close to the surface and is strip-mined; the sulphide fields are found in hard rock and are deep-mined. The costs of mining and character of the skills involved differ considerably. Although the laterite areas are found in abundance and are easier to mine because of their closeness to the surface, they are lower in nickel

---

[37] *Fortune*, Vol. 100 (August 13, 1979), p. 196. For background on Inco, see "Inco: A giant wakes up and starts fighting," *Business Week*, May 26, 1973, pp. 44, 48; and "Inco: A Giant Learns How to Compete," *Fortune*, Vol. XCI (January 1975), pp. 104-10, 114, 116.

content and require considerably more energy to process. Inco's investments in Indonesia and Guatemala represent its attempts to protect its product sources. Inco is also studying the mining of manganese sea nodules to determine if that would be technically and commercially feasible. It is estimated that these contain five times as many nickel reserves as do land ores.[38] Other major nickel producers include the number two Canadian company, Falconbridge Nickel Mines, Ltd., Amax, Inc., an American multinational, and the French Société Métallurgique Le Nickel.[39]

The rise of new producing areas and companies, primarily in the tropical countries, has greatly increased supplies of nickel at a time when the demand has declined as a result of decreased capital spending. In particular, the failure of the steel industry to recover has hurt the nickel industry because of the heavy use of nickel in stainless steel manufacturing. A corollary has been the decline of Inco's share of the world market from approximately 70 percent to about one-half that. Canada, which once supplied 85 percent of the world's nickel requirements, now provides only 40 percent.[40] The impact on employment in Canada has been considerable and is, as always, reflected in international union relations.

IMF Activities

Undoubtedly, because its labor force has been so heavily Canadian, Inco has not seen much multinational union activity other than relations between Canadian and American local union affiliates of the United Steelworkers of America, which represents Inco employees in both countries. There is a Steelworkers liaison committee, composed of the various Canadian and West Virginian local unions, which meets from time to time. Terms and conditions of employment in the two countries contain significant differences.

---

[38] Information supplied by Inco.

[39] In 1976, Falconbridge had sales of $490 million and 9,700 employees. It is 37 percent owned by McIntyre Mines, Ltd., of Toronto, which in turn is 39 percent owned by Superior Oil Company of Houston, Texas. Le Nickel is part of the Rothschild Group of companies known as IMETAL, which in 1976 had sales of $1.4 billion and 21,200 employees. Amax, headquartered in Connecticut, is a major producer of several minerals, with 1978 sales of $1.7 billion and 16,564 employees. *Fortune,* Vol. 99 (May 7, 1979), pp. 276-77.

[40] See John Edwards, "Wonder metal loses its glitter," *Financial Times,* November 10, 1977, p. 12; and Charles Pye, "Why Inco layoffs were inevitable," *Financial Post* (Canada), November 19, 1977, p. 22.

The first major attempt to increase cooperation among unionists employed in nickel operations occurred in late 1971, when the Iron and Steel and Nonferrous Metals Industries Department (formerly the Iron and Steel Department) of the IMF, of which the United Steelworkers is a major affiliate, convened its First World Nickel Conference in Lausanne, Switzerland. This meeting, which was held immediately following the 1971 IMF Congress, was chaired by the Steelworkers' national director for Canada and included a large delegation from this union. Other countries represented including New Caledonia, Australia, Colombia, the Dominican Republic, France, India, the Philippines, Venezuela, and Rhodesia.[41] Besides Inco, major companies with which the unions dealt included Falconbridge of Canada and Le Nickel, which operates in New Caledonia, a producing area exceeded only by Canada and the Soviet Union.[42]

Much of the First World Nickel Conference deliberations were devoted to the possible impact on Canadian operations of the continued development of lateritic ore operations in various tropical countries. The great distances between Canada and the tropical countries and the differences between the standards of living in the areas where Inco's older facilities are located and those in such countries as Guatemala, Indonesia, and New Caledonia would seem to preclude any joint bargaining arrangements. Both the Steelworkers and the IMF, however, encourage unionization in these new areas, advise and support unions there, and otherwise attempt to assist them to raise wages and working conditions. This would, of course, be designed not only to improve the standards of living in underdeveloped countries but also to reduce the cost differentials favoring them over their Canadian, United States, and British counionists.

The IMF sponsored a second World Nickel Conference, which was held in Honolulu, Hawaii, April 29-30, 1976. According to the IMF, thirty-four trade union delegates from eight countries attended.[43] Again, a principal concern of the conference, in addition to the exchange of information on labor agreements and social conditions in various countries, was the development of sources of nickel in underdeveloped areas and the consequences of that development upon labor conditions in Canada. The Domini-

---

[41] *Steel Labor*, December 1971, p. 7.

[42] See Edwards, "Wonder metal," p. 12.

[43] See *IMF News*, No. 12/13 (June 1976), p. 1.

can Republic, Brazil, Indonesia, the Philippines, Colombia, and Guatemala were again noted as major sources of new nickel development. Concern was expressed because of the lack of union rights in most of these countries and the need for such countries to adopt standards recommended by the International Labour Organisation.

The Second IMF World Nickel Conference noted that the major existing corporations in the industry, particularly Inco, are the ones expanding in the underdeveloped areas and served "notice to the multinational corporations that the trade union movements in their home countries will view most seriously any exploitation of their employees anywhere in the world." [44]

Despite these strident words, the IMF proposed in fact to improve the exchange of information among affiliates, to provide assistance when needed by affiliates, and to implement, "as needed and practicable, . . . pilot bargaining objectives to provide international trade union services geared to match the mobility of the multinational corporations of the industry . . . specifically in Colombia and Indonesia where special assistance is required to provide trade union strength at mine sites." [45]

The Second IMF World Nickel Conference, reflecting the optimism in the industry, painted a rosy picture of future growth and employment. One year later, however, demand had fallen drastically. By the end of 1977, Inco, caught with a 308 million pound inventory, announced that it would lay off 3,450 employees in Canada and 10 percent of its work force in the United Kingdom.[46] Falconbridge reduced its work force by 1,200 persons.[47] Under such circumstances, opportunities for international union cooperation recede into the background as those affected by layoffs concentrate on their direct problems.

Inco has reported that, "considering the size of producer inventories throughout the world, restoration of a healthy supply-demand balance in the world nickel market will take some

---

[44] *Ibid.*

[45] International Metalworkers' Federation, *Report of Activities to the 24th World Congress*, Vol. 1, pp. 139-41.

[46] Patrick Wallace, "Inco Ltd. Gives Details on Its Ills in Nickel Market," *Wall Street Journal*, November 9, 1977, p. 22; Edwards, "Wonder metal," p. 12; and Pye, "Why Inco layoffs were inevitable," p. 22.

[47] Patrick Wallace, "Falconbridge Planning Sharp Cuts in '78 at Sudbury, Ontario, Nickel Operations," *Wall Street Journal*, December 9, 1977, p. 7.

time." [48] Although an eight-month strike at Inco's Sudbury operations drastically cut down inventories, problems of oversupply are not likely to disappear. International union cooperation in the industry is unlikely to move forward until the industry's health is restored.

THE ALUMINUM INDUSTRY

The aluminum industry is dominated by six multinational firms (see Table IV-4): the Aluminum Company of America (Alcan), Alcan Aluminium of Canada, Reynolds Metals, Kaiser, Pechiney Ugine Kuhlmann of France, and Alusuisse (Swiss Aluminium). Although Pechiney is the largest company by virtue of its investments in other metals and chemicals,[49] it ranks near the bottom of the six major producers in aluminum production.

Because bauxite, the raw material from which aluminum is extracted, was found in the Caribbean area, particularly Jamaica, prior to its discovery in commercial quantities in Australia, Africa, and elsewhere, and because of its proximity there to the North American market, the four major North American companies established mining and, in some cases, smelting subsidiaries in Jamaica, the Dominican Republic, and Guyana. More recently, deposits in Venezuela and Brazil have been developed.

The IMF and its large affiliate the United Steelworkers of America have encouraged, supported, and advised the labor movements in the Caribbean since World War II, including giving advice and technical assistance in collective bargaining. The basis of the political power of Prime Minister Michael Manley of Jamaica was in fact organized and developed with the Steelworkers' and IMF's assistance. By 1970, most of these Caribbean labor movements were sufficiently entrenched to operate with little or no outside help.[50]

The IMF interest in the industry has also been evidenced in conferences such as the latest one held in Munich, West Ger-

---

[48] "Inco Fears Resumption of Normal Production of Nickel is Years Off," *Wall Street Journal*, December 21, 1977, p. 22.

[49] An incident involving another secretariat and Pechiney is discussed in chapter VIII.

[50] For accounts of the Steelworkers', IMF's, and other international unions' interest in the Caribbean, see Jeffrey Harrod, *Trade Union Foreign Policy* (Garden City, N.Y.: Anchor Books, Doubleday & Company, 1972); and Michael Manley, *A Voice at the Workplace* (London: André Deutsch Ltd., 1975).

TABLE IV-4

The Six Major Aluminum Companies, 1978

Company	Headquarters	Sales ($000)	Assets ($000)	Net Income ($000)	Employees
Pechiney Ugine Kuhlmann	Paris	6,130,496	7,217,729	57,981	95,974
Aluminum Company of America (ALCOA)	Pittsburgh	4,051,800	4,167,200	312,700	46,000 [a]
Alcan Aluminium	Montreal	3,771,204	3,886,286	289,391	63,415
Reynolds Metals	Richmond, Va.	2,829,300	2,708,700	117,800	36,200 [a]
Alusuisse (Swiss Aluminium)	Zurich	2,785,994	4,494,477	52,988	36,317
Kaiser Aluminum & Chemical	Oakland, Calif.	2,466,000	2,679,100	145,500	26,865 [a]

Source: *Fortune*, Vol. 99 (May 7, 1979), pp. 272, 274; and Vol. 100 (August 13, 1979), pp. 194, 196.

[a] Average for the year.

many, from October 31 to November 1, 1977. Fifty trade union delegates, representing workers worldwide, met in Munich to discuss economic conditions and what was perceived to be a "profound, structural change" in the industry.[51] Considerable emphasis was also placed on the question of occupational health hazards.

In preparation for the conference, the IMF prepared several documents:

1. "Aluminum—The Leader in Non-ferrous Metals; An Essential for New Technology Economic and Social Development"

2. "Multinational Aluminum Companies; A Brief Survey"

3. "Aluminum Industry; A Review of Collective Bargaining and Social Achievements"

4. "Occupational Health Hazards in the Aluminum Industry." [52]

The conference approach to the aluminum industry served to highlight the problems that the IMF considered to be the most important at the particular time. As far as we can determine, there has been no major confrontation between the IMF and any multinational firm in the industry since that conference.

EMF Activity

The EMF has made some tentative moves into the aluminum industry. It established a "working group" of union officials on Alcan Aluminium Europe, which met in February 1977 to discuss employment matters. Prior thereto, the EMF general secretary had an informal meeting with Alcan's European manager.[53] The EMF plans to set up a second group for Estel, a Dutch-based concern, and Kaiser, which are planning a joint venture to merge their European operations.[54]

---

[51] *IMF News*, No. 22 (December 1977), p. 1.

[52] All documents published by the IMF for the Third IMF World Aluminum Conference, Munich, October 31-November 1, 1977.

[53] European Metalworkers' Federation, *Report of Activities of the Secretariat, 1974-1977* (Brussels, 1977), pp. 92-93.

[54] Michael Van Os, "European Aluminium link planned by Kaiser, Estel," *Financial Times*, July 18, 1979, p. 18; Hubert Thierron, general secretary, EMF, interview in Brussels, May 10, 1979.

THE BALL BEARING INDUSTRY: AKTIEBOLAGET SKF

SKF, headquartered in Göteborg, Sweden, since 1967, is the leading international ball bearing producing firm. The company was founded in Göteborg in 1907 by Sven Wingquist, who later designed the double-row self-aligning ball bearing. In addition to a complete line of ball and roller bearings, the company has expanded into the production of special steels, high-speed steel-cutting tools, and textile machinery components. In 1978, SKF had sales of $2.1 billion and employed 54,468 persons in West Germany (23 percent), Scandinavia (20 percent), Italy (15 percent), Great Britain (12 percent), France (10 percent), North America (10 percent), South America (4 percent), Asia, Africa, Australia (4 percent), and in other European areas (2 percent).[55]

Union Assistance in the United Kingdom

In the summer of 1975, SKF was successful in acquiring a majority shareholding in the Sheffield Twist Drill and Steel Company, the largest United Kingdom-owned producer of high-speed cutting tools. Discussions over the acquisition were complicated by a strong competitive bid by Thorn Electrical Industries, a British conglomerate that owns Clarkson's, a high-speed tool manufacturer and competitor of Sheffield. Employee consultation and union support appear to have been crucial factors in SKF's success in consummating the merger. SKF insisted on having the support of Sheffield's 2,500 employees and the two important British unions, the General and Municipal Workers' Union (GMWU) and the Amalgamated Union of Engineering Workers (AUEW). The GMWU gave immediate support to SKF's position, and the AUEW followed after contacting Svenska Metall, which in turn backed SKF.[56]

World Council and Meeting

A world council for SKF was established at the IMF Central Committee's meeting in Tokyo in October 1975. This action

---

[55] Company information provided to the authors. See also *Fortune*, Vol. 100 (August 13, 1979), p. 196.

[56] For various aspects of the merger negotiations, see "SKF's Successful Bid for UK Firm," *Business Europe*, Vol. XV (August 15, 1975), pp. 257-58; "Sheffield Twist backs Thorn bid," *Financial Times*, July 3, 1975, p. 1; and "SKF bid for Sheffield Twist nears victory," *ibid.*, July 10, 1975, p. 1.

grew out of an earlier meeting in 1975 of SKF's trade unionists organized by the IMF and held in Schweinfurt, Germany. SKF has its largest ball bearing producing facilities in this German region.

On March 18, 1976, Herman Rebhan, general secretary of the IMF, addressed a letter to the SKF Group president suggesting that a meeting take place between a delegation from the IMF, trade unionists representing SKF workers from a number of countries, and top management of the SKF Group to discuss employment security. The IMF expressed concern about the insecurity of workers at some of the SKF plants "due to effects of the present economic situation, the fierce competition on the world ball-bearing market and rationalization programmes." [57] A meeting was requested for some time in May or June 1976. SKF agreed to hold a meeting only with Rebhan and an IMF colleague. The IMF rejected the SKF proposal and insisted that the delegation at the meeting should include at least members of the Swedish unions as representatives with the parent company.[58]

The meeting was finally held on November 8, 1976, in Göteborg when it was agreed that the IMF would be represented by Herman Rebhan and Assistant General Secretary Karl Casserini to be accompanied by the international secretary of Svenska Metall, Jan Olsson. The SKF Group was represented by its president, his two deputies, and representatives of the legal, personnel, and public affairs units.

Information exchanged at the meeting pertained to the general economic situation, its effect on the SKF Group and on the prospects of the ball bearing industry generally, the implementation and results of the SKF Global Forecasting and Supply System (GFSS—which aims to have each individual bearing size manufactured at only one location allowing the company to manufacture fewer types and sizes but in greater volume), and current trends in the sociopolitical field. In addition, the IMF representatives informed SKF Group management about specific local matters to which their attention had been drawn by member unions in Germany, Great Britain, the Netherlands, France, the United States, and Australia. The IMF also submitted a document for the attention of the company regarding occupational hazards in the ball bearing industry. The company

---

[57] Letter from SKF official to the author, October 26, 1977.

[58] Information furnished to the author by the IMF.

representatives received the union documentation and clarified issues raised by the union.

Brussels and Paris Meetings

Subsequent to this meeting, the IMF and the EMF invited union delegates from the SKF Group, who were present at a European Trade Union Confederation meeting in Brussels from December 7 to 8, 1976, to meet and exchange information on the economic and social situation, with particular emphasis on employment problems. Union representatives from Germany, Belgium, France, Sweden, Italy, and Great Britain were present. Werner Thönnessen and Karl Casserini from the IMF and Günter Köpke, Hubert Thierron, and E. Crins were present from the EMF. Casserini presented a report from the IMF to the delegates giving the background of the November 8 meeting held to discuss SKF problems. Individuals from the SKF unions in different countries took part in the discussion. All of the reports expressed a concern with worldwide recession and the aggravation of the employment problems as a result of the "worldwide structural rationalizations which were being implemented in the SKF Group throughout the world at the same time." [59]

Casserini indicated that a worldwide committee on SKF would be organized in 1977 and that a meeting should take place to continue discussion of the problems. It was suggested that the meeting should take place in France, where there had been some problem with "full union recognition." [60]

The IMF World Council for SKF met in Paris on April 3, 1978, under the leadership of Karl Casserini. A meeting was planned originally to discuss a strike situation involving the company in India. The SKF subsidiary in India, Associated Bearing Companies Limited, had been in confrontation with the ABC Employees Union since early 1977.

According to SKF, the Indian strike background concerned two major issues: "failure to reach an agreement in negotiations with the union following the expiration in 1976 of the previous three year contract" and "demands by the union in 1977 for reinstatement of six employees whose employment had

---

[59] IMF unpublished reports provided by the IMF.

[60] *Ibid.*

been terminated." [61] These issues were referred to the Poona Industrial Tribunal by the government of Maharashtra for adjudication, and the union called a strike for December 1977 to increase pressure on management. Efforts to ameliorate the strike failed, and after a prolonged period, twenty-four employees were suspended and served with "charge sheets." [62] The urgency of the world council meeting was reduced because SKF apparently agreed to reinstate most of the suspended employees with the understanding that the remaining workers would be put on special leave with wages pending the outcome of an inquiry into their cases.

During the council meeting, the delegates were given a tour of the Saint-Cyr-sur-Loire plant, and local factory management answered questions. Subsequent to the plant tour, an SKF French head-office staff member was host to the delegates for lunch at a local restaurant. The IMF continued its campaign to have the six terminated employees reinstated. According to both the IMF and SKF, the employees were reinstated early in 1979.[63] The company, however, made the reinstatement with the understanding that the affected employees would be dismissed if disturbances occurred following their reentry into the plant.

Conclusion

The IMF has thus made a major effort to bring together SKF unions around the world and has achieved a meeting with the company. It is likely that future IMF conferences will be held, but it is by no means certain that the company will agree to further meetings with headquarters personnel.

THE STEEL INDUSTRY

Although large steel companies, such as Nippon Steel or U.S. Steel have a few subsidiaries outside of their home countries, the steel industry is basically not multinational in terms of production facilities. Even in Europe, companies, although tied together in the iron, steel, and coal arrangements that preceded the European Community organization, remain heavily

---

[61] Letter from SKF to the author, June 27, 1978.

[62] *Ibid.*

[63] *IMF News*, No. 2 (1979), p. 5; and company personnel, interviews, May 22, 1979.

domestic. Moreover, many steel companies are government owned or controlled. Nevertheless, the IMF has long had an Iron and Steel Department, which has sponsored a number of world conferences. Initially, delegates concentrated on exchanging information about wages and benefits; more recently, the issue has been the worldwide crisis in steel and the role of the IMF and the national unions in preserving employment in the industry. This, of course, means protective activities in favor of developed countries, except possibly Japan, and against Third World countries like South Korea, Taiwan, and Brazil, which are new, very efficient, and low-cost entrants into the industry.

Union Response to the Steel Crisis

The steel industry worldwide did not recover adequately from the worldwide recession of 1973-75. Excess capacity worldwide in the industry, coupled with a worldwide decline in steel demand since 1974, the probability that this demand in the major industrial markets will increase at a slower rate in the future than it has heretofore, and the extreme price competition in the world trade are considered to be major contributors to the current crisis.

In September 1977, United Steelworkers (USW) officials attended the Fifty-seventh Congress of Tekko Roren, the Japanese steel union. At this meeting, the USW treasurer, Frank McKee, cited the close relationship that exists between the two unions, and he proposed orderly market arrangements. McKee stated that the USW position with regard to the United States and to other steel-producing countries is an "orderly marketing arrangement that will allow steel imports but not to the point of disrupting any domestic markets, harming the economic viability of any steel industry, nor to the point of imposing economic hardship on steel workers anywhere." He emphasized that international union cooperation was very important—in fact, more important than national concerns. He referred to the joint projects with the IMF and the recent Japanese-North American Metalworkers Conference held in Hawaii in 1976.[64]

The United Steelworkers hosted the latest World Iron and Steel Conference for the IMF, in Pittsburgh in June 1976. According to the IMF 1977 Congress report, 150 representatives from thirty countries attended. The emphasis of the conference was the demand for worldwide government cooperation in the

---

64 "Common interests unite American, Japanese Steel Workers: USWA's McKee," *Steel Labor*, October 1977, p. 4.

steel industry as a countermeasure to the dangers of private cartelization by the big steel producers. The IMF is also supporting the European Miners and Steelworkers Union Liaison Committee with the European Community. This committee was established to work out proposals and ways for the European Community to prevent steel recessions.

The Pittsburgh conference developed a six-point action plan which covers the following areas:

1. Full employment in the steel industry. This would include a worldwide survey of investment projects in iron and steel. These investments would be looked at with regard to their effect on the employees, and in addition, a list of proposed plant closures would be established and the union advised at the earliest possible date;

2. Social protection of steelworkers in world trade;

3. Use of government committees and those of the Organization for Economic Cooperation and Development, International Labour Organisation, and European Community to advance union views. This point would also encourage worldwide cooperation in steel through GATT or a world steel conference, provided the unions have representation;

4. Collective bargaining policies for social progress with social protection;

5. Democratization at the workplace and throughout the industry. Since the IMF believes that the steel industry is becoming multinational, it feels that the industry must have binding international control measures. In addition, the IMF believes that it should meet with multinational steel companies to discuss problems relating to total global activities. This would include discussions of the repercussions of central decision making on the plant level; and

6. Improvement of health and safety in a better working environment.[65]

The IMF in its latest congress report describes the role it played at the UNIDO meeting on steel held in Vienna in February 1976.[66] UNIDO (United Nations Industrial Development

---

[65] International Metalworkers' Federation, *Report of Activities to the 24th World Congress*, Vol. 1, pp. 143-46.

[66] *Ibid.*, p. 27.

Organization) is designed to assist less-developed countries in infrastructure building and industrialization. Because steel is considered the basic industry needed for rapid industrialization in developing countries, the main issue at this first consultative meeting was how to increase steel production in the less-developed countries from 6 percent to 30 percent of the world output by the year 2000. The IMF representatives questioned this objective because it would increase steel's overcapacity, create employment and social problems, and cause unfair competition through low wages. As a result of the IMF's intervention, it is reported, the meeting's final report included a statement that steel consumption and steel production in developing and less-developed countries would be carefully coordinated to avoid overcapacity worldwide.

The IMF has established a Working Party on Steel in response to what it sees as a trend toward multinational steel companies, as well as regional developments in the European Community's policy measures.[67] The EC policy measures, the IMF reports, include approval of two agreements for a northern and southern grouping of several steel plants in Germany and the approval of a steel multinational (ARBED) in Luxembourg. Another important development is EUROFER, the Community-wide private association of steel industrialists. These trends, the IMF feels, need to be monitored on a worldwide basis.

An emergency meeting of the Working Party on Steel was held in April 1977 in Frankfurt, Germany. At this meeting, the IMF reviewed its position, which includes: opposing any national assistance and pricing practices for exports which disturb the market, opposing dumping practices, insisting that national and international companies make personnel and employment decisions in cooperation with the trade unions, and, finally, calling for an international steel conference. This would be a tripartite world conference of the major steel-producing countries; developing countries would also be able to participate. In line with the third point of its six-point plan, the IMF brought its world steel conference proposal before the Ad Hoc Steel Committee of the Organization for Economic Cooperation and Development (OECD). This committee has been set up just recently to study the international problem in the steel industry,

---

[67] *Ibid.*, p. 28.

with particular emphasis on two areas: the international structuring of the industry and the control of international trade. The committee did not reach a conclusion on the IMF proposal. It discussed the possibility that, at some future meeting of the committee, it might consult with union representatives. Many delegates of the committee, however, said that it should not get involved in what they called "other initiatives," and they refused to consider a possible meeting with the unions as a preparatory meeting for a world conference on steel.[68]

THE SHIPBUILDING INDUSTRY

The shipbuilding industry has much in common with steel. Both industries provide considerable employment, comprise primarily national rather than multinational concerns (many of which are government owned), and are in deep crisis because of overcapacity exacerbated by the entry of Third World countries into the industry. The shipbuilding industry's problems and the possible solutions to its crisis involve national economies, nationalized corporations, international government organizations, and both international trade secretariats and regional unions. The governments have been pursuing individual solutions to the problems, while groups such as the European Community and the OECD have been trying to find solutions within a broader framework. The international unions, in the meantime, are applying pressure for more direct participation and discussion with these other groups, which could set the precedent for tripartite action both within this industry and others.

Although there are many factors that have contributed to the current worldwide crisis in the shipbuilding industry, one factor seems to occupy a key position—overcapacity. A report on overcapacity in world shipbuilding issued in mid-December 1977 by the Central Intelligence Agency's National Foreign Assessment Center states:

> Output in the depressed world shipbuilding industry will continue to fall until the early 1980s when production will be about one-third the peak 1975 level of 34 million grt [gross register tonnage]. The decline stems from speculative overbuilding in the early 1970s and

[68] "The OECD Ad Hoc 'Steel' Committee is Looking for Greater Transparency in Market Factors and Crisis Factors in the Steel Industry," *Europe*, October 3/4, 1977, p. 7.

the worldwide economic recession—set off by the massive 1973/74 oil price hikes—which deflated demand for both tankers and bulk carriers.[69]

The supply/demand relationship of tankers and bulk carriers is so unbalanced that an elimination of the tanker surplus is unlikely before 1985 at the earliest. The National Foreign Assessment Center report also states:

> Although bulk cargo shipments declined with the onset of the worldwide recession in 1974, orders for bulk carriers nearly doubled in 1975 and remained strong in 1976 as owners converted orders from unneeded tankers to bulk carriers rather than pay cancellation fees. The recession, speculative ordering, and conversions of tanker orders created a surplus of bulk carriers . . . that will increase over the next year or two as orders are completed.[70]

Another factor contributing to the worldwide crisis is the market-sharing relationship among the shipbuilders in Western Europe, Japan, and the developing countries, such as South Korea, Taiwan, Yugoslavia, and Brazil. At present, Japan has over a 59 percent share of the world market. Even with this share of the market, Japan is complaining of unfair competition from the developing countries such as South Korea and Taiwan. In addition, shipyards in Brazil are operating at full capacity and report $300 million in foreign orders. In 1974, Brazil was not listed among the top fifteen shipbuilding countries; now, it is third after Japan and the United States.[71] Although many of the developing countries' yards are operating at full capacity, yards in the United Kingdom are at 70 percent capacity; France is operating at 50 percent capacity; and Sweden has dropped from second to fifth place as a leading shipbuilding nation.

IMF Activity

The IMF Shipbuilding Department, with Lars Skytøen, president of the Norwegian Metalworkers' Union, as its president, is reported to be increasing its activities in light of future retrenchments in the industry. Until recently, its activities were on an ad hoc meeting basis, with an IMF Asian Regional Ship-

---

[69] "World Shipbuilding Crisis Could Go Beyond Mid-1980," *Shipyard Weekly*, December 15, 1977, p. 1.

[70] *Ibid.*

[71] "A Move to Divvy Up the Orders for Ships," *Business Week*, December 5, 1977, p. 37.

building Seminar held in Singapore in May 1975. This was preceded by an IMF Shipbuilding Conference in Tokyo in the spring of 1973. More recently, however, a Working Party on Shipbuilding has been established.[72]

This working party, made up of more than thirty delegates from affiliates in twelve shipbuilding nations, plus the EMF, met with the president and secretary of the OECD's Working Party No. 6 on Shipbuilding in November 1976. At this meeting, the IMF presented a catalog of proposals to the OECD. This "laundry list" of proposals included the following:

> elimination of the use of dangerous vessels; development of new types of ships for greater safety; preservation of the natural environment, energy saving and better transport services; development of new products for which production facilities in shipyards are particularly suitable; reconversion measures for immediate job saving and long-term employment stability; spread of orders and work to obtain the maximum possible employment security in the framework of economic cooperation and planning in world shipbuilding; regular information on labour market development in shipbuilding and in industrial areas with shipbuilding concentration; fight against speculation; rejection of protectionism through effective employment saving programmes; worldwide coordination of investment; worldwide reduction and control of state subsidies; recommendation of the need, under international supervision, to use state aid as a temporary measure for indispensable social protection; tripartite consultations and planning measures with effective trade union participation at national level, and tripartite discussions at international level; fair labour conditions; fair share of increased productivity and maintenance of a price level permitting the shipbuilding industry to face up to its responsibilities for employment and income guarantees; abolition of overtime, compensation for unavoidable overtime with corresponding time off; reduction of working time without loss of income; application of social plans providing for early retirement, retraining and transfer to other jobs, as well as recognition of the full negotiating rights of trade unions in all aspects concerning employment security and the future development of the industry.[73]

The OECD Working Party reportedly expressed some positive response to these union proposals but pointed out that many of the measures requested were outside of the OECD's objectives as it viewed them.

---

[72] International Metalworkers' Federation, *Report of Activities to the 24th World Congress*, Vol. 1, p. 32.

[73] "IMF Demands OECD Guidelines for Social Policy to Safeguard Employment in Shipyards," *IMF News*, No. 1/2 (January 1977), p. 1.

A second meeting was held with the two working parties in March 1977, at which time, Herman Rebhan, general secretary of the IMF, presented a paper that reiterated the IMF's November 1976 demands and included additional proposals. In this paper, the IMF disagrees with the forecasts that the OECD had used; the IMF's figures are more optimistic and predict an increase in tonnage in the early 1980s. The new proposals include spreading orders and work to maximize employment. This would be done under the OECD's aegis, and market developments would be watched. Other new measures include work conversion proposals and control of shipbuilding prices to prevent unfair trade practices. In addition, state aid, although temporary, would be used to help in the adaptation process.

Rebhan reiterates several earlier proposals, including steps regarding new technological development, but he adds that, because companies would not ask for the more expensive ships, the governments should intervene and tell owners of their responsibilities. Finally, Rebhan calls for concerted efforts by all responsible parties and for tripartite meetings. Specifically, he states:

> In this common endeavor the trade unions must be associated at all levels and in the various procedures. They must be able to follow and contribute at all stages, from assessment of the situation, the elaboration of policies and recommendations to their application. Tripartitism has been established in various OECD member countries, to win the battle of survival and lay the foundation for future social progress in a prosperous shipbuilding industry.[74]

EMF Activity

At the November 1976 meeting of the IMF Working Party on Shipbuilding and the OECD Working Party No. 6, the EMF, which also was present, submitted a memorandum on the shipbuilding industry in Europe and a summary of the survey that it had done on wages, working hours, and complementary systems of social security in a number of European shipyards. This 1976 survey is an updated, although abbreviated, version of the report on working conditions in shipyards in the European Community that Günter Köpke, then general secretary of the EMF, had prepared in 1974 at the request of the Commission

---

[74] Herman Rebhan, "Statement . . . on behalf of the IMF Working Party on Shipbuilding to the OECD Working Party No. 6 on Shipbuilding," March 22, 1977, p. 12.

of European Communities. The latest memorandum, presented by Köpke, calls the European Commission to task for what the EMF believes to be a policy aimed solely at reducing production capacities. According to the EMF, this policy of limiting production capacities should include provisions for maintaining full employment, reducing subsidies, enforcing environmental measures, and coordinating negotiations between the EC, Japan, and certain Eastern countries on capacity reduction.[75]

The memorandum also criticizes the commission for not analyzing the effect that its proposed employment cutbacks would have on the various regions. It also states that the EMF is "categorically opposed to the establishing of a link between the reduction of production capacities and the reduction of employment."[76]

The EMF, as did the IMF, urged the establishment of a tripartite conference and called for the same steps as those called for by the IMF: reducing subsidies, collecting Community-wide information on production and employment programs, and developing regional manpower policies.

On November 23, 1977, the EMF rejected the commission's action program proposals, which were sent to the Council of Ministers. According to the EMF, the production estimates are too low, and announcing a 46 percent reduction in production capacity could result in plant closures and mass dismissals in economically weak coastal regions of various countries. In addition to opposing the plans, which affect more than one hundred thousand workers, the EMF stated that it was irresponsible of the commission to submit proposals to the council that only consider industry interests and do not, at the same time, present a general plan for wage and employment guarantees for all European shipbuilding workers. The EMF felt that consulting with high-ranking government officials is not the way to develop policy:

> Without direct participation of workers and their metal unions, on an equal basis, in the preparation and decision making, any real Community policy which aims to overcome the crisis in the European shipbuilding industry is certain to fail. This is why the EMF demands that a tripartite conference be convened at European level as quickly as possible in which all parties concerned should participate: government representatives, the Commission,

---

[75] Memorandum of the European Metalworkers' Federation on the Shipbuilding Industry in Europe, November 23, 1976, p. 2.

[76] *Ibid.*, p. 4.

industrialists and trade unions, in order to discuss existing problems.[77]

The Executive Committee of the EMF met in Brussels from March 19 to 20, 1979, to discuss further problems in the shipbuilding industry. The committee decided "to advocate that a catalogue of demands for improving the safety of tankers be applied," such as requiring that tankers be limited to 100,000 to 150,000 dead weight tonnage, that tankers charging chemicals be equipped with a double hull, and that the maximum capacity of a loading tank not exceed ten thousand cubic meters. In addition, the committee also "examined and approved the outline of a 'scrap and build' programme for ships."[78] In regard to this program, the EMF proposed:

1. A 2 scrap for 1 build ratio as a basis, modified in accordance with a formula to be devised for ships over 50,000 compensated grt.

2. Shipowners scrapping and building on this basis to be eligible for special credit terms or a scrap premium or a combination of the two.

3. The premium or credit to be provided by the country in which the new ships are built. Flexibility could be allowed to each member country in the exact form of support to be given within an agreed ceiling and common guidelines.

4. Community funds to be provided to assist in the cost of these national payments as part of the overall policy of supporting and developing national shipping and shipbuilding industries. This would avoid excessive concentration of new orders in any one country.

5. The scheme to be introduced by the Commission for shipowners and shipbuilders in member states. But Japan and other shipping and shipbuilding countries be invited to operate similar schemes, with safeguards against low cost competition damaging European shipyards.

6. The scheme to be limited to 60 million dwt of ships scrapped over the 3 year period 1979-1981.

7. Owners to be allowed to scrap approved ships where it is most advantageous to them, but consideration to be given to a separate support scheme for the European shipbreaking industry in order to enable it to offer prices comparable to those in the Far East.[79]

---

[77] EMF Press Release, November 23, 1977.

[78] "Shipbuilding and Protection Against the Pollution of the Seas," EMF Press Release, March 21, 1979, p. 2.

[79] "Scrap and Build," EMF Executive Committee Report, February 11, 1979, p. 7.

Interestingly enough, the European Community's Economic and Social Committee issued an "Opinion . . . on Problems Currently Facing Community Shipping Policy, Particularly Maritime Safety, the Growing Importance of the New Shipping Nations, the Development of Flags of Convenience and the Discrimination against Certain Flags" on April 4, 1979, and it appears to have been influenced in large measure by the work of the EMF.[80] The committee's proposals include much of what the EMF demands and the harmonization of pay and working conditions on board ships with the right of Community inspectors to uphold established standards. Acting in concert, the EMF and European Community, of course, are interested in protecting jobs in the industry through a program that offers subsidies to shipbuilders and further restrictions on flags of convenience.

The EMF's shipbuilding demands are meant to harmonize with those of the International Transport Workers' Federation (ITF), which, as we shall note in chapter XVII, has waged a long fight to eliminate flags and crews of convenience from the seas. The EMF worked closely with the Transport Committee of the European Trade Union Confederation in developing these proposals which have a fourfold aim: (1) create shipbuilding needs by scrapping existing ships; (2) bring the resultant work to European shipyards; (3) create jobs for European maritime employees by eliminating use of less-developed country personnel now working on flag-of-convenience ships; and (4) establishment of a tripartite directing body through the European Community, in which the EMF is the accredited representative for employees.

WESTERN EUROPEAN METAL TRADES EMPLOYERS' ORGANIZATION

The Western European Metal Trades Employers' Organization (WEM) is an international organization composed of European national metal trades federations in the principal countries of Western Europe. The WEM has always been reluctant to meet with its labor counterpart, the EMF, to discuss employment and social

---

[80] European Economic Community, Economic and Social Committee, "Opinion . . . on Problems Currently Facing Community Shipping Policy, Particularly Maritime Safety, the Growing Importance of the New Shipping Nations, the Development of Flags of Convenience and the Discrimination Against Certain Flags," Brussels, April 4, 1979.

issues, but it was persuaded to have one meeting, which occurred in Brussels on November 14, 1975. The WEM agreed to this meeting apparently as a tactic to discourage individual company meetings with the EMF, which had already had several meetings, as described in this and the following chapter, with Philips, VFW-Fokker, and Continental Can of Europe.[81]

The agenda for the WEM-EMF meeting proposed discussions of the following:

(a) structure and tasks of the WEM and the EMF,

(b) employment situation in the European metal industries, and

(c) value of such contacts for the parties.

Prior to the meeting, the WEM declined to agree to institutionalize such meetings on an annual or other regular basis. The WEM also stipulated that all discussions be general in character and avoid anything that might be characterized as bargaining. The meeting followed this stipulation.

Following the meeting, however, there were a number of press reports concerning it that disturbed the WEM. During the premeeting discussions, the WEM insisted that, if there was to be a press release, there should be agreement on its mechanics and content. The EMF countered by declaring that it did not favor a press release. Since press reports following the meeting all contained the same general context, the WEM felt that this understanding had been violated. The EMF's position was that its executive had merely answered questions of individual reporters and naturally responded in the same manner to each. Whatever the facts, the WEM has declined to meet again with the EMF, which has also been unable to generate meetings with individual companies in recent years as well.

CONCLUSION

Multinational bargaining has not occurred in the industries examined in this chapter and, for most, does not seem any closer than it was a decade ago. Paradoxically, it could occur in two industries in which multinational corporations are largely absent

---

[81] This section is based upon several interviews with the former general secretary of the EMF and the secretary general of the WEM, and on correspondence with both.

—aerospace and shipbuilding. In the former, the Airbus Industrie Consortium has established an environment in which international cooperation among companies and countries could be extended to a tripartite arrangement. In shipbuilding, overcapacity problems, plus the drive of European Community bureaucrats for Community-wide tripartitism, open the way for European agreements. In both industries, government ownership and/or control of production facilities are likely to result in political support for union aims.

In these situations, the EMF, with its restricted European charter, is the likely beneficiary, rather than the IMF, with its much more diverse worldwide commitment. As we shall see in the following chapter, the EMF has also come closer than the IMF to multinational bargaining in the electrical and electronics industries.

CHAPTER V

The Electrical and Electronics Industries

Changes in technology and industrial structure in the electrical and electronics industries have created a variety of employment conditions to which the International Metalworkers' Federation (IMF) has responded in the past decade. An Electrical and Electronics Department was established by the IMF in 1967 under the chairmanship of Paul Jennings, then president of the American International Union of Electrical Workers (IUE), to collect information and monitor activities of multinational firms. The department is now directed by Copresidents T. Tateyama, president of Denki Roren (All Japan Federation of Electrical Machines Workers' Unions), and W. Wamsteeker, national secretary of Industriebond-NVV, the Netherlands. Administration and coordination of the department's affairs are conducted in Geneva under the direction of Werner Thönnessen, assistant general secretary of the IMF. Assistant General Secretary Karl Casserini also participates in the operation of particular company councils such as the one created for Singer.

Prior to his departure as an IMF assistant general secretary in 1977, Daniel Benedict, a former employee at the General Electric facility in Lynn, Massachusetts, was very active in the department and instrumental in arranging meetings and conferences to discuss the multinational firms. Some evaluation of the effectiveness of the world council, or working groups, idea was made by the IMF in 1979, and it appears that specific companies are being targeted for special attention.

The IMF's overall program in the electrical and electronics industries has included three world conferences (October 1970, the Hague; March 1976, Geneva; and October 1978, Geneva); two Latin American conferences (June-July 1971, Mexico City; and November 1978, Colombia); and two Asian seminars (May 1974, Tokyo; and June 1978, Singapore). In addition, several working groups for multinational companies, or world councils, have been established including those for General Electric, International Telephone and Telegraph, Singer, Brown Boveri, Honeywell, and International Business Machines. Westinghouse was targeted as a particular company for study at the world conference in 1978. (See Table V-1 for statistics on these concerns.)

WORLD COUNCILS/WORKING GROUPS

Subsequent to the establishment of the Electrical and Electronics Department, several world councils, or working groups, were organized to bring together unions representing employees of particular companies as had been done for automobile unionists in previous years. The discussion below concentrates on the work of some of the more active councils.

General Electric Company

The General Electric World Council held its first International Union Conference in Bogotá, Colombia, April 18-19, 1969; a second one in London in 1971; and a third in New York City in March 1973. The 1969 and 1973 meetings were timed to antedate the opening of triennial negotiations between General Electric (GE), the largest electrical machinery company in the world, and a coalition of unions. Among the unions, the IUE has the largest membership in GE. Messrs. Jennings and Benedict repeatedly stressed that their aim was to include unions from other countries within this coalition.[1] They succeeded in doing so to the extent of having foreign unionists attend a few negotiating meetings as nonparticipating visitors.

Over the objections of General Electric and other companies, National Labor Relations Board rulings, sustained in the courts,[2] permit unions certified to represent a particular bargaining unit to include representatives of other unions or other bargaining units on their bargaining committees provided that the fiction is maintained that these outside representatives are representing the unit then bargaining. General Electric deals with two unions on a multiplant, national basis: the IUE and the United Elec-

---

[1] See, e.g., "Bargaining Tables that Circle Earth," *IUE News*, February 4, 1971, p. 7.

[2] General Electric Co., 173 N.L.R.B. 253 (1968), *enforced*, General Electric v. NLRB, 412 F.2d 512 (2d Cir. 1969).

TABLE V-1

Twenty-one Major Companies in the
Electrical, Electronics, and Data Processing Industries, 1978

Company	Headquarters	Sales ($000)	Assets ($000)	Net Income ($000)	Employees
IBM	Armonk, N.Y.	21,076,089	20,771,374	3,110,568	325,517
General Electric	Fairfield, Conn.	19,653,800	15,036,000	1,229,700	401,000 [a]
Philips' Glöeilampen-fabrieken	Eindhoven	15,121,166 [b]	16,210,669	327,117	387,900 [b]
Siemens [c]	Munich	13,864,726	14,907,304	322,021	322,000
Matsushita Electric Industrial [d]	Osaka	10,020,545	9,700,225	416,695	95,487
Western Electric	New York	9,521,835	6,133,617	561,200	161,000 [a]
Hitachi [e]	Tokyo	9,153,283	11,064,047	304,390	138,690
Générale d'Electricité	Paris	7,004,167 [b]	5,893,547 [b]	56,848 [b]	152,000 [b]
Westinghouse Electric	Pittsburgh	6,663,300	6,317,600	243,400 [f]	141,776 [a]
RCA	New York	6,600,600	4,872,900	278,400	118,000
AEG-Telefunken	Frankfurt am Main	5,998,428	5,146,892	(182,305)	131,500
Xerox	Stamford, Conn.	5,901,900	5,577,900	476,900	104,736
Toshiba [e]	Kawasaki City	5,755,536	7,474,305	9,212	100,000
Thomson-Brandt	Paris	5,057,736	6,431,385	53,152	114,600

Table V-1 (continued)

Robert Bosch	Stuttgart	4,798,189	3,811,640	109,133	118,320
Schneider	Paris	4,704,937	12,754,319	1,044	109,000
Brown Boveri	Baden, Switzerland	4,562,236 [b]	7,607,359 [b]	N.A.	98,500 [b]
General Electric Co., Ltd.[e]	London	4,214,096	4,347,770	278,997	191,000
Sperry Rand [e]	New York	3,649,487	3,286,610	176,619	88,275
Honeywell	Minneapolis	3,547,800	2,826,100	201,400	86,328
Singer	New York	2,469,200	1,435,400	62,800	81,000

Source: *Fortune*, Vol. 99 (May 7, 1979), pp. 270-89; Vol. 100 (August 13, 1979), pp. 194-203.

[a] Average for the year.

[b] Also includes certain subsidiaries owned 50 percent or less, either fully or on a prorated basis.

[c] Figures are for fiscal year ending September 30, 1978.

[d] Figures are for fiscal year ending November 20, 1978.

[e] Figures are for fiscal year ending March 31, 1978.

[f] Reflects an extraordinary charge of at least 10 percent.

trical, Radio and Machine Workers (UE), from which the IUE seceded when the UE's Communist domination caused its expulsion from the CIO in 1949. In addition, GE deals with numerous other unions on a local basis. To form a united coalition front, representatives of the unions that have bargaining rights on a local basis have sat in on the national IUE negotiations since 1966.[3]

In 1969, Daniel Benedict also sat in on a few of the GE-IUE negotiating sessions. He did not attempt to participate in any discussions.[4] In 1972, a meeting of the General Electric World Council was held, as noted, just prior to the commencement of GE-IUE negotiations. The IUE asked if the world council group could attend the initial negotiating session. Because the IUE could have brought them in any case as IUE *representatives* and because General Electric could not then legally object (provided that the outside unionists conformed to the court interpretation in their conduct, as discussed below), the company gave its assent.

Foreign unionists attending the opening of General Electric negotiations on March 22, 1973, included those from West Germany, South Africa, Mexico, Colombia, Venezuela, and Argentina, besides Benedict. In addition, German and Mexican union representatives attended the UE negotiations that day. Both IUE and UE groups had their pictures taken with the company negotiators. No substantive discussions occurred on the first negotiating day for the 1972 contract; the international contingent made no speeches, did not otherwise participate in the negotiations, and did not appear again at the negotiations.

Prior to the 1972 negotiations, Jennings told the *Wall Street Journal* that the forthcoming appearance of the IMF council members from abroad was " 'a very important symbol' to remind GE of the backing that the negotiators have." [5] Certainly,

---

[3] For the background on this coalition movement and on General Electric employee relations, see William N. Chernish, *Coalition Bargaining*, Industrial Research Unit Major Study, No. 45 (Philadelphia: University of Pennsylvania Press, 1969), esp. chapter VI; and Herbert R. Northrup, *Boulwarism* (Ann Arbor: Bureau of Industrial Relations, University of Michigan, 1964).

[4] In the *IUE News*, February 4, 1971, it is stated that Benedict "sat in on several GE negotiations sessions." In July 1971, the *IUE News* reported that Benedict "participated in the 1969-1970 GE and W[estinghouse] coordinated bargaining in the U.S." The first statement is accurate.

[5] Byron E. Calame, "Import Curbs Could Hurt U.S. Labor's Ties to Unions Abroad, AFL-CIO Officials Say," *Wall Street Journal*, February 27, 1973, p. 4.

it was symbolic only. General Electric is not strong in Europe, and the IMF council is largely a Central and South American group. It is difficult to believe that employees in those countries would give up income to support their much better-compensated brothers in the north. What has been important to unionists there is the technical and financial support from United States unions and the IMF, which, as in the case of the automobile unions, has resulted in greater bargaining sophistication in dealing with General Electric within their countries. The only overt foreign support for the IUE cause in relation to General Electric, exclusive of Benedict's and the foreign union representatives' "symbolic" presence, occurred during the 1969-70 strike, when the IMF "made a small token contribution in Swiss francs to the IUE strike fund . . . [and] the Japanese electrical workers council contributed $5,000; the presentation took place at a picket line in Newark, N.J." [6] Although one author termed the Japanese action as "perhaps more significant" [7] realistically than that of the IMF, both appear symbolic at most.

If, however, the IMF, or any other group, would attempt to alter the bargaining structure with General Electric by insisting that GE bargain about matters pertaining to plants not included within the IUE bargaining unit (or any other legally defined bargaining unit for which those bargaining were the duly certified agents), such an attempt would be contrary to the court order that has compelled General Electric to admit outsiders chosen by the IUE to the bargaining sessions. For the law, as interpreted by the courts, requires that the outsiders maintain the legal fiction that they are IUE representatives and that they bargain only for matters pertaining to the IUE bargaining unit. If, at a GE-IUE bargaining session, union representatives persisted in attempting to bargain about, for example, labor conditions in the General Electric plants in Colombia, the company not only could refuse to discuss the matter but would be able to bring a charge against the American union involved of refusal to bargain in good faith.[8]

---

[6] Richard L. Barovick, "Labor Reacts to Multinationalism," *Columbia Journal of World Business*, Vol. V (July-August 1970), p. 42.

[7] *Ibid.*

[8] This charge would be brought pursuant to section 8(b)(3) of the Taft-Hartley Act.

The General Electric operations in Colombia have been a favorite source of IMF publicity about the company because a former plant manager there permitted an international union committee and Benedict to tour the facility. The unionists claimed to have found conditions below those elsewhere. In an interview with the *New York Times,* Benedict claimed that the IUE "confronted" GE repeatedly during the 1969-70 negotiations with alleged GE malpractices in Colombia and that, because it was "too embarrassing" for GE, the practices ceased.[9] The reporter did not contact the company, whose negotiators told the authors that Colombia or Bogotá were not mentioned in the negotiations; that one day a claim was made of poor treatment of workers outside of the United States, to which the reply was made that the company negotiators were familiar with United States but not foreign laws; and that no other like reference could be found in the negotiation minutes. The company denied the allegations reported in the *New York Times.*[10]

The IUE and IMF personnel have claimed several other international actions, none of which we have been able to confirm. For example, it has been alleged that, during a 1965 strike at GE's plant in Rome, Georgia, IMF pressure prevented GE from sending "struck work" overseas.[11] The company denies that any such interference occurred or was a factor in the strike. An IMF regional paper merely stated that Jennings sent a cable asking the IMF for support and that the "IMF asked Brother Jennings to assure the strikers of its decided support."[12]

During a 1971 strike at a GE plant in Ireland, John Shambo, a Schenectady, New York, IUE official, who also heads the IUE General Electric Conference Board, visited the strikers after attending a Zurich union meeting. According to Jennings, this resulted in GE's recognizing not only the Irish union "but also other unions in other parts of the world who saw this fight as their own."[13] In fact, the Irish Transport and General Workers'

---

[9] Clyde H. Farnsworth, "Big Business Spurs Labor Toward a World Role," *New York Times,* December 26, 1972, pp. 53-54.

[10] Company interviews, January 25, 1973.

[11] *IUE News,* September 29, 1966, p. 12.

[12] *Metal,* April-May-June 1965. This is the organ of the IMF Regional Office for Latin America and the Caribbean, published in Mexico City.

[13] Speech before the World Conference of General Electric, Bogotá, Colombia, April 18, 1969, p. 5.

Union put up a picket line at GE's plant in Shannon, Ireland, after it had agreed to a representation election and was rejected by the employees as a representative by a three-to-one majority. Despite acts of violence, the picket line failed to deter employees from working. After some months, the issue was settled through mediation by the Irish minister for labor, with the company agreeing to meet with the union officials a few times per year to discuss plant conditions generally. The union was not recognized as a bargaining agent, but such relations have continued.[14]

Claims such as those made in reference to the Irish situation and unsupported statements in various sources, such as "the IUE . . . has intervened frequently with U.S. embassies on behalf of Latin American unions negotiating with General Electric,"[15] cloud the fact that multinational bargaining is nowhere near at hand at General Electric. That GE is not a major operator in the European Economic Community and that its plants in South America continue to avoid the union attempts to achieve common expiration dates indicate that it may be many years before such bargaining is approached, whatever symbolic acts occur in the ensuing years. Moreover, Benedict is no longer on the IMF staff, and Jenning's successor as IUE president, David Fitzmaurice, has obviously been much less interested in international labor matters. Finally, the IUE's active support of protective tariff or quota legislation[16] raises serious questions about the solidarity of unions involved in the GE or other IMF Electrical Department councils.

Honeywell, Inc.

In 1971, the IMF designated Honeywell as a prime target for its first worldwide collective bargaining agreement.[17] An active

---

[14] Based upon documents and interviews in 1969, 1973, and 1974 with General Electric personnel and with the Irish Transport and General Workers' Union vice-president, May 15, 1979.

[15] Barovick, "Labor Reacts to Multinationalism," p. 43. This article, by the Washington editor of *Business Abroad* and *International Reports*, repeats many exaggerated and unsupported claims of union successes with multinational companies.

[16] See, e.g., Calame, "Import Curbs"; and articles in the *IUE News*, which have taken a very strong protectionist line for several years.

[17] See Monty Meth, "World Unions Pick Their Target," *Daily Mail* (London), April 15, 1971; and Ian McGregor, "Multinational Companies Will be Under Spotlight at Metalworkers Congress," *Times* (London), October 25, 1971.

Honeywell World Council has been unable, however, to obtain a meeting with Honeywell management. It has conducted meetings since 1971, attended by representatives from France, Germany, Italy, the Netherlands, the United Kingdom, and the United States.[18] After the initial meeting in March 1971 in Geneva, Switzerland, an IMF representative journeyed to Minneapolis, site of Honeywell's headquarters, to advance the idea of a meeting with Honeywell, but the company declined to meet with him.[19]

In 1973, the *Wall Street Journal* carried a story indicating that Honeywell would deal with the IMF coalition, purportedly based on an interview with Honeywell Bull, then a subsidiary in Paris:

> It'll take three to five years for them to really get together. But there are distinct signs that it's coming, says a spokesman for Honeywell Bull. . . .
> One distinct sign pointing toward the future is that Honeywell, which has so far dealt strictly with national unions on labor questions, now says it is prepared in principle to talk with unions on an international basis.[20]

Honeywell emphatically denies this report and attempted without success to have the *Wall Street Journal* publish this statement issued the next day:

> Honeywell today denied a report published in the *Wall Street Journal* on April 23 that it agreed in principle to talk with unions on a multinational basis. The Company's policy continues to be to deal with a union only in regard to the bargaining unit which that particular union is certified to represent.[21]

Honeywell did have one brush with the IMF during a strike in the French Bull subsidiary in late 1972 and early 1973. Like many walkouts in France and Italy, this strike was not a complete one. About 50 percent of the work force would report one day, 30 percent another day, etc. In the same article in which

---

[18] See, e.g., *IMF News*, No. 33 (September 1972), p. 4; and No. 34 (September 1973), p. 2.

[19] Letter from a Honeywell executive to one of the authors, January 25, 1972.

[20] Neil Ulman, "Talk of the Globe. Multinational Firms Face a Growing Power: Multinational Unions," *Wall Street Journal*, April 23, 1973, p. 1.

[21] Letter from Charles E. Brown, vice-president, Honeywell, Inc., to one of the authors, April 24, 1973. Honeywell no longer controls Bull, nor is it responsible for its management.

it incorrectly states Honeywell's bargaining policy, the *Wall Street Journal* reports the union version of what happened. Its story maintains that Honeywell sought to import workers during the strike from other European countries, but none came because they were advised not to by IMF affiliates.[22]

In actual fact, Honeywell did import workers from Cologne, West Germany, but sent them home after about ten days following a threat by IG Metall, their German union, that "something would be organized" if they remained in Paris.[23] Soon thereafter, the strike was settled when agreement was reached between Honeywell Bull and the Communist Confédération Générale du Travail (CGT), which left the IMF affiliate and Honeywell World Council member, the smaller Christian Confédération Française Démocratique du Travail (CFDT), little to do but to accept the results.[24]

In the United States, Honeywell operates a sizable number of nonunion plants and bargains individually with various unions in other plants on a strictly local basis. At its largest plant in Minneapolis, the bargaining agent is the Teamsters, which is not affiliated with the IMF and has not joined other United States unions that are attempting to alter Honeywell's bargaining policies.

In January 1974, however, the president of the Teamsters of Minneapolis Joint Council 32 wrote the president of Honeywell requesting again that Honeywell agree to a meeting with representatives of the IMF. The request further noted that it was being transmitted at the suggestion of the secretary-treasurer of the International Brotherhood of Teamsters, who had recently been designated a vice-president of another international trade secretariat, the International Federation of Chemical, Energy and General Workers' Unions (ICEF). Honeywell declined again, citing its fundamental philosophy of delegating the authority for primary labor relations to the local level.[25]

In France and Italy, IMF-affiliated unions are minority ones. The dominant French union, as noted, both nationally and at

---

[22] Ulman, "Talk of the Globe," p. 1.

[23] Interview in Paris, August 1973.

[24] *IMF News*, No. 6 (February 1973), p. 2. The claim of the IMF that the "most militant" of the CFDT stayed out and won additional demands is denied by the company and does not seem realistic in view of the CFDT's small size and relative weakness.

[25] Company personnel, interviews, January and March 1974.

Bull plants there, is affiliated with the Communist CGT. In Italy, two unions affiliated with the Confederazione Italiana Sindacati Lavoratori (CISL) and the Unione Italiana del Lavoro (UIL) are members of the IMF Honeywell World Council. Both are much smaller in Italy and in Honeywell plants than the Confederazione Generale Italiana del Lavoro (CGIL), the Communist union. All three are now working together under Communist leadership. Thus, in the three key countries where Honeywell operates—the United States, France, and Italy—the affiliates of the IMF Honeywell World Council are in a minority representation position. Obviously, this weakens the council's potential to achieve multinational bargaining. In addition, since Honeywell no longer controls or manages Bull, the IMF's interest seems to have lessened.

Singer

The initial interplant union contacts at Singer occurred in May 1972, when a six-week strike took place at Singer's sewing machine factory in Clydebank, Scotland. The dominant union involved at Clydebank, one of fourteen manual worker unions, was the Amalgamated Union of Engineering Workers (AUEW), with Gavin Laird as the shop stewards' convenor (chief steward). During the course of the strike, Laird contacted union officials at Singer's plant in Monza, Italy. According to Laird, the idea of approaching their union counterparts in Europe stemmed from Singer management's comparison of the Clydebank and Monza facilities regarding output and efficiency. The Italian union officials promised assistance to Laird, and an exchange of information through letters took place. A letter was received from the Monza union convenor stating that they were attempting to persuade their workers to ban overtime in support of the Clydebank strike. This letter described operations at the Monza plant, including hours, staffing, production, benefits, and salaries. In addition, copies of the 1971 and 1972 labor agreements were supposedly included.

After the strike was over, Laird stated that he intended to get in touch with other union officials at Singer's locations in France, Germany, and Brazil to ensure that these groups would resist any efforts by Singer management to transfer work out of Clydebank during a strike. In July 1972, during vacation shutdown of Clydebank, Laird was reported to have visited the Monza and Turin factories to discuss common union problems.

The personnel manager in Monza allowed Laird to meet in the plant with the union officials, believing that the company was obligated to do so under union conditions in Italy, and plans were made to have reciprocal meetings at Clydebank with the Italian shop stewards. The Italian delegation was refused permission to enter the Clydebank plant in September 1973. Laird, however, arranged to have the group enter the plant during lunch hour. Before disciplinary procedures could be invoked against him, Laird quit Singer and became a full-time union official with the AUEW.

Although there appears to have been only an exchange of letters between Clydebank and Monza, the visit by Laird in Italy and the brief lunchtime visit by the Italians at Clydebank were sufficient for the Clydebank union to find that the labor grading on one new job was one step higher in Italy, and they were subsequently able to gain this higher grading at the Clydebank location.[26]

The IMF Picks Singer as a Target. The initial transnational union contacts were made by individual Singer union officials, but shortly thereafter, the IMF began an initial push for transnational activity, selecting Singer as one of its multinational corporation targets. This strategy was first announced at the 110-member IMF Central Committee meeting held in San Francisco in November 1972.[27]

In addition to setting up working parties for multinational bargaining, the committee outlined a five-point program that included coordinated bargaining and common expiration dates, support to local unions in conflict with multinational companies, and multinational meetings with companies to discuss standards and practices. The IMF held a conference in London in December 1972 concentrating on the activities of multinational electrical and electronics companies, and Singer was selected again as one of the primary negotiating targets, along with Westinghouse and GE. At this meeting, emphasis was placed on employment security and resistance to plant closures and worker dismissals.[28]

Interunion Contacts Continue. In January 1973, Singer management in New York was advised of a letter that the union at Singer Nikko in Japan had received from the Japanese Council of Metalworkers' Union (IMF-JC). The letter describes the

---

[26] Material herein is based on interviews at Singer during 1975 and 1976.

[27] *IMF News*, No. 46 (December 1972), p. 8.

[28] *IMF News*, No. 1 (January 1973).

1972 meetings between Singer in Scotland and Italy and states that the IMF, "using the Anglo-Italian Union conference as a foothold," was planning an expanded conference in early 1973 to include the United States, France, Britain, Italy, Germany, the Netherlands, Belgium, Turkey, Sweden, Latin America, and Japan. According to Singer Nikko, its union did not react to the letter other than advising management that the letter had been received.[29] This conference did not take place in 1973 but did take place on November 6, 1974, as discussed later.

In May 1973, the Singer factory in Bonnières-sur-Seine, France, was visited by two union representatives from the Clydebank factory. They were not admitted to the factory, and according to management reports, they met with their French counterparts in a local bar.

There appears to have been no further known contact between the various Singer plants until mid-1974, when two CGT union representatives from the Bonnières plant visited Clydebank. The Bonnières plant manager was unaware of the visit until a Clydebank employee appeared at the Bonnières plant and requested a similar meeting. It was then that the Bonnières plant manager realized that the two Frenchmen had requested and received three days leave for union education, during which time they went to Clydebank. A report of their visit to Clydebank was given to Bonnières' management, and it stated that an information exchange by mail would be maintained between these union representatives of the two plants and that an interfactory meeting would be held in Monza during the last quarter of 1974. The objectives of such action would be to suppress piecework salary, to avoid production transfers except when employment is guaranteed, and, lastly, to discuss health and safety.[30]

In July 1974, following the Clydebank visit, an announcement appeared in the French press that contacts had been made with the CGT and the British Singer union to set up an international meeting. The announcement also said that the CGT considers organizing unions in multinational companies for common action a priority item and will put it on the World Federation of Trade Unions' International Conference agenda.

Although the Clydebank management did not consider this interunion exchange to have accomplished anything, Singer cor-

---

[29] Interviews at Singer during 1975 and 1976.

[30] *Ibid.*

porate management in the United States did issue a directive in September 1974 that union representatives from Singer factories in Europe were not to be admitted to other Singer locations when their motives (actual or potential) were to make a concerted effort to develop a union program of action or to seek joint meetings with company officials on an international basis. The reason for this prohibition was, United States Singer felt, that any granted request for permission to visit or be admitted to a Singer factory in another country indicates that the company is willing, or feels compelled, to deal with unions on an international basis.[31]

IMF Working Party on Singer Meets. The first meeting of the IMF Working Party on Singer was held in London on November 6, 1974.[32] Twenty-two participants from the Netherlands, the United Kingdom, the United States, Germany, Italy, France, Spain, and Turkey attended. The main topic was employment security since reduction in working hours had recently been announced in several Singer locations. Reports on employment, wages, working conditions, and trade union rights were given by the representatives from the various countries. According to the Clydebank shop stewards' report, two plants in Italy—Monza and Leini—were on twenty-four-hour weeks, and in Leini, only essential overtime was being worked; in Holland, the plant at Nijmegen (business machines) was scheduled to close in January 1975. Singer plants in Germany at Karlsruhe and Blankenloch reported no mass dismissals, but declining employment and short-time hours. The French representative was from the CFDT, and since the CGT is the main union in the Bonnières plant, no information was available. The representative from Turkey stated that his plant was unaffected by the situation. The United States representative indicated that Singer plants in the United States were not well organized and that a meeting had been called of all associated unions to establish a coordinating committee.

At this meeting, a twenty-five-page detailed report was distributed that describes the Singer company, its development worldwide, financial analyses, and product diversification and gives a prognosis of Singer's future, which according to the union report cannot be as bad as reported since "attempts by management to distort financial reports are an old ruse. . . .

---

[31] *Ibid.*

[32] *IMF News*, No. 35 (November 1974), p. 3.

Since the company is not so badly off as their reports try to indicate there is no sound basis for the company to resort to dismissals or resist pay increases." [33] According to Singer management's analysis of the report, most of the information was culled from annual reports, a current prospectus, business publications, and press releases. There are errors and omissions in the list of company locations. The report also attempts to evaluate the current drop-off in profits and the comparative financial position with that of other companies.

Gavin Laird took an active part in this meeting and proposed a set of priority actions. It was agreed that the delegates would urge trade unions in various countries to cooperate with the IMF and

> 1) To exchange information on company operations, investments, extension, finances and collective bargaining; 2) To press for full disclosure of information in all Singer subsidiaries, both through collective bargaining and legislation; 3) Through IMF to urge setting up of a coordinating committee on Singer, with representatives in each country to whom information can be routed, to encourage increased understanding and cooperation; and 4) To pay special attention to pressing problems, such as employment security right now, with common policy and support against plant closures, as well as other forms of protection of jobs and incomes, including measures to avoid lay-offs, to compensate workers for time off, to reduce overtime, to reduce outside subcontracting and to avoid workers in one country being played off against those in other countries.[34]

Singer Closings Continue. Just one month after the November 1974 meeting, Singer workers in the soon-to-be closed Nijmegen plant demonstrated before the Parliament building in the Hague. The eventual closing of Nijmegen was first discussed in 1972, when a reorganization took place. Declining sales and production transfers were leading to the dismissal of five hundred workers. Attempts were made by the Dutch Ministry of Economic Affairs, the United States ambassador, and various businessmen to see if the plant could be sold. A termination agreement costing 40 million guilders was agreed upon. Prospective buyers were not encouraging, but finally Tealtronic, a Swiss-based, British-owned company agreed to take over the operation of Singer Nijmegen. Four hundred of the five hundred

---

[33] Report prepared for the meeting of the IMF Working Party on Singer, London, November 6, 1974.

[34] *IMF News*, No. 35 (November 1974), p. 3.

employees were hired by the new firm, and Singer's severance liability dropped to 10 million guilders. Also Singer reportedly received less than it had asked for the grounds, building, and machines.

Singer management learned that an IMF meeting had taken place in Bogotá, Colombia, in October 1974 with the Singer union, which is another IMF affiliate. There was also an indication that attempts were being made to coordinate Singer bargaining and other union activities in four countries in Latin America, with activities headquartered in Peru. This was a localized effort of a militant leader in Peru who came to power under a new law providing a seat in the company management meetings.[35]

In April 1975, an article about Singer appeared in *L'Unita,* the Italian Communist newspaper. The article cites poor working conditions at Leini, lack of investment capital, and outmoded equipment and also refers to redundancies at other Singer locations in the United States, Belgium, the Netherlands, and Scotland.

A year later in April 1976, Singer's European unions held a "European Works Council" meeting in Monza, Italy, to discuss the plant closings. Union delegates from Monza, Milan, Leini, France, Clydebank, and Germany were present. In addition to the IMF involvement, it was suggested that the European Metalworkers' Federation (EMF) be contacted. A demonstration was planned for May 6, 1976, which resulted in fifty employees going out for one hour in France; another thirty-eight French employees went out for three hours, while fifteen hundred Italian workers were out for one-half day in the Monza plant. There was no response from Germany or Scotland. Following this demonstration, the IMF contacted the IUE in Washington, D.C., and asked for their support in the United States. There was no follow-up to this request.

IMF Singer Group Meets Again. Another IMF meeting was held in September 1976 to discuss the continuation of Singer closings.[36] According to the IMF, Singer employment had declined from 122,000 to 98,000 since 1974. Delegates from the United Kingdom, Germany, and Italy attended. The German delegates outlined the severance arrangements for their employees of Blankenloch, where employees were given an average of two to three weeks' pay for each year of service, while the

---

[35] Information furnished by Singer.

[36] *IMF News,* No. 19 (October 1976), p. 5.

British delegates reported on work-sharing plans and attrition rates. Although the Leini plant had been closed, employees "sat in" on the cafeteria, which according to Italian law is legal. The Italian delegates spoke of a metalworkers' strike called for September 24, 1976. This resulted in a one-hour strike in Monza and a one-hour strike in Milan, where the company's sales headquarters is located. A telegram of protest was sent to Singer management in Pakistan, where the managing director, according to the IMF, had been trying to break the union after having its general secretary arrested and dismissed. The Labour Court upheld the company when it dismissed the union leader for misconduct in resorting to an illegal strike and urging others to strike the company.[37]

Latest Developments. The Leini (white goods) plant problem was finally resolved in May 1977. The plant, at which employees had been staging a cafeteria sit-in, was sold to an Italian state agency (GEPI), which was to integrate the plant into a private company. At one time, there were twenty-four hundred employees manufacturing ovens, refrigerators, and washing machines at Leini.

An announcement was made in December 1977 that Singer would sell two other European subsidiaries in its ongoing effort to cut back on peripheral business involvements. Singer Nikko, the 50 percent owned subsidiary in Japan, also announced that it would discontinue its rifle manufacturing and concentrate on sewing machines.[38]

Clydebank's Impact on Singer Worldwide. The Clydebank facility continued to have problems. In November 1977, it was announced that the Clydebank work force, approximately five thousand, would be reduced by 20 percent to achieve higher productivity and more mobility. The Clydebank plant accounts for about 20 percent of Singer's total world sewing machines sales and is an almost totally integrated location. The plant has felt increasing competitive market pressure from Japanese, Korean, Taiwanese, and Eastern European sewing machine producers, with a steadily increasing loss in sales. Clydebank supplies fourfifths of its annual output for export, with 40 percent going to the United States and the rest going to Europe, Australia, and New Zealand. Clydebank also produced for the United Kingdom

---

[37] Information provided by Singer.

[38] "Singer-Nikko will stop rifles and concentrates on sewing machines," *Japan Economic Journal*, December 20, 1977, p. 13.

market. With its operations in Clydebank, Monza, and Brazil, Singer has been able to retain 40 percent of the United States market despite pressure from Japan and Taiwan.[39]

The Amalgamated Union of Engineering Workers' convenor has been claiming that Singer management has not been putting capital investment into Clydebank and that there continue to be discrepancies between Singer Clydebank and Singer Europe. There appears to be a debate between the union and Singer's European division president regarding the feasibility of producing electronic machines at Clydebank. The electronic machine is presently produced at Karlsruhe in West Germany, and since that plant has not felt the pressure from the Far East, then obviously, according to the union, electronic machines are the answer, and Clydebank should be reequipped to produce them.

Economic difficulties at Singer on a worldwide basis led to a sourcing study that was conducted by the company in the first half of 1978 to determine future manufacturing requirements. During the course of this study, the Second IMF World Meeting on the Singer Company was held in London on April 8, 1978. The purpose of the meeting was to focus on the "possible implications of the international sourcing study at present being undertaken" by Singer. The IMF pledged its support to any plant that would be threatened with closure as a result of the sourcing study.[40]

On announcing the results of its sourcing study on June 22, 1978, Singer indicated that twenty-eight hundred jobs would be lost at the Clydebank factory. The unions, of course, rejected the proposal as "totally unacceptable and unpalatable." [41] The company's announced plans would have meant the loss of five hundred jobs immediately, with the largest number being lost through attrition. The company's plans to invest approximately $16 million in the Clydebank facility gave the union some hope that more severe long-run job effects could be avoided. In addition, the company announced that the unions could prepare alternative plans to save jobs that would be considered by the company.

---

[39] Christopher Dunn, "Electronics the key for Singer plant," *Financial Times*, November 16, 1977, p. 12.

[40] *IMF News*, No. 4 (1978), p. 2.

[41] *Financial Times*, June 23, 1978, p. 1.

Based on the company's suggestion that the union present an alternative arrangement for saving jobs, the shop stewards at the company hired a consulting firm to do a study on the possible alternative future for the plant. P. A. Management Consultants was retained for a ten-week intensive study at a cost of approximately $150,000. The Scottish Development Agency agreed to finance about two-thirds of the cost of the study, and the union at Clydebank voted to contribute approximately $1.00 per week per member for ten weeks to make up individual donations of approximately $10.00.

The report of the consultants hired by the unions was issued on October 30, 1978, and recommends that production of industrial machines should be retained at Clydebank, but on a reduced scale with concentration on the most successful models. The plan projects a saving of approximately one thousand jobs of the twenty-eight hundred that were originally scheduled for elimination, and it also includes recommendations for an investment by the company of approximately $5 million in addition to the $16 million it had already proposed to spend on modernizing the sewing machine operation at Clydebank. The recommendations of the consulting agency were overwhelmingly received by employees at factory meetings and forwarded for management review.[42]

In an effort to demonstrate some coordination of the unions' interests, the IMF held a meeting in Glasgow of shop stewards from the Clydebank plant, local officials, and national trade union leaders upon the issuance of the report. The IMF claimed that its role "will be increasingly important at the later stages of negotiation at the level of the multinational group and in the case of structural rationalization plans affecting Singer locations in other parts of the world."[43]

On November 29, 1978, the company issued its response to the union proposition and indicated that it would continue to produce two industrial sewing machine models and some spare parts at Clydebank and that the new proposal would save approximately 335 jobs. The company also indicated that it would be prepared to invest an additional $2 to $4 million beyond its estimated $16 million needed for the basic restructuring of Clydebank by

---

[42] "Struggle for Job Security with a Multinational Group," IMF Studies, No. 7 (Geneva: International Metalworkers' Federation, 1979), pp. 5-7.

[43] *IMF News*, No. 10 (1978), pp. 1, 2.

1982.[44] The company management challenged the union-commissioned report's claim that 1,000 jobs could be saved. Hugh Swan, deputy convenor at the Clydebank plant, indicated that he was very disappointed that management had rejected the total recommendations of the report that the union had commissioned. On the other hand, the union refused to enter into confrontation with the company about the matter or to seek the IMF's cooperation in coordinating union activity at Singer plants in Europe and the United States.[45]

There were further confrontations at the Clydebank facility in 1979, with union reluctance to accept the company's reorganization plans, and some strike activity threatened the proposal for continued operations. It appears that the union efforts were responsible for saving jobs and some industrial lines at Clydebank that otherwise would have been eliminated. The role of the IMF, however, seems to have been minimal in the total picture. This can be best explained by the apparent lack of interest among local and national union officials in Clydebank who did not view IMF support as being particularly helpful in this case.

Other United States Electrical Companies

Westinghouse Electric Corporation, the second largest American concern in this industry, is more broadly based in Europe than is General Electric; however, it was not the target of any significant multinational union activity until 1978.

In 1969, during the period when Daniel Benedict sat in on a few General Electric negotiations, he visited Pittsburgh, the headquarters of Westinghouse, while negotiations were in progress, but he did not sit in on the negotiations.[46] In the ensuing years, no international unionists attended Westinghouse negotiations or, as far as we are able to determine, visited Pittsburgh while they were in progress. The IMF World Conference for the Electrical and Electronics Industry, held in Geneva on October 24-26, 1978, named Westinghouse as a multinational target company and presented an "Outline for IMF

---

[44] *Wall Street Journal*, November 30, 1978, p. 44.

[45] *Financial Times*, November 30, 1978, p. 46.

[46] According to the *IUE News* ("Bargaining Talks That Circle Earth," February 4, 1971, p. 7), "In last year's GE and Westinghouse negotiations, Daniel Benedict . . . sat in on several GE negotiating sessions . . . and was in Pittsburgh during some of the *W* talks."

Action on Westinghouse Electric Corporation." Under the initiative of the American International Association of Machinists and Aerospace Workers (IAM), IMF affiliates were asked to collect information on Westinghouse operations to be presented to the conference. Information requested included number of employees, products manufactured, market position, investment plans, financial data, unionization rate, negotiating patterns, compilation of collective agreements, and analysis of collective bargaining achievements in major areas. Affiliates in Belgium, Ireland, and Sweden responded to the first request, and the IAM prepared a "Review of the Parent Company," which included a "Description of Operations" and "Financial Analysis." An IMF Working Party on Multinational Companies is being planned to consider the program on Westinghouse as a target company, as well as "to draw-up general guidelines and methods for target companies in general." [47] As far as we can determine, the parent company has not been approached by the American unions or the IMF in regard to this matter.

Texas Instruments, which operates nonunion in the United States, is another company that the IMF, and particularly Benedict, has claimed has been forced to act because of IMF pressures. In a *New York Times* interview, it was reported that:

> Some 1,500 Curaçao women integrated circuit workers wanted to organize a union in the new Texas Instruments plant; the company was opposed and the women struck last September. Workers at the company's plants in West Germany, Italy and the Netherlands supported them by refusing production transfers and after two weeks the company gave in to the women.[48]

The company maintains that there was no stoppage at Curaçao. When some supervisors imported from South America tried to take over an existing union, the company shut down for vacation, sent the supervisors home, and has since negotiated amicably with the union. The only union pressure in Europe was an exchange of "solidarity" telegrams between leaders in Curaçao and Europe with no impact or publicity in Europe.[49]

The IMF joined with another international trade secretariat, the International Union of Food and Allied Workers' Associations

---

[47] "Outline for IMF Action on a Multinational Target Company" (Paper prepared for the Third IMF World Conference for the Electrical and Electronics Industry, Geneva, October 24-26, 1978), p. 3.

[48] Farnsworth, "Big Business Spurs Labor."

[49] Telephone interview, January 23, 1973.

(IUF), to sponsor "a working party" meeting for unions dealing with International Telephone and Telegraph (ITT). Twenty delegates from nine countries met in Geneva on July 6, 1972, to launch an ITT council and to hear reports on such matters as company structure and finances. Emphasis in the resolutions passed by the delegates is on exchange of information and opposition to work transfer from one country to another.[50] Apparently nothing since has developed. ITT has a firm policy of local bargaining and would oppose multinational union approaches.

The IMF, in collaboration with the International Federation of Commercial, Clerical and Technical Employees (FIET), the white-collar employee secretariat, has held conferences on white-collar and computer workers, in which interest in International Business Machines has been expressed.[51] In view of the lack of unionization in IBM, however, it is unlikely that the IMF will pursue such activity.

Brown Boveri

Brown Boveri, the large Swiss-based heavy electrical machinery concern, announced a general management reorganization, effective January 1, 1970, in part centralizing managerial control over some operations that were formerly highly decentralized. Later in 1970, the IMF's Daniel Benedict telephoned the company headquarters in Baden, Switzerland, requesting to pay a "visite de politesse" in order to become acquainted with the new organization of the company. The company agreed to the meeting without ascertaining what the proposed agenda might be or who would represent the IMF. Company management discovered only a few days before September 4, 1970, the day of the meeting, that Benedict and Karl Casserini, then the IMF's economist, would be accompanied by members of union and workers' committees from the various European countries in which Brown Boveri has operating facilities and that the IMF agenda covered basic employee relations and investment policies

---

[50] *IMF News*, No. 27 (July 1972), p. 2; International Union of Food and Allied Workers', *Documents of the Secretariat, 17th Congress, Item 5: Report on Activities—8 Multinational Companies* (Geneva, 1973), p. V-8/18.

[51] See, e.g., *IMF News*, No. 34 (November 1974), p. 1; No. 10 (1978); *FIET Newsletter*, No. 12 (December 1978), pp. 1-2; No. 1 (January 1979), p. 5.

of the company.[52] A previous informal meeting between IMF officials and Brown Boveri representatives had included no national unions or plant work representatives.[53]

Besides Messrs. Benedict and Casserini, the IMF delegation included one union and one Brown Boveri plant worker committee representative each from Germany, Norway, and Austria, the secretaries of the Swiss Metal and Watchmakers' Union, plus one worker committeeman from the Baden plant, one representative each from the French CFDT and the Force Ouvrière, and one each from the Italian CISL and the UIL. The IMF proposed agenda included the following:

—International policy of the Brown Boveri Group and its repercussions on the management and labor organization of its member companies;

—Basic mission and major tasks of the newly created Group Staff, Management Development;

—Business prospects and possible implications for employment as a result of the new organization;

—Personnel policy and social security plans in different Brown Boveri factories;

—Personnel and social problems connected with mergers and acquisitions in which Brown Boveri might be involved;

—Efforts to put everyone on salary; and

—Possibilities of future negotiations on specific problems aiming at a better information of IMF on B.B.C.'s business policy and its consequences on the labor side; possibilities of continuous consultations.[54]

The meeting was relatively short, and most of the topics were discussed only in a general way. Both parties attest to the friendly atmosphere which prevailed at the meeting, but no additional meetings have been held or scheduled. The reason, as in the case of Philips, is apparently the different objectives of the parties.

In its press release concerning the meeting, the IMF states that there was "agreement to meet yearly and, when important

---

[52] This section is based on communications and interviews with company and IMF personnel.

[53] See *IMF News*, No. 33 (December 1969); No. 30 (September 1970).

[54] Letter from G. Bütikofer, director, Brown Boveri & Cie, to one of the authors, October 23, 1973.

problems arose, to renew contacts." [55] Brown Boveri management, however, states:

> No promises were made. Especially there was no agreement on future negotiations or regular consultations. . . . A subsequent press release by the IMF created some disturbances not only in Brown Boveri subsidiaries but also in other business circles, because the announcement made believe that our top management had agreed to institutionalize meetings and talks at the level of IMF.[56]

Perhaps the key to this disagreement lies more in the different objectives of the parties than in what occurred. The IMF makes no secret of the fact that it regards such meetings as an initial step toward multiplant bargaining. The company, however, is dubious of the efficacy of meetings with this objective. Our impression is that the company is particularly concerned about inferences that it is engaged in a collective bargaining relationship with the IMF and that decisions concerning plant employee relations have resulted from the September 1970 meeting. It claims to have taken no such action and believes that claims made otherwise have been "harmful."

As an example of such claims, the company notes that, between April 1970 and April 1971, it put all Swiss blue-collar employees on salary with all the rights of salaried workers. In addition, hours have been made variable with considerable employee choice. The company told the authors, "The relevant management decision was the result of an intensive study which lasted several years and had absolutely nothing to do with IMF's visit." [57] The changes were, of course, discussed with union representatives at the national level.

The IMF did not take direct credit for this change, but an issue of the *IMF News* reports that it was done "in the framework of negotiations between plant representatives of the Swiss Metal and Watchmakers' Union and the Brown Boveri Company." [58] Charles Levinson, secretary general of the ICEF, also attributed these innovations to "recent negotiations" between

---

[55] *IMF News*, No. 30 (September 1970), p. 2.

[56] Letter from G. Bütikofer to one of the authors, October 23, 1973.

[57] *Ibid.*

[58] *IMF News*, No. 41 (December 1970), p. 1.

the Swiss unions and the company.[59] The implication in these reports that it was not the company's initiative apparently makes Brown Boveri management wary of future meetings. Such meetings are, of course, desired by the IMF not only because they are a step toward multinational bargaining but also because, with Brown Boveri headquartered in a non-European Economic Community country, the IMF, not the EMF, is exerting coordinating leadership in the Community. The EMF, which exerted such leadership in the cases of Philips and Fokker-VFW, is, of course, affiliated with the European Trade Union Confederation and maintains only "fraternal relationships" with the IMF.

Robert Bosch

Bosch is a leading electrical and automobile parts manufacturer headquartered on the outskirts of Stuttgart, Germany. A joint venture with Siemens is maintained for the production of appliances. The company had sales of $4.8 billion and employed 118,320 people in 1978, with the majority located in Germany (see Table V-1). Two Italian plants employ a total of 3,000, and there are 7,000 employed in Brazil and 2,000 in Argentina. Additional plants are located in India, France, Spain, Turkey, and South Carolina, U.S.A. Other plants in the United States carrying the Bosch name have not been affiliated with the German company since World War II.

The company has been involved in two incidents entailing some international union activity. A strike in its plant in Bergamo, Italy, occurred on April 28, 1975, following the company's efforts to dismiss 200 of the plant's 2,000 employees. The planned reduction of forces was based on the economic position of the plant, which had incurred a loss of about DM 28 million in its latest three years of operation. A group of outside left-wing radicals invaded the plant and forced the employees, including management, to leave.[60] The occupation ended in July, when the company agreed with the works council to dismiss only 160 people. The Italian unions contacted IG Metall but without any reciprocation or success. There was some leaflet action, and the sales office was shut down for a

---

[59] Charles Levinson, *International Trade Unionism*, Ruskin House Series in Trade Union Studies (London: George Allen & Unwin Ltd., 1972), pp. 320-21.

[60] *Die Zeit*, No. 25 (July 18, 1975).

brief period, but these activities did not lead to any curtailment of business.

The second incident occurred in Spain and was the result of a strike that began in the fall of 1974. During the strike, the company dismissed six strike leaders who were active in an IMF affiliate. The union contacted the IMF and also IG Metall headquarters in Frankfurt for assistance. A meeting of Bosch's Spanish management with Daniel Benedict, an assistant general secretary of the IMF at that time, and a representative of IG Metall occurred in Madrid in November 1974, resulting in an agreement to reengage five of the six persons. The dispute was not settled, however, until April 1975, when it was agreed to give some redundancy pay to the sixth man, who was the leading agitator, but not to take him back into the company.[61]

In addition to the foregoing, there has been some transnational activity by the unions on an irregular basis. The works council in the French plant meets about once a year with its counterpart in the company's largest German plant. Visits from the Swedish works councils to Germany have also been made. These activities are not viewed as significant by the company, but they do indicate that international union and works council contacts may well grow over the years ahead.

Siemens

Siemens, headquartered in Munich, Germany, is the sixth largest electrical manufacturer in the world, with a product line covering virtually the entire electrical field from turbines to light bulbs.[62] About one-quarter of Siemens's goods were manufactured outside of Germany in 1975, and this percentage is growing as Siemens expands overseas, particularly in the United States.

The company has been involved in two matters pertaining to international union activity.[63] These incidents both reflect the company's efforts to confine local issues and to refer them to the works councils with which it has had an effective relationship over the years.

Early in 1975, a clash over grievances occurred on the shop floor in Colombia between a union member and the foreman.

---

[61] Interviews in Stuttgart, Germany, September 16, 1975.

[62] Neil McInnes, "Conservatism Pays Off: Staid Old Siemens AG is Enjoying Renewed Growth," *Barron's*, September 29, 1975, pp. 9, 17-18.

[63] Interviews in Munich, Germany, September 17, 1975; May 24, 1979.

As a result of loud shouting, the union man was seriously warned not to behave in such a manner in the future. The union viewed the company's actions as an effort to suppress its views and asked the IMF for assistance. Eugen Loderer, president of both IG Metall and the IMF, wrote a letter on IMF stationery, dated January 23, 1975, to Peter von Siemens protesting the matter. (Loderer and Siemens were personally acquainted because both serve on the supervisory board of Mannesmann Aktiengesellschaft, an iron and steel concern.) In response to this letter, an employee member of the Central Works Council at Siemens and vice-chairman of the supervisory board made an investigative trip to the Colombian plant and subsequently addressed a letter on April 3, 1975, to Loderer containing his interpretation of the situation. Furthermore, the works council representative asked Loderer to deal directly with him and the council in regard to any future problems. Points made in the letter to Loderer contained the following: (1) Colombian law grants the right to organize by the union and to deal with management on the local level; (2) no grievances as suggested by Loderer seemed to exist; (3) nothing was found to support the claim that union people and union proposals were being suppressed; (4) in regard to the clash between the foreman and the union member, Siemens attempted to reconcile differences based on local regulations pertaining to union affairs; and (5) in regard to overtime, another grievance, nothing was found to support the union's claim. In essence, the works council member who reviewed the situation in Colombia advised Loderer that "there is nothing to the claims as made and please contact me the next time there is a problem." [64]

A second incident involving Siemens occurred in Greece. An effort to bring local matters in Greece to the international scene has been made by a Greek metalworkers' union member who was formerly with the IG Metall in Frankfurt. On March 7, 1975, Loderer addressed a letter to Peter von Siemens pertaining to conditions in Greece. This communication was given to the local works council people in Munich who advised Loderer that he should defer to them and that he should not contact top management at Siemens. A representative of the works council went to Greece to investigate the matter in June 1975, and he found no conflicts that deserved international union involvement.

---

[64] Interviews at Siemens, September 17, 1975.

In regard to transnational union activity and visits of works council members across national borders, the works council from South America has come to Germany on invitation, but there has been no encouragement of continuing mutual exchange. There have also been some limited cross-border meetings between the works council members in Austria and Germany. Such contacts are not, however, on a regular basis, nor are any other such meetings of union or workers council members regularly held.

CONFERENCES AND SEMINARS

In addition to its work in developing particular councils and/or working groups for selected multinational firms in the period 1970-77, the IMF has conducted conferences and seminars to highlight problems in the electrical and electronics industry. As noted earlier, three world conferences, two Latin American conferences, and two Asian seminars have been held in the past decade. These conferences and seminars, which bring together a large number of delegates, play an important role in the IMF's overall program of information and assistance to affiliated unions. Major themes at these meetings generally center on economic and social trends in the regional, national, and worldwide electrical industry; developments in the industry's multinational corporations; wages and working conditions; and trade union rights. Problems associated with nuclear energy were discussed extensively at the secretariat's most recent sessions.

Although the IMF's conferences and seminars are conducted around general themes pertinent to the industry, the framework for approaching multinational firms is sometimes developed. Herman Rebhan, general secretary of the IMF, concluded his speech to the world conference in October 1978 with the following statements:

1. Since we are facing international capital, we have to increase and intensify our cooperation, building on our experience in the struggle with multinational corporations in this industry as well as in others.

2. The multinational company councils have to be activated and coordinated with our other activities. I am sure that this conference and the forthcoming meeting of our working party on multinational companies will contribute to this goal.[65]

---

[65] Remarks prepared by Herman Rebhan, general secretary, IMF, for the Third IMF World Conference for the Electrical and Electronics Industry, Geneva, October 24-26, 1978.

Rebhan's comments indicate that the company councils may be activated. Westinghouse has been named as a special target, but it remains to be seen whether further action will be taken.

IMF ELECTRICAL INDUSTRY ACTIVITIES— CONCLUSIONS AND IMPLICATIONS

The IMF has thus established the union organizational framework for bargaining on a multinational basis in the electrical machinery industry as it has in automobiles. It has made what it regards as the initial step toward bargaining—limited contact between its multinational union committees and major companies. Will these admittedly "symbolic" meetings grow into something more substantial? Perhaps, but it does not appear that any such developments are on the near horizon.

There is, first of all, no inclination among the electrical machinery concerns that have been the target of the IMF to accede to a multinational bargaining arrangement. Electrical concerns lack the integrated production that might encourage broader bargaining boundaries. Such companies produce a wide variety of products in various facilities. Although there is some plant interdependence, a strike in one does not have the same impact, for example, that a shutdown of an auto parts facility has on automobile assembly plants. Consequently, electrical machinery companies on the IMF target list see nothing to be gained by acceding to IMF aspirations and much to be lost. They may be expected to continue to oppose multinational bargaining.

There is another basic reason why IMF is not likely to accomplish its objective in the near future. In the European Economic Community, where the climate is most favorable for possible bargaining arrangements, the IMF finds itself in a secondary position. There the dynamics of the movement have been seized by the regional organization, the European Metalworkers' Federation. As our discussion below demonstrates, it is the EMF that has moved closest to the union goal.

ACTIVITIES OF THE EUROPEAN METALWORKERS' FEDERATION

In 1963, unions in the various metals industries located in the European Economic Community (EEC) countries formed the Metal Committee of the European Confederation of Free Trade

Unions in the Community (ECFTU). The Metal Committee thus maintained a relationship with the International Confederation of Free Trade Unions (ICFTU) through the ECFTU, but no direct affiliation with the IMF, although the latter apparently supported the organization of the committee.[66]

In 1973, unions in the expanded EEC formed the European Trade Union Confederation (ETUC) as a replacement for the ECFTU. The ETUC specifically rejected affiliation or any formal relationship either with the secretariats or with the ICFTU and equally specifically rejected efforts to place the word *free* in its name. The ETUC has since been in the forefront of the union confederation amalgamation movement in the EEC, which has brought the now deconfessionalized Christian and free union confederations close to amalgamation and has initiated discussions with the Communist ones as well. Most free and Christian unions in the EEC, including the Communist Italian CGIL, are now ETUC affiliates.[67] (In Italy, Communist and free unions are working together, and their merger is a possibility. Thus, the ETUC represents a strong movement toward regional unity but international separatism.)

In that framework, the Metal Committee, now known as the European Metalworkers' Federation (EMF) in the Community, affiliated with the ETUC despite IMF efforts to bring it into its fold, as we have noted in previous chapters.

The establishment of the EMF and its affiliation to the ETUC led to questions pertaining to such actions and their potential impact on the IMF. While it appeared at first that the IMF-EMF relationship would be strained, IMF President Eugen Loderer, who is also vice-president of the EMF, stated at the Stockholm Congress in July 1974 "that the tension with the EMF—European Metalworkers' Federation—was now overcome and that the Central Committee [of the IMF] had stated its agreement with the EMF in principle, as it was not a rival organization,

---

[66] In conversation with the authors, other secretariat officials have been highly critical of the IMF for not insisting upon an affiliation arrangement with the Metal Committee. These other secretariats have striven to establish industry groups in the EEC that are directly affiliated with the appropriate secretariat. Nevertheless, there is much regional separatist sentiment among such groups, which is a cause of concern for several secretariats.

[67] See, e.g., Selig S. Harrison, "Labor's Ties Abroad Wearing Thin," *Washington Post*, April 8, 1974, pp. A1, A9; and *Industrial Relations—Europe Newsletter*, Vol. II, No. 21 (August 1974), p. 1.

and would have European contacts only." [68] The IMF will continue to operate the auto councils, and it remains to be seen what kind of coordination of other activities will occur.

The move to create the EMF and its affiliation to the ETUC are significant for multinational bargaining because, since 1967, the EMF has been quite persistent in its avowed aim of pushing key European multinational concerns toward multinational bargaining arrangements. Among these has been the Philips company.

Philips

No company has had more detailed experience in multinational union discussions than Philips, the giant multinational electrical manufacturer headquartered in Eindhoven, the Netherlands. The fifth largest industrial concern outside of the United States,[69] Philips in 1978 employed about 390,000 persons in at least twenty countries, of whom more than 250,000 were located in the EEC.[70] Philips's management has long prided itself on leadership in providing superior wages, benefits, and working conditions for its employees.[71] The company operates on a decentralized management principle (referred to as a "federal organizational" structure in Europe), with a great deal of autonomy vested in the national groups. "This particularly holds true for personnel and industrial relations policies, which have to follow national legislation in the field of labour and social security and have to fit in the national labour market situation, industrial relations structure and climate and take into account national characteristics and preferences." [72]

Philips's contacts with European trade unions began in 1967, when it received a "request to hold informative discussions

---

[68] *IMF News*, No. 23 (July 1974), p. 2.

[69] "Philips: A Multinational Copes with Profitless Growth," *Business Week*, January 13, 1973, p. 64.

[70] P. L. Dronkers, "A Multinational Organization and Industrial Relations: The Philips Case" (Address before the International Industrial Relations Association, Third World Congress, London, September 1973), p. 1. See also Table V-1. The authors have interviewed Philips executives and the general secretary of the EMF annually since 1973 and are grateful to both for supplying information for this case study.

[71] See, e.g., John P. Windmuller, *Labor Relations in the Netherlands* (Ithaca: Cornell University Press, 1969), pp. 235, 310, 372-74.

[72] Dronkers, "A Multinational Organization," p. 1.

with representatives of European trade unions in the metal and electrical engineering industries" belonging to the EMF and other bodies.[73] The company complied with this request believing that it was consistent with its support of the EEC and economic integration. It was thought in 1967 that the EEC would be able to move Europe toward economic unity and that economic harmonization should be accompanied by some form of social harmonization. Furthermore, the company expected that mutual gains would be made by itself and the unions if each clearly understood its respective objectives, policies, and plans in the social field. Philips further thought that an informal meeting with the unions would give its representatives an opportunity to explain the company concept of "federal organization" and national autonomy in decision making.

Four meetings between Philips and the EMF have occurred since 1967:

> *The first* was largely concerned with the subject of Philips production policy in EEC countries and with the Philips decision making process. Philips officials with the help of relevant data were able to prove the union fears about unequal distribution by a "power centre in Eindhoven" of the then prevailing redundancy in Philips plants were not justified. The echo in trade union circles was positive as this was the first time the management of an international firm was prepared to meet and amply to inform European union representatives.

> In *the second* meeting (1969) in connection with the unions' concern for workers affected by transfer of production between EEC countries the company promised that—should there be substantial moves within that area—the European union representatives would be informed.

> In *the third* meeting (1970) a union paper regarding social consequences of rationalisation and restructuring of production was discussed.

> During *the fourth* meeting (1972) the accent was on information provided as to the economic situation and prospects, personnel planning and policy, whilst at the request of the unions the social consequences for workers in case of shorter working hours and redundancies were discussed.[74]

The foregoing meetings were obviously intended by the company to be solely for orientation and information pertaining to matters of mutual interest to it and to employees and the unions.

---

[73] *Ibid.*

[74] *Ibid.*, p. 2.

Equally obvious, however, is that the EMF saw the opportunity to consummate an international collective bargaining agreement with Philips. According to the London *Times*:

> Herr Günter Köpke, West German secretary of the European Metal Unions Committee, told a news conference in Brussels . . . [in September 1970] . . . that it was the intention of his 15-man labour delegation to sign an international collective bargaining agreement with Philips. Eventually, he said, such a contract would cover conditions of labour, including wages and hours.
>
> Herr Köpke made it clear that at first he would expect to sign an accord concerned only with general principles. He could not say how long it would take to get a full agreement. "But we are not prepared to wait for years," he added.[75]

In response to Köpke's remarks, P. L. Dronkers, director of personnel and industrial relations at Philips, reacted as follows:

> The company has no present intention of signing an international collective bargaining accord of the kind outlined by Herr Köpke. The group intends to continue its current practice of negotiating individual agreements in separate countries where it operates, with individual trade unions and employers associations, except in Holland where Philips bargains with the unions collectively.
>
> Secondly . . . the three meetings which Philips' Board of Management have had with European trade union organizations had been of an "informal and informative" nature only and had not discussed anything so specific as an international collective bargaining agreement.[76]

The EMF sought to make multinational collective bargaining the major thrust for the proposed fifth meeting of the parties, which was scheduled for May 1973. It proposed that the company should be prepared to discuss, in terms of all Philips employees in Europe, 100 percent wages in case of shorter working hours and the same redundancy rules in the case of such events as mergers and reorganizations. In addition, the EMF suggested that an IMF representative would appear at the meeting as an observer.

These proposals were rejected by Philips executives, who repeated "their point of view that they were not able nor prepared to conclude material agreements on an EEC level. Not able because of the autonomy of the national Philips organizations." [77]

---

[75] Anthony Rowley, "After the Talks with Philips . . . A Step to Cross-border Unions?" *London Times Business Supplement*, October 21, 1970.

[76] *Ibid.*

[77] Dronkers, "A Multinational Organization," pp. 3-4.

The company further explained that a multinational labor agreement might be in conflict in the EEC vis-à-vis national and government policy. In regard to IMF participation, Philips took the position that this violated earlier agreements with the EMF to deal only with EEC matters.

The Philips position was reiterated by Dronkers in his address to the International Industrial Relations Association in September 1973. In response to a letter from one of the authors, Köpke agreed that the Dronkers paper "is from the company point of view in the most important points correct," but he emphasized the EMF belief "that despite the actual position of Philips we will come to multinational collective bargaining." He further stated that "our reason to insist on" IMF participation "is that the Philips activities around the world should be considered by an IMF representative when the EMF has meetings on European level with Philips." [78] After several informal discussions, the long-delayed fifth meeting was scheduled for May 30, 1975, in Eindhoven. It was, however, cancelled the evening before by the EMF because Philips insisted that the agreement to limit EMF representatives to its own officials and those of EEC unions be adhered to. The EMF had listed an IMF assistant secretary as a member of its delegation and refused to exclude him, perhaps as a result of IMF pressure.

At this writing, no further meetings between the parties have been held except for brief introductory sessions between Köpke and Hubert Thierron and the new personnel manager of Philips who replaced Dronkers in 1978. In July 1977, Hubert Thierron was elected to replace Köpke as general secretary of the EMF. Thierron served as assistant general secretary to Köpke and holds similar views on the importance of contacts with multinational firms.

In its issue of February 15, 1979, the publication *Multinational Service Fortnightly*, which is located in Brussels, states that "there is now a real possibility that regular meetings between senior executives of the Dutch multinational company Philips and Europe's metal-working trade union may resume in 1979." [79] We can state categorically, after meeting both with Philips executives and with the general secretary of the EMF,

---

78 Letter from Günter Köpke, general secretary, EMF, to one of the authors, October 4, 1973.

79 *Multinational Service Fortnightly*, February 15, 1979.

that no such meetings are being planned. [80] What actually occurred was that the EMF sought to induce Philips to resume these meetings, which have not been held since 1972, but the company declined to do so.

Our impression is that the company does not see such meetings as productive and does not feel that, at least for the immediate future, they would be in the best interest of the company or industry in general. The EMF, of course, is very determined to obtain a resumption of these meetings, since its failure to do so is seen as a definite setback for its collective bargaining program.

Thus, we may expect considerable pressure to be put on Philips by the EMF and some of its constituent unions in an effort to reverse the decision of the company. Already the EMF has begun an information campaign among European employees of Philips stressing prospective reductions in employment. On May 28, 1979, the EMF announced:

> On *Wednesday, 30th May 1979,* the metalworkers' unions affiliated to the European Metalworkers' Federation—E.M.F. will jointly organize a campaign to inform all the workers employed in *PHILIPS plants in Europe* and make them aware of the situation, drawing their attention to employment problems and the need to obtain objective and concordant information everywhere and at all levels in respect of the future of the PHILIPS group in Europe.[81]

The foregoing is part of an effort by the EMF to find a series of common demands involving Philips plants throughout Europe in order to attempt to coordinate those demands as a pressure tactic against the company. Nevertheless, it is not believed that there will be any change in the company's posture in the near future unless there is a dramatic course of events that could cause the company to reappraise the situation.

It is apparent that the EMF feels that Philips is a prime target for a bargaining relationship. It is equally clear that Philips approached these meetings with the idea that it could satisfy the unions with a good faith demonstration of its willingness to provide information, its openness, and the fairness of its wage and personnel policies. This, of course, ignores the drive by unions, whether local or international, to achieve parity of

---

[80] Interviews in Eindhoven and Brussels, May 7 and 11, 1979.

[81] European Metalworkers' Federation Press Release, May 28, 1979. The EMF released copies of the various leaflets with a press statement, June 11, 1979.

decision making with management and to develop an organiza-tion and a framework of operations that require consultation and mutual consent *before* policies are determined and actions taken rather than after the fact. For union leadership, informational meetings are valuable only as a stepping-stone to what is re-garded as a necessary bargaining relationship between parties of at least equal stature.

Thus, the Philips-EMF relationship is stalled at a crossroads. In any effort to arrange future meetings, the company will in-sist on a formal agenda and formal minutes of the proceedings. The EMF has accomplished its first objective of securing meetings on a multinational basis and now desires to accomplish its prime objective. Managements considering an invitation to meet with a multinational union group should understand clearly that the Philips type of meeting is, from the union point of view, a transi-tory phase only.

AEG-Telefunken/Zanussi

AEG-Telefunken, headquartered in Frankfurt am Main, Ger-many, is a large producer of electrical products, including do-mestic appliances, consumer electronics, industrial components, and office machines. Western Europe is the major market for the company's products; however, expansion is occurring in other parts of the world. The company employs approximately 131,500 people, with only about 25,000 located in foreign subsidiaries outside of Germany.[82]

AEG-Telefunken has had limited contact with the international trade union movement. Its cooperation with the largest Italian firm manufacturing domestic appliances, Industrie A. Zanussi S.p.A., Pordernone, and its decision in December 1973 to acquire a 20 percent minority interest in that company have aroused con-cern in the European Metalworkers' Federation. In its *Report of Activities* for 1971-74, the EMF notes that a coordinating com-mittee for AEG-Telefunken/Zanussi had been approved on March 2, 1972.[83] Apparently the initiative for the move was supported by IG Metall, AEG-Telefunken works councils, and the Italian metalworker unions at Zanussi. The EMF claims that there was a need for cooperation because the company had "extended

---

[82] *Fortune*, Vol. 100 (August 13, 1979), p. 194.

[83] European Metalworkers' Federation, *Report of Activities, 1971-1974* (Brussels, 1974), pp. 57-58.

its control over the largest Italian household appliance manufacturer with 35,000 employees and introduced a fundamental reorganisation programme in the Italian plants." [84]

There has been one meeting of the coordinating committee, held on September 15, 1972, at Frankfurt, when "delegates from IG Metall and three Italian metalworkers unions, including representatives from the plants, had the first direct exchange of information and created a trade union link." [85] The agenda for the meeting included the following:

—Structure and activity of AEG/TELEFUNKEN-ZANUSSI.

—The employment situation and trade union representation in the plants.

—Relations with the management. [86]

When the authors visited with AEG-Telefunken management in Frankfurt on February 11, 1975, it was obvious that they had not seen the EMF report containing an announcement of the meeting. [87] The company verified through a works council member that the meeting referred to was held when Italian union representatives came to Frankfurt under the tutelage of Günter Köpke. The works council is not interested in further meetings, and according to the company, IG Metall does not wish to push the company into a relationship with the EMF because wages are quite high in Germany, and if they were to get into an international exchange with the Italians, it might result in a reduction of German wages.

Subsequent to the foregoing meeting, some exchange of information between the German and Italian unions has occurred, and the EMF wrote to AEG-Telefunken in 1973 "proposing a discussion on the relations between AEG-Telefunken and Zanussi and their repercussions on the employment situation, particularly in Zanussi plants." [88] The company has not responded to this request and holds firmly to the belief that there is no necessity to meet with the EMF. It does not appear likely that the company will have such a meeting.

---

[84] *Ibid.*, p. 57.

[85] *Ibid.*

[86] *Ibid.*

[87] Interviews in Frankfurt, Germany, February 11, 1975.

[88] European Metalworkers' Federation, *Report of Activities*, p. 58.

COMMUNIST ACTIVITIES

The Communists have been much less active in the electrical and electronics industries but did sponsor international union activities in at least one major instance. This also involved Philips.

A strike against a Philips plant in Colombia was called in 1976 by a Communist union there. Representatives for Philips's plant unions from Venezuela, Mexico, and Peru met with the Colombian union in Bogotá in May 1976. Cuban representatives did not come to this meeting but allegedly funded it. A second meeting set for early 1977 did not occur because the Communists lost control of the Venezuelan union, and the Peruvian leaders could not obtain visas. No permanent organization or council resulted.[89]

CONCLUSION

The record in the electrical and electronics industries appears to indicate that multinational bargaining is not a realistic goal. Evidence suggests that the companies in the industries, as well as national unions in some instances, are opposed to multinational agreements. There are, of course, employment problems in the industries that will continue to attract considerable union interest. Intense competition leading to company restructuring, plant closures, and employee redundancies will promote transnational union interest in controlling the multinational firms. The IMF and the EMF will continue to host conferences and seminars where information will be exchanged and employee problems discussed. Decisions may be taken by the unions to challenge intergovernmental bodies such as the Organization for Economic Cooperation and Development to develop and implement effective company regulations that are perceived to be necessary to minimize potential employment problems. It is not likely that the company world councils created by the IMF, for example, will lead to demands for multinational bargaining but rather to insistence on the preservation of job security at the national level.

---

[89] Information from confidential sources.

PART THREE

The Glass, Chemicals, Rubber,
Petroleum, and Related Industries

CHAPTER VI

The Glass Industry

Probably nothing sparked interest in multinational bargaining as much as the well-propagated claims of the International Federation of Chemical, Energy and General Workers' Unions (ICEF) to the effect that, in 1969, it successfully coordinated multinational union action so that gains were won in several European countries and that the American affiliate of Saint-Gobain was forced to yield to the demands of the United Glass and Ceramic Workers (UGCW), an AFL-CIO affiliate. We concur with the statement of the ICEF secretary general: "There have been few comparable trade union events to which the international media have accorded so much attention. . . ."[1] After examining the detailed record, however, we conclude that the results claimed by the ICEF cannot be supported by credible evidence. A final section analyzes minor Communist attempts at multinational action.

THE ICEF

The ICEF is one of the oldest of the secretariats. Founded in 1907 as the Factory Workers' International, it assumed the name International Federation of Industrial Organizations and General Workers' Unions after World War II and has changed its name twice more since: to the International Federation of Chemical and General Workers' Unions (ICF) in 1965, and then adding the word *Energy* and changing its abbreviation to ICEF in 1976. "ICF" and "ICEF" are used interchangeably throughout this book since much of what is described and analyzed occurred prior to 1976.

The ICEF claims jurisdiction in the atomic energy, cement, chemical, glass, paper-manufacturing, petroleum, rubber, and re-

---

[1] Charles Levinson, *International Trade Unionism*, Ruskin House Series in Trade Union Studies (London: George Allen & Unwin, Ltd., 1972), p. 8. Levinson's Saint-Gobain story is found on pages 8-21.

lated industries. Following the demise in 1976 of the International Federation of Petroleum and Chemical Workers (IFPCW), a rival secretariat,[2] the ICEF laid claim to all energy-affiliated workers as well.[3] ICEF affiliates were largely concentrated in Europe until recent years. Today, it also has major affiliates in the United States, Canada, Japan, and several less-developed countries. In 1977, it claimed an affiliated membership of 4.5 million.

THE FLAT GLASS INDUSTRY

The flat glass sector of the glass industry has been the recipient of most of the ICEF"s claims of multinational glass union activity, although the ICEF and other union coalitions have made some attempts at action both in the pressed glass and fiberglass sectors. The flat glass industry, particularly in Western Europe, the locale of most of the ICEF"s claims, is highly concentrated. The main products—window, plate, automobile, and other safety glass—are dominated in Europe by three companies. Pilkington Brothers, Ltd., is the prime company in the United Kingdom and is the developer and patent holder of the "float" process, which has outmoded all previous production processes. Saint-Gobain-Pont-à-Mousson, the ancient French firm, and BSN-Gervais Danone, the newly assembled French group, control the bulk of the market in France, Austria, Belgium, West Germany, Italy, and the Netherlands. Such concentration, of course, facilitates union activity across borders by creating international union communities with common interests and common company targets. Table VI-1 sets forth the salient statistics of these three companies and compares them to those of the two largest American flat glass companies, Libbey-Owens-Ford and PPG Industries, and to the largest Japanese concern.

THE ICEF AND SAINT-GOBAIN

Saint-Gobain—Europe's largest glass manufacturer—is a multinational concern with sizable interests in chemicals and build-

---

[2] The story of the jurisdictional dispute between what formerly was known as the ICF (now ICEF) and the IFPCW is found in Herbert R. Northrup and Richard L. Rowan, "The ICF-IFPCW Conflict," *Columbia Journal of World Business*, Vol. IX (Winter 1974), pp. 109-19.

[3] The move into energy by the ICEF seems certain to bring it into conflict with two other secretariats, the Public Services International and the International Metalworkers' Federation.

TABLE VI-1

The Six Largest Flat Glass Companies, 1978

Company	Headquarters	Sales ($000)	Assets ($000)	Net Income ($000)	Employees
Saint-Gobain-Pont-à-Mousson	Paris	7,598,170	7,685,545	91,783	157,766
BSN-Gervais Danone [a]	Paris	3,196,294	1,321,593	10,052	57,366
PPG Industries	Pittsburgh, Pa.	2,794,000	2,335,400	132,100	37,400
Asahi Glass	Tokyo	1,745,870	2,296,802	61,771	11,942
Libbey-Owens-Ford	Toledo, Ohio	1,107,128	725,254	65,800	20,997
Pilkington Brothers [b]	St. Helens, U.K.	844,546	1,231,527	61,340	32,600

Source: *Fortune*, Vol. 99 (May 7, 1979), pp. 272-73, 278-79; Vol. 100 (August 13, 1979), pp. 194, 201.

[a] Includes Glaverbel-Mecaniver, a flat glass subsidiary controled by BSN-Gervais Danone and in which BSN has placed all its flat glass operations in Europe.

[b] Figures are for fiscal year ending March 31, 1978.

ing materials. It has facilities in all major Western European countries and in many other parts of the world. Unlike the United States glass companies, among which dominance of the different industry sectors is divided, Saint-Gobain is strong in all four—the flat glass, pressed glass, fiberglass, and container sectors.

In 1958, Saint-Gobain acquired a majority interest in the American Window Glass Company, which had three window glass plants (Arnold and Jeannettee, Pennsylvania; and Okmulgee, Oklahoma). These and two Tennessee plants—a patterned glass factory purchased earlier in Kingsport and a newly constructed plate glass facility in Greenland—made up American Saint-Gobain. This corporation was considerably smaller than the flat glass giants—Libbey-Owens-Ford (LOF) and PPG Industries (formerly Pittsburgh Plate Glass)—and did not, until very recently, emulate them in serving the automobile industry as its major customer.[4]

Saint-Gobain as a Target

In the 1960s, Saint-Gobain was the target of a highly publicized but unsuccessful takeover by a much smaller French-based concern, Boussois-Souchon-Neuvesel (BSN). During the same period, Saint-Gobain was being criticized by the Italian government and unions for its disinclination to expand in labor-troubled Italy; by the key German union, which was anxious to win expanded tenure and severance arrangements for its glass members that it had already won in the chemical industry; and by American unionists who wanted to win parity of wages and benefits for American Saint-Gobain employees with those achieved by LOF and PPG workers. All in all, Saint-Gobain seemed to be an ideal target because of a combination of events not likely to happen again.[5]

Preparing for such an opportunity, the ICEF at its 1967 congress set "coordinated international bargaining with multinational corporations" as a "top-priority policy objective."[6] At

---

[4] The third largest United States flat glass concern is Ford Motor Company, which consumes the bulk of its product internally.

[5] Ralph Reiser, then president of the United Glass and Ceramic Workers (UGCW), interview in Columbus, Ohio, October 25, 1973.

[6] The language is from "ICF Information," letter to all affiliates from Charles Levinson, April 16, 1969.

the same time, it established "divisions" in various industries, including glass, to bring together information and union personnel for unified industry action and "councils" to do the same for companies. Questionnaires were sent to all affiliated unions representing glass workers, and information was assembled on major glass concerns, particularly Saint-Gobain, Pilkington, Owens-Illinois (the largest United States-based glass bottle manufacturer), and Corning Glass (the leading United States-based blown glass, tableware, and television tube manufacturer). A three-day international conference, held in November 1968 in Geneva, agreed to continue the research, encourage mutual assistance, and attempt to gain ICEF international coordinated bargaining objectives by demanding that company managements meet with the ICEF, by developing a list of demands not likely to provoke complete and immediate managerial rejection, and by looking for favorable opportunities to put the ICEF program into effect.[7] It was clear at the conference that Saint-Gobain was to be the primary target of all these efforts.

Taking on Saint-Gobain was an ambitious project, even granting the difficulties with which the company was then faced. The fact that the unions that met at the November conference in Geneva did not represent a majority of the Saint-Gobain employees either in France or in Italy did not help. In the United States, one of the five Saint-Gobain plants was represented by a rival union. Only in Germany was the ICEF affiliate an unchallenged representative. In fact, the unions present at the conference may have represented as little as 7.5 percent of Saint-Gobain's worldwide employees.[8]

Negotiations in the United States

On November 1, 1968, LOF agreed to a contract that the UGCW called "the biggest and best contract ever negotiated in the long history of the United Glass and Ceramic Workers of America." The contract provided for a minimum increase of one dollar per hour over three years for most employees. This settlement, the UGCW emphasized, "parallels settlements the United Auto Workers made with the Big Three car manufac-

---

[7] See *Glass Workers News*, Vol. 35, No. 7 (March 1969), p. 46, for a conference report and an analysis of company data. This paper is the official organ of the UGCW.

[8] "Labor Shaping Up for Global Conflicts: U.S.-European Threat to S. Gobain," *Business International*, Vol. XVI, No. 16 (April 18, 1969), p. 122.

turers," a pattern the UGCW had historically attempted to follow.[9]

When negotiations opened with American Saint-Gobain in Memphis four months later, the UGCW pushed hard for the LOF pattern, plus some additional benefits, including a forty cents per hour "catch-up" to equalize American Saint-Gobain wages with LOF wages. The UGCW also forewarned that, whatever the economic position of American Saint-Gobain, Saint-Gobain should "send over a boat load of francs" because the overall corporation was the target of a multinational union coalition. American Saint-Gobain explained that the parent company would not bail it out again, as had been done for several years, and that it must now "sink or swim" on its own. Moreover, the company emphasized that the automobile industry was not its prime customer and that, therefore, it should not be required to follow the LOF pattern. It also noted the special problems of its plant in Arnold, Pennsylvania, closed since February 1, 1969, and indicated that the plant might never reopen if relief on labor costs was not granted. It stated further that, if it were to meet the LOF pattern, some overall cost reductions would be required, including a manpower reduction of about 2.5 percent.[10]

The UGCW had already recognized American Saint-Gobain's special needs in one instance by agreeing to a subpattern contract covering the new plate glass plant at Greenland, Tennessee, which was still in a shakedown status.[11] Yet, even though American Saint-Gobain offered a pattern-oriented package equal to slightly more than $1.06 per hour for a three-year period, the UGCW

---

[9] "LOF Workers Win Big," *Glass Workers News*, Vol. 35, No. 4 (December 1968), pp. 3-4.

[10] These comments on negotiations are based on interviews with Ralph Reiser, now president-emeritus of the UGCW, and correspondence with E. C. Good, vice-president of personnel of the former American Saint-Gobain Company, on materials supplied by each, and, where noted, on available secondary sources. The figures for the "catch-up" of forty cents per hour are found in *Glass Workers News*, Vol. 35, No. 9 (June 1969), p. 10. The basic facts of the negotiations are not in dispute.

[11] The cloud then hanging over this plant and over American Saint-Gobain's earnings potential was that it was the last built that was based on the old glass-making technology, which has since been completely outmoded by the Pilkington float process. For a company that had moved into the black only in 1968, after several years of losses, including a $1.47 million deficit in 1967, to have spent $40 million on an outmoded technology was a bitter blow to hopes of future improved earnings. See Gregory H. Wierzynski, "The Eccentric Lords of Float Glass," *Fortune*, Vol. LXXVIII, No. 1 (July 1968), p. 91; and *Business Week*, April 12, 1969, p. 58.

refused to lower its demands to that figure. Instead, it requested an adjournment of negotiations for one month as of March 15, the date that the contract expired, with the union members to remain on the job without a contract, so that the UGCW delegates could attend a meeting of the ICEF Saint-Gobain unions in Geneva. Before that conference, the UGCW reached an agreement with PPG, which it called "the biggest and best ever negotiated with this company" and one that "exceeds by several cents the settlement negotiated with LOF." [12] Thus, when the ICEF Saint-Gobain meeting opened on March 29 in Geneva, American Saint-Gobain remained the sole UGCW target.

The Geneva Meeting

Delegates present, besides Reiser and two other UGCW representatives, included those from Belgium, the French Confédération Française Démocratique du Travail (CFDT), Switzerland, Germany, Sweden, Norway, and one from each of the two ICEF Italian affiliates. The delegates formed an "ICEF Saint-Gobain World Council" and agreed that (1) no agreement would be concluded in one country without consultation and approval of a standing committee representing the delegates; (2) if a strike occurred, all unions would provide financial assistance to the strikers; (3) shipments would be prevented from plants that were represented to struck plants; and (4) if a prolonged strike occurred, all Saint-Gobain plants would stop overtime work.[13]

Yet, just before the March 29 meeting in Geneva, unions representing the bulk of Saint-Gobain's French employees settled for a 3.5 percent wage increase, considerably less than the 10 to 12 percent they had initially demanded.[14] Moreover, by the time the March 29 meeting was held, agreement was close in Germany and was achieved during the first two weeks in April. The German employees of Saint-Gobain won a 7.5 percent wage increase and the job security provisions regarding severance pay and tenure that had previously been obtained by the same union

---

[12] *Glass Workers News*, Vol. 35, No. 7 (April 1969), p. 1.

[13] See United Glass and Ceramic Workers, *The Challenge of Change: Officer's Report to the 10th Constitutional Convention*, Miami Beach, July 27-30, 1970, p. 13. See also Levinson, *International Trade Unionism*, pp. 13-14.

[14] "French Wage Increases at Saint-Gobain Aren't as Big as Unions Ask," *Wall Street Journal*, March 28, 1969.

(Industriegewerkschaft Chemie-Papier-Keramik, known as IG Chemie) for its membership in the chemical industry. After this agreement was signed, the secretary general of the ICEF wrote Reiser:

> After consultation with all committee members except yourself, there was agreement that our German affiliate should go ahead and sign an agreement. . . . Before negotiations began, the union told management that any agreement reached in no way conditioned their full participation in the ICF coordinated campaign and that they would carry out all the measures required in solidarity short of a strike which is precluded if the contract is signed.[15]

In Italy, negotiations continued intermittently, and agreement was reached late in April. The ICEF version is that "the company conceded nearly all the points that were outstanding," including "the recognition by Saint-Gobain of the trade unions as the authoritative body for negotiations on a company-wide basis." [16] The company version is that the contract was "renewed with satisfactory conditions for labor and management." [17]

The Strike and Settlement

In the United States, renewed negotiations between American Saint-Gobain and the UGCW remained stalemated, and the union called a strike on May 1. At that time, American Saint-Gobain was still offering a package approximately equal to the LOF and PPG settlements, the UGCW was pushing for more, and disagreements remained over basic working conditions.

No further negotiations occurred until May 20, when the parties met in Pittsburgh and reached agreement on a package the following day with wage increases and benefits based on the LOF pattern. The Arnold plant reopened after the strike but ceased production on September 26 of the same year; it was officially closed on January 4, 1971, and was sold on September 29, 1971. Some five hundred workers lost their jobs.

The parent company did not rescue American Saint-Gobain. Rather, it sold its controlling interest after the strike to Nelson Loud and Associates, an investment firm, which refinanced and reorganized the company. It is now known as ASG Industries, Incorporated. At that time, Certain-Teed Products Corporation, in which Saint-Gobain had long held a minor interest, acquired a

---

[15] Letter from Charles Levinson to Ralph Reiser, April 10, 1969.

[16] Levinson, *International Trade Unionism*, pp. 18-19.

[17] Intracompany correspondence in authors' possession.

26 percent interest in ASG Industries. More recently, Saint-Gobain has purchased a controlling interest in Certain-Teed, but Loud and Associates have maintained its majority ownership in, and control of, ASG Industries.

ICEF Impact on Negotiations

Was the ICEF coalition against Saint-Gobain effective, decisive, or merely propaganda? To answer this question realistically, an assessment of results is required both country by country and overall.

In France, the ICEF could claim little success. The CFDT affiliate could have refused, under the French system, to sign the 3.5 percent wage package that had been accepted by the Confédération Générale du Travail (CGT), but it could not have gained more.[18] The agreement would have been put into effect anyway.

In Italy, the claim that Saint-Gobain recognized the ICEF's affiliates—branches of the Unione Italiana del Lavoro (UIL) and the Confederazione Italiana Sindacati Lavoratori (CISL)—"as the authoritative body for negotiations on a company-wide basis" cannot be substantiated. Negotiations in Italy, as well as in Germany, are on an industrywide, not companywide, basis. In Italy, all union groups—the CISL, the UIL, and the Communist Confederazione Generale Italiana del Lavoro (CGIL)—are involved in these negotiations. In a letter to the authors, the vice-président directeur général of Saint-Gobain states that the company "has never recognized the UIL and the CISL as its sole negotiating partners, and the unions for their part have never asked for separate negotiations." [19]

In Germany, the key issue was the demand by IG Chemie for acceptance by the glass industry of the tenure and severance rules it had already negotiated in the chemical industry. Given the broad nature of German bargaining and the fact that the same union and some of the same companies were involved in both glass and chemicals, it seems that it would have been difficult for the German glass industry to refuse to give in to this demand.

Although it was claimed that the German settlement was "particularly in the United States . . . the basis for further negotiations" with Saint-Gobain, we have found no support for this claim.[20] All UGCW communications, including the official

---

[18] Levinson, *International Trade Unionism*, p. 10.

[19] Letter dated February 11, 1974.

[20] Levinson, *International Trade Unionism*, p. 17.

one announcing the strike to all union members, stress the union's determination to achieve parity for American Saint-Gobain workers with those of LOF and PPG. This is made very clear in a letter from Reiser to all striking employees (May 8, 1969), setting forth the list of UGCW demands, including "the severance pay plan presently in effect for the PPG and LOF workers and which is also in effect for the Cutters' League employees of the American Saint-Gobain Corporation."

Reiser believes that the threat of foreign union assistance was helpful in the United States, although he readily concedes that it was "a weak thing to hang your hat on." He believes, however, that Saint-Gobain, beset with difficulties on all sides, chose to concede to the LOF and PPG pattern rather than to put the union coalition to the test, although it had previously refused to do so without some union concessions on work rules.[21]

The ICEF claims more. Its secretary general wrote:

> After twenty-six days of strike, the company finally capitulated and informed the union that it was ready to engage in serious negotiations with full authority to reach decisions. As a result, a very satisfactory agreement was reached on all the terms demanded by the union; the results were almost identical, except for minor elements, with the original demands. These included:
>
> 1. Overall improvements amounting to a nearly 9 per cent per year increase over a period of 3 years, or a total of 27 per cent.
>
> 2. A $1.06 per hour wage increase and 17 cents per hour increase for fringe or security benefits including improved health insurance, medical insurance, pension scheme, etc. The total comes to an overall increase of 9 per cent per year for three years, or 27 per cent for the term of a 3-year contract. The union succeeded in getting severance pay for the first time. If a worker had 10 years' service in a plant and was dismissed, he would get about $1,300 severance pay in addition to his unemployment indemnity from the government. For incentive workers, an increase in incentive rates of between 10 and 15 per cent was achieved.
>
> 3. Another important achievement was in regularizing work loads of production units among the 15-man teams working on 9 machine units. The workers and the local union themselves were together authorized to draw up schedules and equalize the work loads.[22]

The company position is substantially different. The personnel executive of the former American company provided information

---

21 Interview in Columbus, Ohio, October 25, 1973. This statement is reiterated in substance in current reports by UGCW publications.

22 Levinson, *International Trade Unionism*, p. 20.

to the authors showing that it had offered a package of slightly
more than $1.06 per hour on March 15 and that the final settle-
ment figure after twenty-one days of strike was for just $0.005
more.[23] The company emphasizes that the improved pension and
welfare items were "on the table" by March 15 and did not
change during the strike. Company data show that, when negotiations began, the UGCW was demanding improvements that
would have cost $1.683 per hour, and that, when the strike
began, the union demands would have cost $1.687 per hour. The
Glass Workers News claims that the estimated cost of the settlement was $1.14 per hour,[24] but in view of all accounts of what
items constituted the settlement and of the UGCW agreement
that the company's prestrike offer was worth $1.06 per hour, the
settlement figure was most likely between $1.06 and $1.07 per
hour.

The severance pay provision, which the *Glass Workers News*
states was "similar to the plan in effect for the PPG and LOF
workers," is greatly exaggerated by the ICEF account. A severed
worker with ten years of service would receive $626.88, not
$1,300 as claimed.[25] Moreover, since LOF and PPG already had
severance pay and American Saint-Gobain itself had given it to
a craft union (the Glass Cutters' League), it is difficult to believe
that it was an issue over which the company would risk a strike.[26]

The company position on the rules changes is the following:

> Here three changes were made regarding the work loads. We
> reduced 35 (actually resulted in 38) employees from the work
> force, changed an antiquated system of pay based on speed of
> draw to a new method and changed the break-off procedure so the
> glass cut at this new point was ready to be packed rather than
> having to be recut again. For this, yes, we said as long as you
> adequately man the machines you can arrange your own relief

---

[23] Letter from E. C. Good, vice-president of personnel of the former
American Saint-Gobain Company, to one of the authors, December 3, 1973.

[24] *Glass Workers News*, Vol. 35, No. 11 (August 1969), p. 4. How the
union computed this figure could not be ascertained.

[25] Severance pay under that contract was based on pension credits, which
did not begin until two years' service had been accumulated. Using the figures
in *Glass Workers News* (August 1969, p. 4), which are corroborated by the
company, it is calculated as follows: 10 years minus 2 times $78.36 = $626.88.
Where Lovinson got the $1,300 figure could not be ascertained.

[26] A letter from Reiser to all American Saint-Gobain employees (May 8,
1969) notes that the Glass Cutters' League members who worked for American
Saint-Gobain were covered by the same provision demanded by the UGCW.

> schedule. He's [Levinson] right, it was damn important for *us*.
> Even the Union vocally blamed [the company] for trading a flea for
> an elephant.[27]

Thus, the company position is that it won the manpower reduction it was demanding. It further notes that it would have required additional manpower and cost concessions to keep the Arnold plant operating and that the refusal of the UGCW to grant those concessions ended any opportunity for this plant to survive. The union's position is that this plant, like others in window or sheet glass, was doomed by foreign competition in any case.

Aftermath

Although it is not possible to reconstruct what might have happened if the ICEF-coordinated activity had not occurred, we conclude that such coordinated activity was without significant influence on the course of negotiations in Europe. In the United States, the potential for pressure from Europe seems to have at least encouraged, if not precipitated, strike action by the UGCW. But the results of the strike do not appear to have gained the union much, if anything, for its members over and above what the company was offering prior to the strike. If this analysis is correct and even if the Arnold plant would have closed regardless of union strike action, then international coordination resulted in a net loss for American Saint-Gobain employees. The union did not win the forty cents per hour catch-up pay, and it did agree to a significant manpower reduction, in addition to losing five hundred members at the Arnold plant.

Since 1969, the ICEF has been able neither to arrange a meeting with top Saint-Gobain officials nor to mount another coordinated action against the company. Company executives make no secret of their refusal to recognize or to meet with any ICEF group, and they emphasize their commitment that "human and social problems," including those involving unions, be settled at the local or national levels.[28]

---

[27] Letter from E. C. Good, vice-president of personnel of the former American Saint-Gobain Company, to one of the authors, December 3, 1973.

[28] Statement of Roger Martin, president of Saint-Gobain, at The Wharton School, November 6, 1973, in response to a question posed by Andrew J. Schindler, then research assistant for the Industrial Research Unit's multinational project, following Martin's lecture; and interviews with company officials in Paris in August 1974 and June 1975.

According to the current president of the UGCW, the ICEF Saint-Gobain World Council no longer exists.[29] Moreover, the ICEF's largest Italian affiliate disaffiliated in July 1973, leaving it largely unrepresented in Italy.[30] With Saint-Gobain no longer in control of an American glass company and with the non-ICEF Communist unions dominant in France and Italy, the opportunity for ICEF action against, or for bargaining with, Saint-Gobain in the foreseeable future appears very limited.

Despite the apparent lack of success of ICEF activities involving Saint-Gobain, either in 1969 or thereafter, shrewd ICEF public relations and the failure of many researchers and reporters to probe beneath the flood of press releases created an image that made the 1969 Saint-Gobain activity the byword for "successful" trade union action.

THE ICEF AND PILKINGTON

Pilkington, based in St. Helens, near Liverpool, England, is the smallest company listed in Table VI-1 in sales. Nevertheless, it controls the patents to the float process, the method by which almost all installations built since 1962 have made flat glass. Pilkington licenses to other companies, including the giants listed in Table VI-1, which provides it with substantial royalty income from all over the world.

Pilkington itself supplies about 90 percent of the flat glass sold in Britain and, in addition, has plants in Canada, Australia, New Zealand, India, South Africa, and Argentina. It has majority interests in two companies in Sweden and, prior to the recent business recession, was planning float plants there and possibly in Argentina. Pilkington also produces fiberglass and pressed glass products and photochromic prescription lenses and sunglasses; it has a 3 percent interest in BSN.[31]

---

[29] David C. Hershfield, *The Multinational Union Challenges the Multinational Company*, Report No. 658 (New York: The Conference Board, 1975), p. 29.

[30] This affiliate, Federchimici, was a branch of the CISL. The disaffiliation letter, dated July 20, 1973, was sent to both the secretary general and the president of the ICEF and signed by Danilo Baretta, secretary general of Federchimici. A copy is in our files.

[31] See Pilkington Brothers, Ltd., *Report and Accounts for the Year Ended, 31st March 1974; A Review by Sir Alastair Pilkington, Chairman of Pilkington Brothers, Ltd.* (St. Helens, 1974), circulated with the company's report and accounts; and Wierzynski, "The Eccentric Lords of Float Glass," pp. 90-92, 121-24.

Pilkington first came to the attention of the ICEF in 1970, when a group of employees at St. Helens formed a breakaway (rival) union to the General and Municipal Workers' Union (GMWU) representing them and instigated a jurisdictional strike that lasted for seven weeks. The strike leaders were discharged, and they appealed to the British dockworkers to refuse to handle glass imported from Saint-Gobain for Pilkington's regular customers. At the same time, the ICEF urged French and British unions to boycott Saint-Gobain shipments to Britain. Neither the British dockworkers nor any other British nor French unions took supportive action.[32]

At the November 1972 meeting of the ICEF Glass Industry Division in Geneva, a Pilkington World Council was established. Following that, the representative of the Association of Scientific, Technical and Managerial Staffs (ASTMS), a union representing some Pilkington employees, issued a statement charging that the company's licensing and investment policies had encouraged it to close plants at home and invest abroad, and demanded a meeting with the world council and union representative on the Pilkington Board of Directors to "monitor developments which are going to have an impact on our membership." In reply, Pilkington noted that it had six factories and a head office in St. Helens, far more than it had anywhere else.[33]

The union did get its meeting. Following the ICEF congress in Geneva in November 1973, the Pilkington World Council, as part of the ICEF Glass Industry Conference, met near St. Helens. At the request of the GMWU, the largest union representing Pilkington employees, company officials permitted the delegates to tour their newest plant. On November 12, 1973, David F. Pilkington (director in charge of personnel and related matters), R. S. Aitken (head of personnel relations), and two associates met with the delegates. Present in the union group, besides Levinson and delegates from the two already noted British unions, were representatives from the UGCW, which holds bargaining rights in the Pilkington Canadian plant, and union delegates

---

[32] Saint-Gobain and Pilkington officials, interviews in Paris and St. Helens, July 1974. There is no mention of any relevant dock or glass stoppages or boycotts in the British or French press as of this period that we could find.

[33] "Union Warns of Glass Jobs Threat," *St. Helens Newspaper and Advertiser*, November 28, 1972, p. 1.

from Argentina, Germany, and France, although there are no Pilkington plants in the last two countries.[34]

There was no agenda, but the company delegates carefully controlled the discussions. Mr. Pilkington made it quite clear in a short talk that he was not recognizing the council and reiterated that statement in response to a request from Levinson. He did not rule out future meetings but emphasized that negotiations within a national setting with appropriate unions were company policy. The union delegates emphasized that they wanted regular meetings annually, but they received no company commitment.

Since the world council meeting, ICEF-affiliated unions have attempted twice to use their council affiliation to assist in obtaining objectives. The UGCW mounted an organizing campaign for salaried workers at the Scarborough Works, Canada, where it represents hourly workers. It claimed that St. Helens workers would support demands for higher salaries, but its campaign, which received no discernible support from the British workers, was unsuccessful. In July 1974, a general walkout at St. Helens was followed by salaried workers' "guerilla" (selected) strikes, which were initiated by the ASTMS in an attempt to win salary adjustments. When the company threatened layoffs in retaliation, the ASTMS asked the ICEF to prevent the company from importing glass into Britain and to request "sympathetic action" in all Pilkington subsidaries throughout the world. Nothing appears to have come from these requests.[35]

Actually, international union action against Pilkington is certain to be difficult. Operating in Europe only through subsidiaries in Sweden, Pilkington plants are too isolated and far-flung to be involved easily in multicountry union joint action. Indeed, Pilkington is primarily a British company; it is multinational only in a limited way insofar as its manufacturing operations are involved. Our impression is that, although Pilkington may meet

---

[34] Our description of the meeting is based on the following sources, which are in basic agreement on the facts: interview with company officials (who supplied relevant supporting documents) in St. Helens, July 1974; Reiser, telephone interview, November 19, 1973; and article by Joseph Roman, president, United Glass and Ceramic Workers, *Glass Workers News*, Vol. 40, No. 3 (March 1974). Reiser and Roman were at the November 12, 1973, meeting.

[35] Pilkington officials, interviews in St. Helens, July 1974; "Guerilla Strikers Get 'Lay-Offs' Threat from Firm," *St. Helens Reporter*, July 26, 1974. There is no record of any action at any Pilkington plant in response to this request that we could find in the press or ICEF literature.

again with the world council, it does not envisage such meetings as essentially in the company interest and is not likely to be anxious to do so.

For its part, the ICEF, having won a propaganda victory with the meeting, is not likely to have a second one high on its agenda unless its British affiliates regard such a meeting as helpful to them, and here again, this does not seem too likely in the near future. As a result of the severe downturn in the automobile and construction industries in 1974-75, the glass industry was hard hit. Pilkington's work force suffered a decline, and short weeks were very common. In July 1975, Pilkington announced the closing of a plant making glass funnels for television tubes. The official of the GMWU, whose efforts had made the ICEF-Pilkington meeting possible, called for import controls to protect the industry against foreign competition, especially Japanese.[36] Such divergency of interests among ICEF affiliates, plus the limited multinational manufacturing activities of the company, would seem to limit any immediate interest of the ICEF or of the key British unions in continuing to press Pilkington for international contacts, especially in periods of economic downturn.

BSN-GERVAIS DANONE

BSN-Gervais Danone is a company group headquartered in Paris. It was assembled by Antoine Riboud, who first achieved widespread notice in 1969 by his unsuccessful attempt to win control of Saint-Gobain. Originally a collection of various glass container concerns known as Souchon-Neuvesel, it merged with Boussois, a flat glass maker—becoming BSN—and then won control of glass makers in Belgium, the Netherlands, Italy, Germany, Spain, and Austria. In addition, BSN has become a major factor in the food, beverage, and packaging businesses in Western Europe and has interests in Africa and Latin America.

In the takeover of the Belgian glass concern Glaverbel in 1972, BSN encountered opposition both from Saint-Gobain, which owned 15 percent of the Belgian concern, and from Belgian unions, worker representatives, and government officials who were fearful that a merger would result in lost jobs. To surmount this problem, BSN's then top glass executive, Philippe Daublain, met with representatives of affiliates of the Belgian Christian unions [the Confédération des Syndicats Chrétiens

---

[36] Kenneth Gooding, "Pilkington to Close Plant After State Aid Refusal," *Financial Times*, July 3, 1975, p. 1.

(CSC)] and socialist unions [the Fédération Générale du Travail de Belgique (FGTB)] and negotiated a "Format of the Agreement Relating to the Problems of Employment within the Framework of the Merger of BSN/Glaverbel," issued November 9, 1972.[37] This format of agreement "verifies" that a new entity, "Glaverbel-Mecaniver," would be created, into which all BSN flat glass holdings, including Glaverbel, would be placed, and it sets forth "General Principles," "Modalities [qualifications] of Application of these Principles," and "Mutual Pledges," all couched in quite general terms. The principles include the pledge of BSN to expand its float glass capacity, develop new techniques and markets, expand window glass production by "traditional procedures of fabrication," and establish a committee of labor and company representatives to meet once a year.

The "Modalities of Application" refer to specific production and expansion plans; maintenance, "saving unforeseeable circumstances," of the 1972 labor-force size into 1974; consideration of relative situations in each country without being "either rigid or automatic" in determining the investments in the course of the next five years; and establishment of a multinational association of unions within four months to meet with the company. The "Mutual Pledges" include various agreements on cooperation and good relationships.

To the company, this document meant principally that its representatives would meet regularly with union representatives of its employees in various European countries and advise them of its investment plans and policies. It would be surprising, however, if unions did not regard it as an initial step toward collective bargaining.

The ICEF Meeting

The FGTB glass union is an affiliate of the ICEF, and one of its regional officials is an ICEF vice-president. Seizing an obvious opportunity, the ICEF secretary general convened a meeting of Belgian, French, and German affiliates in BSN glass plants in June 1973 and then invited the company to hold the first promised meeting of the Glaverbel-Mecaniver multinational union-company group at his office in Geneva.[38] After some negotiations on the

---

[37] Copy in authors' possession.

[38] "Report of Activities of the Secretary-General, the 15th Statutory Congress, Geneva, 7th-9th November 1973, Documents," *ICF Bulletin*, October 1973, p. 89.

composition of the union committee, the meeting was held there on September 24, 1973; the company acted as host, however, and invited the delegates, including many from unions that were not ICEF affiliates. Daublain and François Destailleur, BSN director of social relations, represented the company. The labor side included representatives affiliated with the Belgian FGTB and CSC; unions in Germany and Austria; the socialist, Catholic, and Protestant unions in the Netherlands; and plant union members affiliated with the French CGT and CFDT.

The meeting was apparently harmonious, and again, the company gave the union representatives information regarding the company's general position in the industry and the possible course of investments during the next ten years. Discussions also took place concerning a possible protocol on a multinational basis similar to the one signed with the Belgian unions. According to the company, a joint press release was written, and Levinson was to release it.[39]

Levinson, however, issued his own—according to the company, different—press release, which was widely circulated.[40] It states in part that "for the first time an international firm has agreed to discuss its investment policies with the unions from several countries." Then, after noting the presence of Daublain and the union representatives, the ICEF statement declares that the ICEF had organized the meeting and that "unions—ICF to be precise—and management have come together to discuss a format for a permanent negotiation on the subject."

In contrast to the ICEF release, the Belgian unions' release states merely that Daublain discussed his company's views in regard to employment problems, that a fruitful exchange of views occurred, and that future prospects for a possible agreement were discussed.

The ICEF press release upset the company sufficiently to have Daublain issue a question-and-answer press release of his own. In it, he denies discussing investment policies and states that the company officials "gave the unions information regarding the position of Glaverbel-Mecaniver in the flat glass industry on the world plane. We explained what investments were in course, and we indicated the probable evaluation in this field over the next ten years." He further emphasized that "Mr. Levinson was not

---

[39] Interview in Levallois-Perret (formerly the headquarters of BSN), July 1974; also Daublain's press release (statement).

[40] These press releases are in the authors' possession.

the instigator of that meeting. It was held on our initiative."
He deplored "extremely venomous" attacks on multinational companies.

Daublain did, however, favor "the principle of an annual information meeting concerning the problems of employment linked
with investments," and he stated that the creation of a strong
international union was a "likely prospect" and was "necessary."
He recognized that "national feelings are at least as strong
among unionists as among others [and] . . . social conditions
and legislation differ from one country to another" so that if
the "international union movement at the confederal level seems
too difficult to put into effect at the moment, one can . . . imagine
that the union representatives of a multinational firm will get
together on a determined subject such as employment."

Perhaps even more interesting was this question and answer:

> Do you envisage the possibility of concluding a works agreement
> on the international level?
>
> Yes, concerning the problem of the balance of employment. And I
> believe that we are the first Frenchmen to undertake action along
> these lines.

Daublain explained his affirmative reply by noting the history
of the Glaverbel merger (described above).

After this incident, additional meetings were held between a
committee representing the unions and employees in Glaverbel-
Mecaniver's flat glass plants, but at the company's insistence, the
ICEF was not officially represented. After some protests by the
Belgian FGTB representative, this exclusion was accepted by the
unions.[41] Meanwhile, the demand for flat glass declined precipi-
tously as its two main industry customers, automobile manufacturing and building construction, fell into a severe recession.
With several technically outmoded facilities and with world demand at a low point, BSN moved to close some Glaverbel plants
and ran into the emotional and political reaction that has become
increasingly common in Europe whenever a plant shutdown is
announced.

Plant Closings

In January 1975, BSN announced the closing of a technically
obsolete Glaverbel window glass plant in Gilly, Belgium. The
workers reacted by demonstrating, engaging in a twenty-four

---

[41] Documents relating to the meetings are in the authors' files.

hour general strike in Glaverbel plants, and occupying the Gilly plant and locking out management. They even began selling glass on the open market. Considerable political support in the Belgian Parliament developed for the workers, despite the depressed glass market and the fact that Glaverbel could supply its customers from a nearby facility, which, unlike the Gilly plant, utilized the modern float method pioneered by Pilkington.

The climax of the demonstrations came on February 17, 1975, when several hundred Belgian workers journeyed to France under FGTB and CSC leadership and were joined by French workers and unions to demonstrate in front of the BSN headquarters. French worker delegations came particularly from two plants: Wingles (Pas-de-Calais), where 450 of a total of 875 faced dismissal if two window glass furnaces were shut down, and Boussois, where heavy layoffs were also occurring. The CFDT, which had taken a strong stand against plant closures in France, was much more active at the demonstration than the Communist CGT, but radical and Communist organizations from Belgium that had begun and fanned the agitation were also present, as were a Belgian Communist deputy and representatives of Force-Ouvrière, a third French labor federation. The previous week, a delegation from Gilly had participated in a demonstration in Paris led by the CFDT, opposing shutting down the Wingles operation.

Riboud and Daublain met with the demonstrators in a hectic meeting in the company cafeteria and agreed to go to Belgium to negotiate with them and Belgian authorities concerning the plant closing. After several tumultuous meetings in which the Belgian ministers of labor and economic affairs participated, an agreement was signed on February 26, 1975, providing for shutting down the furnace but keeping the plant open. The agreement further provides that approximately 50 workers were to be retained, that another 100 would be given other jobs in nearby Glaverbel plants or elsewhere in the region, and that, within one year, additional activity would be created to provide jobs for 300 to 370 persons, as compared with a plant force of about 480 prior to the furnace shutdown. During the "transformation year," Glaverbel and the Belgian government agreed to set up a fund to guarantee income to workers at their present level. Male employees of at least 58 years and female employees of at least 53 years were to be permitted to take early retirement. Glaverbel also agreed to participate in studies to promote employment in the region.[42]

Thus, the Belgian unions, pushed by radical groups and aided by the Belgian government, used direct action to thwart an economic decision by management and prevent the shutdown of an obsolete facility. Not only did BSN not close its facility, it took, in effect, some responsibility for helping to maintain employment in a region.

The demonstrations and plant seizure at Gilly were initiated and led by insurgent left-wing groups, but both the FGTB and CSC leadership quickly became involved and apparently took over without ICEF or other international involvement. There were, to be sure, joint demonstrations of the CFDT, other French unions, and the Belgian CSC and FGTB in Paris and Levallois-Perret. A union delegation from Boussois also visited Gilly on January 30, and three days before, a joint meeting of Gilly and Boussois union delegations occurred at Boussois. Moreover, on January 13, 1975, BSN officials met with the international union committee, which had been reconstructed some months before without ICEF participation, and advised the committee of its plans to close Gilly's furnaces.

Nevertheless, the final negotiations were strictly among the company, the Belgian unions, and the Belgian government, with no international involvement. The French and Belgian unions demonstrated together but did not work together for solutions, and the Gilly and Wingles problems were not put together by the unions for any kind of multinational final action or solution.

In mid-May 1975, Glaverbel-Mecaniver management announced that it would be forced to shut down one of the two furnaces at the Houdeng, Belgium, plant because of huge unsold inventories. This action was expected to affect about one-half of the 560 workers employed there. The employees protested, starting a partial strike and occupying for one day a national employment office at nearby La Louvière, and won support from members of the Belgian Parliament. Not desiring another Gilly situation, Glaverbel management met with the CSC, the FGTB, and the strike committee and worked out a generous agreement. It pro-

---

[42] There was extensive press coverage of this affair. See, e.g., *Le Monde*, February 20, 1975, *Le Soir*, February 26, 1975; *France Nouvelle*, March 3, 1975; *La Vie Française d'Opinion*, February 20, 1975; *La Voix du Nord* (Lille), February 19, 1975. François Destailleur, directeur de la coordination des relations sociales, BSN-Gervais Danone, also provided a very helpful chronology and agreement summary.

vided for alternate weeks of work for all employees; 90 percent of take-home pay for those on alternate weeks off until December 1975, when a government program to do the same thing would become effective; an outside work program provided by the company for those not otherwise taken care of; and severance payments for all those who resigned.[43]

The Agreement on Employment Problems

Following the press release controversy, BSN officials met with the union committee from Austria, Belgium, France, Germany, and the Netherlands on September 19, 1974, and January 13, 1975. Then, at a meeting on May 27, 1975, an agreement on employment was signed by union and plant representatives from the five countries.[44] It provides for a Permanent Employment Commission composed of representatives of the general management of Glaverbel-Mecaniver and of each of its three operational entities—Benelit, which includes operations in Belgium and Holland; Boussois, those in France; and Flachglas, Delog-Detag, covering those in Germany and Austria—and of one delegate from each union in a country, with a minimum of two delegates per country.

The agreement emphasizes that national companies and unions will continue to handle basic social affairs as they have in the past, that the commission will not cause superior conditions in any country to be reduced, and that it will not diminish the significance of negotiations between management and labor in each country. The primary job of the commission is to examine technical, social, and economic matters in a quest to maintain employment. Its agenda in so doing includes "information and discussion" on the problems of investment, disinvestment, and other activities of the company, with emphasis on maintaining an equilibrium among the countries in which BSN operates. Before meetings of the commission, which are to be held twice per year, an agenda is to be established by a representative of the general management and a designated union correspondent. Pertinent documents are to be made available to participants two weeks before each scheduled meeting. At the February 1976 meeting, for example, the company reported on the employment

---

[43] "Accord à Glaverbel-Houdeng," *Le Rappel*, June 3, 1975.

[44] "Protocole Relatif aux Problèmes de l'Emploi," Boitsfort, May 27, 1975. The name of the commission was changed in late 1978 to "Commission d'Information Economique et Sociale."

effects of the closing of a number of plants that occurred without incident and on plans to install new equipment.

As management representatives pointed out to the authors, this was an agreement on procedure and information and was confined to the subject of employment or matters affecting employment. Moreover, the commission was given no power to alter decisions once made and thus has no collective bargaining function.

Nevertheless, it does seem that, by signing the agreement, BSN took a long stride toward multinational collective bargaining and joint labor-management decision making. The agreement itself states that "the general management does not exclude the principle of negotiating within the Permanent Employment Commission about an international convention with equivalent effects in favor of the workers employed in the countries covered by the three operational entities." The meetings remained informational and consultative through 1977, in part perhaps because employment in the European glass industry was much depressed. Despite the Gilly and Houdeng affairs, news of other plant closings were received without upset by the labor members of the commission.

The commission meeting climate has not changed, although business and employment have improved since 1976, and BSN has announced several plant expansions. A serious problem of another kind developed at Gilly. Employees who have received pay for not working have shown reluctance to accept employment at the newly constructed BSN plant there, despite its close proximity. Some could be permanently unemployed as a result.

Despite such problems, management believes that it can maintain the current character of the commission, and events seem to support this view. It was BSN, not the unions, which created the commission, and the initiative remains with the company. Moreover, the unions may not support international collective bargaining. They clearly regard the agreement as a significant precedent in their relations with multinational companies, but they may not be anxious to transfer their authority to an international body.

Union disunity is another negative factor that could preclude a move toward multinational bargaining. Both the CGT and the CFDT unions refused to sign the protocol. After interviewing all the parties, Professor Rojot concluded that the CGT's refusal was consistent with its Communist philosophy. He also stated that the poor relations between the glass unions of the CGT and the CFDT made the latter fearful of signing because of being charged with class collaboration by its Communist rival. CFDT officials also mentioned the exclusion of the ICEF as a reason.[45] Because they are not signatories to the agreement, CFDT and CGT officials do not participate in the commission's sessions or activities. Interestingly, the participating unions, led by the commission secretary, a Belgian union official, have apparently insisted that only signatories to the agreement can participate in the commission's work.

Thus, the only French unions that are signatories to the agreement are the Confédération Générale des Cadres (CGC), the salaried union; and the two smaller federations, CGT-Force Ouvrière and the Confédération Française des Travailleurs Chrétiens (CFTC). This minority representation, plus the probable reluctance of the unions to cede authority to an international body, when combined with management's determination to avoid a bargaining relationship could well be decisive in maintaining BSN's unique international agreement as an informational and consultative one.

Boussois Strike

A seventeen-day strike occurred in the Boussois subsidiary of BSN in March 1978. Apparently attempting to gain a reentry into the BSN relationship, Charles Levinson issued a circular letter claiming that the ICEF's

> colleagues in the CFDT want us to extend their appreciation for the effective international support developed, particularly to our Belgian and German colleagues in GLAVERBEL, whose boycott of transfer of float glass to France contributed significantly to the successful termination of the dispute. We also want to thank other colleagues, and particularly the British members in Pilkington for their assistance and support during the dispute.[46]

This was flatly denied by BSN officials, who reported that they were able to supply customers from their German and Belgian subsidiaries without interference or action to stop such shipments. Moreover, they affirmed that settlement was reached

---

45 Jacques René Rojot, *International Collective Bargaining: An Analysis and Case Study for Europe* (Deventer, the Netherlands: Kluwer Publishers, 1978), p. 149. More recently, we understand that the CFDT glass union is reconsidering its refusal to sign the protocol.

46 ICEF Circular Letter No. 69/78, April 27, 1978, p. 1.

by negotiations between Boussois management and the unions with "absolutely no international pressure or influence." [47] Pilkington officials also confirmed that "there [was] no evidence of action in any of our factories which prevent[ed] contact with Boussois or stop[ped] glass supplies to Boussois customers." [48]

The commission met after the strike, but no discussion relating to the stoppage occurred other than a brief note by the company that the strike had reduced Boussois sales. The failure of unions in Germany and Belgium to give any support to the Boussois strikers, as well as the lack of discussion of the issue during commission meetings, may be in part attributable to the lack of CFDT and CGT participation in the commission. Nevertheless, it does provide a clear example of the distinction between the information exchange as practiced within the commission and any collective bargaining arrangement.

OTHER COMPANIES AND ACTIVITIES

There have been some minor attempts to involve other companies in multinational union activities, both in the flat glass and in other glass industry branches. A Communist-led coalition, as well as the ICEF, has been involved.

LOF and PPG

In his report to the October 1976 ICEF Congress, the secretary general announces that "world councils" would be formed the following month for Libbey-Owens-Ford and PPG Industries, neither of which has a substantial share of its business outside of North America.[49] As far as we can determine, no such action has occurred. In the same report, it is stated that the ICEF's Glass Division would meet in December 1976 in Toledo, Ohio,[50] a city in which LOF, Owens-Illinois (the leading glass container company), Owens-Corning Fiberglas (which is discussed below),

---

[47] Letter from François Destailleur, directeur de la coordination des relations sociales, BSN-Gervais Danone, to the authors, June 26, 1978. Translated by the Industrial Research Unit.

[48] Letter from David F. Pilkington to the authors, July 5, 1978.

[49] "Executive Committee. Activities Report of the Secretary General. List of Membership," *ICF 16th Statutory Congress*, Montreal, October 27-29, 1976, p. 97. Hereafter cited as *ICF 16th Statutory Congress*.

[50] *Ibid.*, p. 39.

and the American Flint Glass Workers Union (a small American union) all have headquarters. The meeting apparently was not held.

Saint-Gobain and the Communists

In France and Italy, where the Communist-led federations, the CGT and the CGIL, respectively, are the dominant groups, there has been cooperation between their glass affiliates, part:cularly in Saint-Gobain's French and Italian plants. Representat:ves of these unions meet frequently and exchange information but thus far have not attempted any joint action. They did put out a statement urging nationalization both of Saint-Gobain and BSN when the latter attempted to win control of the former,[51] and Saint-Gobain, in particular, was high on the Commun:st-social:st list for nationalization if the left coalition were to have won control of the French Parliament in 1978.

The CGT affiliates participated in consultations when BSN took over German flat glass companies [52] and, as noted, in the early discussions that led to the unique BSN international consultative agreement. By not signing the agreement, the CGT glass union cut itself off from international activity within that company. BSN has no plants in Italy.

Corning

Corning Glass Works, headquartered in the small northern New York State town of Corning, is another glass company that the ICEF has pursued. The world leader in pressed glass for television, tableware, and other uses, Corning in 1978 had sales of $1.3 billion, 25,900 employees,[53] and plants in many countries.

In July 1969, the ICEF secretary general sent a telegram to Corning headquarters protesting "anti-union authoritarian policy of Argentine management refusing Argentine employees just wage demands. . . ." The telegram, which apparently referred

---

[51] "The Boussois Souchon Neuvesel—Saint-Gobain Shares Operation," translated press release, n.d. (1969?), in authors' possession.

[52] Ernst Piehl, *Multinationale Konzerne und internationale Gewerkschaftsbewegung* (Frankfurt am Main: Europäische Verlagsanstalt, 1974), p. 110.

[53] *Fortune.* Vol. 99 (May 7, 1979), pp. 278-79.

to a wage dispute at Corning's plant in that country, was not answered.[54]

In his report to the 1976 congress, the ICEF secretary general claims that, in October 1975, he had protested to Corning headquarters against its redundancy program and had instituted "overtime bans and refusal of extra work during period of strike" and "boycotts of transfer of stocks and inventories—both actual and preparatory." [55] These claims, as the next chapters show, were made in regard to a host of companies and have been found by our research to be basically figments of imagination. The company has no knowledge of any such overt ICEF actions.[56]

What did happen in October 1975 was that the ICEF attempted to contact Corning through a union with which it has bargaining relationships—the American Flint Glass Workers Union (AFGWU). The AFGWU affiliated with the ICEF in 1973 and, in October 1975, transmitted to Corning an ICEF request to convene "a world meeting of ICF affiliates and senior company officials to discuss the restructuring of the company and its implications to the long-range security of the workforce." Corning declined and so notified the AFGWU.[57]

Another mention of Corning came in a 1978 ICEF letter which states that "letters and cables expressing thanks for effective support have been received" from numerous organizations, including those concerned in "a number of disputes in the United States and Canada involving such companies as Dow Chemical, Corning Glass and others." [58] Perhaps this communication refers to the negotiations that were completed at the end of 1977 between Corning and the AFGWU, but Corning officials report that they know of no ICEF communications during these negotiations.[59]

---

[54] Letter from Corning executive to the authors, February 22, 1977.

[55] *ICF 16th Statutory Congress*, pp. 100, 102.

[56] Letter from Corning executive to the authors, February 22, 1977.

[57] *Ibid.*

[58] ICEF Circular Letter No. 59/78, March 28, 1978, p. 1.

[59] Letter from the vice-president of industrial relations, Corning Glass Works, to the authors, July 7, 1978. Dow also could find no reason for the reference.

The 1977 U.S. AFGWU Strike

The American Flint Glass Workers Union is a small American craft union that includes among its members the craftsmen who repair forming molds that are used to make glass bottles and jars. In most bottle and jar plants, the much larger Glass Bottle Blowers Association (GBBA) is the bargaining agent for the bulk of the employees. The ratio is about 1,000 GBBA members to 40 AFGWU members. Bargaining with both unions has traditionally been on an industrywide basis, with AFGWU negotiations following six months after those with the GBBA, although in recent years, Owens-Illinois, by far the largest bottle and jar producer, with 1978 sales of $3.1 billion and 64,588 employees,[60] has bargained separately with the GBBA.

In 1977, a peaceful settlement between the industry and the GBBA was concluded in March, but the AFGWU struck on September 16 and remained on strike until October 14, when a settlement was reached raising the industry wage offer from $1.60 per hour to $1.90 but in return granting the companies the right to have each AFGWU member tend two tape-run engraving machines instead of one.[61]

During the strike, most GBBA members crossed the AFGWU picket lines after the first few days of the strike. Owens-Illinois, for example, had eighteen of twenty plants operating, with supervisors performing needed work ordinarily done by AFGWU members. The membership of the GBBA includes such craftsmen as electricians and pipe fitters, who were understandably not sympathetic to their AFGWU brethren's receiving larger wage increases than they did.

As noted, the AFGWU is an ICEF affiliate. The GBBA was also once an ICEF affiliate but, in the 1960s, disaffiliated and affiliated with the now defunct International Federation of Petroleum and Chemical Workers. Since the latter's demise, the GBBA has declined to affiliate with the ICEF. The ICEF secretary general sent out a series of circular letters dealing with the strike in order to have "affiliates with membership in the glass container industry . . . refuse all exceptional requests for overtime, and to monitor stocks to prevent their diversion to the

---

[60] *Fortune*, Vol. 99 (May 7, 1979), pp. 272-73.

[61] John L. O'Shea, vice-president, Owens-Illinois, Inc., telephone interview, December 9, 1977.

U.S. market during the currency of the strike." [62] When the strike was over, he conveyed the AFGWU's "sincere thanks for the very helpful support received" from "glass workers' unions around the world" and attacked GBBA officials for their failure to demonstrate "solidarity with the workers on strike." [63]

In fact, if there was any union support from around the world, it was unconsequential. There was not a shortage of bottles or jars since most plants kept operating. Owens-Illinois, the largest company, received no communications from unions abroad, found no notice of the strike in its foreign plants, and no mention of the ICEF or international union involvement at the bargaining table.[64]

As for the GBBA, its then president sent out a telegram to all of its glass container local unions urging them "not to perform any work that is normally performed by AFGWU members" but advising that they had "a legitimate contract and . . . requesting that [they] honor the contract and continue working." [65] According to the current GBBA president, this "telegram has always been sent as a policy of this . . . union to honor our contracts which have been negotiated." [66] It should also be noted that, under United States law, if the GBBA local unions had engaged in strikes in support of the AFGWU and thus broken their contracts with companies, they could have been subject to court action and heavy financial penalties.

Owens-Corning

A final action in the glass industry came from an initiative of the CGT and involved Owens-Corning Fiberglas. This company was established as a joint, equally owned venture by Corning and Owens-Illinois, but the founders together now control less

---

[62] ICEF Circular Letter No. 104/77, October 4, 1977. See also the earlier letter, No. 89/77.

[63] ICEF Circular Letter No. 117/77, November 1, 1977.

[64] John L. O'Shea, vice-president, Owens-Illinois, Inc., telephone interview, December 9, 1977.

[65] Telegram from Harry A. Tulley, then president of the GBBA, to all glass container local unions, September 16, 1977 (Tulley retired December 1, 1977), copy in authors' possession.

[66] Letter from James E. Hatfield, president of the GBBA, to the authors, January 9, 1978.

than 50 percent of the equity. In 1977, Owens-Corning had sales of approximately $1.9 billion and 24,400 employees.[67]

In addition to its plants in the United States and elsewhere, Owens-Corning has two plants in Europe—Battice, near Ver- viers, Belgium, and the other at L'Ardoise, near Avignon, France. In April 1976, representatives of unions affiliated with the CGT and the CFDT in France and the FGTB and the CSC in Belgium met in Laudun without international secretariat or other inter- national union coordination.[68] The CGT has played an important role in such international union actions and was the host, as well as the initiator, of this one.

1978 Communist Meeting

The Communists also claim to have sponsored a meeting of French and Belgian glass workers employed by Saint-Gobain and BSN in September 1978 and further assert that delegates of non-Communist unions also participated in this gathering. A declaration was issued calling for an "international demonstra- tion." We understand, however, that the non-Communist groups had separate meetings, and this seems to be confirmed by the fact that the report published by the Communists berates Force- Ouvrière for its refusal to participate in "international coordi- nation outside of the ICEF." [69]

CONCLUSION

The glass industry, in Western Europe particularly, has thus been the scene of several ICEF claims that careful research cannot substantiate, plus occasional meetings sponsored by Com- munist-led unions. Of much greater significance is the multi- national union-management committee of BSN-Gervais Danone, which, insofar as we have been able to determine, is unique.[70]

It is also important to note that the BSN union-management committee has no secretariat or other international or regional

---

[67] *Fortune*, Vol. 99 (May 7, 1979), pp. 276-77.

[68] "Les travailleurs belges et français de Fiberglas réunis en front commun," *Le Drapeau Rouge*, April 29, 1976.

[69] *Information Bulletin* (ICPS), November 1978, pp. 20-21.

[70] On September 15, 1979, BSN announced the sale of all of its flat glass operations in Germany, Austria, Belgium, and the Netherlands to Pilkington, effective early 1980. Whether and in what form the multinational union consultation arrangements will be maintained remains unclear.

group representation. To be sure, the action of the ICEF secretary general in antagonizing management by issuing a press release that exaggerated his role led to his ouster from the committee. Yet the absence of international union involvement may suit national unions best in any case if international bargaining arrangements are developed. This is so because international industrial relations would require a transfer of power from national unions to the international bargaining group and, therefore, perhaps from one official to another, a fact that is certain to cause national union officials at least to pause before acting.

On the other hand, if the national union officials see international bargaining as helpful to them and to their causes and if such bargaining involves no transfer of power to an organization which, like a secretariat, has needs and aims of its own but rather to a committee of national unions, then this might be easier for these unions to accommodate. Thus, the BSN-type arrangement may more nearly be a model for future international union-management arrangements than other more highly publicized ones that include secretariat or regional union representation.

CHAPTER VII

Akzo and the Plant Closing Issue

The International Federation of Chemical, Energy and General Workers' Unions (ICEF) has claimed a wide variety of actions against numerous chemical and pharmaceutical companies, including most of those listed in Table VIII-1. This chapter examines the history of multinational union activities involving Akzo, based in Arnhem, the Netherlands, and the following chapter deals with other chemical and pharmaceutical companies.

Akzo has been chosen as a special case study for two reasons. First, its experience represents a test of the theory that the emergence of mutual goals in various countries, such as avoidance of layoffs (redundancies) and plant closings, could bring unions from various countries to act jointly against a multinational firm;[1] and second, the claims of successful action against Akzo, made by the ICEF secretary general, rank with similar claims made in regard to Saint-Gobain and Michelin (see chapters VI and IX) in terms of press coverage and factual supportability.

AKZO'S RETRENCHMENT PLAN

Akzo was formed by a merger of two Dutch concerns that were already industrial combinations: Algemene Kunstzijde Unie NV (AKU) and Koninkijke Zout-Organon NV (KZO). In the United States, Akzo controls Akzona, which includes American Enka and International Salt, among other operating companies. In 1978, Akzo ranked fifty-third in sales volume on the *Fortune* list of manufacturing companies outside of the United States and, as set forth in Table VIII-1, ranked fourteenth among the free world's chemical companies. In 1975, 1976, and

---

[1] B. C. Roberts has succinctly propounded this theory. See his excellent article "Multinational Collective-Bargaining: A European Prospect?" *British Journal of Industrial Relations*, Vol. XI (March 1973), especially p. 10.

1977, however, it suffered severe losses.[2] Akzo's economic troubles have centered in the European synthetic fibers business of its largest subsidiary, Enka Glanzstoff.[3]

The slump in the fibers market in the early 1970s prompted Akzo management to make a study of the situation. The conclusion was that "measures for a further concentration [of manufacturing facilities] are of vital importance to the Group's survival." [4] Accordingly, on April 6, 1972, plans were announced to close facilities in Breda and Emmercompascum, the Netherlands; one in Fabelta, Belgium; another in Wuppertal-Barmen, Germany; and one in Feldmühle, Switzerland. An estimated 5,000 to 6,000 employees were affected by the announcement. In 1972, Akzo's worldwide employment was 101,000, of whom 83,700 were in Western Europe.[5]

The company's press release announcing the closings emphasized that the plants would be phased out over a period of time, e.g., one year in the case of Breda. It promised employment, where possible, in other Akzo plants to displaced workers and offered to help those not placed to find employment elsewhere. Akzo further indicated that the Emmercompascum employees would be absorbed by the nearby Emmen plant and that it was negotiating to sell a part of the Wuppertal-Barmen facility to "a well-known European producer," which would mean the "pos-

---

[2] *Fortune*, Vol. 100 (August 13, 1979), p. 195; Akzo's annual reports for 1975, 1976, and 1977. See also Table VIII-1.

[3] The basic information for this section is based on extensive field interviews in the Netherlands in July 1973 and 1974, plus two books written in Dutch—Aad Van Cortenberghe and Jeroen Terlingen, *Enka Dossier; Handboek Voor Bezetters* (Utrecht and Antwerpen: A. W. Bruna & Zoon, 1972); and Albert Benschop and Ton Kee, *De bedrijfsbezetting van de Enka-Breda* (Nijmegen: Socialistiese Uitgeverij Nijmegen, 1974)—on a number of documents supplied by Akzo management; and on field interviews in Europe, summer 1973. The books, both written by socialist union adherents from a union point of view, give vivid accounts of the action. Other sources are Ernst Piehl, *Multinationale Konzerne und internationale Gewerkschaftsbewegung* (Frankfurt am Main: Europäische Verlagsanstalt, 1974). Dr. Piehl was on the research staff of the Deutsche Gewerkschaftsbund (DGB), the German Confederation of Labor, and has been appointed senior policy official for the European Trade Union Confederation; and Pierre Hoffmann and Albert Langwieler, *Noch sind wir da!* (Reinbek bei Hamburg: Rowohlt, 1974).

[4] "The Situation in the Chemical Fibre Industry," duplicated document, March 30, 1972. English version provided by Akzo management.

[5] Enka Glanzstoff Press Release, April 6, 1972 (English version provided by Akzo management); and Akzo, *1972 Annual Report* (Arnhem, the Netherlands, 1973), p. 9. All Akzo annual reports referred to are the English versions.

sibility of continued employment" for a "large number" of the three thousand employees. For anyone in any of the closed plants not continued in Akzo employment, "a release arrangement" (severance pay) was promised. Finally, Akzo pledged to inform unions of closings in all affected countries and to seek advice from various local and central works councils.[6]

Reaction to Plant Closing Plan

The Akzo announcement created an uproar in all the countries involved as the works councils and the unions appealed to the national authorities and to the bureaucrats of the European Community to save their jobs. Pressure was especially strong on the Netherlands' government to intervene. In light of these developments, an agreement was reached among the Dutch government, the company, the Dutch and German trade unions, the Central Employees' (Works) Council[7] of Enka-Netherlands to appoint a "Committee of Outside Experts" (COE) to examine the company plans and to report to its principals its "Views on the Restructuring Plan."[8]

The sharp reaction to its "restructuring plan" obviously surprised the Akzo management. The chairman of the Akzo Supervisory Board stated at the general meeting of the shareholders on May 10, 1972, that "it is alarming to find that clear and practical arguments meet with so little response in present-day society."[9] In answer to the criticism that unions and works

---

[6] Enka Glanzstoff Press Release, April 6, 1972.

[7] John P. Windmuller points out that, in the Netherlands "at the level of individual industries, labor's influence is of a somewhat lesser order [than at the level of national, social, and economic decisions]. . . . Below the industry level . . . the influence of unions declines rapidly . . . the contribution of unions to the personnel policies of individual enterprises is either remote and derivative or nonexistent . . . most unions have no shop-level or worksite structure through which they could attempt to exert direct influence on working conditions. Work-place representation belongs by long tradition, reinforced in 1950 by law, to an independent institution, the works council. . . . It is in no sense a part of the union structure. In this regard, . . . the Netherlands shares a common heritage with other Western European countries. It also shares to a large extent a set of common problems growing out of the divided structure of employee representation." *Labor Relations in the Netherlands* (Ithaca: Cornell University Press, 1969), pp. 399-400.

[8] Press Release and Report Issued by Committee of Outside Experts, August 18, 1972, p. 2. English version provided by Akzo management.

[9] Speech made by J. R. M. van den Brink at the general meeting of shareholders of Akzo NV, held in Amsterdam on May 10, 1972. Akzo Press Release, p. 1. English version provided by Akzo management.

councils had not been notified prior to the announcement, the chairman pointed out that so many such bodies were involved that it "would have been asking too much to demand from them secrecy for a longer period." Since, however, a gradual, not an abrupt, closedown was involved, he declared "there is now every opportunity for codetermination and consultation." But he assured the shareholders that he expected that "the investigation by independent experts" would "confirm his view" of the economic situation and the necessity of the proposed actions.[10]

The Committee of Outside Experts did confirm in its August 18, 1972, report that Akzo management could not be blamed for the excess capacity in the synthetic fiber business, and it agreed that "drastic measures" were required. The committee also found that the reduction of capacity plans was based on proper data and "realistic assumptions." It found, therefore, that, "in terms of business economics, the plan is well-thought out . . . and has been drawn up with care." But the committee declared, "This does not settle the question. Where such drastic closedowns are concerned, as the ones envisaged for Breda and Barmen, social, technological and economic factors should be weighed with extra care." It recommended that a cutback in all production facilities, instead of closing some, be considered and that governments or industry, acting as a cartel, allocate production.[11]

The Enka Glanzstoff Board of Management agreed to study carefully the COE report, but it pointed out that the COE proposals had already been the subject of much analysis and discussion with Akzo management both before April 6 and thereafter. It concluded: "This did not result in the discovery of fresh possibilities for the reorganization and rationalization of Enka Glanzstoff by other means." [12] It warned that failure to proceed could jeopardize the entire company. Meanwhile, the nylon textile filament plant in Switzerland was closed,[13] and the

---

[10] *Ibid.,* pp. 1-2.

[11] Press Release and Report Issued by Committee of Outside Experts, p. 1.

[12] Provisional comments of the Enka Glanzstoff Board of Management on the Report of the Committee of Outside Experts (COE), August 17, 1972.

[13] Letter from B. Klaverstijn, head, Public Relations Department, Akzo NV, to the authors, October 25, 1973.

Enka-Netherlands Central Works Council appeared to be leaning toward accepting the company proposals.[14]

Sit-in and Closing Cancellation

On September 18, 1972, the Breda plant employees, who were the largest, most directly affected group, occupied the plant. Short strikes, including a sit-in, also occurred at Wuppertal, Germany, but the agitation was led by members of the Netherlands Catholic Trade Union Federation (NKV). Other groups, including those affiliated with the socialist National Federation of Trade Unions (NVV) and the Protestant National Trade Union Federation (CNV) were also involved. Since Breda is a Catholic area, the NKV has the largest membership there, although it is smaller than the NVV in the Netherlands as a whole.[15]

The authors of the book *Enka Dossier* state that it was an open secret that the sit-in would occur. Middle management personnel (who in Europe are generally as security conscious as are blue-collar workers) apparently looked the other way. A German workers' delegation attempted to participate in the sit-in at Breda but was prevented by the occupying Dutch workers from entering the plant. The sit-in lasted one week. As a result, Akzo abandoned its plans to close the Breda plant and therefore could close none except for the already shut facility in Switzerland, since it is bound by provisions of its merger rules, insisted upon by various countries, to treat equally Belgian and German plant groups with Dutch ones. Instead, the company

---

[14] Benschop and Kee, who provide a day-by-day account of the events, report protests by the NKV Breda group against rumors that union officials or works council members were agreeing with the need for plant closings. *De bedrijfsbezetting*, pp. 28, 123.

[15] According to Professor Windmuller's excellent study, "Dutch workers remained devoutly loyal to Calvinist Protestantism in the north and to Roman Catholicism in the south. This devotion a few decades later became the basis for the creation of confessional trade unions whose viability and power of attraction would far exceed that of Christian labor movements in most western European countries." *Labor Relations in the Netherlands*, p. 5. In 1972, the socialist NVV had 39.4 percent of the 1,583,000 union members in the Netherlands; the Catholic NKV, 25.3 percent; the Protestant CNV, 15.1 percent; and other trade unions, 20.2 percent. Data from *Statistical Yearbook of the Netherlands*, 1972, reproduced in *Industrial Relations-Europe Newsletter*, Vol. I, No. 9 (September 1973), supplement, p. 2. In 1975, the NVV and the NKV agreed to a merger to form the FNV. The CNV decided not to join the FNV (Federation of Netherlands Unions).

adopted the proposals for cutbacks in each facility. Employment in the chemical fibers section of Akzo actually decreased by 6,800 in 1972,[16] but, except for Switzerland, plant closures were avoided.

Aftermath

In retrospect, it is quite clear that Akzo management underestimated the impact and emotional reaction to what it regarded as a sensible business decision. In the Netherlands, workers historically have not rebelled lightly. Professor Windmuller has noted that "Dutch workers are often imbued with a sense of respect, even of deference toward their superiors." [17] To the Dutch worker, as to his European counterpart, however, job security is the most significant issue; and a plant closure, the most direct, flagrant attack on job security. As Professor Roberts has noted: "Where jobs are at stake, there has been a positive and militant response." [18] In reflecting on what happened, the Akzo management reported that it called off the restructuring plan because

> forced implementation would have caused Akzo more damage—both immediately and in the longer run—than the so-called linear curtailment of production that has now been accepted. It should be noted that the extensive and repeated talks with consultative bodies, such as works councils and groups of personnel within and outside the chemical fibres sector, and with the trade unions, failed to win support for our plan. In these talks, the strategy designed to safeguard the long-term interests of our company and our employees was overridden by—in themselves quite understandable—short-term considerations. Moreover, these talks took so long that a well-nigh unbearable and much-deplored strain was placed on the employees involved. The events have taught us that we should allow even more scope in our policy and decision making to the shifting opinions in society.[19]

The Akzo *1972 Annual Report* notes that the financial consequences will be "more unfavorable" because it did not close the plants and that it will be necessary "to actively continue the rationalization measures in our Western European chemical fibre companies." [20] It also indicates that business was improving. In September 1973, Akzo announced that it was doubling

---

16 Akzo, *1972 Annual Report*, p. 9.

17 Windmuller, *Labor Relations in the Netherlands*, p. 416.

18 Roberts, "Multinational Collective-Bargaining," p. 10.

19 Akzo, *1972 Annual Report*, p. 9.

20 *Ibid.*, p. 6.

the texturizing capacity for polyester filament fibers at the Breda plant.[21] According to a company spokesman: "The number of spinning machines will *not* be increased; the process, however, is going to be adapted to a new technology which yields a substantially higher output." [22] Between the announcement of the abortive restructuring plan (April 8, 1972) and the beginning of the sit-in (September 18, 1972), about four hundred employees voluntarily terminated at the Breda plant. This created a shortage of labor for certain production jobs at Breda and caused Akzo, with the consent of the works council and unions, to request Dutch government approval to import fifty to one hundred Spanish workers. By November 1973, the government had approved the first fifty.[23] This turn of events, however logical or explained, naturally confirmed in the minds of those who were opposed to the closedowns that their position was correct. The upturn, nevertheless, proved to be of short duration.

THE ROLE OF THE INTERNATIONAL ORGANIZATIONS

Once the objectives of the occupation of the plant had been won, various organizations began to claim credit for the results. Foremost among these was the ICEF (then, the ICF). Its claims were accepted by *Business Week*[24] and the *Wall Street Journal*,[25] among other publications, but find little support from observers closer to the action. Benschop and Kee's day-by-day account of the event, issued by a Dutch socialist publisher, lists one meeting attended by the ICEF's secretary general, Charles Levinson, and unions affiliated with the ICEF from Germany (Industriegewerkschaft Chemie-Papier-Keramik—IG Chemie), the Netherlands (Industriebond-NVV), Belgium (textile workers affiliated with the Fédération Générale du Travail de Belgique

---

21 *Times* (London), September 1, 1973, p. 21.

22 Letter from B. Klaverstijn to the authors, October 25, 1973.

23 *Ibid.*

24 Initially, *Business Week* gave no credit to the ICEF but one month later acclaimed its great success. Cf. "International Outlook," *Business Week*, September 30, 1972, p. 52; and "Multinationals: A Step Toward Global Bargaining," *Business Week*, October 28, 1972, p. 52.

25 "Michelin Plant Strike Sparks New Walkouts," *Wall Street Journal*, October 9, 1972. This article refers to the ICEF's "triumph" at Akzo and then gives the ICEF completely unsupportable credit for action at Michelin. This is discussed in chapter IX, below.

—FGTB), and Switzerland (Gewerkschaft Textil-Chemie-Papier). This occurred on April 16, 1972, well before the sit-in. There is no other mention of the ICEF in this book.[26] Piehl also notes this meeting and states that a second one between German and Dutch unions also occurred in September in Dortmund, Germany, at the congress of the IG Chemie, at which the ICEF secretary general was present.[27] In addition, he quotes Levinson as telephoning and telexing unions in the United States, Canada, and Brazil to engage in solidarity actions, such as refusal to work overtime, in order to put further pressure on Akzo.[28] Given the lack of freedom at that time for trade union action in Brazil, the weakness of textile unions in the United States, and the fact that the chairman of Akzona, Akzo's United States holding company, knew "of no activity on the part of the ICF involving . . . operations in America" either at this time or in connection with a plant closing in North Carolina a few years later, one must conclude that, if such ICEF communications were sent, they merely constituted a posturing act.[29]

At about the same time as the ICEF meeting, the Dutch Catholic (NKV) and Protestant (CNV) and Belgian Christian (Confédération des Syndicats Chrétiens—CSC) unions held a meeting under the aegis of the World Confederation of Labour, the Christian overall union organization. Again, no other mention of this organization occurs in any analysis of the events leading to the plant occupation.[30]

Nevertheless, there was international union cooperation. The company has confirmed to the authors that, during the discussions of its closure plans, it met twice with multinational union

---

[26] Benschop and Kee, *De bedrijfsbezetting*, pp. 26-27. See also their day-to-day summary, pp. 118-43. The Swiss unionists apparently dropped out of all meetings after this one.

[27] Piehl, *Multionale Konzerne*, pp. 192-93, 196.

[28] *Ibid.*, p. 197.

[29] Letter from Claude Ramsey, chairman and president, Akzona Incorporated, to the authors, October 27, 1976. In his report to the 1976 ICEF Congress, Levinson himself places much emphasis on the lack of freedom of union action in Brazil. See "Executive Committee. Activities Report of the Secretary-General. List of Membership," *ICF 16th Statutory Congress*, Montreal, October 27-29, 1976, pp. 47-49. Hereafter cited as *ICF 16th Statutory Congress*.

[30] Apparently, the denominational unions from Switzerland did not attend those meetings. See Benschop and Kee, *De bedrijfsbezetting*, p. 27; and Piehl, *Multinationale Konzerne*, p. 193

delegates: once with a Dutch and German group and once with these two nationalities and Belgian unionists. These union delegations included neither the ICEF nor other international organization representation.[31]

The fact that the ICEF had no recognized role in this Akzo situation appears to be confirmed by the "Report of Activities" of the secretary general to its 1973 congress, which states:

> Some companies like Michelin, Akzo, Eastman Kodak, Montedison, Du Pont, Shell, Esso, Hoffmann-La Roche, etc., are openly hostile and opposed to direct international relations at the level of the company.[32]

In the same report, the ICEF secretary general claims to have had informal meetings "with top officers of a certain number of companies," including Akzo.[33] But in response to the written question "Did the company or its representatives ever meet with Levinson?" Akzo's official spokesman stated, "No." The same company answer was given to the question "During the discussions [of the proposed closedowns] did the company or its representatives ever meet with a committee of trade unionists with Levinson present, or sponsored by ICF?"[34] Since Akzo readily confirmed, as already noted, that it did meet once with representatives of Dutch and German unions and once with Dutch, German, and Belgian unionists, it seems logical to credit its version.

The company's version is also supported both by the detailed account of Benschop and Kee and by the authors of *Enka Dossier*. The latter sums up as follows:

> On 16th April the world is surprised with a very brave sounding declaration of the International Chemical Workers Union. To this organization belong: the Industriebond (NVV) (Holland), the Textile Workers Centrale (Belgium), the IG Chemie (Germany), the Gewerkschaft Textil-Chemie-Papier (Switzerland). In the

---

[31] Letter from B. Klaverstijn to the authors, October 25, 1973. Piehl and Benschop and Kee also record these meetings and make no mention of ICEF representation.

[32] "Report of Activities of the Secretary-General, the 15th Statutory Congress, Geneva, 7th-9th November 1973, Document," *ICF Bulletin*, October 1973, p. 88.

[33] *Ibid.* In his 1976 activities report, Levinson implies that he rejected an Akzo management offer to meet with him. See *ICF 16th Statutory Congress*, pp. 91-92.

[34] Letter from one of the authors to Akzo, September 12, 1973; and letter from B. Klaverstijn to the authors, October 25, 1973.

declaration it is noted that the results of a failing Akzo/Enka management are being onesidedly unloaded on the workers. Against this kind of management of the company all unions affiliated with the ICF *in the world* will fight, together with the representative bodies of personnel. Akzo/Enka-Glanzstoff is summoned to agree immediately with the demanded investigation by an independent committee. Termination of personnel and stopping of production has to be postponed until the results of the investigation have been worked out. In the declaration, a world conference of all unions who are dealing with Akzo locations is being announced, with the objective to establish a permanent committee to watch and guide this multinational concern. . . .

On hindsight, it must be noted that this declaration both literally and figuratively for the major part appeared to be paper only.[35]

There were power struggles and conflicts among unions and works councils during the controversy and after as several strove to take credit for the action. Most of the credit, however, appears to belong to the Catholic NKV members and leadership in Breda. They led the direct action, despite a more cautious approach by the NKV national organization, and pushed the plant occupation as a means of saving their plant when the Enka Central Works Council appeared about to agree to a modified company plan for its closure. After the plant was seized, other unions cooperated, and the ICEF allegedly sent its ineffectual communications to Brazil, Canada, and the United States.

All this is clearly set forth by the authors of *Enka Dossier*. Their testimony is more pertinent when it is noted that one of the authors, Van Cortenberghe, is employed by a socialist paper (*Het Vrije Volk*) and the other, Terlingen, works for the union journal of the NVV (now the FNV), the socialist union federation whose affiliate, Industriebond, is in turn affiliated with the ICEF. We believe that *Enka Dossier* correctly sums up the role of the ICEF as one which "both literally and figuratively for the major part appeared to be paper only."[36] The same, of course, may be said of the Christian federation, which, however, has apparently made no claims to the contrary.

After the confrontation at Breda, the ICEF announced that it was forming an "ICEF Akzo World Council" composed of unions representing Akzo employees all over the world. It was not until 1975 that this council held its first meeting, as discussed below.

---

[35] Van Cortenberghe and Terlingen, *Enka Dossier*, pp. 57-58. Translated by the Industrial Research Unit.

[36] *Ibid.*

Significance of Action

The significance of the matter lies, of course, not in inflated international union claims, but rather in the fact that a multinational company was forced to alter drastically an economic plan of action. Unions under the leadership of the members of the NKV, the Dutch Catholic Union at Breda, assisted by an ad hoc international coalition of unions, put pressure on the Dutch government to intervene and then took direct action when no agreement was achieved by the intervenors. As a result, only in Switzerland, where unions are less of a factor, was a plant closed. Job security is the key worker issue in Europe, and to the European worker, security means work in the plant where he is now employed. But the ability to stave off economic realities in a competitive and cyclical industry by political and union action is not limitless—as another downturn in the fibers market amply illustrated.

NEGOTIATING A NEW STRUCTURE, 1975-77

The recovery of the chemical fibers business lasted until mid-1974, then gave way to a sharp recession. In Akzo's *1973 Annual Report*, it is stated that the company's "objective to maintain [its] leading position in *chemical fibres* in Western Europe calls for investments to raise capacity, notably for products exhibiting continued strong growth. . . . Outside Western Europe, investments for expansion [continue] to be predominant."[37] One year later, however, Akzo's annual report states that the second half of 1974 was featured by "sales problem that led to cutbacks in production with attendant losses due to undercapacity operation."[38] The following year saw no relief. With a general recession, the fibers losses could not be offset. Akzo incurred a general deficit (see Table VIII-1) and paid no dividends to shareholders. In early 1975, it had 23,000 employees—about one-third of its Western European work force—on short time.[39]

---

[37] Akzo, *1973 Annual Report* (Arnhem, the Netherlands, 1974), p. 7.

[38] Akzo, *1974 Annual Report* (Arnhem, the Netherlands, 1975), p. 10.

[39] *Ibid.*, p. 11. Short time, or reduced workweeks, are used instead of layoffs in many countries. Usually in such cases, government social insurance makes up much of the wages lost by employees on reduced workweeks. The cost of dividing the work to the company is, however, substantial. For a general discussion of this point, see Gordon F. Bloom and Herbert R. Northrup, *Economics of Labor Relations*, 8th ed. (Homewood, Illinois: Richard D. Irwin, Inc., 1977), pp. 512-29.

Enka also cut its work force by 4,200 persons in 1975, largely by attrition.[40] Heavy layoffs were likewise effectuated by its United Kingdom subsidiary,[41] British Enkalon, and by American Enka, which also closed a North Carolina plant. Meanwhile, Akzo sought a permanent solution for its overcapacity problem that could not be thwarted by union and/or political action. It employed the management consulting firm McKinsey & Company to make a study of Enka's markets and to recommend appropriate action.

ICEF World Council Request and Meetings

On May 15, 1975, Jan de Jong, executive of Industriebond-NVV, the largest union in the Netherlands, wrote the chairman of Akzo requesting a meeting with the ICEF world council to discuss (1) investments and consequences for employment, (2) products and location of Akzo facilities, and (3) Akzo's existing and planned personnel policies. The letter further notes that the Akzo World Council had had its first official meeting on April 24-25, 1975, and had determined that it would be desirable to establish "a framework for discussion" between the Board of Directors of Akzo and the ICEF Akzo World Council. De Jong further states that he and W. Beck, representing Germany's IG Chemie, would be willing to meet with Akzo officials and explain their request in greater detail. Akzo replied sympathetically, indicating willingness to meet for discussions, expressing interest in an international company-union discussion, but also emphasizing the need first to discuss the form and content that would make such a meeting helpful.[42]

The preliminary meeting requested by de Jong was duly held. The primary issue of contention was not whether there would be international meetings, but who would represent the employees. De Jong and Beck demanded that the ICEF Akzo World Council be designated the appropriate representative. The company found this unacceptable because it would exclude the significant Catholic (NKV) and Protestant (CNV) unions of the Netherlands, the Christian union (CSC) of Belgium, as well as

---

[40] Akzo, *1975 Annual Report* (Arnhem, the Netherlands, 1976), p. 9.

[41] Rhys David, "Heavy Staff Redundancies Feared at British Enkalon," *Financial Times*, September 11, 1975, p. 8.

[42] Copies of correspondence in authors' possession. Translated by the Industrial Research Unit.

various unions of salaried personnel, and the works councils, and because it would include in the discussions an organization (ICEF) that purported to speak for a group that included countries and unions beyond the area—the Netherlands, Germany, and Belgium—where the problem was concentrated. In the end, Enka Glanzstoff management invited specific employee representatives to meet with management to discuss the McKinsey report and included in the invitation all union and works council representatives in plants affected but excluded Levinson or any other ICEF or other international organization representative.[43] When, after the first meeting, reports were issued that Akzo had met with the ICEF world council, the company took great pains to deny this publicly and to issue a list of those present.[44]

The first meeting occurred in Arnhem, August 29, 1975. It was preceded by three days by a union meeting in Amsterdam sponsored by the ICEF Akzo World Council. Prior to these meetings, McKinsey & Company issued its report, which saw little or no prospect for improvement in several of Enka's fibers businesses, especially in the nylon filament and rayon lines. The unions asked for, and later received, additional information both from Enka and from McKinsey, and the latter's report was thoroughly examined in a nine-hour session.

On September 12, a second meeting of the same parties was held in Arnhem. The unions received all of the information that they requested but remained opposed to the decisions reached— namely, for a gradual closing of facilities in the Netherlands, Germany, and Belgium and the use of attrition as much as possible to handle redundancies but with some permanent layoffs necessary for the balance of six thousand excess employees in Enka plants.

A third meeting between the international union group and Enka management was scheduled for October 20, but it was

---

[43] From the start, Akzo was anxious to make this an Enka Glanzstoff, not an Akzo, matter.

[44] Apparently, IG Chemie announced that the ICEF Akzo World Council was meeting with Akzo, for Enka issued a sharply worded press release rebuttal, "Keine Enka Glanzstoff—besprechung mit ICF-Weltrat" ("No Enka Glanzstoff talks with ICF World Council"), Enka Glanzstoff Press Release, August 29, 1975. Among the journals that incorrectly list Levinson's presence at the first meetings are *Economist*, September 6, 1975, pp. 100, 102; *Times* (London), September 12 and 14, 1975; and *CCH Common Market Reports— Euromarket News*, September 3, 1975. The *Financial Times*, September 11 and 15, 1975, accurately notes no ICEF presence at the meeting.

never held. On October 8, the unions met at Düsseldorf, Germany, and announced that the Akzo plan was unacceptable. Enka's management then called off the October 20 meeting as "having lost its point" and announced that it was requesting national meetings in the three countries.[45] Akzo management was also quite disturbed by the announced intention of the ICEF-affiliated unions to obtain from the company agreements to consult regarding investment strategy and policy as the quid pro quo for agreement on restructuring and by the rather clear desire on the part of these unions to make the Enka matter a test case for international bargaining.[46]

Union Divisions

Despite threats by the ICEF of international union action if Akzo did not return to international consultations,[47] no such actions occurred, and further, the unions soon split wide apart. The Central Works Council of Enka-Netherlands approved the company's restructuring program by a vote of fourteen to twelve, "despite heavy union lobbying for a confrontation." [48] The Catholic (NKV) and Protestant (CNV) unions entered into direct national negotiations, and IG Chemie did likewise, being so required pursuant to the German Shop Constitution Law. Isolated, despite support from the then Dutch prime minister for international consultation,[49] Industriebond-NVV retreated from its confrontation position and began national talks but

---

[45] Michael Van Os, "Enka Calls Off Meeting," *Financial Times*, October 15, 1975, p. 25.

[46] Akzo Press Release, November 5, 1975 (English translation supplied by the company). Others regarded these meetings as "an important precedent." See "Multinationals, Bargaining on an international scale," *Business Week*, October 27, 1975, pp. 38-40; and Paul Kemezis, "A Multinational vs. United Unions," *New York Times*, November 2, 1975, sec. 3, pp. 1, 6.

[47] "Charles Levinson, general secretary of the ICF, claims that the international group has the support of workers as far away as Brazil and the International Brotherhood of Teamsters in the U.S. where Akzo controls American Enka Co. . . . But a German union official at the talks (with Akzo) says no international support has been asked for and that multinational strikes or boycotts are not under discussion." "Multinationals, Bargaining on an international scale," p. 40.

[48] "Akzo: Divided we fall," *Economist*, November 1, 1975, p. 85.

[49] Prime Minister Den Uyl made a nationwide speech supporting the Industriebond-NVV position in November 1975. He was sharply rebuked by Akzo officials in a counterrelease.

later demanded that a tripartite tribunal be appointed to supervise Akzo operations.[50]

In Belgium, the government acted to save the jobs in Akzo's Fabelta subsidiary by pursuing a majority interest therein.[51] This effectively eliminated any Belgian union interest in international action. By late October 1975, the ICEF was talking about the experience as a learning one and "an important step forward." [52] Previously, the ICEF secretary general was quoted as believing that, "if the unions can force formal negotiations with Akzo, it would set a work precedent and increase pressure on other multinationals." [53]

No other union agreements were reached on the company program during 1976, but no union action occurred to prevent Akzo from making forced reductions. Total Akzo employment declined in 1975 and 1976 by 14,300. Of this decrease, 3,800 was attributable to the deconsolidations of businesses, particularly in Fabelta (Belgium). The fibers sector of Akzo accounted for 9,300 of the remaining 10,500 lost jobs.[54] Akzo's *1976 Annual Report* confirms its withdrawal from the polymide (nylon) hosiery business.[55]

---

[50] Michael Van Os, "Enka reduces union opposition," *Financial Times*, November 7, 1975, p. 20; "Dutch labor ranks split," *Chemical Week*, November 26, 1975, p. 22; and Paul Kemezis, "Unions: Setback Abroad," *New York Times*, February 1, 1976, sec. 3, p. 12. A bill was introduced in the Dutch Parliament by NVV supporters which in effect would put Akzo into receivership under a tripartite board. No action occurred.

[51] The Belgian government took a 60 percent interest in Fabelta by investing $7.5 million and assuming $11 million worth of debts. Akzo retained a 40 percent interest. The Belgian company now markets Enka products, mainly carpet yarn and tire cord in Belgium, and Enka sells Fabelta's output of nylon and acrylic fibers outside of Belgium. The agreement calls for technical information exchanges and joint research. See "Belgium buys into fibers," *Chemical Week*, February 18, 1976, p. 19. Discussion at the time that this deal was consummated indicated that the interest of the Belgian government was increased because the Fabelta plant scheduled for closing was in the Flemish sector of Belgium, and Akzo was simultaneously expanding a non-fiber chemical plant in the Walloon sector. Fear not only of unemployment but also of disturbing the delicate balance between these groups was involved.

[52] Kemezis, "Unions: Setback Abroad," p. 12.

[53] Kemezis, "A Multinational vs. United Unions," pp. 1, 6.

[54] Akzo, *1976 Annual Report* (Arnhem, the Netherlands, 1977), p. 12.

[55] *Ibid.*, p. 4.

In 1976, Akzo again failed to make a profit (although it reduced its losses) and paid no dividends. Faced with economic
realities, the Dutch unions and works councils, negotiating separately, came to final agreement in April 1977 with the company,
which compromised on a planned reduction of 400 instead of 600
persons. This included 110 to be laid off at Breda and the closing
of the Emmercompascum plant by August 1, 1977, which involved
300 employees, who would be eligible for transfer elsewhere. In
addition, the headquarters of the Enka division was consolidated
in Wuppertal, Germany, thus eliminating some jobs in Arnhem.[56]
Except for some exchange of information, the Dutch and German
unions have apparently made no further attempt to act in concert. The economic situation in fibers worldwide has remained
severely depressed into 1979.[57]

The ICEF returned briefly to the scene in late 1977, when
Akzo closed a money-losing, strike-ridden plant in Limerick,
Ireland. The Irish Transport and General Workers' Union called
upon the ICEF for assistance.[58] The usual publicity letters were
issued, but the idea that unions in fiber plants in other countries
would, at this time, support their brethren across national boundaries could certainly not be seriously entertained, and Akzo remained as totally disinterested in entertaining any relationship
with the ICEF in regard to Ireland as it has in regard to other
countries.

CONCLUSION

The obviously depressed economic situation in fibers, plus
Akzo's decision to utilize attrition and to confine redundancies as
much as possible, contributed, as the unions claimed, to a disinclination on the part of national union officials and employees
to pursue further confrontations or international actions in the
second Akzo employment curtailment. Yet each national group
was clearly only peripherally interested in what was happening
elsewhere, despite the fact that all were involved in a common
crisis. Moreover, in the first crisis, the international action was

---

[56] Rhys David, "Akzo Attacks Fibre Losses," *Financial Times*, May 11,
1977, p. 26; and "Afsluitend Overleg Met Vakbonden Over Aanvallende
Maatregelen," Enka Glanzstoff Press Release, April 7, 1977.

[57] See, e.g., our discussions of Rhône-Poulenc, Hoechst, and Monsanto in the
following chapter.

[58] "Levinson's ICF enters the Akzo Limerick contest," *Industrial Relations
Europe*, Vol. V (December 1977), p. 1.

certainly overblown by the publicists. In fact, it was the local Breda workers and the Catholic union there that contributed the decisive action. Effective international assistance was again peripheral and largely symbolic, and that of the ICEF on paper only.

Although each Akzo experience involved consultations between a multinational corporation and a committee of unionists from three countries, the results do not seem to have expanded the potential of multinational bargaining, nor have they gained participation in international consultations for an international secretariat. This is true despite the fact that layoffs and plant shutdowns—the key European security issues—were involved in all three countries. Solutions, however, remained national after international meetings produced no results.

Moreover, attempts of the various national unions to work with an international secretariat and to forge a common front failed not only because of the divergent interests of the national unions but also because of competition among international groups. Thus, the Catholic and Protestant unions of the Netherlands and the Catholic unions of Belgium have had different international relationships than do the socialist unions affiliated with the ICEF. The latter, therefore, was not acceptable to the denominational unions as a coordinator; moreover, the ICEF could not speak on behalf of the works councils or the white-collar unions.

Of equal importance is that the ICEF's objectives clearly were to maximize publicity and to gain a bargaining role for multinational unionism. Such objectives were seen by some national unions as in conflict with, or at least peripheral to, their primary task of saving as many jobs as possible for their members. In addition, the attempt of the ICEF to establish such a precedent clearly upset Akzo management and probably added to the pressure in the management community on Akzo to avoid international commitments even with an ad hoc international union committee on which the ICEF had no representation. Thus, the attempts of the ICEF to insert itself into the situation undoubtedly contributed to the breakdown of international union-management consultations, although it seems that national pressure would have precluded in any case effective international union-management bargaining and/or consultations.

CHAPTER VIII

Other Chemical and Pharmaceutical Companies

Besides its alleged involvement in the problems of the glass industry and in those of Akzo, the International Federation of Chemical, Energy and General Workers' Unions (ICEF) has claimed effective action against most of the major chemical, rubber, and petroleum companies in the Western world, and several in other industries as well. In addition, Communist-oriented unions have attempted to set up international arrangements in these industries. This chapter examines the ICEF's and other organizations' claims in the balance of the chemical industry, and following chapters deal successively with the rubber and petroleum industries. The discussion that follows groups the companies involved by nationality and area—Belgian, French, German, Swiss, British, American, Australian, and Japanese.

SOLVAY

Solvay et Cie, headquartered in Brussels, is a major chemical company with 1978 sales of $3 billion and 44,967 employees.[1] Its primary operating areas are in Western Europe, but it also has significant operations in Brazil, the United States, and Australia.[2] The Communist unions and the ICEF both have attempted to coordinate multinational union activity of Solvay employees. Neither group has achieved a meeting or other relationship with Solvay management.

The Communist Group

The Communist group is the larger and older of the two multinational organizations of Solvay unions. Its initial meeting in

---

[1] *Fortune*, Vol. 100 (August 13, 1979), p. 195.

[2] See *Solvay 1977*, Annual Report (Brussels, 1978). English edition.

TABLE VIII-1

Twenty-three Major Companies in the
Chemical and Pharmaceutical Industries, 1978

Company	Headquarters	Sales ($000)	Assets ($000)	Net Income ($000)	Employees
Hoechst	Frankfurt am Main	12,068,207 [a]	11,486,197 [a]	107,559 [a]	179,546 [a]
Bayer	Leverkusen	11,392,483 [a]	12,169,549 [a]	203,857 [a]	179,000 [a]
BASF	Ludwigshafen/Rhine	10,732,452 [a]	8,719,148 [a]	210,170 [a]	115,408 [a]
E. I. du Pont de Nemours	Wilmington, Delaware	10,584,200	8,070,300	787,000	132,140
ICI	London	8,701,411	10,540,265	577,791	151,000
Union Carbide	New York	7,869,700	7,866,200	394,300	113,371
Eastman Kodak	Rochester, N.Y.	7,012,923	6,801,067	902,284	124,800
Dow Chemical	Midland, Mich.	6,887,623	8,789,120	575,224	53,500
Montedison	Milan	6,814,872 [a]	9,594,206 [a]	312,733 [a,b]	126,878 [a]
Pechiney Ugine Kuhlmann	Paris	6,130,496	7,217,729	57,981	95,974
Rhône-Poulenc	Paris	5,655,495	6,270,312	52,872	107,219
Ciba-Geigy	Basel, Switzerland	5,029,609	8,577,106	202,716	75,294
Monsanto	St. Louis, Mo.	5,018,700	5,035,700	302,600	62,851
Akzo Group	Arnhem, Netherlands	4,938,418	4,254,620	11,251	83,200

Minnesota Mining & Manufacturing	St. Paul, Minn.	4,661,666	4,088,370	85,000
DSM c	Heerlen, Netherlands	4,632,616 a	4,256,331 a	31,890 a
W. R. Grace	New York	4,309,588	3,268,438	66,800
Johnson & Johnson	New Brunswick, N.J.	3,497,334	2,382,369	67,000
Allied Chemical	Morristown, N.J.	3,267,956	3,227,949	31,979
American Home Products	New York	3,062,633	1,862,181	49,619
Solvay	Brussels	3,026,782	3,473,707	44,967
Mitsubishi Chemical Industries	Tokyo	2,993,264	4,272,277	15,280
Warner-Lambert	Morris Plains, N.J.	2,878,496	2,666,982	58,000

Source: *Fortune*, Vol. 99 (May 7, 1979), pp. 270-73; Vol. 100 (August 13, 1979), pp. 194-95.
a Also includes certain subsidiaries owned 50 percent or less, either fully or on a prorated basis.
b Loss.
c Government owned.

1962 may have been the first such meeting of a "world council" or, in this case, actually a European one.[3] At the initiative of the Communist unions in France (Confédération Générale du Travail—CGT) and Italy (Confederazione Generale Italiana del Lavoro—CGIL), representatives of unions in Solvay plants in France, Italy, Belgium, and Austria have met sporadically since 1962, with meetings known to have occurred in 1968 and in each year since 1971 except 1974. Representatives from German plants attended the 1972 meeting but withdrew thereafter because of the opposition of the German union Industriegewerkschaft Chemie-Papier-Keramik (IG Chemie) to participation in a Communist-dominated group. Individual unionists from Germany and the Netherlands have, however, attended other meetings, and more recently, Spanish unionists have become prominent in the group. Actually, only Communist union officials have participated on an official basis; others have attended various meetings as individuals. The ICEF secretary general has been invited to several meetings since 1972 but has refused. He has also sent out circular letters advising ICEF affiliates not to participate.[4]

At its 1968 meeting, this group formed the Permanent Union Committee of Coordination for Solvay Plants. Its exact composition is not known, other than that it has had representation of French, Italian, Spanish, Portuguese, and Belgian unions. Its leaflets appear mainly during strikes or other confrontations. It has, however, attempted to coordinate demands against the company at least twice, has several times attempted without success to meet with company officials, and continues to demand such meetings.

After the meeting that was held in Paris, June 4-5, 1971, a list of demands was agreed upon, with the understanding that each union would submit the demands to the company at its various locations. The demands included one for the formation of a Solvay European works council to discuss matters "per-

---

[3] Ernst Piehl terms the 1962 Solvay union meeting "Die wahrscheinlich älteste Initiative" at union coordination. See his *Multinationale Konzerne und internationale Gewerkschaftsbewegung* (Frankfurt am Main: Europäische Verlagsanstalt, 1974), p. 109.

[4] See, e.g., ICEF Circular Letter No. 44/78, March 3, 1978; No. 17/78, January 25, 1978. Copies in authors' possession. Unless otherwise noted, this account is based upon interviews with company, government, and union officials, Brussels and Paris, April 1972, August 1973, July 1974, January 1975, May 1976, May 1977, May 1978, and May 1979, plus documents and press clippings related to the various meetings.

taining to employment, investments, and other points of interest to labor," plus others involving both the accomplishments and the aspirations of almost all of the various national unions. For example, retirement at age sixty and the forty-hour week were French proposals, and the demand for vacation of four weeks at double salary was the Belgian standard.[5] The Belgian white-collar unions, the first to negotiate with the company following the June meeting, presented the demands in November 1971 to the Belgian plants' management. The company, however, declined to agree to "non-Belgian" approaches or to discuss questions concerning nonplant issues for which the union delegation was not "competent." [6]

Meeting at La Louvière, Belgium, September 30 and October 1, 1972, this Communist-led group decided to submit a similar list of demands to the Direction-Générale of Solvay of Europe.[7] This was done, but the company refused either to discuss the demands or to institute any relations with the committee. Some of these issues were later raised at Belgian and French locations when local collective bargaining issues were discussed, and have been reiterated at the group's meetings each year.

The secretariat work for the Communist Solvay coordination committee was handled prior to 1979 by Guy Riboux and Maurice Verschoren, the permanent secretary and national secretary of the Syndicat des Employés Techniciens et Cadres de Belgique (SETCa), which is the salaried employees' union of the Fédération Générale du Travail de Belgique (FGTB), the Belgian socialist federation. The salaried employees' union of the Confédération des Syndicats Chrétiens (CSC) is also an affiliate of the coordination committee. Riboux is reputed to be a Communist. With officials from French and Italian unions affiliated with the CGT and the CGIL, he and, more recently, Verschoren formed the key personnel of this group. The key Italian participant until recently was Christopher Gilmore, an Englishman who has been active in Communist international union affairs in the chemical and rubber industries and has lived in Italy for a

---

[5] Copy of list in authors' possession.

[6] Letter from Solvay management to one of the authors, January 28, 1974.

[7] An open letter, in authors' possession, dated November 27, 1972, from the Délégation Syndicale Solvay & Cie to the personnel of Solvay lists these demands and the committee's aims.

considerable period.[8] Gilmore is now on the staff of the European
Trade Union Institute, the research and information arm of the
European Trade Union Confederation (ETUC).

In 1975, the coordinating committee began a series of meetings to plan a major conference the following year. Meetings
of these key personnel were held in Charleroi, Belgium, December
9-10, 1975, and in Lyon, France, February 13-14, 1976; the
"International Conference of the Solvay Group Europe" was
scheduled for Brussels, May 15-16, 1976, with key personnel
from Belgium, France, and Italy meeting also on May 14. Efforts to gain the participation of the ICEF were again unsuccessful.

Billed as the "Second European Conference" of Solvay's represented employees, the meeting was rather unsuccessful in
achieving unity among the unions involved. There was no participation from Germany, the United Kingdom, or the Netherlands, with the unions from the latter two countries being
"excused." Unionists from Austria and Spain, however, were
present, as well as those from Belgium, France, and Italy. The
conference passed the usual resolutions for solidarity and issued
demands for a meeting with Solvay officials for the improvement of the job market and for early retirement. In addition,
as most union meetings in the chemical industry have done in
recent years, the conference demanded changes to protect
workers' health in the industry.[9]

The Communist coordinating committee held meetings in 1977,
again without success in demanding company recognition. Then
on March 7, 1978, the committee met in Utrecht, the Netherlands. It listed a number of problems allegedly confronting
workers in Solvay plants and noted the refusal of the company
and its president, Jacques Solvay, to meet with it, as evidenced
by a letter dated February 16, 1978, from the company to
Verschoren. The committee then set March 30, 1978, as a
"European Day of Action" in Solvay plants.

On March 30, short strikes of one hour occurred in two
Belgian, one Portuguese, and three French plants, and of two

---

[8] Gilmore's background is summarized in our discussion of the rubber tire
industry in the following chapter.

[9] For reports on the May 15-16, 1976, meeting, see "Faire bloc face
à la multinationale capitaliste," *Le Peuple* (Belgian socialist newspaper),
May 17, 1976; and "Solvay: La construction d'une délégation européene,"
Combat (FGTB), May 17, 1976. A report on the 1977 meeting is found in
Le Journal & Indépendence, November 14, 1977.

hours in an Italian plant. The largest participation involved eight hundred Italian employees. In the other plants, those demonstrating were a small minority. In Brussels, a few salaried employees demonstrated for a few minutes, as did some employees at the commercial and technical center. Petitions embodying the committee's demands for recognition were presented to the company at several plants. No stoppages occurred in Germany, Austria, the Netherlands, or the United Kingdom. Despite the meager results, the March 30 demonstrations resulted in considerable publicity exaggerating what occurred.[10] The Communist coordinating committee also serves as a mechanism for information exchange for the unions involved.

The Communists have been very active in Spain and Portugal. The Belgians have assisted Spanish strikers at Solvay plants there on several occasions. They have also sponsored trips of Spanish unionists to Brussels. The 1977 meeting was held in Barcelona in November and included in its demands the reinstatement of employees discharged from Spanish Solvay plants for illegal strike activity. A leaflet issued by the Portuguese union at the Solvay plant in Povoa, Portugal, told of financial assistance from the Spanish unions during a strike in Povoa in October-November 1978 and described the work of the coordinating committee. The 1979 meeting of the committee was held on March 30, 1979, in Lisbon. The Portuguese took over the secretariat shortly before this because Verschoren and the SETCa had changed their allegiance to the ICEF, as described below, leaving the white-collar affiliate of the Belgian CSC as the only non-Communist affiliate of the coordinating committee. The 1979 meeting, set on the anniversary of the "European Day of Action," established committees under the chairmanship of the CGIL from the Solvay Rossignano plant and the CGT from the Tavaux factory to examine general conditions of work and wages and the effects of vinyl chloride, respectively.[11]

---

[10] Our account is based upon discussions with various observers in Brussels, May 1978, plus company reports. We also have copies of the committee's press releases and *Information*, the publication of the Trade Unions International of Chemical, Oil and Allied Workers (ICPS), No. 2, April 25, 1978, pp. 10-12. The ICPS is a secretariat-department of the Communist World Federation of Trade Unions (WFTU).

[11] Various press releases and communications of the unions involved are in authors' possession. See also *Le Drapeau Rouge* (Belgian Communist paper), April 10, 1979.

Apparently, no request for a meeting with the company was made after this meeting.

The ICEF Solvay World Council

Levinson had promised for several years to establish an "ICEF Solvay World Council." It finally met for the first time in Brussels in October 1975. Alphonse Van Uytven of the FGTB was named chairman. Later, he was succeeded by Michel Nollet, also of the FGTB. The unions affiliated with the French Confédération Française Démocratique du Travil (CFDT) did much of the preliminary work for the meeting. Other unions represented included IG Chemie (Germany), Industriebond-NVV (the Netherlands), and an Austrian one. Belgian representatives were full-time union officials, but no plant union representatives were present. There were no delegations from Italy, Switzerland, the United States, Australia, or Latin America. The SETCa was represented at the beginning of the meeting but was asked to withdraw when its representatives affirmed their intention of continuing their participation in the Communist coordinating committee.[12]

The ICEF meeting passed resolutions on various subjects, including establishing contact with the company, which, as already noted, has declined to meet with either the ICEF or the Communist group. Like the Communists, the ICEF has pushed the industrial health issue. In one situation, the ICEF Solvay World Council attempted unsuccessfully to pressure Solvay headquarters to intervene to have a worker reemployed in Brazil. The former employee claimed that he was discharged because he was suffering from an illness attributable to polyvinyl chloride, whereas in fact, the dismissal was based upon poor performance.[13]

In February 1978, a two-year agreement was reached between Solvay management and unions representing factory and staff personnel at the plant in Jemeppe, Belgium. Despite having ratified the agreement, factory workers at Jemeppe went on strike and remained out until April 20, 1978, when they returned without any concessions on the part of management.

---

[12] ICF Circular Letter No. 196/76, December 2, 1975.

[13] An ICF letter, November 23, 1975, gives the secretariat's version of this incident. The Centrale Générale of the FGTB issues an information bulletin for the ICEF Solvay World Council, but we have found only one issue thus far.

Although the ICEF thanked affiliates "who have already responded effectively to our advance requests . . . for solidarity in support of the strike of Solvay's employees at the Solvic-Jemeppe plant," [14] company officials wrote the authors that they "did not have any knowledge of any activity by the ICEF at this time, and did not have any contact with Mr. Levinson, or any other international committee." [15]

The SETCa Joins the ICEF

In September 1978, Maurice Verschoren, national secretary of the SETCa and chairman of the Permanent Union Committee of Coordination for Solvay Plants, and Michel Nollet, national secretary of the Centrale Générale-FGTB, held a joint meeting of regional representatives and union delegates from four Solvay factories. According to the press reports, Verschoren and Nollet "decided to unite their efforts at the international union level." [16] The form that this unity took was Verschoren's and the SETCa's defection from the Communists to join the ICEF.

At a meeting in Geneva, December 6-7, 1978, the ICEF reconstituted its Solvay group into the ICEF Solvay-Laporte Permanent World Council. (Laporte is a British company in which Solvay has a 25 percent ownership and 50-50 joint ventures in peroxygen factories around the world under the name "Interox." Laporte operates Interox factories in the United Kingdom, Japan, and the British Commonwealth or former Commonwealth countries; Solvay operates them in Europe and elsewhere.) Forty delegates were allegedly present from thirteen countries. Demands were made for multinational bargaining, job security, and "safer" working conditions, but only the Portuguese asked for a company meeting, which Solvay rejected. Nollet remained as chairman; Verschoren was designated cochairman.[17]

The reconstituted ICEF council held a second meeting in Damparis, France, near Tavaux, where a Solvay plant is located, May 21-22, 1979. Only French and Belgian delegates attended, with Nollet and Verschoren again presiding. Despite a

---

14 ICEF Circular Letter No. 69/78, April 27, 1978, p. 2.

15 Letter to the authors, October 2, 1978, translated by the Industrial Research Unit.

16 *Le Peuple*, September 27, 1978, translated by the Industrial Research Unit.

17 *Le Drapeau Rouge*, December 15, 1978. See also ICEF Circular Letter No. 139/78, October 11, 1978, and No. 173/78, December 21, 1978.

request to attend, the Communist CGT was excluded, which is ICEF policy. No mention was made of Laporte, nor were any British, German, or Dutch delegates present. Despite a request from the ICEF that all affiliates demand management recognition of its world council, such requests were apparently not pursued. Again emphasis was on industrial health and safety, employment, and the need for control of multinationals through the ICEF— the usual ICEF conference discussion topics and conclusions to which the local press afforded considerable coverage, including a televised press conference with Levinson.[18]

THE FRENCH CHEMICAL COMPANIES

The ICEF has claimed successful international action against three major French chemical companies—Rhône-Poulenc, Pechiney Ugine Kuhlmann, and L'Air Liquide. What actually occurred is described in this section.

Rhône-Poulenc

Rhône-Poulenc, one of France's largest privately owned manufacturing concerns and one of the twelve largest chemical concerns in the world, was founded in 1895. A series of mergers in recent years have greatly added to its size. Headquartered in Paris, Rhône-Poulenc in 1978 had 107,219 employees, about 70 percent of whom were in France; 12 percent in Brazil, where it is the leading chemical company; and the balance throughout the world, including the United States, where its subsidiary is Rodia, and the United Kingdom and Commonwealth countries, where it has absorbed May and Baker. It manufactures a large number of chemicals, pharmaceuticals, films, and textile fibers. Recent organizational and marketing problems have caused Rhône-Poulenc to fall behind Pechiney Ugine Kuhlmann in sales volume.[19]

In his report to the 1973 ICEF Congress, the secretary general lists a Rhône-Poulenc World Council as founded in September 1971, the third earliest so created.[20] We have ascertained that

---

[18] ICEF Circular Letter No. 55/79, April 26, 1979; "I.C.E.F.: Deux journées de travail . . . ," *Le Progrès*, May 22, 1979; "I.C.E.F.: Deux journées de travail . . . ," *Le Bien Public*, May 23-24, 1979; "A Damparis: Conseil Mondial syndical . . . ," *La Croix Jurassienne*, May 24, 1979; "Un contre-pouvoir à la multinationale?" *Les Dépêches*, May 23, 25, 1979; "Solvay: importante réunion internationale," *Syndicats*, June 16, 1979.

[19] Information from company annual reports. See also Table VIII-1.

[20] "Report of Activities of the Secretary-General, the 15th Statutory Congress, Geneva, 7th-9th November 1973, Documents," *ICF Bulletin*, October 1973, p. 75. Hereafter cited as *ICF 15th Statutory Congress*.

such a council does exist and usually meets annually in Geneva. Attendance seems to be confined to the CFDT chemical union in France, IG Chemie in Germany, and the Transport and General Workers' Union in Britain. Apparently no unions attend from the United States, South America, or any other country where Rhône-Poulenc has plants, including those in the host country, Switzerland. The company reports that, at the bargaining table, there have been no repercussions of, nor question raised concerning, these meetings.[21]

The ICEF secretary general has stated that, in return for support given by British workers to the CFDT while on strike against L'Air Liquide (which is discussed below),

> the CFDT Chemical Workers in the French, chemical, multinational giant Rhône-Poulenc, responding to an appeal of ICF, received the fraternal thanks of the 1,800 British members of the Chemical Workers' Union on strike against May and Baker, a wholly owned, British subsidiary of Rhône-Poulenc, for their prompt supporting action against the parent. Other affiliates also supported the strike, especially in the direct May and Baker subsidiaries in the Commonwealth. In his wire to ICF announcing the end of the strike, Bob Edwards, MP, President of the British Chemical Workers' Union stated: "May and Baker strike ended with 16 percent increase all round stop this victory largely due to your massive international intervention for which eternal thanks." [22]

Rhône-Poulenc officials acknowledged that they were indeed sent numerous letters, telegrams, and cables not only during the noted May and Baker strike but during one in France in November 1973. They merely acknowledged receipt thereof. There were no other overt union actions during these strikes or during a third one in Switzerland noted in the 1973 ICEF "Report of Activities." [23]

The ICEF secretary general has claimed that the ICEF supported the November 1973 French strike and a British one of May 1974 by "messages of support," "intervention and protests to parent," "consumer boycotts and information campaigns," and "documentation, statistics, company data for use in collective

---

[21] Interview in Paris, June 27, 1975. Rhône-Poulenc has sold all its Italian holdings and does not operate there.

[22] Charles Levinson, *International Trade Unionism*, Ruskin House Series In Trade Union Studies (London: George Allen & Unwin, Ltd., 1972), p. 114. The "British Chemical Workers' Union" referred to is obviously the Transport and General Workers' Union, of which Edwards was long a representative.

[23] *ICF 15th Statutory Congress*, p. 84.

bargaining." [24] Whatever documents were sent or data provided, there is no evidence of any boycotts or consumer campaigns but only of leaflet action and letters largely from French unions, which were handled by the company as noted above. Moreover, because the ICEF does not appear to have a statistical or research department, it is not clear what data it could provide of this nature.

It is the policy of Rhône-Poulenc to leave social matters (employee and union relations) to national and subsidiary managements. The company is highly decentralized, and the various subsidiaries in France, as well as those in other countries, operate their employee relations as separate entities. The company has given no serious thought to meeting with the ICEF or to discussing multinational union relationships, a fact which the ICEF's 1976 "Activities Report" seems to confirm.[25]

Pechiney Ugine Kuhlmann

Pechiney Ugine Kuhlmann (PUK), headquartered in Paris, is the result of the mergers of several metal and chemical companies. It is now one of the largest producers of aluminum, copper, and stainless steel, as well as a major factor in other metals and chemicals. Besides plants in Western Europe and many interests, including mines in underdeveloped areas, PUK operates mines in Australia and has several plants in the United States, including those of its Howmet subsidiary, a manufacturer of aluminum and other metal products and medical equipment. In 1978, it had sales of $6.1 billion and 95,974 employees.[26]

The International Metalworkers' Federation (IMF), not the ICEF, is the prime secretariat for PUK. The IMF has had three worldwide "aluminum conferences" at which PUK has been

---

[24] "Executive Committee. Activities Report of the Secretary-General. List of Membership," *ICF 16th Statutory Congress*, Montreal, October 27-29, 1976, pp. 97, 98, 102 (hereafter cited as *ICF 16th Statutory Congress*). See ICEF Circular Letter No. 119/77, November 1, 1977, for typical and pro forma request for "solidarity action" in regard to Rhône-Poulenc.

[25] Company interviews in Paris, June 1975 and May 1977; and *ICF 16th Statutory Congress*, p. 92. In this report, the ICEF secretary general accuses Rhône-Poulenc, among other companies, of making concessions to national unions in order to weaken "their support of the international program" and thus continuing to avoid meeting on an international basis.

[26] See "Pechiney Ugine: Merging to Gain Muscle," *Business Week*, January 8, 1972, pp. 44-47; and Table VIII-1.

discussed.[27] Nevertheless, the ICEF attempted to intervene in a matter involving a PUK aluminum plant. On June 26, 1972, the ICEF secretary general wrote Pierre Jouven, then president of PUK, alleging that PUK had closed the aluminum plant at Noguères, France, without treating the employees properly. He warned that the pressures of the international labor movement would be brought against PUK and accused the company of failing to practice modern and responsible collective bargaining and of behaving as if the company had divine power over the lives of the workers.[28]

The letter was referred to the president of L'Aluminum Pechiney, who, on June 30, 1973, wrote Levinson that he was ill-informed or the victim of the "great volume of inaccurate information spread by the press," because the workers, not the company, were responsible for the plant closing. He pointed out that picket lines, not the company, were preventing workers from entering the plant and that, moreover, before the strike began, the decision had been made to commence cooling the furnaces when the unions refused to furnish employees to maintain them. Any other decision would have risked serious damage to the furnaces and a long plant shutdown. Besides, the aluminum group president noted, this was the first work stoppage, including a long one in 1968, in which the unions took this attitude. The issue involved demands of the Noguères plant workers for an additional 15 percent increase over and above an increase of a like amount already offered by the company, plus other benefits.

Levinson apparently made no attempt to answer this reply, but in his report to the 1976 ICEF Congress, he lists two actions against PUK, both involving a facility at Lyon: the first allegedly occurring during a strike in April 1974; the second, two months later. In April, he claims, the ICEF sent messages of support to the strikers, intervened with the parent company, and boycotted the transfer of stocks. He claims to have also done all these things in June and to have waged a public informa-

---

27 "Multinational aluminum companies; a brief survey" (Report presented at the Third IMF Aluminum Conference, Munich, October 31-November 1, 1977). The report is a detailed analysis of the worldwide business operations, labor contracts, and plant social conditions at major aluminum companies, including PUK.

28 Copies of correspondence in authors' possession. A detailed description of the strike, entirely from the union point of view, is found in Michel Beaud, Pierre Danjou, et Jean David, *Une Multinationale Française: Pechiney Ugine Kuhlmann* (Paris: Editions du Seuil, 1975), pp. 204-10.

tion campaign.[29] We have been unable to find any evidence of such overt activities.

L'Air Liquide

L'Air Liquide Group, headquartered in Paris, is primarily engaged in the production and supply of industrial gases; but also provides technology, gases, and manufacturing equipment for welding applications; constructs facilities and equipment required for its operations; and produces various related chemicals. L'Air Liquide operates in fifty-three countries, including Japan, Australia, Canada, the United States, South America, and Africa. It is very strong in France, where it has the bulk of the business in its field. Because of the nature of its products and their high capital intensity, L'Air Liquide employs only approximately 24,000 employees in about four hundred plants worldwide, with sales of $1.6 billion.[30]

Both in his book *International Trade Unionism* and in his reports to the ICEF congresses, the ICEF secretary general has claimed effective action against L'Air Liquide. The book thus states:

> One of our French affiliates, the Chemical Workers' Federation (CFDT) in March 1970 conveyed thanks to ICF affiliates in ten countries which responded to an appeal for solidarity demonstrations, stoppages, etc. at Air Liquide foreign plants for their members on strike in eight Air Liquide installations in France. The message stated that "this solidarity permitted the French workers to win important wage increases, reduction in working time as well as the introduction of monthly salaries instead of hourly rates beyond a certain category and the possibility of its total application before the end of 1970."
>
> Air Liquide workers in Belgium, Holland, Germany, and Italy effectively frustrated the company's efforts to divert production from its foreign plants in these countries into France during a widespread stoppage of Air Liquide French operations in May 1971.[31]

The facts of these two disputes appear to be that, in 1970, L'Air Liquide was negotiating with various unions in France

---

[29] *ICF 16th Statutory Congress*, pp. 98, 99, 102.

[30] Based on various company reports and interviews, Paris, June 1975, April 1976, and May 1977. See also *Fortune*, Vol. 100 (August 13, 1979), p. 197.

[31] Levinson, *International Trade Unionism*, pp. 114-15.

when they suddenly struck. The company was caught completely unprepared and after three weeks conceded virtually all the union demands. The company did so primarily as a result of the pressure of various manufacturing and construction concerns that were threatened with shutdowns because of low inventories of industrial gases and the lack of sources of supply other than L'Air Liquide. The company received various ICEF-inspired telegrams from unions in Europe, Africa, and Australia supporting the CFDT union, which was one of those striking and was also involved in an attempt to prevent supervisors from working in the Caen plant by a sit-in and by mass picketing.

The ICEF secretary general felt it necessary to write L'Air Liquide on April 7, 1970, certifying that the cables of support were genuine and not sent by the CFDT and, further, "that if in the future workers of L'Air Liquide were to find themselves in such an unfair situation again, the answer would be stronger and more extensive." [32]

In 1971, the French unions struck again, and a flood of telegrams was once more sent to the company. This time, however, the company was prepared. It had made what it regarded as a good offer to the union, built up its inventories, utilized management personnel, and it did import some products from Italy, Belgium, and Spain. Fear of refusal to deliver imports and lack of adequate transport precluded major reliance on imports during the strike; this time, however, after three weeks, the unions ended their strike on terms close to the company's offer. There have been no such strikes since 1971.

L'Air Liquide did not reply to any telegrams or other communications from the ICEF or from its affiliates during either strike, both of which were apparently settled on the basis of the relative bargaining situation then prevailing. The power of striking unions to interrupt transport of industrial gases would seem to make the import of products during a strike difficult, if not impossible, thereby rendering any international union action largely superfluous, even if it were to include something more than communications. By preparing for the 1971 strike, L'Air Liquide management overcame the transport problem.

---

[32] Copies of telegrams and cables and of Levinson's letter in authors' possession. For an account of the Caen situation, see *Paris Normandie*, February 25 and March 3, 1970. The company used helicopters to supply and to remove products from the Caen plant.

Two other international incidents occurred as a result of events in Morocco. In the first one, a night porter was discharged in November 1972 for sleeping on the job with a woman, and a strike occurred in plants at Meknes, where the incident occurred, and at Casablanca. Because it was reported (inaccurately) that he was a union steward, he received support from the ICEF and its affiliates, including the chemical union of the CFDT and the headquarters of the Belgian FGTB. The letter from the CFDT affiliate stated expansively that it could "envisage a very considerable reaction on the part of L'Air Liquide workers in the whole world in order to stop such a situation." The FGTB, less grandiosely, wrote that it was informed by the ICEF that the strike resulted because a union official had been discharged as a result of his union activities; it then announced its solidarity with workers in underdeveloped countries and its disapproval of the company's action. The ICEF secretary general also sent the company a telegram demanding that the "union delegate" be reinstated.

In fact, the discharged employee was not a union delegate, but he was so reported in a Moroccan union paper. The Moroccan Ministry of Labor intervened, and the matter was settled by affirming the discharge but assisting the employee to obtain a job in another plant. The strike lasted one week at the Meknes plant and five days at Casablanca.[33]

In his report to the 1973 ICEF Congress, the secretary general reports successful French union support for the Moroccan strike.[34] Actually, the only international impact that occurred was that the Belgian manager of L'Air Liquide explained to the FGTB what actually had happened in its Moroccan facility.

A very similar occurrence in March 1977 resulted in a telegram from the ICEF secretary general "in the name of five million members" and a letter from the chemical union of CGT-Force Ouvrière to L'Air Liquide's headquarters. In this case, a Moroccan supervisor was discharged by the native Moroccan management because he left his job before a holiday earlier than he was allowed. The ICEF and CGT-FO communications incorrectly state that the man was a union steward and that French insensitivity to Moroccan customs and union animus were involved, whereas in fact, he was not a union steward and,

---

[33] Copies of documents in authors' possession; company personnel executives, interview in Paris, June 1975.

[34] *ICF 15th Statutory Congress*, p. 83.

as noted, was discharged by Moroccan, not French, management. The company did not answer the communications.[35]

THE GERMAN CHEMICAL COMPANIES

After World War II, I. G. Farben, the German chemical colossus, was broken up, and three major chemical companies emerged: Hoechst, Bayer, and BASF (Badische Anilin & Soda Fabrik). In 1978, these companies (see Table VIII-1) ranked first, second, and third, respectively, in chemical worldwide sales, with each having more than $10 billion in sales and more than 100,000 employees. Each of the companies operates throughout the world and is strong in pharmaceuticals, as well as in chemicals.

Despite the size and visibility of these companies, they have been involved in very few international union actions. Labor negotiations in Germany are in the hands of the industry employer associations, and thus, the companies are shielded from direct union confrontations. Works councils handle many of the plant relations, again providing some barrier to union action, although employee members of these councils are usually union adherents. The three chemical giants also pride themselves on their employee relations and provide a host of employee services and benefits while also paying wages substantially above the employer association's negotiated rate.

There is another reason why the German chemical companies (as well as those in other industries) have rarely been the object of international union activity: apparently, the German union officials have not desired it. These union officials take an active part both in the "secretariats" and in the regional European federations. The presidents of IG Chemie and IG Metall are also presidents of the ICEF and the IMF, respectively. German unions are heavy financial contributors to the secretariats and to the regional federations. German union officials have not encouraged multinational unions to be active within their country but rather have insisted on handling problems themselves.

The ICEF secretary general announced (incorrectly) to the 1973 congress that Hoechst and Bayer councils would be formed in December 1973 and January 1974, respectively,[36] but there

---

[35] Copies of documents in authors' possession; company personnel executives, interview in Paris, May 1977.

[36] *ICF 15th Statutory Congress,* p. 78.

was no mention of BASF. Meanwhile, councils, at least on paper, were formed for most other large, non-German chemical companies, but not for Hoechst, Bayer, BASF, or other German companies.

This changed in 1976. At the IG Chemie Ninth Federal Congress in September of that year, the delegates adopted a resolution "to promote and to intensify ICF World Council activities in the Federal Republic." The resolution further identified "crucial points of the task" as

1. The exercise of proper influence on the ICF office to make sure that in cases of support calls caused by conflicts, the following requirements are being fulfilled
   —in cases of conflicts and actions early, sufficient and reliable information must be given about the respective situations in the companies, place, time, nature and extent of the conflicts and actions, as well as the affected groups of employees.

2. All affected employees in the participating companies must receive constant and proper information about intended and executed actions of the ICF unions.

3. In cases of conflict or action it is necessary that all participating ICF unions put qualified representatives as advisors at the constant disposal of the ICF world council.

The resolution then stated its "reasons":

> There is a constant increase of cooperation and interlocking of interests among multinational companies—e.g., AKZO, BASF, Bayer, Hoechst, Schering, etc. They grow faster than other companies. The systems of planning and controls in these multinational companies are constantly being improved and more centralized.
>
> Compared with this, employees and their unions have no equivalent systems for the enforcement of their social interests. For these reasons it is of vital importance to form ICF world councils which could bring about an effective counterweight.[37]

From November 29 to December 2, 1976, at a meeting in Bad Homburg, Germany, which followed the ICEF congress held one month earlier in Montreal, the councils for the three companies were created. The president of each council was the chairman of each company's respective works council and, in all cases, is a member of IG Chemie. Werner Beck, an IG Chemie official, was designated copresident of all three councils, as were Norman Goldstein of the U. S. Teamsters Union for Bayer and Hoechst and

---

[37] Copy of minutes in authors' possession. Translated from the German by the Industrial Research Unit.

J. A. Thomas of the U. S. International Chemical Workers Union (ICWU) for BASF. Alternates included an IG Chemie representative in each case, a Brazilian for BASF and Hoechst, and a Belgian for Bayer.[38] The control of international union activities in the German chemical industry thus remains firmly within IG Chemie.

Since these world councils were created, there has been some upsurge of ICEF activity regarding German companies. Prior thereto, the main event of significance was the strike at the Turkish plant of Hoechst, which is discussed below. Before 1977, there were not even many examples of letters, telegrams, or leaflet actions involving these companies. The few that did occur include the June 1971 period, when short strikes upset the usual calm of the German chemical industry. The secretary general of the ICEF sent each of the companies the usual letters affirming "worldwide" union support of IG Chemie and condemning the management attitudes. On other occasions, works councils of Bayer in Germany and the Netherlands urged joint meetings but, in the face of management opposition, dropped the proposal. A Belgian strike involving the same company resulted in some leaflet action in Germany. BASF has received requests for information from the American Oil, Chemical and Atomic Workers (OCAW), and German works councils in three companies have requested information about the companies' operations in South Africa and in underdeveloped countries. The companies usually give general replies to such inquiries, and they have not been followed up.[39] As we note below, such activity has been increasing.

The Hoechst Turkish Strike

Hoechst has a pharmaceutical plant in Istanbul that employed about 320 persons in 1969, and five years later, over 400. In 1969, it was struck by the union Kimya-Is. This union also had contacts with plants of three American firms—Abbott, Pfizer, and the Wyeth Division of American Home Products—and with a plant of Hoffmann-La Roche, the Swiss firm (which it struck

---

[38] "ICEF-Welträte für Bayer, BASF und Hoechst gegründet," IG Chemie-Papier-Keramik Press Release, XII/93, December 6, 1976.

[39] Company interviews in Germany, February and September 1975. See also *ICF 15th Statutory Congress*, p. 82. The secretary general's report to the 1976 ICEF Congress made no mention of any activity concerning the three companies.

four years later, as described below). A rival union, Petro-Is, dealt with a plant owned by Squibb, an American firm, and was strong in the petroleum industry. Kimya-Is is affiliated with the ICEF; Petro-Is was an affiliate of the ICEF's now defunct competitor, the International Federation of Petroleum and Chemical Workers (IFPCW). The Hoechst contract expired first, and Kimya-Is was using it as the target to set new labor arrangements for the Turkish pharmaceutical industry. According to the ICEF secretary general:

> A notable example of international solidarity at the company level was the victory of Kimya-Is, with the help of ICF, in a dispute with a pharmaceutical subsidiary of the German Hoechst Co. To support the Turkish colleagues of Hoechst, the German IG Chemie Union sent DM 10,000 for strike relief. Former IG Chemie Vice-President and chief negotiator with Hoechst, Karl Küpper, travelled to Turkey to help the strikers. Through his efforts the conflict was taken up at the company's headquarters in Frankfurt. This helped finally to force the company to comprehend that it was no longer facing an isolated, relatively weak organization in Turkey, but one supported by the ICF and by the 600,000 strong IG Chemie-Papier-Keramik, its principal bargaining counterpart in Germany. This realization led to a final settlement after a strike which lasted nearly ninety days. Kimya-Is succeeded in winning demands which for Turkey set new precedents in collective bargaining: sixty-five strike days paid for at new rates, bipartite union-management committee to decide upon all dismissals, substantial pay increases, and numerous associated concessions.[40]

Our investigation reveals that this was a period of considerable student unrest, large union demands, and nationalistic feelings directed in part against foreign-owned companies. Violence and some fatalities occurred in these uprisings. Plant unrest was exacerbated by the low wages and benefits there, which sharply contrasted with what immigrant Turkish workers were receiving in Germany and other Western European countries.[41] Kimya-Is was anxious to win a decisive victory not only because of these factors but also because of its rival union situation that was fanned by the ICEF-IFPCW controversy.[42] In addition, Kimya-Is

---

[40] Levinson, *International Trade Unionism*, pp. 113-14.

[41] For an excellent analysis of the experience and impact of Turkish workers abroad, see Suzanne Paine, *Exporting Workers: The Turkish Case*, University of Cambridge, Department of Applied Economics, Occasional Paper 41 (Cambridge: Cambridge University Press, 1974).

[42] For details, see Herbert R. Northrup and Richard L. Rowan, "The ICF-IFPCW Conflict," *Columbia Journal of World Business*, Vol. IX (Winter 1974), pp. 109-20.

was torn internally by leadership rivalries and was affiliated with a federation known as DISK, which had a strong left-wing, anti-foreign company orientation. All this added to its militancy and the extremity of the union demands.

Kimya-Is bargainers demanded not only sizable wage increases but also control over all discharges. The company strongly resisted this latter demand and countered with a generous wage offer that was rejected, and Kimya-Is struck. The strike lasted eighty-eight days and ended in a considerable increase in wages and improvements for the union in the terms of contract. It did, indeed, accomplish the union objective of setting off a major Turkish wage explosion and major improvements in working conditions and rights, as well as an increase in union prerogatives. Specifically, the settlement included the following:

a) wage increases of 100 percent over three years;

b) a new fourteenth month bonus;

c) increased transportation allowances;

d) a retroactive contract so that the strikers were paid for sixty of the eighty-eight days;

e) recognition of Kimya-Is as the exclusive bargaining agent in matters of disagreement and labor conditions, and meetings of the representatives of the company and union once per month to discuss job matters;

f) creation of a committee of two members selected by the union and two by the company, with a chairman selected by these four members to review disciplinary matters;

g) rejection of the union demand to determine normal and/or collective layoffs and dismissals; and

h) approval of Hoechst's demand for a long-term contract—three years and four months.

The extent to which international pressures played a role in the strike outcome is difficult to gauge. Küpper did, indeed, travel to Istanbul and make a contribution of DM 10,000 to the strikers. Moreover, he acted as the representative of Wilhelm Gefeller, then president both of IG Chemie and the ICEF.[43] The Turkish situation was discussed in Germany by Hoechst and IG Chemie officials, and Küpper's trip was well publicized. Hoechst officials

---

[43] Gefeller has since retired and has been succeeded in both positions by Karl Hauenschild.

insist that the company adhered to its policy of leaving union matters and labor dispute settlement in foreign-based subsidiaries to the national managers there and affirmed that policy in discussions with IG Chemie officials. Moreover, Hoechst personnel insist that the intervention of IG Chemie and the ICEF made the strike settlement neither easier nor more difficult.[44]

After analyzing these reports, we conclude that the publicity given to the Küpper trip and the IG Chemie donation gave both the ICEF and IG Chemie a vested interest in claiming a greater effect than could be justified by their intervention. Local union and government pressures and the unrest then prevalent in the country and the union contributed the most toward the substantial union gains. It is likely, however, that the international support evidenced by the Küpper trip and the IG Chemie contribution helped somewhat both to strengthen the union's hand and to convince the company and/or its local management to pay a heavy price to end the strike.

World Council Recognition Attempt

Early in 1977, the chairman of the ICEF-BASF World Council, Rudi Bauer, then also chairman of the BASF Works Council, formally requested that BASF meet with and presumably recognize the world council as a "social partner." The company declined both to meet and to grant such recognition, because these actions would be contrary to its policy of decentralizing industrial relations in order to conform with the national economic and social requirements of the countries in which it operates.[45]

Neither Bayer nor Hoechst received similar requests. This may indicate that the request for recognition was Bauer's own initiative or that of the BASF Works Council rather than an IG Chemie action. If similar requests are, however, made of Bayer or Hoechst, it is likely that these companies will likewise decline to meet with or to recognize ICEF bodies for the same reasons.

The BASF World Council has also been active in Spain where workers in the several BASF plants have been attempting to establish a coordinating council (Comisión Volante—literally, a "flying commission") in conjunction with the world council.[46]

---

[44] Interviews in Frankfurt, Germany, September 1975; letter to the authors, April 24, 1975.

[45] Documents in authors' possession. ICEF Circular Letter No. 167/78, December 15, 1978, enclosed a questionnaire relating to Bayer, but we have heard of no results or actions generated therefrom.

[46] We have in the files a German translation of an undated (1977) statement of the BASF Spanish union group (UGT) about these efforts.

In a circular letter issued in October 1977, Levinson thanks affiliates for solidarity actions in support of a strike in one of these plants,[47] but a company personnel executive wrote the authors that there had been no strike in any of its Spanish plants in 1977.[48]

Also in October 1977, the ICEF secretary general issued a circular letter claiming "IG Chemie Local Union Denounces BASF Hiring Older Workers for Jobs Exposed to Cancer Hazards."[49] The alleged statement was attached to the circular letter. Actually, it was issued by the works committee, the administrative organ of the BASF Works Council, which claims that most of its members are IG Chemie stewards, not by a "local union," which does not exist.

The statement makes no such charge as alleged by the circular letter. Rather, it reads: "The representatives of the BASF work force firmly reject the idea advanced by some doctors that work places involving health hazards should be filled by older workers."[50]

Apparently, this suggestion referred to possible health hazards to pregnant women. BASF affirmed that the charge that IG Chemie accused the company of such actions is groundless.[51]

Still another incident occurred as a result of a labor dispute in early 1978 in Morocco. The ICEF issued several circular letters in the matter and claimed that the dispute was settled because of "the effective intervention with plant management in the Federal Republic of Germany on behalf of our Moroccan colleagues" by Rolf Brand of IG Chemie, president of the ICEF Hoechst World Council and chairman of the Hoechst National Works Council.[52]

Actually, the strike began on January 21, 1978, over wages and was settled on February 7, 1978, with the assistance of mediation by the Moroccan government. During the strike, an official in the German embassy in Morocco contacted the company and IG Chemie about possible international implications if the

---

[47] ICEF Circular Letter No. 106/77, October 6, 1977.

[48] Letter to the authors, January 30, 1978.

[49] ICEF Circular Letter No. 110/77, October 18, 1977.

[50] *Ibid.*, attachment.

[51] Letter to the authors, January 30, 1978. In ICEF Circular Letter No. 162/78, November 23, 1978, it was again charged that BASF had a disregard for industrial health problems.

[52] ICEF Circular Letter No. 69/78, April 27, 1978. See also No. 58/78, March 28, 1978.

strike was prolonged. Levinson also contacted IG Chemie. Brand interested himself in the matter after twice being contacted by IG Chemie, but he did not act until after the strike was terminated.[53]

Hoechst Dutch Plant Redundancies

In January 1978, Hoechst, which has a strong concentration in the troubled synthetic fibers industry, announced that it would close the portion of its facility in Vlissingen, the Netherlands, devoted to the production of raw material for polyester fiber. About 150 of the 1,000 employees of the plant would be redundant. Hoechst also was unable to assure that further layoffs would not occur.

Industriebond-NVV, the Dutch union, took a strong position that Hoechst should close a West German facility instead, but the company declined, noting that it had reduced employment there by about four hundred persons. The union stated that it would agree to a reduction of force only if it could be demonstrated that it was less costly to manufacture the materials in West Germany. The works council also advised against closure and charged that the Hoechst Board provided insufficient data to enable the council to make a recommendation to management.

When Hoechst moved to activate its program, the union obtained a temporary restraining order against the move and sought to obtain additional information from Hoechst regarding the relative costs of production.[54] As part of its evidence, Industriebond presented an interview with Charles Levinson which supposedly demonstrated that, contrary to the statements of company representatives, the European Common Market Fibre Cartel would effectively handle problems caused by the overcapacity in the industry.[55] After further hearings were held, however, the Dutch union withdrew its petition as it became clear that the court had no jurisdiction in the matter.[56]

---

[53] Letter from Hoechst personnel executive to the authors, June 16, 1978.

[54] There have been numerous press stories about this case. See, e.g., *Financieel Dagblad*, June 15, 1978.

[55] See ICEF Circular Letter No. 105/78, July 18, 1978, p. 2.

[56] This was widely reported in the Dutch press for September 1, 1978. See also "Unions drop attempt to take German company to court," *European Industrial Relations Review*, No. 58 (November 1978), p. 4.

BRITISH COMPANIES

The United Kingdom boasts several major chemical companies, most of which, like British Petroleum, Shell, and Unilever, have the major share of their activities in other fields, and are discussed in later chapters. Imperial Chemical Industries, however, based in London, one of the world's five largest chemical companies, with factories throughout much of the world (see Table VIII-1), has been an ICEF target; and two other companies have been mentioned in ICEF literature.

Imperial Chemical Industries (ICI)

The ICEF's interest in ICI seems to have been instigated by David Warburton, national industrial officer of the British General and Municipal Workers' Union. The ICEF established an Imperial Chemical Industries Permanent World Council at a meeting in Geneva, March 10-11, 1975. Warburton was named cochairman with Bob Edwards, a Labour member of Parliament and then, but since retired, an officer of the British Transport and General Workers' Union, who has been active in several other ICEF councils. Karl Hauenschild, president both of IG Chemie in Germany and of the ICEF, chaired the meeting. Other unions represented included ones from Argentina, Austria, Australia, France, Japan, and the Netherlands. Although Warburton told the press that "the unions at the Geneva conference represented more than 90 percent of the company's labour force," this statement seems very much exaggerated. The press statement also indicates that this ICEF council will attempt to put the company on the defensive by alleging health hazards in its plants, because ICI is an important producer of vinyl chloride.[57] Levinson has made much of this issue in recent years.[58] Both British unions involved wrote ICI asking recognition of the ICEF-ICI World Council. ICI rejected the request.

Another incident involving ICI that has come to our attention occurred after it acquired Atlas Chemical Company in Wilmington, Delaware, now known as ICI, United States. This concern, in turn, took over the operation of a government munitions plant

---

[57] "Workers of the World Unite to Deal With ICI," *Manchester Guardian*, March 13, 1975.

[58] The ICEF sponsored a major meeting on this subject in Geneva in 1974 and managed to have the World Health Organization as its cosponsor. See *ICF 16th Statutory Congress*, p. 107.

in Indiana in which it found union relations in a critical state of disarray. The American union concerned is the International Chemical Workers Union. In the course of various controversies involving this situation during early 1974, Warburton received messages from the American union and issued a number of press releases and telegrams to ICI London headquarters demanding, without success, that it intervene in the American dispute.[59]

In his report to the 1976 ICEF Congress, the secretary general claims ICEF action involving disputes at ICI plants in Britain during a strike in May 1974, in Spain and Argentina in May 1975, and again in Spain in July 1975.[60] The company has no record of any communication from the ICEF in regard to the situation at British plants in 1974 (nor has British Petroleum), where the issues, which involved conditions for shift workers, were peacefully settled; a British union (not the ICEF) inquired about conditions at an ICI Argentina plant; and two unions (again not including the ICEF) inquired about arrests of strikers at a Spanish ICI subsidiary, but this case was not at Zaragoza as reported by the ICEF.[61]

As have other companies in the chemical fibers business, ICI has had some plant reductions and layoffs. In early 1977, it decided to shut down some nylon facilities in Germany and so advised the works council. Through chemical industry sources, the authors heard rumors that an ICEF-ICI World Council meeting was scheduled in Hannover, Germany, to protest this action. Apparently, the rumors were incorrect or the meeting was cancelled, for it never took place.

Other British Companies

We have already noted the probable temporary involvement of Laporte Industries with the ICEF in connection with Solvay. A much smaller London-based concern, it had sales of $204 million and 4,655 employees in 1977.[62] Glaxo Holdings, also London-based, is a multinational pharmaceutical and food manufacturer;

---

[59] Copies of documents in authors' possession. According to the International Chemical Workers Union, relations in the Indiana plant have since improved. See *The Chemical Worker*, January and February 1975.

[60] See *ICF 16th Statutory Congress*, pp. 98, 100, 102.

[61] Letter from ICI personnel executive to the authors, February 15, 1977.

[62] *Laporte 1977*, Annual Report (London, 1978), p. 2; and *Laporte 1977 Report to Employees* (London, n.d.), n.p.

it had, in 1978, sales of $993 million and 30,901 employees.[63] Levinson has several times announced his intention of establishing a world council for this company [64] but has not done so.

THE SWISS CHEMICAL AND PHARMACEUTICAL COMPANIES

Basel, Switzerland, is the home of three of the world's largest chemical and pharmaceutical manufacturing companies: Ciba-Geigy, the largest of the three and the second largest Swiss company after Nestlé (see Table VIII-1); F. Hoffmann-La Roche, the number one company worldwide in ethical drug manufacturing; and Sandoz, the smallest of the three, but a giant in its own right, with 1978 sales of $2.4 billion and 35,168 employees.[65] The ICEF has attempted on several occasions, but without success, to establish contact both with Ciba-Geigy and with Hoffmann-La Roche, but Sandoz has only recently been mentioned as an ICEF target.

Ciba-Geigy

The ICEF claims to have taken several actions in regard to Ciba-Geigy. In the book *International Trade Unionism*, it is noted that Ciba "has outstandingly good labour relations" in Basel, but it is alleged that this is not true in its plants in France and Britain. It is further alleged (without stating the time or place) that the French management was forced to reinstate "plant representatives whom it had previously dismissed" after a two-week strike. The inference is that this was done after intervention at the company's headquarters by Adolf Knecht, then national secretary of the Swiss Federation of Textile, Chemical, and Paper Workers' Union (GTCP) and a member of the ICEF Executive Board. The company denies both that it was forced to reinstate plant representatives in France or that Knecht, with whom, it affirmed, it has had excellent relations, intervened in any French matters.[66]

---

[63] *Fortune*, Vol. 100 (August 13, 1979), p. 200.

[64] The most recent was at the inception of the June 1978 "ICEF World Energy Division Conference," which is discussed in chapter X.

[65] *Fortune*, Vol. 100 (August 13, 1979), p. 196.

[66] Levinson, *International Trade Unionism*, pp. 115-16; and company interviews in Basel, February and September 1975.

In his report to the 1973 ICEF Congress, the secretary general lists among "international trade union actions" one in October 1972 in which the ICEF allegedly intervened in "support of union action against antiunion policy" of Ciba-Geigy in Great Britain.[67] No other details are given.

Such vague statements are, of course, virtually impossible to track down. What is likely is that a letter or telegram was dispatched to the company's Basel headquarters during a strike or labor negotiations in Britain. Certainly, the company took no action as a result of alleged ICEF pressure; for, as noted below, it has a consistent policy of dealing only with national unions.

Also in October 1972, the ICEF announced the formation of a Ciba-Geigy World Council, headed by and composed largely of Swiss union officials, with representatives also from Germany and England.[68] After this, a spokesman of Ciba-Geigy gave an interview that was published in the company newspaper for November 6, 1972. His responses made it very clear that Ciba-Geigy had no interest in or intention of meeting with or developing any relationship with the ICEF or its world council. He noted that ICEF affiliates represented "only a small minority" of the employees of the Ciba-Geigy Group and that "the structure of our Group leaves open no possibility for negotiations with . . . [ICEF]. This holds also for informative talks." [69]

In support of his position, the spokesman cited Ciba-Geigy's policy of leaving personnel relations to the various national managements. He spoke of the different labor and social policies in various countries and mentioned the potential conflict of a centralized personnel policy with national industrywide bargaining that exists in many countries, the depressing bureaucratic impact of attempting to lay down international social policies, and national legal restraints. In conclusion, he expressed the belief that Ciba-Geigy's refusal to meet with and to deal with the ICEF would have no adverse effect on its "positive and fruitful" relationships with Swiss union officials who are key figures in the ICEF world council.

---

[67] *ICF 15th Statutory Congress*, p. 83.

[68] *Ibid.*, p. 76.

[69] "Ein Weltgewerkschaftsrat für CIBA-GEIGY? Die Firma nimmt Stellung," *CIBA-GEIGY Zeitung*, November 6, 1972.

The ICEF has claimed additional successful intervention with Ciba-Geigy, claims which again cannot be supported. Thus, in his report to the 1976 ICEF Congress, the secretary general states that, during a strike at the Ciba-Geigy plant in the United States, which lasted from January 1 to April 15, 1974, the ICEF sent messages of support and solidarity, intervened and protested to the parent company, provided public information campaigns and media materials, and also provided documentation and company data for use in collective bargaining.[70] The director of industrial relations for the company in the United States declared that, to the contrary, no communication was received from the ICEF either in Basel or in the United States, and no such communications surfaced during the strike. The then president of the ICWU, of which the strikers were members, went to Europe for an ICEF meeting during the strike, but no communications or other overt action pertaining to the strike resulted.[71]

The same ICEF report lists action of a similar nature against production transfers in the United Kingdom.[72] In fact, there was some restructuring of Ciba-Geigy's photographic group, but no communication was received from the ICEF by the company,[73] nor was there any publicity given to the matter insofar as we can determine.

There has thus been no change in the company's position. Ciba-Geigy officials have not been in direct contact with the ICEF; they do not consider the ICEF world council—now, as noted below, apparently combined with that of Hoffmann-La Roche—a partner for discussion; and they have continued to emphasize that the company's personnel policy lies in the hands of its domestic general managers and that corporate headquarters staff does not interfere in local matters.

Works Council Meetings. In addition to ICEF attempts, there have been two international meetings sponsored by works councils of Ciba-Geigy. The first occurred in Italy in 1978 and involved the Italian and Spanish works councils from this company. Apparently, the meeting concentrated on an exchange of information and plans for a larger meeting the following year.

---

[70] *ICF 16th Statutory Congress*, pp. 98, 102.

[71] Telephone Interview, February 1, 1977.

[72] *ICF 16th Statutory Congress*, pp. 100, 102.

[73] Letter from Ciba-Geigy officials to the authors, February 17, 1977.

The 1979 meeting was held on May 3 in Barcelona. Prior to the meeting, efforts were made to contact the French and Portuguese, as well as the Italian and Spanish works council groups, and there were some rumors that the Swiss were also urged to attend. Requests were also made to the company to provide paid leave, to share the costs of travel, and to provide conference room facilities. The company declined all of these requests, maintaining that it was a matter of indifference whether the meeting was held and that it would give no recognition, support, or information in behalf of such meetings.

The results were not promising. The French did not come or reply to the requests. The delegates who did come from Spain, Portugal, and Italy apparently decided that it was not worthwhile, and no further meetings were scheduled. Apparently, no mention was made of Swiss attendants or participation. These meetings did not involve the ICEF or other international organizations, but the Communists may well have played a role.[74]

Hoffmann-La Roche

Levinson also claims to have initiated successful actions involving Hoffmann-La Roche. One, concerned with the strike in Madrid in July 1973,[75] involved press releases implying that the ICEF was involved in the strike, although there is no evidence that this was the case. Apparently, no communications were sent to the company's Basel headquarters, nor were other company facilities contacted in any way.

The other involved a rather long strike in Turkey. The secretary general's report to the 1973 ICEF Congress states:

> Consumer and public information campaigns are being carried out more frequently. Several conflicts were largely resolved by the weight of such campaigns in the press, radio, TV, and among the company's employees. The efforts of Brother Adolf Knecht, Central Secretary-Treasurer of the Swiss Gewerkschaft Textil-Chemie-Papier in Zurich and its branch offices in Basel, on behalf of the Turkish La Roche strikers was a notable first in Switzerland, as were the resultant gains won by the Roche workers in Turkey.[76]

---

[74] Documents from meetings in authors' possession; company personnel department, interviews in Basel, May 18, 1979.

[75] *ICF 15th Statutory Congress*, p. 84.

[76] *Ibid.*, p. 87.

This situation concerned a strike in the Hoffmann-La Roche Istanbul plant in the spring of 1973; other drug companies were also involved. The Turkish union demanded a wage increase of 96 percent, the company offered 28 percent, and nonbinding arbitration pursuant to Turkish law proposed 44 percent. Both parties declined to accept this last proposal, but the final settlement wage increase came to 56 percent.

Between the arbitration and the final settlement, the ICEF became involved. A single leaflet was distributed in Basel in the name of the "ICF Hoffmann-La Roche World Council," and Adolf Knecht, who, as noted, was then a prominent Swiss union official, was induced to duplicate the efforts of his German counterpart in the Turkish Hoechst strike in 1969 [77] by sending to strikers a contribution of 10,000 Swiss francs. In addition, the Turkish newspaper *Halkçi*, June 7, 1973, carried this story under the heading "Workers and Unions":

> When the union of the Chemical Workers at Roche, Pfizer and Abbott ceased work, ICF decided to support these strikes. For this reason, the workers of the companies in Switzerland, Sweden, England, France, America, and Canada blocked supplies and did not work any overtime.[78]

There is no apparent factual basis for this statement. All three companies operate nonunion in the United States, and none has a plant in Sweden. None of the companies could find any evidence of disruption of work or interference therewith at any time during the strike.[79] Since then, Hoffmann-La Roche's Turkish plant has been a major target of union activity, which has forced its wage level substantially higher than that of competing firms, but no similar international involvement has occurred.

Levinson has also made much of the drug-pricing disputes that have involved Hoffmann-La Roche and several European governments. Indeed, he claims credit either for the ICEF or for its affiliates in initiating such action.[80] This, of course, is impossible

---

[77] See the above section "The German Chemical Companies."

[78] Translated for the Industrial Research Unit.

[79] Interviews in North Chicago, New York City, and Basel, April and September 1975.

[80] See Charles Levinson, *The Multinational Pharmaceutical Industry* (Geneva: International Federation of Chemical and General Workers' Unions, [1974]), esp. pp. 43-47, 52.

to verify. Finally, following the disaster at a plant owned by Hoffmann-La Roche in Seveso, Italy, an attempt was made to arrange a discussion of safety issues with an ICEF group, but the company declined to meet with the ICEF. On October 13, 1976, in an interview over the Australian Broadcasting Corporation, Levinson denounced the company for failing to meet him.

Combined World Council. The ICEF also listed a Hoffmann-La Roche World Council formed in 1972 and headed, as in the case of Ciba-Geigy, by a Swiss unionist.[81] It seems to have been relatively inactive, for ICEF literature has not publicized its meetings. Then in February 1976, prior to the eighth meeting of the chemical subcommittee of the International Labour Organisation, the ICEF Chemical Industry Division met.[82] As part of this conference, a combined Ciba-Geigy and Hoffmann-La Roche World Council meeting was held in Geneva with Ewald Kaeser of Switzerland as president. The meeting condemned the labor policies of the companies, requested that Levinson send expressions of solidarity to employees of the companies in Chile and Spain, and again voted to seek talks with the companies, which, as noted above, have not occurred and are not likely to occur.

Since this time, the ICEF secretary general has claimed a number of actions of "support and solidarity in response to requests for assistance during multinational company disputes and strikes." Thus, he claims that "letters and cables expressing thanks for effective support have been received from such organizations as . . . the Spanish U.G.T. (Unión General de Trabajadores) in dispute with Hoffmann-La Roche and Sandoz Companies." [83] Hoffmann-La Roche replied to our inquiry that there was "no strike in our branch in Madrid during the course of 1977 and 1978." [84] Sandoz was, however, involved, as noted below.

The ICEF and a Swiss union official who is on the ICEF Executive. Board also sought to interfere in a British labor relations matter involving an attempt by the Association of Scientific, Technical and Managerial Staffs (ASTMS) to gain

---

81 *ICF 15th Statutory Congress*, p. 76.

82 *ICF 16th Statutory Congress*, p. 33.

83 ICEF Circular Letter No. 59/78, March 28, 1978.

84 Letter from company personnel coordinator to the authors, June 27, 1978.

recognition for white-collar employees in plants of Hoffmann-La Roche. The company's policy is to refuse to recognize unions until they can show a 51 percent membership, which the ASTMS was unable to do. ICEF Secretary General Charles Levinson wrote a circular letter in February 1979 criticizing the company's policy as antiunion and urging affiliates to communicate with the company's headquarters, because "past experience has also proved that protests via different national operations of the company where affiliates are strongly organized can have a positive cumulative effect upon attitudes at company headquarters."

Ewald Kaeser, national secretary of the Swiss GTCP and a member of the ICEF Executive Board, sent the ASTMS a resolution allegedly passed by an assembly of workers in Basel supporting the ASTMS position, and attempted to intervene with the company. He was told, of course, that it was none of his concern. The company did not change its position.[85]

Sandoz

The problems at the Sandoz Spanish affiliate in Prat arose in early 1978 because of declining sales. The Spanish company management, in accordance with Spanish law, requested governmental approval to reduce weekly working time. Before any governmental action, however, the local representative of the socialist UGT was contacted by the employees, who were apparently fearful, especially in view of widespread layoffs and workweek reductions in the area, that the company was planning to close the plant. The UGT representative then wrote to the ICEF secretary general about his fears, and the latter, in turn, requested Ewald Kaeser to intercede with the company.

Kaeser, who negotiates with the company for employees of its Swiss plants, did so. He was told by the chief Sandoz personnel officer that what went on in Spain was not the Swiss union's concern but that the information would be given to him as an individual. Meanwhile, business improved at the Prat plant so that layoffs were no longer contemplated. This information was given to Kaeser by telephone and apparently passed on by him to the ICEF secretary general. Levinson then sent a telegram to the UGT representative stating that "central management

---

[85] ICEF Circular Letter No. 19/79, February 9, 1979; letter from Charles Levinson to Roger Lyons, ASTMS national officer, February 28, 1979; and company personnel coordinator, interview in Basel, May 18, 1979.

Sandoz Prat denies any plans for reduced working time or plant closures." This was the full extent of ICEF and Swiss union "intervention." [86]

THE UNITED STATES CHEMICAL COMPANIES

As the ICEF has increased its activities within the United States, it has organized world councils for, and published claims of having influenced, the major United States-based multinational chemical concerns. These claims are scrutinized in this section.

E. I. du Pont de Nemours

Based in Wilmington, Delaware, Du Pont is the largest American chemical company and one of the five largest in the world. A Du Pont World Council was organized in London, March 7-8, 1974, at a meeting attended by delegates from twelve countries. Thomas E. Boyle, then president of the AFL-CIO International Chemical Workers Union (ICWU) was named chairman, and a representative of the Teamsters also participated.[87] Since then, Boyle has been succeeded in both positions by Frank D. Martino. It is not known how many representatives of Du Pont employees actually participated because the meeting was held in conjunction with other ICEF meetings.

After this meeting, the ICEF secretary general was quoted by a London newsletter writer as saying, "Du Pont would not be allowed to continue their international investment programme if they maintain their policy of anti-unionism." The same article reports that "Levinson sees this move as 'one of the most important multinational company actions we have so far taken'" and goes on to state that a prime aim of the ICEF's American affiliates (Teamsters and the ICWU) "will be to establish strong union organisations on those sites which are . . . in the hands of independent unions dominated by loyal Du Pont employees." [88]

Actually, an effective ICEF Du Pont World Council would be most difficult to arrange. A majority of the employees at Du

[86] Letter from Sandoz personnel executive to one of the authors, July 4, 1978; UGT letter to the ICEF, February 10, 1978; and ICEF telegram to the UGT, February 22, 1978.

[87] *The International Chemical Worker*, April 1974, p. 1.

[88] *Chemical Insight*, Mike Hyde's perspective on the international chemical industry, No. 50 (late March 1974), p. 1.

Pont's more than one hundred plants and laboratories in the United States are nonunion; workers in about thirty other plants are represented by local independent unions. The ICWU, an ICEF affiliate, represents only five Du Pont plants in the United States and two in Canada, and other AFL-CIO unions represent two additional plants. The Teamsters have no representation in Du Pont.

As part of his long and unsuccessful campaign to induce local independent unions of Du Pont employees to affiliate with his organization, Thomas E. Boyle, former president of the ICWU, offered in 1971

> as an officer and Co-chairman of the Chemical Section of the Geneva-based International Federation of Chemical and General Workers' Unions, to do my best to bring about a world-wide meeting of all unions having bargaining relationships with Du Pont. The idea has already received endorsement from some of the foreign unions involved, with the promise of almost total cooperation.[89]

A similar proposal was apparently sent to officers of the local independents by Boyle in which he announced that "this matter has already been broached to the president and secretary-general of the ICF with only details to be worked out."[90] Nothing, however, came of these efforts. Meanwhile, Du Pont workers in Kinston, North Carolina, overwhelmingly voted against union representation by the ICWU, and those at Chattanooga rejected representation by the Teamsters, another ICEF affiliate.

The first ICEF activity regarding Du Pont that we have uncovered occurred in 1971. At that time, the employers' federation and chemical union in West Germany were bargaining, and a four-hour strike occurred. Some Du Pont employees were involved. The secretary general sent a telegram pledging support by American unions. This telegram was put into a union handbill.[91] It is difficult to understand, given the union weakness in Du Pont, how such support could be generated.

A second "intervention" occurred in late 1977 when the ASTMS was successfully unionizing supervisors at Du Pont's Northern Ireland complex. Levinson wrote a circular letter castigating the

---

[89] Mimeographed circular from Thomas E. Boyle, president, International Chemical Workers Union, to "Members of Du Pont Independent Unions," October 1, 1971. Copy in authors' possession.

[90] Copy in authors' possession.

[91] Interviews in Wilmington, Delaware, and Geneva, Switzerland, July 5 and August 31, 1973.

company for its opposition to such unionization and promising the worldwide support of Du Pont unions in support of ASTMS.[92]

In the United States, the major current attempt to unionize Du Pont is being carried on by the United Steelworkers, following that union's 1973 merger with District 50, then an independent union. The latter organization had almost as many chemical workers enrolled—about seventy-five thousand—at the time of the merger as had the ICWU.[93] The Steelworkers' main initial thrust was to attempt to take over the local independent unions of Du Pont and more recently to organize Du Pont's plants in the south. Thus far, the only result has been that the employees at the one Du Pont plant represented by the Steelworkers voted to decertify the union.

District 50 maintained a nominal affiliation with the ICEF, but the Steelworkers did not continue that affiliation after the merger. The Steelworkers were not represented at the 1976 ICEF Congress. Although fifteen "observer" delegate seats were reserved for a "Du Pont Council'" delegation,[94] the only Du Pont employee representatives present were from Germany and the two Canadian plants represented by the International Chemical Workers Union.

The ICEF position in Du Pont could, however, improve materially in the future. Pursuant to the 1976 amendments to the German codetermination law, which allows unions to select a proportion of the worker delegates to supervisory boards of corporations (formerly the plant employees elected all such delegates), IG Chemie nominated Levinson to Du Pont's German company's supervisory board. He was duly elected and made vice-chairman of the board. This has undoubtedly enhanced his prestige and that of the ICEF. The propaganda value has been utilized to the fullest, as would be expected.[95] Levinson's election to Du Pont's German company's supervisory board could possibly also induce the Steelworkers to affiliate with the ICEF for its

---

[92] See Nick Garnett, "Du Pont document angers ASTMS," *Financial Times*, November 4, 1977, p. 12; and "Du Pont and ASTMS. Ways of making you vote," *Economist*, November 5, 1977, p. 120.

[93] The ICWU has since lost a considerable number of members to the unions, particularly in Canada, and today may have less than sixty thousand.

[94] *ICF 16th Statutory Congress*, last unnumbered page listing delegations.

[95] See, e.g., ICEF Circular Letter No. 144/77, October 18, 1977, and No. 83/78, May 29, 1978; "The trade union jet set," *Economist*, October 15, 1977, p. 89; and "A critic at Du Pont," *Business Week*, October 17, 1977, p. 48.

chemical union members. It continues to reassess a long-held position of declining to do so but has taken no action.[96]

Union Carbide

The secretary general of the ICEF has claimed without reference to dates that he acted to prevent New York-headquartered Union Carbide, the second largest United States company, from shipping chemical products from Europe during a strike in the United States. He asserts that, through discussion with Union Carbide's international division in Lausanne, Switzerland, he did this on behalf of ICEF's affiliate the ICWU. He also refers to a "consumer information campaign." [97]

The reference must be to the strikes at Union Carbide in 1966-67, in which the prime issue was an attempt by a coalition of fourteen unions under the leadership of the AFL-CIO Industrial Union Department to force Union Carbide to bargain with the coalition on a coordinated, multiplant basis. The strikes failed in their purpose, with settlements achieved on the traditional plant-by-plant relationships and contract expiration dates set farther apart than they had been hitherto. The ICWU was involved only in one small plant in Sisterville, West Virginia. The 250 workers there struck for two hundred days without achieving any alteration in the bargaining structure.[98]

The ICEF secretary's claim that he achieved an agreement with the company officials not to ship products overseas is contradicted by those officials.[99] They confirm that he contacted the management of Carbide's European affiliate and that Carbide did draw upon its European sources of ferro alloys to supply the needs of

---

[96] In a letter dated March 21, 1974, to the authors, Walter J. Burke, then (but since retired) secretary-treasurer, United Steelworkers, states that his union, long a major affiliate of the International Metalworkers' Federation, was not and had no plans to become an affiliate of the ICEF. In a letter dated October 12, 1977, however, Lynn R. Williams, international secretary, states: "We have not sought affiliation with [ICEF]. . . . We . . . continue to review the possibility of affiliation with the ICEF." On July 9, 1979, Williams wrote the authors that "our position in relation to possible affiliation with the ICEF remains as set out in my letter of October 12, 1977."

[97] Levinson, *International Trade Unionism*, p. 113.

[98] This strike is fully described in William N. Chernish, *Coalition Bargaining*, Industrial Research Unit Major Study, No. 45 (Philadelphia: Industrial Research Unit, The Wharton School, University of Pennsylvania, 1969), pp. 110-31.

[99] Letter to the authors, October 22, 1973.

customers in the United States. Beyond that, however, the facts appear quite different.

During the strike, the AFL-CIO Executive Council declared a boycott against Carbide products, and Levinson promptly proclaimed an extension of it worldwide. In neither case was a boycott effective, perhaps because much of Carbide production is not sold to the consumer. Levinson contacted Carbide's Switzerland office to offer to suspend the boycott if management would assure him that product would not be diverted to America from European sources. No assurances were given, and some product did continue to be diverted, all of which was nonchemical. With only two relatively small chemical facilities included in the plants on strike, at which near normal production was maintained by salaried employees, Carbide did not divert chemical production from Europe. The AFL-CIO Industrial Union Department considered the strike "its greatest failure to date." [100]

Since then, the ICEF has twice promised to form an ICEF Carbide World Council—first in February 1974, then in May 1977,[101] but we have found no evidence that this has occurred. Then in 1978, Levinson attempted to utilize the industrial health issue to obtain a meeting with the company. Signing his name "Dr. Charles Levinson," he wrote the chairman of Union Carbide Europe calling his attention to the alert issued by the United States Occupational Safety and Health Administration on the dangers of NIAX Catalyst ESN as a possible cause of urinary dysfunction in exposed workers. He requested that this official supply him with (1) names and addresses of all companies "around the world" to which ESN was sold; (2) all brand names under which ESN was sold; and (3) all plants outside the United States in which it was manufactured. He then noted that the ICEF had established an International Coordinating Committee for Occupational Health matters, and stated:

> Separately from our request for information concerning ESN, therefore, but looking to the longer-term future of preventing or alleviating other health problems, I believe a meeting at international level under the auspices of our Coordinating Committee between the ICEF member unions and responsible officers of the company to discuss the regularization of such measures could be very constructive. Certainly, such a recognized channel of com-

---

[100] Chernish, *Coalition Bargaining*, p. 109.

[101] See *ICF 15th Statutory Congress*, p. 78; and *ICF 16th Statutory Congress*, p. 97.

munication and action could have saved time, money, lives, and more generalized media publicity as in the present case.[102]

Levinson also enclosed a circular letter "alerting" ICEF affiliates to the possible danger.[103]

Union Carbide's European Company chairman replied, enclosing a statement issued by the parent company's New York headquarters on April 13, 1978, which noted that all affiliated companies and distributors were supplied with the United States government information about the chemical and that the company was making further tests on it to determine its possible health impact.[104] Levinson immediately wrote back noting that the Carbide "letter does not respond to our explicit request for a meeting . . . nor did it contain any indication of whether these sales were being suspended worldwide and what companies had been receiving them." The company replied that "all sales of NIAX Catalyst ESN were suspended worldwide and all customers were informed on the subject. We, therefore, see no need for a meeting." [105]

Eastman Kodak

In late 1974, the ICEF announced the formation of an Eastman Kodak World Council. Its only meeting occurred October 17-18, 1974, in Geneva; ICEF Executive Board members were already there in connection with the abortive merger meetings with the board of the now defunct International Federation of Petroleum and Chemical Workers.

Eastman is the world's largest maker of photographic equipment and a major producer of chemicals as well. Headquartered in Rochester, New York, with major plants in Tennessee, Colorado, and Texas, and other facilities in various locations in the United States, Eastman is noted for its generous wages, benefits, and profit-sharing plan. No union represents its employees in the United States. In its plants outside of the United States, such as in Canada, Mexico, Australia, Germany, the United Kingdom,

---

[102] Letter from Charles Levinson to J. C. Stephenson, chairman, Union Carbide Europe S.A., April 17, 1978.

[103] ICEF Circular Letter No. 66/78, April 17, 1978.

[104] Letter from Stephenson to Levinson, May 3, 1978, with attached Union Carbide Press Release.

[105] Letters from Levinson to Stephenson, May 12, 1978; and Stephenson to Levinson, May 30, 1978.

and France, Eastman deals with unions in accordance with the pertinent national laws where such unions have gained representation rights.

The AFL-CIO ICWU, which, like other American unions, has had no success in attracting Eastman employees in the United States, did succeed in 1945 in organizing the Eastman plant that has been located in Toronto, Canada, since the turn of the century. In 1976, however, the ICWU was replaced as bargaining agent there by Local No. 9159, United Steelworkers of America; then in January 1977, the employees left the Steelworkers and formed an independent union.[106]

On November 8, 1974, the ICEF issued a press release calling on members in the United Kingdom, France, Australia, Mexico, and the United States to "support the first strike since the Kodak Council's formation." [107] On the previous day, after union members voted to reject a company wage and benefit offer, the ICWU had struck the Canadian plant, the first strike in its seventy-six-year history. The ICEF asked affiliates to refuse overtime, prevent shipments from going into Canada, etc.[108] Because the Canadian plant is a self-contained operation and because, in any case, shipments that might be sent in would most likely come from the United States, where no Eastman employees are unionized, it is understandable that the company could report that it was unaware of any overt union action except letters of solidarity from other unions to the striking one.[109] The company also reported that retailers noticed no impact of a boycott of Kodak products instituted by the striking local union.[110] The plant was operated during the strike by bargaining unit members who crossed the picket line and by salaried personnel. The strike ended on December 23, 1974.[111]

---

[106] Letter from company personnel executive to one of the authors, January 26, 1977; "Canadian Kodak Workers Leave Steelworkers," *The Chemical Worker*, March 1978, p. 9.

[107] ICF Press Release, November 8, 1974. This action is also mentioned in the secretary general's report to the 1976 congress. See *ICF 16th Statutory Congress*, p. 99.

[108] ICF Press Release, November 8, 1974.

[109] Letter from company official to one of the authors, December 6, 1974.

[110] Letter from company official to one of the authors, January 26, 1977.

[111] *The International Chemical Worker*, January 1975, p. 2.

The ICEF has reported other alleged actions against Eastman Kodak. Thus, the secretary general's report to the 1973 ICEF Congress claims support in regard to a purported previous Canadian strike.[112] In fact, although there were threats of a strike, none actually occurred. Also in the book *International Trade Unionism*, it is stated:

> Also in May [1971], and in response to an appeal by ICF headquarters, the British Transport and General Workers' members and the German IG Chemie members working in the US Kodak subsidiaries, helped to prevent the shipment of film into France where the company's employees were on strike at the film-producing plant at Vincennes in the suburbs of Paris.[113]

The company, at our request, checked its files and found no evidence of overt action in Britain or Germany during the strike.[114] Moreover, the Transport and General Workers' Union (TGWU) was not the representative British union at Kodak Ltd. in 1971, for there was then a works association representing British Kodak workers. In addition, the union representing workers at Kodak AG, Germany was, and is, IG Metall, an affiliate of the International Metalworkers' Federation, not IG Chemie, which is an ICEF affiliate.[115]

In his report to the 1976 congress, the ICEF secretary general reports that the ICEF rendered assistance during Kodak strikes in France and Britain in January 1975 and during a second French Kodak strike in May 1976.[116] According to the company, there were no strikes at Kodak plants in France or Britain in 1975, nor was there any strike in France in 1976.[117]

Communist Activity. In May 1977, a meeting of Kodak union representatives from Britain, France, Spain, and Italy was held in Paris. The meeting was hosted by affiliates of the Communist CGT and was apparently organized by Communist party affiliates and/or sympathizers. The only English language story concerning it appeared in the British Communist party's news-

---

[112] *ICF 15th Statutory Congress*, p. 83.

[113] Levinson, *International Trade Unionism*, p. 115.

[114] Letter from company official to the authors, September 18, 1975.

[115] Letter from company official to the authors, January 26, 1977. IG Metall did, however, participate in the ICEF world council meeting, sending four delegates. *IMF News*, No. 25 (August 1974), p. 3.

[116] *ICF 16th Statutory Congress*, pp. 99, 101.

[117] Letter from company official to one of the authors, January 26, 1977.

paper.[118] The Association of Cinematograph, Television, and Allied Technicians, which won representation for a minority of employees at Kodak's British facility where the majority of workers are represented by the TGWU,[119] was involved in the meeting.

According to the newspaper story, the delegates vowed to prevent the restructuring of Kodak work and the alleged transfer of production from Britain to France. Much of the conference's attention was directed toward support of a strike in Britain at Grunwick Processing Laboratories, a film-processing company in North London where another British union was on strike for about two years in a vain attempt to win recognition.[120]

At the time of the Communist-sponsored Paris meeting, Kodak was indeed in the process of restructuring its operations, transferring some work from some plants to others, and reducing employment by attrition. According to what we have learned, about forty delegates from the United Kingdom, France, Italy, and Spain attended the meeting. The objective was to facilitate cooperation among the unions to oppose the restructuring and to encourage the exchange of economic and social information.

The delegates also voted to stage a concerted demonstration at Kodak plants during the week of May 30, 1977. Unions in each country were to decide upon the character of the demonstration. The only thing that occurred was a short protest meeting—less than one hour—of shop stewards at the camera plant in Stevenage, one of the three British Kodak facilities.[121]

The Dow Chemical Company

The Dow Chemical Company, headquartered in Midland, Michigan, is the fourth largest United States chemical producer, while worldwide, it ranks in the first ten.[122]

---

[118] Charles Brewster, "International Action Against Kodak," *Morning Star*, May 16, 1977.

[119] "ACTT Scores Victory," *Financial Times*, October 30, 1975, p. 16.

[120] This strike was the subject of numerous news stories, articles, and even books. Attempts to induce cooperation of unions internationally were without results.

[121] Eastman personnel executive, telephone interview, December 13, 1977.

[122] See Table VIII-1. In formation on the Dow ICEF World Council meeting is from various confidential interviews.

Dow is a truly multinational company. In 1975, for example, 44 percent of its sales were outside of the United States, and 41 percent of its 53,100 employees were based in other countries. Dow has forty-five manufacturing locations in the United States, including those of joint ventures, plus sixteen more in Canada. In Europe, it has major manufacturing facilities in Belgium, France, Germany, Greece, Italy, Portugal, Spain, Sweden, the United Kingdom, and Yugoslavia. It has plants in Morocco, Iran, Australia, New Zealand, Hong Kong, Indonesia, Japan, and four other Asian and six Latin American countries. Dow has adopted a considered policy of employing nationals to operate its facilities in the various countries. Thus, in 1975, 99 percent of its employees in Canada, 95 percent of those in Latin America, and 99 percent of those in Europe were citizens of the countries where they worked.[123]

In the United States, most of Dow's facilities operate non-union, but the two largest—Midland, Michigan, and Freeport (near Houston), Texas—are organized. The United Steelworkers, by virtue of its absorption of District 50, holds bargaining rights at Midland; a council of craft unions bargains at Freeport. The small ICWU also has bargaining rights at a few of the other facilities in the United States and Canada.

In Europe, Dow has maintained a relatively low profile and has not been heavily unionized. Not until 1976 did the ICEF attempt to convene a meeting of Dow union representatives, and this one seems to have been uneventful. It was called in late 1975 and met in Geneva on January 30, 1976, as part of the meeting of the ICEF Chemical Industry Division. A Dow World Council was formed at this meeting but apparently has not met since then.

About fifty people attended the meeting, including representatives from unions in Austria, Canada, France, Germany, Japan, Morocco, the Netherlands, Sweden, Switzerland, and the United States. The delegations were quite uneven; the largest number, twelve, came from Japan, five came from Germany, and no more than two from any other country attended. Most delegates were union representatives, not Dow employees. From the United States, the OCAW, which was then in the process of affiliating with the ICEF after years of support of the International Federation of Petroleum and Chemical Workers, sent a representative, but the United Steelworkers and the craft

---

[123] See *1975 Dow Annual Report to Stockholders* (Midland, Michigan, 1976).

unions, which represented the largest United States facilities, did not. Unions in the United Kingdom, Belgium, Italy, and Spain and those in Latin America, Asia (except Japan), Australia, and elsewhere in the Pacific were also not represented. Elwood D. Swisher, then a vice-president of the OCAW, but now retired, was elected council chairman, although the OCAW then represented only one Dow Canadian facility and one small United States one with 120 employees. The OCAW has since been decertified by the employees in the latter.

The only concrete results of the meeting appear to have been agreements to meet regularly (which has not occurred) and to exchange information. From what we could learn, reports were made by American, German, and Dutch delegates; it was emphasized that strikes by unions in one country to support workers in another were deemed impractical. The German and Dutch delegates argued that political strength to solve international problems was a sounder approach.

The secretary general of the ICEF gave an introductory speech, stressing his current role as an opponent of health hazards in plants and pollution of the environment and also of the alleged power of multinationals to move jobs and production facilities from one country to another and to set different wages and working conditions. Yet, unlike many such meetings, no grandiose press statement was issued. In view of its unrepresentative makeup, particularly for the United States, the Dow World Council is not likely to be very active in the near future. By mid-1979, it had not met again.

The only other mention of Dow by the ICEF that has come to our attention was a paragraph in a 1978 ICEF circular letter, which includes Dow among companies allegedly involved in disputes. Affiliates of the ICEF allegedly thanked other affiliates through the ICEF for "effective support." Dow officials know of no dispute in that period and certainly were unaware of any such activity.[124]

Monsanto

St. Louis-based Monsanto is a major American chemical multinational [125] but has not apparently been very high on the ICEF

---

[124] ICEF Circular Letter No. 59/78, March 28, 1978; Dow personnel department officials, interview in Philadelphia, June 8, 1978.

[125] See Table VIII-1 for sales and number of employees.

list. Its name does not appear in the index of Levinson's book *International Trade Unionism* or on pre-1979 ICEF lists of world councils. Monsanto has, however, had two brushes with the ICEF, both involving job security, Europe's most critical labor issue.

Wales Plant Reductions. In late December 1971, Monsanto announced that it would shut down several units at its plant in Ruabon, Wales. Some 250 terminations, about one-fourth of the work force, were involved, of which 100 were in silicon operations. Since the company was retaining its silicon operations at Ghent, Belgium, British unions and the press claimed that this was a transfer of production, and they used it as an example of what would happen if Britain joined the Common Market, a move which the unions were then opposing. The publicity resulted in a conference between Monsanto and British government officials, which satisfied the latter that the shutdown was caused by a business downturn, not a production move. Termination issues and benefits were discussed with local union representatives.

In January, Monsanto officials began receiving numerous communications from the ICEF secretary general, who was attempting to organize a high-level meeting among top Monsanto officials, Jack Jones (then the head of the TGWU in Britain) and other British union officials. The company declined, noting that it had settled the matter with British union and government officials.

Nevertheless, Levinson persisted. He called company executives from the airport on one occasion and demanded a meeting, threatening a press conference criticizing Monsanto unless the meeting was held. Monsanto management refused, and no press conference was held.

At this point, a Monsanto manager who was tangentially involved in the situation and who had met Levinson at a conference was approached by him and agreed to lunch with him. Levinson then issued a press release stating that he had intervened and solved the problem. According to his version, Monsanto was warned of a "strong reaction of ICF affiliates around the world . . .":

> The communications between the European management and ICF proved understanding and cooperative. A vice-president promptly travelled from California to London and met with union officials and the Welsh Minister of Labour. As a result of these discussions

and the intervention at the level of the parent, agreement was reached which was unanimously endorsed by the lads in the plant. The agreement provided for an acceptable process of transfer, accelerated retirement and other conditions which removed much of the hardship and discrimination which were originally present. Further, the company agreed to continue its operations in Wales and did not close down the plant.[126]

The ICEF secretary general then issued a press release claiming that, together with the TGWU, it had countered a Monsanto plan to transfer facilities from Wales to the Netherlands and to California. *Business Europe,* a management publication, reported this claim in a lead story without contacting the company.[127]

Monsanto reacted strongly to the *Business Europe* article and succeeded in getting this publication to print a short story entitled "Monsanto Disputes ICF Claim," which recites the following facts, which could easily have been checked beforehand:

—Monsanto had no plans to shut down completely the Wales plant.

—Monsanto had no plans to move plants from Wales to California or to the Netherlands.

—The questions of termination benefits were settled beforehand with the local unions involved.

—Neither Levinson nor the ICEF was consulted or involved in the bargaining over terminations, or present when Monsanto officials discussed their plans with officials of the British government.[128]

In addition to these points, our investigation has determined that Monsanto's only California vice-president is a regional representative who is not a corporate officer and has no authority to represent the company on any matter outside of his territory. He did not travel to Europe to meet with union officials or anybody else. Monsanto's headquarters are in the St. Louis, Mis-

---

[126] ICF Circular Letter No. 45/72, June 13, 1972.

[127] "European unions step up global strategy to counter multinational companies' power," *Business Europe,* August 4, 1972, p. 241.

[128] *Business Europe,* August 25, 1972, p. 272.

souri, area, as they always have been, and that is where the corporate staff is located.[129]

Nylon Plants Closings. The shakedown in the European man-made fiber industry resulted in Monsanto's retrenching by closing its nylon plants there and thus following the example of Akzo, Hoechst, Rhône-Poulenc, Montedison, Du Pont, and others that had cut back operations. The Monsanto announcement, made early in May 1979, affected some 2,300 jobs; 1,500 in the United Kingdom, where four facilities are located, and the balance in two plants in Luxembourg and Germany.[130]

During the first week in April and therefore before any announcement was made, Charles Levinson, who was in the United States, twice telephoned Monsanto's world headquarters in St. Louis and demanded that rumors of plant closings be denied or that discussions be initiated with the ICEF and the various unions on an international basis. Otherwise, he promised to return to Europe to organize a campaign to prevent these closures. His telephone call was handled by a Monsanto public relations staff member who advised him that the matter was still under consideration.[131]

The ICEF Monsanto Permanent World Council was organized at a meeting in Luxembourg on April 20, 1979, at which John Castegnaro, president of the Onofhängegen Gewerkschaftsbund Letzeburg (OGBL), was made chairman. No British or American unionists were present at this meeting, and the only German unionist present was from IG Chemie, whereas the German Monsanto employees principally involved in the nylon situation are represented by Gewerkschaft Textil-Bekleidung (the Textile and Clothing Workers' Union). A cable was sent to Monsanto headquarters demanding a meeting to discuss the closure and safety matters and threatening strikes and civil suits if the company refused. The ICEF also added threats to prevent diversion of

---

[129] Based on interviews with Monsanto officials in St. Louis and Brussels, May and August 1973, and a reading of the company's annual reports. Despite the retraction by *Business Europe*, the *Wall Street Journal*, two years later, repeated in a lead article the Levinson version of the story. See Richard F. Janssen, "Global Clout. How One Man Helps Unions Match Wits with Multinationals," *Wall Street Journal*, June 17, 1974, p. 1.

[130] Sue Cameron, "Monsanto to Close Europe Nylon Plants," and "Why Small is not Beautiful for Monsanto," *Financial Times*, May 10, 1979, pp. 1 and 8, respectively; "Monsanto to Shut Europe Nylon Units," *New York Times*, June 23, 1979, p. 28.

[131] Our facts are based upon various documents relating to the case that have come into our possession.

production to other plants and to ban overtime.[132] These were, of course, not only idle threats but would be ridiculous to institute against a company whose problem is insufficient business. The company did not reply.

Levinson did, however, gain access to a meeting with the company when, late in May, he appeared with Castegnaro as an advisor of the OGBL for a discussion of the Luxembourg plant closing at a tripartite meeting that had been called by the Duchy's then prime minister pursuant to that country's legislation. Anxious to mitigate any impact on the business climate, the prime minister kept the discussion within strict limits. The company then made it clear in private discussions both with the union and the government that Levinson and the ICEF represented no one and that his presence might inhibit any sale of the plant to another company. Levinson did not appear at the next tripartite meeting on June 6, but he was again present (albeit silent) at the final tripartite meeting on June 20, after which discussions on handling the plant closings began directly between the company and the Luxembourg unions, with the Duchy's Ministries of Labor and Economics as nonparticipating observers. Meanwhile, both in the United Kingdom and in Germany, Monsanto handled closure issues and alternatives with union and works council representatives whose concern was with their particular plants, not those elsewhere. No ICEF involvement occurred in these countries.

American Cyanamid

Headquartered in northern New Jersey near New York City, American Cyanimid is a large multinational chemical, pharmaceutical, and related products company; it had sales of $2.7 billion and 43,968 employees in 1978.[133] Subsidiaries include Lederle Laboratories and Formica. Cyanamid, like Monsanto, was an early ICEF publicity target. In a situation involving a strike at the Lederle Laboratories Division, the ICEF secretary general wrote:

> In the case of Cyanamid a number of affiliates published product lists and directives to abstain from purchasing such products in

---

[132] ICEF Circular Letter No. 56/79, April 25, 1979. The ICEF had previously attacked Monsanto on industrial health issues. See ICEF Circular Letter No. 18/78, January 23, 1978.

[133] *Fortune*, Vol. 99 (May 7, 1979), pp. 274-75.

their journals as part of a worldwide campaign. The conflict ended with full satisfaction of ICWU's demands.[134]

No details of time or place are given. Reference, however, is clearly to the strike that occurred at Lederle's facility in Pearl River, New York, beginning on August 30, 1969, and not ending until January 24, 1970. The Geneva, Switzerland, correspondent of *Dun's Review*, an American business magazine, reported that "Charles Levinson is fashioning an increasingly powerful global labor group." He added:

> So far, however, ICF's most effective weapon has been the consumer boycott. It used one earlier this year, for instance against American Cyanamid whose Pearle River . . . Lederle division was battling ICF affiliate International Chemical Workers Union over plant-by-plant bargaining methods. ICF persuaded affiliates in Sweden and Germany, where large Cyanamid plants are located, to sponsor consumer boycotts of Cyanamid products. A long strike ended with Lederle reportedly meeting union demands.[135]

In actual fact, the strike in question lasted five months; the employees returned to work without any significant increase in wages and benefits over what the company had offered prior to the strike; and, above all, the union's attempt to alter the company's plant-by-plant bargaining posture failed. In 1979, Cyanamid, as it always has, continues to bargain on a plant-by-plant basis in the United States, with contract expiration dates scattered both throughout the year and in different years.

During the strike, Levinson sent a telegram to the president of Cyanamid indicating that, if the company's manner of bargaining was not changed, it could expect a worldwide boycott of Lederle products. The company neither replied to the telegram nor experienced any loss of sales. To the best of their knowledge, company officials believe that no one from *Dun's Review* ever attempted to contact them for their story.[136]

Two other mentions of Cyanamid operations by the ICEF have occurred. In the secretary general's report to the 1976

---

[134] Levinson, *International Trade Unionism*, p. 113.

[135] "Labor's Global Organizer," *Dun's Review*, November 1970, p. 67.

[136] One of the authors was in close touch with Cyanamid officials during this strike. The facts concerning the above statements are easily provable by local press reports during the strike and by a review of Cyanamid labor contract expiration dates. It was the *Dun's Review* article, perhaps one of the most irresponsible of many of the same type written by business journals, that initially spurred our current research into the ICEF activities and claims.

congress, it is stated that, during a strike at a Formica plant in France, the ICEF sent "messages of support and solidarity" and intervened and protested "to parent and/or subsidiary." [137] The report also states that a "Formica World Council" would be formed in the spring of 1977.[138] In response to a query, company officials wrote the authors that "we can find no evidence of any activity by Charles Levinson in December 1975." [139] We have found no record of such a world council being formed.

The remaining incident concerned a Cyanamid West Virginia operation in which lead is utilized. The company barred women of childbearing potential from certain operations because of potential damage to a fetus. Five women later sued the company claiming that they were forced to be sterilized or lose their jobs.[140] In fact, the company had agreed to provide jobs elsewhere in the plant with no wage loss, and the company doctor had advised the women not to initiate the action.[141] Levinson used the incident to write a circular letter castigating the company, alleging that similar "discrimination" was "widespread as a tactic," and urging all affiliates "to notify the Secretariat" of such incidents.[142]

NL Industries

NL Industries, Inc. (formerly National Lead Company), is a New York-based multinational firm with interests in the chemical, pigment, and specialty metal industries. In 1978, it had sales of $1.9 billion and 24,700 employees.[143]

In February 1976, the OCAW struck an NL titanium dioxide plant in New Jersey. On August 3, 1976, after the OCAW af-

---

[137] *ICF 16th Statutory Congress*, pp. 100, 102.

[138] *Ibid.*, p. 97. Levinson listed Formica as a French company, although he shows the Cyanamid connection. At that time, Cyanamid owned only a minority interest, but it has since acquired full control.

[139] Letter from Harold T. Walker, manager, Labor Relations, American Cyanamid Company, to the authors, January 19, 1977.

[140] See Gail Bronson, "Bitter Reaction. Issue of Fetal Damage Stirs Women Workers at Chemical Plants," *Wall Street Journal*, February 9, 1979, p. 1.

[141] Company executive, interview in Wayne, N.J., June 28, 1979.

[142] ICEF Circular Letter No. 21/79, January 17, 1979. Levinson also claimed that a strike of the ICWU at Bound Brook, New Jersey, forced Cyanamid to accept "a thorough revision of health procedures at the plant." In fact, the issues involved wages. See ICEF Circular Letter No. 20/79, February 16, 1979.

[143] *Fortune*, Vol. 99 (May 7, 1979), pp. 271-75.

filiated with the ICEF, the secretary general of the ICEF wrote affiliates claiming that the issues in dispute were "representation and attempts to transfer production facilities to other more hospitable parts of the United States." He then states:

> We ask our affiliated organizations in Europe representing membership in National Lead Industries, Inc. to monitor and prevent the shipment of Titanium Dioxide to customers not normally serviced by the units. National Lead Inc. has produced a brochure for worldwide distribution in which it assures its customers that it can continue to supply them with Titanium Dioxide despite the strike in the United States because of the increased output of their European plants and particularly their German plants. We, therefore, request our colleagues in Germany, Belgium and Norway to intervene and prevent the shipment of production to the United States and to other parts of the world not normally catered for. The company often called Kronos has Titanium Dioxide operations in the following locations: Germany-Nordenhan, Leverkusen, Belgium-Longerbrugge, Norway-Fredrichsted. This strike appears destined to be of long duration for the Company obviously is seeking a show down on the issue with the Union. We, therefore, appeal for immediate intervention to boycott shipments by this Company of Titanium Dioxide.[144]

It is correct that the strike was destined to be a long one. It lasted one year and was marked by violence during its first six months when the company operated the plant. In September 1976, the plant was closed because the company did not need the production. The issues, however, involved plant manning and work rules, plus the insistence on the part of the company that more economic methods be instituted.[145] Given the heavy capital investment in such a facility, companies do not find it feasible "to transfer production to other more hospitable parts of the United States."

As to the reaction of European unions to the ICEF boycott request, the company reported in November while the strike was continuing:

> To date there has been no manifestation of any response among our European Titanium Dioxide plants to Levinson's request of August 3, 1976. Moreover, our European management group is not aware of any such reaction of interest expressed by the Euro-

---

[144] ICF Circular Letter No. 100/76, August 3, 1976, pp. 1-2.

[145] M. L. Moore, director, Employee Relations, NL Industries, Inc., telephone interview, December 10, 1976. See also "Sayreville, N.J., successful in shutting down NL Industries plant," *Oil, Chemical & Atomic Union News* (OCAW), December 1976, p. 4.

pean locals to this request. Such is not to say that there will not be cooperation with Levinson's request, but only that it has not occurred to date.[146]

No further Levinson communications were apparently issued, and no interference with production, or even expressions of interest, occurred in other plants during the balance of the strike, according to company records.

Schering-Plough

The Schering-Plough Company in the United States is an independent pharmaceutical concern that developed after being seized from its German forebearers both in World War I and World War II. There is no relation to its large German former parent or to other companies bearing the name "Schering" around the world. In Europe, its operations, established since World War II, are under the name "Essex," after the county in New Jersey where Schering has long been headquartered. In the early 1970s, Schering merged with Plough, a manufacturer of several popular nonprescription drugs and other products. In 1978, it had sales of $1.1 billion and 17,900 employees.[147]

Besides its several plants in the United States, Schering has facilities in France, Spain, Italy, Belgium, Australia, Brazil, Argentina, Mexico, Colombia, and Chile. In the United States, the Schering plants are almost completely nonunion, but Plough's are heavily unionized. Abroad the situation varies.

Schering's only brush with the ICEF and Levinson occurred during a strike at its plant in Caen, France, in 1973. On December 20 of that year, Levinson addressed a letter to the company's "Managing Director" (no such title exists in the United States) in New Jersey announcing that he had "examined the conflict carefully and consider[s] that the demands of the French employees are extremely justified and moderate." He further declared that "the position adopted by the French management is ill-advised and obviously reflects an attitude of arrogance," and promising full support of "five million members of ICF" to the strikers, he urged that the corporate officials intervene.[148]

In fact, the strike lasted fifteen days in December 1973. The issue was the size of the cost-of-living adjustment. Only about

---

[146] Letter from M. L. Moore to one of the authors, November 8, 1976.

[147] *Fortune*, Vol. 99 (May 7, 1979), pp. 278-79.

[148] Copy in authors' possession.

100 of the 270 employees went on strike. The situation was complicated because of new union representatives (both the CGT and CFDT were involved) and the illness of the personnel manager. Settlement was achieved with a bonus over the company offer but below the union demands. The strike ended on December 21, 1973, one day after Levinson wrote his letter and five days before the company received it. No reply was issued by the company.

Eli Lilly

Eli Lilly and Company is a major American pharmaceutical company headquartered in Indianapolis. In 1978, its sales totaled $1.9 billion, and average employment was 25,400.[149] Lilly operates worldwide, with manufacturing facilities in several European and Latin American countries, Taiwan, Japan, Australia, and New Zealand.[150]

Eli Lilly is noted for its generous wage and benefit policies and operates nonunion in the United States. Elsewhere, it deals with unions where employees desire it or the national law so requires. Not surprisingly, therefore, international unions, with one exception, have not attempted to contact Lilly management.

That exception occurred in late 1976 in Spain, where a female employee in the personnel department tried to unionize the plant after becoming friendly with the local official of the socialist UGT. The latter contacted the ICEF secretary general, who, apparently unaware that Lilly plants are overwhelmingly nonunion, sent a telex to the management in Spain, threatening strikes in Lilly plants around the world unless the discharged employee was reinstated. Lilly management did not answer the telex, and of course, nothing resulted from the idle threat.[151]

AVON PRODUCTS IN AUSTRALIA

Avon, headquartered in New York City, is the world's largest cosmetics company. In 1978, it had sales of $2 billion and 31,000

---

[149] *Fortune*, Vol. 99 (May 7, 1979), pp. 276-77.

[150] Eli Lilly and Company, *Annual Report 1977* (Indianapolis, 1978), p. 44.

[151] Lilly personnel officials, interviews in Indianapolis, June 1978.

employees.[152] Avon has facilities throughout the world. With few exceptions, it markets its products directly to the consumer, utilizing representatives who are often housewives, "moonlighters" (those holding second jobs), or others working part-time.

Avon operates nonunion in the United States and in most countries where it is able to do so under national legislation or policy. The company prides itself on having factories and warehouses that are immaculate and on paying wages and benefits that are at least competitive. Considerable emphasis is also placed by the company on treating employees well and on its concern for their problems. As a result, Avon's policy of operating nonunion has not been seriously challenged in most countries.

Australian Organizing Campaign

In Australia, however, a determined attempt was made to unionize Avon and several other cosmetics and drug firms by pressuring managements to agree to provisions that would require union membership as a condition of employment. This problem arose in 1971 and continued over a period of nearly four years. It involved an attempt by the ICEF to intervene and successful legal action by Avon to prevent a crippling boycott.

Avon's Australian factory is in a suburb of Sydney. Such drug companies as Hoffmann-La Roche, Pfizer, Abbott, Eli Lilly, Upjohn, Bristol-Meyers, and Richardson-Merrill also operate in the general area. In 1971, the Australian Workers' Union, the Shop Assistants' and Warehouse Employees' Federation of Australia, and the Seamen's and Packers' Union set out to unionize these and other pharmaceutical firms. The approach was to demand that each company write a letter to the employees encouraging union membership and to give union representatives an opportunity to meet with the employees in small groups in order to induce them to unionize.[153]

Most companies involved did agree to this procedure, but despite winning over some employees in a few companies, the

---

152 *Fortune*, Vol. 99 (May 7, 1979), pp. 274-75.

153 We are grateful to G. H. Sorrell, Dennis Mortimer, and Linda Walters of the University of Sydney for research on this case, and J. Alvin Wakefield, vice-president, Personnel, Avon Products, Inc., and members of his staff for answering numerous questions about the case.

union drive has been generally unsuccessful, and in Avon, particularly so. The Avon managing director did write a letter urging that employees give serious consideration to union membership and offered the unions twelve in-plant meetings with employees on various days in April 1971. After seven of these meetings, the unions gave up because the response was so poor.[154]

The unions nevertheless continued their pressure on Avon to sign an agreement. In June 1972, following the promotion of the Australian managing director to an executive position in New York and the appointment of an executive from Avon's British facility to succeed him, the unions demanded that the company agree to a contract that would require all Avon employees to become union members as a condition of employment. Noting that it had sent two letters to employees urging that they consider union membership and had offered the unions twelve days for meetings with employees, the company replied that it "totally rejects the suggestion" made by the unions that it had pressured employees "to discourage them from exercising their individual right to belong to any organization." It therefore advised the unions that "no individual can or should be compelled to join or not to join any organization against his or her will," and therefore, it "cannot be a party" to the proposed agreement.[155]

The Boycott and Court Order

The unions continued their drive sporadically during 1973 and 1974. In the fall of 1974, the Trades and Labour Council of New South Wales coordinated the union drive. After meetings with management and mediation by the New South Wales Industrial Commission, another letter was sent to employees in October 1974 encouraging them to consider union membership. Like the previous letters, its contents were agreed to beforehand by the unions, but it had no apparent effect. Then on December 23, 1974, the traffic manager of Avon was informed that a ban (boycott) had been imposed on the movement of all Avon goods. The ban was very effective. The trucking

---

[154] Copies of all documents and letters noted in the text are in authors' possession, including various union and company memoranda relating to these events. There are no serious disagreements in union and company sources on the basic facts involved.

[155] Letter from company to the Shop Assistants' and Warehouse Employees' Federation of Australia, July 28, 1972.

employees, dockworkers, and others participated, and Avon goods were tied up in various depots and warehouses and on the docks.

Avon had long been aware of such a possibility and had decided that an action under labor legislation in Australia would achieve no relief. It therefore moved under the common law of contracts to enjoin the boycott on the grounds that it interfered with the fulfilling of contracts by transport companies, warehouse proprietors, and others. Conspiracy was also alleged, and evidence presented that $500,000 (Aus.) in goods and materials were tied up by the ban.[156]

On December 31, 1974, Judge Isaacs of the Supreme Court of New South Wales overruled the unions' objection to themselves as parties. He further ruled that he was satisfied that the unions had combined and conspired to disrupt and to injure the business operations of Avon and had induced breach of contracts and had wrongfully interfered with contracts between Avon and other companies. Accordingly, he issued injunctions restraining the unions from directly or indirectly continuing the bans, which were preventing Avon's receiving delivery of goods, and from combining to restrict the business of delivery or warehouse companies.[157] The bans were lifted, and Avon remains nonunion in Australia, as do most of the other drug companies in the Sydney area, although union organizing efforts have continued.

ICEF Involvement

About this time, the ICEF was attempting to achieve increased membership affiliation in Australia and had induced the

---

[156] For an analysis of legal action under Australian civil law, rather than labor law, prior to the Avon case in order to overcome such boycotts, see J. H. Portus, "Civil Law and the Settlement of Disputes," *Journal of Industrial Relations* (Australia), Vol. 15 (September 1973), pp. 281-95. In 1977, the Trade Practices Act of 1974 was amended to subject secondary boycotts of this nature to legal attack under the antitrust laws.

[157] Avon Products Pty. Ltd. v. Federated Clerks' Union of Australia (N.S.W. Branch). The ban was lifted on January 4, 1975. On January 8, 1975, settlement terms were reached between Avon and the union solicitors (lawyers), and this was signed before the Registrar of the Supreme Court, New South Wales, on that date. Letter from J. Alvin Wakefield, vice-president, Personnel, Avon Products, Inc., to one of the authors, May 20, 1977. For further documentation on the boycott, see "The Avon Lady Won't Call this Christmas," *Daily Commercial News and Shipping List* (Sydney), No. 24854 (December 16, 1974); and "Ban Ties Up Cosmetics," *The Australian*, December 19, 1974.

Australian Workers' Union to affiliate with it. In his report to the 1976 congress, the secretary general claims that, in January 1975, he sent "messages of support and solidarity," effectuated "boycotts of transfer of stocks and inventories—both actual and preparatory," and provided "public information campaigns and media materials." [158] In fact, a circular letter was dispatched from Geneva dated January 13, 1975.[159] This was almost two weeks after the judge issued his ruling, one week after the boycott had been permanently lifted, and five days after a final decree was agreed upon and filed with the Registrar of the Supreme Court.

In the circular letter, Levinson asks the ICEF affiliates to send telegrams of solidarity to the Australian Workers' Union. The executive of this union reported to one of our interviewers that "only about six such communications were received." [160] The circular letter also requests that a "Consumer Information Campaign on Avon products should be begun." The company reported that "Avon *did not* experience any disruption in normal business activity either in Australia *or* at any other overseas location as a result of any action taken by the ICF (now the ICEF) in support of local union attempts to organize Avon employees in Australia." [161] On the other hand, officials of Australian unions give the ICEF credit for assisting them to obtain information about other drug companies that have plants in the Sydney area.[162]

ACTIVITY IN JAPAN

Until the demise of the International Federation of Petroleum and Chemical Workers in 1976, the Japanese chemical unions were split in their affiliation between the ICEF and the IFPCW, and the petroleum unions were affiliated with the latter. Now these Japanese unions are all affiliated with the ICEF and have, in addition, formed a coordinating and liaison body, the ICEF-JAF, to which most are also affiliated.

---

[158] *ICF 16th Statutory Congress*, pp. 99, 102.

[159] ICF Circular Letter No. 5/75, January 13, 1975.

[160] Interview, spring 1976.

[161] Letter from J. Alvin Wakefield to one of the authors, May 20, 1977. (Emphasis in original.)

[162] Interviews in Australia by cooperating group, University of Sydney, spring 1977.

We have found reference to only two claimed ICEF actions. The first involved Kanebo, the huge textile and synthetic fiber company.[163] Like other such Japanese concerns, Kanebo has experienced declining revenues as a result of competition from Korean, Taiwanese, and Southeast Asian firms and as a result of the worldwide glut in the synthetic fiber market. This has forced the company to reduce production and to take other measures to curtail its activities and employment not only in Japan but in other countries where it operates. In May 1975, the ICEF secretary general claims, the ICEF protested to the company against its "anti-union policy," sent "messages of support and solidarity," and intervened and protested "to parent and/or local management in solidarity with stoppage in other countries."[164] Our information indicates that the usual cables were sent during some restructuring of operations and some labor difficulties in Southeast Asia.[165]

The other ICEF claim involves Goka Roren, the Japanese Federation of Synthetic Chemistry Workers' Unions, and a subsidiary of the German Pieroth Company. In a circular letter, the president of Goka Roren is quoted as declaring that "decisive" assistance was received from the ICEF and the IG Chemie in settling a dispute.[166]

Our investigation determined that the strike occurred in late March and early April 1977 and lasted about two weeks. It involved a dispute over whether the pay system for certain field employees, presumably sales personnel, should be on a commission or fixed-rate basis. It was settled by local negotiations.[167] Indeed, it is difficult to conceive, given the nature of Japanese labor relations, that local arrangements would not be determinative.

CONCLUSION

The claims of the ICEF secretary general that major corporate activity, policies, or actions in the chemical industry

---

[163] The ICEF has assumed jurisdiction of synthetic fiber workers in Japan and elsewhere, although such activity would seem within the purview of the International Textile, Garment, and Leather Workers' Federation.

[164] *ICF 16th Statutory Congress*, pp. 100, 102.

[165] Company personnel, interview in Tokyo, June 1976.

[166] ICEF Circular Letter No. 106/77, October 6, 1977.

[167] Information supplied by German contact.

were influenced by the ICEF's coordinating role across national boundaries obviously cannot be supported by our research. Rather, these claims appear to be, almost without exception, either exaggerations or total figments of a fertile imagination, combined with an exceptional flair for publicity.

On the other hand, the election of the ICEF secretary general to the supervisory board of the Du Pont German company is a genuine triumph for him, a major public relations coup, and an advance for the international trade union movement. As we discuss in our concluding chapter, it seems obvious that the international secretariats and others interested in the expansion of international union influence have determined that their opportunity for enhanced power and influence stems largely from their ability to attract government support and to use government mechanisms. Codetermination is an obvious such mechanism that can be manipulated for that purpose.

Levinson has also correctly understood that industrial health and safety is an issue that can unite unions over national boundaries. The ICEF has sponsored meetings on this subject that have attracted officials of various national governments and of the World Health Organization; this issue, as noted several times in the chapter, has been stressed whenever the opportunity has arisen. This point will also be clear in the following chapters dealing with rubber, petroleum, and related industries.

CHAPTER IX

The Rubber Tire Industry

Major companies in the rubber tire industry have long been among the great multinational corporations of the world. The huge investments required in plants, transport costs, different wheel sizes of automobiles manufactured in different countries, and nationalistic policies of many governments which demand domestic production of automobiles and related parts—all ensure that a relatively small number of companies exist in this industry, and that such companies will have plants in many countries. Table IX-1 gives the salient information for the largest tire companies. Many tire concerns are also major producers of chemicals, other rubber products, and, in some cases, other automobile parts.

The International Federation of Chemical, Energy and General Workers' Unions (ICEF) has conducted as active a propaganda campaign in the rubber tire industry as it has in the glass and chemical ones. Indeed, its rubber tire division is one of its most active, and it has established "world councils" for most of the key European and American tire companies. As in the case of the glass and chemical industries, it will be seen that most ICEF claims of action against these companies cannot be substantiated.

The Communist rival group, the Trade Unions International of Chemical, Oil and Allied Workers (ICPS), is also active in the rubber industry. Headquartered in Budapest, Hungary, it has affiliates in France and Italy, where the two largest federations —the Confédération Générale du Travail (CGT) and the Confederazione Generale Italiana del Lavoro (CGIL)—are Communist-dominated, in many developing countries, and, of course, in Eastern Europe and in the Soviet Union. Although the CGIL has resigned its World Federation of Trade Unions (WFTU) membership, CGIL affiliates continue to attend and to participate in meetings of the ICPS. Moreover, the refusal of the CGT to provide the WFTU secretary general, announced at the 1977 WFTU Congress, does not extend to the WFTU branches. A Frenchman remains general secretary of the ICPS.

TABLE IX-1
The Ten Largest Companies
in the
Rubber Tire Industry
1978

Company	Headquarters	Sales ($000)	Assets ($000)	Net Income ($000)	Employees
Goodyear Tire and Rubber	Akron, Ohio	7,489,102	5,231,103	226,127	154,013
Dunlop-Pirelli Union	London/Milan	5,056,147	N.A.	N.A.	165,457
Firestone Tire and Rubber	Akron, Ohio	4,878,100	3,486,400	148,300 [b]	112,000
Michelin	Clermont-Ferrand	4,605,493	6,087,472	136,976	120,000
Uniroyal	Middlebury, Conn.	2,735,856	1,870,960	5,883	49,241
B. F. Goodrich	Akron, Ohio	2,593,533	1,930,551	70,110	40,609
Bridgestone Tire	Tokyo	2,393,438	2,232,401	80,573	30,134
General Tire and Rubber	Akron, Ohio	2,198,220	1,701,085	115,519	42,000
Continental Gummi-Werke [a]	Hannover	1,017,117	813,574	2,633	24,593
Yokohama Rubber	Tokyo	909,368	920,123	2,705 [b]	12,491

Source: *Fortune,* Vol. 99 (May 7, 1979), pp. 270-75; Vol. 100 (August 13, 1979), pp. 195-201.
[a] These data do not show the fact that Continental has purchased the European operations of Uniroyal.
[b] Loss.

In addition to the activities of the ICEF and the ICPS, there have been several direct contacts, meetings, and even some formal activities between national unions in regard to companies during the last decade. In addition, the Communists have sponsored "shop stewards committees" apparently to take advantage of the loose union organization in Britain and the Communist infiltration of leadership there as a means of achieving international cooperation between British unions and the unions that the Communists control in France and Italy. Shop stewards committees have been especially active in international union attempts to pressure Dunlop-Pirelli and Michelin, the subjects of the first two sections of this chapter.

DUNLOP-PIRELLI

On January 1, 1971, London-based Dunlop and the Italian concern Pirelli joined to form the Dunlop-Pirelli Union.[1] A general decline in the European tire and rubber business, particularly in Italy,[2] developed soon thereafter, resulting in redundancies (permanent layoffs) in Britain and short-time working both in Britain and in Italy. Unions blamed these layoffs on rationalization pursuant to the merger, and international activity on the part both of the ICEF and of a Communist-led shop stewards committee followed.

ICEF Action

In June 1972, the ICEF secretary general, Charles Levinson, addressed a letter to the chairman of the Dunlop group of companies demanding that he meet with an international delegation of unionists representing "a Permanent Dunlop-Pirelli World Council" to discuss "international investment strategies . . . particularly in respect of possible repercussions on jobs." A similar letter was sent to Pirelli.[3]

---

[1] A more detailed account of the earlier attempts of the ICEF to involve Dunlop and Michelin is found in our article "Multinational Collective Bargaining Activity: The Factual Record in Chemicals, Glass, and Rubber Tires," Parts I and II, *Columbia Journal of World Business*, Vol. IX (spring and summer 1974), pp. 112-24 and 49-63.

[2] See "Multinationals: The unhappy union of Dunlop-Pirelli," *Business Week*, November 4, 1972, p. 38. Pirelli has suffered a loss in nearly every year since its union with Dunlop.

[3] The Industrial Research Unit has a file of documents and other materials pertaining to this case in which the letters quoted are included.

Noting that the list of unions involved in the world council included many with which Dunlop had no dealings and excluded the large unions in its French and Italian facilities, the company declined through its personnel director either to recognize or to meet officially with the ICEF group. The personnel director, however, did meet informally with Levinson and agreed to a later meeting between Levinson, the cochairmen of the Dunlop-Pirelli World Council, Bob Edwards of the British Transport and General Workers' Union (TGWU) and Egidio Quaglia of the Italian Federchimici,[4] representing the union side, and the personnel directors of Dunlop and Pirelli, representing the management side.

This meeting was scheduled for March 1973 but was never held. Initially, it was postponed because of the illness of the then personnel director of Dunlop. Then on July 30, 1973, Federchimici's secretary general, Danilo Baretta, wrote the president and secretary general of the ICEF to "give you notice of our formal decision of ending our affiliation" to the ICEF.[5] Since then, the ICEF "Permanent Dunlop-Pirelli World Council" has ceased to exist except on paper and has had no meeting to our knowledge. The only Dunlop-ICEF contact since then occurred in October 1976, when the ICEF's European Committee held a meeting in Birmingham, England. Dunlop permitted the visitors to tour one of its plants and provided a luncheon for them.[6] As we note below, the ICEF has more recently attempted to inject itself into Dunlop labor problems.

---

[4] The full name of Federchimici is Organizzazione Sindacale Fra i Lavoratori Chimici ed Affini. It is an affiliate of the Confederazione Italiana Sindacati Lavoratori. Since this date, the chemical affiliates of the three Italian federations have merged into a coordinated organization. The dominant position in the coordinated group is clearly held by the Communist-run Confederazione Generale Italiana del Lavoro. Edwards is now retired from the TGWU. He continues as a Labour member of Parliament.

[5] This is a translated quotation from the letter, a Xerox copy of which is in our case file. Basic disagreement between the ICEF and its Italian affiliates arose over the moves in Italy toward unification of Italian Communist and non-Communist unions. In ICF Circular Letter No. 115/76, September 8, 1976, and in his report to the 1976 ICF Congress, Levinson claims to have "disaffiliated from ICF" Federchimici and other Italian unions over this issue, but, of course, the disaffiliation initiative came from the Italian unions. See "Executive Committee. Activities Report of the Secretary General. List of Membership," *ICF 16th Statutory Congress*, October 27-29, 1976, Montreal, p. 20. (Hereafter cited as *ICF 16th Statutory Congress*.)

[6] *Comité Européen du Caoutchouc*, October 7-8, 1976, Birmingham (mimeo).

Communist Shop Stewards

Meanwhile, the Communists, who had organized a Dunlop-Pirelli Shop Stewards Committee as early as 1970, moved into action. This committee, which has met several times since then, has been expanded to cover other countries, especially France, and other companies, including Michelin and Goodyear, but originally it was an Italian-British, Dunlop-Pirelli organization. In Britain, John Miller, the TGWU officer for the rubber industry, an admitted member of the Communist party, was the key union official involved. Thus, the TGWU has a foot in both the ICEF and the Communist camps in the rubber tire industry.

In Italy, CGIL affiliates provide assistance, and there is probably close WFTU liaison. The key official in Italy is an Englishman, Christopher Gilmore, who is most likely a member of the Communist party. He has served as international director of the CGIL chemical union. He is a former official of the Radical Students Alliance and is married to a daughter of Petro Ingrao, a prominent member of the Italian Communist party. He is now director of information for the European Trade Union Institute, the research arm of the European Trade Union Confederation.

The shop stewards group, headed by an "International Shop Stewards Steering Committee," came into prominence through its "Day of Shame," or "Eurostrike," a widely publicized strike on June 9, 1972, called to protest layoffs (redundancies). This action, organized by shop stewards, affected about 7,500 of the then 54,000 British Dunlop workers, with only one small belting plant shut down. No British trade union officially supported the action. In Italy, where protest meetings are frequent and a certain number permitted without loss of pay, a two-hour demonstration drew 80 percent of the Pirelli work force around Milan. A British shop steward from Speke (Liverpool), the plant that did shut down in England, spoke at the Milan meeting.[7]

The Communist group has grown in scope since 1972, although it, like the ICEF, has received no company recognition. Before examining this group's later and larger action, it is necessary to bring the Michelin story forward.

---

[7] Vincent Hanna, "A false step on the shop floor," *Sunday Times* (London), May 28, 1972; Ian Murray, "Only one in four at Dunlop heed 'Eurostrike' call," *Times* (London), June 10, 1972; interview with the then Dunlop personnel director, London, September 3, 1973.

MICHELIN

As has been described in our analysis of the glass and chemical and pharmaceutical industries, the ICEF has taken credit for a number of international labor actions in which, upon careful investigation, we have found little or no ICEF involvement. Nowhere is this better illustrated than in the stories generated about the ICEF's relations with Michelin, the large French tire multinational. Now the number one tire company in France and Germany, and second only to Pirelli in Italy and to Dunlop in Britain, Michelin recently has opened two plants in Nova Scotia, Canada, and two in South Carolina, is building a third in that state, has purchased a plant in Denver, is negotiating a plant site in Brazil, and has plants in Spain and Africa. Wholly owned and controlled by the Michelin family, this company is the developer of the radial tire.

ICEF Claims

On October 9, 1972, the *Wall Street Journal* reported:

> A strike by 135 workers in a wire mesh department at a Michelin plant in Clermont-Ferrand, central France, for a wage increase of one U.S. cent an hour, has triggered sympathy strikes at a number of other wire mesh plants in Europe.
> The strikes and a refusal by some other employees to work overtime are intended to keep Michelin from making up lost production in other plants.
> Michelin warned it may be forced to cut production at Clermont-Ferrand.[8]

Not long after this story, *Business Week* carried an article giving the ICEF full credit for the strike's resolution in a manner satisfactory to the workers and terming it the most effective of the international secretariats.[9] This story has been repeated by the *New York Times*,[10] again in the *Wall Street Journal*,[11] and

---

[8] "Michelin Plant Sparks New Walkouts," *Wall Street Journal*, October 9, 1972, p. 10. Michelin officials denied to the authors that they had ever "warned" that they might "be forced to cut production at Clermont-Ferrand," claiming that was the ICEF's, not their, statement.

[9] "Multinationals: A step toward global bargaining," *Business Week*, October 28, 1972, p. 52.

[10] Clyde H. Farnsworth, "Big Business Spurs Labor Toward a World Role," *New York Times*, December 26, 1972, pp. 53-54; and Gerd Wilcke, "Multinational Labor Leader," *New York Times*, February 18, 1973, sec. 3, p. 9.

[11] Neil Ulman, "Multinational Firms Face a Growing Power," *Wall Street Journal*, April 23, 1973, p. 1.

by publications throughout the world. If the ICEF did cause Michelin to alter its policies of not recognizing unions unless required or, indeed, even of not discussing its labor policies publicly,[12] it would have been quite a feat. Actually, however, the facts tell a very different story.[13]

The Clermont-Ferrand works of Michelin employ approximately 27,000 workers. Unions there, as in most Michelin plants, are not very strong, but the largest by far is a part of the Communist CGT. An ICEF affiliate, the Confédération Française Démocratique du Travail (CFDT) also is represented there by one of its unions but is much smaller. On September 12, 1972, 113 of the 150 workers in the reinforced fabric section (known as the "PK shop") went on strike and stayed out until October 16, 1972. The PK shop workers demanded wage increases equivalent to approximately ten cents per hour. On October 9, Michelin management offered the strikers wage adjustments varying from one to six cents per hour. The workers' committee rejected this increase and, then, on October 16, returned to work with nothing but a vague promise from management to negotiate in the future. There is no evidence that the ICEF was on the scene, and Michelin officials did not talk to Levinson.

There is, moreover, no record of any sympathy strikes being "triggered" elsewhere in Europe, nor is there any evidence that Michelin sought to import materials from other countries to offset the effect of the PK shop walkout. We have ascertained that German Michelin plants were not requested to work overtime for this purpose, nor did the unions in Germany resist overtime, stop work, or become directly involved in any overt manner during this strike. The same is true in Italy, where, as in France, the dominant union group in Michelin operations by far is the Communist CGIL, which does not cooperate with the ICEF. Neither is there any record of overt British union action at this time; and in Spain, the unions were then too weak and too much under the Franco government's surveillance to have been a part of any international economic pressures.[14]

---

[12] See "Tight-Lipped Michelin Comes to London," *Sunday Times* (London), May 28, 1972.

[13] The facts set forth here were gathered through numerous interviews with management, union, and government personnel in Europe in August 1973, in addition to the sources cited.

[14] There was, for example, no mention in the German, Italian, or British press of any incident involving Michelin workers in their countries that we could find.

In fact, Michelin had no need to import materials from anywhere. At another French Michelin plant in Bourges, the largest
union group, as at Clermont-Ferrand, is the Communist CGT. It
permitted supplies to flow from this plant into Clermont-Ferrand
to offset loss of work from the strike, and the workers at
Clermont-Ferrand and the unions there allowed them to come
in with only token opposition.

Perhaps the most significant reason why the PK strikers received very little support from any union group or from other
employees at Clermont-Ferrand is that they are somewhat of an
elite group, which has not cooperated with other employees in
the past. On one occasion, for example, they had management
lock them into the plant in order to remain at work while a
large segment of the plant was on strike. When the PK shop
employees struck, their picket lines were given meager support.

We have been unable to find any evidence to support the
widely printed story of a major ICEF involvement and/or
triumph regarding the strike of 113 workers in the 27,000-man
Clermont-Ferrand plant of Michelin. The company did not alter
and has not since altered its policy of refusing to recognize the
ICEF and of declining to meet with Levinson. In fact, in his
report to the 1973 ICEF Congress, the ICEF secretary general
reported that no meetings with Michelin had occurred; rather,
he stated that Michelin is one of the companies that is "openly
hostile and opposed to direct international relations at the level
of the company." [15]

The Clermont-Ferrand incident was not the first claim of
ICEF success regarding Michelin that appears unsupportable.
In *International Trade Unionism,* this paragraph is included:

> In February 1971, the French CFDT workers in Michelin demon-
> strated and stopped work at several French Michelin plants in
> support of the German Michelin workers in Bad Kreuznach. The
> latter formally acknowledged the decisive contribution that this
> action made towards winning the strike.[16]

Since the French Michelin workers are much less unionized
than are their German brethren, and since, as noted, the dominant
union in the French Michelin plants is the Communist CGT and

---

[15] "Report of Activities of the Secretary General, the 15th Statutory Congress, 7th-9th November 1973, Geneva, Documents," *ICF Bulletin,* October
1973, pp. 87-88. (Hereafter cited as *ICF 15th Statutory Congress.*)

[16] Charles Levinson, *International Trade Unionism* (London: George Allen
& Unwin, 1972), p. 115.

not the smaller ICEF affiliate the CFDT, it is difficult to believe that the CFDT was capable of aiding the German Michelin workers or would stop work for that purpose. Rather, we understand that the French CFDT sent telegrams of solidarity and that the German union responded effusively when its controversy was settled.

As in the case of Dunlop-Pirelli, the ICEF has organized a world council for Michelin unions. Although it still continues to meet, it is not too representative of Michelin workers throughout the world. Not only is the largest organized group in France a part of the Communist CGT, but in addition, Michelin plants there are probably not much more than 25 percent unionized. In Italy, the ICEF can at most claim affiliation only of the chemical workers union of Unione Italiana del Lavoro (UIL). In Canada and the United States, the new Michelin facilities remain nonunion.[17] In Great Britain, ICEF affiliates have considerable strength in Michelin plants as they do in those of Dunlop, but as will again be noted below, the largest British union, the Transport and General Workers' Union, also cooperates with the Communists. Only in Germany is there an ICEF affiliate that is truly representative of the bulk of the rubber workers in Michelin —Industriegewerkschaft Chemie-Papier-Keramik (IG Chemie).

Communist Activity

Following a series of sit-down strikes and plant occupations over an eleven-month period, Michelin in late 1973, like several Italian companies, including Fiat and Pierelli, agreed to a contract giving Italian unions the right to discuss investment and modernization covering its five plants and fifteen thousand employees there.[18] Before this agreement was completed, it was

---

[17] While the first two Michelin plants were being built in South Carolina, Levinson told his constituents that "with the cooperation . . . of the International Federation of Building and Woodworkers (IFBWW) [another secretariat] and our American affiliates and U.S. construction unions, the [Michelin] Council is examining the means of delaying or even stopping the construction of these costly plants until Michelin is ready to meet at the world level to discuss and change its irresponsible investment programme and anti-union policies." *ICF 15th Statutory Congress*, p. 87. In fact, the plants were completed on schedule by Daniel International, the second largest open shop (nonunion) contractor in the United States.

[18] "Secretive Michelin to Discuss Its Plans with Unions," *New York Times*, October 15, 1973, p. 57.

supported by what the *New York Times* called a strike of British workers against Michelin and a one-day demonstration of French unions involving fifty thousand workers.[19]

In Italy, these strikes were coordinated by the CGIL and involved all the unions there. In France, the CGT organized the demonstration. The *Times* article exaggerates the French participation in which the CFDT also joined. Approximately 20 percent of the workers at Clermont-Ferrand responded to a twenty-four-hour strike call, and about 20 percent of the production workers at other French Michelin establishments observed work stoppages of one or two hours.[20]

The British were apparently "invited" to participate and did so with some demonstrations. These were organized by left-wing groups not under the ICEF's leadership.[21]

THE COMMUNIST "DAY OF ACTION" IN THE EUROPEAN RUBBER INDUSTRY

The redundancies (permanent layoffs) and short workweeks in the European rubber tire industry, a result of the downturn in automobile production following the sharp increase in petroleum prices, led to a broader attempt at international action by the Communist-dominated "International Shop Stewards Steering Committee." The Dunlop-Pirelli Union in Britain and Italy was the main target, but this demonstration, which occurred on October 22, 1975, reached other countries and companies as well. Again, a key figure, if not the leader of the demonstration, was Christopher Gilmore, referred to above.

---

[19] *Ibid.* The agreement, which the Industrial Research Unit has translated, clearly requires consultation before decisions are made but thus far has not seemed to have resulted in any codetermination over investment decisions. The potential for this is greater for an Italian-based company than for a company like Michelin which has its major investments elsewhere. For an analysis of such agreements, concluding that "it seems likely that the whole mechanism of information will be mainly a public relations exercise," see the authoritative British publication *IDS International Report*, No. 32 (September 1976), pp. 1-3. As of 1979, this remained an accurate description.

[20] See, e.g., AFP dispatches (France), covering period September 15-October 20, 1973; *L'Humanité*, September 24, 1973; and others of this period. See also "Turin Cardinal Campaigns for Workers' Job Security Pay," *International Herald Tribune*, October 25, 1973, p. 4.

[21] Information obtained from interviews in London, September 3-5, 1973.

Predemonstration Meetings

The October demonstration followed the pattern of the 1972 one. It began with a union stewards conference in Turin, Italy, in May 1975, which was attended by delegates from five countries. This was followed by a conference in Liverpool, England, on September 11, 1975. Eighty-one delegates registered for this second meeting, of whom fifty-seven came from the United Kingdom, eleven from Italy, nine from Germany, and four from France.[22]

Of the eighty-one delegates who registered, forty came from Dunlop plants, sixteen from Michelin, eight from Pirelli, six from Goodyear, four from British Leyland, one each from Firestone, Continental (Germany), and Innocent-Leyland (Italy), and two from unknown German companies. Gilmore and Sinclair Philip, of the University of Grenoble, France, which is near Geneva, Switzerland, were the other two who signed the delegate list. The TGWU, which gave the meeting at least its tacit support, provided the most delegates of any union, thirty-two in all. The General and Municipal Workers' Union (GMWU) opposed participation in the meeting (as it did in the previous ones of this nature), but five delegates from the GMWU were present, as were nine from the Amalgamated Union of Engineering Workers (AUEW) and some from numerous other British unions. Significantly, the meeting occurred prior to the recent series of union elections in the United Kingdom that turned a sizable number of Communists and leftists out of office, particularly in the AUEW.

The German delegates, all from IG Chemie, listed themselves as observers since their union opposed any participation. French delegates, besides Philip, included three from the CGT; all Italians but one came from the chemical affiliate of CGIL. Present also, and addressing and reporting on the meeting, was Eric Heffer, a left-wing Labour member of Parliament.[23]

---

[22] Copy of registration list and official meeting report in authors' possession. "Report on the International Conference, Held on Thursday, 11th September 1975 in the N.U.R. Club, Deane Road, Liverpool 7" (mimeo).

[23] For his report, see Eric Heffer, "Rubber Workers Take International Action," *Tribune*, September 19, 1975, p. 1. The *Tribune* is considered the organ of the British Labour party left. See also *La Vie Ouvrière* (CGT), April 28, 1976, pp. 27-29.

Gilmore headed the Italian delegation; Stan Pemberton, TGWU president (the position is not full-time), who is a Dunlop worker and is apparently a member of the General Council of the Trade Union Congress, and Charles Parker, a shop steward at Dunlop's Liverpool plant, played leading roles for the British; and M. Jacqueson, reportedly an official of the CGT, for the French. The German delegation's leader was not noted. The theme throughout was minimum redundancies, no factory closures, and joint action against all multinationals and the entire industry. The key action of the meeting was the passage of a resolution "that on the 22nd October 1975 a complete one day stoppage be held of all Workers covered by representation at the Conference." [24]

Impact of October 22, 1975

On October 22, 1975, the impact of the strike varied from country to country and plant to plant. In Britain, Dunlop estimated that 4,524, about 10.2 percent of its employees, responded to the strike call. As had occurred in 1972, the Dunlop plant in Speke (Liverpool) was closed for one day, but in addition, three other Dunlop plants were also shut down this time. Because these plants were working on short time, the actual impact on production was negligible.

Elsewhere in Britain, the only impact reported was a one-hour stoppage on each of the three shifts at the Goodyear plant in the Glasgow, Scotland, area. Other Goodyear plants and those of Michelin, Firestone, and Uniroyal in the United Kingdom were unaffected.[25]

On the European continent, the impact varied considerably. German unions opposed any involvement, and no stoppages were reported. Likewise, there was no response to the strike call in Spain or in the Benelux countries. In France, the only plants affected were two of Michelin. At the huge Clermont-Ferrand works, an estimated 17 percent of the 27,000 workers struck for four hours; at Bourges, about 10 percent engaged in a similar strike. There was also a demonstration in the Clermont-Ferrand town square.

---

[24] "Report on the International Conference," p. 2.

[25] The facts herein are based on numerous news articles, plus correspondence with the companies involved.

Italy was the most seriously affected, but the timing of the strike to coincide with other stoppages obscures its effectiveness; Pierelli factories in southern Italy were unaffected, but those in northern Italy had about a 40 percent response to a four-hour strike call, except for the Bicocca and Milan plants, where the response was closer to 80 percent. Michelin factories were also affected. Its two Turin area plants had a four-hour stoppage of all workers; at Cuneo, 65 percent of the workers stayed out for four hours; at Alessandria, 50 percent struck for three hours; at Fossano, 56 percent struck for two hours; and at Trento, 50 percent struck for one hour.

Several smaller Italian companies were affected by total or partial stoppages lasting for four hours. American-owned Italian factories were apparently not affected.

October 22, 1975, was also the date of a major union demonstration in Italy for job security. Thus, 50 percent of the Fiat employees and about the same percentage of all employees affiliated with the Industrial Union of the Province of Turin struck to dramatize their job security demands. To what extent the Italian rubber strikers were cooperating with an international action or striking for more local interests is thus in doubt.

Much of the discussion at the meeting in Liverpool on September 11, 1975, concerned the George Angus Company facility in Naples, which had been occupied and apparently operated by workers since August 1975, after the shareholders decided to liquidate it. The factory, which makes seals for the automobile and appliance industries, was referred to as a Dunlop plant but actually was a joint venture run by an Italian firm in which Dunlop supplied engineering expertise, not management. When its wage costs allegedly exceeded sales revenues, Dunlop withdrew from the arrangement.

Overall, the strike demonstrates the interest of the Communists in using their shop stewards apparatus in the rubber industry when it seems useful. It also shows their heavy infiltration of key spots in British unions. Their followers closed down Dunlop plants by blocking gates and by denying employees access. Combined with their control of the leading federations in Italy and France, their hold on key positions in British unions could be a problem for multinational companies and for free governments elsewhere, but there has been no repetition of such stoppages as of early 1979.

ICEF Position

On the international scene, the secretary general of the ICEF issued a circular letter stating that "no ICF member is to participate" and that "member unions" should so "enlighten their representatives in the companies . . . that this . . . is a maneuver of the Communist party." [26] He also announced that the ICEF's small affiliate in Italy, the chemical union of the UIL, would not participate.

Previously, the Communist group had castigated the ICEF, calling it a "bureaucratic organization which had divisive policies excluding thousands of Rubber Workers." It stated further that "employers treat the ICF with contempt" and gave as an example the failure of the ICEF to take action when, as noted above, following the well-publicized meeting of its Dunlop-Pirelli World Council, it failed to obtain a meeting with management to discuss investment policies. [27]

Actually, of course, the degree of success of this Communist maneuver was based on the party's strength and following among key union officials in various countries. In Italy, where Communist power is the greatest in the Western world, politically and within the unions, the strike had the largest following, but it also coincided with a national effort; in Britain, it was significant because of Communist infiltration of key union positions; in France, it was much weaker because, even though the Communists control the largest union federation, union strength is much less than in Italy or Britain; and in Germany, the strike was ignored because the powerful labor movement there so decreed.

MICHELIN—1975-79

Following the demise of General Franco and the relaxation of authoritarian controls in Spain, most companies operating there experienced strikes. Led by the CGT, the French and Italian unions engaged in a series of stoppages in late 1975 and 1976 at various Michelin factories in support of the Spanish. These included a series of shift strikes at Vannes, shorter demonstrations at other French plants, and a general demonstration at all French and Italian Michelin plants on March 18, 1976. Participation by the workers varied widely and was never com-

---

[26] ICF Circular Letter No. 169/75, September 17, 1975.

[27] "Report on the International Conference" (Afternoon Session), p. 2.

plete. On April 12, 1976, a fifteen-minute demonstration occurred in four of the six Italian plants, with employee participation varying from one-third to less than 2 percent.

Meanwhile in Spain, the strikes subsided. One of the four Michelin plants, Vitoria, was never struck; a second, Valladolid, was back in full production by March 23; and at the other two, Aranda and Lasarte, the workers drifted back by late April and early May.[28]

The ICEF Michelin World Council held a meeting at CFDT headquarters in Paris in March 1976 on the Spanish situation. Besides the French and Levinson, the only representatives present came from IG Chemie in Germany and the Fédération Générale du Travail de Belgique (FGTB), the Belgian socialist federation.[29] They resolved that each national organization should engage in solidarity action, but no discernible action resulted.

Clermont-Ferrand Strike

Late in 1977, a rumor circulated in Clermont-Ferrand that the company would put workers on rotating, rather than fixed, shifts. Agitation grew quickly, and a strike occurred that was the most severe in the company's history. Officially, it lasted three weeks, although plant operations were resumed after three days, and generally, full production was reached soon thereafter. Both the Communists and the ICEF issued the usual appeals for solidarity. French unions claimed that the strike thwarted a pending company action; the company insisted that no shift changes were contemplated.[30]

Italian Developments

Following a strike in early 1978, the CGIL hosted a meeting in Turin, Italy, for European unions in Michelin plants. Actually, most delegates came from Italy and France. Little action, or even publicity, resulted.

Also in 1978, the ICEF accused Michelin of moving to close an older Italian plant. In fact, Michelin apparently was reducing employment by attrition but not closing the plant.[31]

---

[28] Information from the company; and "Face au Géant Michelin," *Syndicalisme CFDT*, June 1976.

[29] "Le Conseil Mondial Michelin de l'ICF Appelle a des Arrets de Travail en France la Semaine Prochaine," AFP Dispatch, March 9, 1976, Paris.

[30] Based upon press reports and company interviews.

[31] Information supplied by the company.

SEMPERIT AND ARMSTRONG

Semperit and Armstrong are smaller European and American rubber companies, respectively, which have done business with each other, but have no other relationship. They have, however, been linked by ICEF claims of involvement, as discussed below.

Semperit

Semperit is a tire, rubber products, and chemical manufacturer headquartered in Vienna, Austria. Its major facilities are in Austria, Germany, and Dublin, Ireland. Michelin had a major interest in Semperit.[32] In 1976, Semperit had sales of $402.8 million and 13,574 employees.[33]

In his report to the 1973 ICEF Congress, the secretary general reports:

> In the case of Semperit, following a three-week strike of 600 employees of its Dublin Plant, which the direct intervention of Alfred Teschl, Central Secretary of the Austrian Chemical Workers (Gewerkschaft der Chemiearbeiter), helped resolve, discussions took place between Vice-President John F. Carroll of the Irish Transport & General Workers, Alfred Teschl, ICF Secretary General Charles Levinson, and the Managing Director and Vice-Director of Semperit in Vienna. This was followed by a second meeting in Ireland, which included both this group plus Semperit's Shop Stewards and the Irish Management. The negotiations were for transferring from the Austrian collective agreement a clause governing all collective and individual dismissals, except for serious breaches of discipline, through a joint Committee composed of an equal number of union and management representatives.[34]

After investigation of these events, acquisition of pertinent documents, a field investigation in Dublin by a research correspondent, and an interview with the key Irish union official involved, we have ascertained that Teschl of the Austrian union

---

[32] Robert Ball, "The Michelin Man Rolls into Akron's Backyard," *Fortune*, Vol. XC (December 1974), p. 143, reports that Michelin controlled Semperit. In 1973, control was vested in a Swiss holding company, Semkler, in which Michelin had a 30.9 percent interest. In early 1979, the holding company was abolished. Michelin still maintains a large investment in Semperit.

[33] *Fortune*, Vol. XCVI (August 1977), p. 235. Semperit apparently did not achieve sufficient sales to be included in the *Fortune* listing published in 1978. It has suffered heavy losses in recent years.

[34] *ICF 15th Statutory Congress*, p. 89.

did, in fact, approach the company in Vienna early in September 1972, apparently as a result of a request by the Irish Transport and General Workers' Union (ITGWU), the largest union in the Republic of Ireland. The ITGWU is affiliated with the ICEF, as well as with several other secretariats, and may have contacted Teschl through the ICEF or directly. Teschl spoke with Carl F. Rueger, then chairman of the Semperit Board of Management, and I. H. Kogert, a member of that board. At that meeting, Rueger and Kogert agreed to Teschl's request to convene a joint meeting with the management of the Dublin plant and the ITGWU.

Two meetings occurred in Dublin shortly thereafter on September 26, 1972. Rueger and Kogert, plus three members of the Semperit Dublin plant management, met with an international union group at the Intercontinental Hotel at 3:00 P.M. (1500 hours). On the union side were the secretary general of the ICEF, Teschl, two representatives of the ITGWU, and five plant union representatives.

At 4:00 P.M., a second meeting was held at the Dublin Semperit plant, which Rueger and Kogert did not attend but at which the Dublin-based management personnel were present. All union representatives, including Levinson and Teschl, who were at the Intercontinental Hotel meeting, plus nine additional local union representatives (stewards), attended the second meeting. At the latter meeting, a subcommittee was appointed to establish a disciplinary board, modeled on the agreement between Semperit and the Austrian union, for the purpose of handling violations of plant rules. Only Irish personnel were on this subcommittee, and no international involvement occurred after the second meeting.

It is apparent from the minutes of these meetings that Semperit management hoped that the transfer of the Austrian procedure to Dublin would reduce the number of strikes which plague Irish industry. On the other hand, the union representatives saw the potential for giving themselves a decision-making role rather than just a consultative role in the plant. The Austrian agreement provided for minor disciplinary actions to be determined by a committee composed of six representatives, two each representing the employer, the works council, and the staff (managerial personnel) council.

Despite this auspicious meeting, nothing whatsoever resulted. The ITGWU balked at the proposed joint disciplinary procedure concept, preferring adjudication by a governmental labor court under Irish law. John F. Carroll, vice-president of the ITGWU, who was present at the meeting, told the authors that it proved to be a "non-event," with no subsequent discussions. He also stated that both his organization and the Austrian union had communicated with each other on two occasions about support in pending labor troubles but that, again, each time there was neither follow-up nor action.[35]

Thus, it is quite correct that Levinson did, in fact, meet with the then top Semperit management in company with an Austrian union official and officials of the ITGWU. He was also present when an agreement was reached to establish a new disciplinary procedure, but the agreement was not effectuated, and no further meetings have been held since those on September 26, 1972, between Semperit management and a multinational union group. The ICEF secretary general has, however, claimed that, through his office, employees at Semperit's Dublin plant interfered with shipment of tires to an American tire company, Armstrong, in support of strikers who had closed the latter company's plants.

Armstrong

Armstrong Rubber Company, headquartered in New Haven, Connecticut, operates four tire facilities in the United States. It is a major supplier to Sears, Roebuck and Company. In 1978, Armstrong had sales of $377 million and employed 5,765 persons.[36]

For some years, Armstrong has purchased certain lines of tires from Semperit, which have been shipped from the latter's Dublin plant. In his report to the 1973 congress, the ICEF secretary general states:

> When the URW struck four Armstrong factories, the Irish workers of the Austrian Semperit subsidiary, members of the Irish Transport and General Workers Union, boycotted the shipment of tires which the Austrian Company was producing in its Dublin plant for Armstrong.[37]

---

[35] John F. Carroll, vice-president, Irish Transport and General Workers' Union, interview in Munich, Germany, May 15, 1979. Both Carroll and the authors were then attending the European Trade Union Confederation congress.

[36] *Fortune,* Vol. 99 (June 18, 1979), pp. 158-59.

[37] *ICF 15th Statutory Congress,* p. 88.

The strike in question by the United Rubber Workers began on July 12 and ended on August 4, 1973. It was discussed in a front page story of this union's journal for July 1973, but no mention was made of any ICEF or ITGWU involvement. Inquiry of Armstrong Rubber Company elicited a letter from the chief personnel officer, who stated that Armstrong purchases from Semperit have at times suffered from delivery delays and that some such delays did occur in July 1973. He then declared:

> We have made inquiries of our purchasing and marketing personnel who have immediate administrative responsibility for the relationship with Semperit and they have no knowledge of the involvement of any labor organization in the delay of receipt of any tires manufactured by Semperit for Armstrong. We know of no instance, prior to the receipt of your correspondence, where it has been implied that Armstrong may have been the subject of labor sponsored boycott activity.[38]

In response to an inquiry, Semperit's Dublin plant management stated flatly that "there was no interference with our production by virtue of the problem at Armstrong." [39] Finally, Armstrong also reported that there had been no ICEF or international union activity during the 1976 strike, discussed below, or at any other time.[40]

THE ICEF AND THE U.S. TIRE COMPANIES, 1967-75

The United States rubber and tire companies include several of the largest such concerns in the world, including Goodyear, the world leader. Goodyear and three other large concerns, Firestone, Uniroyal, and B. F. Goodrich, make up the American "Big Four." Two other majors are General Tire and the already discussed Armstrong Rubber Company. Uniroyal, like Armstrong, is headquartered in Connecticut; the others are in Akron, Ohio.

Goodyear and Firestone have long had extensive overseas manufacturing operations. The 1975 annual report of the former listed such facilities in thirty countries outside the United States; the report of the latter for the same year listed facilities in twenty-five countries. Uniroyal and Goodrich also have important overseas installations but have pulled out of European

---

[38] Letter from G. Robert Millar, vice president, Armstrong Rubber Company, October 31, 1974.

[39] Reply of Semperit management to correspondent's question.

[40] G. Robert Millar, telephone interview, October 25, 1976.

tire production. General also has several overseas facilities, including joint ventures; Armstrong is solely a United States producer.

Early Activities

The first claim of the ICEF in regard to United States companies apparently occurred in 1967, when, following a lengthy industry strike, it was reported that

> the ICF, by a Congress resolution stood ready to support the rubber workers if called upon.
>
> In fact, President Peter Bommarito [of the URW] reported that a wire from the ICF indicating its readiness to organize a boycott of European subsidiaries in the event they attempted to import tires into the United States to break the strike, impressed management during the negotiations "and was effective as if the boycott was [sic] applied." [41]

Actually, American concerns had stocked warehouses when the strike began but did, without interference, import some tires from abroad. Most rubber executives apparently had never heard of the ICEF before 1970.[42] In the final negotiations to end the Goodyear strike of that year, Bommarito indicated the possibility of a worldwide boycott, but it never went beyond this initial comment.[43]

In May 1971, apparently in reference to Goodyear and Uniroyal, both of which had operations in Turkey, *Newsweek* ran the following:

> In [Levinson's] view, international unions often can make progress by exploiting their own national power bases. "For example, in Turkey, U.S. rubber companies were resisting unionization. . . . We got the parent union to intervene with the parent companies in Akron. Management then realized they were no longer dealing with a small, powerless union in Turkey." [44]

In fact, rubber workers in Turkey were unionized when the government there relaxed its ban on union efforts in the 1960s, There is no objective evidence that American tire companies were "resisting unionization" or especially that their policies were changed by pressure brought through the ICEF.

---

[41] "ICF Information," August 1967, p. 1.

[42] Based on numerous conversations with the U.S. rubber tire company officials and personal notes of one of the authors during 1967 strike.

[43] Interviews in Akron, Ohio, April 6, 1972.

[44] "Labor: The Global View," *Newsweek*, May 17, 1971, p. 78.

Since 1967, an ICEF Rubber Division has been active, headed by Bommarito.[45] In the 1973 "Report of the Activities of the Secretary General," it is stated:

> Another important step in ICF's developing strategy was the coordination with the United Rubber Workers' negotiations in 1973 with the U.S. rubber giants including Goodyear and Firestone and later Armstrong. To build international support before the dispute occurred and strengthen the Rubber Workers' position during the bargaining, the ICF Secretary General, at the request of the United Rubber Workers, participated in the bargaining policy meetings of the Union in Cincinnati, Ohio. A plan for international support of the URW in the negotiations and in the event of a strike at either Goodyear—subsequently chosen as the target company—or Firestone was approved at the Goodyear and Firestone Council meetings, held in Paris in March, 1973. Attempts to increase special production in Italy and Luxembourg were stopped. Very favourable agreements were reached, particularly in improved pensions for rubber workers—with a minimum of plants being on strike.[46]

Levinson appeared at the URW prenegotiation policy meetings in January 1973 and made a speech to the delegates. Goodyear and the URW settled their contract peacefully, but the company was unaware of any interference or even discussions relating thereto at its Luxembourg or Italian plants. Firestone, which had a short strike, also reported no concern or interference at its European facilities.[47]

Turkish Problems

At the prenegotiation meetings between Goodyear and the URW in January 1973, a URW representative gave a Goodyear official a copy of a telegram pledging URW support for the workers in Turkey in their current negotiations with Goodyear. The ICEF announced that URW intervention had forced a settlement. In fact, the Turkish workers at Goodyear had settled at least one day *prior* to the dispatch of the telegram. Moreover, the Turkish negotiations had never reached a crisis stage

---

[45] See, e.g., *United Rubber Worker*, October 1971, pp. 1, 3; *ibid.*, February 1972, p. 8; *ibid.*, September 1972, p. 8; *ibid.*, February 1973, pp. 1, 3; and *ibid.*, March 1973, pp. 1-2. Since then, Bommarito's appearances at ICEF functions and Levinson's visits to the United States have continued to be portrayed in major stories in this monthly journal.

[46] *ICF 15th Statutory Congress*, pp. 87-88.

[47] Telephone interviews, November 1973. No mention is found of any international involvement in the *United Rubber Worker* story on the contract settlements which appeared in the April 1973 issue.

because the Uniroyal plant there had already settled with the same union, and both Goodyear and the Turkish union expected to, and did, follow the Uniroyal pattern.[48]

A similar development occurred in 1975, this time involving both Goodyear and Uniroyal. The latter company has received a number of communications over the years from the ICEF but has not responded. Then, in late January 1975, Bommarito addressed a letter to Uniroyal, as he did to Goodyear, enclosing a communication from a Turkish labor official about a strike involving Uniroyal and Goodyear plants there and promising "all the support possible" to the Turkish union from the "ICF Rubber Industry Division and the Multinational Council of which I [Bommarito] am chairman." A Uniroyal labor relations manager reviewed the situation and was able to reply in mid-February that the strike had been settled earlier and prior to the inquiry.[49]

Goodrich and General Tire

The Goodrich and General Tire Companies were first mentioned in ICEF publicity in 1976. In his report to the ICEF congress of that year, the secretary general declares that he had sent messages of support, provided media information, and intervened with company headquarters in regard to strikes in Mexico involving these two companies and Firestone in October 1973 and strikes involving Goodrich alone in Canada in May 1974 and in Europe in January 1975. A claim that products were boycotted is also made in regard to the Canadian dispute.[50]

In response to our inquiry, Goodrich advised that there was an industrywide strike in Mexico in October 1973 and that, "while it is entirely possible that Mr. Levinson sent messages of support and so on, no impact was made whereby any members of management recall him specifically." Insofar as Europe and Canada are concerned, Goodrich reported that there was no strike in its facilities in Europe during January 1975 or in Canada during May 1974. Firestone and General likewise ad-

---

[48] Goodyear, telephone interview, January 1973.

[49] Correspondence in authors' possession.

[50] *ICF 16th Statutory Congress*, pp. 97-99, 102.

vised us that they had received no communications from the ICEF at the time.[51]

Australian Venture

In May 1974, Levinson was in Australia at the invitation of the since defeated Labour government there. At that time, he talked to a meeting of the Federated Rubber and Allied Workers Union and promised assistance in collective bargaining with subsidiaries of Goodyear, Firestone, and Dunlop.[52] This is duly recorded in his report to the 1976 congress with a claim that "boycotts of transfer of stocks and inventories—both actual and preparatory" had occurred.[53] In fact, no overt act occurred, nor was the ICEF mentioned in the negotiations that followed.[54]

Canadian Strikes

On February 28, 1974, URW local unions in Canada struck Firestone and, on April 25, 1974, struck Goodyear also. The strike involved some three thousand employees. The Canadian Section of the URW urged a public boycott of the products of both concerns, noting that tires were being imported into Canada from the United States and Europe. URW headquarters and the ICEF supported the boycott request.[55] It was totally ineffective. Workers in United States plants, also members of the URW, produced tires for Canada. The companies had capacity to do so because of the severe recession in the automobile industry that followed the huge increases in the price of oil engineered by the oil-producing countries.

---

[51] Letter from Goodrich union relations representative to one of the authors, February 7, 1977. In telephone interviews, February 16, 1977, and January 3, 1979, Firestone's then chief personnel executive and General's present one stated that no communications were received from the ICEF at company headquarters during the Mexican strike.

[52] *Rubber, Plastic and Cable Industries Journal*, May 1974, p. 3.

[53] *ICF 16th Statutory Congress*, pp. 98, 102.

[54] Former personnel director, Dunlop, interview in London, July 9, 1975; and Goodyear, telephone interview, August 10, 1976; and Firestone, telephone interview, February 16, 1977.

[55] See the *United Rubber Worker*, August 1974, pp. 1, 6; *ibid.*, September 1974, pp. 8, 12; and *ibid.*, October 1974, pp. 1-2. See also *ICF 16th Statutory Congress*, p. 99.

THE 1976 BIG FOUR STRIKE

The URW struck the Big Four tire companies for four months beginning in April 1976.[56] The strike lasted much longer than URW officials originally expected. The union made it clear prior to the strike that it expected a combination of pressure from a tire-short automobile industry and the federal government's concern about heavy layoffs to pressure the tire industry into an early settlement and further that an international boycott under ICEF auspices would prevent any relief in the form of imported tires. Neither of the union strategies worked as planned.[57]

Although the four largest American companies were struck, as much as 45 percent of the United States tire production was unaffected. Firestone, Uniroyal, and Michelin had nonunion plants that kept producing throughout the strike. The URW locals at General Tire Company refused to join the strike,[58] as did those of Kelly-Springfield, a Goodyear subsidiary, and of Dunlop.[59] Plants of Lee Tire, another Goodyear subsidiary, of Dayton and Seiberling, both Firestone subsidiaries, and smaller

---

[56] The discussion of the 1976 strike reproduces information from the authors' article "Multinational Union Activity in the 1976 U.S. Rubber Tire Strike," *Sloan Management Review*, Vol. 18 (spring 1977), pp. 17-28.

[57] See, for example, Ralph E. Winter, "Rubber Workers Strike Enters Sixth Week Amid Signs Pressure for Settlement Lags," *Wall Street Journal*, May 27, 1976, p. 5; and "Auto makers shake the URW's strategy," *Business Week*, June 21, 1976, p. 33.

[58] The failure of the General Tire locals to join the strike was a special blow to the URW strike leadership since General supplies about 12 percent of the original equipment market. President Bommarito had announced that the General Tire locals would strike when their contract expired on May 15, 1976, but the local unions extended their contracts under a provision providing that they would receive the same settlement as the strikers. Bommarito was quoted as saying, "It looks like a crack in our united front . . . I don't know what happened." See "A rift threatens rubber negotiations," *Business Week*, May 31, 1976, pp. 21-22. Levinson incomprehensibly wrote that the "agreement with General Tyre [*sic*] . . . represents the first breakthrough against the solid front of management." ICF Circular Letter 101/76, August 4, 1976.

[59] Bommarito also indicated that the key Kelly-Springfield local at Cumberland, Maryland, would strike, but it followed the General Tire action, as did other locals of this Goodyear subsidiary, of Dunlop, and of Mohawk. See "Firestone Official Says Auto Firms' Tire Stock Will Last Until August," *Wall Street Journal*, June 8, 1976, p. 11; Philip Revzin, "How a Union Leader Stays Busy Keeping Strikers Spirits Alive," *ibid.*, July 8, 1976, p. 1; and "Auto makers shake the URW's strategy," p. 33.

companies such as Mohawk and Cooper remained at work, while another smaller company, Mansfield Rubber, was struck less than one day.[60] Armstrong's five plants remained at work until July 1 and then were struck until August 28. Companies moved molds from struck plants in order to produce needed tires, placing them both with their nonstriking domestic and with their foreign subsidiaries. No company has reported any difficulties in having tires produced or shipped in such situations.

Even the struck plants were not idle; salaried and supervisory employees operated them at reduced levels, concentrating on the lines in short supply. Moreover, the automobile companies not only had large stocks on hand prior to the strike but also temporarily reduced original equipment needs by 20 percent by shipping new cars without the spare tire. Customers received a credit slip entitling them to the tire when the strike was over.

International Action Plans

International action was promised by Bommarito before the strike commenced. Thus, in December 1975, the *United Rubber Worker*, official journal of the URW, announced:

> Rubber Industry labor leaders from throughout the world will also be in Cincinnati, [Ohio], January 21-24, to attend a meeting of the Rubber Division Council of the International Federation of Chemical and General Workers' Unions (ICF).
> The international delegation, expected to include unionists from Germany, Sweden, France, England, Australia, Brazil, Holland, Japan, and Luxembourg, will have as one of its objectives the establishment of an International Solidarity Action Program in support of the upcoming URW negotiations.[61]

Actually, no foreign delegates came to the Cincinnati meeting.[62]

On April 26, 1976, immediately after the strike started, Bommarito, accompanied by a reporter from the *Akron-Beacon Journal*, the leading paper in the United States rubber capital, journeyed to Geneva for a meeting of the ICEF Rubber Division. According to this reporter, unions from Sweden, Geneva, Austria,

---

[60] "Mansfield Tire Struck by Rubber Workers; Walkout Soon Ends," *Wall Street Journal*, June 17, 1976, p. 4.

[61] *United Rubber Worker*, December 1975, p. 1.

[62] No official reason for this reversal of plans appeared in the *United Rubber Worker*, but apparently the Geneva meeting, described below, was substituted.

Switzerland, France, and the United Kingdom attended the meeting, and cables pledging support were received from Japan, Turkey, and elsewhere.[63] Stories appeared in the *New York Times* and in syndicated columns throughout the United States, as well as in the Akron press, about the potential worldwide widening of the strike.[64]

Firestone was selected as the target for the worldwide action, and a boycott was placed against its products. Delegates from Firestone, the second largest such concern in the world, have attended ICEF meetings, and a Firestone World Council does exist. Except for some communications about Spain,[65] however, this company had not been a key ICEF target prior to this strike, although it has been a major one since then. The AFL-CIO joined the ICEF in support of the Firestone boycott, but few results followed, or could be expected, from such an action. Tires that Firestone produced during the strike undoubtedly were shipped to automobile concerns, and most of its other products are likewise not sold directly to consumers. After the first blush of publicity, news stories about the strike gave little mention to the Firestone boycott, which by all evidence was totally ineffective.

ICEF Claims and Companies' Posture

At its April 26, 1976, Geneva meeting, the ICEF Rubber Division voted to ban overtime in order to prevent foreign subsidiaries of the struck companies from making up output lost by the strike, to monitor shipments to the United States, and to prevent them if possible. In a series of "Circular Letters," the ICEF urged "intensification of monitoring of subsidiary shipments," declared the boycott both of Firestone and Goodyear

---

[63] See the articles in the *Akron-Beacon Journal* by Stu Feldstein, who accompanied Bommarito to Geneva, April 25, 27, 28, and May 2, 1976; also Bruce Larrick, "Boycott . . . Goal is to make Firestone suffer worldwide," *ibid.*, April 22, 1976.

[64] "Unions in Foreign Subsidiaries to Help Rubber Strikers in U.S.," *New York Times*, April 27, 1976, p. 17; "Rubber Boycott May be Widened," *ibid.*, April 28, 1976, p. 42; and "Stretching the Strategy: Rubber Walkout Test of Possibility of Multinational Union Global Strikes," syndicated column of Victor Reisel, for release April 21, 1976.

[65] See note 45 above and quotation relating thereto, note 50 above, and note 76 below. The communications referred to, one by telephone, one by letter, concerned strikes in 1975 in Spain and were transmitted by Bommarito. Firestone advised him that, since it had only a minority interest in these facilities, it could do nothing. Telephone interview, February 16, 1977.

was "having a real effect," and declared that "recent checks at American ports indicate that no supplies of tires have been getting through." Because there was a "likelihood of a new desperate effort to break the blockade," ICEF affiliates were urged to contact the International Transport Workers' Federation and the AFL-CIO International Longshoremen's Association and Seafarers' International Union, "who will refuse to unload the tires in American ports." [66] Speaking to the 1973 congress of IG Chemie in Hamburg in September after the strike was terminated, the ICEF secretary general stated that "the positive, fantastic results of the longest rubber industry strike in U.S. history were, in part, due to your [IG Chemie and others] solidarity actions such as cut back in overtime, transportation boycotts, and many, many more solidarity actions." [67] Similar claims are made in the secretary general's report to the 1976 congress. There he claims:

> This [ICF] appeal met with an active and enthusiastic response from ICF affiliates throughout and duration of the lengthy URW strike. In fact, the sustained solidarity of ICF rubber affiliates during the long strike constituted an important advance in ICF's action program against multinationals.[68]

The companies tended from the beginning to downgrade the potential of importing tires. Thus, a vice-president of B. F. Goodrich commented: "We typically don't even ship tires across the ocean because they're too bulky. . . . And there's no prospect of our scheduling overtime over there because the market is soggier there than it is here." [69]

Analysis of Claims

Tires were imported in anticipation of, during, and after the strike in order to supply customers (see Figures IX-1 and IX-2,

---

[66] ICF Circular Letter No. 85/76, June 30, 1976. See also No. 71/76, June 16, 1976, and No. 101/76, August 4, 1976.

[67] *Tagesprotokoll des 10. Ordentlichen Gewerkschaftstages der IG Chemie-Papier-Keramik in Hamburg*, September 1976, p. 25. In the same talk, it was promised that the following Friday a boycott would support a strike of Bantu workers in South Africa, and on the previous Friday, all shipments to South America would be boycotted. We found no record of either occurring. Translations by the Industrial Research Unit.

[68] *ICF 16th Statutory Congress*, pp. 33-34.

[69] Peter J. Pestillo, quoted in "The rubber talks have gone flat," *Business Week*, May 24, 1976, p. 40.

below). We have been unable to find a single instance of interference with shipments of tires in Europe, in Japan, or in the United States. There is no discussion of such interference of the ICEF or of the rubber strike in the publications of the International Transport Workers' Federation, the transport secretariat,[70] or recorded action by the International Longshoremen's Association in United States East and Gulf Coast ports or by the Longshoremen's and Warehousemen's Union in West Coast ports.[71] The only instance of overt action reported in the *United Rubber Worker* is an alleged sympathy strike of Peruvian rubber workers, which our research indicates did not occur.[72]

The ICEF action never had complete support. As already noted, its backing in France is minor, and, in Italy, marginal at best. In addition, the secretary of the ICEF Rubber Division, a Luxembourg unionist, declined to attend the April Geneva meeting. During the strike, Goodyear's large Luxembourg facility peacefully negotiated a new agreement providing basically what was required by law.[73] Public avowals of support elsewhere in Europe were very limited, and little appeared in the press.[74]

In Japan, the situation was similar. For the record, Japanese unions promised to prevent shipments of rubber tires to the United States.[75] The Japanese Federation of Rubber Workers

---

[70] See the *ITF Newsletter*, March-December 1976, in which there is no mention of the rubber strike, or of the ICEF.

[71] Such actions would, of course, make the boycotting union in the United States liable for National Labor Relations Board and court action, and potentially heavy financial damages. Levinson admitted this in his report to the 1976 congress. *ICF 16th Statutory Congress*, p. 89.

[72] *United Rubber Worker*, July-August 1976, p. 5. We have checked through several sources and find no record of such stoppage or report thereof.

[73] The ICEF called this contract a breakthrough. ICF Circular Letter No. 101/76, August 4, 1976.

[74] Besides subscribing to numerous European papers and journals, the authors were in Europe during April and May 1976, and one of the authors was in Sweden during June 1976. There appeared a letter of support from a union in a Swedish paper, a story on ICEF action in the French journal *Intersocial* and little else. A leaflet distributed in Turkey was also brought to our attention. The article in *Intersocial*, May 1976, was an interview with the ICEF secretary general, who mentioned the boycott but quickly changed the subject to industrial health.

[75] The Japanese unions allegedly pledged "'severe' control of inventories at U.S. rubber companies' foreign plants to keep them from being diverted to America." Stu Feldstein, "More Foreign Unions Vow Aid to URW," *Akron-*

Unions translated the ICEF and URW documents and submitted them to each enterprise union affiliated with it and to the presidents of each tire company in Japan. The Ohtsu Tire and Rubber Company, in which Firestone then owned 19.77 percent of the stock, simply replied that it was taking no action to assist United States users of rubber products. Similar responses were made by other companies. Some Japanese rubber enterprise unions did not even press the matter this far and did not discuss it with their members.[76] As summed up by an executive of one major Japanese rubber company:

> As we see it, the ICF proposals achieved nothing in Japan. A boycott is meaningless as very few U.S. tires are imported into Japan and if you understand the Japanese national mentality, you will appreciate that any request to curb exports would fall on a deaf ear.[77]

The Import Data

The U.S. Department of Commerce records each tire imported by country and by major tire category. These data provide absolutely no support whatsoever for any boycott claims. Table IX-2 shows imports of passenger tires by month and principal country for 1976, and Figure IX-1 summarizes these data. The number of passenger tires imported each month jumped substantially in March, leveled back, but remained well above the January figure throughout the strike. Some of these imported tires were undoubtedly for foreign cars. All major American companies manufacture them abroad, but some make them here also. In addition, however, we have ascertained that molds were sent abroad so that American tires could be manufactured there, and there was no report of interference by unions or employees. The March jump in imports was in anticipation of the widely expected strike.

Of special significance in these data are the Canadian figures. Imports from Canada rose substantially in March and then, after a drop from this high, jumped by August to a figure almost twice that of January. The same cars are made on both sides of the

---

Beacon Journal, April 28, 1976, pp. A1, 20. Actually, although the Big Four have relations with several Japanese tire companies, they have no controlling interest therein.

[76] Rubber tire firms, interviews in Tokyo and Nagoya, June 1976.

[77] Letter to authors, October 6, 1976.

border by American-based automobile companies and thus take the same size tires. Obviously, locals of the URW in Canada built many tires for the United States market while their union brothers were on strike—exactly the reverse of what happened in 1974 during the already described strike of URW locals at Canadian Goodyear and Firestone plants.

Unlike passenger car tires, those for trucks and buses made in different countries are likely to be uniform in size and are less likely to be manufactured by smaller companies. Moreover, they are a high-profit line. The strike of the Big Four, coupled with the brisk demand for small trucks and vans, caused a shortage of these tires that was met by imports (Figure IX-2). Some of these imports came from Big Four plants in Europe; others from Michelin, then planning a truck and bus tire plant in South Carolina, now in production, and anxious to serve better its American customers; from depressed Pirelli in Italy needing sales; and from Japanese companies and others.[78] As shown in Table IX-3, Canadian factories supplied a major share of these imports, with almost nineteen times as many truck and bus tires crossing the border in September as in January. In addition, every major tire-manufacturing country exported considerably more to the United States as the strike progressed. Moreover, to fill depleted stocks, American companies continued to import after the strike ended, thus depriving the returned strikers of some overtime work. Demand in the immediate poststrike period was also affected by the Ford Motor strike.[79]

OIL CRISIS IMPACT AND INTERNATIONAL UNIONISM

The oil crisis, with its impact not only on total and type of automobile sales and therefore on sales of tires but also on the costs of tires since synthetic rubber has a petroleum base, has resulted in considerable changes in the tire industry. In addition, the shift in demand from bias-ply to radial tires has fur-

---

[78] "Detroit is getting tires from other sources as well. Domestic auto workers have made spot purchases of European-made tires such as Michelin and Pirelli. And Canadian tire supply lines have been extended further across the border, acknowledges General Motors." "Cause for Optimism," *Chemical Week*, August 18, 1976, p. 13.

[79] Telephone interviews, October 27 and November 1, 1976. After the strike, companies imported particularly their lines of tires for sizes in smaller demand so that they could concentrate on heavy demand lines in domestic plants. The sharp drop in October imports reflects the Ford strike, since Ford is a major truck producer.

TABLE IX-2
Passenger Tires Imported to United States by Month and Principal Nation Source, 1976

Country	January	February	March	April	May	June	July	August	September	October	November	December
Canada	184,814	225,817	301,593	248,986	227,061	278,539	340,234	352,793	351,583	323,163	233,809	226,928
Brazil	4,020	2,800	12,064	19,265	84,960	21,473	23,169	31,474	36,118	22,787	28,606	20,490
Sweden	4,637	3,232	12,660	1,840	2,760	8,264	1,668	9,812	4,579	10,279	1,700	12,075
United Kingdom	47,638	22,689	76,341	78,280	103,315	102,882	69,926	59,748	37,429	25,888	38,723	35,613
Ireland	17,866	11,295	49,439	18,800	41,046	25,949	27,377	27,300	18,661	21,781	9,688	27,893
Netherlands	2,281	5,386	9,348	3,913	3,840	10,311	7,302	15,365	30,590	11,383	13,383	14,955
France	161,187	151,367	169,292	246,827	178,184	198,073	183,751	124,739	166,670	109,364	201,190	184,618
West Germany	111,113	88,805	193,365	45,331	91,051	72,704	86,949	72,702	90,627	81,059	116,479	119,725
Spain	91,300	127,988	189,079	61,258	91,085	105,716	93,617	109,223	97,914	58,864	122,296	137,880
Italy	197,007	145,295	178,318	287,510	108,105	162,416	130,850	118,132	54,141	93,850	82,983	110,601
Israel	14,389	27,531	43,544	36,416	35,370	40,691	37,087	50,240	37,796	27,870	38,937	53,187
Japan	58,577	33,446	73,121	54,645	45,362	49,721	73,775	71,486	87,407	80,661	90,401	86,597
All Countries *	925,812	858,686	1,328,922	1,178,784	1,107,080	1,102,115	1,094,387	1,065,314	1,028,667	887,894	999,897	1,065,470

Source: U.S. Department of Commerce, Bureau of the Census, Foreign Trade Division.
* Also includes tires imported from Mexico, Belgium, Austria, Switzerland, Yugoslavia, Australia, New Zealand, Egypt, East Germany, Uruguay, the Korean Republic, China, Hungary, Czechoslovakia, India, and Denmark.

TABLE IX-3

Truck and Bus Tires Imported to United States
by Month and Principal Nation Source, 1976

Country	January	February	March	April	May	June	July	August	September	October	November	December
Canada	11,710	14,484	20,641	86,779	68,643	128,121	114,149	160,670	221,805	52,784	72,181	62,956
United Kingdom	10,357	8,540	32,084	28,096	34,462	30,500	29,170	41,388	28,245	25,472	35,554	43,346
France	39,607	42,182	62,170	81,840	69,315	77,723	71,740	69,039	46,352	28,797	43,000	55,599
West Germany	8,057	10,671	29,479	19,306	13,520	14,010	9,107	17,346	9,972	12,194	21,804	15,415
Spain	957	999	2,786	292	467	1,298	1,524	654	8,037	130	3,889	1,916
Italy	7,229	5,912	7,059	15,686	9,381	12,901	18,685	22,082	16,252	12,491	26,368	20,292
Israel	1,740	8,421	5,345	7,800	5,397	7,894	8,941	13,450	17,053	16,510	14,915	27,052
Korean Republic	5,428	1,666	14,217	14,078	6,410	6,394	17,751	11,054	23,742	20,741	34,581	35,806
Japan	54,834	37,222	59,550	37,099	32,409	40,806	65,174	80,559	74,024	80,821	102,607	91,442
All Countries*	144,809	185,972	242,328	252,084	247,895	324,319	346,392	422,247	453,555	260,494	370,917	366,685

Source: U.S. Department of Commerce, Bureau of the Census, Foreign Trade Division.
* Also includes tires imported from Mexico, Guatemala, Costa Rica, Jamaica, Venezuela, Peru, Chile, Sweden, Denmark, the Netherlands, Belgium, Austria, Hungary, Switzerland, Poland, India, Malaysia, the Philippines, and China.

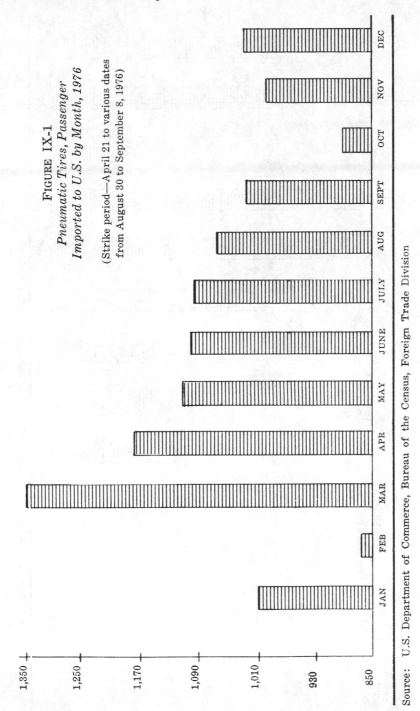

FIGURE IX-1
*Pneumatic Tires, Passenger
Imported to U.S. by Month, 1976*

(Strike period—April 21 to various dates
from August 30 to September 8, 1976)

Source: U.S. Department of Commerce, Bureau of the Census, Foreign Trade Division

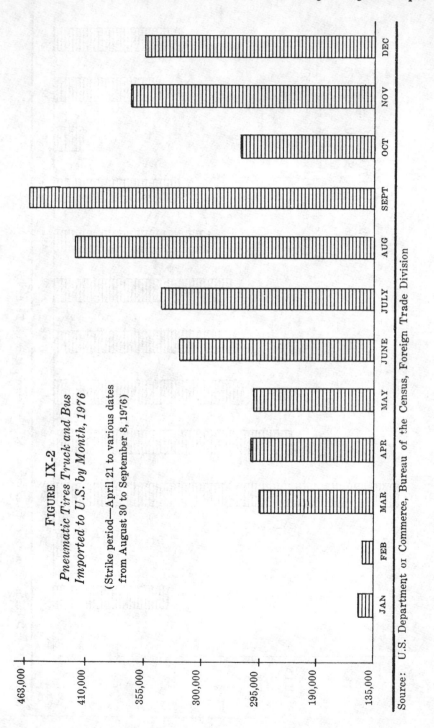

FIGURE IX-2
*Pneumatic Tires Truck and Bus
Imported to U.S. by Month, 1976*

(Strike period—April 21 to various dates
from August 30 to September 8, 1976)

Source: U.S. Department of Commerce, Bureau of the Census, Foreign Trade Division

ther upset existing consumption, sales, and manufacturing patterns and has resulted in overcapacity of manufacturing facilities.[80] A number of tire manufacturers have therefore been forced to restructure their activities, to reduce employment, and to close plants. This has caused labor relations problems and has encouraged both the ICEF and the Communist groups to attempt to take advantage of situations involving Firestone, Dunlop-Pirelli, Goodyear, and Uniroyal.

Firestone

The utter failure of ICEF action to affect production and distribution during the 1976 United Rubber Workers strike apparently led to some coolness between that union and the ICEF. Allegedly, the URW paid no affiliation dues to the ICEF for one year. This was apparently a temporary chill, however; for both soon again made Firestone, beset with the recall problems and plant closings, a key target.

Swedish Plant Closings and the OECD. On November 14, 1977, Lennart Nyström, an officer of the Swedish blue-collar union federation, LO, wrote to Henri Bernard, then general secretary of the Trade Union Advisory Council (TUAC) of the OECD, alleging "a successful use of the OECD Guidelines." According to Nyström, Firestone decided early in 1977 to close one of its three Swedish plants, located at Tvååker, and to transfer production to the two others, located at Borås and Viskafors. The local management agreed to negotiate the changes with the trade unions, but "these negotiations were meaningless since the local management had no real capacity to take any decisions nor to negotiate any agreements to change what in reality had been decided in the U.S." When the local unions were unable to effectuate negotiations with representatives from group management in Akron, Nyström reported that the LO's affiliated union Sv. Fabriksarbetareförbundet contacted Firestone's headquarters and "asked for negotiations with representatives of the management authorized to make decisions" based on the OECD guidelines, paragraph 9, under the chapter on "Employment and Industrial Relations." [81] The company, according to the LO, did not respond to the union's demand.

---

[80] See, e.g., "Tire makers face flat sales in the 1980s," *Chemical Week*, May 30, 1979, pp. 16-17.

[81] Letter from Lennart Nyström to Henri Bernard, November 14, 1977. The OECD guidelines are discussed in Part Seven of this book.

The LO's affiliated union then sent another letter to the company in Akron repeating the demand and threatening to take up the matter with the Swedish government unless there was a positive reply from the company. The ICEF was also contacted, and "the trade secretariat sent out a communication to all its member unions . . . worldwide, condemning Firestone's action." [82] According to Nyström, "this worked and on October 19, real negotiations took place between our affiliated union and a representative of the group management of Firestone. These negotiations also resulted in an agreement on how the changes should be handled." [83]

Enar Agren, president of the Swedish Factory Workers' Union, claimed also that: "This time we got a prompt answer and a date for negotiations was fixed for the end of October. Participating in these negotiations were a representative for the Firestone group's executive, two for the Swedish company management and a representative for the Employers' Confederation's general group." [84]

In response to the foregoing claims, the chief personnel officer of the company wrote that "throughout this discussion the Firestone Tire & Rubber Company took the position that the Firestone-Viskafors board of directors and its management have the responsibility for conducting the necessary business activities of Firestone-Viskafors, and they have full authority to conform to the legal requirements in Sweden." [85] He further stated that, in October 1977, Firestone changed its managing director in Sweden, and expressed the belief that the arrival of the new managing director was a basis for the union's claim that the company sent a representative for the purpose of negotiating with the union. He further wrote that "this claim is totally incorrect. The matter in its entirety was negotiated by our Swedish organization." [86] Further communications with the company underscore the fact that a new managing director was sent to Sweden to deal with the company's general problems and not

---

[82] Article by Inez Backlund in the *LO Newspaper*, No. 33 (1977) (translated by Erica Stempa).

[83] Letter from Lennart Nyström to Henri Bernard, November 14, 1977.

[84] See Backlund article above.

[85] Letter from J. H. Zimmerman, vice-president, Firestone, to the authors, February 10, 1978.

[86] *Ibid.*

to deal specifically with the union situation.[87] The new managing director decided to close the plant in order to improve the general economic position of the company.

The LO claims that, during negotiations, Firestone's group executive insisted that the plant be closed and that he responded favorably to the union's demand for the company to provide replacement work for the closed plant and to give severance pay to those who lost their jobs. The company agrees that severance pay was provided but denies that any replacement work was promised and points out that it certainly had not been provided.[88] Nevertheless, the official union report claims a victory:

> Even though we didn't succeed in saving the Tvååker factory, we see the negotiations as a success from the union's point of view. This example shows too how we can use the guidelines and our International trade secretariats to scare companies into negotiating. The OECD guidelines have many shortcomings, but we think they can be utilized nevertheless, and the possibilities they open up should be taken advantage of.[89]

Of interest is the fact that Charles Levinson does not share the LO's enthusiam for use of the OECD guidelines but has repeatedly deprecated their significance, seeing them as competitive with his efforts. Thus, he has written:

> It is, of course, the basic intent of multinational companies to avoid and beat off any attempt to develop a countervailing force which would involve their own employees through their democratic trade unions because that means dealing with problems specifically and concretely, rather than distilling them into the level of abstractions and platitudes around "Minimum Codes," which of course have very little impact on the real questions or affect multinational companies in any way.[90]

The Firestone Swedish case is of special interest because (1) it demonstrates how a given situation can be interpreted in two entirely different ways, and (2) it provides a clear example of how unions attempt to use the OECD guidelines to support their particular interests.

Switzerland and North America. In late March 1978, Firestone announced the closing of its bias-ply passenger tire plants in

---

[87] J. H. Zimmerman, telephone interview, February 20, 1978.

[88] J. H. Zimmerman, telephone interview, December 22, 1978.

[89] See Backlund article above.

[90] ICEF Circular Letter No. 59/78, March 28, 1978, pp. 1-2.

Pratteln, near Basel, Switzerland, and Calgary, Canada, and the phasing out of the same production in Akron, Ohio. The closing of Switzerland's only tire plant caused considerable adverse press, and governmental reaction in Switzerland was based primarily on the alleged failure of Firestone to consult with or to notify government officials or employees beforehand and the precipitous manner in which the announcement was made. Press reports also noted, however, that with Switzerland's virtually nonexistent unemployment, those displaced would have no difficulty in finding suitable employment.[91] Other press reports implied that the case would be taken before the OECD.[92] The principal union involved —an ICEF affiliate, Gewerkschaft Textil, Chemie, Papier (GTCP)—led a one-and-a-half-day strike, rare for Switzerland, to protest the allegedly "deceitful conduct" of Firestone.[93]

On March 28, 1978, the ICEF secretary general issued an "Urgent Request for Solidarity" against Firestone demanding that affiliates "convey expressions of solidarity" to the Swiss union involved, "immediately initiate [a] boycott of production transfer to Switzerland of all Firestone tires from your country," and "apply [a] ban on all overtime and refuse to work extra hours in extraordinary production schedules." The same circular letter states that this issue was "of critical importance to ICEF affiliates in the rubber and tire industry generally."[94] The letter further charges without evidence that Firestone would be importing tires from the Soviet bloc into Switzerland. Interestingly, no mention is made in this circular letter of the closings of the Calgary or Akron facilities.

The ICEF circular letter was followed up by Peter Bommarito, who also threatened a boycott. He was reminded that past boycotts (during the Canadian strike of 1974 and the United States strike of 1976) were completely without effect. Bommarito also announced a demonstration in front of Fire-

---

[91] See, e.g., "Firestone (Schweiz) stellt Produktion ein," *Neue Zürcher Zeitung*, March 23, 1978; "Scharfer Gewerkschaftsprotest gegen den Firestone-Entscheid," *ibid.*, March 25/26, 1978; "Höhere Radio- und Fernsehgebühren—Firestone," *ibid.*, May 11, 1978; "Schweizer Firestone-Werk wird endgültig geschlossen," *Handelsblatt*, May 15, 1978; and "Trouble in Baselland: Firestone wants out," *Business Week*, May 1, 1978, p. 30.

[92] "Der 'Multi-Kodex' der OECD," *Neue Zürcher Zeitung*, May 13, 1978.

[93] "Trouble in Baselland: Firestone wants out," p. 30.

[94] ICEF Circular Letter No. 58/78, March 28, 1978. See also "Boykott von Ostblock-Autoreifen?" *Frankfurter Allgemeine Zeitung*, April 27, 1978, p. 15.

stone headquarters to coincide with the April 1978 visit of the Swiss ambassador and his staff to the United States, coming to Akron to urge Firestone to reconsider its decision. The demonstration "never occurred and the two-day meetings with the Swiss representatives were conducted without interference, on a business-like basis." The company has also confirmed that it has "felt no impact" of any alleged boycott.[95] No mention of the alleged boycott or demonstration appears in the *United Rubber Worker*.

Nevertheless, the agitation over the Swiss plant closing continued. The ICEF Firestone World Council met in Madrid on June 21, 1978, in conjunction with the ICEF Executive Board meeting. It resolved to ask Bommarito, who did not attend the meeting, to attempt to arrange a meeting between Firestone executives and the ICEF world council.[96] Bommarito did attempt such an arrangement, but Firestone executives declined.[97]

On August 4, 1978, the ICEF secretary general sent out a circular letter asking affiliates whether, in order to force the company to meet with the world council, they would (1) carry out "a one-day solidarity demonstration strike," (2) "carry out a total ban on overtime," (3) be "prepared simultaneously to carry out a consumer boycott and/or a consumer information campaign against the company," or (4) "suggest complementary and additional measures."[98] Six weeks later, the secretary general indicated that he had received no replies to this inquiry.[99] By the end of 1978, the company reported that no overt action by ICEF affiliates anywhere in the world had occurred and that, in the United States, as a result of the recall of the Firestone "500" radial tire, members of the United Rubber Workers were working considerable overtime.[100]

Meanwhile, the Swiss GTCP filed a suit against Firestone and has demanded damages over the closing of the Pratteln plant. The

---

[95] Letter from J. H. Zimmerman to the authors, May 30, 1978.

[96] ICEF Circular Letter No. 120/78, August 4, 1978; ICEF Press Release, No. 4/78, June 20, 1978.

[97] J. H. Zimmerman, telephone interview, November 7, 1978.

[98] See ICEF Circular Letter No. 120/78, August 4, 1978.

[99] ICEF Circular Letter No. 132/78, September 20, 1978, p. 3; and No. 151/78, November 15, 1978.

[100] J. H. Zimmerman, telephone interview, December 22, 1978.

case had not as yet been heard by the Swiss courts as of mid-1979.

Finally, the ICEF secretary general promised to issue and to disseminate widely "a Firestone File," which would highlight and specify "the endless violations of contract obligations, legal responsibilities and the immoral and antisocial behavior characteristic of Firestone, which continues to arrogantly refuse all requests for responsible discussions with the ICEF Permanent Firestone World Council at world level." [101] Neither Firestone nor we have seen this document, which, if issued, has certainly not been "widely disseminated."

Spanish Issue. At its June 1978 Madrid meeting, the ICEF also charged that Firestone was failing to negotiate properly with Spanish unions which were then on strike, and issued the usual threats of worldwide action.[102] URW President Bommarito was requested to seek a meeting between Firestone [103] and the world council to discuss this issue, as well as the one involving the plant closure in Switzerland. As noted, this request was declined by the company.

Dunlop-Pirelli

The Dunlop-Pirelli Union, as already noted, has been beset with problems ever since its inception in 1971. Pirelli in particular has had an unbroken string of losses since 1973.[104] Now Dunlop in the United Kingdom has found itself with losses resulting not only from the general problems in the tire industry but additionally from the decline in the British automobile industry.[105] In the first quarter of 1979, for example, 57.5 percent of the new automobiles sold in the United Kingdom were imported. In addition, British Leyland, Dunlop's largest original customer and once the leader in the United Kingdom market, saw its share of new car sales drop to 17.7 percent while Ford

---

[101] ICEF Circular Letter No. 132/78, September 20, 1978, p. 3. See also No. 120/78, August 4, 1978; and No. 101/78, July 12, 1978.

[102] ICEF Press Release No. 4/78, June 20, 1978; ICEF Circular Letter No. 88/78, June 26, 1978.

[103] *Ibid.*

[104] Rupert Cornwell, "Pirelli facing 'serious' deficit," *Financial Times*, March 29, 1979, p. 19.

[105] Barry Riley and Nick Garnett, "Dunlop discloses $47M European tyre loss," *Financial Times*, April 20, 1979, p. 22.

captured 33.6 percent. Moreover, over one-half of the Ford cars sold in this period were imported rather than manufactured in the United Kingdom.[106] As the leading British tire manufacturer, Dunlop is particularly hard hit by this trend, but other companies, as noted, are also having problems.

To cope with its problem, Dunlop decided to close one of its oldest, least productive, and most labor strife-ridden plants— Speke, on Liverpool's Merseyside—which involved a loss of 2,333 jobs, and to reduce its labor force at Fort Dunlop (Birmingham) by 500 and at Inchinnan (near Glasgow) by 240 persons.[107] This caused a series of strikes in several Dunlop plants and boycotts of Dunlop materials led by the TGWU, whose president, John Pemberton, was being laid off at Speke.[108] (The presidency, as noted, is not a full-time job in the TGWU.)

ICEF Involvement. Charles Levinson, secretary general of the ICEF, tried to insert himself into the problem and wrote several circular letters urging solidarity,[109] but no action occurred as a result. The TGWU-led pickets did interrupt work at other plants, but in at least one case, the employees at a plant authorized shop stewards to organize the breaking of picket lines if necessary to maintain production.[110] The dispute apparently ended in May 1979 with the agreement of Dunlop to establish a joint union-company working party to study the possibilities of introducing new products in the Merseyside-area plants of the

---

[106] Kenneth Gooding, "Record April sales for new cars," *Financial Times,* May 10, 1979, p. 17.

[107] "Dunlop Announces Rationalisation and Investment Programme for Tyres," Dunlop Press Release, January 19, 1979; "Now Dunlop plans Speke Shutdown," *Sunday Telegraph* (London), November 12, 1978, p. 22; and Kenneth Gooding, "Dunlop will make 3,100 redundant at tyre plants," *Financial Times,* January 20, 1979, p. 32. For an analysis of the labor problems at Speke and the failure of unions there to cooperate, see the interview of K. J. Johnson, Dunlop director of administration, *Liverpool Daily Post,* April 4, 1979.

[108] "Dunlop faces one-day strike," *Financial Times,* February 20, 1979, p. 18; Nick Garnett and Rhys David, "Dunlop faces closure dispute," *Financial Times,* April 5, 1979, p. 1; Garnett, "Helicopter used to avoid pickets," *Financial Times,* April 24, 1979, p. 13; and "Dunlop's Latest," *The Record* (TGWU), April 1979, p. 3.

[109] See, e.g., ICEF Circular Letter No. 39/79, March 20, 1979; No. 43/79, March 21, 1979; No. 44/79, March 21, 1979; and No. 52/79, April 2, 1979.

[110] Nick Garnett, "Dunlop workers act against picket lines," *Financial Times,* April 25, 1979, p. 7.

company.[111] Meanwhile, the Speke tire plant was closed. Dunlop had already announced that, at Speke, it would continue its belting division with 400 employees and would move its golf ball facility to a nearby site with a reduction of employees from 280 to 200.[112]

Although Levinson's efforts in regard to the Speke closings were totally without impact, he did find the occasion useful to advertise his new book, *Vodka Cola*. He charged on British television, as well as in his circular letters, that Dunlop's troubles were attributable to imports from Communist countries that had purchased technology particularly from Pirelli, and this resulted in considerable publicity for him and for the book.[113]

Meanwhile, a strike against a Pirelli operation in Belgium occurred for several weeks in February and March 1979. The ICEF claimed that only the solidarity of its affiliates prevented Pirelli from shutting down the facility, and this again gave Levinson the opportunity to advertise his book.[114] The matter actually was a dispute over wages, which was resolved without any non-Belgian intervention.

Communist Activity. Prior to the ICEF involvement, a meeting was held by TGWU officials (particularly the Speke group) with their counterparts in France and Italy, probably under Communist auspices. They organized a supposed international strike on March 7, 1979; about 50 percent of Dunlop's United Kingdom employees struck, but there was no action on the European continent. Support from Dunlop factories there never involved more than telegrams to the company's headquarters.

A second strike scheduled for April 11 was cancelled. Then on May 2-4, the Communists sponsored a meeting in Torino, Italy, at which they set up an International Union Coordination Group

---

[111] *Ibid.*; "Joint talks agreed at Dunlop," *Financial Times*, May 15, 1979, p. 13.

[112] "Dunlop Announces Rationalisation."

[113] The book, published by Gordon and Cremonesi, was reviewed in the *Financial Times*, March 27, 1979, p. 10. Like Levinson's previous writings, it is virtually devoid of citations despite considerable use of figures and statistics, which therefore cannot easily be checked. Pirelli and Dunlop do not import tires from Eastern Bloc countries; Pirelli has four contracts with Communist countries providing for production of tires under license or the building of tire-manufacturing facilities. Obviously, if Pirelli had not won these contracts, other concerns would have.

[114] ICEF Circular Letter No. 47/79, March 26, 1979.

for Dunlop-Pirelli, Michelin, Firestone, and Ceat, and promised an international strike for Dunlop and Pirelli plants on May 14.[115] Nothing occurred, perhaps because the agreement on the aftermath of the Speke closing had already been achieved.

Goodyear

The world's largest tire manufacturer, Goodyear, has also closed a facility in the United Kingdom, its long labor-troubled plant in Drumchapel, Glasgow, Scotland, and in addition has been reducing employment at its other British plants, located in Craigavon, Northern Ireland, and in Wolverhampton. The closure at Drumchapel followed the refusal of the work force to work the Friday night shift, to improve absenteeism or otherwise to improve productivity, which the company stated was less than one-half that of other plants in Europe, including the remaining two in the United Kingdom where the company has been receiving better employee and union cooperation.[116] Belated attempts of the Glasgow employees and unions to alter their adamant refusal to work at an acceptable pace did not change the company decision,[117] and the plant is now closed. Because of the workers' attitude, the company received few, if any, unfavorable comments for the first international plant closure in its history.

On the other side of the world, Goodyear negotiated an amicable agreement in April 1979 with its sales organization employees in Japan. An ICEF circular letter claimed that Goodyear's "antiunion stance" was reversed by an ICEF cable to the company's Japanese headquarters.[118] Anyone familiar with the Japanese labor relations scene will understand that such matters are invariably settled within the enterprise and that a cable of this nature, if sent, would be of no consequence.

---

[115] "The European Strikes for the Crisis in the Rubber Industry are Going to Start," translation of an article appearing in the *Corriere della Sera* (Milan), May 5, 1979, p. 12.

[116] "Goodyear Unit to Close Scottish Plant, Cites Lagging Productivity," *Wall Street Journal*, February 21, 1979, p. 20; and Ray Perman, "Goodyear calls off rescue of Scottish plant," *Financial Times*, February 21, 1979, p. 1.

[117] "New talks on Goodyear," *Financial Times*, February 26, 1979, p. 1.

[118] ICEF Circular Letter No. 63/79, May 4, 1979.

Uniroyal

On May 9, 1979, the URW struck the unionized tire plants and some other product plants of Uniroyal in the United States.[119] Thus, Peter Bommarito, president of the URW, maintained his record of never having a critical negotiation with the Big Four rubber companies without striking at least one of them since he led his first negotiations in 1967. Uniroyal had one nonunion tire plant and several other facilities continuing in full operation, and some tires were produced by salaried personnel in the struck plants prior to the end of the strike on June 17.

The issues in this strike were directly affected by the guidelines determined by President Jimmy Carter. Bommarito announced beforehand that he would pay no attention to them; Uniroyal insisted that they must be maintained. The matter was further complicated by the fact that Bommarito insisted that an agreement was reached earlier and then reneged upon by Uniroyal at government insistence. Once again, the ICEF called upon the unions in Europe and elsewhere in Uniroyal plants to assist the American strikers;[120] once again, there is every evidence that absolutely nothing resulted from this call and that the ICEF had nothing to do with the settlement of the dispute.[121]

Uniroyal previously announced that it was selling its European tire plants to Continental Gummi-Werke, and negotiations to accomplish this transaction are proceeding. The plants involved are located in Germany, Belgium, France, Great Britain, and Luxembourg.[122] Uniroyal has also closed a number of plants in the United States, with the result that it may now rank fourth, instead of third, in United States tire sales. These plant closings were also issues in the 1979 negotiations and strike and resulted

---

119 Reginald Stuart, "Uniroyal is Struck by Rubber Workers," *New York Times*, May 10, 1979, p. A16; and Stuart, "Uniroyal Agrees to 3-Year Accord, Paving Way for Industry Settlement," *ibid.*, June 19, 1979, p. A19.

120 "Uniroyal Inc., Union Preparing to Resume Contract Negotiations," *Wall Street Journal*, May 18, 1979, p. 5; and ICEF Circular Letter No. 70/79, and No. 71/79, both of May 14, 1979.

121 While in Europe during May 1979, the authors found no evidence whatever of any ICEF action and saw no communications relating to it. Uniroyal European personnel managers interviewed in London, May 9, 1979, and in Brussels, May 22, 1979, reported that they had heard of no ICEF action or even of any communications relating to it.

122 "Uniroyal Agrees to Sell European Tire Operations," *Wall Street Journal*, April 18, 1979, p. 5.

in an agreement to give the URW prior notice of future closings and the right to negotiate concerning them.

CONCLUSION

The record indicates that, despite claims to the contrary, neither the ICEF nor the Communist group has been able to develop effective multinational action in the rubber tire industry. The 1976 U.S. Big Four strike is the most obvious example of the disparity between union claims and actual events. Clearly, there have been no international boycotts, no monitoring of shipments by European or Japanese union members, no cooperation with the International Transport Workers' Federation or with American longshore and maritime unions to prevent tire imports into countries where rubber plants are on strike, and no sympathy actions in 1976 or at any time before in support of ICEF activity anywhere, its claims to the contrary notwithstanding.

This chapter again indicates that most claims of multinational union actions are more imagined than real and that purported support of one union for another over national boundaries almost invariably has amounted to little more than leaflet action or letters or telegrams of support to the unions and idle threats to the companies. To expect European, Japanese, and other national union groups to support a strike of very well-paid American workers when key locals of the striking union in the United States and Canada stayed on the job and helped make up the lost production is, on its face, rather extraordinary, especially since there has been no real precedent for mutual support in this industry.

Union officials and members who hear these reports of great success in international action must know that they lack a factual basis. Certainly, the members of IG Chemie who listened to the ICEF secretary general praise them for monitoring and blocking tire shipments to the United States know that they did none of these things. Such claims once called attention to the work and potential of the international union movement. One wonders whether a continuation of such a policy, instead of a straightforward approach to effective information exchange, can serve any constructive purpose.

The demonstrations of the Communist-supported shop stewards organization, while sensational in a different form, also appear to lack the continuity and stability to build viable international union cooperation. Such disruptions can apparently be maintained over a long period in Italy, for short periods in France, and here and there in Britain. But the Communists have no support in Germany or in the United States, and disruption, with its resultant loss of work and pay, does not gain long-term adherents. The strength of the Communists in Italy and France is in itself a major barrier to multinational union cooperation in the Western world, for it exacerbates the divisions in the labor movement.[123]

We must conclude that international union cooperation, despite claims to the contrary, has not been a serious factor in labor disputes in the rubber tire industry and was virtually nonexistent except on paper in the long 1976 strike in the United States. It seems reasonable also to conclude that the prospects for more effective multinational union cooperation are not bright. Union divisions, divergence of national union interests, employee disinterest in losing work and pay because of problems elsewhere, the demonstrated ability of companies to handle a long stoppage and to avert product shortages, the increase in the number of nonunion plants in the United States and Canada, and the overemphasis of the international union movement in this industry on publicity and sensation instead of a basic program and organization to support it are some of the obvious reasons for this conclusion. It therefore follows that the prospects for multinational rubber industry labor-management information meetings and/or bargaining sessions are poor for the foreseeable future.[124]

---

[123] Considerable time is spent by each group warning of the other's moves. Thus in October 1976, the ICEF secretary general warned affiliates against a plan led by the CGIL, the Italian Communist-dominated federation, to organize a Firestone Tire and Rubber Company meeting in Europe. See ICF Circular Letter, No. 133/76, October 31, 1976.

[124] At the ICEF's sixteenth congress, held in Montreal in October 1976, its secretary general issued a press release reiterating his claims of effective ICEF action in the 1976 United States rubber strike and stating that collective bargaining between multinational companies and unions would begin within two years. Evidence to support such a prediction was not given, and the two years have now come and gone.

CHAPTER X

The Petroleum Industry

Because oil must be obtained where deposits exist and because it is a product in universal demand, the petroleum companies have been among the earliest and most internationalized corporations. The petroleum companies include the largest multinationals in the world plus enormous nationalized concerns in both the petroleum-producing and the developed countries. Table X-1 lists key data for the seventeen largest petroleum corporations as reported by *Fortune* magazine. In sales, they are all among the fifty largest companies in the free world.[1]

Multinational unionism in the petroleum industry has been historically sharply split. Two international trade secretariats carried on a bitter jurisdictional dispute for twenty years: one, the International Federation of Chemical, Energy and General Workers' Unions (ICEF), survives; the other, the International Federation of Petroleum and Chemical Workers (IFPCW), suspended all operations by the end of 1976.[2] The ICEF has since gained many of the IFPCW's former affiliates but, as we note below, not all.

The Communists have always been active in the petroleum industry, and particularly so since the demise of the IFPCW. The Trade Unions International of Chemical, Oil and Allied Workers (ICPS) has moved rapidly to gain followers in Africa; Asia; the Near East; and Latin America, where the IFPCW was strongest and where the ICEF has traditionally not been a significant factor.

The World Confederation of Labour, the former Christian Federation, has its main strength in Latin America. Its Latin

---

[1] *Fortune*, Vol. 98 (August 1978), p. 184.

[2] The story of the jurisdictional dispute between what formerly was known as the ICF (now ICEF) and the IFPCW is found in Herbert R. Northrup and Richard L. Rowan, "The ICF-IFPCW Conflict," *Columbia Journal of World Business*, Vol. IX (Winter 1974), pp. 109-19.

TABLE X-1

The Seventeen Largest Companies in the Petroleum Industry, 1978

Company	Headquarters	Sales ($000)	Assets ($000)	Net Income ($000)	Employees[e]
Exxon	New York	60,334,527	41,530,804	2,763,000	130,000
Royal Dutch/Shell Group	The Hague/London	44,044,534	42,422,370	2,084,653	158,000
Mobil	New York	34,736,045	22,611,479	1,125,638	207,000
Texaco	White Plains, N.Y.	28,607,521	20,249,143	852,461	67,841
British Petroleum	London	27,407,620	26,532,763	853,057	109,000
Standard Oil of California	San Francisco	23,232,413	16,761,021	1,105,881	37,575
National Iranian Oil[a]	Tehran	22,789,650[b]	15,147,063	15,178,157[b]	67,000
Gulf Oil	Pittsburgh, Pa.	18,069,000	15,036,000	791,000	58,300
Standard Oil (Indiana)	Chicago	14,961,489	14,109,264	1,076,412	47,011
ENI[a]	Rome	12,565,727[c]	20,916,568[c]	367,892[c,d]	120,884[c]
Française des Pétroles	Paris	12,509,942[c]	11,537,181[c]	60,305[c]	43,994[c]
Atlantic Richfield	Los Angeles	12,298,403	12,060,210	804,325	50,716
Continental Oil	Stamford, Ct.	9,455,241	7,445,165	451,340	42,780
Petróleos de Venezuela[a]	Caracas	9,137,238	8,376,250	1,449,209	29,882
Petrobrás (Petróleo Brasileiro)[a]	Rio de Janeiro	9,131,228	11,227,151	1,214,516	58,020
Elf-Aquitane[a]	Paris	9,115,703	12,590,744	332,336	38,000
Tenneco	Houston	8,762,000	10,134,000	466,000	104,000

Source: *Fortune*, Vol. 99 (May 7, 1979), p. 270; Vol. 100, (August 13, 1979), p. 194.
[a] Government owned.
[b] *Fortune* estimate.
[c] Also includes certain subsidiaries owned 50 percent or less, either fully or on a prorated basis.
[d] Loss.
[e] Wide variation in number of employees in relation to assets is attributable in part to inclusion of nonpetroleum subsidiaries in data.

American regional organization, Central Latinoamericana de Trabajadores, is also active among petroleum workers in this area.

IFPCW ACTIVITIES, 1954-76

The IFPCW was founded in 1954, largely by American trade unionists, and it remained American-run until its demise, although its second president was a Venezuelan and its third, a Lebanese. The IFPCW's first president and its key founder was O. A. Knight, then president of the U.S. Oil Workers International Union—later to become the Oil, Chemical and Atomic Workers (OCAW). The secretariat's general secretary from 1954 to 1973 was Loyd A. Haskins, formerly Knight's assistant, and from 1973 until the organization's demise, Curtis Hogan, also a former OCAW staff person, held the position. The IFPCW's headquarters was always in Denver, Colorado—first in the OCAW building, then in a building of its own. The OCAW always paid the salary of Haskins. In 1973, the IFPCW claimed an affiliated membership of 1,369,307 workers affiliated in 108 unions from sixty-two countries.[3]

The founders of the IFPCW originally believed that they would merge with and absorb the ICEF, which in the 1950s was known as the International Federation of Industrial Organizations and General Workers' Unions and which then had virtually no affiliates outside of Europe. In 1963, however, Charles Levinson became secretary general of this rival organization and soon began the public relations campaign that made the ICEF well-known. Levinson quickly persuaded his executive board to disavow a previously agreed upon IFPCW-ICEF merger plan and, refusing any accommodation, successfully fought the IFPCW until the IFPCW ceased operations after the withdrawal of AFL-CIO support and the disaffiliation of the OCAW.

Levinson's campaign against the IFPCW was materially aided by the IFPCW's tactical errors. Wilhelm Gefeller, then president of Industriegewerkschaft Chemie-Papier-Keramik (IG Chemie), was anxious to head a secretariat. Knight and Haskins, underestimating the future power of the German unions, declined to offer him a key post in the IFPCW. Levinson, however, worked

---

[3] Report of General Secretary Loyd A. Haskins to the Seventh World Congress of the International Federation of Petroleum and Chemical Workers, Singapore, October 1973, p. 5. Hereafter cited as IFPCW Seventh World Congress.

out a deal. Gefeller became president of the ICEF, and IG Chemie dropped its affiliation with the IFPCW and persuaded the Dutch to do likewise. Thereafter, the IFPCW was not a factor in European international unionism. Moreover, in the underdeveloped areas, where its activities were concentrated, the IFPCW had made little effort to collect dues. As a result, it was easily criticized for its dependence on grants from government sources, even though most were funneled through AFL-CIO-controlled institutes. When the AFL-CIO dropped its support, the IFPCW had no power and few resources to remain viable.

IFPCW Company Activities

The IFPCW initially considered its mission that of assisting in the unionization of workers, and it performed this task well. Its first success was the recognition of Shell refinery employees on the Caribbean island of Curaçao. The secretariat was aided by a probably illegal picket line put up by the U.S. Seafarers' Union in United States Gulf of Mexico ports. The IFPCW helped unions to get started in Latin America, in many African countries, in Southeast Asia, and even for a period in Iran and the Near East.[4]

IFPCW staff and officials expended their energies achieving recognition for these unions, training their leaders, and developing their bargaining capabilities. In so doing, they earned the respect of petroleum management not only because of their effective representation and training of their constituents but also because, under IFPCW leadership, trade union tactics and aspirations were substituted for the revolutionary ones of the Communists and other radicals who competed for worker allegiance in these areas.[5]

Typically, therefore, Haskins, Hogan, or other IFPCW staff entered a situation quietly in search of an agreement, not publicity. They frequently served as advisors and consultants in local negotiations and sometimes, with management's approval, as actual negotiators. Often they recruited assistance from developed countries. Thus, for the first contract in Curaçao, they

---

[4] This information is taken from the officers' reports and proceedings of IFPCW congresses and from numerous interviews with Messrs. Haskins and Hogan.

[5] Based upon many comments of petroleum industry personnel directors.

imported an experienced Dutch trade unionist, who knew the language, was familiar with Shell, and was acceptable to the company and the union. He assisted in the negotiation and in winning the IFPCW its first major success.[6]

Lack of World Councils

Attempts to form world, or even regional, councils for bargaining in the petroleum industry have not been successful. The ICEF-IFPCW jurisdictional dispute was a longtime obstacle. Another is the wide dispersion of operating units, and political problems and funds to finance meetings all pose problems. In one case, the IFPCW and ENI, the Italian company, attempted to develop a multinational union contract for petroleum employees in Africa. Both parties had agreed that it might be desirable, but they gave up the attempt because of the multitude of local laws, regulations, and customs that were involved.[7]

Another obstacle to multinational bargaining in the petroleum industry is the wide difference in unions' organizational structure in various countries. In the United States, there is one dominant union—the OCAW—and many local independents—the Teamsters, the Operating Engineers, and other AFL-CIO affiliates. In Germany, petroleum workers are part of the major chemical union. They are covered by a contract governing four hundred thousand workers, of whom only a small percentage are in petroleum operations. In Britain, there is no petroleum union. Refinery and other oil workers belong to a host of craft unions, plus the Transport and General Workers' Union. In the underdeveloped countries, petroleum workers are usually the elite— the first to have organized and the highest paid. They are anxious to maintain their status.

In his report to the 1973 IFPCW Congress, retiring General Secretary Haskins criticized the "world council" approach to multinational concerns, as advocated by the ICEF. He had supported instead "coordinated national industry-wide bargaining."

> In countries such as the United States, Canada, Venezuela, Japan, and India, the industry-wide method is used. No other method has been found to be as effective. North American unions, in their earlier stages of development, used the company council method.

---

[6] Report of General Secretary Loyd A. Haskins to the Second World Congress of the International Federation of Petroleum Workers, Rome, 1957, pp. 2-5; Loyd A. Haskins, interview in Denver, Colorado, May 1973.

[7] Loyd A. Haskins, interview in Denver, Colorado, May 1973.

They eventually found it necessary, however, to abandon this method in favor of industry-wide coordinated bargaining.

Weaknesses are inherent also in the worldwide company council method. A primary weakness is that a worldwide council program works at cross purposes to the various national programs. Each company that is taken out of a national program to participate in a worldwide council program weakens the national program. If thirty to forty worldwide councils were formed under separate collective bargaining programs, every national program would be diluted and eventually destroyed. The establishment of such councils becomes counterproductive and weakens the strength of organized labor.

We believe it necessary to completely organize our fields of jurisdiction in each country into strong national unions with strong national collective bargaining programs. IFPCW's role is then to coordinate the national programs in such a manner as to simultaneously apply maximum pressure upon all multinational and national companies for purposes of ensuring a successful outcome to negotiations.[8]

In line with this approach, the IFPCW, by research and communications, attempted to make affiliates aware of what companies provided in their contracts all over the world. As one company executive noted several years ago:

> On the whole, [our] regional and operating organizations have not experienced any serious difficulties as a result of efforts by IFPCW to create multinational instruments for purposes of collective bargaining or assisting local unions to achieve objectives they could not reach alone. At the moment we are more concerned perhaps by the moves being made by unions to secure national legislation or ILO resolutions and recommendations limiting the activities of multinational companies. However, we believe that international union bodies will work hard, and make some progress, in the years ahead, to develop machinery facilitating coalition bargaining across national lines. Their leaderships are committed; it may be the principal raison d'etre of their organizations; and a number of well-financed national unions, especially in the U.S. and Europe, feel a need to raise wage and work standards in other areas to protect the living standards of their own members.[9]

The IFPCW did attempt to encourage transnational activity to some extent. The boycott of United States ports in the Curaçao dispute has already been noted. In 1967, during a long strike involving Exxon in Jamaica, the IFPCW urged its affiliates in the Caribbean and in Venezuela to refuse to load products destined for Exxon customers there. The Venezuelan

---

[8] IFPCW Seventh World Congress, 1973, pp. 8-9.

[9] Letter to the authors, January 5, 1973.

union failed to act, but the one on Aruba, where Exxon has its largest refinery, did delay some shipments.[10]

Similarly in 1970, during a strike of Esso, Shell, and British Petroleum workers in Malta, the IFPCW called for a boycott by Italian unions.[11] The strike was settled before any action could occur. In 1973, the IFPCW vigorously endorsed the Shell boycott discussed below.

The IFPCW leadership always had considerable doubt about the efficacy of this approach and believed that it often hindered, rather than effectuated, settlements. Hence, such boycott threats were used more to counter the ICEF's public relations than for any real impact. Particularly toward the end of the IFPCW's active endeavors, one had the impression that this was true as the IFPCW sought to compete with the ICEF. Certainly, IFPCW officials were skeptical that such activity would contribute to the end desired.[12]

ICEF APPROACHES

The ICEF has generally followed the same tactics in the petroleum industry that were used in the other industries that we have examined. Any labor dispute involving a major petroleum company thus becomes the vehicle for a flood of telegrams demanding of the company's chief executive and/or regional manager that the "antiunion" activity cease and threatening a worldwide reaction if the union demands are not promptly met. Whether the communications are acknowledged, answered, or ignored, the ICEF secretary general claims "effective action" against a multinational company.

In December 1971, for example, Texaco's German affiliate was involved in a wage dispute with IG Chemie. An ICEF telegram to Deutsche Texaco warns that "action would be taken against the company on an international level" unless an agreement was promptly reached.[13] Texaco ignored the telegram, and the

---

[10] Information from company officials; and Loyd A. Haskins, interview in Denver, Colorado, May 1973.

[11] *Ibid.*

[12] Thus the ICEF loudly claimed boycott activities in the Malta dispute and in the U.S. Shell strike, both noted below.

[13] "Union Federation Warns Deutsche Texaco," *Times* (London), December 1, 1971.

strike was eventually settled without any "action . . . on an international level" or any other level.[14]

Major American and European petroleum companies, such as Exxon, Shell, Mobil, and others, have received similar communications when labor disputes have occurred and generally have reacted in a like manner. For example, during a dispute involving Exxon in Rotterdam, Levinson added a request for a meeting to settle the problem. Exxon declined the request.[15] A similar telegram to a number of concerns involved in a controversy in Malta was simply ignored.[16]

Elf-Aquitaine

In February 1976, the French 100 percent state-owned Elf-Erap Company was merged with the French 54 percent state-owned Société Nationale Elf-Aquitaine, with the government maintaining a 71 percent interest. The predecessor company, Elf-Erap, had an incident with ICEF in 1971-72.

In 1971-72, a Senegalese company in which Elf-Erap had a minority interest and to which it provided technical assistance had labor trouble that culminated in the occupation of the refinery in Dakar by the workers. At that time, the Senegalese comanager of the refinery had just been nominated general manager of the company.

The secretary general of the ICEF sent Elf-Erap a telegram "on behalf of 4,000,000 members," and an affiliate of the Confédération Française Démocratique du Travail at the company's French refinery branch called on the management to resolve the issue and issued a few leaflets to that effect. In fact, the matter was settled by action of the Senegalese government, which evicted the union members from the plant.

The company has had no direct contact with the ICEF. Since the Senegalese incident, neither the ICEF nor any other international union organization has attempted to contact the company.[17]

---

[14] Texaco personnel executives, interviews in Houston, Texas, July 12, 1973.

[15] Exxon and Shell personnel executives, interviews in New York and London, June and September 1973.

[16] See "Congress Reports I: Activities Report of the Secretary General," *ICF 14th Statutory Congress*, Folkets Hus, Copenhagen, October 22-24, 1970, p. 31. This was, of course, the same dispute in which the IFPCW issued claims as noted above.

[17] Letters from director of personnel, Elf-Aquitaine, August 22 and October 26, 1976.

British Petroleum and Texaco

In the report to the 1976 congress, the ICEF secretary general claims strike and collective bargaining support against a number of petroleum companies: British Petroleum (BP) in May 1974 during a strike in Britain and in April 1976 during a Belgian strike; Texaco during a strike (that was accompanied by violence) in Trinidad in April 1975, and in a collective bargaining situation in Panama; and in several instances involving Shell, which are discussed below. In all the cases, it was reported that "messages of solidarity" and "intervention and protests to the parent company" were sent; that, in two cases, "manifestations, token work stoppages, solidarity movements at work place" occurred;[18] that, in the Texaco Trindad strike and BP Belgian dispute, "overtime bans and refusal of work during period of strike" were instituted at company plants in other countries; and in addition that, in the Texaco Trinidad situation, the ICEF was able to effectuate "boycotts of transfer of stocks and inventories both actual and preparatory"—in order to put pressure on the company.[19]

"Messages of support and solidarity" may have been sent to the unions involved, and protest letters may have been sent to the headquarters of BP and Texaco, but, when questioned, company personnel executives were unaware of any.[20] Neither we nor the companies, however, were able to uncover any record of any stoppage, overtime ban, boycott, or overt action in support of the incidents noted at the Texaco and BP plants.[21]

On October 6, 1977, the ICEF secretary general dispatched a circular letter that, among other things, contains this paragraph: "The Spanish UGT has asked us to convey their appreciation for the solidarity actions in regard to recent strike actions against Saint-Gobain, British Petroleum, the American Union Carbide and the Spanish subsidiary of German BASF.[22]

---

[18] This is the language of the report. What it means is perhaps purposely unclear.

[19] "Executive Committee. Activities Report of the Secretary General. List of Memberships," *ICF 16th Statutory Congress*, Montreal, October 27-29, 1976, pp. 98-102. Hereafter cited as *ICF 16th Statutory Congress*.

[20] E.g., a BP personnel executive wrote the authors: "One thing I am fairly certain about . . . is that at the BP Head Office in London we cannot recall any communication being received from the ICF." Letter dated April 14, 1977.

[21] We have searched general and union newspapers of this period, as well as queried the companies, and find no record to support ICEF claims.

[22] ICEF Circular Letter No. 106/77, October 6, 1977.

At our request, the British Petroleum personnel office checked its files and reported that it was unable "to trace any evidence of the activity claimed by Levinson in respect of the very small BP company in Spain and . . . unable to trace any evidence of any communication addressed to us here in London by the ICEF." [23] Moreover, the company's Spanish executive was "unable to identify either any strike action which involved BP Spain or any evidence of correspondence received from Mr. Levinson." [24]

Occidental Petroleum

With 1978 sales of over $6 billion and 33,161 employees, Occidental Petroleum Company, headquartered in Los Angeles, is the thirteenth largest American petroleum company and the thirty-third largest American industrial corporation.[25] Its chairman, Armand Hammer, is especially noted for his contacts and business relationships in the Soviet Union.

In the late summer of 1978, Occidental was involved in a dispute over a refinery closing in Antwerp, Belgium. The ICEF issued a press release blaming the company for violating, on the basis of a "technical argument," an agreement to negotiate. The release then states:

> The ICEF Secretary General cabled Armand Hammer, chairman of Occidental Petroleum, at headquarters, Los Angeles, California, U.S.A., for discussions at the international level. A similar cable was sent by the Belgium regional Labour Department representative. The company ignored even receipt of the cable—as was to be expected. . . . ICEF affiliates have . . . been asked to boycott the transfer of products by surface tankers and rail during the full period of the strike.[26]

We found no evidence of any boycott. In fact, Occidental directors closed and wrote off the value of the refinery in July 1978 because it had operated at a substantial loss since 1974 and was used only intermittently. The closing precipitated a general Belgian refinery strike in September 1978 and an occupation of the refinery by Belgian workers that did not end until August 1979 when Occidental, pursuant to Belgium's extreme employee termination law, agreed to severance pay totaling more than $10 million. In August

---

23 Letter to the authors, December 30, 1977.

24 Letter to the authors, January 13, 1978.

25 *Fortune*, Vol. 98 (May 7, 1979), pp. 270-71.

26 ICEF Press Release No. 6/78, September 12, 1978, pp. 1-2; see also ICEF Circular Letter No. 126/78, September 12, 1978.

1979, the refinery was sold to a smaller American concern, Coastal States Gas Corporation.[27]

Shell as a Target

Shell was especially an ICEF target during the early 1970s. An ICEF Shell World Council was organized in November 1972.[28] Its organizational meeting in London included only unions from Germany, Norway, Sweden, the Netherlands, and the United Kingdom. Unions in Shell plants outside of Europe were then almost all affiliated with the IFPCW.

In December 1972, Levinson wrote the chairman of the Shell group in London asking for a meeting with the ICEF world council. This was denied, but a Shell personnel officer did meet Levinson twice—on March 21, 1973, and June 20, 1973—to tell him informally that Shell saw no purpose in such a meeting and that labor relations were matters for its national affiliates.[29]

A second ICEF Shell World Council meeting was held in Nunspeet, Netherlands, June 28-29, 1974. This one, better attended than the previous one, but again an entirely European affair, included representatives from the Netherlands, France, Germany, Italy, Norway, Sweden, Switzerland, Ireland, and the United Kingdom. It passed resolutions against petroleum price increases, for joint action during strikes, and in favor of a meeting of the council with Shell management. No such meeting, however, was requested, and none has been held to date.[30]

The 1973 OCAW strike against Shell in the United States gave the ICEF an opportunity to expand its petroleum support beyond Europe. The ICEF offered to support a boycott of Shell in Europe, and the OCAW accepted the aid. Wide publicity resulted,[31] but no boycott occurred. Shell operated all of its United States plants during the strike with salaried and supervisory employees. At its annual meeting in Houston, on April 26, 1973, the president of Shell (United States) presented information

---

[27] "Occidental Will Sell Its Belgian Refinery to Coastal States," *Wall Street Journal*, August 8, 1979, p. 6; and "Coastal States' Leap into Global Oil Refining," *Business Week*, August 27, 1979, pp. 39, 41.

[28] *ICF 16th Statutory Congress*, p. 95.

[29] Shell personnel department, interview in London, September 3, 1973.

[30] ICF Circular Letter No. 83/74, July 5, 1974, contains the secretary general's report on this meeting. Various interviews with Shell management in London, 1973-78.

[31] Numerous press clippings in our files attest both to Levinson's excellent publicity and to the failure of press and business journals to go beneath self-serving press releases and interviews.

showing that, despite the boycott promised by the ICEF and despite the IFPCW's efforts in publicizing the strike, sales and earnings had risen during the strike.[32]

Since this meeting, the ICEF Shell World Council has apparently not met. The only other ICEF references to Shell prior to the Energy Division Conference described below are four claims of "solidarity actions" similar to those described above involving BP and Texaco, which the ICEF secretary general reported to the 1976 ICEF Congress. They allege support of the Italians in negotiations in December 1973, of Australians in May 1974, and of Dutch demonstrations against price increases in June 1974.[33] Again, this support did not amount to much more than solidarity letters to the national unions.

ICEF Energy Division and Conference

In 1976, the OCAW, having already disaffiliated from the IFPCW, affiliated with the ICEF.[34] A. F. Grospiron, president of the OCAW, was named cochairman of a new ICEF Energy Division and chairman of its Oil and Petrochemical Committee. Jan de Jong of the Netherlands Industriebond was appointed the other cochairman.

The new division held its first meeting at the Royal Festival Hall, London, June 13-15, 1978. About ninety persons attended, including twenty from Japan, a large group from the United Kingdom, and the balance from such countries as the United States, Australia, Germany, and Greece; an observer delegation from Egypt also attended.

The meeting attracted little newspaper attention and does not seem to have accomplished a major purpose. In addition, there apparently was considerable disagreement—especially between Grospiron, on the one hand, and British and European unionists, on the other—on the best approach to multinational corporations. On the first day of the conference, Grospiron presented papers entitled "Industrial and Economic Characteristics of the Energy Problem" and "Industrial Structure of the Petroleum Industry and Its Relationship to Collective Bargaining in

---

[32] Information package on strike and annual meeting, Shell Oil Company, 1973.

[33] *ICF 16th Statutory Congress*, pp. 98, 99, and 102.

[34] *Ibid.*, p. 24.

[35] See *Union News* (OCAW), August 1978, p. 1. Much of the information discussed here is based upon confidential interviews with conference participants.

North America," and he sought to draw a parallel between the first convention of local unions in the United States oil industry in 1918 and the meeting at hand.[35] Although the OCAW's monthly newspaper featured Grospiron's speech with the headline "Worldwide Unity of Energy Unions a Necessity," Grospiron actually advocated only better communications among energy unions in different countries and was reportedly very skeptical about the prospects for multinational bargaining, apparently stating that it could occur only if there were simultaneous advantages to participating national unions.

Surprisingly, Levinson was also reported to be defeatist about the prospects for multinational bargaining in the petroleum industry. He apparently complained that it was too easy for multinational companies to reject his requests for meetings at company headquarters level because national unions were not supporting such requests or delegating power to the ICEF.

In the debates, there were considerable differences among delegates about the relative advantages of industrywide bargaining versus companywide bargaining; an apparent majority of the delegates favored the latter. These differences spread over to the international sphere to add to the lack of unity on approaches to multinational companies. In large measure, the differences mirrored the distinction between the approach of the now-defunct IFPCW and the traditional one of the ICEF. The OCAW and other former IFPCW affiliates tended to favor the coordinated national company approach, which characterizes the OCAW's bargaining in the United States. Reports presented by national delegations, such as the Japanese, emphasized this.

Grospiron, with apparent AFL-CIO backing, asked unions present to assist in organizing Exxon, whose North American refineries are largely represented by local independent unions or are nonunion. Exxon was also a principal target for attack by other conference delegates. In his report to the 1976 ICEF Congress, Levinson had already announced that world councils would be formed for Exxon and Mobil.[36] It was indicated at the conference that the Exxon council and ones for Glaxo Holdings, the British pharmaceutical group, and for two unspecified German companies would be formed.

Apparently this did not occur, perhaps because of the fundamental disagreements on approaches as noted above. The ICEF's report on the proceedings does not even mention Exxon and

---

[36] *ICF 16th Statutory Congress*, p. 97.

indicates that organizing the world councils was still in the planning stage. Thus, it states that "it was of the greatest importance that an appropriate structure be created" to develop, among other programs,

a priority list of target companies for the creation of ICEF Multinational World Councils in which to develop short-term and longer-term policies according to the requests of affiliates, particularly those representing workers in the parent companies. Among the companies suggested for the creation of such multinational company councils were Texaco, Mobil Oil, BP, Shell, Petrofina, and perhaps ENI. Others could be established according to circumstances and conditions as they develop and as requested by major affiliated organizations representing employees in other multinational energy companies.[37]

As surprising as the exclusion of Exxon in the targeted group is the inclusion of Shell for a prospective world council. According to the secretary general's report to the 1976 congress, a Shell World Council had existed since November 1972 and, as noted above, had had two meetings. In any case, to our knowledge, no world council in the petroleum industry has been formed, nor has one met since the June 1978 Energy Division Conference.

More agreement was achieved on other matters. Levinson, as has been his usual policy for several years, dwelt extensively on health and safety matters. There was agreement to attempt to exchange information so that the best practices could "serve as guides for harmonizing the best conditions upward at the world level."[38] Levinson also allegedly stressed his election as vice-chairman of the supervisory board of DuPont's German subsidiary as the beginning of a new era of industrial democracy. Also, the conference went on record in favor of the Dutch-originated demand for a five-shift system in continuous operations, "since only such a system makes possible the introductions of the 35- and 32-hour week."[39] Moreover, the conference endorsed a 35-hour week "or less"; a "substantial reduction in working time," including the elimination of overtime; and hours reduction as "a primary means of eliminating the hazards and dangers to the physiological and psychological health of workers and their families."[40]

---

[37] ICEF Circular Letter No. 118/78, July 31, 1978, p. 5. This circular letter contains the reports and summary statements of the Energy Division Conference.

[38] *Ibid.*

[39] *Ibid.*, p. 3. See also ICEF Circular Letter No. 7/79, January 24, 1979.

[40] ICEF Circular Letter No. 118/78, July 31, 1978, p. 3.

In early 1979, the ICEF's strength in the petroleum industry was further reduced when the OCAW Executive Board apparently decided that, as a result of financial constraints, it would consider disaffiliation from the ICEF. To prevent this, the ICEF secretary general excused the OCAW from affiliate dues payments for 1979. This meant a loss of approximately $84,000 for the ICEF.

ICEF Latin American Problems

The ICEF has never been strong in Latin America, and since the demise of the IFPCW, this situation has not materially changed. FEDEPETROL, Venezuela's most powerful union and the clear leader of petroleum unions in South America, was a firm supporter of the IFPCW. Its late president, Luís Tovar, became the second president of the IFPCW in 1966 and remained in that post until his death shortly before the IFPCW's demise. Since then, FEDEPETROL has declined overtures to affiliate with the ICEF but instead has attempted to interest the OCAW in forming a petroleum workers' federation for the Western Hemisphere. The OCAW has proved unresponsive. In turn, FEDEPETROL has sought again, thus far unsuccessfully, to organize a Latin American federation.[41]

Mexico, the second largest—and potentially the largest—petroleum producer in Latin America, also has a dearth of ICEF activity. A 1977 Wharton Industrial Research Unit study found that eleven members of the industrial union that includes petroleum workers did attend the 1976 ICEF Congress in Montreal, but the Mexicans are unrepresented as officials on any ICEF committees, and there seems to have been little ICEF presence in Mexico over the years.[42]

Compounding the ICEF's Latin American problems, the United States Glass Bottle Blowers Association (GBBA), an AFL-CIO and former IFPCW affiliate, has organized Latin American petroleum union seminars and used the Spanish initials of the

---

[41] Cecilia M. Valente, *The Political, Economic, and Labor Climate in Venezuela*, Multinational Industrial Relations Series, No. 4d (Philadelphia: Industrial Research Unit, The Wharton School, University of Pennsylvania, 1979), pp. 217-18.

[42] James L. Schlagheck, *The Political, Economic, and Labor Climate in Mexico*, Multinational Industrial Relations Series, No. 4b (Philadelphia: Industrial Research Unit, The Wharton School, University of Pennsylvania, 1977), p. 130.

IFPCW (FITPQ) for the conferences' organizations.[43] Funding for these meetings came from the American Institute for Free Labor Development (AIFLD), the largely United States government-financed, but AFL-CIO-controlled, union training and assistance organization.

All this has led to ICEF action on several fronts: a crescendo of denunciations of the GBBA and AFL-CIO leadership;[44] an announced willingness to accept grants, such as those from the AIFLD, which it formerly spurned; great stress on its "aid" to an affiliate in Peru; and attempts to form a Latin American federation under its auspices.

The GBBA-led meeting was held in Lima, Peru, June 26-28, 1978, and was quite well attended. During this month, the ICEF Executive Board met in Madrid and adopted the policy of accepting outside grant funds,[45] the same policy for which the ICEF had so harshly criticized the IFPCW for so long.[46] On July 6, 1978, A. F. Grospiron, president of the OCAW, wrote AFL-CIO President George Meany emphasizing that he was not supporting the creation of a Western Hemisphere petroleum union federation, advising Meany that the ICEF had now agreed to accept outside funds, and hoping that this would settle differences between the AFL-CIO and the ICEF.[47]

Meanwhile, the ICEF has been busy attempting to cement its relationship with the Peruvian Federation of Petroleum Workers, one of its few petroleum industry affiliates in Latin America. The secretary general claimed that, partly because of a telegram from him, a six-month strike against PETROPERU, the state-owned oil company, was settled satisfactorily for the employees.[48] It is difficult to give credence to such a claim.

The Wharton Industrial Research Unit's study of Peru found that two other unions there had become ICEF affiliates but that the

---

[43] See ICEF Circular Letter No. 99/78, July 11, 1978; No. 123/78, August 21, 1978; and No. 57/79, April 27, 1979.

[44] See, for example, *ibid.*

[45] For an account of the executive board meeting and its decisions, see ICEF Circular Letter No. 100/78, July 12, 1978, esp. pp. 4-5.

[46] See Northrup and Rowan, "The ICF-IFPCW Dispute."

[47] This letter is attached to ICEF Circular Letter No. 123/78, August 21, 1978.

[48] ICEF Circular Letter No. 111/77, October 14, 1977; and No. 120/77, November 1, 1977.

ICEF had not developed any programs for Peru.[49] In contrast, this study found that, "of all the secretariats with affiliations in Peru, IFPCW was by far the most active." [50] The ICEF has not filled the gap left by the demise of its rival, but it is now apparently hoping to develop a Latin American council of its affiliates and to use its Peruvian affiliates as a basis for that council. A Peruvian unionist has been employed to sell this program to others in South America, and presumably, it is hoped that AIFLD funds will be available for supporting activities. Unless the Venezuelan and Mexican petroleum unions support the move, it will have little impact. In late 1978, the ICEF ran its first two seminars in Latin America—one in Brazil, the other in Peru.[51] It remains to be seen whether this small start will be continued.

The Latin American scene is also the major stronghold of the World Confederation of Labour, the former Christian organization. Its regional affiliate, Central Latinoamericana de Trabajadores (CLAT), headquartered in Caracas, Venezuela, conducts a large educational and agitative program among workers, but its main strength lies in other industries.[52] In Colombia, however, one of the oil workers' groups is affiliated to a national confederation that is in turn affiliated with the CLAT, but there is no record of any multinational activity in relation to corporations by this or any other CLAT union.

COMMUNIST ACTIVITIES

The Trade Unions International of Chemical, Oil and Allied Workers (ICPS) has not actively sought involvement with multinational companies, especially prior to recent years. Ernst Piehl, who surveyed Communist activity of this time, recorded no ICPS activity in the petroleum industry.[53] More often, the Communists have utilized special committees or ad hoc organi-

---

[49] Nancy R. Johnson, *The Political, Economic, and Labor Climate in Peru*, Multinational Industrial Relations Series, No. 4c (Philadelphia: Industrial Research Unit, The Wharton School, University of Pennsylvania, 1978), pp. 132-33.

[50] *Ibid.*, p. 130.

[51] ICEF Circular Letters No. 127/78 and No. 128/78, both of September 14, 1978.

[52] See, e.g., Schlagheck, *The Political, Economic, and Labor Climate in Mexico*, pp. 137-45, for CLAT activity in the automobile industry.

[53] Ernst Piehl, *Multinationale Konzerne und internationale Gewerkschaftsbewegung* (Frankfurt am Main: Europäische Verlagsanstalt, 1974), pp. 106-7, 109-10.

zations instead of secretariats belonging to the World Federation of Trade Unions in their attempts to coordinate union activities internationally, and this has been increasingly the case in the petroleum sector. In recent years, the decline of the IFPCW, the failure of the ICEF to fill the resultant vacuum in the underdeveloped countries, and the obvious strategy of the Soviet Union to enhance its power in undeveloped areas have led to a step-up of Communist activities, particularly in Africa, the Arab countries, and the Mideast. The revolution in Iran will undoubtedly encourage such Communist activity further, for the emerging unions there apparently have strong Communist leanings and/or leadership.[54]

Using their friends in Iraq and Algeria, the Communists held the "World Conference of Trade Unions in the Oil Producing and Consuming Countries" in Baghdad, Iraq, in December 1977 after an International Conference of Oil Trade Unions in Algiers the preceding March. Success in attracting other than Communist unions was, however, limited.[55]

The Communists have also established an Arab Federation of Oil, Mines and Chemical Workers, which works closely with the ICPS, as does the International Confederation of Arab Trade Unions.[56] Iraqi and Algerian groups are the backbone of these organizations, but in the future, the Iranians could well play a prominent role.[57]

In Latin America, as already noted, the Communists are quite active, especially in Peru, where once the IFPCW was extremely prominent.[58] In other countries, such as Venezuela and Mexico, they are largely agitative groups and do not control the major

---

[54] See, e.g., *Information Bulletin* (ICPS), November 1978, p. 31; September 1978, p. 7; Youssef M. Ibrahim, "Khomeini Leads, But Not Everyone Follows," *New York Times*, February 18, 1979, p. E1; "A Shadow on the Iranian Revolution," *World Trade Union Movement* (WFTU), No. 4 (1979), pp. 6-10; Karen Elliott House, "Iran's New Regime Steps Up Its Efforts to Determine Foreign, Domestic Problems," *Wall Street Journal*, February 20, 1979, p. 6; and "A Spreading Threat to Iran's Oil," *Business Week*, June 15, 1979, p. 38.

[55] The documents of the conference are in our possession. They emphasize the Communist commitment to achieve hegemony in Africa and the Near East and contain the usual condemnation of the West and of multinational corporations.

[56] See, e.g., *Information Bulletin* (ICPS), November 1978, pp. 4-6; and *Flashes from the Trade Unions* (WFTU), April 12, 1978, p. 3.

[57] See, e.g., *Flashes from the Trade Unions* (WFTU), December 22, 1978, p. 3.

[58] Johnson, *The Political, Economic, and Labor Climate in Peru*, pp. 111-50.

collective bargaining organizations in key petroleum installations.[59] In the Far East, with their base in Vietnam, the Communists are working to establish a presence, but their role is still limited.[60] Former affiliates of the IFPCW in Japan, South Korea, and Southeast Asian countries have affiliated with the ICEF. Communist political successes in Africa have aided union penetration there, and such semisatellite Communist states as Angola, the Congo, and Mozambique are regular participants in ICPS conferences, with delegates from Nigeria often present also.

Petroleum conferences sponsored by the ICPS or other international Communist organizations concentrate mostly on political denunciations of the West and of corporations but pay little heed to collective bargaining or labor relations coordination. The ICPS does send telegrams of support during strikes, but much of the multinational activity is handled directly by the Communist-controlled French Confédération Générale du Travail and Italian Confederazione Generale Italiana del Lavoro. Thus, in the already noted controversy regarding the shutdown of a Belgium refinery by Occidental Petroleum, the ICPS sent a telegram, but the CGT petroleum unions sent a delegation to meet with Belgium refinery unions.[61]

CONCLUSION

Multinational union activity in the petroleum industry has involved numerous conferences, considerable assistance from developed countries' unions to those in underdeveloped countries, and much political indoctrination. Multinational bargaining, however, has neither been approached nor seems likely as the companies see no reason for agreeing to it; many national union officials are not at all convinced that it would be beneficial to their organizations and themselves; and there is no indication that employees desire it.

---

[59] Schlagheck, *The Political, Economic, and Labor Climate in Mexico,* chapter IV; and Valente, *The Political, Economic, and Labor Climate in Venezuela,* chapter V. The Communists have, however, been working hard to expand their strength in the Caribbean, using their base in Cuba as a focal point. See, e.g., *Flashes from the Trade Unions* (WFTU), December 6, 1978, p. 8; and *Information* (Trade Unions International of Agriculture, Forestry and Plantation Workers), January 1979, n.p.

[60] *AAFLI News,* December-January 1979, p. 2.

[61] *Information Bulletin* (ICPS), September 1978, pp. 1-2, 29.

CHAPTER XI

The Paper, Graphical, and Building Materials Industries

Both the International Federation of Chemical, Energy and General Workers' Unions (ICEF) and the Communists have been active in the paper industry; a small secretariat, the International Graphical Federation, has attempted multinational contacts in the graphical industry; and the ICEF and a third secretariat, the International Federation of Building and Woodworkers, are found in cement and building materials. This chapter examines multinational activities in these industries.

THE PAPER INDUSTRY

Both the Communist Trade Unions International of Chemical, Oil and Allied Industries (ICPS) and the ICEF have been active in the paper industry. Neither has accomplished a meeting with a major corporation or successfully coordinated union policy over national boundaries, although both have attempted to accomplish these actions. In addition, national unions have had direct contacts with unions in other countries and have been brought together by government groups. Table XI-1 sets forth the basic statistics for the ten largest paper-manufacturing companies.

The Communist Group

The Communist group (ICPS) had its first meeting in Hastings, England, September 30-October 3, 1970. Host for the meeting was the British Society of Graphic and Allied Trades (SOGAT), then led by a general secretary, Vincent Flynn, who was probably a member of the Communist party and certainly a strong Communist sympathizer and adherent. Delegates present were from the Soviet Union, Germany, the paper unions of

TABLE XI-1

The Ten Largest Forest Products Companies, 1978

Company	Headquarters	Sales ($000)	Assets ($000)	Net Income ($000)	Employees
International Paper	New York	4,150,200	4,099,200	234,200	51,306
Flick Group	Düsseldorf, Germany	3,803,583	3,879,991	34,628	45,939
Weyerhaeuser	Tacoma, Wash.	3,799,441	4,463,619	371,138 [c]	46,040
Champion International	Stamford, Conn.	3,632,420	2,856,104	168,688 [c]	42,975
Bowater	London	3,002,207 [b]	2,083,555 [b]	69,296 [b]	36,500 [b]
Reed International	London	2,919,845	2,193,250	30,220 [d]	82,800
Boise Cascade	Boise, Idaho	2,573,110	1,981,947	132,800	35,704
Crown Zellerbach	San Francisco	2,456,013	1,963,709	112,094	32,238
St. Regis Paper	New York	2,300,154	2,111,190	126,514	31,800
Statsföretag Group [a]	Stockholm	2,278,736	4,099,829	113,638 [d]	43,690

Source: *Fortune*, Vol. 99 (May 7, 1979), pp. 270-75; Vol. 100 (August 13, 1979), pp. 194-96.
Note: Both the Continental Group and the American Can Company have major forest products divisions.
[a] Government owned.
[b] Also includes certain subsidiaries owned 50 percent or less, either fully or on a prorated basis.
[c] Reflects an extraordinary charge of at least 10 percent.
[d] Loss.

the French Confédération Générale du Travail (CGT), and the Fédération Générale du Travail de Belgique (FGTB), as well as from the SOGAT. The meeting was declared for worldwide unity and solidarity of the paper unions but accomplished nothing concrete other than establishing a largely inactive "Standing Consultative Committee of Hastings" and issuing a solidarity declaration.[1] Since then, "the Hastings declaration" has been much heralded by the Communists as meaning unity of unions under their banner.

The Communist group has had two other meetings but without the SOGAT's participation. When Flynn retired in the early 1970s, he was succeeded by W. H. (Bill) Keys, who, although in the left wing of the British trade union movement, is not a Communist. Under the leadership of Keys, the SOGAT dropped its affiliation and financial support of the ICPS. The SOGAT had been affiliated with the ICEF as late as 1970 but either disaffiliated or was expelled as a result of its affiliation with the Communist rival ICPS. In 1974, the SOGAT, having disaffiliated from the ICPS, reaffiliated with the ICEF.[2]

Since then, the attempts of the ICPS either to involve non-Communist unions or to develop international actions against the paper industry have been rather unsuccessful. For example, at the most recent meeting of the "Standing Consultative Committee of Hastings," held in Sofia, Bulgaria, in September 1977, the only delegations from non-Communist countries came from Italy and France, where the Communists control the dominant union federations; Belgium; and Japan, where Communists have strength in public employee unions.[3] The principal decision reached at the Sofia meeting was to appeal to national pulp and paper industry unions to hold a "Day of Action and Solidarity" on Thursday, December 15, 1977, "as a means for more

---

[1] Eugene Novacelov, "Towards International Coordination of Trade Union Activity," *World Trade Union Movement* (WFTU), December 1970, pp. 17-19.

[2] The SOGAT was listed as an ICEF affiliate at the latter's 1970 congress, but not at its 1973 congress, and then again listed as an affiliate at the 1976 congress. The SOGAT is the former National Union of Printing, Bookbinding and Paper Workers and took its present name when it merged with the National Society of Operational Printers and Assistants in 1964. This merger later broke up, with the latter union seceding and resuming its former name. The printing group in the SOGAT was affiliated with another secretariat, the International Graphical Federation, between 1974 and mid-1977.

[3] *Information Bulletin* (ICPS), November 1977, p. 11. Forest lands are publicly owned in Japan, so that the unions representing forest workers deal with the government.

effective coordination of trade union activity on the international level." [4] According to the official announcement:

> The purpose of this coordinated initiative is to support the following claims which may be adapted to the specific situation in each country:
>
> 1) full employment. A ban on all dismissals where no provision has been made for equivalent reclassification;
>
> 2) improvement of working conditions;
>
> 3) reduction of working hours;
>
> 4) the safeguarding and development of the paper industry in each country.
>
> The Conference calls on the different trade union organizations to determine the best forms of participation of the workers in the day, such as short work stoppages, meetings in the plants and solidarity meetings.[5]

In general, December 15, 1977, passed unnoticed in the Western world's and Japan's paper industries. In Italy, there was a meeting in Milan at which a French union official addressed those assembled. There were also some short work stoppages as are so customary in Italy.

Although the Communists claim there were work stoppages in France, we are unable to find any record of their occurrence either in the general or union press. A careful reading of the official report on the "Day of Action and Solidarity" shows that an attempt was made to link events that occurred two weeks before to the action day. On December 1, 1977, a rather unsuccessful and poorly supported general strike led by the Communist CGT occurred in France. Undoubtedly to cover up the absence of overt developments on December 15, the ICPS literature combined in its general coverage of events for December 15 the stoppages and demonstrations that took place in the French paper industry on December 1.[6]

The ICPS also reported a mass meeting on December 13 in Tokyo.[7] This was a general demonstration, but it did not occur on December 15, nor did it particularly involve the paper indus-

---

[4] *Ibid.*, pp. 10-11.

[5] *Ibid.*, p. 11.

[6] *Information Bulletin* (ICPS), February 1978, pp. 9-15, and for France, esp. p. 15.

[7] *Ibid.*, p. 9. For comments of the ICEF on this Communist activity, see ICEF Circular Letter No. 17/78, January 25, 1978, p. 3.

try. No overt action was reported in Belgium or anywhere else in the free world and, of course, not in the Communist dictatorships.

The ICEF Pulp and Paper Division

The ICEF held its first paper industry conference in Geneva in 1971 [8] and has held several since, including two in London, November 1975 and June 1976,[9] which were hosted by the SOGAT, and one that was scheduled in Geneva, October 23-25, 1978, but may not have been held.[10] Between 1968 and 1978, the then president of the U.S. United Paperworkers International Union (UPIU), Joseph Tonelli, and the president of the Swedish Svenska Pappersindustriarbetareförbundet, now Roine Carlsson, presided as cochairmen over the Pulp and Paper Division. Both have also been vice-presidents of the ICEF, and Carlsson, now first vice-president, is a member of the ICEF Management Committee, the top policy organization between congresses. After Tonelli's conviction for embezzlement in November 1978, he was removed as UPIU president. He may be replaced in the ICEF position by Bill Keys of the SOGAT, who recently has played a leading role in ICEF matters. In dues paid, the UPIU has been the largest ICEF affiliate in the paper industry and the third largest affiliate in general.[11] The Canadian Paperworkers Union, now also an ICEF affiliate, seceded from the UPIU in 1975.

Early ICEF Activities Involving Paper Companies. In 1971, the Wisconsin-based firm Kimberly-Clark was beset with a series of strikes. At the September 1971 Pulp and Paper Division conference, Kimberly-Clark, described in an ICEF circular letter as "one of the most viciously anti-union, anti-labor companies in the world," was one of the companies selected for the

---

[8] "Industrial Division Conferences," *ICEF Bulletin,* January-February 1972, pp. 36-46.

[9] "Executive Committee. Activities Report of the Secretary General. List of Membership," *ICF 16th Statutory Congress,* Montreal, October 27-29, 1976, pp. 34-36 (hereafter cited as *ICF 16th Statutory Congress*); and *CCH Canadian Industrial Relations and Personnel Developments,* No. 49 (December 3, 1975), p. 851.

[10] ICEF Circular Letter No. 100/78, July 12, 1978, p. 4; No. 42/78, February 28, 1978; No. 50/78, March 16, 1978, all announcing an October meeting. We have, however, found no evidence either in ICEF or SOGAT literature that the meeting was actually held.

[11] *ICF 16th Statutory Congress,* p. 134.

formation of a permanent world council and as a target of an action program. Two paper unions based in the United States had allegedly previously established a "North American Joint Kimberly-Clark Council," and a meeting was scheduled for November 1971 in Geneva.[12]

It is not believed that the November 1971 meeting in Geneva was held, because the strikes were settled. Since then, there has been no evidence of any activity on the part of this "North American Council," but it is nevertheless listed as one of the ICEF's "permanent world councils" in the 1976 report of the secretary general.[13]

In November 1973, a world council for New York City-based St. Regis Paper Company, with Tonelli as chairman, was announced.[14] No overt action has apparently occurred involving this company. There is no mention of St. Regis in the secretary general's 1976 report.

Also in the 1973 secretary general's report, it is announced that world councils were scheduled to be formed for the Norwegian firm Borregaard AS; the Swedish company Billeruds AB; and New York-based International Paper Company, the world's largest forest products concern but an almost entirely United States and Canadian one.[15] No such councils were formed. In both 1976 and 1978, a council for International Paper was again promised for some future date, as was one in 1977 and 1978 for Reed International, a London-based firm that has facilities in Europe, Africa, Australia, and North America.[16] One for Bowater, then the current most intensively ICEF-targeted paper company, had already been formed.

Bowater Corporation Limited. In addition to its facilities in the United Kingdom, London-based Bowater, the third largest forest products company in the world and probably the most international one, operates throughout Western Europe, in the

---

[12] ICF Circular Letter No. 27/71, October 6, 1971. At that time, there were two major unions in the North American paper industry. They have since merged, but as noted, the Canadians now have a separate organization.

[13] *ICF 16th Statutory Congress*, p. 94.

[14] "Report of Activities of the Secretary-General, the 15th Statutory Congress, Geneva, 7th-9th November 1973, Documents," *ICF Bulletin*, October 1973, p. 77. Hereafter cited as *ICF 15th Statutory Congress.*

[15] *Ibid.*, p. 78.

[16] *ICF 16th Statutory Congress*, p. 97; ICEF Circular Letter No. 100/78, July 12, 1978, p. 5.

United States and Canada, Australia, New Zealand, and the Far East.

In November 1975, the ICEF Pulp and Paper Division met for three days in London. The conference was cochaired by Carlsson and Keys. It was there again resolved to form world councils in the industry, with Bowater as the first. Among the objectives of the Bowater Council are the folowing:

> In order to eliminate obstacles and advance international coopera-
> tion in collective bargaining and disputes, [council] affiliates are
> urged to remove or qualify no-strike provisions or prescriptions
> [sic] of secondary actions in collective agreements and legislation
> where it pertains to multinational companies. Affiliates are also
> urged to increasingly try to establish similar termination dates for
> collective bargaining agreements from country to country as a
> means of facilitating joint action and cooperation.
>
> *   *   *
>
> A common objective of all affiliates must be to achieve official
> recognition by the company as a discussion partner and eventually,
> as a bargaining agent on international problems, especially global
> investment programme and employment. . . .[17]

Other objectives for the Bowater World Council include extending "workers' control or participation in management decision-making" with the "ultimate objective . . . to extend such systems multinationally to the international centre of the enterprise." [18]

Prior to the November 1975 meeting, a strike involving nearly twenty-five thousand paperworkers occurred in Canada, shutting down most of the North American newsprint mills. The delegates voted support of the strikers,[19] and at the request of the delegates from the Canadian Paperworkers Union, the conference resolved that officials of the SOGAT should discuss the strike with the management of Bowater and Reed because the Canadian union had alleged that these companies were in the forefront of opposition to the union's huge wage demands. SOGAT officials apparently brought the matter up with Bowater, but without any concrete proposals or without at that time mentioning the world council action. Nevertheless, the ICEF claims to have

---

[17] Bill Keys, "International Solidarity Action Agreed By World Paper Unions," *SOGAT Journal*, January 1976.

[18] *Ibid.*

[19] "Striking Paperworkers Get International Support," *CCH Canadian Industrial Relations and Personnel Developments*, No. 49 (December 3, 1975), p. 851.

sent protests to the company headquarters, sent messages of support and solidarity to the unions, and boycotted transfer of stocks.[20] It may have done the first two, but it surely accomplished nothing in the way of boycotts. Newspapers in the United States and Canada printed without interruptions, using Canadian mill inventory stocks and United States and foreign sources without any union disruption.[21]

In early 1976, Bowater management was advised by SOGAT officials that the ICEF would be forming a Bowater World Council at a meeting in London in June and was asked to meet with the council members.[22] By then, the nature of the council and its objectives had been publicized in the *SOGAT Journal*. Nevertheless, Bowater officials were apparently persuaded that they could have an informal, or exploratory, meeting with the council without a commitment to recognize or to deal with it as such, and so agreed.

The ICEF, however, communicated this willingness to meet as Bowater's virtual recognition of the council. This allegedly upset not only Bowater officials but also former President Tonelli of the UPIU. Apparently, Tonelli was not at the November meeting. We have been advised that he felt that he was insufficiently consulted, both as president of a major union dealing with Bowater and as cochairman of the ICEF Pulp and Paper Division, and that he was not given a role appropriate to his status in the undertaking. The result was that Bowater withdrew its previous concession to meet with the ICEF body shortly before it convened in London, June 1-3, 1976. Moreover, Tonelli did not attend this meeting either.

In his report to the 1976 ICEF Congress, the secretary general states that discussions between top international management of Bowater and SOGAT officials

> were under way for a meeting between management and a delegation of the ICF Permanent Bowater World Council. Following such a meeting, it is expected that other multinational companies will meet with delegations of the Paper World Councils—thus instituting an important new stage of development in the action program.[23]

---

20 *ICF 16th Statutory Congress*, p. 100.

21 Based upon numerous discussions with paper and newspaper industries' executives and a close following of the Canadian strike.

22 The ICEF secretary general reported that the Bowater Council was formed in November 1975 (*ICF 16th Statutory Congress*, p. 95). This seems also the gist of the *SOGAT Journal* story, note 17 above.

23 *ICF 16th Statutory Congress*, p. 35.

As of mid-1979, no such meetings had occurred. Moreover, even the ICEF secretary general was not optimistic. In March 1978, following a meeting of the ICEF Pulp and Paper Division's Steering Committee, he wrote:

> The Steering Committee noted the stiff opposition of multinational employers to the recognition of collective bargaining at the international level. Permanent World Councils previously established for Bowater and International Paper had not so far succeeded in achieving a breakthrough in this respect and detailed planning was necessary to develop more active means of pressuring management towards this end. In any event, however, it would be affiliates themselves who would provide the impetus and support for such activities at international level coordinated through the ICEF Permanent World Councils.[24]

Yet in the same letter, he maintains that the "coming period would see a breakthrough by means of the World Councils into the next phase of real international activity." [25] No such "breakthrough" has occurred insofar as Bowater is concerned, and we have been unable to ascertain that an International Paper World Council has even been formed.

Reed International. The 1975 Canadian strike also saw Reed visited by SOGAT officials in an endeavor to put pressure on this British-based multinational. Reed had by then diversified into various paper consumer fields and held widespread operations outside of the United Kingdom. It now owns the London newspaper the *Daily Mirror.* More recently, it has considerably retrenched. It was hinted that the *Daily Mirror* might have labor trouble if a Canadian settlement was not reached, but the company declined any central headquarters action, and nothing overt occurred.

In 1976, Reed purchased a Dutch paper company. The Dutch works council sent a union official to interview company and SOGAT officials before approving the transaction. This prompted SOGAT officials to inquire about investments abroad while plants were being closed and employment was shrinking in Reed United Kingdom plants. The company pointed out that the British plants were declining because of the need to convert to waste paper raw materials and to reduce dependence on Canadian and Scandinavian pulp. This seemed to end the matter at this time.[26]

---

[24] ICEF Circular Letter No. 50/78, March 16, 1978, p. 3.

[25] *Ibid.*

[26] Reed International personnel office, interviews in London, May 12, 1977.

Reed International, as noted, remains on the ICEF's list to form a world council. No action has occurred, and it is very unlikely that Reed would either welcome or recognize such a move.

Roles of the SOGAT and the UPIU

Neither the Communists nor the ICEF have accomplished serious international coordination in the paper industry. Their future ability to do so is likely to be influenced strongly by the attitudes of two key unions—the SOGAT and the UPIU.

The SOGAT clearly plays an important role since its general secretary, Bill Keys, is obviously interested in international activity. Moreover, his interests go beyond the ICEF. In 1978, for example, the SOGAT exchanged visits with the Russians,[27] the French CGT,[28] and the Swedish unions.[29] Only the last are ICEF affiliates.

There remains a strong pro-Communist, anti-ICEF group in the SOGAT. Only a promise by Keys that it will stay affiliated with the ICEF "while it is useful to us" staved off a resolution by an SOGAT official who was a delegate to the 1976 ICEF Congress to withdraw from the ICEF on grounds that it "was not a genuine international body." [30] Direct contacts with Communist union groups, which still permit Keys to play a key role in the ICEF, are apparently a compromise with the extreme left, which would prefer affiliation to the ICPS.

Unlike the SOGAT, the UPIU is playing down international union affairs. In the last years before his ouster as UPIU president, Tonelli attended few ICEF meetings, and the UPIU failed to pay its ICEF affiliate dues. His successor, Wayne E. Glenn, was not at the October 1978 meeting. Glenn's assistant has advised the authors that "for the time being our relationship with the ICEF is on the back burner. . . . At some time in the future we may take a more active role in the ICEF, but for the immediate future, we do not foresee any involvement

---

27 "Warm Welcome in Siberia," *SOGAT Journal*, October 1978, pp. 12-13.

28 Bill Keys, "Why We Need Stronger Links with European Unions," *SOGAT Journal*, November 1978, p. 2.

29 "Sweden . . . employers and unions are highly organized," *SOGAT Journal*, November 1978, pp. 6-7, 22.

30 "No move yet to pull out of union international," *SOGAT Journal*, July/August 1978, p. 24.

other than to monitor their activities." [31]   By not paying dues for several years, the UPIU has in effect disaffiliated from the ICEF. Without the backing of the UPIU, ICEF world councils will lack significant representation and strength.

European Community

The European Community (EC) constantly encourages and sponsors international tripartite meetings. Two such meetings have been held in the paper industry. A European Pulp and Paper Employers Federation (CEPAC), composed of the industry trade associations in the various EC countries, has represented the employers; the ICEF has provided at least some of the union representatives and found one meeting "potentially useful." [32]   An employer association representative who was present describes that meeting as "really something of a non-event." [33]   It is, however, most likely that such meetings, as well as those in the United Kingdom, which have established tripartite Sector Working Groups in pulp and paper, and in other industries, do stimulate interest among unions in further contacts with their fellow organizations in other countries. Any effective multinational union activity in the paper industry does not, however, appear likely in the immediate future, even with EC official support.

THE GRAPHICAL AND PUBLISHING INDUSTRIES

Although there are some very large firms in the graphical and publishing industries which operate in several countries, most companies in these industries do not rank with industry's giants in sales, number of employees, or scope of operations. As a result, there have been far fewer attempts at multinational union-management consultation or transnational union cooperation in these industries as compared with such industries as chemical, glass, rubber, automobile, and electrical machinery. Nevertheless, there have been two significant actions to date which we have found: a series of meetings between an interna-

---

[31] Letter from William Casamo, assistant to President Wayne E. Glenn, UPIU, to the authors, January 5, 1979.

[32] ICEF Circular Letter No. 50/78, March 16, 1978, addendum.

[33] Letter to the authors, January 18, 1978.

tional trade union secretariat [34] and an international employer association, and assistance from a German union to a British one involved in a dispute with the *Times* of London.

The Master Printers and the IGF

The International Master Printers Association (IMPA), headquartered in London, is an organization of national or trade associations in the graphical trades. In 1977, eighteen national associations were affiliated to the IMPA, fifteen of which were from European countries. [35]

The International Graphical Federation (IGF) is a small international trade union secretariat, headquartered in Berne, Switzerland. It was founded in 1949 by an amalgamation of former international organizations that had become virtually defunct as a result of repression in the 1930s and World War II. The IGF's affiliates are primarily European. Its staff consists of a general secretary, an assistant secretary, and one office secretary. In 1978, the last year for which data are available, the IGF reported thirty-four national union affiliates from twenty-five countries, with a total membership of 626,077, about 85 percent of whom were from Europe. The IGF's income in 1978, mostly from affiliate dues payments, was 452,400.50 Swiss francs. [36]

The IMPA and the IGF have had three formal meetings and several contacts between their managing executives. Formal contacts between the two organizations began on November 20, 1970, when an IMPA delegation composed of representatives from France, Switzerland, the Netherlands, and Austria, plus the IMPA's director, a British national, came to Berne to meet with an IGF delegation comprised of representatives from Britain, Austria, Switzerland, and West Germany, plus the IGF general secretary, a native of Germany.

---

[34] The structure, operations, finances, and memberships of the international trade secretariats, together with their role and activities, are summarized in a forthcoming book by the authors to be published by Management Centre Europe, Brussels.

[35] "International Master Printers Association," *Yearbook of International Organizations*, 17th ed. (Brussels: Union of International Associations, 1978), p. A 1444.

[36] International Graphical Federation, *Report of Activities for the Period 1 January 1976 to 31 December 1978* (Berne, 1979), pp. 59, 72.

According to the IGF report of the meeting:

> The two delegations specially emphasized two points which held promises of closer cooperation and further discussion in the future: a) Industrial training in the graphical industries, an important problem at a time of far-reaching technical changes; b) Structural developments and an examination of economic conditions in the world generally and the European Community in particular.[37]

A second meeting, again with a European multinational committee representing both sides, was held in Berne on July 5, 1971. The IGF report succinctly summarizes the "views put forward during the discussions" as follows:

> a) Steps should be taken to ascertain whether the governing bodies concerned (the IMPA Council of Administration and the IGF Executive Committee) were prepared to approve the proposed cooperation.
>
> b) It should be made clear that the proposed cooperation would serve the advantage of employers and employees alike.
>
> c) Both the IMPA and the IGF have member organizations outside Europe. No advantage should be sought for our European members to the detriment of our overseas members.
>
> d) Difficulties in reaching agreement are a general experience in international work. It would therefore be unrealistic to suppose that cooperation between the IMPA and the IGF at international level would be an exception to this.
>
> e) Problems of organization and finance might arise; for example, in filling the seats on the proposed sub-committees and the joint committee, in the financing of travelling expenses and the payment of per diem allowances.
>
> f) The value of IMPA/IGF cooperation will be essentially determined by mutual exchanges of information. It was proposed to promote the exchange of technical information.
>
> g) The proposed joint committee should refrain from issuing instructions. This meant that the joint committee should not deal with questions affecting wages, conditions of work, etc., these being the preserve of the affiliated national organizations.
>
> h) There was general agreement that too much eagerness to achieve quick progress might jeopardize everything. The objective was to proceed cautiously in seeking out the areas of common interest. All proposals concerning suitable subjects for discussion should be fully explained and documented.
>
> The representatives of the IMPA and the IGF at their second meeting on 5th July, 1971, decided to submit the following decisions to their governing bodies:
>
> —It would be desirable to explore the idea of a joint committee at European level and, if there were agreement on this point,

---

[37] International Graphical Federation, *Report of Activities for the Period 1 January 1970—31 December 1972* (Berne, 1972), p. 17.

—that it would be expedient to set up a small preparatory working party (two or three representatives from each of the two organizations) which would investigate, in the light of the existing problems, whether the idea of a joint IMPA/IGF committee could be translated into practice.[38]

Multinational committees of the two organizations met a third time in Berne on January 29, 1973. "Without actually reaching any tangible results," the parties discussed industrial training and various technical, safety, and related problems. IMPA representatives stated that further discussion of the items considered would not be possible without obtaining the views of organizations affiliated with it.[39] This was the last meeting of the two committees.

Meetings to discuss a possible resumption of the committee talks were held between the IMPA director and the IGF general secretary on June 28, 1973, in Berne and on August 23, 1974, in Bedford, England. Then on March 26, 1975, the IMPA director wrote the IGF that further discussion with it could be resumed "provided that we first receive from you written assurances that it is not the IGF's intention that the discussions should lead to any international agreements or to recommendations for submission to our national organizations, but that it is your wish that we should exchange views and information on questions of mutual interest." [40]

A further meeting of the two organizations' executives in London on April 23, 1975, failed to break the impasse. Then on November 26, 1975, the IGF wrote the IMPA that it could not give the assurance demanded by the latter

> simply because we never intended to seek international agreements with you or even recommendations for submission to member organizations. (There may come a time when both our organizations think these things are desirable but we recognize that, even if so, that time is a long way off.) You will, we feel sure, see our dilemma. We cannot give you the written assurance your people demand, for the simple reason that, to do so, would imply that we intended to do what we didn't intend to do. On the other hand, our inability to give such an assurance is not, obviously, to be taken to mean that we intend to do what we hadn't any intention of doing. Nevertheless, we can be categoric about this: we will be glad to go on

[38] *Ibid.*, p. 18.

[39] International Graphical Federation, *Report of Activities for the Period 1 January 1973—31 December 1975* (Berne, 1975), pp. 26-27.

[40] *Ibid.*, p. 27.

exchanging views and information with the IMPA. Our Executive Committee consider contacts between the IMPA Director and the IGF General Secretary as being useful and wish to continue them.[41]

Informal exchanges between the general secretary of the IGF and the director of the IMPA have continued on a limited basis. The IGF would like to cooperate with the IMPA to form a graphic trades committee within the European Community, but thus far, the IMPA has not been interested in such joint action.[42] The IMPA's views, as set forth by its director, are that relations between the two organizations should remain as they are—highly informal and limited. Thus, he wrote one of the authors:

> IMPA has had contacts with the IGF over the past few years. Our policy at the present time is not to hold any formal meetings between representatives of our Association and the IGF, principally because we have found it impossible to find subjects which both our members and theirs would like to discuss at international level.

> In the nature of things, almost anything which the IGF would like to discuss with representatives of our organization would impinge on the sensitive areas of industrial relations, and we believe that any discussions we have at international level, even for the expressly limited purpose of exchanging views, would be likely to make the negotiation of national agreements more rather than less difficult.

> We shall, nevertheless, maintain informal contacts with the IGF and we have, for instance, already agreed to provide them with the documentation from the World Print Congress in Singapore.[43]

The IGF-IMPA meetings and contacts are the only examples of such which we have found between an international trade union secretariat and a multinational employer association in manufacturing industry. It would appear, however, that the formal meetings will not be repeated and that even informal contacts between the IMPA director and the IGF general secretary are, and will be, both quite infrequent and very narrow in scope.

---

[41] *Ibid.*, pp. 27-28.

[42] Heinz Göke, general secretary, IGF, interview in Berne, September 28, 1977. See also IGF, *Report of Activities 1976-78*, p. 40.

[43] Letter from G. Wilson, director, IMPA, to one of the authors, April 4, 1978.

The Times Controversy

A long series of disputes with various printing unions over manning and work practice issues induced the famous *Times* of London to shut down the paper in November 1978. The newspaper remained closed into late 1979. When negotiations were reopened in April 1979, it appeared that a solution to the issues might be found, but no agreement was reached.

The *Times* management thereupon decided to publish a weekly in Germany and distribute it to countries outside of the United Kingdom. It normally distributes about thirty-five thousand copies of its three hundred thousand circulation in foreign lands. A small, largely nonunion printer in Darmstadt, West Germany, set the edition, and it was scheduled to be printed for the first week in May 1979 by the plant, also nonunion, operated by the Tercüman Newspaper Group of Turkey, which prints a European edition of a Turkish newspaper for the many Turkish "guest workers" in Europe.

At this point, the British National Graphical Association, a key union involved in the *Times* dispute, appealed to the IGF for assistance. The IGF transmitted the request to "black" the *Times* to various European unions, including the powerful and militant German union Industriegewerkschaft Druck und Papier, whose president is also president of the IGF. About three hundred demonstrators, including groups described as "leftwing extremists with records of being present when violence occurs," and Turkish nationals opposed to the policies of Tercüman camped by the plant in Zeppelinheim, near Frankfurt, apparently to make good the IG Druck und Papier promise that it would "make every effort possible" to prevent distribution of the *Times*. Following some acts of violence and attempted sabotage and threats of additional such troubles for any future printings and distributions, the *Times* management abandoned, at least temporarily, its German publishing attempt, although several thousand copies were in fact printed and distributed.[44]

---

[44] For an account of these events, see the following articles in the *Financial Times*, April and May, 1979: "European unions advised to black Times overseas edition," April 24, p. 13; Pauline Clark, "Times plans to publish paper in Europe before election," April 25, p. 14; and several by Guy Hawtin, "German company has type-set European edition of Times," April 26, p. 14; "German print union hope to halt Times weekly edition fades,"

Following these events, both Ter Druckerei, the Turkish-owned printing concern, and the Verband Hessischer Zeitungsverleger, the Hessen newspaper publishers' association, initiated legal action against IG Druck und Papier and its president for "violent obstruction" in the prevention of the *Times* publication.[45] The official position of IG Druck und Papier is that a solidarity strike is in accord not only with the union's statutes and its international obligations as an affiliate of the IGF but also with German law, since the obligation of German unions to maintain peace applies only to a union's own bargaining issues and not to action in support of other German or foreign issues.[46] Whatever the merits of this issue, there is apparently no precedent for such an action under German labor law. In any event, the industry could maintain its case under civil law rather than labor law and is reported to be doing so, charging illegal obstruction to commerce.

Meanwhile, the *Times* claimed that it had offers from numerous concerns in several countries to print its international weekly,[47] while an IG Druck und Papier official commented: "If they do succeed in finding [a printer] . . . , we shall picket them, too. . . . They will not find it particularly easy to print here." [48] Even if nothing further is accomplished by IG Druck und Papier, however, it has provided one of the few actual direct and effective sympathy actions across national boundaries that our seven-year research has uncovered.

April 28, p. 3; (with John Lloyd), "Times suspends W. German print after protests," April 30, pp. 1, 18; and "The Turkish and left-wing connections," May 1, p. 18. For a German view, see "Hensche: Solidaritätsstreik ist rechtlich unumstritten," *Handelsblatt*, No. 85 (May 3, 1979), p. 6. (The whole episode was thoroughly covered by German television.) See also John Vinocur, "London Times Is Due in Frankfurt Today," *New York Times*, April 29, 1979, p. 4; and Vinocur, "London Times Abandons Attempt to Put Out Paper From Frankfurt," *New York Times*, April 30, 1979, p. A-4.

[45] Guy Hawtin, "W. German union to be sued over Times demonstrations," *Financial Times*, May 2, 1979, p. 20.

[46] "Hensche: Solidaritätsstreik," p. 6.

[47] John Lloyd, "Times considers 30 printing offers," *Financial Times*, May 23, 1979, p. 20.

[48] Hawtin, "The Turkish and left-wing connections," p. 18.

Conclusion

Printing is going through tremendous technological changes that are vastly reducing employment in all graphic trades and publishing. This in turn has caused shrinking membership in unions (as well as in the IGF), wiped out craft union demarcations, and caused severe labor disputes. That involving the *Times* is but one of many examples on both sides of the Atlantic. Nevertheless, the dramatic events involving the *Times* and the more mundane meetings between the IMPA and the IGF involve special circumstances that are not too likely to be repeated in the near future in the graphical and publishing industries.

CEMENT AND BUILDING MATERIALS

For the building materials industry, the multinational reach is relatively limited, but an increasing number of companies do operate on an international basis. Two international secretariats have asserted jurisdiction in this industry: the ICEF and the International Federation of Building and Woodworkers (IFBWW). The latter is, like the former, Geneva-based. Its affiliates are primarily European unions, but it does have others in North America, Australia, and elsewhere.[49]

ICEF Cement Industry Activities

The ICEF's interest in building materials is concentrated in its Cement Industry Division, of which the chairman and co-chairman, respectively, are Thomas F. Miechur, president of the small U.S. Cement, Lime & Gypsum Workers' Union (CLGW),[50] and Walter Horeis of the German Industriegewerkschaft Chemie-Papier-Keramik (IG Chemie). The ICEF's Cement Industry Division appears to be the most inactive of its divisions. It has held no general meetings or conferences and only one meeting of its steering committee. The division officers were first listed at the 1976 ICEF Congress. The CLGW had once been an

---

[49] For further knowledge of the IFBWW, see our forthcoming book published by Management Centre Europe.

[50] The Cement, Lime & Gypsum Workers' Union has less than forty thousand members in the United States and Canada, but the union is a power in the United States and Canadian cement industries.

affiliate of the ICEF, disaffiliated in 1968, and reaffiliated in 1974. It sent two delegates to the 1976 ICEF Congress.[51]

The 1978 Steering Committee Meeting. The ICEF Cement Industry Division Steering Committee met for the first time in Houston, Texas, October 14-15, 1978.[52] The meeting preceded the nineteenth convention of the CLGW. The only foreign unionists present were Jean De Nooze of Belgium and Marcel Hupel, Force Ouvrière, France. ICEF Secretary General Charles Levinson was present and occupied much of the time with his usual exaggerated claims of actions against multinational companies. He also spoke in the same vein to the convention (e.g., "We are involved in supporting each other in collective bargaining and strikes on the average of 15 to 20 a month . . ."). Previously, he had claimed that ICEF "effective and constructive solidarity . . . contributed substantially in the settlement of cement negotiations in the United States"[53]—a statement for which there is no factual support.

The steering committee meeting took note of the number of European cement companies that had entered North America, but its only reported action was a discussion of a forthcoming

---

[51] No mention was made of the cement industry in "Industrial Division Conferences," pp. 36-46. The cement industry was not reported on to the 1970 ICEF Congress. See "Congress Reports I: Activities Report of the Secretary General," *ICF 14th Statutory Congress*, Folkets Hus, Copenhagen, October 22-24, 1970 (hereafter cited as *ICF 14th Statutory Congress*). The disaffiliation of the CLGW is reported on page 7 of this document.

In his report to the 1973 ICEF Congress, the secretary general states that, for the cement industry division, "Co-chairman to be designated at next conference." There was no report of any cement industry conference activity. See *ICF 15th Statutory Congress*, p. 23.

For a listing of the officers of the ICEF Cement Division, see *ICF 16th Statutory Congress*, p. 31. On page 38 of the same document, it is stated: "Other industrial conferences and working party meetings took place for the glass industry, pulp and paper industry and the cement industry," but no particulars are given. The Cement, Lime & Gypsum Workers' Union is listed as an affiliate and Miechur and one other officer of this union as delegates on the next to last (unnumbered) page of delegate listings. *Voice*, the official journal of CLGW, reported in February 1978, p. 5, that "CLGW has been a member of ICEF since 1974."

[52] According to *Voice*, prior to this meeting, the division's "work has been done by correspondence" (February 1978, p. 5). See also ICEF Circular Letter No. 75/78, May 10, 1978; and No. 84/78, May 29, 1978.

[53] "ICEF's Levinson tells how multinationals work," *Voice*, November 1978, pp. 8-9, 18-19; "First international cement meeting held in U.S.," *ibid.*, pp. 9, 18; and ICEF Circular Letter No. 82/78, May 30, 1978.

committee meeting in Europe and an organization program for the ICEF in Latin America.[54] It would seem, therefore, that the main purpose of the meeting might well have been to gain CLGW Executive Board and membership support for President Miechur's international activities and the costs thereof, including those of ICEF affiliation.

Holderbank Financière Glaris (Eternit). The ICEF's biggest, if short-lived, success in the cement industry involved Holderbank Financière Glaris, which operates cement and building material firms in several Western European countries under the Eternit name and also has sizable interests on other continents. It is headquartered in Niederurnen, Switzerland, and in 1978 had sales of $1.05 billion and 17,044 employees.[55] In his report to the 1973 ICEF Congress, the secretary general announces that, in March 1974, a world council would be established for "Holderbank."[56] This was actually formed two years later on March 22, 1976, and is listed among the councils in the 1976 ICEF Congress report, with Walter Horeis of IG Chemie as chairman.[57]

The Holderbank-Eternit World Council, formed at a March 22, 1976, meeting in Geneva, was hosted by the ICEF but participated in also by the IFBWW. The chief promoter of the meeting, in addition to the ICEF, was the Fédération National des Salariés de la Construction et du Bois—a Confédération Française Démocratique du Travail (CFDT) organization affiliated with both secretariats. Unions from Belgium, West Germany, Italy, the Netherlands, and Sweden, in addition to France, apparently also attended. The purpose, according to an IFBWW report, was "to counter the firm's decision to cut back its labour force."[58] Various Eternit operations have, according to a management journal, "undertaken a programme of reorganization and rationalization that has significantly changed the group. . . . at Eternit NV [Belgium], the number of workers fell by 300

---

[54] *Voice*, November 1978, p. 18.

[55] *Fortune*, Vol. 100 (August 13, 1979), p. 200. See also "Replacement-Cost Accounting Spurs a Belgium Firm to Action," *International Management*, Vol. 32 (November 1977), pp. 47, 49.

[56] *ICF 15th Statutory Congress*, p. 78.

[57] *ICF 16th Statutory Congress*, p. 96.

[58] International Federation of Building and Woodworkers, *Report of the General Secretary, April 1, 1975—March 31, 1976* (Geneva, 1976), p. 12.

to 2,400 through dismissals, early retirement and attrition." [59]

Following the meeting, the ICEF asked the headquarters of Holderbank for a meeting with the new world council. The company agreed to a meeting, which was held on July 2, 1976. Union reports state that the ICEF secretary general and delegates from Belgium, Sweden, and West Germany were present, and the company representatives included Stephen Schmidheiny, director of Eternit AG, Switzerland. According to a Swiss union journal:

> The [union] delegation was of the opinion that the discussion should be handled in an open and constructive manner. In contrast to the negative and adverse tendency displayed by most multinational companies at meetings with the ICF Councils, the attitude of Mr. Schmidheiny must be emphasized. He said he was well aware that within international economic development there is an increasing need to deal with problems at the international level. Mr. Schmidheiny also said that at the international level companies should strive for better ways of communications and discussion than in the past.
>
> Both delegations agreed, that if future discussions were conducted in the same concrete and objective manner as this meeting was, they could very well be a significant contribution to international relations between the union representatives and the headquarters of multinational companies. [60]

This union report, and the absence of any company rebuttal, implied that the Holderbank group was in favor of international union-management consultation and/or negotiations and that additional such meetings were planned. This the company has denied, indicating that it will have no more such contacts. [61] The company agreed to the meeting primarily with the hope that it could avoid being attacked over the health hazards of asbestos microscopic fiber, a principal raw material in its manufacturing process. [62] In this, it was doomed to disappointment.

Johns-Manville and Asbestos

Johns-Manville, based in the Denver, Colorado, area is a major manufacturer of building materials, paper, and other products

---

[59] "Replacement-Cost Accounting," pp. 47, 49.

[60] Translated by the Industrial Research Unit from the internal newsletter of the Swiss union Gewerkschaft Textil-Chemie-Papier (GTCP), September 7, 1976.

[61] Letter from a company executive to the authors, January 18, 1977.

[62] *Ibid.*

and the largest manufacturer of asbestos in the world. In 1978, Johns-Manville had sales of $1.6 billion and 25,800 employees.[63] The discovery that asbestos fibers may cause cancer has caused severe problems for Johns-Manville, as well as for the Holderbank group. It has also provided the ICEF with an obvious opportunity.

On May 9, 1979, a circular letter was dispatched calling for the creation of a permanent world council for Johns-Manville and appending a questionnaire about unionization in its plants. The same circular letter proposed a second meeting of the Eternit group and a general conference of affiliates from the two companies to deal "with the question of asbestos exposure world-wide." [64] This was followed two days later by "a public challenge to the Johns-Manville Corporation . . . to come clean on its past safety record and to enter into discussion with the trade unions internationally on the future of the industry. It was further claimed that the "convening of the ICEF Johns-Manville and Eternit World Councils is planned to advance such discussions to the international level as a matter of urgency." [65] As of mid-1979, we are not aware that these meetings have occurred, but we are advised by Johns-Manville management that it has heard nothing.[66]

Other ICEF Cement and Building Materials Activities

Besides these events, the ICEF has claimed to have intervened with the parent Eternit company in strikes involving its subsidiaries in Sweden and France.[67] Actually, such intervention involved the sending of letters or telegrams, which were neither significant in affecting the outcome of any controversy nor replied to by the company.

The only other ICEF activities in these industries have been "interventions" in the form of nonsupported claims by the ICEF secretary general based on letters or telegrams sent to various companies. In particular, the Indian National Cement Workers'

---

[63] *Fortune*, Vol. 99 (May 7, 1979), pp. 276-77.

[64] ICEF Circular Letter No. 65/79, May 9, 1979.

[65] ICEF Circular Letter No. 65/79, May 11, 1979.

[66] Vice-president of labor relations, Johns-Manville, telephone interview, August 14, 1979.

[67] *ICF 16th Statutory Congress*, pp. 88, 97. Similar claims were made in regard to the French concern Ciment LaFarge.

Federation has elicited a number of Levinson telegrams and circular letters in support of its strikes. Thus, the secretary general's report to the 1970 ICEF Congress claims that assistance from the ICEF "obliged" the company "to recognize and bargain with the union which it previously refused to do." [68] In his report to the 1976 congress, the ICEF secretary general claims that, in October 1973 and in May 1975 in collective bargaining situations involving the Indian National Cement Corporation and "several cement firms" in India, he sent "messages of support and solidarity" and "documentation, statistics, company data for use in collective bargaining." [69] Also in October 1977, the secretary general reported a telegram from the president of the India National Cement and Allied Workers' Federation, which indicated that a cable from the ICEF "was very much in time and effective. . . . strategically worded . . . the last straw on the camel's back . . ." which won a national agreement for arbitration.[70]

We have not been able to verify any of these assertions. Given, however, the doubtful impact of a cable from Geneva on a labor dispute on the other side of the world, the absence of an ICEF research department, and the demonstrated consistency of gross exaggeration in ICEF reports, one can be understandably skeptical that in these, or in any other cement industry labor disputes, the ICEF has been a factor in the outcome.

The IFBWW and the Dillingham Corporation

Dillingham was formed in 1961 through the merger of two family-owned Hawaiian companies. It is now a diversified company, headquartered in Honolulu, Hawaii, which operates in four principal industry groups: maritime, including a fleet of over one hundred tugs and barges, shipyards in Hawaii, Oregon, Australia, and New Zealand, and a 50 percent interest in a worldwide dry bulk shipping operation; resources, including marketing liquid petroleum gas, mining, and building facings, paving materials, and precase concrete structural members; construction in the United States, Canada, and the Pacific; and property ownership and management. Dillingham had revenues of

---

[68] *ICF 14th Statutory Congress*, p. 30.

[69] *ICF 16th Statutory Congress*, pp. 97, 100, 102.

[70] ICEF Circular Letter No. 106/77, October 6, 1977.

$920 million and employed about twelve thousand persons in 1978.[71]

Dillingham's contacts with international unionism occurred as a result of a dispute with an Australian construction union over a mining project. In June 1975, the Federated Furnishing Trade Society of Australia, Victoria Branch, "banned" an Australian subsidiary of Dillingham, which was building a multistory office building in Melbourne. The union ban stopped the final glazing on this building and affected another project; a Dillingham joint venture, D. M. Minerals, was mining zircon and rutile on Fraser Island,[72] an island off Queensland on which an Australian national park exists. Considerable publicity concerning the strike was generated through the intervention of the IFBWW, to which this Australian union is affiliated.

Background. Dillingham and its partner had permits from the Queensland state authorities for the Fraser Island operation, which was subject to strict environmental safeguards, including reshaping sand dunes, revegetation, and other restoration. The Australian Department of National Resources monitored the company's mining activities in conjunction with the Queensland Department of Mines. No breach of agreement had been found or export licenses refused because of an alleged breach.[73]

Approximately 8 percent of Fraser Island was included in D. M.'s mining leases granted or under application. About 20 percent of the island was included in the parks, with additional land planned to be added. In 1971 and 1972, D. M. Minerals donated acreage to the park. More than 70 percent of Fraser Island was reserved for forestry and had been logged for over a century. D. M.'s mining permits were granted after exploration, which began in 1962, and a public inquiry in 1971. Other mineral-sand mining has occurred on the island since 1972.

In July 1975, the Australian Commonwealth Government established a commission to inquire into the environmental impact

---

[71] Dillingham Corporation, *1978 Annual Report* (Honolulu, 1979); and Dillingham Corporation, *A Special Report: Where it is, Where it is Going* (Honolulu, 1977).

[72] This reason for the strike was given in a union officer's statement that is recorded in an official transcript of proceedings involving the dispute, dated October 9, 1975.

[73] This background information is found in the documents put together by D. M. Minerals, which include statements by all parties, and several articles from the *Financial Times* and the *Australian Financial Review*, as well as from Australian governmental documents.

of the mining operation. Although D. M. Minerals cooperated with the inquiry in supplying geological and environmental information, it declined to supply information of a financial and commercial nature and sought court determination of the right of the commission to demand such information.

In December 1975, the commission made an interim report in which it suggested that government decisions relating to export and in particular any proposed decision on whether to grant "blanket approval" for exports be deferred until the commission's final report was provided. D. M. Minerals had been granted blanket export approval with respect to certain leases on December 13, 1974. It was pointed out by the government that, to be assured of continuing blanket export approvals, the company must fulfill its obligations under the relevant mining lease conditions to protect the Fraser Island environment. Following receipt of this approval, D. M. Minerals committed itself firmly to the mining of its Fraser Island leases on a long-term basis. By the time the environmental inquiry was announced on March 25, 1975, sales contracts had been exchanged; contracts and subcontracts for services and facilities were entered into; capital expenditure on plant and equipment was made, with further capital expenditure being approved and committed; and physical operations on the site of the leases had commenced.

The interim report was no criticism of the company, but it was used by the union to justify its position. Meanwhile, the general secretary of the union declined an invitation to visit the mining operation and observe the facts for himself.

The IFBWW Involvement. The Federated Furnishing Trade Society called its strike even before the government commission issued its interim report. It was followed in January 1976 by a circular letter from the general secretary of the IFBWW claiming that the strike was called to force the company to "observe" environmental restrictions and alleging that Dillingham's operation "has in several cases violated the environmental conditions under which its mining lease was granted." The IFBWW circular letter requests national unions to send letters of support to the striking union and to ask Dillingham to observe environmental standards.[74] Copies of the letter were widely disbursed and received considerable press notice.[75] A copy was

---

[74] IFBWW Circular No. 3/76, n.d., but issued in January 1976.

[75] See, e.g., "Dilco Mining Job Incurs Union Wrath," *Honolulu Star Bulletin,* February 16, 1976, p. A-11.

also sent to the chairman of Dillingham with a letter stating that "this dispute concerns your Australian mining subsidiary's apparent violations of the environmental code. . . . [It] has refused to alter . . . practices to meet the stipulated environmental standards." [76] To a union official, the IFBWW secretary wrote:

> Essentially, what we and our Australian affiliate want is that Dillingham agree to cooperate with the ongoing government inquiry into its Fraser Island mining operations and to cease mining until that inquiry is completed. While we feel that the environmental damage being done by the mining is serious enough, we also resent the firm's apparent indifference to Australian public opinion and to the many trade-union representations made to it. . . . We would be very grateful for any help . . . in bringing this long dispute to a close: the glaziers organized by our Australian affiliate have been off the job now for over three months. We think things are now beginning to move in our direction as the international wire services have picked up the story and are beginning to print articles on it.[77]

The chairman of Dillingham responded that he was pleased to be able to set the record straight, since "it is often true that persons with responsibilities such as yours, are, of necessity, unable to observe geographically remote areas personally. If you were thus able, I believe that you would seriously question the information that you have been given." He supplied the IFBWW general secretary with considerable factual material, expressing the hope that the latter would "wish to share it with those who received copies" of the IFBWW circular letter. The Dillingham chairman also expressed the hope that the IFBWW general secretary would agree that "the dissemination of misleading information is counter productive to working out a solution to our current difficulties with your Australian affiliate." [78] Other Dillingham executives contacted union officials to acquaint them with the nature of the dispute and to point out, among other things, that a number of Australian union officials, other than the general secretary of the striking union, had visited the

---

[76] Letter of John Löfblad, general secretary of the IFBWW, to chairman, Board of Directors, Dillingham Corporation, January 12, 1976.

[77] Letter from IFBWW official to United States union official, February 16, 1976.

[78] Letter from Lowell S. Dillingham, chairman, Dillingham Corporation, to John Löfblad, general secretary of the IFBWW, February 17, 1976.

Fraser Island project and commended the company on its environmental work and restrictions.[79]

The IFBWW letter attracted no material trade union support outside of Australia. In the United States, the IFBWW's nine affiliates, although contacted twice by February 16, 1976, did not even reply.[80] A few did contact the company for an explanation of the situation. Company officials provided the same information that was sent to the IFBWW, and this ended the matter insofar as these unions were concerned. Unfortunately, however, the strike of the Federated Furnishing Trade Society and the IFBWW publicity strengthened the antimining forces in Australia.

After more than one year, the Federated Furnishing Trade Society finally suspended its ban in August 1976. There has been no sand mining on Fraser Island since the export licenses were refused, and the whole of the island is now part of the national estate—that is, a national park. Restoration and rehabilitation by D. M. Minerals of those areas mined prior to December 1976 are now nearing completion. In January 1978, after the announcement by the government of New South Wales that it would also forbid all future mining in national parks in that state, thus effectively curbing Dillingham's operations in areas where it had leases, Dillingham announced that it was going out of the mineral-sand mining business.[81]

The discontinuance of these Dillingham operations on Fraser Island and in New South Wales resulted in the liquidation of a business begun in 1967 and the termination of 350 employees.[82] Meanwhile, Dillingham has a claim of $25 million now before the Australian government to recover losses resulting from the government's action in closing down the Fraser Island operation. Some $10.3 million in losses were suffered in 1977 as a result of these events. The Australian government has announced that it will pay the company $4.5 million, which, according to the company, "is entirely inadequate and is tantamount to expro-

---

[79] For example, the director of industrial relations of Dillingham flew to Washington, D.C., to answer an inquiry by a vice-president of the International Union of Operating Engineers in regard to the IFBWW circular.

[80] Letter from the IFBWW, note 78, above.

[81] Dillingham Corporation, *News Release,* January 1978.

[82] *Ibid.*

priation without fair compensation." [83] The matter still remained
unsettled as of mid-1979.

U.S. Steel and the Steelworkers

A final type of international union activities has been direct
assistance provided by the United Steelworkers of America over
national boundaries. Universal Atlas Cement, a subsidiary of
United States Steel Corporation, has a facility in the Bahama
Islands. The United Steelworkers has provided a consulting
service over the years for the Bahamian union involved. At the
same time, U.S. Steel sends corporate personnel to assist in the
bargaining.[84] This Steelworker activity is similar to its support
of Caribbean bauxite unions, which at one time was a regular
activity but more recently is much more infrequent.

Conclusion

Multinational union activities in the cement and building
materials industries are largely based upon secretariat attempts
to take advantage of particular situations or to support a national affiliate. There seems little prospect that any permanent
relationships are likely to develop from such incidents.

---

[83] *Ibid.*; and *News Release*, September 22, 1977.
[84] Interviews in Pittsburgh, Pa., January 29, 1976.

PART FOUR

The Food, Beverage, and Tobacco Industries

CHAPTER XII

Nestlé and Unilever

The food and allied products industry group manufactures and processes a wide variety of food, beverages, and tobacco products. In addition, service industries, particularly hotels and restaurants, are part of this group. It includes some major multinational companies (see Table XIII-1), the largest of which are British-Dutch Unilever and Swiss-based Nestlé, the subjects of this chapter. Many food companies are, however, small, localized concerns.

The principal international union in the industry is the International Union of Food and Allied Workers' Associations (IUF). Founded in 1920 as the International Union of Food and Drink Workers, the IUF was largely a European organization prior to World War II. In the 1950s, the IUF merged with, or took over, existing tobacco and hotel and restaurant secretariats and acquired its current name and structure in the following decade. Claiming only 2.1 million affiliated members in 1977, it remains one of the smallest of the major secretariats and has often suffered from severe financial problems because it receives regular dues from only 1.5 million members.[1] Nevertheless, by adroit use of its resources, the IUF has managed to gain a reputation as a significant advocate of multinational union-management consultation and bargaining. A large grant from the Swedish unions has at least temporarily alleviated the IUF's financial problems.[2]

The IUF has rivals in both the Communist and deconfessionalized Christian camps. The Communist World Federation of Trade Unions has a Trade Unions International of Food and Allied Workers, which is composed largely of Eastern European groups but also has affiliates in France and Italy and, like all Communist

---

[1] International Union of Food and Allied Workers' Associations, *Executive Committee Meeting and 18th Congress* (Geneva, 1977), Item (14) Budget. (Hereafter cited as *IUF 18th Congress*.)

[2] This grant is discussed below.

groups, is active and often well financed in the underdeveloped areas of Asia, Africa, and Latin America. The former Christian World Confederation of Labour's World Federation of Workers in Food, Tobacco and Hotel Industries (WFFTH) has affiliations in the Benelux countries, Quebec, and Latin America. The IUF is, however, far more active in pushing relationships with multinational companies than is either of its rivals. This chapter discusses the IUF's attempts to gain a relationship with Nestlé and Unilever. The following one discusses multinational union activities in other food, beverage, and tobacco companies.

THE IUF AND NESTLÉ

Nestlé, S.A., based in the small town of Vevey, is the world's second largest food company (see Table XIII-1). Today, Nestlé branches, subsidiaries, and affiliated companies operate throughout the free world and developing countries.

The IUF has worked diligently to develop a relationship with Nestlé, but after a promising start, its efforts have been much less successful. The first reported incident occurred in 1971, when Dan Gallin, IUF general secretary, addressed to "The President, Nestlé Alimentana, S.A." a letter expressing concern about layoffs at the subsidiary SOPAD factory at Gap, France, and about the impact on employees in France of a pending merger between Nestlé and Ursina-Franck, a Swiss food firm. As is his usual policy, Gallin asked affiliated unions to prepare similar letters and to send them to Nestlé headquarters.[3]

In the book *International Trade Unionism*, it is implied that the IUF moves induced Nestlé to grant additional severance benefits to employees at Gap and to postpone the Ursina-Franck merger.[4] Nestlé, however, has denied this and pointed out that it replied to the IUF that the care of Gap employees was a local matter and that local arrangements had "as . . . always" been "properly taken into consideration." The Gap plant was closed and the merger with Ursina-Franck finalized without further communications from the IUF.[5]

---

[3] Letter from Dan Gallin to Nestlé president, January 21, 1971; and IUF letter to all affiliates, January 21, 1971—both in authors' possession. The company has since dropped the word *Alimentana* from its name.

[4] Charles Levinson, *International Trade Unionism* (London: George Allen & Unwin, Ltd., 1972), pp. 121-22. No source is given for this claim.

[5] Letter from Nestlé executive to the authors, May 30, 1973.

The June 13, 1972, Meeting

The IUF's major, but temporary, breakthrough followed eighteen months later when a delegation met with Nestlé officials at company headquarters in Vevey, Switzerland, on June 13, 1972. This meeting was preceded by a conference of unions representing Nestlé employees in Geneva during May 17-19, 1972, and participated in by forty-five representatives from twenty unions. Although this represented a widespread assemblage, key unions, such as those from the United States, were not present.

At the conference, information concerning the company, its plants, employees, and unions was discussed, and a tour of Nestlé's chocolate plant at Broc, Switzerland, was made with the company's cooperation. The delegates agreed to form a permanent Nestlé World Council, to seek a meeting with Nestlé management to discuss overall views, and to request implementation of policies adopted at the conference. As in most cases, emphasis was placed on job security and employee rights in mergers and plant closings.[6]

Upon the IUF's assurance that these talks could not become a substitute for the relations of the companies manufacturing or selling Nestlé products with the unions at national levels, Nestlé agreed to the meeting requested.[7] From our discussions with company officials, we understand that Nestlé was concerned about its public relations and image throughout the world. With only 3 percent of its sales in its headquarters country, Nestlé management is wary of bad publicity and anxious to avoid union attacks. The company's reputation generally is that of affording a high degree of job security, paying wages and benefits that compare favorably to industry and/or labor market, and recognizing the role of unions in representing employees. It sought to apprise the IUF of its policies in order to avoid future misunderstandings and, thus, to enhance its reputation by appearing reasonable and responsive.

---

[6] The discussion of the conference and of the IUF-Nestlé meeting is based on correspondence with the parties, interviews with Nestlé personnel in Vevey and Geneva, Switzerland, August 1973, and on documents supplied by both parties.

[7] "First Meeting between an IUF Delegation and the Management of Nestlé," IUF Press Release, Geneva, June 16, 1972.

At the June 13, 1972, meeting, the IUF was represented by its general secretary, two assistants, and representatives from unions in Switzerland, Belgium, Mexico, Germany, Britain, and France; the company, by its executive manager, general director of manufacturing, and two other officials. The meeting was amicable, but the company made it clear that it would neither engage in anything approximating bargaining nor supply information to the IUF beyond what is supplied to stockholders. Nestlé reiterated its position of recognizing and bargaining with national or local unions, except where such unions are completely political in nature, and striving to avoid employee layoffs. The IUF stressed parity in wages between office and production workers and between sexes and full union participation in wage and benefit determination, and it "invited" the company to supply information before decisions were made that might affect employment and working conditions.[8]

Meeting Aftermath

Although an agreement was reached that further such meetings could take place, none has occurred. The relationship between the parties soon became strained concerning the character of such meetings. Nestlé held firmly to the position that it would provide appropriate information to, or exchange information with, the IUF but would not deal with the IUF as a bargaining agent for its employees or those of any subsidiary. All matters relating to employee relations are deemed the concern of management in the country involved. The only point on which the IUF received assurance was the promise by the company that, if a subsidiary "without any justification" adopted a clearly antiunion attitude, Nestlé headquarters management would intervene and request the local management to conform to general company policy.

The IUF immediately attempted to capitalize on the political and publicity victory achieved by inducing Nestlé to meet. To keep its affiliates informed, it began publishing a mimeographed *Nestlé Bulletin* in five languages.[9] These bulletins often feature unflattering descriptions of Nestlé policies. Moreover, the IUF attempted soon after the meeting to intervene with top Nestlé management in substantial company subsidiary labor policies and

---

[8] *Ibid.* Also interviews and correspondence with company officials.

[9] As of February 1979, twenty-five issues of this bulletin had been published.

actions. The result was an increasingly strained relationship, which was not improved by an informal meeting between two Nestlé personnel executives and Gallin and his chief assistant during an International Labour Organisation tripartite conference on November 3, 1972, in Geneva.[10]

The several IUF attempts to intervene with Nestlé top management involved, in part, two developments shortly after the June 1972 meeting. The first involved methods of bonus payments by Nestlé's French subsidiary, SOPAD. The IUF telephoned the Vevey headquarters but was advised that this was a local matter. It appears that an objective of the IUF in this instance, besides expanding its relationship at the top, was to influence the company to give greater weight to the IUF French affiliate, the food union of the Confédération Française Démocratique du Travail (CFDT), which, of course, is smaller than the food branch of the Communist Confédération Générale du Travail (CGT).[11]

The IUF's second venture in expanding its role was to protest the company's announcement that it was planning to build a dairy plant in Greece. Although its protest was couched primarily in terms of the lack of civil liberties and union rights in Greece and the possible impact on plant production in other countries, the IUF's basic demand was that it receive information before such a company decision is made. The company replied in a letter and in the informal meeting of November 3, 1972, that its decisions could not involve political interference in a country and that, if it did not expand in Greece, another company would. The plant was completed on schedule and began operations, interestingly enough, after democracy was restored in Greece. Paradoxically, if Nestlé had heeded the IUF, the result would have been fewer employees for the now unionized Greek food workers.[12]

---

[10] On November 3, 1972, Gallin addressed a letter to the members of the Nestlé World Council setting forth his views on the widening split with Nestlé management.

[11] Company and IUF sources and interviews.

[12] In an interview with the *New York Times*, Gallin contended that the IUF "threatened to cut production in other countries if the decision [to build the plant in Greece was] . . . not rescinded." There is no evidence either that this threat was actually made or that it could have been effectuated if made. See Clyde Farnsworth, "Big Business Spurs Labor Toward a World Role," *New York Times*, December 26, 1972, pp. 53-54. Nestlé officials have stated that they were not contacted by the reporter before this article was printed. The article also contains questionable claims by other secretariat officials concerning several companies.

On January 28, 1973, just prior to the Seventeenth IUF Congress, the Nestlé Permanent World Council met and voted to request a second meeting with Nestlé management. Nestlé, however, declined to agree to a meeting without having beforehand a proposed agenda setting forth the matters that the IUF wished to discuss. Rather than comply, the IUF withdrew its meeting request.[13] Later in the year, a matter erupted in Peru that greatly increased the friction between the two parties.

The Perulac Strike

The Peru incident occurred in the factories of Perulac, which manufactures and sells Nestlé products. A strike occurred over the terms of a new agreement, April 5-12, 1973, at the Maggi factory in Lima and was ended through government arbitration. While the Maggi factory was on strike, Perulac employees at Chiclayo and Cajamarca struck in sympathy.[14]

On April 18 and 19, 1973, and again beginning on April 26, union workers at the Chiclayo and Cajamarca plants struck. They claimed that they had been discriminated against because nonunion employees had been paid during the strike and the union workers were not. The company claimed that it was adhering strictly to Peruvian law, which requires payment to all those who report to work during a strike, whereas those on strike lose their right to be paid. On May 2, the Peruvian government sided with the company by declaring the strike illegal.

On May 3, Enildo Iglesias, IUF Latin American secretary, who is headquartered in Montevideo, Uruguay, arrived in Lima. He visited Perulac's managing director, who advised him that the strike was illegal and a local matter and that, therefore, Perulac would not negotiate with him. Iglesias then traveled to Chiclayo and Cajamarca to support the strikers. After Perulac's managing director informed the authorities of his presence, Iglesias was arrested, held in jail for forty-eight hours, and expelled from the country on May 7.

---

[13] IUF and company documents and correspondence.

[14] The Perulac strike story is based upon numerous documents and information supplied by both Nestlé and the IUF. The basic facts are not in dispute between the parties, but interpretations and nuances are, of course, quite different.

IUF Action during the Strike

Subsequently, the Peruvian government issued an order for an end of the strike in seventy-two hours. The strikers at Cajamarca returned to work; those at Chiclayo did not but occupied the plant instead. After some tense weeks, the strike ended on May 23, 1973.

Throughout the strike, the IUF made it a key matter. On May 2, prior to the arrival of Iglesias in Peru, Gallin and two other IUF representatives met informally with representatives of the Nestlé personnel department in Morges, a small town between Geneva and Vevey, to review both the Peruvian situation and other matters. Maintaining that the Peruvian case was a local dispute, the company declined to interfere. After the Iglesias affair, Nestlé maintained its position despite numerous calls from the IUF that were received by the Nestlé personnel staff. The IUF sent "practically [its] entire reserves . . . for the purpose of assisting striking unions" (about $4,000), and it also collected small contributions from affiliates for that purpose.[15] Gallin wrote that among the things at stake were "the credibility of the IUF, as a machinery for practical international solidarity, so far as both Nestlé and the unions in Peru and in other countries are concerned." [16]

Obviously, Nestlé also considered the Perulac strike a test. If the IUF were to be able to force its hand in this matter, it certainly would continue pressure whenever a labor dispute involving a subsidiary occurred and thus effectively move toward a collective bargaining relationship. Top Nestlé management, therefore, refused to become involved. The IUF's telephone calls were answered with a "polite but firm insistence" that no discrimination against union members had occurred in Peru and that the issues were local matters subject to local negotiation and determination.[17]

The Strike Settlement and Aftermath

In terms of the strike settlement, the outcome was clearly a company victory. It did not pay wages to the strikers for any of

[15] Letter from Dan Gallin to all unions with membership in Nestlé and to all members of the Nestlé World Council, May 17, 1972, p. 2.

[16] *Ibid.*, p. 1.

[17] Correspondence from and interviews with Nestlé officials, Vevey, July and August 1973.

the period that they were on strike. During the strikes, non-strikers were compensated according to Peruvian law; some of the compensation was for work performed at home and away from the Chiclayo plant while it was occupied. The settlement terms for the Chiclayo and Cajamarca workers were identical to those paid to the Lima employees under the governmental arbitration, and this settlement had been available to these two plant groups prior to the strike.

Nevertheless, the IUF claimed victory because the Lima settlement included the payment of a lump-sum bonus to the union. The IUF claimed this "would allow it to pay the workers for strike days." [18] Yet the Lima employees received the same settlement prior to the strike, and the workers who struck received nothing additional to make up for the time lost.[19]

Since the strike, relations in the Peruvian plants of Nestlé appear to have become mutually satisfactory. The Peruvian dictatorship has greatly restricted union activities; nevertheless, Nestlé's local management continues to deal with the unions in plants there, and a new agreement was signed in 1975 that the IUF termed mutually satisfactory.[20] The IUF is undoubtedly desirous of maintaining its Peruvian affiliates, in part because Peru and Mexico are the only two Latin American countries in which it has known affiliates in Nestlé plants.[21]

The Perulac strike widened the rift between Nestlé and the IUF. The IUF felt that the actions of Perulac management were "antiunion" and that, therefore, Nestlé headquarters management should have intervened.[22] Nestlé management believed that the IUF's intervention and financial support lengthened the strike considerably.[23] This basic dispute on the role of each party has

---

[18] IUF Press Release, May 28, 1973, p. 1.

[19] The IUF's claim was given currency by a European-published management newsletter that wrote its story without consulting Nestlé. After the company protested, the editor wrote a correction with an apology to Nestlé and to the readers. See *Industrial Relations-Europe Newsletter*, Vol. I, No. 6 (June 1973), p. 7; Vol. I, No. 11 (November 1973), p. 6.

[20] *IUF 18th Congress*, Item IX(a), p. 13. The IUF attributes the improved relationship to the appointment of a new Nestlé managing director.

[21] *Ibid.*, "Minutes of the Congress," p. 51.

[22] This theme ran through all IUF communications and is summarized in the IUF's *Nestlé Bulletin*, No. 10 (June 4, 1973), pp. 4-5.

[23] Nestlé officials made their feelings plain to the IUF (*ibid.*, p. 4) and in correspondence to and interviews with the authors.

since been widened further by developments involving Nestlé subsidiaries and the IUF's affiliates in the United States.

Conflict over Stouffer

Nestlé has four major subsidiaries in the United States— Stouffer Foods; Libby, McNeil & Libby; The Nestlé Company, Inc.; and Alcon Laboratories, a pharmaceutical concern acquired in 1977. Libby and The Nestlé Company now operate under a holding company, Nestlé Enterprises; Alcon is a subsidiary of a Nestlé-owned French cosmetics company; and Stouffer operates as an independent subsidiary of the top headquarters company and, like Alcon, is independent of Nestlé Enterprises. Stouffer, a hotel, restaurant, and frozen food company, was acquired just prior to the beginning of the abortive IUF-Nestlé relationship. Stouffer has always operated nonunion and attempts vigorously, and thus far successfully, to remain so.

At a Nestlé World Council meeting called to consider action in regard to the Perulac strike but actually convening after the strike was settled, it was decided to support a drive by the Hotel and Restaurant Employees and Bartenders International Union in the United States to unionize Stouffer hotels and restaurants.[24] Within one year, an IUF North American office was established in New York City, and considerable comment and criticism were directed at Nestlé for not altering Stouffer's policies.

Laurent Enckell, perhaps second only to General Secretary Dan Gallin in the IUF administrative organization, was appointed IUF North American representative. Enckell participated in organizing drives involving Stouffer; these, however, proved unsuccessful. Stouffer employees voted against representation by the Hotel and Restaurant Employees Union in National Labor Relations Board elections, twice in Atlanta and once in Cincinnati.

These NLRB election losses and Stouffer management's campaigns to urge employes to remain nonunion resulted in repeated demands by the IUF for meetings with top Nestlé management.[25] No such meetings were granted, but Nestlé's then managing director did in fact consent to a meeting with Edward T. Hanley, president of the Hotel and Restaurant Employees, and

---

[24] *Nestlé Bulletin*, No. 10 (June 4, 1973), pp. 6-7.

[25] See, e.g., *Nestlé Bulletin*, No. 11 (October 1, 1973); No. 12 (December 1, 1973); and No. 13 (February 19, 1974).

Enckell in Vevey on June 12, 1974. According to both parties, no action resulted from this meeting.[26]

The Hotel and Restaurant Employees' drive to unionize Stouffer has apparently been aborted because the union, and particularly its president, has been the subject of a governmental investigation of its financial practices.[27] Undoubtedly, the IUF's interest in this union's effort has also been diminished by the union's failure to pay the IUF any affiliation dues since 1975, and only partial dues in that year, a fact that forced the IUF to operate at a deficit during this period.[28]

The Coalition Drive against The Nestlé Company, Inc.

Coalition or coordinated bargaining in the United States involves the coordinated effort of several unions, each of which may have bargaining rights at one or more of a company's plants, to compel the company to bargain with the unions as a group on a multiplant basis. Unions thus coordinating their efforts usually attempt to push the company toward common termination dates of local union-management agreements and strive to secure similar or identical provisions for other terms of the agreements and thus lead toward one overall contract.[29]

The United States Nestlé company has historically negotiated its labor agreements on a local basis with some eight unions.[30] By 1974, however, this approach was threatened. An independent union at the largest United States plant, the chocolate facility in Fulton, New York, affiliated with the Retail, Wholesale and Department Store Union, AFL-CIO (RWDSU), an active IUF affiliate. The RWDSU, which also represents two other Nestlé

---

[26] *IUF 18th Congress*, Item IX(a), p. 14.

[27] See, e.g., Seymour M. Hersh, "Culinary Union is Facing U.S. Inquiry on Finances," *New York Times*, July 25, 1976, pp. 1, 29. For a critique of the failure of the U.S. Department of Labor to pursue this inquiry vigorously, see "How Washington Winks at Corruption in Unions," *U.S. News and World Report*, January 23, 1978, pp. 62-64.

[28] See *IUF 18th Congress*, Item 14, p. 9; and financial reports for 1977 and 1978 (in authors' possession).

[29] For an analysis of this union approach, see William N. Chernish, *Coalition Bargaining*, Industrial Research Unit Major Study, No. 45 (Philadelphia: Industrial Research Unit, The Wharton School, University of Pennsylvania, 1969).

[30] This section is based on a 1976 research paper prepared by Steven S. Plice, then a research assistant, Industrial Research Unit.

plants, requested the AFL-CIO Industrial Union Department (IUD) to coordinate a coalition attempt against Nestlé, and Laurent Enckell was invited to participate. The various unions representing Nestlé employees met with Enckell and IUD officials and agreed on demands that included common contract termination dates. Official of unions representing employees in one plant sat in on negotiations in other plants,[31] and the International Association of Machinists struck the chocolate plant in Burlington, Wisconsin, in an endeavor to gain a common termination date with the Fulton plant. Although this strike lasted four months, it did not succeed in its purpose, nor did Nestlé agree to change its local bargaining policies or agree to any common contract termination date.

Nestlé has since reorganized and strengthened its United States industrial relations organization, and this, plus the failure of the union coalition to achieve its purposes, has tended to reduce, at least temporarily, the unions' interest in a coalition approach. The RWDSU can, however, be counted upon both to press union coordination and to assist the IUF where possible. In December 1977, for example, the president of the RWDSU attempted without success to arrange a meeting between IUF General Secretary Dan Gallin, who was attending the AFL-CIO convention, and an executive of the United States Nestlé company. Enckell will apparently continue to push bargaining coordination at Nestlé as a means of adding to the pressure on the company's Swiss headquarters to recognize the IUF.[32] Enckell's activity in this regard is unique in that this union coalition effort is the only one in the United States in which a secretariat official has a role.

The Second IUF Nestlé Conference

The key role that the IUF ascribes to Nestlé is indicated by other involvements. Strikes in France and Italy have resulted in several attempts to obtain a contact with the headquarters management. Enckell assisted the Jamaica National Workers' Union in presenting a case involving Nestlé to an arbitration board.

---

[31] Under United States law, a union has the right to choose any representative. Thus, if a representative of another union sits in on a negotiation, he must be accepted, provided that he avows to be representing, not his union, but the one that has bargaining rights. If, however, he raises issues involving another bargaining group, he has no rights, and management is not required to deal with him on such issues.

[32] *IUF 18th Congress*, Item 6(c), pp. 1-3.

There have also been occasional informal meetings between Nestlé executives and Dan Gallin. The latest of these occurred in 1978, when Gallin and Günter Döding (president of the German food workers union, Gewerkschaft Nahrung-Genuss-Gaststätten, vice-president of the IUF, and a member of the supervisory board of a German Nestlé subsidiary) met with the Nestlé managing director in Vevey.

Gallin alluded to a rapproachment in his report to the 1977 IUF Congress.[33] Therefore, when elaborate preparations were made for a second Nestlé conference to be held in late 1978, it was expected that the IUF would request another formal meeting with Nestlé management.

The conference was held in Geneva from October 27 to 29, 1978. Prior thereto, affiliates were requested to prepare reports on Nestlé's operations and employee relations in their countries, based upon an IUF survey questionnaire. Reports were also submitted by regional IUF representatives in Asia and Latin America. The IUF also prepared a summary report on overall company business policies and included in it strident criticisms of Nestlé's business practices.

The IUF claimed that the conference was attended by forty-two delegates and observers, representing twenty-three unions in twenty countries.[34] Emphasis was on "glaring differences . . . between what is practiced in each country in terms of recognition, information, consultation, and general acceptance of unions by the company," [35] as well as variations in benefits, job security provisions, etc.—not a surprising situation in view of the different legal, social, economic, and political environments around the globe.

We understand that delegates were requested to keep files on key Nestlé subsidiary staff persons so that those considered difficult for the unions would be known and so that authorities of countries could be pressured not to give them work permits if transferred to another country. Delegates were also requested to sign a document committing them to support an international strike if called by the Nestlé World Council. Even if this docu-

---

[33] *Ibid.*, Item IX(a), p. 15. Gallin stated: "Informal contacts between the company and the IUF were resumed at the end of 1976 to explore the possibilities of solving some of the pending problems." Nestlé officials have affirmed that such meetings have occurred.

[34] *IUF News Bulletin*, Vol. 48, No. 12 (1978), p. 5.

[35] *Ibid.*

ment were signed, however, participation in such an endeavor would be subject to national legislation and to approval by the national and local unions involved.[36]

The conference revealed a split between unions from developed and underdeveloped countries. Those from the former indicated no major problems in their relations with Nestlé companies, which they found generally good. Hence, these unions opposed any confrontation, nationally or internationally. The delegates from underdeveloped areas were apparently strongly left-wing and pushed for more direct and, occasionally, extreme positions regarding the company. These positions were deflected by a decision to have the IUF study alleged problems in Latin America and in the Far East and then determine what to do about them.

Unlike the 1972 Nestlé conference, the 1978 one was not followed by a request for a meeting with Nestlé management. This may well reflect the position of key unions in developed countries that there are no general claims to discuss with the company and that what issues exist can best be handled locally or nationally. In addition, we understand that Nestlé has made it clear that it has no interest in any formal arrangement that would recognize the IUF in a representative capacity for its employees. Perhaps also the IUF was committed so deeply to its campaign against Unilever relating to South Africa (see the discussion of Unilever which follows) that it did not have the resources to push for a Nestlé meeting. In any case, the official conference report stressed the need for greater coordination of the union efforts at the national level "which was considered a necessary prerequisite for effective international action." [37]

The official conference report also sets forth no Nestlé meeting aspirations:

> Future activities within the IUF group of Nestlé unions will be coordinated by a working party made up of one representative each from Switzerland, Germany, France, the United States and the Scandinavian countries. The IUF secretariat will continue to publish the *Nestlé Bulletin* and to engage in research and information activities.[38]

---

[36] This and subsequent paragraphs are based upon confidential interviews with conference participants.

[37] *IUF News Bulletin*, Vol. 48, No. 12 (1978), p. 5.

[38] *Ibid.* See also International Union of Food and Allied Workers' Associations, *Second IUF Conference of Nestlé Workers* (Geneva, 1978).

It is not likely, however, that the IUF will permanently alter its aspirations for a formal relationship with Nestlé. It is more likely that Gallin will attempt to maintain informal relationships in the hope that a time will come when they can be formalized and the IUF can assume a formal bargaining or representative role.

UNILEVER

Unilever, the world's largest company in food manufacturing and the twelfth largest manufacturing company in the world on the 1979 *Fortune* list,[39] is a British-Dutch concern, headquartered in London and Rotterdam. Its principal American companies have been Lever Brothers and Lipton, U.S.A., but in early 1978, it also acquired National Starch and Chemical. Its 1978 sales exceeded $18.8 billion, and it has a strong position in chemicals, as well as in food (see Table XIII-1).

Formation of a World Council

In 1973, the International Union of Food and Allied Workers' Associations and the International Federation of Chemical, Energy and General Workers' Unions (ICEF) jointly established a Unilever World Council. The first meeting occurred in Geneva from June 6 to 8, 1973. These dates corresponded with the opening of an International Labour Organisation conference, which the meeting sponsors hoped would "facilitate the participation of some delegates from distant countries."[40] The meeting was preceded by analyses of Unilever businesses and profit positions, number and locations of plants, and personnel and labor relations practices. It appears that the IUF compiled nearly all these data using both reports from affiliated unions and published materials.[41]

The attendance at the June meeting was apparently disappointing. Ten countries were represented, a majority being IUF affiliates, plus three observing delegations. Australian, Canadian, and American delegates, as well as delegates from several other countries, were not present. A "permanent IUF/ICEF Unilever

---

[39] *Fortune*, Vol. 100 (August 13, 1979), p. 208.

[40] Letter announcing joint IUF/ICEF Unilever Council meeting, February 23, 1973, p. 1.

[41] The various reports issued to the delegates are on file in the Industrial Research Unit library.

Council" was established, and the first issue of the *Unilever Bulletin* was issued in mimeograph form on June 20, 1973.[42] Most of the conference time was directed to delegates' reporting on conditions in their respective countries. Six issues of the bulletin concerning Unilever had been published by early 1976 and were apparently jointly issued by the ICEF and the IUF. Then in November 1976, the IUF alone began issuing the bulletin in a new format, entitled *Unilever Information*. Five issues had appeared by June 1978. It would appear that, although the joint world council exists, the bulletin is now exclusively an IUF function.

Incidents in Italy and Spain

One matter that was reported to the first world council meeting involved pressure by the IUF to alter Unilever action. In September 1972, a telegram was sent to Unilever's Rotterdam headquarters by the IUF protesting what was considered to be the company's decision to close a small tomato paste factory in Parma, Italy. A Dutch IUF affiliate also expressed its concern to Unilever management.[43]

Unilever claims that its Italian company had decided that tomato paste no longer fitted into its product line and had made arrangements to sell the factory, if a satisfactory buyer could be found to continue the business. While negotiations were in progress with a prospective buyer, a rumor was circulated that the plant would be closed by a property developer. This led to the IUF response. Unilever is still operating the plant.

The second incident involved a union in Spain, where organized labor then operated in the shadow of illegality. On August 10, 1973, the IUF and the ICEF sent a joint circular letter to affiliates in the Netherlands, the United States, Belgium, the United Kingdom, and Germany concerning a strike at a Unilever facility near Madrid in which, pursuant to then Spanish law, five strike leaders had been suspended following a wage dispute. The affiliated unions were requested, "in the name of the IUF/ICEF Unilever Council," to intervene with the managements of their national companies to express their support of the Spanish workers and pressure Unilever to settle the dispute. The affected

---

[42] Summary of meeting and minutes in authors' possession.

[43] Copy of IUF telegram in authors' possession; and interview in London, September 3, 1973.

strikers were reinstated by an agreement reached pursuant to Spanish conciliation procedure prior to the company's receipt of the IUF/ICEF communications.[44]

Second Meeting and U.S. Strike

The Second IUF/ICEF Unilever World Council Meeting was held in London from March 5 to 6, 1974. On March 15, four United States Unilever (Lever Brothers) plants were struck by the International Chemical Workers Union, an ICEF affiliate. The president of this union attributed in part the "final success" of the strike, settled on March 28, to "effective international cooperation and solidarity." Although there appears to be no factual basis for the claim that the strike length or settlement was affected by any international action, the claims were repeated by a consultant's newsletter as showing "the ability of the international union movement to mobilize and react quickly." [45] This same newsletter also erroneously reported that Unilever management had met with the IUF/ICEF council in Geneva in June 1973. Even the secretariats had never claimed that such a meeting had occurred; in fact, Dan Gallin, general secretary of the IUF, wrote a letter, reprinted by this publication, emphasizing that no such meeting occurred.[46]

On March 28, 1976, *De Tijd,* a Dutch newspaper, reported that a meeting had been held between Unilever-Netherlands and Industriebond of the Dutch Socialist Federation of Trade Unions (NVV), which is affiliated with both the IUF and the ICEF. It was further reported "that Unilever had agreed in this meeting not to export goods to the United States during the strike and that the NVV representative, Mr. Van Hattem, communicated this position to Charles Levinson, secretary-general of the ICF." According to the paper, "Levinson said that efforts would now be made to bring pressure on the Unilever in the United Kingdom through the British trade unions." This paper also reported, however, that "a Unilever spokesman pointed out that there could not possibly be any question of conceding to the

---

[44] Circular letter and company communications in authors' possession.

[45] *Industrial Relations-Europe Newsletter,* Vol. II, No. 17 (April 1974), p. 7.

[46] *Ibid.,* Vol. II, No. 18 (May 1974), p. 1.

NVV demands since Unilever Nederlands did not export to the U.S.A. at all." [47]

Actually, no such meeting between Unilever and NVV affiliate representatives occurred. What happened was that a Dutch union official telephoned the company to find out if any products sold by Lever Brothers Company in the United States were now exported from Europe. After receiving an answer in the negative, the Dutch unionists issued a statement of solidarity with the American strikers! [48] Nothing in fact resulted, nor was there any overt reaction by British unionists who were also contacted by Levinson. [49]

IUF Meat Industry Meeting

Besides its participation in the joint world council with ICEF, the IUF has attempted to coordinate other national union activities involving Unilever, again without noticeable success. Thus,

> fifteen delegates from eight food workers' unions in Belgium, Denmark, France, Germany, the Netherlands, and the United Kingdom, affiliated to the International Union of Food and Allied Workers' Associations (IUF), met in Amsterdam, September 19 to 20, 1975, for an exchange of information and consultations on the growing unemployment in the meat industry. [50]

The meeting was called largely at the instigation of Dutch trade unions, which claimed rationalization was reducing jobs in the Netherlands. IUF General Secretary Dan Gallin was present.

From what we have learned, there was some discussion of attempting to obtain a meeting with Unilever for a multinational committee, but instead the delegates decided first to seek redress for their grievances at the national levels. The plan apparently called for national unions to meet with Unilever personnel concerning Unilever's investment plans in the meat industry, for each union to keep the others informed about results, for a second

---

[47] Translation from *De Tijd*, March 28, 1974.

[48] This account is based on several interviews in London, Brussels, and the Netherlands with persons who desire to remain anonymous. In fact, an examination of the product mix and brand names of Lever Brothers, U.S.A., and Unilever, NV, will show different products, brand names, etc.

[49] Despite the complete lack of evidence that the ICEF was involved in this situation, the *Wall Street Journal* reported that action by Levinson was crucial. See Richard F. Janssen, "Global Clout: How One Man Helps Unions Match Wits With Multinationals," *Wall Street Journal*, July 17, 1974, p. 1.

[50] *IUF News Bulletin*, Vol. 45, No. 11 (1975), p. 3.

meeting to occur in early 1976, and for the national unions to seek support for their position regarding the meat industry and employment therein from their respective ministers who represent their countries in the European Parliament.[51]

In December 1975, however, officials of chemical and food affiliates of the French CFDT, which had representatives at the meat plant workers' conference, wrote the Unilever Board in Rotterdam requesting a meeting between the Unilever World Council and the Unilever Board to discuss company investment policies and employment guarantees. The secretary of the Unilever Board replied that industrial relations issues in France are matters for local management.[52]

Second IUF Meat Industry and IUF/ICEF Working Party Meetings

The second meeting of the IUF meat industry group, originally set for January 1976, was held in Geneva on June 28, 1976. No delegates from the United Kingdom attended, and apparently little was decided. The company meanwhile closed one meat plant in Britain and announced the closing of another. In each case, an agreement was reached beforehand with the affected British unions on closure procedures and severance arrangements. Both plants were closed without any stoppage of work or dispute arising.

Following the meat industry meeting, an IUF/ICEF working party was convened in Geneva from June 29 to 30, 1976. There was the usual discussion of company policies, and a decision was made to continue the *Unilever Bulletin*;[53] but as noted below, the meeting was not well attended, and as already discussed, the IUF now apparently is handling the publication without the ICEF's involvement.

Christian Group Meeting

The World Federation of Workers in Food, Tobacco and Hotel Industries, a World Confederation of Labour affiliate, held a congress at Blankenberge, Belgium, September 29 to October 2,

---

[51] Interviews with various sources. See also *IUF 18th Congress*, Item IX(a), p. 16.

[52] Copies of correspondence in authors' possession.

[53] *IUF 18th Congress*, Item IX(a), p. 16.

1975. The IUF was represented as an observer at this meeting.[54] Multinational companies were discussed in detail, and Unilever was especially singled out in a commissioned report by representatives of a radical fringe union known as the SOMO (Stichting Onderzoek Multinationale Ondernemingen/Foundation for the Study of Multinational Enterprises) of Amsterdam. The SOMO has been helping to prepare the "Anti-Reports" with the anticapitalistic Counter Information Services, which regularly attacks large enterprises like Unilever.[55]

Spanish Unrest and ASTMS Booklet

Unilever, like many companies, has received numerous communications from the secretariats, in this case from both the ICEF and the IUF, during periods of industrial unrest in Spain. In addition, national unions in Britain and the Netherlands have charged the company several times with permitting unhealthy or substandard conditions in Spanish factories, a charge that the company has vigorously refuted. The Association of Scientific, Technical and Managerial Staffs (ASTMS), which is trying to unionize Unilever's British salaried workers, has been especially active in this regard. It has also published a booklet claiming that it is moving toward joint action with Industriebond-NVV on negotiations with Unilever regarding salaried employee conditions.[56] Actually, neither union represents a significant portion of Unilever's salaried work force in the two countries, and there have been no actual attempts for joint action.

IUF/ICEF World Council Meeting and Second U.S. Strike

As noted, an IUF/ICEF World Council working group met in Geneva from June 29 to 30, 1976, but the British and Belgian representatives and all non-Europeans were absent. Representa-

---

[54] *Ibid.*, XII(c), p. 2.

[55] S. Gussenhoven, "Meat and Multinational Corporations" (Report prepared for the World Federation of Workers in Food, Tobacco and Hotel Industries World Seminar, Blankenberge, Belgium, September 29-October 2, 1975), pp. 19-24. Also published as "Unilever's World," Anti-Report No. 11, and reprinted in French by the CFDT.

[56] Association of Scientific, Technical and Managerial Staffs, "A Charter for Unilever Staff" (London, [March 1976?]). See also "ASTMS in Dutch Union Link," *Financial Times*, March 3, 1976, p. 12. A foreword in the booklet from Industriebond-NVV states that the latter is "the main union representing staff in Unilever Holland" and has "recognition for white collar workers in most plants and subsidiaries." This is simply not correct.

tives from the Dutch, German, Italian, and French unions were present. Apparently little action resulted, except to consider whether to request Unilever to meet on a multinational basis.

While this meeting was in progress, the International Chemical Workers Union (ICWU) was on strike against four plants of Lever Brothers in the United States after the employees rejected a company offer. This strike began on April 9 and lasted until July 3. The Oil, Chemical and Atomic Workers (OCAW) accepted the same offer at the single plant where it represents Lever Brothers employees, and its members kept working all during the ICWU strike. The OCAW changed its international affiliation in 1976 from the defunct International Federation of Petroleum and Chemical Workers to the ICEF. Nevertheless, an ICEF circular letter was issued criticizing the policies of Lever Brothers and requesting a boycott of the American company's products, most of which are either not produced outside the United States or are known by different brand names in different countries.[57] The ICWU also asked for a boycott in the United States. No noticeable effect resulted either from the ICEF's or the ICWU's requests. The strike ended with terms so similar to those accepted by the OCAW without a strike that no renegotiation of the latter's agreement was necessary.

1977 World Council Meeting

The IUF/ICEF World Council met in London on July 11, 1977, where it concerned itself primarily with the fate of meat plants that had become marginal in the Netherlands.[58] Unilever had previously submitted proposals to Dutch unions and works councils proposing a reduction in the number of employees and new investment. Attempts of the Dutch unions to obtain support from the British or German unions were met with suggestions from these groups that they negotiate with Unilever under Netherlandic law and institutions. After the world council meeting, the Dutch unions proposed and Unilever's Dutch Meat Group agreed to an investigation of the matter by a committee of outside independent experts. The report of the experts, known as the

---

[57] ICEF Circular Letter No. 60/76, May 7, 1976, sent to all ICEF affiliates and members of the joint council.

[58] Pauline Clark, "European unions concerned over Unilever plans for Britain," *Financial Times*, July 13, 1977, p. 23; "Unilever-Wereldraad wil internationaal overleg met concern," *Financieel Dagblad*, July 13, 1977.

"Janssen Committee," upheld the company's basic contention that two plants were uneconomic and had to be closed.

Trinidad Strike

In the summer of 1977, a dismissed worker attempted to force his way into a Unilever plant in the Caribbean island of Trinidad and was injured in a scuffle with guards, who were suspended pending investigation. The union demanded that the security force be discharged and instigated an illegal slowdown ("go-slow"). Then after two weeks, the company reacted by discharging fourteen workers. The union then countered by striking, claiming that a lockout had occurred. The company took legal action against the union, but talks between the union president and the local Unilever company chairman resulted in a settlement. The discharged workers were reinstated, and the demand against the security force was withdrawn.

In September 1977, the ICEF secretary general issued a circular letter charging the company with "schizophrenic industrial relations" by dealing with unions in developed countries and being antiunion in underdeveloped areas, such as Trinidad, where, he charged, seven hundred workers were "locked out." He asked affiliates "to protest to their local management and to express their solidarity with their Brothers in Trinidad." [59] The circular was distributed to the strikers, and the company reported receiving pro forma protests from unions in Japan and the Irish Republic.[60] After the settlement, the president of the Trinidad union sent the ICEF his "thanks" for "national and ICEF international support," which forced the company "to end lockout." [61] In fact, of course, the matter was entirely settled on a local basis.

German Union Correction of IUF Claim

The third *Unilever Information*, issued by the IUF in February 1978, contained the charge that Unilever's German margarine plants were being put on a three-day week. According to the IUF, the short workweek was falsely being blamed by Unilever on the fact that soybeans and grain were not being shipped to the plant from the United States as a result of a waterfront

[59] ICEF Circular Letter No. 99/77, September 17, 1977.

[60] Company correspondence with authors, December 1977.

[61] ICEF Circular Letter No. 106/77, October 6, 1977, p. 2.

(longshore) strike there. The IUF article alleged that Unilever was trying to cover up its purchasing mistakes by blaming other workers.

Actually, no short time was either effectuated or contemplated in any German Unilever plant. One such plant is located in Emmerich, where there is also an Akzo plant; short time in the latter was contemplated but not effectuated as a result of the United States longshore strike. On April 4, 1978, the German food union, Gewerkschaft Nahrung-Genuss-Gaststätten (NGG), sent an official letter to the IUF requesting a correction "in the next issue of *Unilever Information,* because in addition to the works councils, the concern's management, which is also aware of the contents of *Unilever Information,* has complained." [62]

South Africa Campaign

In late 1977, the IUF held an African regional meeting and established an African office. Following this, the Swedish central union federations' (LO and TCO) international committee provided the IUF with funding of 816,000 Swiss francs (about $400,000) per year for six years (1978-84) to develop an "ongoing education program . . . intended for IUF-affiliated unions in Africa, Asia, and Latin America." The funds were provided via the Swedish hotel and restaurant union, an IUF affiliate. [63]

The IUF has long concentrated a lot of attention on Africa, with special reference to multinationals that operate in South Africa. The 1977 IUF/ICEF World Council Meeting passed resolutions regarding Unilever's alleged failure to recognize black workers' unions in South Africa, although Unilever had publicly expressed a willingness to do so if any such union could evidence the support of the employees involved. [64]

The Swedish unions and the IUF continued their attack on Unilever. On May 6, 1978, a Swedish daily paper, *Aftonbladt,* which is owned by the LO, the Swedish federation of blue-collar workers, stated that the Swedish food workers' union was preparing to challenge Unilever in Sweden over its investments and, specifically, that sit-in demonstrations would occur. Three

---

[62] Copy of letter in authors' possession. Quotation is from an English translation of the German original.

[63] International Union of Food and Allied Workers' Associations, *Meeting of the IUF Executive Committee* (Geneva, 1978), Item 3(e).

[64] "Black Unions Score Increasing Gains in South Africa," *Wall Street Journal,* August 29, 1977, p. 6.

days earlier, a Netherlands radio commentator, interviewing a person in Sweden, indicated that sympathy strikes would occur in four Swedish Unilever plants.

The journal of the Swedish food workers' union, issued April 25, 1978, contains a cover cartoon and a lead article castigating Unilever for not recognizing the black union at the plant in Boksburg, South Africa; it further urges the employees of Unilever plants to engage in stoppages to protest, stating, "We do not want Sweden to accommodate within its boundaries a company practicing racial discrimination of the worst kind." [65]

Financed by the Swedish unions and fed by a steady stream of propaganda by the IUF to affiliates, the campaign about South Africa against Unilever seemed to generate a sufficient following by the fall of 1978 for the IUF to announce its "Unilever South Africa Action Week" for October 23-28, 1978. The IUF clearly hoped that there would be major stoppages and demonstrations throughout Europe and proclaimed beforehand that it was assured of widespread national union support, particularly in Europe. The results, as summarized below, fell far short of these expectations. [66]

1. The Federation of Dutch Trade Unions (FNV) organized a "training meeting," permissible under its collective agreement. About sixty Unilever employee representatives attended the meeting. Various works council meetings were held, and Unilever management took steps to correct false statements published in an FNV pamphlet that was based on IUF distortions. Government ministers in the Dutch Parliament were twice asked about Unilever's policies in South Africa and responded factually.

2. In Germany, the NGG distributed a pamphlet, again based upon IUF-supplied misinformation, and the general secretary of the black union involved addressed the German Unilever Works Council. No overt action occurred, and no notices of the "action week" appeared in the press.

3. In France, the CFDT left the initiative to its food and chemical affiliates. They sent a common "open letter" to management of Unilever-France, which was reported on a

---

[65] *Mål och medel*, April 25, 1978, p. 1. All documents in authors' possession.

[66] The Industrial Research Unit has a large file of IUF materials from this event and has interviewed company personnel and examined company releases. This summary is based on these documents, plus materials in the public press.

back page of the CFDT journal.[67] No stoppages and little or no publicity occurred.

4. There were no reported activities in United Kingdom factories, although the IUF had previously announced that the Trades Union Congress was supporting its activities.[68] In May 1979, IUF General Secretary Dan Gallin made an unprecedented public attack on three British unions for their failure to support the IUF's action week. Speaking at the annual conference of the General and Municipal Workers' Union, he stated that the IUF received "absolutely no support" from the GMWU, the Transport and General Workers' Union, or the United Shop, Distributive and Allied Workers' Union, but rather that these unions had been satisfied by a "meaningless" company statement.[69] British union officials defended their position as consistent with the facts.

5. In Italy, there were some meetings but apparently no work stoppages.

6. Two-hour stoppages occurred among hourly workers and supervisors in two Swedish plants. Salaried employees did not take part in the demonstration.

7. In Denmark, a two-hour stoppage by each of two shifts occurred in one plant, and site-meetings were held in two others. Anti-Unilever propaganda was almost as strong in Denmark as in Sweden.

8. On October 25, a two-hour stoppage occurred in one plant in Finland, a slowdown in another, and a token stoppage of fifteen minutes in a third.

9. The IUF's propaganda generated letters and inquiries to Unilever in many other countries but no stoppages.

10. From the North American continent, one American and one Canadian union wrote Unilever. No publicity seems to have been generated in the press.

---

[67] *Syndicalisme* (Confédération Française Démocratique du Travail), October 19, 1978, p. 17.

[68] In a circular letter dated September 23, 1978, the IUF general secretary's office states: "The support of the Trades Union Congress in the United Kingdom and the Dutch Workers' Federation (FNV) in the Netherlands—the two countries where Unilever has its headquarters—has been assured for the campaign."

[69] Nick Garnett, "European official censures UK unions," *Financial Times*, May 23, 1979, p. 12.

Thus, except for letters from various unions to Unilever's general and various country headquarters, plus the short stoppages in the three Scandinavian countries, the so-called action week seems to have precipitated little action and achieved no significant objective, although it gained the IUF some publicity as an active international secretariat.

CONCLUSION

The IUF and the ICEF have thus not moved significantly toward their goal of multinational meetings with Unilever. Unilever, like Nestlé, is proud of its good employee relations and is anxious to have a good reputation for fair dealings with unions and employees. It is therefore quick to act when situations arise that could damage that reputation, but it regards industrial relations problems as ones that should be settled at local or national levels. Unilever has not, as of this writing, shown any disposition to meet with multinational union groups under a secretariat's auspices. Meanwhile, because of their size, both Nestlé and Unilever are likely to continue to be the target not only of the IUF and the ICEF but also of other union groups that will utilize issues such as South Africa and health and safety to attempt to gain their objectives.

CHAPTER XIII

Other Food, Beverage, and Tobacco Companies

Besides Nestlé and Unilever, the International Union of Food and Allied Workers' Associations (IUF) has claimed major initiatives involving Coca-Cola and Seagram and participated in an action involving Brooke Bond Liebig, Ltd., in which another secretariat, the International Federation of Plantation, Agricultural and Allied Workers (IFPAAW) played a leading role. This chapter examines these cases, plus several others, including short-lived ones in which the International Federation of Chemical, Energy and General Workers' Unions (ICEF) and the International Metalworkers' Federation (IMF) were involved.

COCA-COLA

The Coca-Cola Company, headquartered in Atlanta, Georgia, is the world's largest soft-drink company. In 1978, it had sales of $4.3 billion but only 36,100 employees (see Table XIII-1). Most of its business is done through independent franchises, which bottle the company product with syrup supplied by the company and made with a secret formula.[1] Employees of the bottlers are not, therefore, Coca-Cola employees except in the relatively few instances in which the company owns the bottling operation. Nevertheless, by virtue of its size and its worldwide sales, Coca-Cola is continually watched by the IUF, which in 1973 claimed a major victory in allegedly forcing the company to reopen a plant in Rome, a story that the company has emphatically denied.

According to the IUF, the 336 workers at the ARIB bottling plant in Rome struck on October 4, 1971, to protest a plant

---

[1] Coca-Cola discontinued bottling in India when the government of that country demanded the right to purchase a majority interest in its Indian operation and to obtain knowledge of its formula.

TABLE XIII-1

Seventeen Major Companies in the
Food and Allied Industries, 1978

Company	Headquarters	Sales ($000)	Assets ($000)	Net Income ($000)	Employees
Unilever	London; Rotterdam	18,893,176	11,119,234	531,337	318,000
Nestlé	Vevey, Switzerland	11,001,848	9,095,004	416,131	147,000
Procter & Gamble	Cincinnati, Ohio	8,099,687	4,983,817	511,668	55,600
Beatrice Foods	Chicago, Ill.	6,313,888	2,560,012	221,538	84,000
Esmark a	Chicago, Ill.	5,827,184	2,116,649	80,100	45,000 b
Kraft	Glenview, Ill.	5,699,900	2,300,900	184,000	46,881 b
General Foods	White Plains, N.Y.	5,376,204	2,433,024	169,506	49,000
Taiyo Fishery	Tokyo	4,518,317	2,091,616	7,003	13,750
Coca-Cola	Atlanta, Ga.	4,337,917	2,582,809	374,692	36,100
Colgate-Palmolive	New York	4,312,054	2,384,983	175,572	56,600 b
PepsiCo	Purchase, N.Y.	4,300,006	2,419,369	225,769	95,000
Ralston Purina	St. Louis, Mo.	4,058,400	1,897,900	154,600	70,000
Borden	New York	3,802,559	2,165,738	135,827	39,600 b
Consolidated Foods c	Chicago, Ill.	3,535,567	1,662,939	100,633	80,900
General Mills d	Minneapolis, Minn.	3,243,000	1,612,700	135,800	66,574

| CPC International | Englewood Cliffs, N.J. | 3,221,800 | 1,860,700 | 147,300 | 42,000 |
| George Weston Holdings [e] | Toronto | 3,035,662 | 1,338,625 | 41,655 | 104,130 |

Source: *Fortune*, Vol. 99 (May 7, 1979), pp. 270-89; Vol. 100 (August 13, 1979), pp. 194-203.
Note: BAT Industries, R. J. Reynolds, and Philip Morris also have large food operations; their statistics are given in Table XIII-2.

[a] Figures are for fiscal year ending October 31, 1978.
[b] Average for the year.
[c] Figures are for fiscal year ending June 30, 1978.
[d] Figures are for fiscal year ending May 31, 1978.
[e] Figures are for fiscal year ending March 31, 1978.

closure. Subsequently, a meeting was held in Rome by representatives of all Italian labor federations (the Confederazione Generale Italiana del Lavoro, Confederazione Italiana Sindacati Lavoratori, and Unione Italiana del Lavoro), which agreed not to permit other Coca-Cola plants in Italy to send their products to Rome.

According to the IUF account, the company at first refused to discuss the matter since the plant was closed. Workers occupied the plant until March 1972, when the police forced them out; then, 120 strikers continued to camp on the street around the plant. Under the auspices of the prime minister, an agreement was signed in June 1972 whereby 200 former employees were rehired and the plant "would continue in operation." [2]

The IUF version of this story was summarized in the *New York Times* [3] and later discussed by the then vice-president of Coca-Cola Europe in answer to a letter from one of the authors:

> As I was involved for some time in the liquidation of ARIB S.p.A. in Rome, I feel that from the very beginning there has been no failure on our part to communicate to all concerned the facts and figures relevant to the case. The Food Workers' Federation's claim which you quote in your letter represents the very subjective view of that Federation's Secretary, but the facts in which you are interested are, to the best of my knowledge, the following:
>
> (a) After the liquidation of ARIB S.p.A. there has been no direct negotiation between Management and Unions; not that this was feared or considered undesirable but, simply, it was felt that the Liquidator who has been appointed in accordance with local laws was solely qualified to implement the liquidation procedures.
>
> (b) When, at a certain point in time, the local authorities offered to intervene, we worked in close contact with them and, as far as we know, they, in turn, did the same with the local Unions.
>
> (c) As a result of this co-operation with local authorities we were able to arrive at what we consider a satisfactory solution, i.e.
>
> (i) ARIB's liquidation proceedings will be completed and there is no question of re-opening ARIB S.p.A.
>
> (ii) A new Bottler will be appointed in the Rome territory as soon as certain—rather complex—local conditions are met.

---

[2] See International Union of Food and Allied Workers' Associations, *17th Congress, Documents of the Secretariat* (Geneva, 1973), Item V(8), pp. 15-16. (Hereafter cited as *IUF 17th Congress.*)

[3] Clyde H. Farnsworth, "Big Business Spurs Labor Toward a World Role," *New York Times*, December 26, 1972, pp. 53-54.

> This will be a new bottling operation which is expected to function on a streamlined, economically viable basis.[4]

After this letter was received, we verified that this bottling plant was closed and liquidated, and then a new franchise was granted. The new plant is operating successfully. One reason is that truck operations were subcontracted so that the bottler has very few employees.[5]

Since the Rome incident, the IUF has sent numerous communications to Coca-Cola headquarters involving labor problems in Guatemala, Spain, Kenya, and other locations.[6] The Coca-Cola Company does not respond because its position is that the bottlers are independent and that, therefore, the Coca-Cola Company has no jurisdiction in labor matters. The company does occasionally buy out a franchise that is having difficulty. This is what happened in Rome, but after closing down the plant there, a new franchise was awarded, and an independent bottler is now in operation, as noted.[7]

SEAGRAM

The IUF has always claimed jurisdiction in the liquor and beverage industry but has seemed to stress this area since the mid-1970s. As in the case of the tobacco industry, discussed later in this chapter, IUF literature devotes much attention, regarding the liquor industry, to matters of health, advertising, taxation, and the effect on employment of government action regarding these matters. One can conjecture that the IUF regards these areas as possible avenues for IUF-industry cooperation and, therefore, for successful industry contacts, or that it believes that fear of bad publicity in union relations and its

---

[4] Letter from S. S. Dolfi, formerly vice-president, Coca-Cola Europe, to the authors, February 23, 1973.

[5] S. S. Dolfi, interview in Atlanta, February 15, 1978. Dolfi is now executive assistant to the president.

[6] *IUF News Bulletin*, Vol. 46, No. 2 (1976), p. 6; Vol. 47, No. 1 (1977), p. 10; Vol. 47, No. 4 (1977), p. 3; Vol. 47, Nos. 6-9 (1977), pp. 3-4; Vol. 47, Nos. 10-12 (1977), p. 10; Vol. 48, Nos. 6-7 (1978), pp. 5, 6-7; and Vol. 48, Nos. 8-9 (1978), p. 10. Much of this material refers to Guatemala, where serious labor trouble has occurred and a union official was murdered. See also "Guatemala: Government Contracts," *Latin America Political Report*, Vol. XIII (February 2, 1979), p. 39.

[7] Charles Hodgson, general counsel, Coca-Cola Export Company, telephone interview, December 12, 1975.

impact on companies' public stance might induce them to meet with the IUF.

The IUF has had Beverage Workers' Conferences [8] and has listed a number of companies as possible targets, including, besides Coca-Cola, Tuborg-Carlsberg and Seagram. The IUF had previously issued a resolution attacking Seagram for allegedly failing to agree to union demands at a French plant,[9] but it was in a Canadian dispute that the IUF attempted a major involvement.

Seagram, controlled by the Bronfman family, is one of the largest distillers of alcoholic beverages in the world, with major facilities in the United States, Canada, and many Western European and other countries. Its corporate headquarters is in Montreal, and a second headquarters is in New York. Its 1978 sales were $1.3 billion, and it then had 15,000 employees.[10]

The Canadian Dispute

Seagram operated seven distilleries and related operations in Canada, which for many years had a master agreement with the Distillery, Brewery, Winery, Soft Drink and Allied Workers' Union, which is affiliated with the AFL-CIO, the Canadian Labour Congress (CLC), and also with the IUF. In 1973, however, the local union in the Seagram operations in the Vancouver, British Columbia, area announced that it would negotiate separately. After the other six local unions under the master contract had settled, the British Columbia local union called a strike that lasted five months and resulted in a settlement that was twenty-two cents per hour superior to that negotiated pursuant to the master agreement. Consequently, as had been agreed in negotiations with the Distillery Workers, the master agreement was reopened and adjusted to the higher British Columbia settlement.[11]

During the strike and in the settlement negotiations, the secretary-treasurer of the British Columbia Federation of Labour, who was a former official of the Retail, Wholesale and Depart-

---

[8] See *IUF News Bulletin*, Vol. 45, No. 5-9 (1975), p. 2.

[9] *Ibid.*, p. 4.

[10] *Fortune*, Vol. 100 (August 13, 1979), p. 198.

[11] The history is in part related in British Columbia Distillery Company Limited v. Distillery, Brewery, Winery, Soft Drink and Allied Workers' Union, Local 604, decision of the Labour Relations Board of British Columbia (March 27, 1975).

ment Store Union (RWDSU), assisted the striking Distillery Workers' local union. After the strike was over, the local disaffiliated from the Distillery Workers and affiliated with the RWDSU, which was duly certified to represent the employees of Seagram's British Columbia operations by the Labour Relations Board of British Columbia. The RWDSU, like the Distillery Workers, is an affiliate of the AFL-CIO, the CLC, and the IUF.

Labor relations at the British Columbia operations continued to be poor after the 1973 strike settlement. The company complained of low productivity, which is corroborated by an RWDSU official who agreed that the local union's members "were as unenthusiastic as possible" and had refused to work overtime.[12] In addition, the company charged that besides slow-downs, there were thirty-six incidents of sabotage during the six months prior to May 31, 1975.[13] For its part, the RWDSU claimed that the company reacted with a "hard line" and failed to recruit skilled mechanics to fix new equipment.[14]

When the local union declined to be moved by the company's demand that it improve conditions or be "faced with drastic action," the company shut down the bottle and packaging shops in February 1975 and laid off eighty employees. The RWDSU countered by picketing other Seagram operations in British Columbia and shutting them down.

The RWDSU also complained to the Labour Relations Board of British Columbia. The board ruled in a split decision that Seagram's plant closing was an illegal lockout and ordered Seagram to reopen the plant and to reinstate the employees. The board also ruled unanimously that the RWDSU picketing and strike were illegal and ordered the RWDSU to end these activities.[15] The union complied, but Seagram declined to accept the order. The company did, however, commence paying wages to the laid-off workers to avoid possible future liability, but it did not bring them back to work.

---

[12] *Ibid.*; and Allan Peterson, international representative, RWDSU, quoted in Richard Osler, "Seagram has dismantled plants in British Columbia, but union fights on," *Financial Post* (Canada), January 31, 1976, p. 24.

[13] *Ibid.*

[14] *Ibid.*

[15] British Columbia Distillery Co., decision of the Labour Relations Board of British Columbia; order of the board in the same matter (April 28, 1975).

The board then sought to have the Supreme Court of British Columbia enforce its award, and the RWDSU asked the same court to sequester the assets of the company as a means of enforcement. The court, however, found the board's order ambiguous and refused to enforce it.[16] The board, without a further hearing, then issued a new order, instructing the company (1) to cease its alleged lockout; (2) to "resume operations at the said Bottling Plant, including bottling, labeling, packaging, and casing operations, to the same extent and in the same manner as the said operations were conducted at that location prior to February 26, 1975"; (3) to reinstate all members of the union who were laid off or terminated; and (4) to maintain operations and employment until a legal lockout or strike occurred.[17]

Again, the company declined to accept the board's order. This time, the first three parts were enforced; however, the fourth was denied enforcement.[18] Again, the RWDSU filed a writ to sequester the company's assets, but it was disclosed that the union had filed a strike notice on April 26, 1975, two days prior to the board's second order and had begun a strike on June 2, two days after the collective agreement expired. This nullified the board's entire order.[19]

IUF Involvement

From February 1975, when Seagram closed the bottling facility, until the strike was settled twenty-three months later, the RWDSU made strenuous efforts to have a boycott initiated against Seagram products, appealing to the AFL-CIO, the CLC, and the IUF for this purpose. Since a boycott was opposed by the Distillery Workers, however, none of these organizations could act. The CLC did ask consumers in Canada not to buy Seagram products, but the company reported that its sales actually increased. In British Columbia, however, Seagram was shut out because the British Columbia Liquor Commission—the

---

[16] Distillery, Brewery, Winery, Soft Drink & Allied Workers' Union—Local 604 v. The British Columbia Distillery Company Limited, Vancouver Registry No. 39040/75 (Supreme Court of British Columbia, April 18, 1975).

[17] British Columbia Distillery Co., order of the Labour Relations Board of British Columbia.

[18] Vancouver Registry No. X7566/75 (Supreme Court of British Columbia, June 26, 1975).

[19] Vancouver Registry No. X7552/75 (Supreme Court of British Columbia, July 6, 1976).

sole customer for distillery product sales in the province—followed its usual policy of refusing to stock products where a British Columbia struck plant is involved.[20]

As noted in our discussion of the Nestlé situation, the RWDSU is very active in the IUF. Considerable pressure was put upon the secretariat to become involved in the dispute. This the IUF attempted to do short of supporting an RWDSU boycott request. On November 6, 1975, IUF General Secretary Dan Gallin wrote Edgar N. Bronfman, president of Seagram, demanding that the company rescind its layoffs and reopen the plant and threatening international union action. This was followed up with a second letter in March 1976.[21] The company did not respond to these letters.[22]

Then at the IUF congress held in Geneva in January 1977, a resolution introduced by the RWDSU calling for a worldwide boycott of Seagram products was passed.[23] The Distillery Workers, unlike the RWDSU, had not sent a delegation to the congress. The IUF boycott resolution had an immediate effect in Sweden, where Seagram products were removed from the shelves. In Austria and Finland, action was also threatened.[24] Meanwhile, however, an agreement was reached with the RWDSU in British Columbia.

Strike Settlement

In December 1976, Seagram sold its main British Columbia plant. This permanently eliminated the jobs of most of the Seagram employees in British Columbia. In late January—almost at the very time that the IUF congress was passing its boycott resolution—agreement was reached ending the strike. Ac-

---

[20] Osler, "Seagram has dismantled plants," p. 24. Strangely enough, this policy is not applied in similar circumstances if the struck plant is located in another Canadian province.

[21] *RWDSU Record*, March 1976, p. 2; *IUF News Bulletin*, Vol. 47, No. 2 (1977), p. 2.

[22] Peter Abbott, vice-president, Personnel and Industrial Relations, The House of Seagram, Ltd., interview in Montreal, April 29, 1977.

[23] Copy in authors' possession.

[24] Peter Abbott, interview, April 29, 1977. The *IUF News Bulletin* claimed that a boycott was instituted in Norway and on the Spanish island of Majorca and was about to begin in France [Vol. 47, No. 2 (1977), p. 2]. Since French unions are very divided, the potential for a French boycott may at least be questioned.

cording to the IUF, "The company agreed to reopen two whiskey distilleries and signed a new collective agreement providing wage increases and benefits estimated at 56 percent in monetary value over wages and conditions prevailing two years ago." [25]

According to the RWDSU, the Seagram workers "returned to work" with the "strongest" contract in their industry. The *RWDSU Record,* the principal journal of the national union, summarized the contract "at some length . . . so that the countless persons and many organizations throughout North America and abroad can know what their support of the Seagram boycott has wrought." "World-wide support" was claimed for this victory, and the statement ended: "All Hail to Solidarity." [26]

The contract is indeed generous in economic benefits. It also provided for first recall of the chief pickets during the strike and for $750 severance pay for those who gave up hope of regaining their jobs. It certainly did not, however, commit the company to reopen plants (which had been sold). Rather, the contract states:

> During the recent negotiations for a Collective Agreement the matter of expansion of the operations of the British Columbia Distillery Company Limited was discussed and certain assurances were given in this regard and they are given in writing herein.
>
> The Company hereby gives an undertaking that, within six months from the date that work is resumed, it will carefully evaluate the feasibility of establishing a bottling operation in British Columbia.
>
> The factors which will determine such feasibility of a bottling operation, which will require a substantial investment and time to become operative, will be:
>
> (a) Employer-Employee relations or in general, the working climate within the on-going operations;
> (b) The degree to which the sales of the Company's products (which have been zero for two years) can be reestablished in B.C.;
> (c) Prevailing economic conditions.
>
> The Union needs to accept in good faith that the Company will examine the situation in the most positive light at the appropriate time and will communicate freely with the Union.[27]

---

[25] *IUF News Bulletin,* Vol. 47, No. 2 (1977), p. 2.

[26] *RWDSU Record,* March 1977, p. 2. See also *IUF News Bulletin,* Vol. 47, No. 3 (1977), pp. 2-3.

[27] "Agreement between the Distillery, Brewery, Winery, Soft Drink and Allied Workers, Local 604 . . . and the British Columbia Distillery Company Limited et al." (February 7, 1977); and attached "Letter of Understanding," p. 2, in authors' possession.

Pursuant to the agreement, Seagram management met with the RWDSU local union in July 1977 and advised it as follows: (1) employee-employer relations had improved substantially; (2) sales of company products in British Columbia had improved, but not sufficiently to justify a distilling operation; and (3) Seagram had ample capacity in Canada to supply British Columbia without reopening an operation there. By July 1979, the company had completed the exodus of all inventory from the closed plant but still had sixty thousand barrels in the warehouse from which they were shipping. Only 21 employees were left, 135 of the pre-strike work force having been dismissed. All employees were scheduled to go by mid-1981, when the warehouse inventory would be depleted. The company and the RWDSU were negotiating at this time, with the union demanding that the plant be reopened and that very generous severance pay be granted.[28] The company, obviously, will not accede to the first and was in a position strongly to resist the second.

Impact of Boycott

The IUF boycott obviously did nothing to save the jobs lost by the strike. The Swedish-IUF boycott lasted two weeks. Even if Finland and Austria or other small countries had followed suit, it is not likely that the company would have felt an impact in the United States or Canada, its largest markets. Nevertheless, because alcoholic beverage manufacturers are unusually vulnerable to union pressure, especially to that exerted through liquor commissions or boards and other governmental agencies, it is not unlikely that unions and the IUF will be involved in similar pressures in the future.

Prior to the strike, the Distillery Workers had become delinquent in dues to the IUF. Since then, this union has paid no dues.[29] It is not known whether the boycott controversy was involved in this union's apparent defection from the IUF.

W. R. GRACE

W. R. Grace, once known for its shipping, banking, and South American industrial activities, has disposed of these investments

---

[28] Peter Abbott, telephone interviews, February 20, 1978, and July 26, 1979.

[29] Data from IUF financial reports in authors' possession.

and is now a major New York City-based conglomerate with activities concentrated in chemicals and consumer products, including restaurants. It also has some food-manufacturing facilities. In 1978, Grace had sales of $4.3 billion and 66,800 employees and ranked fifty-ninth in sales among American industrial corporations.[30]

In 1972, the IUF and the International Federation of Chemical, Energy and General Workers' Unions formed a joint world council, which has held two meetings. The first occurred February 23-25, 1972, in Geneva and was attended by delegates from twelve organizations. A discussion of Grace operations was followed by a directive to the ICEF and IUF secretariats to contact the international management of Grace and to present them with "a common platform of demands." The second meeting occurred in Geneva, September 7, 1972, to discuss the refusal of Grace management to meet with the council. Representatives of only three unions were present. It was decided to communicate the "anti-labor attitude" of Grace to local unions and to hold a "public campaign to inform consumers" throughout the world of the company's attitude. This agitation was planned for the week of October 23-28, 1972, to compel Grace management to engage in a dialogue with the ICEF/IUF council.[31]

The planned day of strife passed without incident at any Grace plant,[32] and no further developments are known to have occurred. Nevertheless, Charles Levinson, secretary general of the ICEF, told the *New York Times* late in 1972 that "a W. R. Grace world council has called for a public campaign to inform consumers of the company's "anti-labor attitude" because of Grace's refusal to meet with union representatives to discuss plans for plant shutdowns." [33]

According to the company:

> The facts in this situation are very simple. We have for many years followed the practice of meeting the needs of our employees through bargaining at the local level. We do this because our business is very diversified, and because industry patterns differ so greatly.

---

[30] *Fortune*, Vol. 99 (May 7, 1979), pp. 272-73.

[31] *IUF 17th Congress*, Item V(8), pp. 9-10. Farnsworth, "Big Business Spurs Labor," p. 54.

[32] W. R. Grace personnel official, telephone interview, February 15, 1974.

[33] Farnsworth, "Big Business Spurs Labor," p. 54.

> The movement to form a Grace World Council is strictly a figment of the imagination of Mr. Charles Levinson. We have had no discussions with him and we do not plan to have any.[34]

In more recent years, Grace has sold its European restaurants but still retains some food-manufacturing plants there. The only incident involving international unions was a communication in early 1978 from the IUF in support of Italian unions striking some of these plants.[35] Although the secretary general of the ICEF listed the IUF/ICEF W. R. Grace World Council as active in his report to the 1976 ICEF Congress,[36] his IUF counterpart noted in 1977 that "no activities have taken place within the [council] for Grace . . ." since 1972.[37]

OETKER GROUP

The Oetker Group, headquartered in Bielefeld, Germany, is a major multinational food and beverage company that also has interests in banking, chemicals, printing, and textiles. An IUF-led Oetker conference occurred in Bielefeld, October 11-12, 1972. The ICEF, the International Graphical Federation, and the International Textile, Garment and Leather Workers' Federation, which have affiliates in the group, sent messages to the conference, which heard reports on labor problems in the group. According to IUF reports, forty delegates representing ten countries were present:

> The participants visited one of the local Oetker establishments and had a chance to discuss, during an informal interview with representatives of the management, some of the problems treated in the course of the conference. R. A. Oetker, president of the company, participated in this meeting along with certain of the manage-

---

[34] Letter from executive vice-president, W. R. Grace, to one of the authors, January 30, 1973.

[35] International Union of Food and Allied Workers' Associations, *Meeting of the IUF Executive Committee* (Geneva, 1978), Item 3(d), p. 5. (Hereafter cited as *IUF Executive Committee*.)

[36] "Executive Committee. Activities Report of the Secretary-General. List of Membership," *ICF 16th Congress*, Montreal, October 27-29, 1976, p. 94. (Hereafter cited as *ICF 16th Statutory Congress*.)

[37] International Union of Food and Allied Workers' Associations, *Executive Committee Meeting and 18th Congress* (Geneva, 1977), Item IX(a), p. 13. (Hereafter cited as *IUF 18th Congress*.)

ment staff. It was agreed to organize an official meeting between representatives of the IUF and the Oetker management for March 1973 to discuss workers' demands.[38]

The planned meeting never occurred, and apparently the Oetker World Council formed by the IUF at the October 1972 meeting has been totally inactive since then.[39]

BROOKE BOND LIEBIG, LTD.

Brooke Bond Liebig (BBL) is a London-based multinational corporation with interests in livestock, plantations, and food and related products. It is a leading tea marketer in England and owns extensive tea plantations in East Africa and Asia. In 1978, BBL had total sales of $1.4 billion and 70,000 employees.[40]

The International Federation of Plantation, Agricultural and Allied Workers is a Geneva-based secretariat that was formed in 1959 as a result of the merger of the European-oriented International Landworkers' Federation, which was organized in 1923, and the Plantation Workers' International Federation, which was organized in 1957. The latter union was composed exclusively of unions from underdeveloped countries; and, the IFPAAW's membership is primarily from these areas. As a result, the IFPAAW is not self-supporting, with as much as 75 percent of its income from sources other than affiliates' dues. Its main income source over the years has been the contributions of the solidarity fund of the International Confederation of Free Trade Unions (ICFTU), with supplemental donations from Dutch, Swedish, German, and American unions and governments.[41] In 1976, the IFPAAW's income from dues totaled only $23,615, whereas $141,251 was received by the ICFTU solidarity fund.[42] Much more was expended from grants from unions and governments in support of the IFPAAW in the Third World.

---

[38] *IUF 17th Congress*, Item V(8), p. 8.

[39] *IUF 18th Congress*, Item IX(a), p. 13.

[40] *Fortune*, Vol. 100 (August 13, 1979), p. 198.

[41] The ICFTU, in turn, receives its solidarity funds from governments through unions. The Friedrich Ebert Foundation, wholly funded by the German government, is a major supporter of the IFPAAW.

[42] Data supplied by Stanley Correa, general secretary, IFPAAW, from reports to the 1976 congress.

Television Impact

Granada Television, with which the IFPAAW was "in contact," [43] stirred international concern for tea plantation workers in Sri Lanka with a single telecast. This British television team, in its "World in Action" series in September 1973, portrayed to the British public its version of the situation on the Brooke Bond and other foreign-owned tea estates. It pictured the overcrowded living quarters, exemplified by a man sleeping on the floor of a boarded-up latrine (on a Lonrho estate); [44] the undernourished and disease-ridden children; the illiterate workers; the ill-equipped dispensers; the very low purchasing power of the Rs219.50 monthly wage [45] that a husband and wife can earn on the plantations; and the discrimination suffered by the Indian Tamils [46] under the Sri Lankan government.[47]

It was not surprising then that, following a Ceylon Workers' Congress (CWC) statement reporting basically the same conditions as Granada Television had broadcast, the ICFTU/ITS working party on multinational companies, during its meeting in Tokyo on October 4, 1973, decided to direct an internationally coordinated attack at the industrial level and to make Brooke Bond **Liebig its principal target.** A consumer boycott of tea in Britain, as well as other international actions, was suggested as a means by which the ICFTU might help to improve the conditions of the plantation workers, especially the Tamils. The consumer boycott was subsequently dropped, however, when it was realized that the action would be ineffective because of the popularity of BBL's tea brands.

Company Meetings

When Brooke Bond Liebig received a copy of these proceedings, it immediately sought information about what action was envisaged for improving conditions on its estates. Confusion

---

[43] Letter from the IFPAAW to its European affiliates, February 4, 1974.

[44] Lonrho is a British company with extensive African interests.

[45] Rs1 = U.S. $0.16.

[46] Indian Tamils are immigrants from India brought to Sri Lanka at the turn of the century, after which they were denied citizenship and thus became hopelessly tied to the isolated plantations.

[47] Carl Wilms-Wright, "Sri Lanka Tea: The Time for Action," *Free Labour World*, Vol. 298 (April 1975), pp. 13-16.

ensued, however, because BBL was inundated with "information" from the ICFTU, the IFPAAW, and the IUF, which also had an interest in the situation. Brooke Bond continued to insist on local collective bargaining as a means to achieve the union goals in Sri Lanka; nonetheless, BBL Chairman Sir Humphrey Prideaux suggested in a March 7, 1974, letter to T. S. Bavin, the IFPAAW general secretary, that a meeting be arranged between himself, Bavin, and an IUF representative.

The IFPAAW and the IUF then agreed to meet Prideaux in London. They requested that the discussion center on the following four major issues: (1) a realistic wage rate for workers; (2) the inadequate and bad housing, resulting in overcrowding; (3) the lack of piped pure water supplies and sanitation; and (4) the high degree of malnutrition prevailing among the women and children.[48]

Prior to this meeting, however, the IFPAAW released to the press more evidence and on March 29, 1974, openly criticized BBL in the *Guardian* and the *Observer*. Thus, this set the scene for the May 4 meeting between the unions, which were represented by Bruce Vandervort (IUF) and T. S. Bavin, and Brooke Bond Liebig, represented by its chairman, Sir Humphrey Prideaux, and its plantation director, P. L. Brazier. The four aforementioned issues were discussed, and each side admitted the difficulties which prevailed. Brooke Bond, however, stated that it would attempt to improve or to replace its labor housing once the operation was again profitable.[49] (Also during this meeting in London, the IFPAAW produced four photographs allegedly depicting intolerable situations at BBL's Daverashola estate, which is actually in South India, not Sri Lanka. Brooke Bond examined the photographs and later reported to the IFPAAW in a June 10 letter that three of the four pictures were not even of Daverashola. Furthermore, BBL noted that the fourth situation depicted had occurred as a result of a shortage of cement.) At the close of the meeting, BBL reiterated its belief in local bargaining and suggested a meeting on the local level.

As a result of BBL's suggestion, a meeting between Brooke Bond Ceylon, the CWC, and the Ceylon Estate Employers' Fed-

---

[48] Letter from T. S. Bavin, then general secretary, IFPAAW, to Sir Humphrey Prideaux, chairman, BBL, March 19, 1974. Bavin is now president of the IFPAAW.

[49] Meeting notes with BBL representative, London, Friday, May 4, 1974.

eration (CEEF) was held on August 20, 1974, in Sri Lanka. BBL was represented by L. Wirritunga, director of Brooke Bond Ceylon; N. Ranasuriya, personnel officer; and L. Perera, estates group manager. The CWC was represented by S. Thondaman, president; M. S. Sellasamy, general secretary; H. Sandrasekara, public relations officer, and S. Renganathan, director of industrial relations. Also present was C. Rajasooriya, deputy secretary of the CEEF. Housing, water supply, medical care, and wage rates were again the topics for discussion. At this meeting, BBL explained in detail the difficulties in solving the problems of the plantation workers, especially the discrimination practiced by the Sri Lankan government against the Tamils. At the end of the meeting, all parties agreed to another meeting to be held in September to discuss the following issues: overpopulation, housing, drugs, medical facilities, crèche and child care, and garden plots.[50]

That second local meeting took place on September 24, 1974. L. Wirritunga (BB Ceylon), L. Perera (Galaha Tea Estates), S. Thondaman, H. Sandrasekara, S. Renganathan, and V. Jayasekera (CEEF) were all present. During this meeting, Brooke Bond agreed to implement a three-year program for the maintenance and improvement of housing and sanitation on the estates. Brooke Bond Ceylon, however, refused to quantify financially what was being spent or even what was going to be spent on housing and sanitation, drugs and disease control, crèches, and food production. Further efforts to obtain this information were to no avail. Brooke Bond responded that "the official repercussions possible following the unauthorized disclosure to foreign organizations of sensitive material affecting national assets do not permit us at this juncture to provide you with the information you request."[51]

This stern position taken at the meeting and in subsequent communications led S. Thondaman to consider Brooke Bond's progress to be unsatisfactory. T. S. Bavin and Dan Gallin, the IUF general secretary, also expressed their dissatisfaction in a letter to Brooke Bond dated December 19, 1974.

---

[50] Notes of discussion between Brooke Bond Ceylon and the Ceylon Workers' Congress held on August 20, 1974. Brooke Bond, previous to this meeting, declined to meet at the international level in Geneva.

[51] Letter from S. E. Satarasinghe to Dan Gallin, general secretary, IUF, December 10, 1974.

On February 4, 1975, a third meeting was held between the CWC and BBL. S. Thondaman, H. Sandrasekara, P. L. Brazier, L. Wirritunga, and S. E. Satarasinghe (BB Ceylon) were present. P. L. Brazier, the plantation director for BBL, was present at this meeting in response to an invitation by the local representatives of Brooke Bond Ceylon. During the meeting, the CWC insisted that Brooke Bond Liebig "state in decisive terms the programmes that [it has] drawn up to improve the standard of living of the workers." [52] Again, Brooke Bond responded that "it was not possible to make long-term programmes as one could not be certain of the fluctuations in the economic situation." [53] Thus, the CWC concluded that the meeting was merely "in the nature of a courtesy chat." [54]

Furthermore, the CWC felt that the fourth local meeting with Brooke Bond Ceylon on March 7, 1975, produced "nothing positive." [55] The meeting did, however, further antagonize the IFPAAW since BBL refused to permit S. G. Correa, then an IFPAAW representative and, since December 1976, the general secretary of the IFPAAW, to attend the meeting.

Then, on March 17, 1975, the British "World in Action" television team presented new evidence revealing in detail how the conditions on the plantations had deteriorated since its first television report in September 1973. Its medical survey uncovered several cases of anemia and hookworm, as well as a few deaths from malnutrition. Brooke Bond Liebig responded by placing full-page advertisements in several British newspapers, including the *Sun*, refuting the allegations made by the Granada broadcast.[56]

End of "Solidarity"

The ICFTU saw this as a direct confrontation between Brooke Bond Liebig and the international free trade union movement. Therefore, it again insisted on dealing with the matter on an international level:

---

[52] Discussion with representatives of Brooke Bond Liebig at Colombo on February 4, 1975.

[53] *Ibid.*

[54] *Ibid.*

[55] Letter from T. S. Bavin to Sir Humphrey Prideaux, March 21, 1975.

[56] Wilms-Wright, "Sri Lanka Tea," p. 14.

It will be up to the international free trade union movement to see what further help can be given to the CWC and the Sri Lankan plantation workers in their fight against exploitation. There have been too many broken promises, too many unfulfilled pledges at a time when sheer physical survival has become evermore difficult. What is apparent is that the plight of the Sri Lankan tea plantation workers presents a test case and a vital challenge to international trade union solidarity.[57]

The ICFTU also saw a need for international union solidarity: "What is clear is that the time for action has come and transnational capitalism must be combatted by transnational labour unity. Nothing less will serve to end the scandalous profiteering being practiced on Sri Lanka's tea plantations today." [58]

The international labor solidarity was eroded, however, when an investigation into the conditions on British-owned tea estates in Sri Lanka was carried out by a group of British members of Parliament. The Department of Trade's report on the visit of members of Parliament revealed that "the subjects chosen [by Granada] were predominantly problem families not typical of the generality of the families on the estates." [59] Thus, Granada was criticized for its failure to put the general conditions into perspective. Again, it should be noted that the IFPAAW earlier stated that it was "in contact with the British Granada Television Co. and important sections of the British Press (OBSERVER) with a view to discreet leakage of sufficient information as to maintain interest." [60]

Further eroding the international labor solidarity movement was the CWC's push for nationalization. The Ceylon Workers' Congress strongly urged the Sri Lankan government to buy the tea plantations. Thus, in May 1975, it was announced publicly that Sri Lanka, after several months of negotiations, had agreed to buy the three estates of Brooke Bond Liebig. With nationalization, however, the Ceylon union lost any effective help from the international secretariats. The IFPAAW and the ICFTU could no longer exert pressure on an "infamous multinational corporation" since Brooke Bond no longer owned the estates.

---

[57] Carl Wilms-Wright, "A Test Case for Labour Solidarity," *Free Labour World*, Vol. 297 (March 1975), p. 17.

[58] Wilms-Wright, "Sri Lanka Tea," p. 16.

[59] United Kingdom, Department of Trade, *Sri Lanka Tea Estates* (London: St. Stephen's Parliamentary Press, 1975), p. 18.

[60] Letter from the IFPAAW to its European affiliates, February 4, 1974.

Nonetheless, the CWC saw it as an improvement for their workers:

> The benefit of the nationalisation of estates should accrue to the workers in the plantations and the masses. This should not be turned into an instrument of oppression of the workers as has been the case on estates acquired by the Land Reform Commission. Our experiences on these estates have belied all our hopes and workers and staff have been arbitrarily thrown out of not only employment but even from their dwellings. Therefore, to avoid a repetition of this episode when nationalisation becomes a fait accompli, workers must unite under one strong organisation and not dissipate their strength by disunity.[61]

But with the British Commons referring the parliamentary delegation's report to the Ceylon Association,[62] the controversy was quickly tabled. Without the British referring the report to a select committee of the Commons and without any effective aid from the IFPAAW, the situation on the former Brooke Bond estates ceased temporarily to maintain the public's attention on an international level. It thus reverted to a local problem to be worked out between the workers and the Sri Lankan government—the new plantation owners.

Impact of Nationalization

Under public management, the conditions of the plantation workers were soon found by the international unions to be "rapidly deteriorating." [63] The government broke up some of the estates to convert them to farm plots for the purpose of growing food but gave much of the land to others rather than to the Indian Tamils. The Ceylon Workers' Congress, which pushed nationalization so strongly, struck in March 1977 against the government's "compulsory resettlement schemes which had the effect of uprooting [Sri Lankan estate workers] without any prior consultation, from the estates on which generations of their families had worked." [64] Communal riots in August 1977,

---

[61] S. Thondaman quoted in *Congress News*, Vol. VIII, No. 6 (August 15, 1975), p. 1.

[62] An independent body of trade interests connected with Sri Lanka but with no official status.

[63] "Beyond Nationalisation," *Free Labour World*, Vol. 317-318 (November-December 1976), p. 26.

[64] *International Trade Union News* (International Confederation of Free Trade Unions), April 18, 1977, p. 2.

which were directed against the Indian Tamils, resulted in arson, looting, and the death of about one hundred persons.[65]

For those who have remained on the plantations, the situation has also deteriorated since nationalization. The use of fertilizers has declined, and old, less productive tea bushes are not being replaced on schedule.[66] In 1968, production declined from a former peak of 503 million pounds to 400 million pounds.[67] Poor management and the uprooting and repatriation of Indian Tamils, who have lived in Ceylon for a century, to southern India, where they add to already severe unemployment problems, have resulted in labor shortages. The Sri Lankan majority ethnic group, the Sinhalese, are not inclined to work on the estates. This has caused the Sri Lankan government to consider the importation of skilled plantation labor *from* India.[68] It has already sent 230,000 Tamils from Sri Lanka *to* India.[69]

The nationalization of the tea estates has thus been counterproductive to the economy and to people of Sri Lanka. The same groups which on television stirred the British public with a study of limited accuracy have not, however, concerned themselves with the increased misery brought to the Tamils in part by those groups' agitation, which helped to pave the way for nationalization and dislocation. Rather, they have continued to criticize Brooke Bond Liebig management's conduct of its plantation labor conditions, this time in India, again making claims that the company challenges as inaccurate.[70]

One British union, the General and Municipal Workers' Union, and the British Labour party supported the charges against

---

[65] William Borders, "Strife in Sri Lanka Abates, but the Tensions Persist," *New York Times*, August 30, 1977, p. 1.

[66] Barry Kramer, "Socialist Sri Lanka Acts to Curb Welfare Outlays, Welcome Back Foreign Firms to Lift Growth Rate," *Wall Street Journal*, August 22, 1978, p. 44.

[67] "Labour problems for Lanka tea estates," *Economics Times* (Bombay), February 1, 1979, p. 6.

[68] "Sri Lanka tea hit by Indian repatriation," *Economics Times*, October 24, 1978, p. 4.

[69] Kevin Rapperty, "Sri Lanka: Labour problems for tea estates," *Financial Times*, January 25, 1979, p. 21; *Economics Times*, February 1, 1979, p. 6.

[70] See *Brooke Bond Liebig and the Indian Tea Estates* (Distributed at the December 8, 1978, annual shareholders' meeting of BBL by the World Development Movement, a self-styled defender of Third World interests); and *Tea Workers Today* (Brooke Bond Liebig), December 1978, also distributed at this meeting.

Brooke Bond at its 1978 annual meeting, while the ICFTU did so in press coverage.[71] The IFPAAW has, however, apparently not done so. Its activities in this situation are now concentrated on raising relief for the Tamils deported to India; on attempts to assist them in organizing and gaining work, a difficult task given its funding levels and the already mass poverty and unemployment in southern India; and on continued support to those still working on former tea estates, with funds provided by the United States Agency for International Development and funneled through the AFL-CIO-controlled Asian-American Free Labor Institute.[72]

THE BORDEN COMPANY

The Borden Company, headquartered in New York, is one of the ten largest food-producing companies in the world and also has major investments in chemicals. Its 1978 sales were $3.8 billion; in the same year, it had 39,600 employees and ranked sixty-eighth in sales among American manufacturing companies.[73]

Both the IUF and the ICEF have indicated an interest in Borden. At its 1973 congress, the IUF recommended that its affiliates should include Borden among the companies for which meetings should be held and presumably world councils formed.[74] Apparently, nothing developed in this regard.

In August 1976, the secretary general of the ICEF wrote affiliated unions as follows:

> Our French CFDT [Confédération Française Démocratique du Travail] colleagues have informed the Secretariat that the strike at the Borden Chemical France subsidiary, which began on 11 May was successfully concluded on 19 May. The colleagues obtained

---

[71] The GMWU and Labour party cast votes for the resolution which was "overwhelmingly defeated." See John Bartholomew, "Brooke Bond rejects plea for workers," *Financial Times*, December 9, 1978, p. 22. See also "Profits soar—but no money for Indian teapickers," *International Trade Union News* (International Confederation of Free Trade Unions), December 15, 1978, p. 3; and "In Sri Lanka, Teaworkers' Development Plan Begins," *AAFLI News*, December-January 1979, p. 1.

[72] Stanley Correa, general secretary, IFPAAW, interview in Geneva, September 19, 1977; and *IFPAAW Snips*, November/December 1978, p. 2.

[73] *Fortune*, Vol. 99 (May 7, 1979), pp. 272-73. See also Table XIII-1.

[74] *IUF 17th Congress*, Item 7, p. 5.

a Fr. 100 a month increase for all and an agreement by the company for a total reorganization of the enterprise to be carried out in close collaboration with the Union. The French colleagues of Lillebonne specially wish to thank our English colleagues for their support and intervention which had a decisive influence on the successful solution of the dispute.[75]

The inquiry at the company produced the following statement from the corporate director of labor relations:

> In essence, I am informed that the economics involved in the strike were relatively a simple part of the problem. We settled for basically what we intended to settle for pre-strike. The more difficult issue was that of redundancies (layoffs). The total reorganization of the "enterprise" referred to in Mr. Levinson's letter was, in effect, an acceptance of the Company's plan to provide for redistribution of the duties and the layoffs which would occur as a direct result of the redistribution.
>
> After the short strike, the union accepted our plan. Mr. Levinson is correct that the ICF did, in fact, write to both the unions at our factories in Norway and England, asking for solidarity and for the blacklisting of any goods to be sent to customers if, in fact, said goods were replacing those previously made in France. However, the strike was settled prior to any such issues arising.[76]

ITT

As noted in chapter V, the IUF participated with the International Metalworkers' Federation in meetings of represented employees of the International Telephone and Telegraph Company (ITT), which has large food and hotel subsidiaries. A meeting organized primarily by the IMF involving twenty delegates from nine European countries met in Geneva on July 6, 1972. A similar meeting of North American unionists was held the previous week.[77] No company contacts have been made by either secretariat since then, and no further such meetings have been held.

---

[75] ICF Circular Letter No. 100/76, August 3, 1976, p. 2. The ICEF secretary general's report to the 1976 ICF Congress in Montreal refers to its alleged "intervention" as having occurred in June 1976. See *ICF 16th Statutory Congress*, p. 101.

[76] Letter from Allan L. Miller, corporate director of labor relations, Borden, Inc., to one of the authors, November 29, 1976.

[77] *IMF News*, No. 27 (July 1972), p. 2; and *IUF 17th Congress*, Item V(8), p. 18.

INTERNATIONAL SLEEPING CAR & TOURIST COMPANY

The International Sleeping Car & Tourist Company (Compagnie Internationale des Wagons-Lits et du Tourisme—CIWLT or "Wagons-Lits") serves sleeping cars and restaurants on European railroads. Because the number of passengers requiring those services has declined considerably, the CIWLT has laid off a large number of workers over the years and concentrates more heavily on hotels and station restaurants. Concern for job security led to a number of meetings by national unions and eventually to the formation of a CIWLT Standing Committee of the European Railway Catering Workers at a 1969 Paris meeting. Several of the unions involved are not IUF affiliates (e.g., unions from the French Confédération Générale du Travail and the Confederazione Generale Italiana del Lavoro), but the IUF secretariat acts as the coordinator. The IUF also publishes irregularly a mimeographed bulletin, *Wagons-Lits*, for the committee. Ten have been issued since 1969.[78]

The committee has met several times since 1969. It now also includes representatives of national dining and sleeping-car employee groups. In 1969, it met with the CIWLT personnel director, and in 1971, the committee met with a delegation of CIWLT management at the company's Paris headquarters. Both meetings were informational in nature, with the CIWLT managing director emphasizing "that problems arising could only be solved at national level." [79]

European railroad companies, all government owned, have a "Pool" management committee which works out railroad schedules, car exchange systems, etc., for European international travel. On January 26, 1978, the union committee met with the Pool management in Milan. Delegates from Austria, France, Germany, Italy, Spain, and Switzerland were present. The union committee was attempting to stop the increasing practice of "coupling"—putting one attendant in charge of two sleeping cars instead of one.[80] In view of the declining business of sleeping cars, this union attempt seems unlikely to succeed even in a government-owned operation.

---

[78] *IUF Executive Committee,* Item 3(d), p. 3. Number 10 was issued in October 1979.

[79] *IUF 17th Congress,* Item V(8), p. 12.

[80] *IUF Executive Committee,* p. 3.

THE TOBACCO INDUSTRY

After absorbing the affiliates of the now defunct International Federation of Tobacco Workers in the late 1950s, the International Union of Food and Allied Workers' Associations created a Tobacco Workers' Trade Group Conference and has seemingly marked the tobacco industry for special attention. The problems of this industry relating to smoking and health, taxation, and export and import policies may have encouraged IUF affiliates to seek international relationships and possible joint action with multinationals. To date, however, the IUF has managed to meet only with one multinational company in this industry.

At the 1970 meeting of the IUF Tobacco Workers' Trade Group Conference in Berlin, a proposal was made to discuss the need for "calling meetings on the subject of international firms . . . for the purpose of planning coordinated action." [81] This theme has been reiterated in Tobacco Conference meetings held in Geneva in 1973 and in London in 1975.[82] Previously, the IUF published analyses of British-American Tobacco Company, the Rupert/Rembrandt Group (Rothmans International), and the United States companies (R. J. Reynolds, Philip Morris, American Brands, and the Liggett Group).[83] The 1970 meeting included on its agenda a discussion of the need for international coordination of collective bargaining demands, and this theme has been recurring since then.

BAT Industries

British-American Tobacco, now headquartered in London, is not only the world's largest cigarette- and tobacco-manufacturing firm but, in addition, a manufacturer of paper and cosmetics and, through more recent acquisitions, a large retailer as well. Its tobacco interests are found in almost two hundred countries; it is a major producer in many lands, and its Brown & Williamson Company ranks number three in the United States. Recent acquisitions have included supermarket and department store chains

---

[81] International Union of Food and Allied Workers' Associations, *16th Congress: Documents and Reports* (Geneva, 1970), "Report of Activities," p. 4.

[82] *IUF News Bulletin*, Vol. 44, No. 6 (1974), p. 2; Vol. 45, No. 5-9 (1975), p. 4; and Vol. 46, No. 12 (1975), p. 4.

[83] These analyses in mimeographed form provide such basic information as profits, plant locations, products, and number of employees.

TABLE XIII-2

Six Major Tobacco Companies, 1978

Company [a]	Headquarters	Sales ($000)	Assets ($000)	Net Income ($000)	Employees
BAT Industries	London	7,750,092	7,111,975	411,061	153,000
Philip Morris	New York	4,968,863	5,608,165	408,581	60,000
R. J. Reynolds	Winston-Salem, N.C.	4,951,700	4,615,500	441,900	37,346
Imperial Group [b]	London	4,043,288 [c]	3,914,080	233,577	101,200
American Brands	New York	3,293,486	2,896,965	211,539	54,520
Rothmans International	Aylesbury, Bucks, U.K.	1,241,024	1,716,913	63,054	17,926
Liggett Group	Durham, N.C.	891,665	762,071	56,820	8,200

Source: *Fortune*, Vol. 99 (May 7, 1979), pp. 270-73, 280-81; Vol. 100 (August 13, 1979), pp. 194, 199.
[a] All companies listed above have substantial nontobacco divisions and subsidiaries. R. J. Reynolds is the largest U.S. company in tobacco sales; Brown & Williamson, a division of BAT, ranks third, and P. Lorillard, a division of Lowes, Inc., fourth.
[b] Figures are for fiscal year ending October 31, 1978.
[c] *Fortune* estimate.

and other companies in West Germany, Brazil, and the United States, where its best known affiliate is the Gimbel-Saks Fifth Avenue chain.[84]

The IUF early claimed a successful contact with British-American. The union version, well-publicized by Charles Levinson and Ernst Piehl on the basis of IUF reports, states that, in 1961 at the request of the IUF, the secretary of the British Tobacco Workers' Union went to Pakistan to assist the Pakistan Cigarette Labour Union in its negotiations with a subsidiary of British-American. The issue was allegedly the discharge of twelve union members. No description of what then transpired or what settlement was made is given either by Levinson or Piehl.[85]

Our investigation confirms that the trip was indeed made but that the British unionist was unable to secure resolution of the matter, in part because his Pakistani confreres would not agree to a compromise settlement that the British representative allegedly thought reasonable. Subsequent pressure was applied to the company to reinstate the workers who had been dismissed for initiating an illegal strike. This pressure took the form of a resolution passed by the IUF condemning the company and of telegrams to BAT's headquarters from IUF affiliates in various parts of the world demanding that the workers be reinstated. Despite some union discussion of industrial action, none in fact occurred, nor were the employees involved reinstated.[86]

A second issue involved the demand of the Pakistani union to be permitted to collect union dues during work hours. Because this was not the practice in Pakistan at this time, the company also refused to accede on this point.

A factor that may have encouraged the IUF to seek action and to give it much publicity was that the Communist World Federation of Trade Unions (WFTU) was then active in Pakistan. It is possible that the IUF feared that the WFTU might have attempted to exploit the situation at the IUF's expense if the IUF did not exhibit a major interest.

---

[84] "Dobson looks beyond Britain," *Business Week*, April 13, 1974, pp. 91-92.

[85] Levinson gives no dates or sources for this occurrence, but Piehl provides the year and the IUF sources. See Charles Levinson, *International Trade Unionism* (London: George Allen & Unwin, Ltd., 1972), p. 120; Ernst Piehl, *Multinationale Konzerne und internationale Gewerkschaftsbewegung* (Frankfurt am Main: Europäische Verlagsanstalt, 1974), p. 94.

[86] This account is based on extensive interviews in London in 1974 and 1975 and on correspondence from our London sources.

More recently, the IUF has attempted twice to contact BAT. In the first instance, a strike occurred in Brazil in March 1979. At this time, there was general unrest in Brazil, with unions at three plants attempting to break through government wage increase guidelines. In twelve other company locations, settlements occurred without strikes. Dan Gallin, IUF general secretary, sent a telegram to BAT's London headquarters falsely accusing the company of refusing to recognize the Brazilian union or to bargain with it, whereas BAT had long done both. German, French, and British unions and other IUF officials all sent similar protests to company headquarters. BAT management ignored all these communications except that from the British tobacco workers, whose officials were informed of the facts. The strike was settled within one week.[87]

The second incident involved an illegal strike in Sri Lanka from December 1978 to February 1979, which was illegal since it occurred after the issues had been referred to government arbitration by the minister of labor. Pursuant to practice there, all strikers were dismissed; 825 of 1,250 were rehired; 300 additional were referred to other jobs as arranged by the company; and about 125, including some arrested by police for violence and intimidation, were discharged. In July 1979, the IUF sent a telex to BAT demanding reinstatement of all strikers. We understand that no reply was made by the company.[88]

A third situation involved the attempt of BAT to move its Benelux headquarters from Amsterdam to Brussels. The company has been thwarted for two years by persistent litigation instituted by a small white-collar union and by Dutch legislation dealing with redundancies and plant closures.[89] Except for reporting on the incident, the IUF does not seem to have attempted to insert itself in the matter, perhaps because the union that instigated the matter is from the Dutch Protestant federation, Christelijk Nationaal Vakverbond in Nederland (CNV), and not an IUF affiliate.

ICEF Involvement. In addition to the IUF, the International Federation of Chemical, Energy and General Workers' Unions

---

[87] Copies of IUF and other union correspondence and telexes in authors' possession; letter from Dan Gallin to all member unions of the Tobacco Workers' Trade Group, March 13, 1979; and interviews and correspondence with company personnel, London, May 1979.

[88] Documents in authors' possession.

[89] "British-American Tobacco Faces Stacked Deck on Corporate Responsibility," *Business International*, December 15, 1978, pp. 393-94; and Charles Batchelor, "BAT Dutch closure blocked," *Financial Times*, June 25, 1979, p. 3.

has also claimed involvement with BAT. This incident arose in early 1976, when Vita Foods, a BAT subsidiary, closed a branch in Hunts Point, Long Island, New York. The Distributive Workers of America, a small left-wing union with membership concentrated in the New York City area but with apparent international pretensions,[90] wrote the chairman of BAT Industries protesting against the action. The chairman of BAT replied stating that this was a matter for the local management to discuss. Subsequently, the head of the British salaried union, the Association of Scientific, Technical and Managerial Staffs, also wrote the BAT chairman indicating support for the Distributive Workers.

The Distributive Workers has been affiliated with the ICEF. In his report to the 1976 congress, the secretary general of the ICEF notes that support had been given for a strike against BAT Industries in New York City. This alleged support was claimed to involve "Messages of support and solidarity," "Intervention and protest to parent and/or local management in solidarity with stoppage in other countries," and "Overtime bans and refusal of extra work during period of strike." [91]

Inquiry at company headquarters elicited the response that no correspondence, inquiry, or other manifestation of ICEF action was received or heard about or otherwise known.[92] Certainly the claim of "overtime bans" is completely unsupported by any evidence whatsoever. Actually, the incident was settled without a strike.

Rothmans International, Ltd.

Rothmans International is part of the tobacco and distilling empire put together by South African industrialist Anton E. Rupert. Among the companies under the Rupert banner are Alfred Dunhill; Carreras-Rothmans in the United Kingdom, which includes the former Carreras Limited and Rothmans of

---

[90] The Distributive Workers was formerly Local No. 65, Retail, Wholesale and Department Store Union. It seceded from its parent in the late 1960s, but its membership, based mainly on small industry and retail establishments in and around New York City, has declined materially in recent years and is probably less than 20,000. In 1979, it merged into the United Automobile Workers.

[91] *ICF 16th Statutory Congress*, pp. 101-2.

[92] Letters from BAT to the authors, May 12, 1976, and January 24, 1977; interviews at BAT headquarters, London, May 10, 1977.

Pall Mall; Turmac and Schimmelpennick of the Netherlands; Martin Brinkmann of West Germany; and Tobacofina of Belgium. Rothmans, or companies associated in Rupert's "Rembrandt Group," also has subsidiaries or interest in companies in various British Commonwealth countries, such as Canada, Australia, New Zealand, Fiji, Cyprus, and Jamaica. Rothmans has only 9 percent of the British domestic cigarette market but nearly 60 percent of the British export market. In addition, Rupert has acquired two small American tobacco companies, Larus & Brother Co. and Riggio Tobacco, and owns a minority interest in the Liggett Group, a tobacco firm with dog food and other product interests. Rupert-controlled liquor and beer brands include J&B Scotch, Wild Turkey Bourbon, Grand Marnier liqueur, and Carling Beer.[93]

Given these far-reaching holdings, it was obvious that Rothmans would attract the attention of the IUF. It appears that the IUF interest was spurred by Günter Döding, then head of the tobacco workers in West Germany [now president of the German food union, Gewerkschaft Nahrung-Genuss-Gaststätten (NGG), and also an IUF vice-president and chairman of its Tobacco Workers' Trade Group Conference]. The IUF requested in 1973, and was given by Rothmans International, information concerning plant locations, employment, and related policies of the various operating subsidiaries. In September 1973, the IUF had a meeting of its Tobacco Workers' Conference, and soon thereafter, Rothmans International consented to a meeting with the IUF, which was held on February 27, 1974, in Brussels.

Rothmans International, a British registered company which then had a service company in Monaco, was represented by its Monaco managing director and two assistants. There was no company person present who normally dealt with trade union relations or who was an industrial relations specialist. The IUF Tobacco Conference was represented by Gallin, Döding, four other German unionists, and one each from the Netherlands, Belgium, and the United Kingdom. There was no formal agenda. As in the case of Nestlé (see chapter XII), the IUF asked for information on investments, forward planning, and particularly for information prior to action. Again, as with Nestlé, the

---

[93] See the cover story "South Africa's Mystery Man: Anton E. Rupert," *Business Week*, September 28, 1974, pp. 80-85; also interviews in London and Geneva, August 1973 and July 1974; later correspondence relating thereto; and *IUF News Bulletin*, Vol. 44, No. 6 (1974), p. 2; Vol. 46, No. 12 (1975), p. 4.

company officials maintained that they could not give the unions information that they did not give to stockholders.

Additionally, the union representatives expressed concern about rationalization of production, displacement of personnel, and diversification, to which, like all tobacco companies, Rothmans has moved since the health issue first affected cigarette sales. IUF representatives also discussed health, taxes, and other social issues but emphasized that their intention was not to interfere where such matters would injure their members. The union delegates, led by the Germans, requested a more formal recognition of the IUF group. The company did not agree to this but did agree to a second meeting to be held early in 1975.

A change in Rothmans's management organization caused the postponement of the second meeting for almost one year. The Monaco office was abolished, the managing director of the service company resigned, the operating companies were decentralized, and various duties that were performed from Monaco were transferred to the London headquarters, with the head of the British company as overall managing director. The director of personnel in Britain was designated to work with a personnel committee, with duties including consultations in regard to union relations involving more than one subsidiary and/or country. As a result, the company's policies demonstrated a greater consciousness of industrial relations and of the need to avoid infringement on national collective bargaining matters. Along that line, the Dutch company was able to negotiate the closure of an obsolete cigar factory in 1974 without any IUF or international involvement.

The IUF and the German unionists did, however, keep insisting that the company fulfill its commitment for a second meeting. To that end, the president of Tobacofina, the Belgian subsidiary, met with Dan Gallin and Günter Döding in the spring of 1975 to discuss the timing of such a meeting. Gallin attempted but failed to gain company agreement to institutionalize such meetings and expressed interest in inviting representatives from all over the world. The company representative raised the question of the representativeness of the IUF, particularly in view of the absence from its ranks of the denominational unions of Belgium and the Netherlands. Nevertheless, a meeting for November 4, 1975, in Brussels was agreed to after additional preliminary discussions.

In the second meeting, the company was represented by persons directly knowledgeable in personnel, labor, and manufacturing, including the personnel directors from the United Kingdom and from one Dutch and one Belgian plant and manufacturing or administrative officials from the other European subsidiaries, with the president of Tobacofina chairing the delegation. As in the first meeting, Döding led the union delegation, and there were three other German delegates (one from the tobacco department of the NGG and the president and vice-president of the Brinkmann AG's Central Enterprise Committee); Mrs. Terry Marsland, deputy general secretary of the British Tobacco Workers' Union, again represented that organization but was also accompanied by the secretary of the union's Carreras-Rothmans branch. The national secretary of the socialist Fédération Générale du Travail de Belgique, an IUF affiliate, represented Belgium, as did the national secretary of the Catholic Confédération des Syndicats Chrétiens (CSC), which is not an IUF affiliate. The Netherlands was represented not only by the secretary in charge of the tobacco department of the socialist Industriebond-NVV, an IUF affiliate, but also by representatives of the Nederlands Katholiek Vakverbond (NKV) and the Protestant CNV, which like the Belgian CSC, have no IUF affiliation. A surprise to the company was the presence of two representatives of the American Tobacco Workers International Union (TWIU)—the president, who is a Canadian, and the first vice-president.[94] J. P. Laviec of the IUF secretariat represented his organization in the absence of Dan Gallin, who was ill.

Company representatives at the meeting emphasized the autonomy of the national companies, the lack of a personnel function at the international corporate level, and therefore the unofficial nature of the meeting and the fact that such meetings could not be institutionalized. Company data on personnel in various subsidiaries, prices and taxes in various countries, and the latest annual report were given to the delegates. The company's stress was on health, taxes, and other factors influencing tobacco sales.

The union delegates expressed interest in investment policies, particularly in the possible transfer of production to low-wage

---

[94] The Tobacco Workers International Union has since merged into the Bakery and Confectionery Workers, now known as the Bakery, Confectionery and Tobacco Workers, and the former president of the Tobacco Workers is the secretary-treasurer of the merged union. He is also a vice-president of the IUF.

countries, and in possible company diversification into nontobacco products but emphasized the desire for a formal IUF-Rothmans relationship. The British and American delegates argued especially for the latter, with the former requesting a common international social policy program. The chairman of the company group indicated that possibly the IUF could help on such common problems as development of a European Community tobacco policy and expressed willingness to resume the dialogue within a year.

The IUF posture before, during, and after this meeting made it very clear that it could not be satisfied with the type of informal exchange of views which prevailed in these two meetings with Rothmans. Thus, the *IUF News Bulletin* commented after the second meeting:

> Another important issue discussed was the nature of these very meetings. Rothmans categorically refused to consider them as negotiations and insisted on their informal character, as they felt the situation was not yet "ripe" to institutionalize them. The IUF delegation pointed out, however, that some issues could not be solved at a purely local or national level and that an international instrument was necessary in such cases. In future these questions should be dealt with on a more concrete and clear basis, since workers and unions could not content themselves with vague informal assurances.
>
> The answers given at this second meeting indicated that some progress had been made since the first one, however, Rothmans International still had a considerable way to go before it took the frank and progressive stand it so readily prides itself on.[95]

A third meeting took place between the IUF group and Rothmans in Hamburg on April 18, 1977. This meeting occurred at the request of the union side, and the agenda was selected by the unions to include (1) diversification, (2) South African relationships, and (3) transfers of production. The company responded briefly to all three points, pointing out that it had built a new factory in England to service the Middle East export trade and that it had nothing to do with the declines in plant employment elsewhere; that it was a South African-controlled corporation and that the management in South Africa was doing all it could to promote equality for blacks; and that diversification was being studied, the subsidiary Dunhill having entered the cosmetic trade and considering entry into the men's wear trade.

This third meeting lasted only two and one-half hours. There

---

[95] *IUF News Bulletin*, Vol. 46, No. 12 (1975), p. 4.

was no demand for a formalized relationship from the IUF, and the union representation was less complete than in any other meeting. Döding and Mrs. Marsland were there representing the German and British tobacco groups, respectively, and there were representatives from the Federatie Nederlandse Vakbeweging (FNV), the merged NVV-NKV group. No North American or Belgian representatives were present. There was also a representative from Denmark, where Rothmans does not have a factory. The general secretary of the IUF was absent and represented by a functionary from his office. The IUF side did not make a request for further meetings.

It thus remains to be seen to what extent the constituent unions of the IUF desire an international agreement and what functions they are willing to delegate to the IUF to achieve such an agreement. For example, although the spokesman for the British Tobacco Workers' Union endorsed the idea at the November 1975 meeting, the extent of support for her position in the United Kingdom may not be complete. The British Tobacco Workers' Union and the Tobacco Industry Employers' Federation have long had an industrywide bargaining arrangement involving Rothmans, Gallagher, and Imperial,[96] which could stand in the way of international bargaining, as could German labor-management institutions. There is also a question of the role of the denominational unions of Belgium and the Netherlands, which are not IUF affiliates but were at the 1975 meeting only. Finally, what role, if any, would be played by non-European unions, including the North American TWIU, remains to be seen. The former president of the TWIU, now secretary-treasurer of the merged Bakery, Confectionery and Tobacco Workers' Union, is allegedly very interested in any international role and, at the January 1977 IUF Congress, held in Geneva, was elected an IUF vice-president. The extension of the IUF-Rothmans discussions beyond Europe, which apparently did not occur during the 1975 meeting, despite the presence of the TWIU representatives, and was not brought up at the 1977 meeting, would obviously add to the diversity of interests of the union delegates and also to the problems of the company in responding to union delegate pressures.

---

[96] Each tobacco company in the United Kingdom also has its own bargaining arrangements. Moreover, staff (salaried employees) unions are not represented in the National Joint Negotiating Committee for the tobacco industry.

Assuming, however, that the union side resolves its problems, the big decision rests with Rothmans. As has been clear in all other instances where informational meetings have been instituted and as the above quotation from the *IUF News Bulletin* clearly indicates, unions regard the informational meeting as only a step toward bargaining. As we have stated in discussing the Philips situation:

> It is equally clear that Philips approached these meetings with the idea that it could satisfy the unions with a good faith demonstration of its willingness to provide information, its openness, and the fairness of its wage and personnel policies. This, of course, ignores the drive by unions, whether local or international, to achieve parity of decision-making with management and to develop an organization and a framework of operations that require consultation and mutual consent *before* policies are determined and actions taken, rather than after the fact. The dynamics of union policy see value in informational meetings only as a stepping-stone to what is regarded as a necessary bargaining relationship between parties of at least equal stature.[97]

There is now some doubt that the IUF will continue to exert pressure to achieve a formal relationship. If it does, then Rothmans officials have only two choices: to break off the contacts altogether, with attendant antagonistic publicity, or to accede to the IUF's demands and thus to open a new area of formal bargaining with attendant demands, pressures, and probably costs.

The American Companies

For almost the last half century, tobacco manufacturing in the United States has been dominated by six companies—R. J. Reynolds, Philip Morris, Brown & Williamson, American Brands (formerly American Tobacco), P. Lorillard, and Liggett & Myers. Despite diversification, altered corporate control, and considerable changes in relative market share, this situation remains true today.

R. J. Reynolds. The sales leader in the American market for many years has been R. J. Reynolds, which has diversified into containership (it owns Sea/Land Services), food products, and other products. Reynolds operates entirely nonunion in its United States tobacco facilities and is the only American tobacco company that does not have an agreement with the Bakery, Confectionery and Tobacco Workers' Union.

---

[97] Richard L. Rowan and Herbert R. Northrup, "Multinational Bargaining in Metals and Electrical Industries," *Journal of Industrial Relations* (Austraila), Vol. XVII (March 1975), p. 26. See also chapter V, above.

The Reynolds international operations, until recently, involved very little but export sales. In 1973, however, Reynolds purchased Macdonald Tobacco Company of Canada and has moved energetically into other areas, including Europe and South America, not only through exporting but through establishing plants as well.[98] Its nonunion character in the United States and its low profile abroad have left it free from any known IUF contact attempts. The latter has been limited to publishing surveys of Reynolds operations and passing resolutions supporting its American affiliate's vain efforts to unionize Reynolds employees.

Philip Morris. The second American company in cigarette sales, the fastest growing, and most internationally oriented of the United States tobacco firms is Philip Morris. Since World War II, its growth has taken it from fifth to second place overall in tobacco and to first in the United States in overseas sales. Philip Morris is also a major factor in beer, owning Miller Brewing Company, in razors and razor blades through its American Safety Razor Division, in homebuilding, in paper and packaging, and in soft drinks through its recent purchase of Seven-Up.

Unlike Reynolds, Philip Morris began manufacturing abroad at an early date. It has plants throughout Western Europe and Latin America, and in Canada, Africa, Australia, and the Far East, plus licensing arrangements in the Soviet bloc and in Japan.

Despite these far-flung operations, there have been only a few attempted IUF contacts with Philip Morris, the first occurring in 1974. A Philip Morris Dutch plant was facing loss of work in December 1974 because the company had shut off exports to Italy. This action was taken because the Dutch facility had been unable to obtain for a considerable time either payments due or consideration of a price increase from the Italian government tobacco sales monopoly. The company reasoned that since a Christmas vacation shutdown was scheduled for the last week of the month, a full month's closing would be the least disruptive way to handle the matter.

This did not prove popular with the employees, and apparently the IUF's Dutch affiliate, Industriebond-NVV, contacted the IUF, and it, in turn, its affiliated unions. Philip Morris received contacts from unions in Switzerland, Pakistan, India, and the United States. Philip Morris headquarters in New York looked into

---

[98] "R. J. Reynolds's Foreign Operations To Be Based in U.S.," *Wall Street Journal,* January 19, 1976.

the matter, and a meeting was arranged between the Dutch unions, including not only the IUF's affiliate (NVV) but the Catholic NKV and Protestant CNV as well, and a representative of Philip Morris Europe, which is headquartered in Lausanne, Switzerland. The IUF was not represented at this meeting.

Meanwhile, the Italian government had begun to settle its debt; and because the company did not see the issue of how it compensated for the sales drop-off as inflexible and also was anxious to avoid union problems at a time when it was expanding facilities in Germany and the United Kingdom, it agreed to keep the Dutch plant open on a reduced basis during December rather than lay off the work force. The IUF claimed credit for the results and also for helping to persuade the Italian government to speed payment and to permit price adjustments, although this cannot be confirmed.[99]

A second attempted IUF contact with Philip Morris occurred as a result of a company study made available to Dutch unions and works councils in 1975, which called for the closing of one of its two facilities, that in Eindhoven, and the expansion and modernization of its other one located in Bergen op Zoom. The employees and unions at the latter were, of course, delighted; those at the former fought and delayed the decision for about two years. They even visited their German counterparts in Munich in the winter of 1977 amid much publicity, but no actual German involvement occurred. Gallin wrote the company asking to meet on European problems, but the company declined. Other attempts of Gallin to contact the company's European or New York offices were not successful. Döding did meet with the Philip Morris European managing director in Munich in 1977, but the discussion pertained mainly to German problems, and neither Gallin nor another IUF functionary was present.[100]

Other Activities in the Tobacco Industry

We have found no IUF involvement with other companies. The Communists have had a tobacco coordinating group and

---

[99] IUF circular letter from Dan Gallin, general secretary, to all affiliated and fraternal unions representing employees of the Philip Morris Company and to other member unions of the IUF Tobacco Workers' Trade Group, January 14, 1975; company officials, interviews in New York, December 3, 1975.

[100] Based on documents and materials supplied by the company and on IUF reports.

have had several meetings. Like all Communist groups, the Trade Unions International of Food, Tobacco, Hotel and Allied Workers, a branch of the World Federation of Trade Unions, has been very active in Africa and the Middle East. Allegedly, Mrs. Terry Marsland of the British Tobacco Workers has contacts with the Communists, as well as with the IUF, but we have discerned no multinational company involvement by this organization.

CONCLUSION

There are a number of reasons why multinational bargaining in the food and allied industries is likely to be difficult to accomplish. Highly diversified companies operate many plants that typically employ a relatively small number of employees. Products of struck plants can often be produced elsewhere, or plants can be operated by supervisors and salaried employees during a strike, thus decreasing the power of unions to gain acceptance of their demands.

The unions in the industry are, moreover, fragmented and provide only irregular support of international action. As a result, the IUF has always been beset with financial problems and has regularly operated under deficits, which has limited its activities. Nevertheless, by inserting itelf into such situations as South African problems, by achieving meetings with Nestlé and Rothmans, and by adroit use of publicity, IUF General Secretary Dan Gallin has become one of the most widely known of the international trade union officials, and the IUF has been propelled to one of the five or six most active international trade union secretariats involved in the pursuit of formal relations with multinational companies. The fact remains, however, that multinational bargaining is not a likely prospect in the food, beverage, or tobacco industries in the foreseeable future, barring some extraordinary development or governmental requirement.

PART FIVE

*The
Services and Communications
Industries*

CHAPTER XIV

The Insurance, Banking, and Retail Services Industries

Insurance companies, banks, and retail operations, such as specialty stores, supermarkets, and car rental agencies, all include in their ranks large companies that operate on a multinational basis. It is, therefore, not surprising that these companies have attracted the attention of the international trade union secretariats. The record to date in these industries is discussed in this chapter.

THE INSURANCE INDUSTRY

International union activities are relatively new in the insurance industry. Most insurance companies do not operate on a multinational basis. Moreover, the industry is predominantly white-collar; in most countries, it has considerably less unionization than has manufacturing; and because it is regulated rather strictly by countries or by divisions of countries, such as states within the United States, the opportunities for change through international union action are somewhat limited. Nevertheless, multinational expansion, notably by European companies into other countries nearby or, more recently, into the United States, has increased. This has induced one trade union secretariat, the International Federation of Commercial, Clerical and Technical Employees (FIET), to expand its insurance industry contacts, and it has apparently made progress after an initial setback.

The FIET is Geneva-based and claims an affiliated membership of six million workers in commerce, banking, insurance, and among industrial, clerical, and salaried employees.[1] Its claims make it one of the three largest secretariats in size, and its strength in membership following, commitment, and finances has substantially improved under the leadership of Heribert Maier, its current general secretary. The FIET has established regional

---

[1] *Introducing FIET* (Geneva, [1977]).

organizations on the various continents and trade groups that operate within those regions. Thus, in Europe, the regional organization is Euro-FIET, and the insurance group operates within Euro-FIET when European matters are concerned. Euro-FIET also acts as a committee of the European Trade Union Confederation.

At its 1970 congress, the FIET determined to establish committees to attempt to deal with multinational firms "chosen on the basis that they employed large numbers of white collar workers in many countries in which FIET has affiliated unions." [2] Two insurance companies were initially placed on this list, the German-based Allianz Versicherungs AG and the Swiss-based Winterthur Schweizerische Versicherungs-Gesellschaft. The FIET's attempted moves involving Allianz never developed beyond reports on the company and meetings of FIET officials with union representatives in Allianz operations.[3] Winterthur, however, became more involved, as did at least one other company.

Winterthur

The leading figure on the union side in the Winterthur involvement has been Alfred Hubschmid, a Swiss unionist who has long been a key official of the Swiss commercial workers' union (Schweizerischer Kaufmännischer Verein—SKV) and as such has also played a leading role in Swiss apprenticeship and training, including the training of insurance agents. In these capacities, he was well known to officials of the Winterthur company, which is based in the Swiss city of the same name and has direct or affiliated operations throughout Western Europe, Canada, and the United States. Hubschmid has also been a leading figure in Euro-FIET's insurance group. He persuaded reluctant Winterthur officials to agree to a meeting with an FIET group, which occurred on November 9, 1971.[4]

---

[2] "Oslo Resolutions," *The Non-Manual Worker in the Free Labour World*, No. 29 (October 1970), p. 3.

[3] See "The Allianz Insurance Group," *The Non-Manual Worker in the Free Labour World*, No. 25 (April 1970), p. 6; and *FIET Newsletter*, No. 10 (October 1977), p. 3. Allianz has recently purchased two American companies, and the FIET has evidenced continued interest. See *Europe*, June 28, 1979, p. 14.

[4] The story of this relationship is based upon FIET sources as cited below, and a letter from the Winterthur personnel executive to one of the authors, September 13, 1978.

FIET representatives at the meeting explained to the Winterthur officials that they were anxious to enter into an agreement for the purpose of harmonizing employment conditions, ensuring that employees be permitted to unionize, assuring that the FIET be apprised of employment conditions, and generally covering all legal aspects of employment on an international basis.

Winterthur, of course, declined such a course. Its representatives pointed out that the insurance business is highly and differently regulated in each country and that, moreover, social and labor problems and policies within its structure are handled on a decentralized basis within each country's legislation and customs. Hence, it would oppose harmonization on an international basis.

Winterthur believed that it gave the FIET no encouragement, but in fact, FIET officials remained convinced that Winterthur would provide them with a major triumph by signing an international labor agreement. Thus, FIET officials noted in the FIET's monthly publication that Winterthur was "an approachable employer." [5] They held this belief not only because of what they conceived to be the results of their November 1971 meeting with the company but also because prior thereto, in September 1971, a Winterthur management representative visited the FIET's Geneva headquarters apparently to discuss the then forthcoming meeting. In any case, the FIET announced that it would "offer Winterthur a general agreement . . . respecting certain general matters of concern—trade union rights, provision of information to staff, mobility, vocational training, etc." [6]

Winterthur had no desire for a second meeting but was equally reluctant to offend Hubschmid. After much persuasion, it did agree to meet with the Euro-FIET international insurance committee again, and the meeting was set for August 30, 1974. Meanwhile, the FIET continued its preparations and its public pronouncements of the purpose of the meeting, which was, as far as it was concerned, very clear. In the words of its general secretary:

> The FIET Winterthur committee, composed of one Swiss, one Belgian, one Austrian, one Swedish and two German colleagues, is preparing a draft collective agreement, to be approved by the workers' representatives in each of the subsidiary companies and

---

[5] "FIET to Offer Winterthur a General Agreement," *The Non-Manual Worker in the Free Labour World*, No. 40 (January-February 1972), p. 7.

[6] *Ibid.*

by the various national unions concerned. After the second meeting with Winterthur's central management at the beginning of next year, we will try to get negotiations on a basic agreement.

An enlarged FIET Winterthur committee, composed of union and company representatives, would then have to negotiate the conclusion of an international collective agreement.

This method seems to many to be unrealistic, at least for the next few years or even decades.

Nevertheless, we should fully support the plan clearly outlined for us by this FIET committee.

The partners to the international collective agreement we are hoping to achieve with this company will be the affiliated unions involved. The agreement, initially, will be based on existing national agreements. In later negotiations, attempts will be made to improve working conditions still further, and gradually to harmonize them upwards. Such an agreement would doubtless contain many provisions on standardization. Whatever the content of such an agreement may be, it will point the way for all of us.

One of the objects of this kind of bargaining is to make clear to the management the advantages of such an agreement for the company. This will not be an easy task, but it is not impossible. Such an agreement will have a positive effect on the social order of the enterprise as a whole. All depends on our state of preparedness and a strong enough level of trade union organization. It would, of course, be unrealistic to imagine that an agreement with a multinational firm could fix identical conditions for every country in which it operates. This is not our aim: cost structures vary too much. And something which cannot be achieved at national level is certainly not possible on an international basis. A global labour system, uniform working conditions the world over, are undoubtedly still a generation away. In our bargaining with the multinational firms, we must be guided by the principle that provisions in an international collective agreement always be superior to those in force at national level. However, should the conclusion of such multinational agreements not be possible at once, then the various national negotiations must be coordinated so that their timing and content are identical. The same obviously applies to trade union actions, insofar as they are feasible.

The multinationals plan and trade on a worldwide basis. We have to do the same, and evolve a counterstrategy that will give us comparable strength in the field of collective agreement policy. This means that we must move from our present *ad hoc* actions and develop a systematic structure for our international negotiations. The system evolved by the FIET Winterthur committee should be used in the case of the other companies to be approached.[7]

On March 27, 1974, the FIET sent a questionnaire to its affiliated organizations in countries where Winterthur operates.

---

[7] International Federation of Commercial, Clerical and Technical Employees, *Report on the 17th World Congress* (London, 1973), pp. 52-53.

The replies were compiled by the SKV and were to be used to frame an agreement with Winterthur. Meanwhile, Winterthur finally became aware of the FIET's well-publicized purpose. Its officials advised Hubschmid that the meeting was cancelled. On August 13, 1974, two weeks before the scheduled meeting, Hubschmid advised his FIET colleagues of the cancellation on the grounds that personnel management at Winterthur was decentralized and that "FIET had no authority to reach agreement." [8] There has been no contact between the parties since 1974.

American Life Insurance Company

The FIET has had one American insurance company contact. It concerned the American Life Insurance Company's decision to close its Beirut, Lebanon, regional office. The FIET claims that, after Lebanese workers occupied the Beirut office to prevent this closing, the general secretaries of the International Confederation of Free Trade Unions (ICFTU) and of the FIET, plus an official of the Lebanese Federation of Insurance Trade Unions, met in Brussels on November 4, 1975, at the ICFTU's offices with an official of American Life [9] and requested a six-month moratorium on the closing. According to the FIET's general secretary, the company granted the six months, but the continuation of the civil war in Lebanon since then apparently negated any desire to keep the offices open.[10]

Victoria-Versicherungs

Victoria-Versicherungs-Gesellschaften is a major multinational insurance company headquartered in Düsseldorf, Germany. Its management has had two meetings with the FIET.

The first meeting occurred in 1978 and involved Heribert Maier; the head of the German Gewerkschaft Handel, Banken und Versicherungen (HBV); and the chairman of the company's works council.[11] The meeting's purpose, according to the company's chief executive, who was present, was to determine

---

[8] International Federation of Commercial, Clerical and Technical Employees, *Report on Activities Covering the Period from 1973 to 1976* (London, 1976), p. 109. (Hereafter cited as *FIET Activities 1973-76*.)

[9] *Ibid.*, pp. 110-11.

[10] Heribert Maier, interview in Munich, Germany, May 15, 1979.

[11] *FIET Newsletter*, Nos. 7-8 (July-August 1978), p. 11.

whether the parties could use German experience to help "colleagues in Spain and Portugal with the setup of democratic partnership relations." [12]

At the second meeting, which was held in May 1979, the chairmen of the company's Austrian and Dutch works councils were also invited. From May 24 to 26, 1979, the FIET committee for Victoria met in Wuppertal, Germany, at the company's training center. According to the FIET report:

> The meeting . . . was paid a visit by the Victoria General Director, Herr H. Schmöle, who was invited to express the company's point of view at the opening session. After a thorough exchange of information, the meeting decided, among other things, to extend activities to a fifth country, Spain, to set up a target of a 10 per cent increase in unionisation of Victoria staff in the coming year and to hold its next meeting in Vienna or Amsterdam, when the main matters to be studied will be rationalisation, recognition of works councils and working conditions.[13]

Schmöle advised the authors that the company did not expect to meet regularly with the FIET and its multinational committee and that the initial meeting was a "totally noncommittal one." [14] It appears from the FIET's report that the company did not involve itself deeply or commit itself at the second meeting.

Maier, interviewed prior to the second meeting, felt quite differently. He stated that the FIET's objective was to have regular multinational meetings with Victoria, at least on an annual basis.[15] It, therefore, remains to be seen whether this situation will develop as that with Winterthur did.

BANKING

Although there are a large number of multinational banks, there has been little multinational industrial relations involvement, in part because of the lack of bank unionization in many countries. The FIET does have a banking committee and has targeted Barclays Bank of London for a possible relationship and has pushed for meetings with American Express. According to the FIET general secretary, a study group for Barclays Bank

---

[12] Letter from Heinz Schmöle, Vorsitzender der Vorstände, Victoria, to the authors, April 17, 1979. Translated by the Industrial Research Unit.

[13] *FIET Newsletter*, No. 6 (June 1979), p. 1.

[14] Letter from Schmöle to the authors.

[15] Maier, interview, May 15, 1979.

has been established, and British union officials have been active in training union leaders in various Third World countries. This has furthered interunion relationships that the FIET hopes will result in a meeting with the bank management.[16]

American Express Company

American Express Company, headquartered in New York City, is the world leader in the credit card and traveler's check markets and, in addition, has significant travel agency, international banking, and fire and casualty insurance businesses. Historically, these various business sections have operated completely autonomously, although current management appears to be "synchronizing the activities of the various divisions." [17] In 1978, American Express had revenues in excess of $4 billion and employed 37,856 persons throughout the world.[18]

The FIET, which, as noted, has attempted for several years to establish a relationship with an international banking concern, has apparently considered the American Express banks in Europe a likely target. Accordingly, efforts have been made by the banking section of the FIET's European regional organization, Euro-FIET, to meet with American Express banking executives. Thus, in the FIET's 1973-76 report, it is claimed:

> AMEXCO.—On 6 February 1976, FIET was represented at a seminar arranged in Hanover by the Gewerkschaft Handel, Banken und Versicherungen, for twenty-five staff members of three firms in Germany belonging to the Amexco group: American Express Bank G.m.b.H. (300 employees), American Express International Banking Corporation Military Banking (under special contract to the American Government for banking operations for soldiers— 1,600 employees) ; and American Express International Incorporated (specialising in travel and credit cards—260 employees). Two special items on the agenda were: a report on FIET activities by the FIET secretariat, explaining our Federation's work facing multinationals; and a discussion with two representatives of the German management of two of the group's member firms.[19]

Also in 1976, the settlement of a labor negotiation involving American Express banking facilities in Greece led to meetings

---

[16] *Ibid.*

[17] A. F. Ehrbar "Hazards Down the Track for American Express," *Fortune*, Vol. 98 (November 6, 1978), p. 96.

[18] *Fortune*, Vol. 100 (July 16, 1979), pp. 162-63.

[19] *FIET Activities 1973-76*, p. 111.

of Greek union officials and an American Express representative. Greek union officials apparently conferred with their German counterparts at the 1976 FIET Congress in Helsinki about establishing an FIET council for American Express. Then in April 1977, an American Express official became aware of a Euro-FIET circular letter announcing a joint Euro-FIET and FIET conference of American Express and European unions for April 27, at which an official of American Express would be present and would discuss the company's "aims of business and personnel politics" [policies?].[20] At about the same time that this official received the circular letter, he also received a letter from the German union conference host inviting him to address the conference. Through local country channels, the invitation was declined.[21] A circular letter issued for the meeting stated very clearly that this meeting was to be the initial move "for the international organization of employees." [22]

The proposed April 1977 meeting ran into other difficulties and was postponed until the next month. Even so, the meeting was not well attended, with apparently only German, French, and Greek unions represented.

A second meeting of what the FIET now calls the FIET Amexco Committee was held in Geneva in May 1978. According to the FIET report:

> Representatives from trade unions and works councils in six countries where the American Express Company operates—Denmark, France, Germany, Greece, Switzerland and the United States—took part in the second meeting of FIET's Amexco Committee, which was held in Geneva on 30 May under its chairman, Günter Volkmar (HBV, Germany). The Committee examined a FIET survey on multinational banks and also: decided to circulate a questionnaire on working conditions in Amexco offices, with special emphasis on the effects of rationalisation; affirmed that the 5-day week, now under attack in some countries, must be maintained; decided to develop contacts with colleagues in other countries where Amexco operates, and supported FIET efforts to obtain international guidelines with binding regulations to control the activities of multinational banks.[23]

---

[20] Copy of document issued by the Gewerkschaft Handel, Banken und Versicherungen (HBV) Hauptverstand (trade, bank and insurance union headquarters), April 1977, in authors' possession.

[21] American Express Company officials, interview in New York, July 13, 1978.

[22] Bilingual document issued by the HBV, April 1977, in authors' possession.

[23] "FIET Amexco Committee Meets while Profits Soar," *FIET Newsletter*, No. 6 (June 1978), p. 1.

Attending the meeting as the United States representative was Don Hofer, vice-president of the Retail Clerks' International Union (now the United Food and Commercial Workers' Union), an AFL-CIO and FIET affiliate, who was reported to be studying European union methods of bank unionization. In the United States, banks are about 99 percent nonunion. In Canada, where this union also operates, bank unionization has made little progress despite a controversial decision by the Canada Labour Relations Board that permitted branch-by-branch organization of banks.[24] American Express does not operate banking facilities in the United States or Canada, but, as clearly indicated in the above quotation, one purpose of the meeting was to give impetus to the FIET's campaign to encourage the United Nations and/or the Organization for Economic Cooperation and Development to establish guidelines for international banking organizations—a move seen by all interested unions as a way toward bank unionization throughout the world. Until such unionization does in fact occur, the FIET's attempt to develop a relationship with international banking concerns is likely to meet with difficulty.

RETAIL TRADE

A number of international trade union secretariats have been active in various retail trade segments. In some situations, the company involved (for example, Bata) is both a manufacturer and a retailer, and the secretariat has, in effect, followed the company from manufacturing to retailing. For supermarkets and department stores, the FIET is the major secretariat, but others have been involved. This section examines development in the retail industries.

Bata Limited

Bata Limited is the central holding company of the shoe-manufacturing and -retailing empire rebuilt by Thomas J. Bata and his father after they were forced to flee the Nazi takeover of Czechoslovakia. There are now more than one hundred companies in the Bata group, all of them privately held except where national governments have insisted on part local ownership. Bata manufactures and/or retails shoes in over twenty

[24] Peter Silverman, "Slow going for CUPE campaign despite 'milestone' contract," *Financial Post* (Canada), October 14, 1978, p. 23.

countries throughout the Western and underdeveloped world. No other shoe concern has such far-flung operations. Its headquarters are in Toronto, Canada.

The International Textile, Garment and Leather Workers' Federation (ITGLWF) is a relatively new secretariat formed in 1970 by a series of mergers involving three smaller, older secretariats with jurisdiction in the textile, apparel, leather, and shoe industries. It is headquartered in Brussels.[25]

In 1971, the ITGLWF embarked on a study of three major multinational companies within its jurisdiction—Bata; Courtalds, the London-based multinational textile and chemical company; and C & A Brenninkmeijer, the privately owned, Dutch-based multinational department store concern.[26] Concerned about the study's accuracy, Bata had its European personnel coordinator meet in 1971 with John Burcham, a student employed on a part-time basis by the ITGLWF to make the study. Then in November 1972, the European and headquarters personnel coordinators met with Charles Ford, ITGLWF general secretary, and discussed the report prepared by the union. Both meetings were in London. The company felt that, with some exceptions, the union study was not unduly adverse.

Meanwhile, Ford made several efforts to meet with the company president, Thomas J. Bata. They already had a basis for a relationship since both were once involved with the work of the Organization for Economic Cooperation and Development (OECD): Bata was chairman of its Business and Industry Advisory Committee while Ford was chairman of its Trade Union Advisory Committee. While they had these respective chairmanships, they did not, however, meet.

After several attempts by Ford, Bata agreed to a meeting, which was held in London on May 23, 1975. Ford raised questions about a strike in Rhodesia in which union officials had been jailed, the shutdown of manufacturing facilities in Sweden, and Bata's strong nonunion position in the United States, where the only one of the company's four plants unionized is a facility in Wisconsin that had been organized prior to its acquisi-

---

[25] Based upon materials supplied by Bata in interviews in Toronto, October 1975, and by the ITGLWF in correspondence, July 1975.

[26] "Three Leading Multinational Companies in the Textiles, Garment and Leather Industries" (Prepared by Eli Marx and John Burcham for the International Textile, Garment and Leather Workers' Federation, First World Congress, Amsterdam, Netherlands, October 16-20, 1972).

tion by Bata. All these points were made in the union report on the company.

Bata declined to go into details on these subjects, emphasizing the company's decentralized structure and the responsibility of national managements for social policies within their countries. Bata also emphasized that the company was not prepared to engage in multinational bargaining or in discussions with committees of unions from different countries.

Commenting upon the meeting, Ford stated:

> Transnational bargaining is of course the ultimate objective of the international T.U. Movement. But it's a long way off!
>
> In the meantime, there is much that can be done through informed talks with responsible people in MNCs to draw their attention to certain personnel practices pursued by their subsidiaries which they may not be fully aware of, and which may damage the worldwide image of the company.[27]

The meeting was cordial and undoubtedly added to the stature of Ford and the ITGLWF, but it is not likely to be repeated. Our impression is that the company sees no advantage in any future meetings and that there are, at least in the immediate future, no compelling pressures that might alter its position.

The ITGLWF has continued its interest in Bata with meetings of union delegates and information reporting; no company involvement has, however, occurred since 1975.

A&P/Tengelmann

In January 1979, Tengelmann, a German retail group, agreed to purchase a substantial interest in the Great Atlantic and Pacific Tea Company (A&P). By late August 1979, Tengelmann had close to majority control.[28] A majority of the A&P employees are represented by the Retail Clerks International Union and the Amalgamated Meat Cutters and Butcher Workmen, which merged in June 1979 to form the largest union in the AFL-CIO, the United Food and Commercial Workers' Union.[29] The Retail Clerks Union was affiliated to the International Federation of Commercial, Clerical and Technical Employees, and it is ex-

---

[27] In a letter to one of the authors, July 30, 1975.

[28] "Tengelmann Begins Boosting A&P Stake Via Small Purchases," *Wall Street Journal*, July 12, 1979, p. 16; and "Tengelmann Group Raises Stake in A&P to 44.2% of Shares," *Wall Street Journal*, August 15, 1979, p. 10.

[29] David L. Perlman, "Convention Puts Seal on Merger," *AFL-CIO News*, June 9, 1979, p. 1.

pected that the merged union will continue an active affiliation to the FIET.

The FIET and the HBV, its German affiliate, arranged for a meeting with Tengelmann's chief executive, Karl Erivan Haub, at Tengelmann's headquarters in Düsseldorf on March 20, 1979. According to FIET General Secretary Heribert Maier, the trade union delegation that met with the company management consisted of himself; Gerry O'Keefe, director of the International and Foreign Affairs Department of the U.S. Retail Clerks Union; Tom Russow, director of organization of the Retail Clerks Union; Bud Lutty, international vice-president of the Meat Cutters and Butcher Workmen; and Helmut Stegmaier, secretary of the HBV.[30] The delegation exchanged views with Haub on "future policies of the A&P in the United States," and the union "insisted that any changing company policies should not bring about social hardships for the employees concerned."[31] Haub had shown an earlier willingness to meet with the unions when he met with the shop stewards of the Tengelmann group in Munich on March 19, 1979.

Further meetings between the FIET, the United States unions, and the Tengelmann management are expected to take place in the fall of 1979. Haub has been invited to visit with the United States union representatives in Washington, D.C.

Other Retail Chains

The FIET has been involved with two other European retail chains. Works council and union members from Austria and Germany, plus FIET representatives, met December 7-8, 1978, in Linz, Austria, with Willi Laschet, director general, and other management staff of Quelle (an Austrian-based company that is one of Europe's largest mail order and department store chains), and exchanged information. According to the FIET, "It was agreed to continue the contacts in a pragmatic way."[32]

In a significant development, Maier was placed on the supervisory board of "bilka" Kaufhaus GmbH, Frankfurt, a subsidiary of Hertel, a leading German department store enterprise.[33] Maier, an Austrian citizen, is the fifth international

---

30 Maier, interview, May 15, 1979.

31 *FIET Newsletter*, No. 4 (April 1979), p. 1.

32 *Ibid.*, No. 1 (January 1979), p. 11.

33 *Gewerkschaft Report*, June 1979, p. 36.

union representative and the third non-German union official to represent employees on a German supervisory board.[34] As is noted in the final chapter, this puts him in a strong position to urge multinational union recognition and bargaining.

THE HERTZ CORPORATION

The Hertz Corporation is the largest car and truck rental concern in the world. Since 1967, Hertz has been a wholly owned subsidiary of RCA, Inc., and, like its parent corporation, is headquartered in New York City. In 1978, Hertz had sales of $938.3 million and employed approximately fourteen thousand persons.[35]

Hertz's multinational operations are primarily in Western Europe, where it employs approximately thirty-five hundred employees, and Latin America. In other areas and in smaller locations in Europe and the Americas, Hertz uses licensees, which are independent contractors.

Hertz's encounter with the international trade union movement occurred as a result of a strike in Denmark in late 1976. Personnel employed by Hertz in Copenhagen were unionized by the HK, a Danish commercial and clerical union, which demanded wage increases of approximately 30 percent. When Hertz offered much less, the union struck. Hertz countered by bringing in six to eight employees from its companies in the United Kingdom, Italy, and France to operate the facilities at Kastrup Airport and downtown Copenhagen. After several weeks, a compromise settlement was reached, and the strike was terminated on November 24, 1976. Meanwhile, however, Hertz reorganized its Danish operation, transferred accounting and other functions to its German company, and reduced its union Danish personnel complement from twenty-two to nine.[36] Company officials claim that they had planned to abolish the Danish central office some months before but agreed that the strike and the higher wages made it more advantageous to do so.[37]

---

[34] Others are Herman Rebhan and Werner Thönnessen of the IMF, Charles Levinson of the ICEF, and Günter Köpke of the European Trade Union Institute. Rebhan and Levinson are not German citizens.

[35] RCA, Inc., *Annual Report 1978* (New York, 1979), p. 12. Employment information supplied by the Hertz Corporation.

[36] See "Labour mobility change after Hertz dispute?" *Industrial Relations Europe*, Vol. IV (December 1976), p. 1.

[37] Telephone interview, London, May 9, 1977.

The secretary of the HK declared that international union support forced Hertz to concede on the wage matter;[38] the company cited as the key reason picketing at the airport business location, harassment of potential customers there, and consequent loss of business.[39] Although it is extremely doubtful that international union pressure had anything whatsoever to do with the company's wage concession, there is no doubt that this dispute, despite involving at most only twenty-two employees, did generate considerable international publicity. The reason was Hertz's use of its employees from other European countries. They kept the operation running; this in turn has led to widespread attempts on the part of various union bodies to declare this a violation of multinational corporate codes of conduct; to the success of union efforts in the International Labour Organisation's draft guidelines on multinational enterprises, as discussed below; and to union attempts to have legislation enacted limiting manpower mobility within the EC during a strike.

Danish unions also brought pressure on their own government, which demanded information from Hertz on the number of employees involved and whether social insurance requirements were being met. Hertz replied that only six employees were involved at the time of the inquiry (formerly there were eight), that they were on loan from other Hertz companies and not on the payroll of the Danish company, that they were fully covered by social security in their own countries, and that such employees remained in Denmark an average of ten days, apparently being rotated.[40] There was thus no violation of Danish law that could be charged.

International Action

The unions have used the incident as a cause célèbre against the American management tactic of attempting to operate during a strike if at all possible. Mass picketing at Hertz's Copenhagen Airport office was dispersed by police.[41] The matter was

---

[38] As quoted in the Danish press.

[39] Hertz Corporation, interview in New York City, March 9, 1977.

[40] Letter from general manager, Hertz Biludlejning A/S, to chief of division, Arbejdministeriet, November 24, 1976, in response to latter's letter of November 19, 1976.

[41] "Strike—break moves spark controversy," *Industrial Relations Europe*, Vol. IV (November 1976), p. 3.

then raised in the European Parliament by a Danish member. A unanimous resolution was passed deploring Hertz's action and asking the European Commission to propose rules to avoid in the future similar "misuse" of the rules governing the free movement of labor within the European Community.[42]

The Danish government raised the question again at the December 1976 meeting of the EC social ministers. A report was requested on "problems" involving workers temporarily in a Community country other than their own. Also in December, Danish union representatives on the EC Advisory Committee on Free Movement raised the issue. It was therefore suggested that the matter be referred to the EC working group on multinational enterprises.[43]

Both international and regional union groups also became involved. The Danish clerical union, HK, is an affiliate of the FIET. FIET General Secretary Maier sent a telegram from the FIET's Geneva headquarters on September 30, 1976, the day before the strike commenced, to the general manager of Hertz Denmark "on behalf of 6 million members," announcing its support of the "effort of HK, our Danish affiliate to conclude collective agreement without delay," and promising that "FIET will intervene with European members of your company." [44] Hertz did not acknowledge the telegram nor did it experience any "intervention" in its other European operations.

Euro-FIET brought the matter before the European Trade Union Confederation, which passed a strong resolution on December 10, 1976, deploring Hertz's alleged actions and then added these paragraphs:

> The ETUC points out that in case this example should spread to other multinational companies, it may have incalculable consequences for the situation of the employees within the EC.
> On this background, the European Trade Union Confederation invites the Council and the Commission to take appropriate action without delay to prevent a repetition of this clear violation of the intentions of the EC regulations on the free movement of labour. In particular the ETUC draws attention to the OECD declaration on the conduct of multinational companies. The example of HERTZ proves that it is indispensable in the eyes of the ETUC that the directives of the OECD should become mandatory.

---

[42] "Labour mobility change," p. 1.

[43] Letter from J. Stenbejerre, Danish Employers' Federation, January 24, 1977.

[44] Copy in authors' possession.

The ETUC is of the opinion that the European Communities and EFTA should now take steps towards the drawing-up of actually binding rules in respect of multinational companies, so as to secure against such attacks on the employment, wages, and conditions of work of European employees.[45]

The unions did not drop the matter there. The Trade Union Advisory Committee of the OECD presented the Hertz case to the OECD as an example of the ineffectiveness of voluntary corporate guidelines for multinationals. The OECD declined to act on individual cases like this one, but then the unions turned to the International Labour Organisation's "Tripartite Advisory Committee on the Relationship of Multinational Enterprises and Social Policy," which convened in Geneva, April 4-7, 1977.

At this ILO committee meeting, the parties did adopt part of the OECD guidelines as a proposed ILO statement. The unions demanded in addition a paragraph that would have encouraged international union actions within multinational corporations. This was rejected, but the committee did agree to the following paragraph:

Multinational enterprises, in the context of bona fide negotiations with the workers' representatives on conditions of employment, or while workers are exercising the right to organise, should not threaten to utilise a capacity to transfer the whole or part of an operating unit from the country concerned in order to influence unfairly those negotiations or to hinder the exercise of the right to organise; nor should they transfer workers from affiliates in foreign countries with a view to undermining bona fide negotiations with the workers' representatives or the workers' exercise of their right to organise.[46]

It is quite clear from conversations with those present that this paragraph was a direct result of the Hertz incident and was not especially objected to by employer delegates, particularly those from European countries where such resistance to union strike action is relatively infrequent. Thus, although an attempt by Hertz, or any other company, to maintain its operation and to provide service to the public during a strike by using some of its employees from other EC countries is evidently

---

[45] *ETUC Resolution on the Hertz Case,* December 10, 1976.

[46] "Tripartite Declaration of Principles Concerning Multinational Enterprises and Social Policy" (Geneva: International Labour Organisation, 1977), Par. 52. In 1978, this paragraph was incorporated into the OECD Code of Conduct also.

violative of a proper code of conduct for multinational corporations, no such corollary conduct by unions has been condemned. European national unions, the secretariats, and European regional union bodies all advocate coordinated union action across national boundaries as indicated by the FIET's threat to "intervene with European members of your [Hertz] company." Perhaps the illogic is based upon the failure of the international unions to achieve such promises, but certainly the illogic and disparate treatment are rather obvious. In the final chapter, we shall discuss further the potential impact of codes of conduct on the prospects for multinational bargaining.

CONCLUSION

The services areas are not too heavily unionized in many countries, but the FIET is obviously determined to make the most of its opportunities. It remains to be seen whether FIET General Secretary Maier can continue to induce companies to meet with his multinational union committees. If he can, he could possibly develop a permanent relationship with a company.

CHAPTER XV

The Telecommunications Industry

The field of telecommunications has not provided a great deal of opportunity for multinational bargaining activities. Most companies in this industry, which provides telephone, telegraph, and telex services, are state owned and/or nationalized and, as such, are heavily regulated by government mandates. International trade union activity that may lead to a disruption of communication services would probably be severely restricted or prohibited in most countries. Also, employees in the industry have considerable job security and are not likely to fear the multinational firm in terms of their continued employment.

One attempt at establishing multinational union coordination in this industry has occurred in recent years. The Geneva-based Postal, Telephone and Telegraph International (PTTI), an international trade union secretariat, initiated discussions with Cable and Wireless, Ltd., headquartered in London, pertaining to a harmonization of working conditions for its affiliates, particularly in the Caribbean area.

PTTI-CABLE AND WIRELESS MEETINGS

Cable and Wireless, Ltd., is a state-owned, privately operated telecommunications company that employs approximately ten thousand people in fifty countries around the world in telephone, telegraph, and telex services; radio stations; and satellite earth stations. In addition, the company maintains sixty-three thousand miles of telegraph and thirty-two thousand miles of submarine telephone cable.[1]

The 1965 Meeting

The company did not experience a great deal of unionization until after World War II, and there was practically no contact

---

[1] Information provided by the company.

with the PTTI until the mid-1960s. In 1965, a director of Cable and Wireless arranged a meeting in the West Indies of branch managers and trade union negotiators "to see whether we could arrive at some formula in regard to the conditions of service which would be acceptable to all our branches in the West Indies." [2] After a lengthy discussion, the company director came to the conclusion that "the trade union officials would not wish to give up their bargaining position to any extent and therefore we could not arrive at overall conditions to cover everyone." [3] There was no follow-up to this particular meeting until 1973.

PTTI Caribbean Regional Conference

A PTTI Caribbean Regional Conference was held in Curaçao in April 1973, at which time the Cable and Wireless matter was discussed. Delegates, whose unions include Cable and Wireless employees in the West Indies, met during the conference on April 6 to consider such matters as common expiration dates, fringe benefits, salaries, general contract clauses, and coordination. It was agreed that a special conference of trade union negotiators should be scheduled to develop specific collective bargaining demands and strategy.

Carl Tull, a PTTI Executive Board member and general secretary of the Communications Workers' Union of Trinidad and Tobago, acted as chairman of the Cable and Wireless group and arranged with the Barbados Workers' Union to serve as host organization at a meeting to be held in Barbados from September 1 to 2, 1973. In preparation for this meeting, Tull made an analysis of various contracts in the Caribbean area and summarized it in a "Table of Allowances Extracted from Industrial Agreements for the Cable and Wireless Industry in the Caribbean Area." This information was circulated to union delegates on August 17, 1973, for review before the September conference.

The Barbados Conference

The Barbados conference was sponsored by the Inter-American Office of the PTTI and attended by delegates from Guyana, Jamaica, St. Lucia, St. Vincent, Trinidad and Tobago, Antigua, Grenada, and Malta. A representative from Malta was included

---

[2] Letter from company official to one of the authors, October 22, 1973.

[3] *Ibid.*

in this Caribbean gathering as a special matter to bring attention to the fact that PTTI "colleagues had so far been unsuccessful in their efforts to obtain a collective agreement and had been forced to resort to arbitration on many occasions" in Malta.[4] The problem in Malta had arisen in part as the result of a Maltese PTTI affiliate formulating unrealistic demands based on the most favorable clauses in a number of Caribbean agreements.

The following items were discussed at the conference, and agreement for action was reached as indicated:

> The first agenda item was a detailed review of all allowances mentioned in every collective agreement. There was a total of eighteen of these, including the 'leave allowance' provision of the Seychelles Cable and Wireless Staff Union collective agreement. None of the other agreements contained this provision. The differences between meal allowance and subsistence allowance [were] carefully defined as [were] the difference between shift allowance and night differential allowance and the difference between officer-in-charge allowance and acting allowance. It was agreed that definitions and specifications for these and the other allowances should be standardized.
>
> . . . the Conference reviewed the expiration dates of their collective agreements and it was noted that the agreements in Guyana, St. Lucia, Jamaica and St. Vincent expired on December 31, 1973, the agreements of Barbados and Trinidad expired on September 30, 1973, Antigua was presently in negotiations and only in Grenada was the expiration date very far removed from the dates of the other agreements—July 31, 1974. It was agreed that an effort would be made to bring these termination dates closer together.
>
> There was considerable discussion of fringe benefit provisions, centered mainly on maternity leave and trade union leave provisions. At the request of the delegates, a comparison was made of these provisions by the PTTI which has been sent to each delegate.[5]

In addition to concluding that, "as far as is practicable, unified proposals would be submitted for forthcoming negotiations by all of the Unions representing workers employed in the branches" of Cable and Wireless, the delegates decided:

> 1) That the Governments in the region should be urged to enact legislation to provide for Tax-free Severance Pay, and also to make provision, by legislation for the introduction of an Agency Shop that is meaningful.

---

[4] Summary Report on Cable and Wireless Negotiations Conference, Bridgetown, Barbados, September 1-2, 1973.

[5] *Ibid.*

2) That there shall be an exchange of collective agreements among participating territories.

3) The Conference viewed with alarm the existing situation affecting our affiliate in Malta, with respect to the absence of a Collective Bargaining Agreement, and the frequent reference to Arbitration, indicating a total disregard for the Collective Bargaining Process on the part of Cable & Wireless.

To this end the Conference decided to support the legitimate efforts of our Brothers in Malta in any future struggle, and requested the PTTI to convey our views to the Head Office of Cable & Wireless in London.[6]

Aftermath of the Barbados Conference

The aftermath of the conference witnessed an exchange of correspondence and one meeting between PTTI representatives and Cable and Wireless management personnel in London.[7] On September 18, 1973, Stefan Nedzynski, general secretary of the PTTI, wrote to W. H. Davies, a director of Cable and Wireless, calling attention to the fact that the Caribbean conference had been held and that the delegates were concerned about the Malta situation. He also stated that, where practicable, unified proposals would be presented in future negotiations. Davies answered this letter on September 25, 1973, agreeing to meet with Zerafa Boffa, president of the Clerical Section of the Malta General Workers' Union and F. H. Edwards of the British Post Office Engineering Union, as representatives of the PTTI, for the purpose of discussing difficulties in Malta, as well as laying the groundwork for harmonization of conditions in all of the company's branches.

Edwards, Boffa, and several Cable and Wireless managers, headed by Davies, met at the company's London headquarters on January 8, 1974. This meeting covered essentially two matters: the Malta situation and a request by the union for a statement of the company's worldwide industrial relations policy and procedures for conducting collective bargaining.

In regard to Malta, company representatives explained why conditions in that country were different from those in the West Indies. The company further indicated why it would not be possible to bargain in Malta over a set of conditions formulated on the basis of Caribbean agreements. Apparently this matter

---

[6] PTTI Press Release, September 3, 1973.

[7] Copies of correspondence in authors' possession.

was resolved, since there was no response from the union
following the January 8 meeting.

Discussions have been pursued on the matter of Cable and
Wireless industrial relations policy. The PTTI requested a
"statement of Company policy defining the collective bargaining
process and Agreements covering your employees working in
Branches of the Company throughout the world." [8] The union
emphasized the fact that "all negotiations between the Company and the Unions should be conducted against the background of an agreed procedure." [9] In answering this request,
Cable and Wireless noted that "we, too, would like to be able
to conduct negotiations with Unions against a background of
an agreed procedure and known policies but in aiming at a
harmonized policy . . . it would obviously need to be a two-way
process, calling for co-operation of the Unions concerned to set
out, and agree, their own policies on various matters." [10] The
company reiterated its position as follows:

> This, we feel, is one of the areas where problems can arise.
> In many of the Company's branches our staff are members of Unions
> which are not specifically telecommunications oriented but rather
> general workers Unions covering a wide range of industries. In the
> past there have been various moves amongst groups of branches,
> particularly in the Caribbean to establish mutual co-operation in
> collective bargaining, but while the Cable and Wireless Union
> members favour moving along such lines, in practice the general
> executives of such Unions, because they are negotiating within
> the limits of policies common to all their members in their ter-
> ritory rather than policies laid down from outside, are rather
> wary of any move which might, in any way, encroach on their
> Union's negotiating rights, and for such reasons moves towards
> closer co-operation in bargaining have not been particularly
> successful.
> It is particularly in those countries or territories which are
> newly independent that Union leaders are most sensitive to any-
> thing which might be regarded as outside control on their rights
> and affairs, and it is therefore very important that we should be
> advised by the local Unions as to the actual mandate given to the
> P.T.T.I. by the local Unions and the extent to which such unions
> are prepared to give their co-operation, and of course, the Unions
> concerned in this matter (of which we presume you could supply
> us with a list of names). In this respect, for the reasons given
> above, neither we (nor the P.T.T.I.) could afford to sit down to

8 Letter from F. H. Edwards to W. H. Davies, January 10, 1974.

9 *Ibid.*

10 Letter from D. A. Graydon to F. H. Edwards, February 19, 1974.

discuss matters affecting Unions unless they have advised us that you have been given a mandate to negotiate and have the full authority to settle agreements.

We have already mentioned that the executives of some Unions are constrained by local conditions and policies and equally this must apply to the Company. Every country or territory has its own peculiarities, and political and economic patterns, and each individual Union will therefore place a differing emphasis on certain aspects of the negotiations as will the Company in considering the claim. The settlement which is eventually reached reflects these emphases and it would therefore be difficult, in considering conditions at different branches, to set a standard for all, unless of course the Company were prepared to look at each condition individually, picking out the branch which had the best settlement on this and reflecting it to all the others. Such a position would, in the circumstances, be completely unviable from the Company's point of view.[11]

CONCLUSION

The PTTI-Cable and Wireless exchange could have set the stage for a continuing dialogue, but it did not. As the general secretary of the PTTI has pointed out to the authors, the PTTI secretariat was more interested in sponsoring multinational bargaining than were the unions involved.[12] Desirous of maintaining their own independence, the various Caribbean island unions just let the matter drop, and the PTTI could not revive interest. This is what the management of Cable and Wireless expected to happen as a result of their experience in 1965, and they simply permitted it to run its course.

---

[11] *Ibid.*

[12] Interview in Munich, Germany, May 16, 1979.

CHAPTER XVI

Radio, Television, and Entertainment

Largely unknown to students of multinational industrial relations, there has developed in the European radio, television, and entertainment industries a series of multinational labor agreements. The parties on the labor side are two international federations,[1] the International Federation of Musicians (FIM) and the International Federation of Actors (FIA), known collectively as the International Federations of Performers (FFF). Founded in 1948 and 1952, respectively, the FFF opened their ranks both to the free world and Communist unions and have attempted to remain nonpolitical. They are, therefore, not affiliated with any central body. For the most part, the FFF have been the exclusive representatives of performers' interests on the international level. An international trade union secretariat, sponsored and financed by the International Confederation of Free Trade Unions, was organized in 1965. Known as the International Secretariat of Entertainment Trade Unions (ISETU), it was quite active for several years but was unable to make real headway against the entrenched FFF. The ISETU now appears to be defunct, with little money and few remaining affiliates. The FFF, in contrast, have gradually reinforced their stability and international recognition over the years.

A special concern of the FFF has always been those technological advances that make possible widespread reproduction or transmission of individual performances, whether it be via records (phonograms), tapes, television and radio broadcasts, or, most recently, video-cassettes (videograms). These issues have been addressed by the FFF in three ways: (1) restrictive or remunerative national agreements; (2) work with international or

---

Philip Miscimarra, Industrial Research Unit research assistant, wrote the original draft of this chapter.

[1] Originally, a third organization existed and worked with the other two. Known as the International Federation of Variety Artists (FIAV), it was founded in 1952 and merged with the FIA in 1974.

451

intergovernmental bodies like the Berne Union, the International Labour Organisation, the United Nations Educational, Scientific, and Cultural Organization (UNESCO), the Intergovernmental Copyright Committee (Universal Copyright Convention), and the International Convention for the Protection of Performers, Producers of Phonograms and Broadcasting Organizations (Rome Convention); [2] and (3) restrictive or remunerative multinational agreements. The sections below briefly describe the development and content of the multinational agreements that the FFF have individually or collectively concluded with the International Federation of the Phonographic Industry, the European Broadcasting Union, and the International Radio and Television Organization.

THE FIM/IFPI AGREEMENTS

The International Federation of the Phonographic Industry (IFPI) was founded in 1933 to promote and defend the national and international rights of producers of phonograms. In practice, this has led to an interest in many legal problems affecting the record industry, especially those connected with copyright. As of 1977, the IFPI represented national groups in twenty-seven countries worldwide, and 550 individual companies in sixty-four countries. [3] Soon after the founding of the FIM, the IFPI concluded that the musicians' international federation shared an interest with producers in controlling the use of records in broadcasting. After a number of preliminary points were agreed upon in negotiations on July 10, 1950, and November 4-5, 1952, the "FIM/IFPI Agreement on the Participation in Broadcasting Revenues" was signed on March 11, 1954.

Nature of Agreement on Broadcasting Revenues

The 1954 "FIM/IFPI Agreement" provided that the "FIM or its affiliated associations shall be entitled to receive 25 per-

---

[2] For an introduction to the work of these copyright organizations and to the background of the Rome Convention, see Edward Thompson, "International Protection of Performers' Rights: Some Current Problems," *International Labour Review*, Vol. 107 (April 1973), pp. 303-14. The Rome Convention was adopted by a diplomatic conference jointly convened in Rome by the International Labour Organisation, International Union for the Protection of Literary and Artistic Works (Berne Union), and UNESCO and lays down regulations for the protection of rights of performers.

[3] *Yearbook of International Organizations, 1978-79*, 17th ed. (Brussels: Union of International Associations, 1978), reference no. A2028 [unpaginated].

centum of the net distributable revenue received by IFPI, its National Groups or members and derived from the broadcasting of its members records." [4] Five percent of the IFPI payments was to be given to the FIM secretariat, subject to the approval of the national recipient(s). The overall agreement was qualified, however, in a number of significant ways.

First, the IFPI's financial obligation to pay 25 percent of its broadcasting revenue to musicians applied only to countries of Europe, although "the principle of participation [was] accepted by IFPI as applying to all countries of the world." [5] The agreement provided for further discussion between the FIM and the IFPI of the implementation of this principle on a country-by-country basis.

The second limiting factor in the agreement is that payments were not to be made in a country unless they were accepted by the country's performing musicians (whether affiliated to the FIM or not) in full discharge of the IFPI's financial liability. This qualification stemmed from an IFPI fear that it might have to deal continuously with competing musicians' groups within a country, each of which might demand payment from broadcasting revenues. The FIM and the IFPI agreed early in negotiations that the 25 percent payments by the IFPI, issued in a *single* amount, would fulfill its national financial obligations. It was further stipulated that a plan for distributing that sum would be settled within each country. [6]

A third very important qualification in the 1954 agreement is that implementation was to end in any country where (1) it became legally compulsory to share broadcasting revenue with musicians; (2) national legislation was introduced enabling musicians to "demand payment in respect of or otherwise exercise control over the broadcasting and public performance of records"; and (3) other private contracts provided musicians with a right to receive payments derived from the broadcasting of records. [7] The provision, designed to prevent the IFPI from being placed in a position of double jeopardy (obligated to pay

---

[4] "FIM/IFPI-Agreement on the Participation in Broadcasting Revenues," March 11, 1954, clause 1.

[5] *Ibid.*, clause 3.

[6] Minutes of a meeting between the FIM and the IFPI, Zurich, November 4-5, 1952, p. 2.

[7] "FIM/IFPI-Agreement," clause 8.

musicians by both the agreement and national legislation), has caused the agreement to be terminated in every country that has ratified the Rome Convention.[8] This is somewhat ironic since a nation's ratification of the Rome Convention, while welcomed by the FIM, eliminates the FIM secretariat's 5 percent share of the IFPI's broadcasting revenue.[9]

The final limitation of the 1954 "FIM/IFPI Agreement" is not explicitly mentioned in any of its provisions: the agreement is not binding on IFPI affiliates. Under the IFPI's constitution, affiliated organizations maintain managerial autonomy. The IFPI, therefore, can only issue recommendations to their members. Generally speaking, the nonbinding character of IFPI agreements has not been an obstacle to implementation. The FIM observed in 1963, for example, that "experiences made so far, show, that the members of IFPI strictly follow the recommendations of their international organization." [10]

Agreement in Practice

The early history of the "FIM/IFPI Agreement" demonstrated that the agreement's nonbinding recommendations were made in good faith. By the spring of 1956, over 800,000 Swiss francs (equivalent at the time to about U.S. $200,000) had been issued to musicians' unions in Germany, Austria, Norway, and Switzerland.[11] The agreement could not be implemented in Italy, the Netherlands, or Ireland, however, and there were also obstacles to its implementation in France.[12]

In 1957, problems arose in Germany when the IFPI asserted that the German Musicians' Union (DMV) had not used pre-

---

[8] Article 7, section 2(3) of the Rome Convention provides, for example, that "the domestic law . . . shall not operate to deprive performers of the ability to control, by contract, their relations with broadcasting organizations"; UNESCO, "The Rome Convention," *Copyright Laws and Treaties of the World* (CLTW Supplement 1962, Item B-1), pp. 1-7.

[9] Rudolf Leuzinger, general secretary, FIM, interview in Zurich, March 23, 1979.

[10] "IFPI/FIM Principles," FIM Circular Letter No. 5/19, May 16, 1963, p. 1.

[11] International Federation of Musicians, *Report on the Activity of the Executive Committee on the 2nd Ordinary Business Period, Spring 1953-Spring 1956* (Zurich, 1956), p. 15. (Hereafter cited as *FIM 2nd Ordinary Business Period*.)

[12] International Federation of Musicians, *Minutes of the 3rd Ordinary Congress, London, May 7-12, 1956* (Zurich, 1956), pp. 8-9.

vious IFPI payments according to the provisions of the 1954 agreement.[13] A similar situation ensued in Switzerland, "owing to the very analogue structure of legislation in the two countries." [14] Eventually, the agreement was terminated completely in Germany when it was superseded by two decisions of the German Court of Justice (May 1960).[15]

The 1954 agreement also ceased to operate in Norway when, on June 30, 1957, an act was passed that mandated payments for every secondary use of a musician's mechanically fixed performance. An agreement was reached, however, in the summer of 1956 that provided for an equitable distribution of IFPI revenue derived from the broadcast of commercial recordings in South Africa. By mid-1962, the 1954 agreement was operative in Austria, Ireland, Italy, the Netherlands, and Switzerland, and the total amount of IFPI payment (since 1954) had exceeded two million Swiss francs.[16]

Limiting Records

In late 1960, the FIM entered into negotiations with the IFPI in an attempt to limit the secondary use of recordings. By March 1963, five "FIM/IFPI-Principles" were agreed upon that condemned all forms of clandestine recording and discouraged several types of secondary use.[17] Again, these principles only took the form of recommendations to IFPI organizations, but, as in the case of the 1954 agreement, implementation did not

---

[13] Clause 6 of the 1954 agreement provides, in part, that "the payments to be received by FIM, its associations or members under this agreement shall be applied for the benefit of performing musicians and shall not in any circumstances be used for any purpose which may be contrary to or adversely affect the interests of IFPI or its members."

[14] International Federation of Musicians, *Report on the Activity of the Executive Committee to the 4th Ordinary Congress, Paris, May 19-23, 1959* (Zurich, 1959), p. 19. (Hereafter cited as *FIM 4th Ordinary Congress.*)

[15] International Federation of Musicians, *Report on the Activity of the Executive Committee to the 5th Ordinary Congress, Geneva, September 17-21, 1962* (Zurich, 1962), p. 17.

[16] *Ibid.*

[17] The five FIM/IFPI principles specifically condemn or discourage (1) clandestine recordings, (2) the use of commercial records in film soundtracks, (3) the use of commercial records in stage productions, (4) the use of film soundtracks or recordings made by broadcasting organizations in commercial records, and (5) the use of commercial records in connection with non-musical live productions.

pose a problem. The FIM reported in 1969, for example, that "experience has shown that record producers are not adverse to the demands made by musicians' unions for closest possible limitation of the use of records for broadcasting purposes." [18] Since May 1973, a sixth principle has been agreed upon which asserts that "existing phonograms (recordings made for the purpose of being issued as discs, tapes, cassettes) should not be used for the making of videograms without the permission of the performers who had made the original sound recording." [19] (At the end of 1971, the IFPI had altered its constitution and name in order to affiliate producers of videograms.)

By 1976, the "FIM/IFPI Agreement" was operative only in Belgium, the Netherlands, Ireland, Switzerland, and partly in Italy. Special arrangements also provided for modified operation of the agreement in France and Israel. As we have mentioned above, the 1954 agreement automatically ended in every country that ratified the Rome Convention, which provides that, if "a phonogram published for commercial purposes . . . is used directly for broadcasting or for any communication to the public, a single equitable remuneration shall be paid by the user to the performers, or to the producers of the phonogram, or to both," subject to domestic law or an agreement between the parties concerned.[20] In 1979, Ireland ratified the Rome Convention, thus ending the agreement in that country. The FIM still retained some influence in the distribution of broadcasting revenue in Rome Convention countries, however, by a 1969 agreement with the IFPI (supplemented during 1978) which still covers the distribution of broadcasting revenue in certain cases.[21]

On January 1, 1977, the "Protocol" to the 1954 agreement became effective increasing the remuneration payable to performers from 25 to 33-1/3 percent of the IFPI's broadcasting

---

[18] International Federation of Musicians, *Report on the Activity of the Executive Committee to the 7th Ordinary Congress, Nuremberg, September 8-12, 1969* (Zurich, 1969), p. 11.

[19] International Federation of Musicians, *Report on the Activity of the Executive Committee to the 9th Ordinary Congress, Stockholm, August 30-September 3, 1976* (Zurich, 1976), p. 15. (Hereafter cited as *FIM 9th Ordinary Congress.*)

[20] "The Rome Convention," article 12, in *Copyright Laws and Treaties of the World*, p. 3.

[21] "FIM/IFPI London Principles," February 14, 1969, clauses 1-3; "London Principle No. 4," December 20, 1978.

revenue.[22] The "Protocol" also makes the FIA a party to the agreement. Other sections provide that no separate national agreements to implement the 1954 agreement will be made in the future; payments to associations of performers (whether or not affiliated to the FIA or FIM) may not be used for any purposes contrary to the IFPI's, the FIM's, or the FIA's interests; and, in countries where the FIM or the FIA derive revenue from the broadcasting of records and the IFPI does not, the record producers of that country shall be entitled to a 33-1/3 percent share of the revenue.

The 1954 "FIM/IFPI Agreement," as revised by the "Protocol," currently operates in Belgium, Israel, the Netherlands, Switzerland, and, possibly, France.[23] By a separate agreement, the FIM and the FIA have decided that the musicians in a country shall be entitled to 29-1/6 percent of the IFPI's broadcasting revenue, leaving the actors with 4-1/6 percent. It was pointed out, however, that "this ratio of distribution is not strictly binding; if on an amicable basis the organizations of musicians and actors can agree on different shares, they are free to do so." [24]

THE FFF/EBU AGREEMENTS

The European Broadcasting Union (EBU), an employers' organization representing broadcasting companies, was founded in 1950 as the successor to the Union International de Radio-diffusion (International Broadcasting Union). The EBU provides a number of services for its members, including advice regarding copyright legislation, contracts, and technical aspects of broadcasting. Its "Eurovision" network, however, which has facilitated relays of television programs among active members since 1954, has had the greatest impact on performers. As of 1977, the EBU had active members in thirty countries within the European Broadcasting Area (as defined by the International Telecommunications Union) and associate members in at

---

[22] "Protocol to the Agreement between the IFPI and the FIM on the Participation in Broadcasting Revenues of 11th March, 1954," November 9, 1976, clauses 1-7.

[23] "Co-operation FIM-IFPI-Protocol to the Agreement FIM-IFPI of March 11, 1954," FIM Circular Letter No. 9/8, January 24, 1977, p. 1.

[24] *Ibid.*, p. 2.

least forty-one other countries.[25] Relations between the FFF and the EBU represent performers' pursuit of many of the same goals described above. There have been several additional issues of FFF concern, however, which are unique to broadcasting. One of the most important has long been the EBU's Eurovision network.

Boycott and Eurovision Agreement

The principles that became the basis of FFF demands regarding Eurovision were originally formulated at an International Conference on Television, jointly sponsored by the then three performers' organizations, the FIM, the FIA, and the International Federation of Variety Artists, which was held in Paris, April 20-21, 1954. Although the organizations present at the conference (twenty-seven unions from twelve countries) acknowledged that the international exchange of television could be valuable in promoting international goodwill, they deplored the fact that "arrangements for such relays [had] been made by European television organizations without any consultation with the performers' international Federations." [26] The participants resolved not to extend any oral or written agreements with television stations after June 15, 1954, if an agreement with the EBU regarding international relays had not been reached. This boycott on Eurovision transmissions was implemented when the FFF representatives did not even meet with the EBU until October 8-9, 1954.

Subsequent negotiations between the EBU and the FFF were not very fruitful, although the boycott was reported, in early 1956, to be a full success: "In eight countries all programs with the collaboration of performers (musicians, actors and variety-artists) that were intended for relay, had to be cancelled." [27] Actually, the boycott appeared to take a toll on both sides. Although a number of EBU transmissions had to be cancelled or altered (at one point, the EBU resorted to television trans-

---

[25] *Yearbook of International Organizations*, reference no. A0598; and *The Europa Year Book, 1971* (London: Europa Publications, Ltd., 1978), Vol. 1, pp. 168-69.

[26] International Federations of Performers, [*Report of the*] *International Conference on Television, Paris, April 20-21, 1954* (Zurich, 1954), "Resolution 1: International Television Relays," p. 11.

[27] *FIM 2nd Ordinary Business Period*, p. 18.

missions in which the sound was recorded),[28] FFF representatives were forced to abandon their bargaining objective of limiting the number of Eurovision relays, accepting instead additional remuneration for the individuals whose performances were exploited to a greater extent.

After a total of six two-day meetings between FFF and EBU representatives had been held, the "Agreement respecting International Television Relays" (hereafter referred to as the Eurovision Agreement) came into force on February 1, 1957. This agreement provided for the originating broadcasting organizations to make supplementary payments to performers (musicians, actors, choristers, singers, dancers, and variety artists) who participate in Eurovision relays. The agreement did not apply to staff personnel (performers who received periodic payments) or to international relays that did not utilize the Eurovision network. As in the case of the "FIM/IFPI Agreement," the Eurovision Agreement was not binding on EBU members but constituted, rather, a recommendation that supplements be paid by broadcasting companies in individual countries.

Implementation of Eurovision Agreement

Although some early problems in applying the Eurovision Agreement led to a meeting of the joint EBU/FFF Committee (provided for under the agreement) in June 1957, television relays by 1959 were reported to be "a well-established cultural factor." [29] By 1966, the Eurovision Agreement's provisions had been incorporated in most European countries into national collective agreements.[30] A notable exception to this rule, however, was the Federal Republic of Germany.

In 1967, FFF and EBU representatives negotiated a "Supplementary Agreement," which replaced the original Eurovision Agreement for a two-year trial period effective January 1, 1968. The basis for this agreement was the performers' desire to eliminate "lump-sum payments" (payments that were not in proportion to the extent of a performance's use). In return for the elimination of both lump-sum payments and the maximum

---

28 International Federations of Performers, Report on a conference held between the EBU and the FFF, Paris, March 22-23, 1956, p. 5.

29 *FIM 4th Ordinary Congress*, p. 20.

30 International Federation of Musicians, *Report on the Activity of the Executive Committee to the 6th Ordinary Congress, Stresa, May 3-7, 1966* (Zurich, 1966), p. 11.

amount of remuneration that had been previously set for relays to broadcasting stations in eight or more countries, the FFF representatives reduced the minimum supplementary payment for a Eurovision relay from 50 percent to 20 percent and agreed to supplements "individualized by country" instead of determined by the number of countries participating in a relay. During the trial period, the FFF noted that the "Supplementary Agreement" was only being applied to a limited extent, with lump sums still being paid by EBU members in certain countries (Italy and the Federal Republic of Germany, for example).[31] As a result, the federations decided to terminate the "Supplementary Agreement" after December 31, 1970. The EBU, in turn, gave notice that it chose to terminate the original 1957 agreement (which was to replace the "Supplementary Agreement" on the same date.

On January 1, 1971, a "Revised Eurovision Agreement" became effective, which retained individual supplements for Eurovision countries but raised the aggregate of all supplements (which would theoretically be applied if every country of Europe participated in a Eurovision relay) from 150 to 192 percent.[32] Supplements for relays that were extended to Eastern European (Intervision) countries were placed at an aggregate total of 70 percent. The revised agreement also increased the minimum supplement for a Eurovision relay from 20 to 25 percent; it extended coverage to include directors and choreographers who do not acquire a copyright for which they are remunerated; and, although acknowledging the fundamental principle that EBU organizations were not to pay "lump-sum fees" instead of the recommended supplements, it allowed the existing practices in the Federal Republic of Germany and Italy to continue.

On August 30, 1973, EBU and FFF representatives negotiated the current Eurovision Agreement, which became effective on January 1, 1974. The 1974 agreement, like previous ones, applies to free-lance performers (including directors and choreographers as described above) who are affiliated via their national unions

---

[31] "Eurovision Agreement," FFF Circular Letter No. F/30, April 28, 1970, p. 1.

[32] International Federation of Musicians, *Report on the Activity of the Executive Committee to the 8th Ordinary Congress, London, May 7-11, 1973* (Zurich, 1972), pp. 16-18. The supplements for Western Europe which are set out in the 1971 revised agreement actually total 188 percent. An additional one percent is added, however, for "developing countries situated in the European Broadcasting Area and not included in the . . . list."

to the FFF. The EBU, however, is to "recommend its members favourably to consider, in the light of their national situation, the application of the provisions . . . to performers who are not members of a Union or who are members of a Union not affiliated to one of the Federations." [33] The 1974 agreement again retained supplements for different countries but increased the aggregate (for Eurovision and Intervision countries) from 258 percent to 292 percent of the base fee. [34] The individual supplements per country may be found in Table XVI-1.

The Eurovision Agreement currently in effect, like the 1954 "FIM/IFPI Agreement," is qualified or limited in a number of ways. It applies only to simultaneous or deferred relays carrying the "Eurovision" identification that are offered on a non-commercial (nonprofit) basis by an active or associate EBU member located in the European Broadcasting Area. [35] It may also be terminated after six months' notice either by the FFF or the EBU at the end of any calendar year. These restrictions, along with several others, certainly affect the administration of the Eurovision Agreement in a profound way. They cannot, however, be easily interpreted as evidence that the agreement itself is insignificant, for its twenty-two-year history and the provision for a joint committee to settle points of dispute demonstrate a strong commitment by the EBU and the FFF to cooperate on the international level.

FFF/EBU Basic (Sound Radio) Agreement

One of the EBU's main fears in negotiating the 1957 Eurovision Agreement was that an agreement covering international television relays would lead to similar union claims in the area

---

[33] "Performing Artists Agreement with the International Federations of Performers, International Television Relays," Supplement No. 5, January 1, 1974, clauses 1 and 2.

[34] Clause 12 of the 1974 Eurovision Agreement provides that "supplements shall be calculated on the basis of the initial fees actually paid to performers for the creation (rehearsal and performance) of the programme as first broadcast by the originating organization to its own audience."

[35] "Authentic Interpretation of the Agreement between the European Broadcasting Union and the International Federations of Performers respecting international television relays," Supplement No. 5, January 8, 1974, clause 5. See also *EBU Review*, Vol. XXV (January 1974), p. 60.

TABLE XVI-1
Supplements Provided by the FFF/EBU Agreement
Respecting International Television Relays
(Eurovision Agreement valid from January 1, 1974)

Country	Supplement (Percentage)	Country	Supplement (Percentage)
EBU Members in			
Algeria	2.0	Luxembourg	4.0
Austria	5.0	Malta	1.0
Belgium	6.0	Monaco	2.0
Cyprus	1.0	Morocco	2.0
Denmark	5.0	Netherlands	7.0
Finland	4.0	Norway	4.0
France	27.5	Portugal	2.0
Federal Rep. of Germany	40.0	Spain	8.0
Greece	2.0	Sweden	7.0
Iceland	1.0	Switzerland	4.0
Ireland	2.0	Tunisia	1.0
Israel	2.0	Turkey	2.0
Italy	27.5	United Kingdom	40.0
Jordan	2.0	Yugoslavia	5.0
Nonmembers of EBU in			
Bulgaria	3.0	Poland	8.0
Czechoslovakia	7.0	Rumania	4.0
East Germany	8.0	USSR	40.0
Hungary	5.0		

Source: *FFF/EBU-Agreement respecting International Television Relays*
(Eurovision Agreement valid from 1st January 1974), clauses
13(a) and (b).

of sound broadcasting. The 1957 agreement provided, therefore,
that it was not to be a precedent for agreements in radio.[36] On

---

[36] Even the present (1974) Eurovision Agreement provides that its recommendations "shall not impugn the principles and practices obtaining in the
field of sound broadcasting at the national or international level, and can
constitute no precedent in this respect. . . . The Federations undertake not to
revoke the present recommendations in order to put in issue the principles
and practices affecting sound broadcasting or to make modifications of the
said principles and practices a condition of a new agreement to supersede
the present Agreement" (clause 3).

this basis, the EBU for several years refused to discuss the international use of radio programs involving performers.[37]

In December 1959, the FIM's Executive Committee decided to boycott the international relay of sound broadcasts emanating from European music festivals, a move that was also supported by the FIA. The EBU, as a result, finally agreed to negotiate the terms of some recorded sound radio broadcasts.

The FFF/EBU sound radio agreement evolved in two stages. After preliminary negotiations were held in July 1961 and July 1962, the "Basic Agreement" was drafted in September 1962, embodying a number of general principles to become effective January 1, 1963. The specific terms and conditions of the agreement, however, were set out in a number of "Rules" that were written in February 1964.

The "Basic Agreement" broadly defines the scope of issues to be covered as "certain types of international exchanges of sound radio broadcasts." [38] The phrase "certain types of exchanges" has included, in practice, those recorded sound broadcasts that do *not* qualify as direct (live) or deferred international relays under the agreement.[39] Protected performers (musicians, actors, singers, chorus artists, and dance and variety artists) only include those who are "engaged at a fee" (free-lance) and are not part of an orchestra that receives "subsidies or other payments from a broadcasting organization of a nature such that they could not continue to exist without them." [40] The "Basic Agreement" also

---

[37] "Use of sound radio recordings outside their country of origin/Basic Agreement and 'Rules' UER/FFF," FFF Circular Letter No. F/11, February 1966, p. 1.

[38] "Performing Artists Basic Agreement on certain exchanges of programmes in sound broadcasting," December 31, 1962, clause 1.

[39] Article 6 of the "Basic Agreement" defines a "deferred international relay" as "an international relay which replaces a direct (live) relay when such a relay cannot be arranged for technical, programme schedule or other imperative reasons, and which fulfills the following conditions: (i) that the relaying organization has requested or accepted the relay before the original broadcast takes place; (ii) that the transmission is made by the relaying organization not later than 30 clear days after the date of the original broadcast and further, if made from a recording supplied by the originating organization, not later than 15 clear days after the date of receipt of the said recording. Only the first transmission by the relaying organization, in the circumstances specified in (i) and (ii) above, shall be deemed to be a deferred relay."

[40] "Basic Agreement," clauses 3 and 4. In a preliminary version of the "Basic Agreement," the following orchestras were specifically mentioned (after the FIM was assured that they were satisfactorily protected by na-

only relates to performers hired by a broadcasting organization itself, provided that the originating organization is an EBU member located in the European Broadcasting Zone (as defined by the European Broadcasting Convention that was in effect during 1963) and that the use is made by a broadcasting organization (which does not have to be an EBU member) located in the same zone.[41]

The "Rules of Implementation for the Basic Agreement," as noted above, were agreed upon by representatives of the EBU and the FFF in February 1964. The most substantive provision, Article 2, sets the following minimum supplements for an individual whose performance is reused according to the terms of the "Basic Agreement": 10 percent for one organization; 20 percent for two organizations; and so on up to 50 percent for five or more organizations.

The "Rules of Implementation" were originally to take effect on July 1, 1964. A number of difficulties arose, however, in drawing up the "Authentic Interpretation" of the rules that was mandated by the EBU's Administrative Council. The problems centered upon clause 6 of the "Basic Agreement," which excludes direct and deferred relays from the rules' application, and clause 8, which asserts that the "status of performers and the uses to which the present Agreement is not expressly applicable shall continue to be subject to national practices or arrangements." According to the FFF, these provisions permitted supplements for simultaneous and deferred relays to be the subject of negotiations at the national level; according to the EBU, clause 6 demonstrated an FFF commitment to forego supplements for such relays. Finally, after a joint committee of FFF and EBU representatives met in January 1965, it was agreed that, when a broadcasting organization applied the "Rules of Implementation for the Basic Agreement," the national unions concerned were not to claim supplements for direct and/or deferred relays. This recommendation was not to affect, however, national agreements or practices to the contrary already in existence at the time that the rules came into operation.[42]

---

tional agreements): Filharmonish Sleskap (Norway), Musikselskabet "Harmonien" (Norway), Orchestre de la Suisse Romande (Switzerland), and Orchestre de Chambre de Lausanne (Switzerland).

[41] *Ibid.*, clauses 5 and 7.

[42] Minutes of the Joint Committee of the EBU and the International Performers' Federations, Zurich, January 28-29, 1965, pp. 15-20.

Ironically, after the obstacles to the "Basic Agreement's" implementation were removed in 1965, very few of the agreement's provisions were incorporated into national contracts. In 1970, the FIA reported that the agreement suffered from "either opposition from the broadcasting organizations or lack of interest (or strength) on the part of the unions representing the actors in the countries concerned." [43] In 1979, however, the EBU noted that a "majority of [its] members actively participating in exchanges have adopted the main lines of the Basic Agreement and the Rules." [44]

Thus, the "Basic Agreement," like that concerning Eurovision relays, appears not to have suffered from its nonbinding character. The "Basic Agreement's" limited scope, however, may nevertheless lead one to the conclusion that it has been less significant than some other multinational agreements in entertainment. Representatives of the EBU and the FFF are currently engaged in discussions regarding the effectiveness of this agreement.

THE FFF/OIRT AGREEMENT

The International Radio and Television Organization (OIRT) is an association of broadcasting companies that was formed in 1946. It is similar to the EBU in that it was founded in succession to the Union Internationale de Radiodiffusion and has a network (called "Intervision") that provides for the international relay of television programs. As of 1977, the OIRT represented organizations in twenty-three countries primarily located in Eastern Europe, Asia, and the Middle East.[45] The Intervision network has been of FFF concern for almost two decades.

---

[43] International Federation of Actors, *Summary of Activities since the 7th Congress, Prague, October 2-8, 1967* (Stockholm, 1970), p. 7. (Hereafter cited as *FIA 7th Congress.*)

[44] Letter from M. Cazé, director, Legal Affairs Department, European Broadcasting Union, September 12, 1979.

[45] *Yearbook of International Organizations*, reference no. A2391. EBU and OIRT members constituted, at one time, a single organization, the International Broadcasting Union (UIR), which was founded in 1925 and succeeded, in 1946, by the International Broadcasting Organization (OIR). In 1949, however, the Western members of the OIR withdrew from the organization due to Cold War tensions and formed the EBU. By 1960, the two organizations had been separate for about ten years (the OIR became the OIRT in 1959), and each had its own broadcasting network: the EBU's Eurovision system primarily operated within Western Europe and North Africa, while the OIRT's Intervision system was functional in Eastern Europe. The two systems could provide for the exchange of programs between

Complementary EBU Agreement

FFF requests for an OIRT agreement regarding Intervision relays date back to July 1960. At the time, the OIRT declined to negotiate an agreement, noting that there was a relatively small number of FFF affiliates in Intervision countries and that the principle of supplementary payments to performers for the foreign use of their programs had not been incorporated in the national contracts of any OIRT affiliates. The OIRT was not opposed to general discussions in principle (FFF representatives did meet with the OIRT on several occasions), but the early discussions did not result in any firm agreements.[46]

In the absence of an OIRT agreement, both the FFF and the EBU were in an awkward position because relays *between* the Eurovision and Intervision networks were technologically feasible but of questionable legality. The EBU could freely relay artistic programs originating within the OIRT countries (subject only to national restrictions or quotas) but could not permit Eurovision broadcasts to be carried by Intervision.[47] In an attempt to eliminate this lack of reciprocity, the FFF and the EBU negotiated a "Complementary Agreement to the Eurovision Agreement," which permitted EBU relays to OIRT countries to commence on July 1, 1965.[48] Participants in the relayed programs received an additional supplement amounting to 10 percent for each relaying OIRT organization. The maximum amount of the Intervision supplements was set at 50 percent of the performers' base fees. The "Complementary Agreement" was revised and incorporated into the "Supplementary Agreement," which was in effect from January 1, 1968, to December 31, 1970. By the time of the Revised Eurovision Agreement (effective January 1, 1971, to December 31, 1973), individual supplements had been set for OIRT countries at an aggregate of 70 percent, a figure which

---

Eurovision countries alone, between Intervision countries alone, or between Eurovision and Intervision countries. See Burton Paulu, *Radio and Television Broadcasting in Eastern Europe* (Minneapolis: University of Minnesota Press, 1974), pp. 58-66, for more information on the OIRT.

[46] International Federation of Actors, *Report of Activity on the Period since the 5th Congress, Paris, June 6-10, 1961* (Paris, 1964), p. 12.

[47] "Additional Agreement Eurovision," FFF Circular Letter No. FFF 10, July 24, 1965, p. 2.

[48] The specific countries listed in article 1 of the agreement are Bulgaria, Czechoslovakia, East Germany, Hungary, Poland, Rumania, and the USSR (European Broadcasting Zone).

was increased to 75 percent in the Eurovision Agreement that went into effect on January 1, 1974.

Although FFF/EBU agreements concerning Intervision served to protect (or at least to remunerate) performers employed in EBU productions that were relayed to OIRT countries, they did not protect artists who participated in OIRT programs that were relayed to other companies within the OIRT or the EBU. During 1967, however, the FFF decided not to extend the EBU agreement concerning the OIRT beyond December 31, 1967, unless the OIRT proposed a draft agreement that would regulate cultural broadcasts *within* the Intervision network. The OIRT met this demand, ultimately resulting in an "Intervision Agreement," which was signed on May 22, 1969.[49]

The Agreement and Its Effect

The FFF/OIRT agreement, like the EBU agreements, applies only to free-lance performers involved in international multilateral relays (i.e., "direct and deferred relays transmitted by at least two television organizations") and recommends that OIRT companies pay them supplements calculated as a percentage of the initial fees paid by the originating organization. During a "transitional period," the specific amounts of the supplements were to be fixed at the national level. It was noted, however, that "the parties should endeavour to unify the system which would subsequently take effect for all television organizations of OIRT participating in Intervision."[50]

It appears that the Intervision Agreement, even more than the FFF/EBU "Basic Agreement," has suffered from a nonbinding character. It was reported in 1973, for example, that "since the individual unions concerned have not claimed that it be applied[,] the agreement has not come into operation."[51] The agreement's lack of application largely results from the fact that most Intervision countries are Communist states. Since the FFF/OIRT agreement is extremely general, a certain amount of union independence is required to set specific terms at the national level.

---

[49] *FIA 7th Congress*, p. 7.

[50] *FFF/OIRT Agreement on Recommendations respecting International Television Relays* (Intervision Agreement) (1969), section V, clause 5.

[51] FIA, *Summary of Activities since the 8th Congress, Amsterdam, September 21-25, 1970* (Stockholm, 1973), p. 11.

In most Communist countries, such independence is, of course, conspicuously absent. There has been no recent information indicating that the FFF/OIRT agreement's extent of application has increased.

CONCLUSION

The agreements described above show multinational entertainment union activity to be advanced beyond that in other industries. In certain respects, the International Federations of Performers have attained a degree of international union solidarity that is completely unprecedented. The most vivid example, perhaps, is the FFF boycott on Eurovision broadcasts that forced the EBU to recommend the payment of supplements to certain participating performers.

The agreements do demonstrate, of course, that solidarity still has not reached the point where unions in more than one country are willing or able to demand identical terms and conditions of employment. None of the agreements even attempt to establish basic absolute compensation levels for performers; they provide only for payments or supplements expressed as a percentage of a performer's initial fee, or as a percentage of a record producer's distributive broadcasting revenue, both of which vary between individual countries. Moreover, since the agreements are not binding in character, the supplements are applied in each country to a varying degree, depending upon the strength (or inclination) of the national unions involved. Thus, there may be some merit in the contention that the performers' contracts described herein are not really multinational agreements but rather multinational principles whose application depends upon the conventional exercise of industrial relations power on the national level.

There are numerous indications that the national barriers to absolute union cooperation in the entertainment field will be slow to fall. Rigid reciprocity agreements among many national unions, for example, provide for only a one-to-one (or other fixed ratio) exchange of foreign and domestic performers. A principle of the "FIM/IFPI London Principles" provides that remuneration due to individual performers that cannot be distributed should nevertheless "remain in the country in which it has arisen." [52] The protection of narrow national interests is also demonstrated by the practice of the American Actors' Equity Association, recently found to be in violation of the National

---

[52] "FIM/IFPI London Principles," clause 3.

Labor Relations (Taft-Hartley) Act, whereby resident members of the union pay substantially lower dues than alien (nonresident) members.[53]

Nevertheless, the agreements of the International Federations of Performers undeniably represent a big step toward multinational collective bargaining in the entertainment field, the closest to that concept that we have uncovered in any industry. This appears to be the result of the traditionally cosmopolitan nature of the entertainment industry; an unusually broad perception of interests by the unions involved; the skillful ability of FFF officials to balance their organization's long-range international goals with the national interests of affiliates; the fact that, as a service industry, the entertainment industry has difficulty in opposing strikes and boycotts; and the fact that European broadcasting facilities are largely government owned and therefore may be susceptible to union pressure. The possibilities for successful industrial action on the international level by entertainment workers may have also increased as a result of the relatively recent organization of technical personnel by the International Federation of Unions of Audio-Visual Workers, an organization that cooperates to a great extent with the FIM and the FIA. The question of how far multinational collective bargaining will proceed in the industry, however, has still not been answered.

---

[53] "High Dues Rate for Alien Actors Barred," *Daily Labor Report*, July 5, 1979, pp. A-13 to A-14. Actors' Equity Association is appealing the administrative law judge's decision to the full National Labor Relations Board.

PART SIX

Transport

CHAPTER XVII

The Ocean Transport Industry

This chapter examines the work of the London-based International Transport Workers' Federation (ITF) in the ocean transport sector where much controversy surrounds the union's campaign to control flags and crews of convenience.

FLAGS OF CONVENIENCE

Although there appears to be no general agreement on either the use or definition of the term, the ensigns of Liberia, Panama, Singapore, Cyprus, and the Somali Republic are those most frequently identified as flags of convenience. Honduras was once an important flag-of-convenience country but now contributes little to tonnage under these flags. Other registries, once considered tax havens but now regarded as quasi-flag-of-convenience registries, include Hong Kong, the Bahamas, Greece, and several small countries in the Pacific area.[1] The ITF lists Liberia, Panama, Cyprus, Singapore, the Somali Republic, Oman, the Bahamas, Bermuda, the Netherlands Antilles, Malta, Lebanon, Cayman Islands, and the Seychelles as flag-of-convenience registries.[2]

Combined, the fleets under flags of convenience total more than 88.4 million gross tons, approximately 25 percent of the world's total merchant fleet. Liberia has the largest merchant fleet in the world,[3] and predictions based on 1978 orderbooks indicate that this country's portion of total world tonnage may

---

Mary J. Immediata, former Industrial Research Unit research assistant, coauthored an earlier draft of this chapter.

[1] R. N. Metaxas, "Flags of Convenience," *Fairplay International Shipping Weekly*, Vol. 251 (May 30, 1974), p. 21.

[2] *ITF Newsletter*, No. 3/4 (March/April 1977), p. 18.

[3] *Lloyd's Register of Shipping Statistical Tables 1975*, tab. 1, pp. 4-5 and tab. 7, pp. 34-35.

increase from 18 to 25 percent by 1978. Total flag-of-convenience tonnage may account for 35 percent of the world's merchant fleet by the early 1980s.[4] The growth of these fleets since World War II—caused by the benefits of a politically neutral flag, attractive fiscal arrangements including low registration fees, low tonnage taxes, and, in some instances, tax exemption, and lower manning costs made possible by the absence of unions and social benefit legislation and regulations concerning the employment of national crews—has attracted the attention of academics, unions, and governmental and other bodies.[5] Because of the high breakage and loss ratios, especially of vessels under new flag-of-convenience registries,[6] and the apparent lack of flag-of-convenience governmental machinery to enforce international safety standards and social conventions, vessel owners are often equated with substandard shipping operators, which may or may not be the case.[7]

CREWS OF CONVENIENCE

Parallel to the growth in size of flag-of-convenience fleets and also attracting the ITF's interest has been the growing employment of seamen from developing countries at lower rates of pay. Although the absence of restrictions concerning the employment of national crews has facilitated their employment aboard these vessels, these crews of convenience are not employed exclusively

---

[4] H. P. Drewry Ltd., *World Shipping Under Flags of Convenience*, Economic Study No. 37 (London, 1975), p. 35.

[5] See B. A. Boczek, *Flags of Convenience: An International Legal Study* (Cambridge: Harvard University Press, 1962); R. N. Metaxas, "Some Thoughts on Flags of Convenience," *Maritime Studies and Management*, January 1974, pp. 162-77; Folke Schmidt, "Ships Flying Flags of Convenience," *Arkiv for Sjørett* [Journal of Maritime Law] (Oslo), Vol. 12 (1972); E. Argifroffo, "Flags of Convenience and Substandard Vessels," *International Labour Review*, Vol. 110 (November 1974), pp. 437-53.

[6] Peter Quaile, "Convenience Flags Account for Half of All Tonnage Lost," *Marine Week*, Vol. 1 (September 13, 1974).

[7] In August 1971, following its inquiry into the collision of two oil tankers, the *Allegro* and *Pacific Glory*, the Liberian government set up a Liberian Maritime Inspection Division to inspect ships flying the Liberian flag. Charles H. Blyth, retired general secretary, ITF, has noted, "Among extremes associated with Flags of Convenience, making generalization hazardous, is that some owners are among the best employers in the world, e.g., the U.S. oil companies, while others are certainly the worst." Address to Company of Master Mariners, London, December 3, 1975.

aboard flag-of-convenience vessels. British flag vessels, for example, have traditionally employed Asian seafarers, at Asian rates, on Far Eastern trade routes. In fact, the lack of a sufficient number of national seamen has at times necessitated the employment of foreign crews.[8] This practice has been accepted during periods of merchant fleet expansion by North European maritime unions whose wages and benefits are on the average considerably higher than the rest of the world; yet, in a severely depressed and contracting industry, the employment of Asian seafarers raises problems for unions whose declining membership is largely unemployed.

The ITF's policy on crews of convenience has been formulated to affect vessels flying what are considered traditionally maritime as well as "convenience" flags: "any shipowner who, without prior consultation and agreement with the bonafide seafarers trade union(s) recognized as such by the ITF, in the country of the flag of the vessel(s), departs from the practice of manning his vessel(s) with the seafarers of that country, shall be deemed to have engaged a crew of convenience."[9] Despite the inclusion of traditionally maritime flag operators in this definition, and occasional boycott activity taken against them,[10] the major thrust of the ITF's campaign has been directed toward flag-of-convenience operators employing crews of convenience.

The ITF's claims that it represents these crews, which have on occasion solicited portside intervention by ITF-affiliated unions, have been disputed by both unions and governments of developing nations, as well as by shipowners signing valid articles of agreement with national maritime boards of the crews' home countries. The development of ITF policy on flags and crews and case studies of companies' responses to the ITF's campaign are discussed below.

---

[8] S. G. Sturmey, *British Shipping and World Competition* (London: The Athlone Press, 1962), pp. 14, 297.

[9] International Transport Workers' Federation, *Report on Activities: 1971-1973* (London, [1974]), p. 161 (hereafter cited as *ITF Reports 1971-73*).

[10] The ITF reported that the Swedish motor vessel *Delos* was boycotted in Sydney, Australia, by Australian unions until the owners agreed to pay the twenty-six member Papuan and New Guinean crew at Swedish rates, increasing wages 633 percent. Swedish maritime unions reportedly boycotted the British flag *Clan Robertson*, employing a Zulu crew, in Gothenburg, Sweden, March 18, 1973. *Ibid.*, p. 112.

THE ITF CAMPAIGN—THE 1950s

Originally established in 1896, the ITF claims more than four million affiliated members organized in 378 unions in eighty-three countries.[11] The secretariat includes eight industrial sections to which affiliated unions may belong, including railways, road transport, inland navigation, ports and docks, shipping, fisheries, civil aviation, and allied industries and services. In addition, and of particular interest in this chapter, a special seafarers' section has been created to represent the interest of seamen. This is the section that has been active in conducting the ITF program against the flags of convenience. The ITF did not commence formulating an official policy on multinational companies until 1974,[12] but the seafarers' and dockers' sections have conducted a joint campaign to enforce union standards on international shipping firms for over twenty-five years.[13]

Setting Up of the Campaign

Prior to 1948, contact between ITF affiliates and management representatives in the shipping industry was limited to participation in the International Labour Organisation's Maritime Conferences and Joint Maritime Commissions. By the time of its second postwar congress, held in Oslo in July 1948, however, the ITF favored direct and independent action. At the urging of dockers' and seafarers' sections, the Oslo congress passed a resolution condemning the registration of ships in Panama and Honduras and calling for "an international boycott of Panama and Honduras ships . . . [to] be applied by both seafarers and dockers, . . . [since] it is only through such drastic action that the menace can be eliminated." [14] A boycott committee was sub-

---

[11] International Transport Workers' Federation, *Report on Activities: 1974-1975-1976* (London, [1977]), p. 23 (hereafter cited as *ITF Reports 1974-76*).

[12] "Resolutions adopted by the Stockholm Congress," *ITF Journal*, Vol. 34, No. 3, pp. 22-23.

[13] See Ken A. Golding, "In the Forefront of Trade Union History, 1896-1971: Looking Back on 75 Years of the ITF," *ITF Journal*, Vol. 31, No. 2, p. 41; and International Transport Workers' Federation, *Reports 1950-1951 and Proceedings of the Stockholm Congress, 1952* (London, [1952]), pp. 72-79. (Hereafter cited as *ITF Reports 1950-51*.)

[14] Text of the resolution cited in Erling D. Naess, *The Great PanLibHon Controversy* (Epping, Essex: Gower Press, 1972), p. 10.

sequently appointed by a joint seafarers' and dockers' conference that met in London in February 1949.[15]

The Panamanian government requested an ILO inquiry into its maritime affairs, and the ITF boycott was not implemented. Following the release of the ILO committee's report in June 1950, a number of shipowners signed collective agreements with the ITF. These may have been the first agreements ever signed between employers and an international trade secretariat. Shipowners generally agreed that many Panamanian vessels in the early postwar period were substandard. Surplus tonnage and low freight markets encouraged a transferral of obsolete tonnage from traditionally maritime flags to the Panamanian government, which, by 1947, had registered two million tons of shipping, had ratified no International Labour Conventions, and had no administrative machinery for the conclusion of collective contracts.

These first agreements set for crews of mixed nationality minimum acceptable standards at the level established by the British National Maritime Board and provided for union organization of crews of flag-of-convenience ships and contributions to a seafarers' international welfare fund. In cases where the majority of the crew was of a single nationality, minimum acceptable standards were to be those set by national maritime board agreements of the majority's home country if those levels were higher than those set by the British National Maritime Board.[16] A special seafarers' section was set up to act as bargaining agent for crews employed aboard Panamanian, Honduran, Liberian, and Costa Rican vessels. The ITF's three-pronged campaign policy is outlined in the secretariat's 1950-1951 report:

> (1) Organization of the crews of Panamanian and such like ships in a Special Seafarers' Section of the ITF;
> (2) Conclusion of collective agreements with owners who are prepared to apply the wage and other standards formulated by the ITF;
> (3) Compilation of an index of substandard ships against which action shall be taken at every opportunity.[17]

---

15 *ITF Reports 1950-51*, p. 74.

16 International Transport Workers' Federation, *Reports 1954-1955 and Proceedings of Vienna Congress, 1956* (London, [1956]), p. 77 (hereafter cited as *ITF Reports 1954-55*).

17 *ITF Reports 1950-51*, p. 73.

A permanent International Fair Practices Committee composed of affiliated seamen's and dockers' union representatives was set up by the ITF 1954 Congress to replace the original boycott committee. In 1955, a comparison of northern European collective agreements was completed, and studies to examine agreements from additional countries and officers' contracts were planned.[18]

Documentation concerning the significance of this early ITF affiliate boycott activity is sketchy. Erling Naess reports only twenty-one separate actions between October 1952 and May 1957. Except for one in Belgium, all of these were taken in the United Kingdom, the United States, and Scandinavia.[19] ITF reports for these years, however, indicate that the number of collective agreements continued to grow. According to one report,

> It has been possible to negotiate the appropriate agreements direct with some shipowners without any recourse to disturbing action or indeed threats of action. These owners, during negotiations, have expressed themselves to the effect that they wished to apply reasonable wages and conditions and they had no objection to entering into collective agreements for this purpose.[20]

By 1956, much of the obsolete tonnage registered under flags of convenience in the postwar years had been scrapped. Flag-of-convenience tonnage, however, had continued to grow from four million tons in 1950 to over eight and one-half million tons by 1955. The ITF acknowledged this rapid growth and reported in 1955 that fully one-third of the tonnage registered under the flags of Panama, Liberia, Honduras, and Costa Rica was less than six years old.[21] Concerned primarily with the maintenance of its active northern European and United States affiliates' wage standards, ITF policy underwent further change;[22] except for speculation about "what conditions on shipboard will

---

[18] English translations of Danish, Finnish, Norwegian, German, and Swedish agreements were included in this ITF study. *ITF Reports 1954-55*, p. 74.

[19] Naess, *The Great PanLibHon Controversy*, pp. 13-14.

[20] *ITF Reports 1954-55*, p. 79.

[21] *Ibid.*, p. 77.

[22] The close collaboration of United States unions in this phase of the ITF's campaign is evidenced by the opening of a New York office "to coordinate the activities of the special section on the North American continent with the activities being pursued in Europe." *Ibid.*, p. 81.

be like in a few years' time . . .," protests about obsolete and substandard vessels yielded to charges of unfair economic competition.[23]

Coalition of Interests

With their own maritime economies and interests affected by increasing tonnage under flags of Panama, Honduras, and Liberia, the governments and shipowners of traditional maritime countries, such as the United Kingdom and the Scandinavian countries, joined the ITF in opposition to their continued growth, although for different reasons. Until late 1958, the ITF actively courted the favor of these groups, appointing a delegation to discuss the effect of flag-of-convenience registry "with other interested parties in the international shipping industry" and publishing a pamphlet "stating the problem in terms of the shipping industry itself, the economic effects on maritime countries, and its relation to western defense through NATO." Prepared in nine languages, this ITF pamphlet was distributed by seafarers affiliates in November 1957 to legislators, shipowners, embassies, and the press.[24] The adoption of the "genuine link" concept by the International Law Commission in 1956, its subsequent incorporation as article 5 in the 1958 UN Convention on the High Seas, and the adoption of the Seafarers' Engagement (Foreign Vessels) Recommendation (No. 107) and the Social Conditions and Safety (Seafarers) Recommendation (No. 108) by the Maritime Session of the 1958 International Labor Conference marked the most significant achievements of this temporary coalition of interests.[25]

The idea of a "genuine link," which has never been clearly defined and the validity of which is not recognized in the United

[23] Boczek, *Flags of Convenience*, p. 69. The Preparatory Technical Maritime Conference, which met in 1956 to discuss the question of flag transfers, noted the change in the nature of the complaint against flags of convenience or necessity. *ITF Reports 1954-55*, p. 79.

[24] *ITF Reports 1954-55*, pp. 79-81; Boczek, *Flags of Convenience*, pp. 64, 74-75; International Transport Workers' Federation, *Reports 1956-1957* (London, [1958]), pp. 73, 76-78.

[25] For analysis and further explanation of these developments, see Boczek, *Flags of Convenience*, pp. 64-79; also, E. Argiroffo, "Flags of Convenience and Substandard Vessels," pp. 443-47; and F. Schmidt, "Ships Flying Flags of Convenience," pp. 77-79.

States,[26] sought to establish an effective bond of control between a state and ships registered under its flag as a principle of international law. Specifically, article 5 of the UN Convention on the High Seas states, "there must exist a genuine link between the State and the ship; in particular the State must effectively exercise its jurisdiction and control in administrative, technical and social matters over ships flying its flag." [27]

The ILO's recommendation concerning the social conditions and safety of seafarers incorporated the UN conference's formula into the body of its own resolution. The recommendation went further, however, by incorporating many of the proposals first forwarded by the seafarers' group at the Preparatory Technical Maritime Conference in 1956. The Seafarers' Engagement (Foreign Vessels) Recommendation, on the surface also a clear victory for the ITF position, advised states to discourage seamen from crewing foreign flag vessels without collective contracts or provisions comparable to the minimum already recognized by shipowners' and seafarers' groups of European maritime countries.[28] These recommendations, however, proved to lack any real influence or effect. The ITF boycott in December 1958, particularly the ensuing actions by American unions discussed below, supposedly on behalf of the ITF, dissipated whatever support the ITF had among governments and shipowners of certain maritime European countries.

1958 Boycott

In conjunction with its portside campaign to conclude collective contracts and its diplomatic activities before international agencies. The ITF's Fair Practices Committee encouraged direct pressure by national affiliates upon the governments of traditional maritime states. When these union representations proved ineffective, the committee, influenced by Scandinavian and United States affiliates, recommended, and the ITF congress approved, plans

---

26 See Walton J. McLeod, "Flags of Convenience Problem," *South Carolina Law Review*, Vol. 16 (1964), pp. 413-16, for discussion of United States position.

27 Text of article 5 of UN Convention on the High Seas quoted in Boczek, *Flags of Convenience*, p. 73.

28 *Ibid.*, pp. 446-49; International Transport Workers' Federation, *Report on Activities: 1958-1959* (London, [1960]), pp. 60-61. (Hereafter cited as *ITF Reports 1958-59.*)

for a four-day boycott of all flag-of-convenience ships not carrying agreements acceptable to the ITF.[29]

The ITF's 1958 boycott, beginning at midnight November 30 and lasting until midnight December 4, marked the first attempt by an international trade secretariat to coordinate industrial action by its affiliates on a world scale and to solicit support from other international trade secretariats as well.[30] Its effectiveness was spotty. The single notable exception was the support received in the United States, where an estimated 42 percent of flag-of-convenience tonnage was effectively owned in 1958 and where American maritime unions were concerned about the consequent reduction in jobs available to their members.[31] The ITF's two largest United States maritime affiliates, the National Maritime Union (NMU) and the Seafarers' International Union (SIU), brought nearly twenty years of jurisdictional disputes to an end and won the support of sixteen other United States unions during the four-day boycott. There is some discrepancy in the numbers of vessels claimed to have been boycotted in the United States. The ITF initially reported that 192 vessels had been detained worldwide, 143 of these in United States ports. NMU and SIU figures, however, indicate only 129 stoppages in nineteen ports picketed. Twenty-five of there were reported in New Orleans, where the boycott was most successful.[32]

Exact figures for Europe are even less complete. *Lloyd's List* reported that nine ships were affected in the United Kingdom,[33] one in Sweden, and several in Belgium.[34] Key nonaffiliated Christian and Communist unions in three important maritime

---

[29] *ITF Reports 1958-59*, p. 64.

[30] According to Omar Becu, then ITF general secretary, "the International Federations of oil workers [the now defunct IFPCW], metalworkers [IMF], and factory workers [presently ICEF] . . . called on their members to take appropriate action to ensure that the boycott also applied to the loading and unloading of tankers and ship repairing." Omar Becu, "Fighting the Pirate Flags," *Free Labour World*, February 1959, p. 60.

[31] Edward A. Morrow, "Seventy-Two Vessels Tied up by Boycott in U.S.," *New York Times*, December 2, 1958, p. 27.

[32] Edward A. Morrow, "129-Ship Boycott is Ordered Ended," *New York Times*, December 5, 1958, p. 62; ITF General Secretary Omar Becu reported that final tabulations showed "over 200 vessels" affected by the boycott in seventeen countries. Becu, "Fighting the Pirate Flags," p. 61.

[33] According to the *New York Times*, the boycott was ignored only in Hull because of high unemployment there. "British unions press boycott," December 2, 1958, p. 27; Morrow, "Seventy-two Vessels Tied Up," p. 27.

[34] Naess, *The Great PanLibHon Controversy*, p. 62.

countries—France, Italy, and the Netherlands—refused to co-operate with the ITF's boycott.[35] There was no boycott in West Germany.[36] Asia, except for the Philippines, and Latin America, except for Cuba and Uruguay, were unaffected. There was no boycott in Africa.[37] Despite the fact that boycott headquarters were located in the Dutch seafarers' building in Rotterdam, Dutch affiliate support was insignificant for reasons discussed below. The boycott received no backing from either shipowners or governments. The International Shipping Federation refused to support it "because it involved a breach of national collective agreements and, in some cases, a breach of international law." [38]

Public Policy Implications of the 1958 Boycott

Although uncertainty regarding the legality of sympathy boycotts in various countries failed to influence the 1958 decision of ITF affiliates, public policy ultimately determined the impact of the boycott. Subsequent court action, undertaken by various owners' groups as a result of the December 1958 boycott, influenced the future course of ITF policy.

In the Netherlands, for example, despite the meager response of Dutch ITF affiliates to the December boycott, shipowners sought injunctive relief in Dutch courts. Ensuing litigation terminated in a decision rendered by the Dutch High Court (*Hoge Raad*) in January 1960. This decision established that striking employees and unions inducing breach of contract could be sued for damages under the 1953 statute on contracts of employment. Similarly, employees and unions enjoined from acting in breach of contract could be fined. This decision, which virtually eliminated the right to strike except in unusual circumstances, affected the course of Dutch labor relations, as well as Dutch support of ITF policy, for the next decade. A similar legal climate also prevented union support of the ITF's worldwide boycott in Norwegian and German ports.[39]

---

35 Becu, "Fighting the Pirate Flags," p. 61.

36 Morrow, "Seventy-two Vessels Tied Up," pp. 1, 27.

37 Naess, *The Great PanLibHon Controversy*, p. 62.

38 OECD Maritime Transport Committee, "Flags of Convenience," *Journal of Maritime Law and Commerce*, Vol. 4, No. 2 (January 1973), p. 251.

39 John P. Windmuller, *Labor Relations in the Netherlands* (Ithaca, New York: Cornell University Press, 1969), pp. 321-25. See Omar Becu's reference to "legal difficulties" in West Germany which precluded any boycott activity there. Becu, "Fighting the Pirate Flags," p. 61.

Twelve Liberian and three Panamanian corporations were denied injunctions to prevent United States union participation in the ITF's four-day boycott, and 129 vessels were immobilized in United States ports between December 1 and 4, 1958, as a result. Subsequent action by American unions attempting to negotiate collective contracts for foreign crews aboard foreign flag and, in at least one case, foreign-owned vessels were less successful in avoiding injunction.[40]

CONCERN FOR PROTECTION AND IMPROVEMENT OF UNION STANDARDS IN THE 1960s

The employment of non-European crews aboard flag-of-convenience ships was an increasing concern to the ITF. General Secretary Omar Becu explained in January 1959 that the protection of union standards had been at the heart of the ITF campaign. He said:

> The main reasons for the growing concern on the part of seafarers' and dockers' unions were that they saw in this growing fleet of merchant ships . . . a strong threat to established standards; and because they recognized that continued development would ultimately threaten the very jobs of their members.[41]

In an effort to respond to the foregoing threats, a joint meeting of seafarers' and dockers' sections held in London, January 22, 1959, evolved a new formula for the conclusion of ITF agreements. The new policy's most important provision stated that "[such] agreements [are] to be concluded through the affiliated unions of the country in which actual control of the shipping operation is vested and, where necessary, by the ITF Seafarers' Section through its Fair Practices Committee."[42] The Fair Practices Committee met from April 13 to 14, 1959, unanimously endorsed the joint sections' resolution, agreed to implement the new policy, and announced the termination of all previously acceptable ITF agreements. This shift in policy reflected the

---

[40] Guy L. Heinemann and Donald C. Moss, "Federal Labor Law and the Foreign-Flag Vessel—An Inversion of the Doctrine of Preemptive Jurisdiction," *Journal of Maritime Law and Commerce*, Vol. 1, No. 3 (April 1970), p. 417. Naess describes the American shipping industry's legal response to American union activity. *The Great Panlibhon Controversy*, pp. 47 ??.

[41] Omar Becu, "Memorandum on Panlibhonco Shipping," January 1959, p. 2, in authors' possession.

[42] *ITF Reports 1958-59*, p. 64.

experience of American maritime unions within ITF councils. Joseph Curran and Paul Hall, presidents of United States maritime unions, had been appointed to the Fair Practices Committee in 1958. Because a majority of foreign flag operators were subsidiaries of American-owned companies, the new policy provided for increased organization of foreign crews by American unions. Agreements, previously acceptable to the ITF, had been based upon the wage level agreed to by the national maritime board of the majority of the crews' home countries—for example, Italian wage levels for crews aboard those flag-of-convenience ships employing primarily Italian nationals.

Under the new policy, if effective control were determined to lie in the United States, an Italian crew's wage levels could be negotiated by American unions.[43] Paul Hall and Joseph Curran, presidents of the powerful SIU and NMU respectively, cooperated in setting up an International Maritime Workers' Union to coordinate the organization efforts. Favorable United States National Labor Relations Board (NLRB) decisions regarding coverage of foreign shipping by the National Labor Relations (Taft-Hartley) Act [44] encouraged this union activity until a series of United States Supreme Court decisions stripped the NLRB of jurisdiction in matters affecting foreign flag shipping.[45] Later Supreme Court decisions withdrew immunity from unions engaging in boycotts of foreign flag ships and permitted courts to enjoin such activity.[46] This has ended, at least for the present time, effective support by American longshore and shipping unions for ITF boycotts of flags or crews of convenience. Es-

---

[43] Edward B. Shils, " 'Flags of Necessity,' 'Flags of Convenience,' or 'Runaway Ships'?" *Labor Law Journal*, Vol. 13 (December 1962), p. 1017.

[44] United Fruit Company and National Maritime Union of America, AFL-CIO, 134 N.L.R.B. 287 (1961). In making this decision, the board relied on its own previous decision, West India Fruit and Steamship Company and Seafarers International Union of North America, Atlantic and Gulf District, AFL-CIO, 130 N.L.R.B. 343 (1961), determining the NLRB's jurisdiction as dependent on "the weight of foreign vs. American contacts" of the subject company.

[45] McCulloch v. Sociedad Nacional de Marineros de Honduras, 372 U.S. 10 (1963). This reversed the NLRB's decision and invalidated the NLRB's means of determining its jurisdiction over foreign ships. The same day the Supreme Court also ruled on Incres S.S. Co. v. International Maritime Workers, 372 U.S. 24 (1963). The same matters were decided, and the court referred to "McCulloch" in its decision.

[46] Windward Shipping Co. et al. v. American Radio Association, AFL-CIO, 415 U.S. 104 (1974).

sentially, the Supreme Court ruled that it was never the intention of Congress to apply United States labor law to foreign flag ships, and therefore the courts were not restricted in the granting of injunctions in labor disputes of this nature.

New Definition of Flags and Crews of Convenience

United States union activity resulted in the return of many Greek ships, lured also by government policy, to the Greek flag and the registration of many newly built American ships under the British flag. In November 1960, Liberia announced that it had lost some two hundred ships to Greece and other nations in an eighteen-month period. Similarly, American owners, who had placed only 9.1 percent of their investments under British flag in 1959, placed more than 13.9 percent under that flag in 1961.[47] Shipowners threatened to transfer additional tonnage to traditional maritime flags.[48]

In response, a September 22, 1961, seafarers' section conference resolved that "flag of convenience registration is not limited to the Panlibhon nations, but applied to registration under any flag for such purposes." [49] For the first time, the ITF declared its right to conclude collective contracts with vessels flying any flag other than that of the country in which effective control resided. Even the British flag, with stringent safety codes, a respected inspection service, and strict licensing requirements, whose national maritime board agreement levels had been accepted by the ITF since 1952, was considered a "convenient" registry subject to ITF boycott activity if American owners employed it to remain competitive. The objectives of the ITF were clearly stated in a 1963 Fair Practices Committee press statement:

> . . . ITF unions are determined to pursue their efforts to ensure that wages and conditions of seafarers on flag-of-convenience ships are adequate and to continue to work towards the aim of forcing all ships back to the flags of countries in which genuine control lies.[50]

---

[47] Shils, " 'Flags of Necessity,' " p. 1025; Edward B. Shils, "The Flag of Necessity Fleet and the American Economy," *Labor Law Journal*, Vol. 13 (February 1962), pp. 156-57; International Transport Workers' Federation, *Reports: 1960-1961* (London, [1962]), p. 69. (Hereafter cited as *ITF Reports 1960-61*.)

[48] *ITF Reports 1960-61*, p. 67.

[49] *Ibid.*

[50] ITF Press Statement, 1963, in authors' possession.

Shortage of staff, difficulty in securing docker cooperation, and the prospect of lengthy and costly legal action prevented implementation of ITF policy except in Sweden and Finland, where boycott activity was legal, the seamen's unions had the full cooperation of militant transport workers' unions, and nonunion labor was relatively unavailable.[51]

The 1963 statement of the Fair Practices Committee is interesting also because it established for the first time the ITF's position on the employment of Asiatic seafarers at lower rates of pay aboard vessels registered in traditionally maritime countries. The press release proposed

(a) improvement of the extremely bad wages and working conditions applying to seafarers in the South-east Asian region; and

(b) prevention of the adverse effects of these substandard conditions on the wages and working conditions of seafarers in European maritime countries.[52]

A proposal to appoint an ITF Southeast Asian representative was passed by the executive board in 1963. A 1964 meeting of the Asian Advisory Council appointed Charles Blyth special ITF representative to Hong Kong to stimulate the development of trade union activity there. Blyth later served as secretary of the special seafarers' section, assistant general secretary, and general secretary of the ITF.

The ITF adopted a policy for Asian seamen in November 1965. The policy, which was reaffirmed by the Fair Practices Committee in March 1968, insisted that Asian seafarers serving on non-flag-of-convenience ships belong to an ITF-affiliated union in the country of the flag and enjoy wages and other conditions negotiated by the union, not less than those provided by ILO Recommendation No. 109.[53] When the Fair Practices Committee attempted to pass a similar resolution in 1972, however, they met with opposition from Indian and Philippine affiliates, who apparently were concerned that the wage rates negotiated by European unions were unrealistic for seafarers from low wage

---

[51] From 1965 to 1968, twenty-seven Panlibhon ships signed agreements with the ITF, all in Sweden and Finland. Naess, *The Great PanLibHon Controversy*, pp. 111-16; International Transport Workers' Federation, *Proceedings of the 29th Congress* (London, [1968]), p. 37.

[52] ITF Press Statement, 1963, in authors' possession.

[53] "Employment of 'Crews of Convenience'" (special seafarers' resolution), *Report on Activities: 1968, 1969, and 1970* (London, [1971]), p. 140.

areas and would threaten their employment opportunities.[54] This opposition has continued and is discussed in a later section of this chapter.

The policy for European flag vessels placed Asian seafarers in the same position in which European unions had found themselves when the 1959 policy for flag-of-convenience vessels temporarily gave American unions the power to negotiate wages for European crews aboard vessels controlled by American company subsidiaries. Conflicting interests of unions from disparate wage areas resulted similarly in strains in international union solidarity. In recognition of this fact, the ITF revised its policy on both flag-of-convenience and crew-of-convenience vessels, permitting its affiliates to "adopt a flexible approach to the problems of wages and conditions." [55] In no instance, however, are wages, hours, and manning levels to be less than those specified by ILO Recommendation No. 109.[56]

THE CAMPAIGN OF THE 1970s

Under pressure from Scandinavian unions backed by a powerful and newly affiliated Australian Waterside Workers' Federation, and supported in some measure by public opinion following the widely publicized collision of two Liberian tankers in 1971, the ITF campaign entered a new phase in 1972. In January 1972, the Fair Practices Committee directed a subcommittee composed of British National Union of Seamen (NUS), Swedish Seamen's Union, and Federazione Italiana Lavoratori del Mare— Confederazione Italiana Sindacati Lavoratori representatives to draft a new ITF collective agreement and requested affiliates in ten key ports to appoint officials to inspect conditions on flag-of-convenience ships on a regular basis. The growth in the number of vessels signing ITF agreements, the steady expansion of the

---

[54] Kingsley Laffer, "Australian Maritime Unions and the International Transport Workers' Federation," *Journal of Industrial Relations* (Australia), Vol. 19 (June 1977), p. 124.

[55] *ITF Reports 1971-73*, p. 107. The ITF's collective agreement now employs two wage scales for flag-of-convenience vessels, one for European affiliates and one for Far East Asia. These scales, which establish basic monthly pay for various occupational groups from master to catering boy, set the rate for able seamen at U.S. $483 per month and U.S. $343 per month, respectively (effective September 1975).

[56] At the time, Recommendation 109 provided for a minimum monthly wage of £25 ($100). The present ILO minimum is £48 ($115) per month.

ITF inspectorate, and the increase in the size of the International Seafarers' Welfare, Assistance, and Protection Fund reflect both the renewed interest in and increased effectiveness of the ITF's campaign since 1972.

By March 1979, the ITF claimed in its *Newsletter* that vessels carried blue certificates indicating that a special agreement with the ITF had been signed. In addition to certain wages (including rates for overtime, Saturdays, Sundays, and public holidays and for cash compensation for unclaimed leave), hours, and conditions, the special agreement also provides for a contribution of $144 per man per year to the ITF's Seafarers' Welfare, Assistance, and Protection Fund. In cases where the crew is of mixed nationality or belongs to a union not affiliated to the ITF, additional fees are levied for enrollment in the ITF's special seafarers' section ($12 per man) and payment of annual membership dues ($24 per man per year).[57] Activities leading to special confrontations and agreements with the ITF are discussed in the following sections. Particular attention is drawn to port activities in Scandinavian countries and in the United Kingdom.

Port Activities in Scandinavia

Since 1972, when the first ITF inspectors were appointed, portside activity has become increasingly effective. In January 1976, the ITF's Fair Practices Committee announced the appointment of an increasing number of inspectors, and in March 1979, the committee reported the appointment of "a number of new ITF ship inspectors . . . including those in Portugal, Spain, Iceland, and the U.K.," bringing the number of countries with inspectors up to eighteen.[58]

These inspectors, who in some cases assume ITF responsibilities in addition to their national union duties, are paid at least in part from welfare fund contributions. When a flag- or crew-of-convenience vessel arrives in port, inspectors board the vessel and request the captain to show an ITF blue certificate as proof that his vessel meets the standards accepted by the ITF. Often no further inspection of the vessel is made. If the vessel does not

---

[57] These rates effective as of September 1, 1975, represent a substantial increase in 1972 rates previously expressed in pounds, which were as follows: £4 enrollment fee, £8 dues payment, £48 contribution to ITF's welfare fund. A further 7 to 8 percent increase was planned for 1976.

[58] "New ITF Drive on Free Flags," *Lloyd's List*, January 29, 1976, p. 1; and *ITF Newsletter*, March 1979, p. 33.

carry a blue certificate, the inspector informs the ship's officer that portside unions intend to boycott the vessel until an ITF special agreement is signed, regardless of wages and conditions on board. Boycott activity of this type has been most effective in Finland, Sweden, Australia, and Canada. Despite the ITF's acknowledgment that conditions aboard United States oil companies' tankers are among the best in the world, these tankers have been targets of ITF affiliate activity.

Gulf Oil Corporation. Shortly before the Fair Practices Committee met to reorganize the ITF campaign in 1972, an incident involving Gulf Oil Company occurred in Skoldvik, Finland. On December 29, 1971, a representative of a Finnish ITF affiliate boarded the *J. Frank Drake,* a Gulf tanker docked at Skoldvik to discharge crude oil at the Neste refinery, and requested to inspect the vessel's ITF blue certificate. The vessel was manned by a nonunion Italian crew covered by wage standards superior to the ITF minimum at that time. Because the ship held no blue certificate, the Finnish Seamen's Union threatened a blockade in port "until the necessary affiliation fees to the ITF had been made." A local union official at Skoldvik, however, "told Gulf's local agents that the ship could sail on the condition that a letter be forwarded to the union stating that the required fee payment would be forthcoming." Upon promise of payment, the ship was permitted to sail December 30, 1971. The union threatened to shut down Fingulf's marketing operation unless a check for the fee was submitted by January 5.

Although a check totalling $3,230 was forwarded to the Finnish Seamen's Union, Gulf refused to recognize ITF jurisdiction over its nonunion crew or to sign an ITF special agreement. Once more, Fingulf's marketing operations were threatened by strike. A meeting between Gulf officials and ITF representatives was held in London on January 7, 1972. At that meeting, the ITF sought no major confrontation, and it appeared that the action of their Finnish affiliate "could well be an embarrassment to them." Gulf signed no agreement with the ITF, and the Finnish union, apparently under pressure from secretariat headquarters, cancelled the threatened shutdown action "after the company made assurances that all seamen on the *J. Frank Drake* were paid wages and benefits equal to the Italian standards set by the union," standards which were already in effect and superior to the minimum set by the ITF.[59]

---

[59] Letter from Gulf Oil Corporation to the authors, September 16, 1974.

Phillips Petroleum Company. In August 1972, a vessel belonging to Philtankers Inc., a subsidiary of the United States Phillips Petroleum Company, was detained in the Swedish port of Malmö. While discharging its cargo of carbon black feedstock on August 22, 1972, the *Phillips Texas*, which carried a crew of nonunion Italian nationals, received an ultimatum from the ITF-affiliated Swedish Seamen's Union. The union, according to Phillips's Malmö agent, "acting on behalf of International Transport Workers' Federation, London," demanded that Phillips sign a "collective agreement" with the ITF requiring Phillips to contribute to the ITF's Seafarers' Welfare Fund and receive in return a blue certificate assuring *Phillips Texas* of immunity from further ITF boycott. This demand was made despite the company's position that wages and working conditions aboard Philtankers Inc. vessels "exceed in every aspect . . . these (ITF) minimum standards" and aboard *Phillips Texas* specifically are "in every way in compliance with the Italian union's standards," and that any payment into a union fund was merely "tribute money." The ITF representative threatened to withhold from the *Phillips Texas* the pilots required by law when leaving the harbor and tugs that were needed that day because of high winds unless the ship's master would comply with the Swedish demands.

Because litigation procedures would have involved several days, at greater final cost to the company than the initial amount demanded (£1,740, or about $4,350), the company signed the ITF agreement. The agreement was signed August 22, and the *Phillips Texas* sailed the following morning with less than an hour's delay.

The *Phillips Texas*'s blue certificate was allowed to expire at the end of a year, and Phillips has had no further contact with the ITF. Interestingly enough, Philtankers had routed one of its Liberian flag tankers, the *Phillips New York*, to Malmö in 1971, and it discharged its cargo and proceeded without incident. Subsequent to the 1972 boycott, the company sent the *Phillips New Jersey*, also of Liberian registry, to Malmö in July 1974 and July 1975; again, the vessel discharged its cargo and departed without incident.[60]

Texaco. Texaco Panama Inc., a subsidiary of Texaco, first encountered the effects of a toughened ITF campaign in the Swedish ports of Malmö and Stockholm in 1972. While docked in the port

---

[60] Information received from director of marine operations, Phillips Petroleum Company, April 2, 1975.

of Malmö on November 2, the Panamanian *Texaco Missouri* was boarded by two union officials requesting that the ship's master enroll the nonunion Italian officers and Indian crew in the ITF's special seafarers' section. The master refused and was threatened with a boycott by local tugboat crews. A protest note was issued by the master "holding the ITF responsible for their illegal intrusion and for any delay or damage to the vessel or third parties as a result of this boycott." The *Texaco Missouri* sailed with pilots on board but without tugboat assistance.

At Stockholm, union officials were denied access to the *Texaco Missouri*. The ITF representatives then informed the terminal that, unless the required ITF enrollment fees and membership dues were paid, the *Texaco Missouri* would be refused tug assistance. Nevertheless, the vessel shifted berth the following day, November 5, with tug assistance. The 29,340-deadweight-ton vessel was berthed with a downstream heading in case further tug assistance was denied. Union demands were reduced, requiring payment only for Indian crewmen. On November 6, Swedish union officials announced that no further action would be taken against the *Texaco Missouri*, which departed the next day after generator repairs.

The Swedish newspaper *Arbelet* reported that Texaco had agreed to ITF wages for all Indian crewmen employed on the *Texaco Missouri*. Company officials denied the report maintaining that, "except for the initial boarding in Malmö when the Master refused to discuss their demands, the ITF was completely denied access to the vessel and no discussions were held with ITF representatives." [61]

In 1974, Finnish maritime unions simultaneously boycotted another Texaco tanker, the 43,000-deadweight-ton *Texaco Iowa*, registered in Panama, and a 78,000-deadweight-ton crude carrier, the *Chevron Frankfurt*, operated by Standard Oil Company of California and registered in Liberia.

On April 29, 1974, the *Texaco Iowa*, which had just completed loading a full cargo of gasoline destined for the United States, was informed that it would face boycott by Finnish maritime unions responsible for the vessel's departure unless an ITF blue certificate were signed for Texaco's entire Panamanian fleet. As the *Chevron Frankfurt* approached its dock at the Neste Oy facility at Porvoo Roads the following day, company officials

---

[61] Information received from Marine Department, Employee Relations Division, Texaco, Inc., May 11, 1976.

were similarly informed that, unless Chevron signed an ITF agreement covering all of their flag-of-convenience vessels, the *Chevron Frankfurt* "would not be given tugs, pilots, and similar services to sail following discharge of cargo." Following negotiations with Texaco lawyers, demands were reduced to cover the two vessels in port only. Both companies, however, still refused to sign an ITF agreement.

Since wages and working conditions on Texaco Panama vessels, including the *Texaco Iowa*, which carried an all-Italian crew, already exceeded ITF standards, Texaco officials believed the sole objective of the Finnish action to be "to force the company to pay dues to the ITF and recognize their jurisdiction." Standards for Chevron's Indian crew were established by Indian National Maritime Board agreement and negotiated with the National Union of Seafarers of India, an ITF affiliate. For these reasons, Chevron officials also maintained that the Finnish action was illegal and that the ITF affiliates had "no authority to collect funds or establish wages in their [the crew's] behalf." [62]

Finnish unions refused to provide either pilots or tugs required by law for ships navigating in Finnish waters. Lawyers for the companies applied twice in writing to the Finnish Maritime Board for permission, which was subsequently granted, to sail without a pilot. The *Texaco Iowa* sailed May 3 without a pilot. A pilot did board the *Chevron Frankfurt*, which also obtained tug assistance, and guided the ship to sea. A total of three days' time was lost.

The International Federation of Petroleum and Chemical Workers, the now defunct petroleum trade secretariat, reported that the ITF was asking for the support of refinery workers in a boycott of all Texaco and Chevron tankers. It also reported that the Finnish union wished to call public attention to "irresponsible actions of the operators of the Panamanian flagship, *Texaco Iowa*, and the Liberian-flag, *Chevron Frankfurt*," which "not only risked the lives of the crews of of the two ships concerned and the safety of other vessels and their crews, but also risked the possibility of a major pollution disaster." [63]

---

[62] Information received from manager, Labor Relations, Texaco, Inc., December 31, 1974, and manager, Labor Relations Department, Standard Oil Company of California, October 22, 1974.

[63] *IFPCW Petrogram*, No. 74-23 (June 7, 1974).

The actions of the operators in this instance were in fact most responsible. The fully loaded *Texaco Iowa,* which had been shifted from dockside to anchorage, was in an extremely hazardous position at Porvoo Roads. For this reason, the Finnish Maritime Board waived the requirement that the vessel sail with a pilot in Finnish waters. The departure was accomplished before darkness, as the board required, and under excellent weather conditions. The *Chevron Frankfurt* sailed with the assistance of both pilots and tugs. No international action of any kind was taken against Texaco or Chevron vessels except in Australia, where maritime unions detained a British flag Texaco tanker "for just a little while," according to then ITF General Secretary Charles Blyth.[64]

Exxon. An Exxon oil tanker, the *Esso Yokohama,* was boycotted in Norrköping, Sweden, between September 26 and October 4, 1975. The vessel carried a Panamanian flag and a Filipino crew led by four senior Italian officers and several Filipino junior officers. Upon arrival in Norrköping on September 25, 1975, the *Yokohama* was boarded by a local member of the Swedish Seamen's Union who acted as an ITF representative in demanding that the ship's master sign an ITF agreement and pay the initiation and other fees. When the master refused to sign the agreement, the terminal workers, employed by the Port of Norrköping, entered into a sympathy action with the Swedish Seamen's Union and halted the discharge of the cargo. The master issued a "Note of Protest" to the harbor master on September 26 stating:

> Before all of the cargo which my ship came to deliver was discharged, the operation was stopped by your representatives. Since 1730 hours on 25th September, I have approximately 2,500 Tons of cargo remaining on board my ship. I consider this a hazardous situation and hold you responsible for any damage to my ship and its personnel that may arise from not having been able to fully discharge.
> I request that you make the necessary arrangement to receive the rest of the cargo.[65]

Because the note was ignored, the ship attempted to leave port but was refused essential tugboat assistance. Exxon rep-

---

[64] Christopher Hayman, "ITF Hots Up the Flag War," *Seatrade,* Vol. IV, No. 9 (September 1974), p. 4.

[65] Note of Protest issued to the harbor master, Port of Norrköping, by the captain of the *MV Esso Yokohama,* September 26, 1975.

resentatives from New York and Gothenburg met in Norrköping on September 28 to discuss the matter with the ITF union representative and the harbor master, and a second "Note of Protest" was issued by the ship's master raising the question of the vessel's safety in port because of weather conditions. Strong winds threatened to blow the ship off the pier, and the master warned that the harbor master would be "responsible for any damage to [the] vessel unless [it was] permitted to leave before strong winds again occur[red]." [66]

Subsequent to the foregoing warning, Exxon's New York representative went to London and joined his European colleague for a meeting with ITF General Secretary Charles Blyth. Blyth's immediate response was that the matter was a local affair and that he had no authority to enter into it; however, when Exxon insisted that there was a safety factor involved in having the ship detained in port, Blyth agreed to have one of his assistants in London contact the ITF Swedish affiliate for an investigation. This action presumably led to an end of the boycott on October 4, 1975. When Exxon officials returned to Norrköping from London, tugboat assistance was made available, and the ship left port still carrying about twenty-five hundred tons of oil.

Interestingly enough, the tugboats were manned by personnel from three different unions, only one of which was the Swedish Seamen's Union. The latter covers the deckhands who stated that they would not participate in assisting the ship's exit, but as a matter of fact, they did appear for work on the morning of the exit. No ITF agreement was signed, nor were any commitments made on the part of the company concerning future activities.

This incident raises the question of whether the company could recover damages in court. Such action has never been taken by shipowners in Sweden. Exxon's local affiliate and company counsel advised that it would be futile to institute legal action in the Swedish Labor Court. Although present Swedish legislation governing collective agreements does not address the question of sympathetic actions supporting foreign primary conflicts, the Swedish Labor Court has determined such support is not illegal provided a primary conflict does not exist abroad. The new Swedish labor law, which was heavily influenced by the unions, will permit unions to take sympathy action without

---

[66] Copy of second Note of Protest also in authors' possession.

restriction concerning previously existing or illegal primary conflicts.[67]

In Sweden, the law does require a seven-day notice prior to work stoppage. Whereas in Norway, neglecting to give proper notice makes boycott action illegal,[68] notice in Sweden is merely an order of instruction, and failure to issue such notice constitutes a misdemeanor. A special clause inserted in the law upon the urging of the Swedish LO, however, provides that the obligation to give notice does not apply to unions planning to boycott flag-of-convenience vessels unless the ship's arrival is announced sufficiently in advance to make such notice feasible.[69] The only alternative for those companies that desire to discharge cargo in Sweden without ITF certification appears to be that of going into ports where exit is possible without union assistance.

Regional Boycott in Scandinavia. It is not surprising that Swedish and Finnish trade unions led the movement for an intensified ITF campaign. ITF officials report that, in 1975, 110 ships were stopped in Sweden alone. In an effort to intensify the campaign along regional lines, the Scandinavian Transport Workers' Federation, a loosely knit organization of Nordic trade unions, most of which are also affiliated with the ITF, headed by the president of the Swedish Transport Workers' Federation, has for several years attempted to organize a Scandinavia-wide boycott of all flag-of-convenience vessels. The failure of this group to implement a successful boycott illustrates further the critical importance of national policy to the ITF campaign.

Scandinavian Transport Workers' Federation (STWF) Boycott. In May 1974, the Scandinavian Transport Workers' Federation congress, meeting three months before the ITF con-

---

[67] Åke Bouvin, "Sympathetic Action in Support of Foreign Conflicts" (Address at Los Angeles Conference, November 7, 1975).

[68] Boycott Act, December 5, 1947 § 2(d). This provision has effectively blocked Norwegian support of the ITF campaign since 1959, when the Supreme Court of Norway ordered the Norwegian Seamen's Union and the Norwegian Transport Workers Union to pay jointly a sum equivalent to £2,894.9 plus 4 percent interest from June 15, 1955, plus legal costs amounting to kr2,000 to Cia Naviera Somelga in consequence of an illegal stoppage of that company's vessel, the *San Dimitris*, on October 14, 1954. English transcripts of the Oslo City Court's decision (December 21, 1957), the Eidsivating Court of Appeal's decision (January 24, 1959), and the Supreme Court of Norway's decision (November 5, 1959) are in the authors' possession.

[69] Folke Schmidt, *Politiska strejker och fackliga sympati åtgärder* (Stockholm: P. A. Norstedt & Söners Förlag, 1969), p. 43.

gress, announced a Nordic boycott of all flag-of-convenience vessels to be enforced by Swedish, Norwegian, Finnish, Danish, and Icelandic trade unions. *Lloyd's List* reported in July that the boycott, scheduled to begin September 1, would "effectively exclude all black sheep owners from a sizeable portion of Europe." [70] In fact, no such boycott ever took place. Isolated actions continued in Sweden and Finland unsupported by unions of other countries.

The latest effort to launch a regional Nordic campaign occurred on May 1, 1976. Announced by the STWF Executive Board on November 16, 1975,[71] the action sought "to persuade shipowners of vessels sailing under flags of convenience to conclude collective agreements with their crews in order to eliminate the threat to the international wage level which under payments could contain." [72] Folke Schmidt, professor of law at the University of Stockholm, formulated the boycott's legal strategy: "The laying down of work by the dockers should . . . not be regarded as a sympathy measure in support of the crew on a vessel sailing under a flag of convenience. It is primarily a question of a measure intended to support the Nordic Seamen's Union in their effort to obtain acceptable wage and employment conditions for *their* members." [73]

The boycott marked the STWF's first attempt to test the legality of sympathy boycotts in Norway and Denmark since 1959, when court settlements in those countries had seriously circumscribed union actions.[74] Potential problems arose in both countries in two areas: the legality of the boycott itself and strict notice requirements. In Norway, the wording of the ITF's collective agreement posed further difficulty.

---

[70] "Convenience Flags to Face Major Boycott," *Lloyd's List*, July 11, 1974, p. 1; "ITF Launches Combined Campaign," *Fairplay International Shipping Weekly*, October 31, 1974, p. 9.

[71] "Convenience Ship Boycott," *Financial Times*, November 18, 1975, p. 7; excerpt from Swedish Press Bureau, Stockholm, November 17, 1975, in authors' possession.

[72] Scandinavian Transport Workers' Federation, Nordic Action Programme for Trade Union Measures Against Ships Sailing Under Flags of Convenience, Circular No. 5, May 1974, p. 5.

[73] *Ibid.*, p. 33 (emphasis added); see also *Business Week*, December 8, 1975, p. 41.

[74] *Svenska Dagbladet* (Stockholm), November 6, 1975. The ITF reportedly offered to assist the STWF by drawing up a register of shipowner addresses.

After consulting with ITF officers, the STWF drew up a "notice of warning" to be issued to all shipowners. The notice informed shippers planning to send vessels to Scandinavian ports after May 1:

> Should you refuse to sign an Agreement acceptable to the ITF and the Scandinavian Transport Workers' Federation, your ship will be placed under boycott when she has entered a Scandinavian harbour. Consequently, the Scandinavian Transport Workers' Federation will call all appropriate members of the affiliated unions mentioned below to take industrial action. You will not be allowed to hire any person to supplement the crew. Your ship will not be handled, towed, loaded or unloaded by any member of these unions or by any worker joining in a sympathetic action.[75]

Four Danish unions, three Finnish unions, three Norwegian unions, and six Swedish unions were listed as supporting the boycott. Copies of ITF policy guidelines on flags of convenience, the ITF's collective agreement, and the special agreement to be signed by owners, promising payment to the ITF's welfare fund and enrollment of nonunion seafarers in the ITF's special seafarers' section, were enclosed with the letter. In Denmark, this letter was supplemented by union-issued notices informing various Danish employer associations of the intended date of boycott in accordance with the provisions of Denmark's collective agreement of 1973. Similarly, Norwegian unions were to inform the Norwegian Employers' Association and the Steamship Forwarding Employers' Association of the intended boycott action.[76] Because trade union membership in Norway is voluntary (a position upheld by the Norwegian courts in the 1959 *San Dimitris* ruling), article 24 of the ITF's special agreement was amended to read as follows in Norway: "All seafarers covered by this agreement who are not members of an appropriate national trade union affiliated to the ITF *may voluntarily* become members of the Special Seafarers' Section of the ITF." [77]

Denmark: Industrial Court Case No. 7745. Despite these precautions by the Danish Engine Crews' Union, the Danish Employers' Federation challenged both the lawfulness of the boycott and the legality of the notices of intended sympathy action

---

[75] Text of letter from Scandinavian Transport Workers' Federation, Stockholm, April 20, 1976.

[76] Scandinavian Transport Workers' Federation, Nordic Action Programme . . ., pp. 21, 35-37.

[77] *Ibid.,* p. 38 (emphasis added).

issued by the Danish Federation of Special Workers' Unions, the Danish Federation of Employees' Unions, and the Federation of Trade Unions in Denmark (LO). The Industrial Court held its first hearing May 6, 1976, five days before sympathy action was scheduled to begin in Denmark.[78]

In Denmark, a conflict between unions or union groups affiliated to the LO and employers organized in the Danish Employers' Association (DAF) is subject to regulation under the Collective Agreement of 1973. Because foreign shipowners do not belong to the DAF, boycott of flag-of-convenience vessels by seamen's groups does not fall within rules prescribed by Danish labor law, but the main conflict, although not subject to various restrictions, must be considered legal under Danish law.

Boycott action by the Danish Union of General and Semiskilled Workers, the Danish Federation of Special Workers' Unions, or the Danish Federation of Employees' Unions in support of such action, on the other hand, is subject to the provisions of the Collective Agreement, since the workers involved are affiliated through their unions to the LO and employed by groups affiliated to the DAF. These actions are subject to the notice requirement explained in reference 78 below.

The DAF maintained in the first place that no lawful main conflict could be initiated simply through the issue of four thousand to six thousand letters, nor could the Danish Engine Crews' Union demand collective agreements for an entire ship complement, nor could the union argue that it desired agreement for its own members, since not one of its members served on the flag-of-convenience vessels concerned. The action, then, was completely outside the scope of the traditional accommodations covered by Danish labor law and could not be declared legal. The court rejected this contention.

Secondly, the DAF argued that there was no basis for sympathy action, whether the main conflict were legal or not. Among its arguments, the employers' group cited the January 1959 court settlement that had outlined conditions under which future sym-

---

78 Section 2, article 4 of the Collective Agreement of 1973 stipulates that, prior to a lawful work stoppage, dual notice must be given to the employer or employer group affected. The first notice must be given fourteen days prior to the intended stoppage; the second, one week prior to the stoppage. *Ibid.*, pp. 21-22. Since the first notices were not sent until April 22 and April 23, respectively, and since the Danish LO did not send its second notice until April 30, the Danish boycott could not have begun until May 7 at the earliest. Transcript of the Judgment of 1st July, 1976 of Industrial Court Case No. 7745 (office copy), p. 2, in authors' possession.

pathy actions against flag-of-convenience vessels would be deemed lawful.[79] Assuming a lawful main conflict, the settlement provided:

> the Danish Employers Association recognizes that the Federation of Trade Unions in Denmark shall be entitled, subject to observance of the notices prescribed in paragraph 2 of the September Settlement, to declare sympathetic conflicts where requested to do so by the International Transport Workers' Federation (ITF) to such an extent and for such a period as the ITF might decide. . . . The Danish Employers Federation further recognizes that the Federation of Trade Unions in Denmark shall be entitled to carry through such sympathetic conflicts *to the same extent as they are in fact carried through in the other countries or in a substantial number of Western European countries which are affiliated to the ITF.*[80]

The DAF maintained and the court upheld that not all the conditions of the settlement were fulfilled. In particular, the court ruled: "Since it has not been contested that no parallel actions decided by the ITF have been started in the Federal Republic of Germany, Holland, and England, the notified sympathetic conflicts cannot consequently be lawfully established." [81] Each of the parties was requested to pay one-half the court costs.

As a result of this action on the part of the Danish Employers' Association, the STWF boycott failed in Denmark and Norway. Actions continued in Sweden and Finland as usual. No action took place in Denmark, and it seems likely that the court's decision has restrained any significant union participation in future regional boycotts. Apparently it is legal for Danish seamen's groups to prevent their members from signing on board flag-of-convenience vessels, but it is unlikely that any Danish seamen are currently employed on such vessels anyway. Without the support of dock and refinery workers, the seamen are powerless to prevent loading and unloading of flag-of-convenience ships calling at Danish ports. The unions in Norway adopted a "wait and see" attitude from May 6 to July 1, 1976, when the Danish case was finally resolved. Flag-of-convenience ships have entered

---

[79] The events leading to this 1959 settlement have been discussed earlier in connection with the ITF's "world wide" boycott in 1958. The September Settlement referred to below preceded the Collective Agreements of 1960 and 1973, but its provisions regarding notice were substantially the same

[80] Text of the settlement cited in transcript of the Judgment of 1st of July, 1976 of Industrial Court Case No. 7745 (office copy), p. 7 (emphasis added).

[81] *Ibid.*, p. 16.

and left Norwegian ports unaffected by the much publicized STWF boycott.

Port Activities in the United Kingdom

Milford Haven, the United Kingdom's most important oil terminal, has been troubled by boycotts since the port's tug operators, who are members of the ITF-affiliated Transport and General Workers' Union (TGWU), issued an ultimatum to oil tanker owners flying flags of convenience in January 1975. The tugmen apparently have threatened to refuse to handle ships unless wage scales of the tankers' crews, regardless of crew nationality or articles of agreement already in effect, are approved by either the NUS or the ITF.[82] This type of boycott is effective particularly at Milford Haven, which is located on the southwest tip of the Welsh coast and can be approached only through a narrow, shallow, six-mile long channel from Angle Bay.

The *Nereide* and *Nemeo*, two 18,000-ton Greek-owned tankers of Liberian registry on charter to Esso, were among the first vessels blacked in January 1975 at Milford Haven. These British coastal trade vessels had recently switched to the Liberian flag. Coastal trade is reserved normally for local union standards, if not national flag standards. The ITF contacted the secretary of the NUS's Milford Haven branch, Joe Barlow, who refused to allow the *Nereide* to berth until the vessel registered under a Greek flag. The *Nereide* left Milford Haven for the British east coast without unloading but returned January 22, still under Liberian flag. Boycott was reimposed and was extended to the *Nemeo*, which had arrived the same day. The owners arrived in Milford Haven on January 24 to discuss the situation with Barlow, as well as with the local secretary of the TGWU. The owners apparently paid £700 in back wages to the crew and "gave a written assurance that they would change to the Greek flag and pay the crews under the country's pay scales which are almost in line with international agreement." No ITF agreement was signed.[83]

Exxon. In November 1975, a 250,000-ton Exxon carrier, the *Esso Singapore*, was detained in Milford Haven by the NUS.

---

[82] "Tugmen in Free Flag Boycott," *Lloyd's List*, January 30, 1975, p. 1; "ITF Blackings Spread to Britain," *Fairplay International Shipping Weekly*, February 6, 1975, p. 15.

[83] "Underpaid Crews—Ships are 'Blacked,'" *Western Telegraph—South West Wales*, January 27, 1975.

The vessel was permitted to unload and leave port after a verbal understanding that the company was paying its Italian crew at Italian rates of pay, whose levels are 99 percent of the ITF minimum of $483 basic monthly pay. A company official met with NUS officers in London and was told that, in the future, more definitive information regarding terms and conditions of employment would be required. NUS officers later approached Esso petroleum officials in London promising not to detain Exxon's ships in the United Kingdom if Exxon's crews, which are not composed of British nationals, would join the NUS. Exxon has always maintained that the conditions on board Exxon vessels match those of the country of the crews' origin and has refused to consider the NUS's approach.[84]

Universe Ranger. In December 1975, a Liberian carrier, owned by Universal Tankers and transporting 273,000 tons of crude oil from the Persian Gulf to Milford Haven for Texaco Refining, was prevented from entering Milford Haven by the refusal of tugmen to assist the vessel until owners agreed to meet with the ITF. Although the *Universe Ranger*, which can enter Milford Haven only several times a month when the tides are high enough to handle the vessel's draught, was under boycott for only two days, unfavorable tides and bad weather resulted in a total nine days lost at a reported cost of $300,000.

Universal Tankers's representatives met with ITF representatives, including General Secretary Blyth and Brian Laughton, at a hotel in London from January 20 to 21, 1976. An agenda drawn up by the shipper included safety, manning capabilities, and terms and conditions of employment. The company's strategy was to exhaust the conference by discussing the first two matters and, when the time came to discuss terms and conditions of employment, by maintaining that there was nothing to discuss. After exploring the question of safety, the ITF conceded that there was no complaint about the *Universe Ranger*, which was less than two years old. A long discussion followed concerning manning capabilities, but the company was able to demonstrate that, because their crews had long service records, there was essentially no crew complaint regarding company policy in this respect. The ITF, too, agreed that Universal Tankers had demonstrated good conditions in that area. Regarding terms and conditions of employment, company representatives maintained

---

[84] Information received from manager, Fleet Employee Relations Division, Exxon International Company.

that, since the mixed West Indian crew employed aboard the
Universe Ranger was already represented by a union, the ITF
had no right to negotiate terms and conditions for them. The
ITF, arguing that the union was little more than a company
union, persisted in its demands that the crew be affiliated with
the ITF's special seafarers' section and be paid according to
the terms of the ITF's collective contract. Company representatives refused to negotiate on these matters. General Secretary
Blyth requested that the company consider the ITF demand and
respond within thirty days. The company responded by letter
nearly a month later maintaining that it could not speak for
the *Universe Ranger*'s union, that it held the ITF responsible
for damages, and that further harassment would lead to court
action.[85]

New Breeze. Milford Haven has not been the only United
Kingdom port troubled by ITF-related union activity. Two further actions took place in 1976 at Cardiff and Eastham. The
latter, which led to court action, has greatly enhanced the ITF's
legal position against owners' seeking injunctions in the United
Kingdom.

On January 23, 1976, Bank Line Limited, a British company,
sold its small dry goods vessel *Rosebank* to Transocean Shipping Company Limited of Monrovia, Liberia. At the time of purchase, the vessel, which was berthed at Cardiff, was renamed
New Breeze and placed under Liberian flag. The British officers
and Indian crew already employed aboard *Rosebank* were retained by the new owners at the same rates of pay. These rates
established by a new contract negotiated prior to the vessel's sale
provided for payment of the nonunion British officers at rates
higher than British National Maritime Board rates; similarly,
the Indian crew members were compensated at the highest rates
allowed by Indian government policy. The new owners made additional payments to an Indian Seafarers' Welfare Fund.

Before the vessel could be delivered to Transocean Shipping's
London agent, Associated Shipping Services Limited, representatives of the NUS at Cardiff approached agency representatives
at the port, demanding that the owners of the now Liberian flag
vessel produced an ITF blue certificate or be "blacked." *Rosebank*,
as a British flag vessel, had not been required to carry a blue cer-

---

85 "Supertanker Held Up by Pay Row," *Financial Times*, December 23,
1975; "ITF Sponsors Boycott of VLCC," *FACS Forum*, February 1976, p. 2;
and conversations with various company officials, March 2 and 11, 1976.

tificate. The vessel was prevented from sailing by the sympathy action of the port's lock operators, who are members of the National Union of Railwaymen, the ITF's second largest British affiliate.

Directors of Associated Shipping Services Limited met with union officials in Cardiff on Saturday, January 24, 1976. Interestingly enough, union representatives present at the meeting were district officers of the Merchant Navy and Airline Officers' Association (MNAOA), a somewhat smaller ITF affiliate than the NUS. The union refused to alter its position that the owners must sign an ITF special agreement, despite the company's contention that wages and conditions about the *New Breeze* were equal or superior to recognized Indian and British rates and the same as those aboard the *Rosebank*. In addition, the union demanded that the company enroll the six nonunion British officers in the MNAOA at a cost of £20 per man. Associated Shipping Services's director signed the ITF special agreement under protest and paid £2,990.35 to the ITF's welfare fund. No special seafarers' section enrollment or membership fees were required since the Indian crew already belongd to an Indian ITF affiliate and since Associated Shipping did enroll the *New Breeze*'s officers in the MNAOA. Following enrollment in the MNAOA, *New Breeze*'s officers demanded to be paid ITF rates. The company agreed to pay the officers a 20 percent increase in basic wages in lieu of overtime pay. At the following port, the entire crew complement was discharged and a new crew hired. The owners also have considered changing the ownership of the *New Breeze* to invalidate the ITF special agreement to bring pay scales back to normal.[86]

It is difficult to understand the ITF's position in cases like the above, except for contributions to its welfare fund, since the issues of substandard wages and working and safety conditions were not involved. The Liberian vessel was not forced back to British flag. Neither did the British officers or Indian crewmen receive long-term improvement in wages. Nor will it be likely that unionized British seamen will in any way gain from the dismissal of *New Breeze*'s officers and crew. The ITF campaign did, however, receive a substantial boost from another 1976 United Kingdom stoppage, which resulted in court action granting the ITF and its officers immunity from injunction.

---

[86] Affidavit sworn by director of Associated Shipping Services, Ltd.

The Role of Public Policy in the United Kingdom—The Camellia.
The *Camellia,* a 30,000-ton oil tanker owned by the Panamanian
Camellia Tanker Ltd. S.A. and managed by Wing On Enterprises, a Hong Kong group, was detained by British unions at
the Queen Elizabeth II docking complex at Eastham during
the period January 29 to February 9, 1976. The vessel was registered in Panama and carried a mixed crew of Pakistanis, In-
dians, and Chinese seamen.

Upon arrival at Eastham, the *Camellia* was boarded by an ITF
representative who made certain demands regarding previous
ITF-related incidents at Haifa, Israel, in which the *Camellia* had
been involved. The British ITF representative insisted that the
owners pay wages due a Filipino crew discharged at Haifa in
June 1975, drop disciplinary action against them, and provide for
their reemployment. The following day, John Nelson, secretary
of the Manchester branch of the NUS and official ITF inspector,
boarded the *Camellia* with a solicitor and received permission
to speak with the crew. Upon employment, crew members had
signed affidavits promising to have nothing to do with the
ITF. On January 20, Nelson returned to demand that the
owners sign an ITF agreement, pay the crews at the rates prescribed by the ITF agreement, provide the difference in back
pay amounting to $142,987, and reimburse the crew members
signed at Piraeus who had paid $400 a piece to a recruiting
agency prior to employment. Nelson informed the ship's master
that the vessel would not leave the docks until these demands were
met. Apparently both tugmen and lock operators were prepared
to support these ITF demands.

By the evening of January 20, 1976, the *Camellia*'s cargo of
crude oil from Venezuela had been discharged; a formal port
clearance notice was issued by the port authority the following
day. On January 22, the crew refused to allow the vessel to sail
or change berth. Following intervention by Nelson, the crew did
permit the *Camellia* to shift berth.

Faced with mutiny and with threats of boycott by TGWU-
affiliated tug and lock operators, the owner first applied in High
Court, Chancery Division, for an injunction restraining ITF-
affiliated unions or representatives from preventing the *Camellia*'s
sailing. The plaintiffs named the ITF and John Nelson as code-
fendants. In a judgment rendered February 6, Justice Templeman
held that the incident constituted a trade dispute within the

meaning of section 29 of the Trade Union and Labour Relations Act (TULRA) 1974. Immunity from tort was granted to the ITF under section 14 and to Nelson under section 13 of that act.

Section 14 grants immunity from tort to trade unions where the actions giving rise to litigation are "done in contemplation or furtherance of a trade dispute." [87] Section 13 confers immunity from tort liability upon those persons who have induced a breach of contract of employment if they were acting "in contemplation or furtherance of a trade dispute." [88] Interestingly enough, a trade dispute, for the purposes of the act, is not confined to domestic disputes but extends "to matters occurring outside Great Britain." [89]

The court of appeal found it unnecessary to consider whether Nelson was acting "in contemplation or furtherance of a trade dispute." The justices found that Nelson had not induced breach of contract but had merely passed on information regarding the *Camellia*'s presence in port. The court based its opinion on the findings of *Thomson* v. *Deakin* (1952), where inducement was defined as involving "pressure, persuasion, or procuration." Lord Justice James held that although "Mr. Nelson hoped for and expected support from members of affiliated Unions (*sic*) . . . [those] affiliated Unions were autonomous and not bound to follow ITF policy." [90]

Even more importantly, the court of appeal's decision marks a significant departure from previous judicial thinking regarding the granting of interlocutory relief and will probably make injunctions increasingly difficult to obtain. In Britain, unlike the United States, the test applied in determining whether an injunction should be granted was not defined by the statute until the passage of the Employment Protection Act (EPA) in November 1975, when section 17(2) of the TULRA was incorporated in schedule 16. Section 17(2) clearly states that a judge, before granting an injunction against union defendants, must "have regard to the likelihood of that party's succeeding at a

---

[87] Trade Union and Labour Relations Acts 1974 and 1976, c. 52, § 14.

[88] *Ibid.*, § 13.

[89] *Ibid.*, § 29(?).

[90] Judgment in the Supreme Court of Judicature, the Court of Appeal (Civil Division), Royal Courts of Justice, February 17, 1976, Camellia Tanker Ltd. S.A. and International Transport Workers' Federation and John Nelson, p. 19.

trial of the action in establishing the matter or matters which would, under any provisions of section 14, 14(2) or 15 [of TULRA] . . . , afford a defence to the action." [91] If the trial court finds that the employer cannot succeed on the merits of the case because the TULRA gives the union or the union officers a defense to an action in tort, the court cannot grant an injunction. In contrast, the judicial standard, established prior to the passage of the EPA by a 1975 patents case *American Cyanamid* v. *Ethicon,* had required only that the plaintiff show "a serious question to be tried," [92] regardless of his chances of winning the case. In the *Camellia* case, the court held that the plaintiff must show "a good arguable case." [93] This standard approaches the United States prima facie case standard. When current British labor law is considered, especially section 13 of the Trade Union and Labour Relations Act, which became law in March 1976, it becomes apparent that employers will find it in most instances more difficult to get an injunction when "a good arguable case" standard is applied.

The difficulty that shipowners will continue to face in Britain in an effort to obtain injunctions against ITF action is further highlighted in a decision by the House of Lords on July 26, 1979, which upheld a court of appeal decision to deny a lower court ruling that granted an injunction in the case of a Chinese-owned ship, the *Nawala.*[94]

The *Nawala* is a 123,000-ton bulk carrier owned by NWL, a Hong Kong corporation. In June 1979, the ship, flying the British flag and containing a crew of thirty-one Chinese, was designated by the ITF to be boycotted at the British port of Redcar, Cleveland. Dockers and tugmen refused to carry out the boycott, and the ship sailed to Narvik, Norway, where it was detained for two weeks before being released under a court order apparently based on a 1959 Norwegian Supreme Court decision

---

[91] Employment Protection Act 1975, sch. 16, pt. III, para. 6.

[92] American Cyanamid Co. v. Ethicon Ltd. [1975], Appeal Cases 369.

[93] Judgment in the Supreme Court . . . Camellia Tanker Ltd. and ITF and John Nelson.

[94] "Lords dismiss appeal against ship blacking," *Financial Times,* July 27, 1979, p. 8; see also Ian Hargreaves, "Law Lords ruling this week on international seamen's boycotts," *Financial Times,* July 23, 1979, p. 4.

prohibiting such boycotts.[95] The shipowners sought an injunction against further "blacking" of the carrier in Britain. A High Court judge granted an injunction against ITF action, but this decision was set aside on appeal, and the court of appeal upheld the judge's refusal to grant an injunction.[96] On July 26, 1979, the House of Lords, without citing reasons, dismissed the appeal against the ship's "blacking." Harold Lewis, ITF general secretary, said, "We have always believed that we were acting lawfully and now we have been vindicated in that belief." Lewis also indicated that, in regard to the flags-of-convenience campaign, "we shall continue to prosecute that campaign with all our vigour." [97]

An Australian Incident

Boycott activity has been a frequent occurrence in Australian ports.[98] Until recently, virtually no relief was possible for the boycotted shipowner except compliance with the ITF's demands. The case presented below, however, indicates not only some of the difficulties shipowners may encounter in Australian waters but also how they may be overcome.

Utah International. Utah International is a major mining concern with large operations in Australia and other areas. Utah is now a wholly owned subsidiary of the General Electric Company. Since May 1977, its Australian affiliate, Utah Development Company, has been in dispute with the Seamen's Union of Australia (SUA) over whether Australian seamen should be employed on UDC-operated bulk carriers.

Utah employs Spanish seamen under the Liberian flag on the carriers involved, which, among other activities, transport coal from Queensland, Australia, to European steel mills. According to the company, if Spanish crews were replaced by Australians, annual operating costs would rise by $23,000 for each Australian seaman employed. Utah has negotiated a labor agreement covering the seamen with the Euzko Langileen Alkartasuna-

---

[95] *FACS Forum*, July 1979, p. 4.

[96] "Lords dismiss appeal," p. 8.

[97] *Ibid.*

[98] For a complete account of ITF activity in Australia, see Laffer, "Australian Maritime Unions."

Solidaridad de Trabajadores Vascos (Basque Workers' Solidarity), which is an affiliate of the ITF.[99]

The dispute began in May 1977, when members of the SUA employed on tugs used to berth carriers at Hay Point, Queensland, refused to handle *Lake Berryessa*, a Utah ship. The company then agreed to a number of SUA demands, which, it claims, increased benefits above ITF standards. At this point, according to the company, the SUA demanded that the Spanish crew be replaced by Australians. After considerable legal maneuvering, Utah filed for an injunction in the Federal Court of Australia, pursuant to section 45D of that country's Trade Practices Act. The Australian government filed an action supporting Utah's request. On December 22, 1977, an interim injunction, still in effect at this writing, was granted forcing the SUA to lift the boycott. An attempt of the SUA to have section 45D set aside was denied by the High Court of Australia on November 28, 1978.[100]

As part of its defense against the SUA's actions, Utah appealed to the ITF to obtain a blue certificate for its ships. It pointed out that it had a contract with an ITF affiliate covering its seamen and that it was paying wages and benefits considerably above the ITF minimum. According to the company, ITF officials declined to provide the certificate because of the objections of the SUA.[101] Utah ships, however, have apparently not been boycotted in European ports.

ITF CONFLICT WITH ASIAN COUNTRIES

The ITF has a total of 413,114 affiliated members in India, 5,484 in Pakistan, and 13,215 in Bangladesh.[102] The special sea-

---

[99] "Utah Development Company and the Seamen's Union of Australia: A Position Paper" (Utah Development Company, July 1978), pp. 2, 4; "Utah's Consortium—The basic facts," *Seamen's Journal* (Australia), February 1978, pp. 38-39; and Larry Kornhauser, "Seamen's Union Unlikely to ban Utah vessel," *Financial Review* (Australia), January 6, 1978, p. 1.

[100] The Seamen's Union of Australia v. Utah Development Company, High Court of Australia, 53 ALJ 83 (November 28, 1978). The opinions herein contain a thorough review of the case. For an analysis thereof, see Brian Brooks, "Decisions Affecting Industrial Relations in 1978," *Journal of Industrial Relations* (Australia), Vol. 21 (March 1979), pp. 90-91.

[101] Director of personnel, Utah International, interviews, San Francisco, March 1, 1978; London, May 7, 1978.

[102] *ITF Reports 1974-76*, p. 24 (ii, viii, xii).

farers' section has been conducting the ITF's campaign against flag-of-convenience ships. In 1973, the ITF negotiated rates with the International Shipping Federation (ISF), a group including individual shipowners and companies employing Asian crews. The ISF agreed to compensate Asian seafarers at the rate of £48 per month, the minimum established by the ILO at that time, despite the fact that the national seamen's unions were demanding less than this rate.[103] When the seamen's association's two-year contract came up for renegotiation in October and November 1973, however, the governments of India, Pakistan, and Bangladesh forbade domestic shipowners on their national maritime boards from offering more than £32 per month and threatened to withhold labor supply from companies employing crews at ILO rates.

An agreement reached between the ITF and the ISF provided that wage rates for Asian crews be set no lower than £48 per month, with "special arrangements" for crews from the Indian subcontinent. These arrangements provided for wage rates to be no less than £32 and for the creation of special funds to be financed by payment of the difference between the £48 standard and the actual wages paid by employers to these seafarers.

The funds thus set up are managed by a committee consisting of the National Maritime Board of India, Indian shipowners, and the Indian seafarers' union. The political clout that this position of management of funds gave the union may well be one of the many reasons for the Indian unions' and government's opposition to the ITF campaign for higher wages for Indian seamen.

The other reasons, however, have meaning in the context of the high unemployment and the low wage structure in India. It is not only the ITF that has found this unusual situation of a country's and its unions' resistance to higher wages for its seamen. When the British working group endorsed the recommendation of the United Kingdom Race Relations Act of 1977 to impose United Kingdom flag rates of £187 a month for

---

[103] In May 1973, the ITF Asian Seafarers' Conference declared its concern for the disparity between rates paid to Asian and other seamen and warned of the "danger of multinational shipping companies holding down the level of wages in Asian countries. . . ." Indian and Pakistani union delegates to the conference, however, expressed concern that a significant increase in crew costs might endanger the employment of their members. *Maritime Worker*, August 5, 1973.

Indian seamen, the Indian government opposed the move because of "enlightened self-interest." [104]   According to the Indian government's estimates, there are about fifteen thousand seamen on foreign vessels, of which about twelve thousand are employed on British ships. The Shipping Ministry maintained that "on a balance of convenience Indian seamen should be paid less." [105] This unusual course of action is explained by the government as a precautionary measure; it felt that, in the face of growing unemployment in Britain and surplus labor availability from developing countries for continental shipping lines, the Indian seamen would be eased out once they lost their attractiveness to the shipowners (i.e. low wages). In addition, the government and the Indian unions also felt that a higher wage for Indian seamen on United Kingdom flag carriers was likely to precipitate a demand for higher wages by seamen working with Indian ships. This they felt would have serious repercussions on the country's shipping industry and employment therein.[106]

This unusual position of Indian seamen has led to conflict within the ITF's campaign against flag-of-convenience ships. The relationship between the Indian government and the ITF deteriorated further when the ITF protested the arrest of George Fernandes, former president of the All Indian Railwaymen's Federation (an ITF affiliate), under the "emergency" rule of Indira Gandhi on June 10, 1976. The Indian affiliates protested strenuously against the ITF's actions and statements. Representatives of four affiliates met in Bombay on August 26, 1976, and adopted a resolution calling for the ITF secretary general's suspension.[107]

It is in this context that the suspension of the National Union of Seafarers of India (NUSI) from the ITF on October 17 and 18, 1978, took place. The boycott organized by the ITF against the Liberian-registered *Camilla M* and *Anna M* during September at the port of Glasgow was resisted by the original Indian crew, which refused to sign the ITF contract calling for higher

---

[104] "British wages for seamen opposed," *Overseas Hindustan Times* (New Delhi), November 23, 1978.

[105] *Ibid.*

[106] *Ibid.*

[107] *ITF Reports 1974-76*, pp. 48-50.

wages.[108] The owners brought a court injunction and were allowed to sail. This action prompted the ITF to demand from the NUSI whether it had suggested to the owners to bring a court injunction for release of the vessels. A strongly worded telegram from the NUSI to the ITF saying that the NUSI "appreciated the glorious boycott at Glasgow, resulting in loss of employment to Indian seamen on two vessels" later resulted in the NUSI's suspension from the ITF.[109] The NUSI with twenty-four thousand members was the largest Indian affiliate of the ITF, and the suspension does weaken the ITF's representation of seamen from developing countries.

Interestingly, another Indian ITF affiliate, the Port and Dock Workers Federation, used the ITF leverage by threatening the Indian government with global boycott of ships visiting Indian ports during the November 1978 major nationwide port strike.[110]

The ITF now faces the problem of evolving a strategy that, without endangering its campaign against flag-of-convenience ships, can accommodate the unique and paradoxical problem of seamen of Asian countries like India, Bangladesh, and Pakistan. In the meantime, the Asian Seafarers' Conference met in Singapore on April 28 and 29, 1979, to establish a pro-tem Secretariat of Asian Seafarers, which "will ensure that policies and actions of the International Transport Workers' Federation do not adversely affect the interest and welfare of Asian Seamen." [111] At the Asian meetings, the delegates demanded that "Asian unions be given full and adequate representation on the various committees of the ITF including its Executive Board"; that the ITF flag-of-convenience policy be reviewed "in consultation with unions whose members are engaged on such vessels"; that the ITF Fair Practices Committee be restructured to include "appropriate representation from these unions"; and that the National Union of Seafarers of India be reinstated.[112]

---

[108] "Camilla M 'still blacked in spite of owners offer,' " *Financial Times*, October 11, 1978, p. 11.

[109] Leo Barnes, general secretary, NUSI, Note on Suspension of NUSI by ITF, Bombay, December 27, 1978.

[110] "Global boycott of Indian ships threatened," *Statesman Weekly* (Calcutta), November 25, 1978, p. 7.

[111] "Asian seamen to set up secretariat," *Asian Wall Street Journal*, May 6, 1979, p. 7.

[112] "Boycott Trade with Vietnam," *Labour News* (National Trade Union Congress, Singapore), mid-August 1979, pp. 1, 16. Despite the title, this article is primarily concerned with the conference of Asian seamen.

The Asian conference emphasized that its purpose was to strengthen, not weaken, the ITF and that its purpose was not to undermine wage standards. Nevertheless, it demanded that ITF policies be carried out so as not to contribute to the shrinkage of employment and not to undermine national collective agreements, and the delegates declined to go to a special ITF congress in Stockholm to meet with ITF leaders.[113] Thus, the creation of the Asian organization clearly is a result of growing hostile relations among seamen from the developed and underdeveloped world and the feeling on the part of the latter that ITF policies have removed work from seamen of poorer nations and given it to those of the richer ones.

CONCLUSION

During the course of its long history, the International Transport Workers' Federation has conducted a variety of activities toward the elimination of what it has perceived to be substandard working conditions in the world shipping industry. In addition to its work before international labor bodies and its efforts to influence national legislation, the ITF has engaged in a direct campaign against flags and crews of convenience. Agreements (blue certificates) have been sought from shipowners covering acceptable ITF wage and safety standards. Success in this area is witnessed by the more than one thousand such agreements claimed by the secretariat as of 1979. These agreements have been arranged, in many instances, under an actual or threatened boycott of a vessel carrying a flag or crew of convenience. Such agreements are almost always made directly with single nationality carriers and thus do not constitute multinational bargaining per se. On the other hand, the ITF is believed to be the only international secretariat that maintains company agreements.

The continued effectiveness of the ITF's campaign, based on boycott activity, will depend on supportive national legislation and the willingness of affiliated and allied unions to take sympathetic action. In those countries where the law and judicial interpretation of public policy are largely protective of the union's efforts—Sweden, Finland, Australia, and the United

---

[113] *Ibid.*

Kingdom—the ITF can expect continued success. Moreover, it now appears that the powerful European metal unions, acting through the European Metalworkers' Federation (EMF), have won the support of the European Commission for a program designed to replace flag-of-convenience and other ships as a means of supporting both European shipping and shipbuilding.[114]

Shipowners, no doubt, will continue to sign blue certificates in those parts of the world where ITF boycotts are effective, because the cost of compliance may be considerably less than the cost involved in pursuing legal action and risking delay in the unloading of a ship's cargo. This, in turn, will greatly enhance the ITF's financial position because, under a blue certificate, payments of $144 per man per year to the Seafarers' Welfare and Assistance Fund accrue directly to its accounts. The fund, which is estimated to contain several million dollars at present, can be used to employ additional inspectors and otherwise to support the campaign against the flags and crews of convenience.

In the past, the ITF has played a constructive role in attempting to improve general standards for seafarers through ILO resolutions, and this will likely continue in the future. The recent series of accidents and oil spills in American and European waters will undoubtedly enhance the ITF's role in this regard. On the other hand, in the decade ahead, the ITF's plans for direct campaigns against flags and crews of convenience, dependent on the boycott for their enforcement, appear to need some reassessment. Certainly, the campaigns analyzed in this chapter indicate some elevation of wage standards for seamen in particular cases, but competition for jobs between nationals of underdeveloped and developed countries, especially in periods of depressed employment, may limit job opportunities for seamen in traditional maritime countries. Some shipowners claim that the flags and crews of convenience are in reality flags and crews of necessity, for it has become economically infeasible to operate under wage and safety standards established in countries like the United States. Unions and governments in some underdeveloped countries are now beginning to react vigorously against ITF boycott policies, and even to form a rival organization to oppose ITF actions. Competition for jobs will thus be

---

[114] See chapter IV.

514 *Multinational Collective Bargaining Attempts*

a matter of considerable importance to the ITF while it develops its strategy to protect standards at the international level.

Thus far, the ITF has not utilized its economic power to enforce standards or agreements in other industries. If it were to do so, it could presumably supply the force that would curtail the movement of products over national boundaries during strikes or even compel manufacturing companies to bargain on a multinational basis. Such action, of course, would again depend upon national legislation. Finally, the ITF has not moved against ships of the Soviet or Eastern bloc. These nations are greatly expanding their maritime role and are in direct competition with ships carrying ITF-affiliated crews.[115] Moreover, the conditions aboard these ships are allegedly inferior to ITF standards and, in many cases, to those of flags of convenience as well. Although the ITF has not ignored this growing threat to the employment of its affiliated members, it has not developed policies to deal with it.

---

[115] "Comecon Competitors Move into Europe's Shipping Lanes," *Business Europe*, Vol. XVII, No. 2 (January 14, 1977), p. 13; and David A. Andelman, "Soviet Union Widening Foothold in World of Far Eastern Shipping," *New York Times*, January 22, 1977, p. 29.

CHAPTER XVIII

The Air Transport Industry

The International Transport Workers' Federation (ITF) is very active in air transport, as well as in ocean transport, and has participated in a number of actions involving airlines. In air transport, however, the ITF is faced with two obstacles: most airlines, except in the United States, are government owned, and thus action against them invokes a direct confrontation with governments; and second, pilots' unions are affiliates of the International Federation of Air Line Pilots' Associations (IFALPA), a unique organization, which, although actively concerned with industrial relations matters, considers itself primarily a professional and technical organization. Therefore, the IFALPA's cooperation with the ITF, as is noted below, is quite limited.

ITF AIR TRANSPORT ACTIVITIES

The ITF offers affiliations to all transport (including air transport) unions. Its affiliates include airline maintenance, service, clerical, and cabin employee unions, plus at least three pilots' unions, which are both ITF and IFALPA members. The world's largest national organization of pilots, the United States Air Line Pilots' Associations (US-ALPA) was likewise a member of the ITF and the IFALPA for a short period during the 1950s.[1]

ITF Attempts at Joint Action with the IFALPA

The IFALPA president and the delegate of the US-ALPA to the IFALPA were observers at the 1977 ITF Congress in Dublin.[2] Here it was suggested that the ITF and the IFALPA adopt a joint

---

[1] Our facts and discussion of IFALPA policies are based upon the separate study of the IFALPA which the Industrial Research Unit will shortly publish.

[2] Captain Thomas Ashwood, secretary, US-ALPA, interview in Washington, D.C., December 1, 1977.

statement on crew complements for the Boeing 7X7,[3] a problem of great concern to pilots. Beyond simple policy statements, however, little joint action occurs. The executive secretary of the IFALPA noted that it would never ask the ITF for assistance nor would it become involved in ITF disputes.[4] Instead, the IFALPA has suggested that the ITF go through the local carrier or pilot group.

KSSU and ATLAS. One area in which the ITF would like to involve the IFALPA is the "pooling" of certain services by two European airline groups—ATLAS (Air France, Alitalia, Lufthansa, Sabena, and Iberia) and KSSU (KLM, Swissair, SAS, and UTA). Under a formal agreement, each of these groups transfers and shares maintenance and other ground services among their members to obtain major cost savings.[5] Thus, for example, one company will maintain all General Electric engines, and another all Pratt & Whitney engines, for all members of the group. Similarly, one will overhaul DC-10s, another Boeing 747s. Only day-to-day maintenance is carried out by the operating airlines, while overhauls, spare parts, etc., are exclusively the province of one of the member companies. The savings on inventories alone is enormous. Similarly, in each country, all reservation service is conducted by the host country; common training programs are developed; and interior aircraft design is coordinated.

The ITF sees such pooling agreements as diminishing employment and has been particularly active among unions in the KSSU group in an effort to offset such activities. A KSSU union group has been meeting for some years under ITF auspices, and the ATLAS union group attended at least one of these meetings.[6] The ITF now claims that the KSSU unions have agreed on a joint formulation of demands and a common strategy. According to the ITF, "KSSU member unions will, within the limits placed on them by national legislation, offer practical support and solidarity to each other."[7] How solid this solidarity is may be

---

[3] International Transport Workers' Federation, *Report on Activities: 1974-1975-1976* (London, [1977]), p. 147.

[4] Captain Laurie Taylor, executive secretary, IFALPA, interview in Egham, England, May 15, 1978.

[5] *Ibid.*

[6] ITF, *Report on Activities*, pp. 144-47.

[7] *ITF Panorama*, Vol. 1, No. 3 (1979), p. 1.

indicated by the comment on the same page of the *ITF Panorama* that "we would respectfully point out to aviation affiliates in companies which at present operate quite independently that it may be their members tomorrow who face the problems that their European colleagues are struggling so manfully to overcome today." [8]

The ITF has also attempted to arrange a meeting with the KSSU companies but has been rebuffed, although it did have one meeting with a KSSU member, Scandinavian Airlines.[9] More recently, it has asked the Organization for Economic Cooperation and Development (OECD) to designate ATLAS and KSSU as "multinational corporations" and therefore subject to OECD guidelines.[10] Presumably, the ITF desires to charge that these organizations are somehow violating the OECD multinational corporate guidelines by not consulting it on their rationalization programs.

Although the IFALPA has evidenced some concern about potential transfers of pilots from one airline to another, it is not ready to give any specific aid to the ITF's efforts.[11] The US-ALPA, for one thing, whose membership comprises one-half the total affiliated membership of the IFALPA, does not see this as a major problem. In the United States, it is not uncommon for one airline to perform major maintenance or overhaul for another, for one airline to lease planes to another to handle seasonal traffic, or for pilots of one airline to take over and fly the planes of another to provide through service. Recently, for example, Braniff, a United States company, and Air France have provided for Braniff to fly the Concorde from Washington, D.C., to Dallas-Fort Worth, Texas. Air France pilots fly from Paris to Washington, and Braniff pilots fly from Washington to Texas. When Braniff pilots take over, the contract between the US-ALPA and Braniff governs. The US-ALPA position, and therefore the major influence on the IFALPA, is that this is the key element, not who owns the equipment.

EC Level. At the European Community level, the ITF has also been seeking the cooperation of the IFALPA in forming

---

[8] *ITF Panorama*, Vol. 1, No. 3 (1979), p. 1.

[9] *Ibid.*; and ITF, *Report on Activities*, pp. 139-40.

[10] We shall discuss the OECD guidelines' import for multinational industrial relations in the final chapter.

[11] Captain Taylor, interview, May 15, 1978.

an EC Joint Advisory Committee for Civil Aviation. As with previous efforts, the IFALPA has avoided any joint actions. Instead of working with the ITF, the IFALPA is consulted separately by the EC on questions concerning airline pilots. Because of the EC's regional nature, the IFALPA is hoping in the future to turn over this responsibility to EUROPILOTE, the IFALPA's European regional affiliate. [12]

Future relations between the ITF and the IFALPA will remain informal. As noted earlier, the main activities of the IFALPA are related to technical/safety problems and not to industrial actions, and the IFALPA especially does not desire involvement in industrial actions initiated by other organizations. This professional association posture will continue to keep the two groups separate.

Aircraft "Captives"

When an airline is involved in a labor dispute, attempts have been made through international trade union secretaries to prevent the operation of aircraft of such companies by refusing to fuel or service the aircraft. Hence the planes are "captured." The ITF and at least one other secretariat have been involved in captures.

ICEF in Australia. In September 1977, flight attendants of Trans International Airlines (TIA), a United States charter carrier, struck. They were supported by TIA pilots and flight engineers until December 1977, when the attendants rejected a proposed settlement. Then the pilots returned to work, and TIA resumed operations with nonstriking employees.[13]

The TIA flight attendants were represented by the Teamsters union, which despite its preeminence in the motor trucking industry, is not an affiliate of the ITF but rather of the International Federation of Chemical, Energy and General Workers' Unions (ICEF). The ICEF secretary general sent a letter

---

[12] International Federation of Air Line Pilots' Associations, *Report of the Thirty-First Conference*, Acapulco, Mexico, March 31-April 6, 1976, Appendix G, pp. 2-3.

[13] See Larry Kornhauser, "Two Aust unions get U.S. strikes backlash," *Financial Review* (Australia), January 9, 1978, p. 3, for a complete write-up of this case.

to all affiliates on November 14, 1977, requesting a ban on TIA flights. Apparently unaware that such ICEF circulars generally receive little more than token support, as was made clear in chapters IV-XI, two Australian unions, thinking that Latin American and European unions were already disrupting TIA service, placed a ban on TIA operations. The Australian Transport Workers Union refused to fuel and the Miscellaneous Workers Union refused to clean and otherwise service TIA planes, thus rendering them inoperative.

This "capture" continued for six weeks until TIA both introduced incontrovertible evidence that only in Australia was support being given to the ICEF request, and began proceedings under section 4D of the Australian Trade Practices Act for an injunction lifting the boycott. At about the same time, the TIA flight attendants reversed themselves and accepted the contract that they had earlier rejected. It remains unlikely that an ICEF request will in the future be accepted in such good faith by the two Australian unions as it was in the TIA case.

Malaysian Airlines System. A dispute beginning in December 1978 involving Malaysian Airlines brought the ITF in conflict with the government of that country as well. The strike took on serious dimensions when the government declared it illegal, and the ITF, whose assistant general secretary was visiting Malaysia, called on all affiliates to boycott Malaysian Airlines. He was expelled from the country, and the ITF's resident Asian representative and nineteen airline employees were arrested, thus exacerbating the matter.[14]

As a result of the ITF's efforts, a Malaysian DC-10 was "captured" for nine days in Sydney, Australia, and "rescued" only after the Australian government ordered the Royal Australian Air Force to provide for its return; and another DC-10 was delayed several hours to Frankfurt, Germany, because union adherents blocked its path and distributed leaflets to passengers

---

[14] See the Malaysian Employers Federation, "What Response From ASEAN to International Trade Union Action?" (Prepared for the First Conference and Seminar, ASEAN Confederation of Employers, Manila, May 12-14, 1979); "Malaysian Unionists Arrested," *AFL-CIO Free Trade Union News*, April 1979, p. 1; Barry Winn, "Imprisonment of Unionists, Imposed Salary Settlement Leave MAS Future Clouded," *Asian Wall Street Journal*, April 17, 1979, p. 1; K. Das, "Getting MAS off the ground," *Far Eastern Economic Review*, May 4, 1978, pp. 26-27; and "Concorde threat paid off for MAS DC-10s to London," *ibid.*, August 31, 1979, pp. 45, 48.

protesting against the detentions resulting from the dispute. The protesting unionists maintained their blockade until the Frankfurt Airport police forced them to retire.

ITF—Final Comment

Most air transport companies are government owned. This brings international trade secretariats into direct conflict with governments when they become involved in airline disputes. The ITF is already under severe criticism by Third World countries for its role in the flags-of-convenience issues. "Capturing" aircraft substantially worsens the ITF relationship with such governments. An increase in such incidents could mean continued conflict in the transport industry.

IFALPA ACTIVITIES

Industrial activities of the IFALPA are limited to the terms of mutual assistance pacts between member associations. The IFALPA does not engage in bargaining, but the pacts among affiliates could conceivably give national unions greater economic power in disputes with major airlines by providing a financial cushion, or even additional overt support. In line with its understanding of international differences, the IFALPA urges that mutual assistance agreements be arranged on a bilateral or multilateral basis among member associations. Regional solidarity funds are also encouraged, as well as accommodation, transport, and finances for stranded pilots in the event of a strike.[15] The IFALPA does not itself request assistance from its affiliates in behalf of another affiliate. It will, however, provide information on industrial matters by transmitting information directly from one affiliate to others.

The Manual

For the purpose of assisting member associations in developing these agreements, an "Industrial (I) Manual" has been formulated by the IFALPA.

It is "intended to cover all arrangements between operators in which the services of pilots from a member association are used in such a way as to threaten the job security, conditions

---

[15] International Federation of Air Line Pilots' Associations, *Introducing International Federation of Air Line Pilots' Associations*, 7th ed. (London, 1977), p. 18.

of service, or safety standards of pilots of another Member Association." [16]

The agreements must be consistent with national and international law while offering help and cooperation to member associations in industrial disputes or if they are subject to intimidation or repression. Various suggested forms of assistance follow:

1. assistance to pilots on strike stranded from home base;
2. requests for recruitment ban (do not replace strikers);
3. nonextension of route mileage and/or carrying capacity in event of a strike;
4. prevent victimization for implementing IFALPA policy;
5. do not advocate sympathy strikes, however, do not take advantage of strikes; and
6. make loans if needed (IFALPA has no strike fund so does not give money to pilots directly).[17]

It has been noted by the IFALPA, however, that implementation of these agreements has been sporadic,[18] which may indicate an unwillingness on the part of some of the larger member associations to participate. Most strike support issues eventually boil down to questions of safety (e.g., the three-man crew discussed below). Clearly, if there is a strike at a particular airport, activities may be significantly disrupted and become hazardous. Also, in order to support a strike effort, it would have to be occurring at an airport which that member association used. If safety problems are not the initial cause of an affiliate's strike, they usually will arise and are then used to justify strike support from other groups.

Implementation Examples and Issues

The following discussion provides some recent examples of these policies in action and the IFALPA's effectiveness in supporting member associations.

---

[16] International Federation of Air Line Pilots' Associations, "Industrial (I) Manual" (London, 1977), p. 5.

[17] *Ibid.*, pp. 2-3; International Federation of Air Line Pilots' Associations, "Administrative (A) Manual" (London, 1977), pp. 3-4. The "Administrative (A) Manual" contains IFALPA key documents.

[18] International Federation of Air Line Pilots' Associations, *Report of the Thirty-Second Conference*, Brighton, England, March 17-22, 1977, p. 1.

French Air Traffic Controllers (1973). In one of the earlier attempts to establish the IFALPA's role during industrial disputes, member associations were requested to refuse to fly over France during a strike of the French Air Traffic Controllers (SNOMAC) that began on February 20, 1973.[19] Mutual aid was requested from the French pilots' group—Syndicat National des Pilotes de Ligne (SNPL). In an attempt to break the strike, the French government brought in military air traffic controllers, who were unfamiliar with the International Civil Aviation Organization's standards. Following a mid-air collision over France and several near misses, the IFALPA felt that the substitution of personnel created safety hazards and requested a ban on flying over or into French airspace by IFALPA members.

Many pilots' associations respected the ban; several others did not. As a result, air traffic continued to flow into and out of French airports. By the 1973 IFALPA conference in March, some member associations had become annoyed because the sacrifices made by their members and their countries' airlines had not been sustained by others.

Canadian Air Traffic Controllers (1976). Later reactions by the IFALPA member associations to industrial actions were not always extensive either. On June 19, 1976, the Canadian Air Line Pilots' Association (CALPA) ceased operations when the air traffic controllers went on strike. Canada was proposing a law that would make it possible to use both English and French in radio broadcasts. Verbal support of the CALPA action was sent by the IFALPA to Canadian government officials. Nothing more could be offered, however, because "the urgency of the situation and the after-normal-working hours time-frame had precluded any rapid IFALPA or Member Associations response."[20]

Bilingualism represents a very serious safety concern to airline pilots. This is why one language, English, is standard at all airports, and this was the issue in the CALPA action. In Quebec, controllers would, for example, speak English to Americans and French to other airline pilots. When a pilot can understand the instructions given to other pilots, he can correct for dangerous situations. An important example would be a con-

---

[19] International Federation of Air Line Pilots' Associations, *Report of the Twenty-Eighth Conference*, Tokyo, Japan, March 14-21, 1973, Vol. 1, Attachment 4 to Appendix A, p. 1.

[20] IFALPA, *Report of the Thirty-Second Conference*, p. P-5.

troller's error giving the same airspace to two different planes. The use of one language assures that pilots are aware of what other pilots are being instructed to do and that they can, therefore, make alterations necessary for safety. This action was fairly well supported by the US-ALPA because it felt that a genuine safety issue was involved.[21] All United States airline pilots, except those of Delta Airlines, refused to fly into Quebec. US-ALPA rules give final authority to the airline system chapters on such matters.

This support was unlike that available to the Mexican air traffic controllers (discussed below) who, in 1978, had two strikes in three months.[22] As noted below, the US-ALPA felt that the airways were unsafe during the first walkout, but all system chapters decided to fly anyway.

Asociación Nacional de Pilotos de Venezuela (1976). A strike against the government by the Venezuelan pilots' association over the safety of Venezuelan airports was called in 1976. Consequently, eight board members of the pilots' association were dismissed by their companies, Avensa and Aeropostal, while several other pilots were arrested.[23] The government also threatened to replace civilian pilots with military personnel. IFALPA officials aided the pilots by making direct contact with Venezuelan government officials, including President Pérez.

The dispute was quite lengthy, and conversations between the IFALPA and the Venezuelan government continued into 1978. Although safety conditions had improved, the Venezuelan pilots had not yet been reinstated at the time of the IFALPA's 1978 conference. Because the argument was with the Venezuelan government, many members of the IFALPA chose to remain neutral.

Associazione Nazionale Pilote Aviazione Commerciale (ANPAC) (1976). An example of indirect pressures on governments occurred during the 1976 strike of the ANPAC for recognition as the representative of Italian airline pilots. Another pilots' group, the FULAT, affiliated to the Communist-controlled Confederazione Generale Italiana del Lavoro, wanted to take over the ANPAC.[24] Political pressure was applied against the

---

[21] Captain Ashwood, interview in Washington, D.C., December 28, 1978.

[22] *Ibid.*

[23] IFALPA, *Report of the Thirty-Second Conference*, p. P-7.

[24] Captain Ashwood, interview, December 28, 1978.

ANPAC, whose right to bargain collectively, as well as its professional standing (by disallowing technical and safety input), was threatened by the FULAT. Support for the ANPAC was offered at the IFALPA's 1976 conference. The federation and EUROPILOTE directly approached the European Commission and the International Labour Office, as well as the appropriate ministries in Italy. The IFALPA's member associations concentrated their efforts on influencing the Italian government in order to keep the pilots' group nonpolitical.

The outcome was favorable to the ANPAC, which claimed that the IFALPA was directly responsible for its success. Although it did not use any financial aid, several offers of assistance were said to have "constituted a very much appreciated, useful and welcome safety margin." [25]

Hellenic Air Line Pilots' Association (1977). When members of the Greek pilots' association involved themselves in an industrial dispute with Olympic Airways, several members of HALPA were dismissed, which prompted the group to strike on March 22, 1977.[26] The HALPA requested mutual assistance from IFALPA members, stating that safety issues were involved, although this was questionable. The IFALPA conference recommended a ban on all operations into Greek airports to demonstrate support. The IFALPA communicated this support directly to the government of Greece and the state-owned Olympic Airways, but its effectiveness was uncertain.

Kenyan Pilots' Association (1977). As with many African pilot groups, the Kenyan Pilots' Association (KPA) has struggled for recognition and survival amidst the relatively unstable and deteriorating economic environment in its country. On February 14, 1977, the East African Airways Corporation (involving the countries of Kenya, Uganda, and Tanzania) went out of business and left many airline pilots unemployed. Approximately two hundred expatriate pilots were involved and were only allowed to take £2,500 with them if they decided to leave Kenya.[27] Following these activities, the Kenyan government formed Kenya Airways Ltd., which refused to hire any KPA members.

---

[25] IFALPA, *Report of the Thirty-Second Conference*, Appendix J, p. 1.

[26] *Ibid.*, pp. A-2, P-7.

[27] *Ibid.*, p. P-8.

Because a recruitment ban would not solve their members' unemployment problem, the KPA felt that it should not be requested. Instead, in order to counter this move by the Kenyan government, it asked all IFALPA members to go through its organization before accepting or attempting to obtain any job with the new airline.

Syndicat National des Pilotes de Ligne (1978). Members of the SNPL vehemently opposed the proposal by Air France to operate with cockpit crews of two instead of three persons in its contemplated new plane, the Boeing 737. The press heatedly attacked the SNPL for putting undue economic pressure on Air France. As a compromise, the SNPL offered to fly three-man crews in the 737s for the same wage rate as a two-man crew. The new planes, however, were designed for only two men, and Air France could not agree.[28]

This problem is part of a broader technological conflict between the IFALPA and various airlines, as well as the United States Federal Aviation Administration (FAA). In the United States, some 737s fly with two-man crews and some with three-man crews. The US-ALPA's official policy does not approve the two-man crews, and the association has strongly pushed the three-man concept. While IFALPA policy claims that a decrease in crew size impairs safety, the FAA and others assert that the increased workload has no impact on crew performance.[29] Although the FAA has found that two-man crews are safe, the US-ALPA strongly contests the basis for this finding.

At the 1978 IFALPA conference, the SNPL stated that it would be the first to oppose this movement to decrease crew sizes and asked for support of other IFALPA members associations. Both the IFALPA and EUROPILOTE have come out strongly against the two-man crew. As a direct result of the SNPL's action, Air France announced that its impending lease agreement for the Boeing 737s was cancelled.

Mexican Air Traffic Controllers (1978). In Mexico, the air traffic controllers struck twice in three months. The first strike lasted only thirty minutes on July 31, 1978, and the second strike, which began on September 16, continued only for two or three days. Although the US-ALPA reviewed contingency plans of various American airlines that flew into Mexico City and other

---

[28] Captain Ashwood, interview, December 28, 1978.

[29] "Editorial," *IFALPA Monthly News Bulletin*, No. 79 (February 1978), p. 1.

ports during the first strike and found them to be inadequate, local chapters of the US-ALPA decided to fly into Mexico anyway. Because the Mexicans were not flying, the air was less crowded and probably fairly safe. During the second strike, the US-ALPA advised its chapters that conditions were safe for flying. This incident illustrates the effect that the US-ALPA's policy of deferring decisions to local chapters can have on requests for strike support. In spite of the fact that the US-ALPA had determined that the airspace around Mexico was unsafe during the controllers' strike, the chapters flew anyway, according to their own judgment.

Trinidad and Tobago Air Line Pilots' Association (1978). Approximately 130 pilots, members of the TALPA, struck the British West Indies Airlines (BWIA) in January 1978. The IFALPA called for an investigation of this strike to understand why management and government decisions had escalated the problem into a major dispute. What began as a "fight to provide even-handed justice for an individual pilot" changed "to a fierce battle to preserve the jobs of all the pilots and the continued existence of the Pilots' Association." [30] The object was "to force the management to reinstate a senior Boeing 707 pilot with an 18,000-hour flying record spanning twenty-five years whom the company had grounded because it said that it had lost confidence in him." [31]

Aid was offered to the TALPA in the form of financial support from the IFALPA member associations and a recruitment ban on the British West Indies. In addition, the IFALPA continued to push for the nonextension of route mileage and carrying capacity. Neither Eastern nor Pan American Airlines put on any new flights, but whether this was a direct result of IFALPA pressures or because they did not want to is unknown.

After the three-and-one-half-month-long strike was ended, some serious setbacks had occurred. First, while the TALPA was on strike, BWIA took the time to review its entire future policy on civil aviation. The result was a merger between BWIA and the Trinidad and Tobago Air Services (TTAS) to form the Trinidad and Tobago Airways. Incidentally, the strike was not supported by the TALPA's TTAS counterparts.[32]

---

[30] *Ibid.*

[31] David Renwick, "Airline Merger Provides a Fresh Start for Trinidad," *Financial Times*, November 27, 1978, p. 32.

[32] *Ibid.*

The TALPA pilots' morale was further dashed when they "eventually went back to work, but were forced to accept conditions in many cases markedly inferior to the ones they enjoyed prior to the walkout." [33] Adding insult to injury, "the Trinidad and Tobago government has amended the law governing labor relations to make civil aviation an essential service which means that the withholding of labor by pilots or others employed in such an industry is now forbidden." [34]

The IFALPA was obviously not successful in supporting the efforts of its members in Trinidad and Tobago. The outcome illustrates some of the practical difficulties that the IFALPA will face if it attempts to involve itself in its affiliates' disputes.

Summary. The IFALPA policy is based upon the premise that so much disparity exists among various economies and societies that any attempts to interfere or to bargain beyond the national level are infeasible.[35] Thus, it tries to play a less direct role when industrial disputes arise. The federation's main activity involves the presentation of pilots' views to governmental officials, the press, and international organizations. Because its conferences are held annually, the IFALPA offers opportunities for coordination of the policies of member associations in an effort to enhance their effectiveness, as evidenced by the preceding examples.

A fundamental reason why the IFALPA is reluctant to become closely involved with affiliates' labor disputes is that the employer of pilots outside of the United States is almost always a government. Unless a clear safety issue is involved, the IFALPA would, in effect, be requesting pilots of one country to pressure the government of another. Overt action in such a situation is difficult to justify and can rarely achieve its purpose. Quiet diplomacy, usually through a country's diplomatic service, is both far more acceptable and more likely to achieve results.

The 1979 Conference Debate

At its annual conference in 1979, an effort was made to strengthen the IFALPA's power in industrial disputes and to permit the IFALPA to call for a general pilot stoppage. The Italian, Spanish, and especially Dutch pilots' associations were

---

[33] *Ibid.*

[34] *Ibid.*

[35] Captain Ashwood, interview, December 1, 1977.

in the forefront of this move. Thus, the president of the Dutch pilots' association stated that the IFALPA members "have shown a deplorable lack of unity" when they were "called upon to stand together for the sake of aviation safety in the context of mutual assistance." He declared also that besides safety, there are "other valid grounds for mutual assistance." [36]

This view was rejected by the majority of pilots' associations led by the US-ALPA, whose delegate declared that there was

> the feeling of a substantial majority . . . that the Federation [IFALPA] . . . should not have the authority to call for a ban on operations. The United States [US-ALPA] had made it clear that they could not and would not accept such an arrangement; their own Executive did not have this authority. During recent . . . situations there have been different interpretations as to whether conditions were safe or unsafe. The Federation [IFALPA] was being used by other organizations to pursue their industrial objectives, through closure of airspace. The Federation should not have that authority or responsibility.[37]

In its review of the 1979 conference, the *IFALPA Monthly News Bulletin* commented upon the split in the federation as follows:

> The technical papers placed before the conference were well received and were almost all accepted with the recommended policy status. There was a different fate in store for the papers . . . dealing with the possible curtailment of operations . . . the debate, voting and ratification procedures revealed a division between those Member Associations which seek to have the Federation present a strong and unified response to those problems which may be amenable to being solved by means of a curtailment of operations, and those other Member Associations which believe that the strengths, weaknesses, social and political circumstance of the Member Associations differ too widely to enable a single concerted and disciplined response to be made when such problems confront the Federation.[38]

Viewing the split as one "which defines a future challenge for the Federation and its Member Associations," the *IFALPA Monthly News Bulletin* emphasized that policies must be developed in this area "which command a wider support than any yet discussed," and promised that its committees and officers "will be making renewed efforts over the current year." [39]

---

[36] International Federation of Air Line Pilots' Associations, *Report of the Thirty-Fourth Conference*, Amsterdam, the Netherlands, March 15-20, 1979, pp. O8-O9.

[37] *Ibid.*, p. A-5.

[38] *IFALPA Monthly News Bulletin*, No. 92 (March/April 1979), p. 1.

[39] *Ibid.*, p. 2.

US-ALPA Role

In any determination of IFALPA policies pertaining to mutual assistance or concerted action, the US-ALPA has a special role. By far the largest IFALPA affiliate, it would be called upon to intervene in most disputes if the IFALPA were operated like the typical international trade union secretariat. The US-ALPA does not believe that it is either appropriate or wise to attempt to utilize power against foreign governments. Moreover, it supports the concept of the IFALPA as a professional organization devoted to promoting pilot welfare primarily through improved air safety. Therefore, it does not envisage the IFALPA as having a very active role in industrial disputes.

On the other hand, the US-ALPA constantly stands ready to improve the bargaining abilities of its fellow IFALPA affiliates by technical assistance. Thus, the US-ALPA maintains without charge a computer bank of wages, working conditions, and contract terms to which twenty-four IFALPA affiliates have subscribed as of January 1979.[40] It provides advice and assistance in a variety of ways when requested by smaller associations. For its benefit, the US-ALPA can use the IFALPA's influence on the International Civil Aviation Organization to increase pressure on the Federal Aviation Administration on issues in which the administration's position is not in accord with that of the US-ALPA. It thus benefits from the support given the IFALPA.[41]

The US-ALPA is extremely wary, however, of requests for boycotts or overt pressures of any kind unless, in the opinion of its governing body, safety is the basic issue. Even then, as already noted, the airline system pilots' chapter involved makes the final determination whether any action is warranted. Given the US-ALPA's size and role, the IFALPA is likely to remain primarily a professional body and only secondly to operate as an international union coordinating group in labor relations matters. Therefore, future overt action in airline disputes across national boundaries is much more likely to involve the ITF without the IFALPA.

---

[40] "IFALPA Computer Survey," *IFALPA Monthly News Bulletin*, No. 90 (January 1979), pp. 4-5.

[41] Captain Ashwood, interview, December 1, 1977.

PART SEVEN

Summary and Conclusion

CHAPTER XIX

The Prospects for Multinational Bargaining

This book has investigated virtually every claim that multinational bargaining has occurred or that international trade union secretariats, regional unions, or coalitions of national unions have banded together to deal with, coerce, or influence company behavior or action across national boundaries. We have found several cases of information exchange between multinational corporations and multinational union groups and a very few instances of regular multinational union-management consultation. We have also found that one secretariat—the International Transport Workers' Federation (ITF)—makes agreements directly with shipping companies and associations, even usurping at times the role of national unions.[1]

Even in North America, where the different local branches of the same union typically represent workers both in the United States and Canada, bargaining is rarely international, even when the same company is involved. The only multinational bargaining arrangements that we have uncovered in our worldwide research are found in the European recording, radio, and television industries. Two little-known international federations—the International Federation of Musicians (FIM) and the International Federation of Actors (FIA)—have had for many years agreements with the European Broadcasting Union, an organization of radio and television companies, nearly all government owned, which provides for higher rebroadcasting fees for performers than those established by an international agreement known as the Rome Convention. For an even longer period, the FIM has had an agreement with the International Federation of the Phonograph Industry governing the use of records in broadcasting. In 1969, the FIA and the FIM also signed an agreement relating to television broadcasts with the International Radio and Television Organization, but this arrangement has not been

---

[1] See chapter XVII.

effectuated. Although these agreements are not technically binding on the national organizations of the parties, the first two have generally been accepted and are the closest approximation to multinational bargaining that we have uncovered in our long search.[2]

These findings are, of course, in direct contrast to the many claims of some of the international unions, particularly the International Federation of Chemical, Energy and General Workers' Unions (ICEF),[3] which has made the most elaborate claims in this regard.[4] Examining the documentary evidence, however, demonstrates beyond a shadow of a doubt that these claims are, at best, figments of a fertile imagination bulwarked by an extraordinary publicity sense and, at worst, downright fabrications. The press has spread these imaginative, and mostly wholly untrue, speculations apparently because they are interesting and sensational; and the academics too often have given them further credence without any effort at verification.[5]

In this concluding chapter, we first examine in greater detail the reasons set forth in chapter II why multinational bargaining has not occurred and then look at national, regional, and international union policies and those of national governments and intergovernmental organizations, which can contribute to making multinational bargaining a reality. We also point out certain corporate policies that could have the same result.

THE OBSTACLES TO MULTINATIONAL BARGAINING

The reasons why multinational bargaining has not developed are quite clear once the institutional settings involved and the basic needs of the social partners are examined. These reasons

---

[2] See chapter XVI.

[3] See chapters VI-XI.

[4] Many of these claims are, of course, found in Charles Levinson, *International Trade Unionism*, Ruskin House Series in Trade Union Studies (London: George Allen & Unwin Ltd., 1972). There is virtually no documentation in this book.

[5] For examples of academic articles that repeat unsupported claims, see J. A. Litvak and B. J. Maule, "Unions and International Corporations," *Industrial Relations*, Vol. 9 (February 1972), pp. 62-71; and Lloyd Ulman, "Multinational Unionism: Incentives, Barriers and Alternatives," *Industrial Relations*, Vol. 14 (February 1975), pp. 1-31. This journal's editors three times rejected articles that would counterbalance these less well-researched ones.

can be summarized under four headings: varying law and practice, management opposition, union reluctance, and lack of employee interest.

Varying Law and Practice

Most commentators on multinational industrial relations tend to see other countries as mirroring the law and practice of their own. Actually, this is very misleading. Even such small neighboring countries as Belgium, the Netherlands, and Luxembourg have strikingly different laws and practices. Countries have different methods and requirements for determining union representation, and different union jurisdictions and structure. Representation by works councils or stewards' organizations, as well as by unions, exists in some countries in different forms but is totally absent in others. Employer associations have varying roles, country by country, and the scope of bargaining is equally varied.

The United States system of majority union rule and exclusive bargaining rights is absent from virtually all other countries except Canada. Much more common is a situation in which union representation is split on ideological or religious lines. Companies in most countries must deal with a union regardless of whether it represents a majority, or even a sizable minority, and regardless of whether other unions also represent employees in the same bargaining unit.

Representation in Europe is also split between unions and works councils. There are no local unions. The works councils, which are independent of unions, have varying authority from country to country but generally are the key local institutions for settling local matters. In some countries, Germany and the Netherlands, for example, works councils have a virtual veto power over management's right to increase hours, to schedule overtime, and to add work shifts, or to reduce hours or employment, to name just a few issues. In Great Britain and Australia, local stewards play a somewhat similar role. Whether works councils or stewards are involved, agreements made by unions are either not compellingly binding or cannot cover areas where the councils or stewards have jurisdiction.

In Japan, unions are organized on an enterprise basis and include virtually all employees, blue-collar, clerical, and managerial, in the enterprise. National organizations are relatively weak confederations, with power residing in the enterprise organizations.

The situation in underdeveloped countries varies considerably, with unions usually closely aligned with the ruling political parties, but in Latin America, many splits along ideological lines exist. The extent and power of unionism in these countries is widely dependent upon legal and political support mechanisms.

Bargaining structure also varies tremendously. In Britain, it is so fragmented that any deals in some companies are subject to almost immediate modification or repudiation by another group in the same establishment. In Australia, compulsory arbitration prevails, but unions can, and do, use the weapons of conflict to push for greater benefits regardless of what the law provides. In some countries of Europe, conditions are set nationally or regionally. In Germany, which comes closest to our exclusive jurisdiction system, bargaining is on a regional basis and covers large groupings; all metals and electricals, for example, in one group bargain with Industriegewerkschaft Metall (IG Metall). The situation varies in other countries, but employers' associations are very much more likely to represent groupings of companies or industries than is the case in the United States. Thus, a bargaining unit for multinational bargaining purposes would be most difficult to establish.

Finally, it should be emphasized that law, rather than bargaining, sets the terms and conditions to a much greater extent in most countries than in the United States. Moreover, many countries limit managerial authority either directly or indirectly by requiring union and/or works council approval of such moves as decreasing employment, shortening hours, reducing shifts, moving facilities, or even altering the product mix. In fact, the scope of bargaining varies considerably from one country to another. Thus, there is considerable variation not only in who the representatives of employees and employers in a multinational bargaining arrangement would be, and what their authority would be, but also in what the scope of the bargaining would be and how the bargaining arrangements would comport with the national law.

Such fundamental variations in law and practice apply to comparisons not only between the United States and other free world countries but even among neighboring nations. Within the European Community, for example, there has been little or no harmonization of basic labor relations law. Most discussions of multinational bargaining tend to ignore such fundamental institutional problems and the difficulties that they place in the path of attempts to bargain across national boundaries.

Management Opposition

Virtually all managements are firmly opposed to multinational bargaining. Most businessmen see multinational bargaining as creating the potential for a complicating factor that would add a third level of risk to work stoppages, not only with no compensatory relief but with considerable additional cost as well. This is difficult to refute.

The varied and complex arrangements which would be required to establish collective bargaining on a multinational basis would seem to demand a three-level structure. This would involve multinational discussions followed by national ones and, in turn, by local bargaining. Companies, as well as unions, would have difficulty in assigning responsibilities and priorities for the three levels. If, however, that were accomplished, the company would face a strike risk at each level of bargaining. Moreover, it is not unlikely that the results of bargaining would be more costly, because each bargaining level would have constituents to satisfy.

The experience under the bargaining system in America appears to add credence to the argument against widening of bargaining coverage. General Motors, Ford, and Chrysler each bargain on a national basis for overall economic and policy issues; they then bargain with local unions on a multitude of local issues involving plant rules, seniority, etc. Initially, national settlements meant a virtual guarantee against local stoppages. More and more, however, regardless of national settlements, strikes have occurred over local issues, sometimes with far-reaching effects on total company production, as local union officials attempt to gain for their members what is important locally, insignificant nationally, but costly, or potentially so, to the corporations.

It is not far-fetched to envision multinational bargaining followed by a few years of labor peace and then a gradual breakdown, as local and national interests, tired of having their desires and aspirations "swept under the rug" by multinational negotiators who see only the large view, institute an increasing number of strikes to satisfy their constituents. It is this vision, combined with a fear of loss of flexibility and decline of bargaining power, that causes nearly all managements to avoid any relationships that might lead to multinational bargaining.

A fundamental weakness of coordinated or coalition bargaining, whether national or international, is its tendency to force wages and conditions on an industry that cannot be borne.[6] Today, most major companies operate in several rather than only one industry. Within one company, some of the products made are often capital intensive, others labor intensive. The wider the bargaining unit, the less it suits the needs of diversity and the more likely that it will result in costs to a segment that cannot bear them. Multinational bargaining by its very nature seems too broad to meet the needs of a varied product mix.

Who would represent management in a multinational collective bargaining arrangement also poses serious problems. As already noted, the practice in many European countries is to have negotiations carried out by staff of employers' associations. Yet their presence would indicate a coverage at the bargaining table far beyond that of a multinational company that might be involved. Moreover, the limits of responsibilities given to an association executive under such circumstances could be difficult to determine. This may be why, except for a single meeting between the European Metalworkers' Federation (EMF) and the Western European Metal Trades Employers' Organization,[7] our research found employer association involvement in multinational union-management activities only in the graphical,[8] entertainment, radio, and television,[9] and shipping industries.[10]

Employee relations policies of multinational corporations appear to be left to the discretion of national and local firm managers to a surprising degree. In our research on multinational industrial relations, we have repeatedly discovered that the central personnel department of a large company has little up-to-date information on developments in foreign-based subsidiaries and no policy regarding multinational union contacts. Moreover, operating personnel have often been found to be

---

[6] See William N. Chernish, *Coalition Bargaining*, Industrial Research Unit Major Study, No. 45 (Philadelphia: Industrial Research Unit, The Wharton School, University of Pennsylvania, 1969).

[7] See chapter IV.

[8] See chapter XI.

[9] See chapter XVI.

[10] See chapter XVII.

making decisions in industrial and union relations matters without consultation with knowledgeable specialists within their own companies.

A case in point is how Rothmans International became involved in meetings with the International Union of Food and Allied Workers' Associations (IUF). The initial company decision to meet with the IUF was made by a since deposed managing director, and the initial meeting was carried out by him and two aides without the benefit of staff expertise or advice. A reorganization of the company then brought more specialized personnel into the consultations, but the original format of the meetings was determined without their assistance.[11] In such a situation, the company is on the defensive if it attempts to rearrange meeting priorities or policy to conform with what industrial relations expertise deems appropriate.

Continental Can's European managing director met with the head of the EMF on an annual basis for a number of years. The company purposely excluded the personnel experts in order to impress upon the union side that industrial relations matters were not to be a concern of the meetings. For the same reasons, representatives of national unions were excluded from these meetings. Here, however, the company was applying a deliberate policy and not just permitting things to happen as they may and possibly blunder into a situation it would come to regret.[12]

A number of other companies have had consultative—not bargaining—meetings with multinational union groups of various kinds. Unaccountably, most have agreed to such meetings without a prearranged agenda. Unless one knows the subjects for discussion in advance, it is difficult to have the right staff present and to be prepared with information and answers. Again, this illustrates the unstructured approach to multinational industrial relations adopted by many corporations. Conversely, those corporations that have thought out the problem and have still decided to meet on a multinational basis with union representatives usually have insisted on an agreed upon agenda and have staff members present who are knowledgeable about the matters to be discussed. This includes key personnel from affected subsidiaries. The meeting chairman is often a top company official who may be the corporation's chief personnel officer. If the

---

[11] See chapter XIII.

[12] See chapter IV.

latter is not the chairman, he is usually a major, or chief, spokesman for the company.

Finally, businessmen fear dealing on a multinational basis because they seriously doubt that unions can develop workable mechanisms for decision making on an international basis. They see a situation where each member union of the multinational union coalition can veto any agreement, but no one can commit the whole group.

Union Reluctance

At a meeting in Davos, Switzerland, key United States, British, and German labor officials emphasized their lack of enthusiasm for multinational bargaining.[13] The reasons for this viewpoint are many. Not the least important is the question of who will represent and/or coordinate an international union group.

Many observers have assumed that the international trade secretariats would be the natural representative, or at least coordinator, of the union side in multinational bargaining arrangements.[14] Yet, although the secretariats have served as a forum for the exchange of information among national unions, they have not managed to extend their activities to the coordination of collective bargaining. Even the International Metalworkers' Federation (IMF), the strongest secretariat in financial support, leadership, and staff, has had little success in the few times that it has attempted to inject itself into collective bargaining establishments.[15] The claims of the ICEF that it has successfully coordinated bargaining efforts of its affiliates across national boundaries cannot be supported by the evidence.[16] Other secretariats, which, like the ICEF, have limited income and

---

[13] Those announcing their opposition to multinational bargaining were Jack Jones, emeritus general secretary of the British Transport and General Workers' Union; Lane Kirkland, secretary-treasurer of the AFL-CIO; and Heinz Oskar Vetter, president of the Deutsche Gewerkschaftsbund. See "Business Forum in Europe Hears Labor News it Likes," *Wall Street Journal*, January 31, 1978, p. 2.

[14] For example, see the excellent article of Professor B. C. Roberts, "Multinational Collective Bargaining, A European Prospect?" *British Journal of Industrial Relations*, Vol. IX (March 1973), pp. 6-11.

[15] See chapters III-V.

[16] See chapters VI-XI.

staffs, are less likely than the IMF to transform information exchange into collective bargaining.[17]

The secretariats' worldwide interests and affiliations also militate against their potential for bargaining coordination. If multinational bargaining is ever to occur, it would seem to require that the national unions involved have a reasonable community of interest. To involve unions from all over the world, including those both from developed and underdeveloped countries, is more likely to preclude bargaining than to further it. Even combining European and American unions adds to the many complications that already exist within such diverse groupings. When the IUF included American and Canadian unionists in its second meeting with Rothmans International, the company, having contemplated a European meeting only, was concerned about how wide such information exchange should extend and what its implications would be.

European regional union organizations, grouped into committees of the European Trade Union Confederation (ETUC), appear better placed to move toward multinational bargaining. This is an avowed goal of the European Metalworkers' Federation, the most active of the ETUC committees. Unaffiliated with the secretariats and more unitary in outlook, the EMF and other ETUC committees have met with a number of multinational companies for information exchange and consultation (not bargaining). But even in these more homogeneous situations, disputes have arisen as to the function of these European regional committees vis-à-vis national unions, or works councils, or even their role relative to the secretariats.

Thus, in the case of Philips, the pressure on the EMF to include the IMF in the meetings, undoubtedly emanating from the largest affiliate of both, IG Metall, whose president, Eugen Loderer, is also president of the IMF and vice-president of the EMF, caused the EMF to forgo the opportunity to resume meetings with the company.[18] And in the VFW-Fokker situation, the Dutch and German works councils were obviously quite willing to assist the company in easing the EMF out of the picture.[19]

---

[17] See, for example, the discussion in chapters XII and XIII relating to the activities of the IUF.

[18] See **chapter V.**

[19] See **chapter IV.**

The ideological and religious split among unions also complicates the representation issue, especially for the secretariats. The IMF, for example, will not accept affiliation of the Communist unions, which are the major bloc in France and Italy, and which, as also do the dwindling Christian unions, have their own, if limited, secretariats. Multinational companies operating in France and Italy, where the largest segment of their employees is likely to be represented by an affiliate of the Communist federation, or with plants in the Low Countries, where the Christian group is strong, would be eliminating major segments of their employees from representation if they recognized a secretariat as a bargaining partner.

The ETUC and its committees, including the EMF, have affiliated the Christian unions and the Italian Communist federation but not the French one. They thus have more, if not complete, representation in the European Community.

Even where completely representative through pertinent affiliated unions, however, the presence of an official from a secretariat or regional union organization, especially in a coordinating role, can bring complicating factors. If bargaining becomes multinational, there would have to be a power transfer from the national unions to the international bargaining authority and, therefore, from some officials to others. Obviously, this is a reason for national union officials to pause before advocating multinational union action. From the individual union official's point of view, such transfer of power could reduce his importance in the eyes of his constituents and therefore reduce his opportunities for maintaining his position against intraunion challenges.

Moreover, the internationalization of union officials is affected by the business cycle, and in times of economic adversity, such internationalism diminishes substantially. Demands for tariffs, import quotas, and the exclusive utilization of domestic products are frequent union policies when unemployment rises and are incompatible with multinational bargaining. If a secretariat or regional union official is the spokesman for a multinational union bargaining group and advocates a position that the rank and file of a national union find contrary to theirs, the political repercussions will rebound to the officials of that national union. Such officials thus have very practical reasons for being wary of multinational bargaining.

Union coalitions across national boundaries are certain to be difficult to manage and to make viable if they occur. One can envisage that decision making within such a coalition would be very difficult, as already noted, because each national union would want to reserve the right to veto any agreement that it found undesirable for its members. At the same time, however, these same national unions would be extremely reluctant to cede authority for agreement to any official, or even to a majority.

If, for example, a company proposal were likely to cause unemployment in one area but increase employment in another, it is difficult to see how the national union representative from the former area could agree; but by opposing it, he would stand in the way of progress for other members of the coalition. The problems of sustaining a multinational union bargaining group are as difficult as those involved in forming it.

Commentators have held that, if unemployment and plant layoffs were key issues, then unions would come together for multinational bargaining.[20] This, too, remains to be demonstrated. Our detailed discussion of the Akzo experience certainly gives no support to this theory. As soon as pressures mounted, or a national solution surfaced, each national union group went its own way, and the union coalition quickly disintegrated.[21]

When BSN-Gervais Danone, the French glass, food, and beverage firm, closed a plant in Belgium and reduced employment in French plants in 1975, French and Belgian unionists agitated together in both countries. When the time came for negotiations, however, there was no multinational involvement.

BSN is the only multinational manufacturing concern that has had a regular multinational consultative arrangement based upon a written accord. The company met biannually with a multinational committee of Belgian, Dutch, French, German, and Austrian unionists. The meetings are purely consultative and involve information exchange, not bargaining. No secretariat or regional union official is involved. The secretary general of the ICEF participated in a formative meeting of the group, but he issued a press release following this meeting that exaggerated his role and the significance of the meeting. The company has since barred him from the meetings.

---

20 See, e.g., Roberts, "Multinational Collective Bargaining," especially p. 10.

21 See chapter VII.

Although the BSN consultative arrangement could well have developed into bargaining, it did not do so. The reluctance of national union officials to cede authority to other representative groups is one reason why it failed to move in this direction. Union rivalry is another. Three smaller unions in France were parties to the BSN agreement, but the two largest declined to participate.[22] With BSN selling most of its flat glass facilities to Pilkington in 1980, the arrangement will cease or be altered.

The significant fact about the BSN consultative arrangement, however, is that it remained in effect for so long a period. It may well be that the absence of outside international or regional union officials contributed materially to this longevity. A coalition of national union figures in an essentially non-decision-making setting involves no loss or transfer of power for the unionists and provides them with some additional prestige and/or stature. Rivalries are thus diminished, and the need to go beyond consultation is blunted by the fear that this would intrude into national power centers. It may well be that such coalitions are a more likely union structure for possible future multinational consultation or even perhaps bargaining than are those led by international or regional union officials.

Lack of Employee Interest

It seems very clear that employee interest in multinational union action is probably close to being nonexistent. The idea that workers of one country will enthusiastically, or even reluctantly, support the cause of their brothers and sisters in another country is a figment of the intelligentsia imagination that persists over the years without either occurring to or permeating the thoughts of those who are expected to lose pay to make it come true. A union official who attempts to commit his members to such sympathetic acts is courting political disaster. Indeed, in the few cases in which action in one country was affected by strikes or overt action in another, that action has usually been effectuated by radical or other so-called activist groups. Such was the situation in which the printing of the *Times* of London was prevented.[23]

Consider the efforts of the IUF to embarrass Unilever by a campaign alleging, quite falsely, that this corporation was mis-

---

[22] See chapter VI.

[23] See chapter XI.

treating black employees in South Africa and refusing to recognize their unions. For almost one year, the IUF directed a strident propaganda campaign, financed largely by Swedish unions and assisted particularly by Scandinavian and Dutch unions. The climax was to come during the week of October labeled an "action week" by the IUF. The net result was numerous communications directed to Unilever management, which spent much costly time answering and correcting the factual errors in the communications that were based upon IUF misstatements; two-hour stoppages in two Swedish plants in which salaried workers took no part; similar strikes at one plant in Denmark and another in Finland; a slowdown in a second Finnish plant; and a fifteen-minute work stoppage in a third. The labor movements of Belgium, France, Germany, the United Kingdom, the United States, and many other countries let the "action week" pass without overt action, and little or no notice even occurred in the national or, in some countries, union press.[24]

We have also noted how the rubber workers in Canada and the United States, members of the same union, supplied each other's markets during the Canadian strike of 1974 and the United States one of 1976; and how, during the latter strike, tires were imported in huge quantities into the United States not only from Canada but also from all countries of Western Europe and several in Asia. United States companies sent molds abroad, and tires were made thereafter without incident or interference.[25] This is typical of most such situations. Claims of international solidarity actions during such strikes rarely amount to more than leaflets promising support, statements of "solidarity" by union officials, or letters from foreign unions to company headquarters officials "demanding" that they agree to the striking union's terms.

THE SUPPORT FOR MULTINATIONAL BARGAINING

The analysis thus far shows rather conclusively that multinational collective bargaining is absent in any real sense on the world scene, that there is no real demand for it from employees, that corporate management quite correctly opposes multinational bargaining as certain to increase costs and to enhance the risk

---

[24] See chapter XII.

[25] See chapter IX.

of strikes, and that many national leaders have good cause to be wary about the potentially adverse economic effects on their union members if they become involved in multinational bargaining.

Is multinational bargaining a dead issue then? The answer is that, for several reasons, its potential is very much alive for the longer term. First, there are persons in positions of importance who see multinational bargaining as a vehicle to increase their prestige and power. These include officials of international and regional labor organizations, bureaucrats of international and regional governmental bodies, and some national labor union and government officials, particularly those in small countries or those out of power on the national scene. Second, the movements toward parity codetermination and toward the establishment of union-controlled "asset formation" schemes not only directly enhance union power but put union officials, including international ones, in a position to seek multinational bargaining with considerable leverage. Third, corporate management, by unthinking or shortsighted decisions and inadequate communications, can encourage, and has encouraged, demands for bargaining at the international level. Finally, and perhaps most important, the development of codes of conduct for multinational corporations or so-called guidelines at the level of international governmental organizations provides both a forum and a means for international unions and bureaucrats to advocate multinational bargaining.

International and Regional Union Officials

For several years, many international union officials have been attempting to position themselves for international bargaining. The likelihood of an international trade union secretariat playing such a role is, however, not great despite the expressed hopes of some of such organizations' leadership. Their member unions seem too diverse and far-reaching and the community of interest too lacking to achieve the unity of purpose and program required for such action. Nevertheless, the secretariats do provide a forum for mutual discussion and encouragement of multinational union action, and also of propaganda in support of it. Moreover, as noted below, recent "commentaries" on the code of conduct (guidelines) proposed by the Organization for Economic Cooperation and Development (OECD) for multinational corporations have given encouragement to the aspirations of some secretariat officials.

Regional organizations, particularly the EMF and possibly in time other industry committees of the ETUC, have affiliates with much less diversity and much more mutuality of interest. The EMF is forthrightly committed to multinational bargaining. Although rebuffed when it has attempted to push corporations toward this goal, it remains quite ready to seize any opportunity that might present itself to accomplish this mission. Of course, the obstacles in its path, including the reluctance of its affiliates and that of corporate management, as already discussed, remain formidable.

International Bureaucracy

International governmental organization bureaucrats constitute significant and influential proponents of multinational bargaining. The tripartite machinery of the International Labour Organisation (ILO) and its overwhelmingly union-oriented staff provide both climate and fertilizer for multinational union-management relationships. The ILO sees as one of its principal functions the promotion of collective bargaining, and multinational bargaining is considered merely an addition to employee and union "rights."

The bureaucrats who most avidly promote multinational industrial relations are of course those attached to the various agencies of the European Community. They obviously see multinational bargaining as a proper culmination of European integration. Undoubtedly also, many EC and other intergovernmental organization personnel as well see themselves playing a greater role if they become involved in multinational bargaining. In any case, the zeal with which EC bureaucrats push multinational tripartite meetings, multinational works councils, and European corporate charters with overt multinational bargaining requirements, and the affinity and close relations of these bureaucrats with the regional union officials stationed in Brussels all point to a steady source of pressure toward internationalizing industrial relations.

When a European industry encounters serious problems, the EC bureaucrats push for tripartite solutions. Shipbuilding is a good example. Bringing together the state-dominated concerns, government, and unions, the EC has promoted solutions which clearly bear the imprint of the EMF.[26]

---

[26] See chapter IV. Günter Köpke, former general secretary of the EMF and now managing director of the European Trade Union Institute, did a basic economic study of the shipbuilding industry for the EC in the mid-1970s.

National Union Officials and Their Political Supporters

There are also a relatively few national union officials and their political supporters who support multinational bargaining. Such support varies in intensity, in time, and by situations. Certainly, the German union officials who nominated international and regional union officials to company supervisory boards further the multinational bargaining concept, but German unions, with superior conditions to other European Community countries, appear unlikely actually to promote such bargaining.

More direct union leadership support of multinational bargaining emanates from union officials of small countries who already play a key role in European regional unions. Thus, the general secretaries of the ETUC and the EMF are from Luxembourg and Belgium, respectively, and the president of the ETUC, from the Netherlands. Undoubtedly, international and regional unions offer a much greater role for small country union leaders than is possible within the narrow confines of their now very limited territories. The Dutch are the most conspicuous in this grouping. Indeed, the largest Netherlandic union, Industriebond-NVV, even went so far as to commit itself to found a multinational trade union.[27] The likelihood that this initiative will find support is clearly minute. Not only are the strong German, divided French, and fragmented British unions largely disintegrated, but also the international trade secretariats and regional unions certainly oppose any new rivals for their territory. The general secretary of the IUF quickly attacked the idea.[28] It does illustrate the attitude of a small, but significant, group.

The possibility that, if they support multinational bargaining, unions will have government support is also present. Again, the Dutch afford the best example. Former Prime Minister Den Uyl urged the OECD to require such bargaining in the guidelines and denounced Akzo in a nationwide speech for refusing such bargaining.[29] Other small country political leaders allied with unions would likely add their support. To the politician, such advocacy permits favors that, on the face, at least immediately, are costless to be granted to supporters.

---

[27] Jeroen Terlinger, "Multinational union experiment?" *Free Labour World*, November-December 1978, pp. 16-17.

[28] See Dan Gallin, "Building international union power," *Free Labour World*, November-December 1978, pp. 18-19.

[29] See chapter VII, note 49.

There is also the possibility that key national union officials, frustrated by their inability to induce a multinational corporation to concede key issues, might seek redress on a multinational level. For reasons already examined, this is not likely to occur. Nevertheless, the possibility is not foreclosed. The form that such a movement might take, again for reasons discussed in the first section of this chapter, could more likely be a coalition of national union officials without the presence of international or regional union officials. Such a coalition, however, would need to develop a workable decision process that we have found to be quite difficult.

Codetermination

A fundamental fact about codetermination as long practiced in the German iron, steel, and coal industries, and to a somewhat lesser extent in large German companies since the law changes of 1976, is that the presence of outside unionists on the supervisory boards (*Aufsichsräte*) changes the corporate decision-making process. The leadership, if not the control, by these outside unionists of most other employee directors on the majority of large company supervisory boards inevitably points toward political decision making at the expense of the economic needs of the corporation. This affords an opportunity for multinational bargaining.

The key aspect of such codetermination allows unions to nominate outsiders to the company supervisory board. Prior to the recent changes in the law, employee supervisory board members were selected from a company's employees, except in the iron, steel, and coal industries. Now, for the first time, major companies in Germany have persons on their supervisory boards who owe their presence and allegiance strictly to the unions that nominated them. Five of these new supervisory board members are international union officials, as listed in Table XIX-1. Three, as noted, are not German citizens.

These international union officials have already made their presence felt. Thus, after the Ford of Germany labor relations director died suddenly in 1978, Rebhan led the employee directors in holding up the appointment of a successor for several months. Thönnessen has also assumed leadership of the employee directors at Standard Eloktrik Loronz, and Levinson is vice-chairman of the Du Pont of Germany Supervisory Board. Meanwhile, throughout Germany, many companies find the union officials on boards are already attempting to increase the authority of the super-

TABLE XIX-1
International Union Officials on German Supervisory Boards

Name	Principal Position	Company Board
Herman Rebhan [a]	General Secretary, International Metalworkers' Federation	Ford of Germany
Werner Thönnessen [b]	Assistant General Secretary, International Metalworkers' Federation	Standard Elektrik Lorenz (ITT)
Charles Levinson [c]	Secretary General, International Federation of Chemical, Energy and General Workers' Unions	Du Pont of Germany
Heribert Maier [d]	General Secretary, International Federation of Commercial, Clerical and Technical Employees	"bilka" Kaufhaus GmbH
Günter Köpke [b]	Managing Director, European Trade Union Institute; formerly General Secretary, European Metalworkers' Federation	Philips of Germany

Source: Supervisory board records.
[a] An American citizen, Rebhan was born in Germany and immigrated to the United States as a child.
[b] German citizen.
[c] Canadian citizen.
[d] Austrian citizen.

visory boards by having such boards assume powers now exercised by the managing boards (*Vorstände*) or works councils.[30]

Such political maneuvering could quite conceivably be used to promote international unionism and multinational bargaining. For example, the union bloc on the supervisory board could decline to support action that management proposes unless the management agrees to a meeting with an international union group. Under German law, the chairman, chosen by the shareholders, has the decisive vote in case of supervisory board deadlocks. Many companies feel, however, that use of this chairman's power against union proposals will result in union retaliation during the bargaining process.

A principal task of the supervisory board is to select members of the managing board. Thus, Germany's codetermination law

---

[30] These comments are based upon interviews in Germany, May 1979.

puts union officials in a position to influence the selection of management and to harass or even to cause the dismissal of managerial personnel whom the union supervisory board members might regard as antagonistic to union aspirations. That such a potential is likely to encourage ambitious lower and middle managers to curry favor with union officials seems rather obvious. Again, management could be pressured into multinational bargaining by such union presence and power.

To date, German union officials have demonstrated no propensity to engage in multinational bargaining. German conditions of work are generally superior to those in other parts of Europe. It is not, therefore, unlikely that German unionists fear that multinational bargaining could do little to improve their situation and might actually retard their economic progress. Nevertheless, by nominating international union officials to German supervisory boards, German union leaders have undoubtedly added prestige to these individuals and the organizations that they represent.

If German unionists ever decide to encourage multinational bargaining, they could certainly induce Volkswagen to be the pioneer. By virtue of their support by supervisory board members representing the 40 percent ownership of Volkswagen of the German Federal Republic and the State of Lower Saxony and the board member representing the Bank für Gemeinschaft, the union-controlled bank which is a large Volkswagen shareholder, employee directors have long been in a position to control Volkswagen's destiny.[31] Under the new German legislation, about two-thirds of supervisory boards are employee—basically union—oriented. Eugen Loderer, president of Industriegewerkschaft Metall, German's largest union, who is also president of the IMF and vice-president of the EMF, has long been vice-chairman and probably the most powerful man on the Volkswagen Supervisory Board. A former IG Metall functionary is Volkswagen's labor director. The future course of Volkswagen bargaining is thus a function of union desires.

Union-Controlled Asset-Formation Plans

A number of plans have been developed in European countries that could, if effectuated, give control of major corporations to

---

[31] For an incisive analysis of union maneuverings on the Volkswagen Supervisory Board, see Alfred L. Thimm, "Decision-Making at Volkswagen, 1972-1975," *Columbia Journal of World Business*, Vol. 11 (Spring 1976), pp. 94-103.

union officials. Briefly, such plans would require that a percentage of corporate profits be turned over to a public corporation in the form of company stock. Union officials would manage the public corporation. After a given number of years, the public corporation would control the companies whose stock it had received.

Such plans have been proposed in Denmark; in Sweden, under the Meidner Plan; in the Netherlands, where it is called "VAD"; and by the European Commission bureaucracy. None have been enacted.[32] If such expropriation of shareholders' equity becomes law, union officials will, of course, have the power to influence corporate decision making toward multinational bargaining if they so choose.

Management Action

Plant closures in Europe result in tremendously adverse publicity for multinational corporations. Often, managements fail to explain completely the needs for such actions, thus compounding the difficulties. A rush of such closures could well trigger support for multinational union action, although, to date, unions have tended to seek national settlements despite international agitation.

Perhaps more serious in terms of promoting multinational bargaining is the increasing tendency in Europe towards solutions of production problems by cartel formation. The depressed man-made fiber industry is a case in point. If a cartel is permitted, it could generate demands for European Community-wide bargaining. Since production and market share would be determined by agreement among those subscribing to the cartel, unions could point out that the producers are also agreeing among themselves to allocate employment and that such allocation should be a matter of collective bargaining. Since the allocation of production and employment is being made on a European Community-wide basis, unions could likewise argue that bargaining should be on this basis. With markets secure and competition stifled, some producers might be willing to accept multinational bargaining to obtain union support for their anticompetitive arrangements.

---

[32] For a thorough analysis of these and related programs, see Geoffrey W. Latta, *Profit Sharing, Employee Stock Ownership, Savings, and Asset Formation Plans in the Western World*, Multinational Industrial Relations Series, No. 5 (Philadelphia: Industrial Research Unit, The Wharton School, University of Pennsylvania, 1979).

CODES OF CONDUCT

Codes of conduct intending to regulate the activities of multinational firms have proliferated since the mid-1970s. Both international and national trade union organizations have been strong proponents of such codes and have lobbied hard for them in all jurisdictions. Intergovernmental agencies, such as the Organization for Economic Cooperation and Development, International Labour Organisation, and the United Nation's Commission on Transnational Corporations, have been very active in the pursuit of an agreed upon set of guidelines for corporate behavior. At this time, the OECD and the ILO have developed and issued codes of conduct, and the UN bodies are continuing discussions with the hope of finalizing a code by 1980. The importance of all of this activity is aptly described by the *Economist* when it suggests that the business world should be watching the working groups at the OECD "like a hawk, because what is at stake here (and in other backrooms at the United Nations) are the rules it will have to live by." [33]

The OECD

On June 21, 1976, a declaration by governments of OECD member countries on international investment and multinational enterprises was issued containing "Guidelines for Multinational Enterprises." These voluntary guidelines cover the following areas: disclosure of information, competition, financing, taxation, employment and industrial relations, and science and technology.

The decision by the OECD to develop a code of conduct for multinational firms has provided areas of confrontation that were not present in the earlier life of the organization. Following World War II and the joining of twenty-four developed nations in 1961, the major objective of the OECD was to promote economic growth and employment in a stable financial environment. Consequently, the OECD has provided a mechanism whereby governments have exchanged useful information, research studies have been professionally prepared, comparative data on international economic conditions have been developed in a reliable manner, and conferences have stimulated new ideas and constructive solutions to problems. The introduction of guidelines now forces the organization into the posture of a regulatory

---

[33] "Rules for firms—and governments," *Economist*, March 31, 1979, p. 60.

agency, and the employment and industrial relations guidelines, in particular, have introduced strong third-party involvement, in the form of active trade union initiatives, in discussions between the multinational firms and governments. It has also provided a forum in which multinational bargaining can be encouraged.

The rationale for the guidelines can possibly be explained on the basis of tremendous publicity given to alleged malpractices on the part of some multinational firms in the early 1970s, union support for guidelines, and a movement by the ILO in the direction of formulating a code of conduct. The OECD evidently desired to issue the first set of guidelines in order to protect business interests as much as possible. At least, in being first, it was felt by some that the OECD might avoid more stringent regulations that may be forthcoming and precedent setting by the ILO and/or the UN.

Committee on International Investment and Multinational Enterprises (CIIME). The issuance of the guidelines led to the creation and activation of various bodies within the OECD. The CIIME is now responsible for the supervision of work conducted under the guidelines. Business interests are represented before the CIIME by the Business and Industry Advisory Committee (BIAC), and labor's interests are represented by the Trade Union Advisory Committee (TUAC).

Representatives on the CIIME are drawn from national government echelons and usually come from agencies whose work pertains to finance and investment. Since the employment and industrial relations section of the guidelines appears to have generated the most activity for the CIIME, it is surprising that practically no labor relations representatives have been appointed to the committee. At the April 25-27, 1979, meeting of the committee, for example, the United States delegation consisted of representatives from the Departments of Commerce, State, and Treasury but no one from the Department of Labor. This same situation was true for most of the countries that sent representatives to the April meeting. The difficulty arising from this situation, of course, is that the significance of technical and very practical labor problems discussed before the committee by trade unionists as well as others may not be fully understood by those with essentially a financial background. Many times, the nuances of industrial relations issues are quite subtle, and they are likely to be overlooked or improperly evaluated by those not in the field.

BIAC. The Business and Industry Advisory Committee of the OECD consists of member organizations in each of the participating twenty-four nations; Committees on International Investment and Multinational Enterprises, Economic Policy, and Energy and Raw Materials; and approximately ten working groups of experts in areas ranging from capital markets to education. In addition, there is a small secretariat staff that operates in Paris, including a secretary general, deputy secretary general, two assistants to the secretary general, and four members of the administrative staff.[34] The Paris office principally handles arrangements for meetings at the OECD, coordinates meetings of the committees and groups of experts, and prepares some staff papers. There is no permanent BIAC staff person, for example, who is an expert in the field of labor and industrial relations and who pursues matters relating to industrial relations on a fulltime basis as is true with their counterpart, the TUAC, although experts from industry have acted as advisors.

TUAC. The Trade Union Advisory Committee to the OECD consists of thirty-six national trade union centers, such as the AFL-CIO in the United States, the Deutsche Gewerkschaftsbund (DGB) in West Germany, and the Trades Union Congress (TUC) in Britain (see Table XIX-2). A secretariat is maintained in Paris with a general secretary, Kari Tapiola, and staff members. Tapiola comes from the Finnish trade union movement, and prior to his position in Paris, he served as special labor assistant to Klaus Sahlgren, director of the UN Centre on Transnational Corporations in New York. The primary mission of the TUAC is to prepare a trade union response to issues arising at the OECD level.

Challenges to the Guidelines

Needless to say, the trade unions in particular were anxious to test the guidelines once they had been issued. In late 1976 and early 1977, two separate events occurred in Europe that led to international trade union activity before the OECD and the ILO. Cases pertaining to the Badger (Belgium) N.V. Company and the Hertz Corporation in Copenhagen, Denmark, created the first real challenges under the OECD guidelines.

The Badger Case. The Badger Company is a subsidiary of Raytheon, a United States multinational company, with head-

---

[34] Business and Industry Advisory Committee, *Report of Activities, 1978* (Paris, 1979), pp. 27-32.

TABLE XIX-2
Trade Union Advisory Committee
List of Affiliates: Membership and Affiliation Fees
(French Francs)
as of January 1, 1979

Organization	Country	Membership	Affiliation Fees
1. DGB	Germany	6,800,000	122,400
2. OGB	Austria	1,620,000	29,160
3. CSC	Belgium	1,100,000	19,800
4. FGTB	Belgium	900,000	16,200
5. CLC	Canada	1,300,000	23,400
6. CSN	Canada	159,000	2,873
7. FTF	Denmark	241,000	4,338
8. LO	Denmark	1,046,000	18,828
9. AFL-CIO	U.S.A.	13,378,700	240,816
10. SAK	Finland	951,000	17,118
11. TVK	Finland	250,000	4,499
12. CFDT	France	1,077,000	19,386
13. CGC	France	300,000	5,400
14. CGT-FO	France	905,000	16,290
15. FEN	France	550,000	9,900
16. GSEE	Greece	105,000	1,890
17. TUC	United Kingdom	10,363,600	186,534
18. ICTU	Ireland	550,000	9,900
19. ASI	Iceland	42,402	756
20. CISL	Italy	1,700,000	30,600
21. UIL	Italy	550,000	9,900
22. DOMEI	Japan	1,300,000	23,400
23. SOHYO	Japan	2,600,000	46,800
24. CGT	Luxembourg	32,000	576
25. LCGB	Luxembourg	18,000	270
26. LO	Norway	680,000	12,240
27. CNV	Netherlands	216,700	3,888
28. FNV	Netherlands	350,000 (NKV)	6,300
		724,000 (NVV)	13,032
29. LO	Sweden	1,800,000	32,400
30. TCO	Sweden	968,000	16,596
31. CNG	Switzerland	106,000	1,908
32. SVEA	Switzerland	15,000	270
33. USS/SGB	Switzerland	475,000	8,550
34. UGT	Spain	—	—
35. STV	Spain	100,000	1,800
36. TURK-IS	Turkey	500,000	9,000
Total			966,472

Source: TUAG.

quarters in Cambridge, Massachusetts. On January 14, 1977, Badger decided to close its office in Antwerp, Belgium, which affected some 250 employees. The company claimed bankruptcy and initially "refused to supplement the assets of its Belgian affiliate, on the grounds of the theory of the limited responsibility of the (Belgian) corporation." [35] The case came in the midst of a Belgian political campaign and was used to generate enormous publicity.

The central question in regard to this case was simply, Must a parent company assume the financial obligations of a subsidiary operating as a limited liability company in a particular country? The Belgian government interpreted the guidelines of the OECD as meaning that the parent company would be responsible for the obligation of the subsidiary. The matter was eventually brought before the OECD by the Belgian government and the International Federation of Commercial, Clerical and Technical Employees.

The CIIME was not anxious to receive the case because there were no procedures established in the guidelines for processing such a case. The committee's responsibility was that of looking only at the general principles of the matter without considering an individual case. An attempted challenge before the OECD, plus tremendous pressure by Badger's clients, the major oil companies, who feared involvement, however, led to negotiations between the Badger Company, the Belgian government, and the trade unions. This, in turn, led to an agreement wherein the Badger Company supplemented the assets of the subsidiary in Belgium to an agreed amount, which was deemed to cover the severance pay liabilities of the Badger subsidiary to its Belgian employees. It should be noted that the Belgium severance pay law not only may be the most generous in Europe but is also quite vague as to amounts. Union and government claims on Badger were substantially modified downward in the final negotiations.

---

[35] Roger Blanpain, "The OECD Guidelines for Multinational Enterprises—the Badger Case," *Journal of the Royal Society for the Encouragement of Arts, Manufactures, and Commerce*, Vol. CXXVI (May 1979), p. 327. Professor Blanpain, who served as an advisor to the Belgian government throughout the case, also authored a book, *The Badger Case and the OECD Guidelines for Multinational Enterprises* (Deventer, The Netherlands: Kluwer, 1977). For the company view, see the article, "The Badger Case: The Company's Side of the Story," *Commerce in Belgium*, October 1978.

The Hertz Case. Hertz's encounter with the international trade union movement and the OECD occurred as the result of a strike in Denmark in late 1976, as explained in chapter XIV. As noted there, a strike over wages led to Hertz's bringing in six to eight employees from its companies in the United Kingdom, Italy, and France to operate the facilities at Kastrup Airport and in downtown Copenhagen. A compromise settlement terminated the strike in November 1976, but meanwhile, Hertz reorganized its Danish operation, transferred accounting and other funds to its German company, and reduced its employment in Denmark.

The TUAC presented the Hertz case to the OECD as an example of the ineffectiveness of voluntary corporate guidelines for multinationals. The essential question that was raised in the case was, Can a multinational firm legitimately transfer employees across national boundaries in order to maintain operations at a struck facility? The OECD declined to act on the individual case, but the unions then turned to the ILO's Tripartite Advisory Committee on the Relationship of Multinational Enterprises and Social Policy, which convened in Geneva on April 4-7, 1977. At this ILO committee meeting, the parties adopted part of the OECD guidelines as a proposed ILO statement. The unions demanded in addition a paragraph that would have encouraged international union action within multinational corporations. This was rejected, but the committee did agree to the following paragraph:

> Multinational enterprises, in the context of bona fide negotiations with the workers' representatives on conditions of employment, or while workers are exercising the right to organise, should not threaten to utilise a capacity to transfer the whole or part of an operating unit from the country concerned in order to influence unfairly these negotiations or to hinder the exercise of the right to organise; nor should they transfer workers from affiliates in foreign countries with a view to undermining bona fide negotiations with the workers' representatives or the workers' exercise of their right to organise.[36]

As is noted below, the Hertz case resulted in more attention during the review of the guidelines in 1979, and it also led to the only textual change as a result of the review. Neither the ILO nor the OECD thought it pertinent to question the right of unions to engage in multinational activities, such as boycotts,

---

[36] Paragraph 52, *Tripartite Declaration of Principles Concerning Multinational Enterprises and Social Policy*, MEO, 1977.

when a primary controversy involves conditions in a particular country.

Other Cases. The Badger and Hertz cases were not the only ones presented to the OECD during the early life of the guidelines. The International Metalworkers' Federation, along with other international trade secretariats, have submitted approximately fifteen cases to the OECD in the hope that this action would establish the right of the trade unions to bring individual cases directly before the CIIME. The committee has consistently refused to review the cases that were presented on an individual basis; however, their presentation has led to the establishment of ad hoc bodies within the OECD that meet occasionally to conduct informal discussions arising from particular cases that are submitted by the trade unions. Companies have on several occasions been unaware that their policies were under review.[37]

Review of the Guidelines

When the guidelines were issued in June of 1976, a requirement was stated for a review that would take place after three years, or by June 1979. This review was completed in May 1979 and a formal report by the CIIME was issued in June 1979.[38] Hearings were conducted by the CIIME during 1978, at which time the TUAC and the BIAC made presentations concerning their respective positions.

The BIAC position can generally be described as one of insisting on no changes in the guidelines on the grounds, first, that there had not been enough experience in three years to evaluate the results of the guidelines; second, that, because some companies had agreed to voluntarily abide by the guidelines, it would be a mistake to "rock the boat" early in the game by attempting to revise the language in the guidelines; and third, that a review, not a revision of the guidelines, was intended for 1979 when the document was first issued in 1976.

The TUAC position pushed very strongly for the right to revise and to introduce changes in the language of the guidelines.

---

[37] We have personally surprised a few companies by advising them of charges that they had violated the guidelines.

[38] OECD, Committee on International Investment and Multinational Enterprises, *The Review of the 1976 Declaration and Decisions on International Investment and Multinational Enterprises*, C(79), 102.

Considerable effort was expended by the TUAC to uphold the right of the trade unions to be recognized and to be able to bring specific charges against multinational corporations before the CIIME.

The Results of the Review. As far as textual changes are concerned, the review of the guidelines led to only one major amendment, and this comes directly from the Hertz case, as previously mentioned. The gist of this matter is covered in paragraph 70 of the published review:

> The Committee also considered the question whether the transfer of employees from a foreign affiliate in order to influence unfairly bona fide negotiations with employee representatives on conditions of employment would be contrary to standards set out in the Employment and Industrial Relations chapter and more particularly to paragraph 8. In the view of the Committee, such behavior, while not specifically mentioned in the Guidelines, certainly would not be in conformity with the general spirit and approach underlying the drafting of the Employment and Industrial Relations chapter. Accordingly, it is recommended that enterprises should definitely avoid recourse to such practices in the future. The Committee, therefore, proposes that this recommendation, which does not imply a major change of the Guidelines, should be made explicit in the text of paragraph 8 by the following addition (amended language [italicized]):
>
> 8. In the context of bona fide negotiations with representatives of employees on conditions of employment, or while employees are exercising the right to organise, not threaten to utilise a capacity to transfer the whole or part of an operating unit from the country concerned *nor transfer employees from the enterprises' component entities in other countries* in order to influence unfairly those negotiations or to hinder the exercise of a right to organise.[39]

Although it is correct that the review process led to a recommendation of only one textual change, the commentary that was provided by the committee and forwarded to the ministers for their consideration suggests a number of very significant advances made by the unions. Several of these commentaries, as contained in the review of the guidelines, are presented below since they indicate the success of the TUAC in influencing the review process, and they indicate the manner in which the unions will attempt to continue to utilize the guidelines toward their own advancement.

> 60. . . . The thrust of these provisions of the Guidelines is towards having management adopt a positive approach towards the activities

[39] *Ibid.*, pp. 35-36.

of trade unions and other bona fide organisations of employees of all categories and, in particular, an open attitude towards organisational activities within the framework of national rules and practices.

61. While not explicitly addressing the issue, the Guidelines imply that the management of MNEs should adopt a cooperative attitude towards the participation of employees in international meetings for consultation and exchange of views among themselves provided that the functions of the operations of the enterprises and normal procedures which govern relationships with representatives of the employees and their organisations are not thereby prejudiced.

62. The Committee has not considered the question of the conduct of collective bargaining at an international level, for which there are no real examples, although there has been some development of trade union efforts to coordinate the approaches to multinational enterprises on a cross-country basis. The question has been raised, however, whether the Employment and Industrial Relations Guideline could put obstacles in the way of recognition by the management of an MNE, in agreement with the national trade unions it has recognised and consistent with national laws and practices, of an International Trade Secretariat as a "bona fide organization of employees" referred to in paragraph 1 of the Guidelines. It is the Committee's view that no such obstacle exists or was intended in the Guidelines.[40]

Analysis of Commentaries. These paragraphs appear designed to encourage union expansion and multinational bargaining. Thus, for example, paragraph 60 would seem to go far beyond the United States National Labor Relations (Taft-Hartley) Act both in encouraging unionization generally and in approving the organization of supervisory, salaried, and managerial employees. Of course, the deference to national legislation is a safeguard, but pressure is induced by such international action to alter legislation to fit the guidelines, especially when, as in this instance, approval has been given by national government representatives.

Paragraphs 61 and 62 clearly support the concept of multinational bargaining. Few employers deem it their obligation to support, encourage, or even cooperate with union or secretariat-sponsored multinational employee meetings, as is proclaimed proper by paragraph 61. The attitude of most companies is that such meetings should be neither encouraged nor discouraged. To cooperate can mean to assist in setting the stage for multinational bargaining and the attendant risks which managements clearly believe are involved. Because international union or-

[40] *Ibid.*, p. 33.

ganizations regard consultation as a prelude to bargaining, such management fears may well be realistic.

Paragraph 62 is a major victory for the international trade union secretariats. In fact, they are federations of organizations, not of employees, and have not hitherto been considered unions as such. A combination of paragraphs 60, 61, and 62 could well be interpreted as meaning that a refusal of a multinational corporation to meet with an international trade secretariat, or an ITS and a committee of national unions, to consult, or even to bargain, on a multinational basis is a breach of the OECD guidelines. The authors have yet to meet a company that voluntarily announced support of the guidelines while believing that the guidelines meant what is apparently implied in these three paragraphs of "commentaries."

The next review of the guidelines is scheduled for 1984; however, there is the possibility of an interim report on activities under the guidelines. The TUAC will undoubtedly push for a review process to take place on a continuous basis rather than at stated intervals, especially in view of the success which it achieved in the 1979 review.

The ILO

In November 1976, the 201st Session of the ILO Governing Body established a tripartite drafting group to draw up a "Declaration of Principles of MNCs and Social Policy." One year later, in November 1977, the 204th Session of the Governing Body endorsed the tripartite declaration. There has been very little confrontation under the ILO declaration. During its meetings in May and June 1979, the governing body was concerned with the selection of a tripartite committee that would be charged with reviewing reports from governments on the implementation of the declaration. Government consultations with employers and workers' organizations are presently being conducted in various countries so that a report on the effects of the declaration can be submitted early in 1980.

The UN/CTC

The Centre on Transnational Corporations serves as a secretariat group to the Commission on Transnational Corporations, which was developed in 1974 under a resolution of the Economic and Social Council of the United Nations. The commission has been operational since November 1975. One of the top priorities of the Commission on Transnational Corporations has been the development of a code of conduct. The first session of the Intergovernmental Working Group on a Code of Conduct at the UN met in January 1977, and the seventh session of the group met from March 12 to 23, 1979. The center has prepared background and working papers for the working group, and at present, the chairman of the working group has formulated the contents of a draft code, and the subject of implementation is now being discussed. In regard to the section of the code pertaining to employment and labor, it has been proposed that it will only be necessary to refer to the ILO tripartite declaration. There will be some pressures, of course, to include more specific language favorable to the trade unions as the drafting process continues, but it appears likely, at this stage, that the ILO document will be accepted as the code in the industrial relations field.

Guidelines—Final Comment

It appears that the multinational corporation will continue to be closely monitored by intergovernmental agencies. Codes of conduct will continue to be a fact of life. The extent to which corporations will be affected by the codes of conduct will depend in large measure on their own decisions on whether they wish to participate in an effort to influence constructively the development and implementation of the code. It is somewhat surprising to learn from the review of the OECD guidelines that employment and industrial relations was "the chapter of the Guidelines to which the Committee has devoted most time" and, at the same time, discover very little expertise in the field of industrial relations regularly present on the review committees or within the responding organizations from the business community to the committee. Standards that are developed on international codes have a way of finding themselves expressed in national legislation at some time in the future. This is perhaps one reason why the business community should pay particular attention to the drafting of such international codes. Another is that the guidelines now appear to be the focal point of the international union organizations' drive toward effective multinational corporation recognition and, eventually, multinational bargaining.

CONCLUDING REMARKS

Multinational bargaining is virtually nonexistent today, and the signs that it will emerge soon are not present. There are formidable obstacles to its development and serious questions whether it would be in the public interest. Nevertheless, there are pressures from various vested interests, particularly international trade union organizations and international government groups, to promote multinational bargaining. Today, pressures emanating especially through the bureaucracy of the European Community and via the OECD guidelines very much keep the potential for multinational bargaining alive.

Index

Racial Policies of American Industry Series

Order from: Kraus Reprint Co., Route 100, Millwood, New York 10546

STUDIES OF NEGRO EMPLOYMENT

Order from the Industrial Research Unit
The Wharton School, University of Pennsylvania
Philadelphia, Pennsylvania 19104

* Order these books from University Microfilms, Inc., Attn: Books Editorial Department, 300 North Zeeb Road, Ann Arbor, Michigan 48106.